Synopsis Purioris Theologiae
Synopsis of a Purer Theology

Studies in Medieval and Reformation Traditions

Edited by

Andrew Colin Gow (*Edmonton, Alberta*)

In cooperation with

Sylvia Brown (*Edmonton, Alberta*) – Falk Eisermann (*Berlin*)
Berndt Hamm (*Erlangen*) – Johannes Heil (*Heidelberg*) – Susan C.
Karant-Nunn (*Tucson, Arizona*) – Martin Kaufhold (*Augsburg*)
Erik Kwakkel (*Leiden*) – Jürgen Miethke (*Heidelberg*)
Christopher Ocker (*San Anselmo and Berkeley, California*)

Founding Editor

Heiko A. Oberman †

VOLUME 187

Texts & Sources

Edited by

Falk Eisermann (*Berlin*)

VOLUME 5

The titles published in this series are listed at *brill.com/smrtts*

Synopsis Purioris Theologiae
Synopsis of a Purer Theology

Latin Text and English Translation

VOLUME 1
DISPUTATIONS 1–23

Volume Editor
Dolf te Velde

Translator
Riemer A. Faber

Editor, Latin Text
Rein Ferwerda

General Editors
Willem J. van Asselt †
William den Boer
Riemer A. Faber

BRILL

LEIDEN | BOSTON

Sponsored by STICHTING AFBOUW KAMPEN

This publication received a generous grant from Stichting Afbouw Kampen (SAK).

Cover illustration: Title page of the *Synopsis purioris theologiae disputationibus quinquaginta duabus comprehensa*, Leiden: Elzevier 1625, Library of the Theological University Kampen. Courtesy Maarten Boersema.

Library of Congress Cataloging-in-Publication Data

Synopsis purioris theologiae = Synopsis of a purer theology / volume editor, Dolf te Velde ; translator, Riemer A. Faber ; editor, Latin text, Rein Ferwerda ; general editors, Willem J. van Asselt †, William den Boer, Riemer A. Faber.
    pages cm. – (Studies in medieval and Reformation traditions, ISSN 1573-4188)
    Includes bibliographical references and index.
    "Latin text and English translation."
    ISBN 978-90-04-19218-8 (volume 1 : hardback : alk. paper) – ISBN 978-90-04-28246-9 (volume 1 : e-book) 1. Reformed Church–Doctrinal and controversial works–Early works to 1800. 2. Theology, Doctrinal–Early works to 1800. I. Velde, Roelf T. te, editor. II. Asselt, Willem J. van (Willem Jan van), 1946- editor. III. Synopsis purioris theologiae. IV. Synopsis purioris theologiae. English. V. Title: Synopsis of a purer theology.

BT70.S918 2014
  230'.42–dc23

2014030877

This publication has been typeset in the multilingual "Brill" typeface. With over 5,100 characters covering Latin, IPA, Greek, and Cyrillic, this typeface is especially suitable for use in the humanities. For more information, please see www.brill.com/brill-typeface.

ISSN 1573-4188
ISBN 978-90-04-19218-8 (hardback)
ISBN 978-90-04-28246-9 (e-book)

Copyright 2015 by Koninklijke Brill NV, Leiden, The Netherlands.
Koninklijke Brill NV incorporates the imprints Brill, Brill Nijhoff, Global Oriental and Hotei Publishing.
All rights reserved. No part of this publication may be reproduced, translated, stored in a retrieval system, or transmitted in any form or by any means, electronic, mechanical, photocopying, recording or otherwise, without prior written permission from the publisher.
Authorization to photocopy items for internal or personal use is granted by Koninklijke Brill NV provided that the appropriate fees are paid directly to The Copyright Clearance Center, 222 Rosewood Drive, Suite 910, Danvers, MA 01923, USA. Fees are subject to change.

This book is printed on acid-free paper.

Printed by Printforce, the Netherlands

*Dedicated to the memory of Willem J. van Asselt (1946–2014),
scholar and friend*

Contents

Notes on Contributors   IX
Acknowledgements   XII
List of Abbreviations   XIV

Introduction   1

Text and Translation

Preface addressed to the most honorable and all-powerful States of Holland and West-Friesland   22

Disputation 1. Concerning the Most Sacred Theology   30

Disputation 2. On the Necessity and Authority of Scripture   48

Disputation 3. Concerning the Canonical and Apocryphal Books   74

Disputation 4. On the Perfection of Scripture, and the Futility of Adding Unwritten Traditions to it   106

Disputation 5. About the Perspicuity and the Interpretation of Holy Scripture   128

Disputation 6. About the Nature of God and his Divine Attributes   150

Disputation 7. On the Holy Trinity   184

Disputation 8. Concerning the Person of the Father and of the Son   202

Disputation 9. On the Person of the Holy Spirit   228

Disputation 10. Concerning the Creation of the World   246

Disputation 11. On the Providence of God   260

Disputation 12. Concerning the Good and Bad Angels   284

Disputation 13. About Man Created in the Image of God 314

Disputation 14. On the Fall of Adam 338

Disputation 15. On Original Sin 350

Disputation 16. On Actual Sin 384

Disputation 17. On Free Choice 406

Disputation 18. Concerning the Law of God 432

Disputation 19. On Idolatry 452

Disputation 20. Concerning the Oath 488

Disputation 21. On the Sabbath and the Lord's Day 512

Disputation 22. On the Gospel 556

Disputation 23. On the Old and the New Testament 574

Glossary of Concepts and Terms 603
Bibliography 615
Scripture Index 632
General Index 648

Notes on Contributors

W.J. (Willem) van Asselt
(1946–2014), Ph.D. (1988) Utrecht University, was Professor of Historical Theology at the Evangelische Theologische Faculteit, Leuven, and Emeritus Associate Professor in Church History at Utrecht University. He was (co-)author or editor of numerous articles and books on the history of Reformed theology, including *The Federal Theology of Johannes Cocceius (1603–1669)* (Brill, 2001), *Introduction to Reformed Scholasticism* (Reformation Heritage Books, 2011), and *Reformed Thought on Freedom* (Baker Academic, 2010).

A.J. (Andreas) Beck
(1965), Ph.D. (2007) Utrecht University, is Professor of Historical Theology and Academic Dean at the Evangelische Theologische Faculteit, Leuven, and the director of the Institute of Post-Reformation Studies there. He is the author of *Gisbertus Voetius (1589–1676). Sein Theologieverständnis und seine Gotteslehre* (Vandenhoeck & Ruprecht, 2007), and author or co-editor of numerous articles and volumes on medieval and early modern history, theology and philosophy.

H. (Henk) van den Belt
(1971), Ph.D. (2006) Leiden University, is Professor of Reformed Theology: Sources, Development, and Context at the University of Groningen. He is the author of *The Authority of Scripture in Reformed Theology: Truth and Trust* (Brill, 2008) and of several articles on Reformed Orthodoxy and on neocalvinism; he also edited *Restoration Through Redemption: John Calvin Revisited* (Brill, 2013).

W.A. (William) den Boer
(1977), Ph.D. (2008) Theological University Apeldoorn, Postdoctoral researcher in Early Modern Reformed Theology at the Theological University Kampen, and Research Associate at the Jonathan Edwards Centre, University of the Free State, South Africa. He is author of *God's Twofold Love. The Theology of Jacob Arminius (1559–1609)* (Vandenhoeck&Ruprecht, 2010), and author or editor of several books and articles on church history and historical theology.

G.A. (Gert) van den Brink
(1974), Ph.D.candidate, Evangelische Theologische Faculteit Leuven, minister in the Hersteld Hervormde Kerk. He is the author of *Herman Witsius en het antinomianisme* (Institute for Reformation Research, 2008), and of several articles on historical theology; he is the co-author of *Scholastic Discourse: Johannes*

Maccovius (1588–1644) on Theological and Philosophical Distinctions and Rules (Institute for Reformation Research, 2009). He has published also in the field of apologetics.

J.C. (Elco) van Burg

(1983), Ph.D. (2010) Free University of Amsterdam (VU), is Associate Professor of Entrepreneurship and Organization at that university. His research has focused on the concept of internal and external calling in the theology of Petrus van Mastricht (1630–1706).

R.A. (Riemer) Faber

(1961), Ph.D. (1992) University of Toronto. He is Associate Professor of Classical Studies at the University of Waterloo, and Director of the Waterloo Institute for Hellenistic Studies. His research interests include Greek and Latin philology and literary criticism, and neo-Latin, and he has published widely in these fields. Most recently he co-edited *Belonging and Isolation in the Hellenistic World* (University of Toronto Press, 2013).

R. (Rein) Ferwerda

(1937), Ph.D. (1965) Free University of Amsterdam (VU). He served as *Rector Gymnasii* in Ede from 1968 until 1993, Visiting Professor of Latin at Hope College, Holland (Michigan) from 1967 until 1968. He is the author of *La signification des images et des mëtaphores dans la pensée de Plotin* (Wolters, 1965), and has published Dutch translations of the works of Aristotle, Democritus, Diogenes Laertius, Empedocles, Plato, Plotinus and Sextus Empiricus. He has translated also the works of Saint Gregory Palamas, into English. He is the author of *Lof der Scepsis* (Klement, 2003).

P.J. (Philip) Fisk

(1959), Th.M. (2008) Westminster Theological Seminary, Philadelphia, is Research Assistant at the Evangelische Theologische Faculteit, Leuven. He is the author of three peer-reviewed articles on issues pertaining to Reformed Orthodoxy, and of two forthcoming articles on Jonathan Edwards against the background of Reformed scholasticism.

A.J. (Albert) Gootjes

(1979), Ph.D. (2012) Calvin Theological Seminary. He has authored *Claude Pajon (1626–1685) and the Academy of Saumur: The First Controversy over Grace* (Brill, 2014), and has published several articles on seventeenth-century French Protestantism. He is also the translator of numerous articles and books on the history of Reformation and post-Reformation theology.

H.-J.M.J. (Harm) Goris

(1960), Ph.D. (1996) Catholic Theological University Utrecht. He is Senior Lecturer at the School of Catholic Theology, Tilburg University. He is the author of *Free Creatures of an Eternal God. Thomas Aquinas on God's Infallible Foreknowledge and Irresistible Will* (Peeters, 1996), and served as co-editor of several books and articles, in particular on the thought of Thomas Aquinas.

H.J. (Jan) van Helden

(1979), MA (Philosophy, 2007) M.Phil. (Theology, 2011) Free University of Amsterdam (VU), Minister of the Nederlands Gereformeerde Kerk at Amsterdam-centrum. He is co-editor of the Dutch theological journal *Soteria*, author of several articles on systematic and historical theology, and is preparing a research project on the relation between the sovereignty of God and human freedom in nineteenth century liberal theology and Dutch neo-Calvinism.

P.L. (Pieter) Rouwendal

(1973), MA (2002) Utrecht University. Independent scholar. He is currently completing a dissertation on *Predestination and External Calling in Geneva, From Calvin to Pictet* (Free University of Amsterdam). He is the (co-)author of several books and articles on church history and historical theology, including *Calvin's Forgotten Classical Position on the Extent of the Atonement: About Sufficiency, Efficiency and Anachronism* (Westminster Theological Journal, 2008), and *Introduction to Reformed Scholasticism* (Reformation Heritage Books, 2011).

R.T. (Dolf) te Velde

(1974), Ph.D. (2010) Theological University Kampen, and currently Postdoctoral Researcher at that university. He is the author of *The Doctrine of God in Reformed Orthodoxy, Karl Barth, and the Utrecht School* (Brill, 2013), and of several articles on systematic and historical theology; he co-edited *Reformed Thought on Freedom* (Baker Academic, 2010).

A. (Antonie) Vos

(1944), Ph.D. (1981) Utrecht University, Research Professor at the Evangelische Theologische Faculteit, Leuven. He has (co-)published widely in philosophy and the history of medieval philosophy, systematic theology and the historical theology from the sixteenth to the eighteenth century, including *Contingency and Freedom* (Springer, 1994), *Duns Scotus on Divine Love* (Ashgate, 2003), and *The Philosophy of John Duns Scotus* (Edinburgh University Press, 2006).

Acknowledgements

On behalf of the research group Classic Reformed Theology (Oude Gereformeerde Theologie), the editors would like to take this opportunity to express their gratitude for the support provided by a number of institutions and individuals. In particular, we thank the Theologische Universiteit Kampen (TUK), the Theologische Universiteit Apeldoorn (TUA), and the Evangelical Theological Faculty of Leuven University (ETF), for sponsoring the research group and its current project, the three-volume edition of the *Synopsis of a Purer Theology*. Besides giving financial support, the involvement of personnel from these institutions served to propel this project in a timely fashion.

We are grateful to the Theologische Universiteit Kampen for extending a visiting professorship to Riemer Faber from January until July 2013; this permitted him to participate more directly in the meetings of the research group, to expedite the editing of this volume, and to continue the work of translation. The professorship was supported also by subsidies from the Koninklijke Smilde Fonds, the Vicariefonds RDO *Balije van Utrecht*, and the University of Waterloo, Canada.

The Theological University Kampen generously sponsored and hosted a symposium on November 28, 2012, called "Synergy and Synopsis: The Advantages of Interdisciplinary Collaboration in the *Synopsis Purioris Theologiae* Project." Additional support for this symposium, and for other activities of the research group, was provided by the *Netherlands School for Advanced Studies in Theology and Religion* (NOSTER). On June 14, 2013, the Scaliger Institute of the University of Leiden kindly served as host for a workshop entitled "Scholastic Disputations and the *Synopsis Purioris Theologiae*." We are grateful to Dr. Martine Zoeteman-van Pelt and Dr. Jacob van Sluis for their participation in this workshop.

We thank Stichting Afbouw Kampen for subsidizing some of the publication costs for this volume; further support has been offered by the Stichting Jagtspoel Fonds and the Studiefonds van de Gereformeerde Bond of the Protestant Church.

The Faculty of Religious Studies (University of Utrecht) and the Faculty of Catholic Theology (Tilburg University) are thanked for allowing the Classic Reformed Theology research group to use their offices for its regular plenary meetings. The purpose of these meetings was to address problems in establishing the Latin text and its meaning, and in matters of translation, annotation, and explanation. For effective organizational arrangement the research group was divided into three teams, each of which was responsible for supervising

the production of the disputations that comprise the *Synopsis*. We would like to thank the leaders of each team for their role in co-ordinating the activities of its members and encouraging them in their tasks: Henk van den Belt and "team Utrecht"; Philip J. Fisk and "team Leuven"; and Dolf te Velde and "team Dordrecht." Dolf te Velde deserves special mention for completing his duties in editing volume 1.

The members of the teams are listed in the Notes on Contributors. In addition to them, we would like to thank several individuals who offered their expertise and time to the project. These include Siebold Schipper, who assisted William den Boer by researching the various editions of the *Synopsis Purioris Theologiae* and checking the accuracy of the reference to Bible-passages. Johan Mouthaan assisted Rein Ferwerda in determining the Latin text; he identified explicit and implicit references to classical authors, church fathers, medieval and contemporary theologians and philosophers. Wilco Veltkamp contributed many of the brief biographies of the students who served as respondents to the original disputations. Ben Wiskerke provided assistance to the volume-editor, Dolf te Velde. Wendy Mayer, Ray Laird, Stephen G. Burnett, and Lillian Wheeler are thanked for their help in finding the sources for several citations. The ongoing support of several others will receive due attention in subsequent volumes.

Finally we would like to thank Arjan van Dijk, Brill's senior acquisitions editor, as well as editor Ivo Romein and series editor Andrew Colin Gow, Texts & Sources subseries editor Falk Eisermann and the editorial board of Brill's series *Studies in Medieval and Reformation Traditions* for their enthusiastic support for this edition, and for their assistance throughout the entire process.

Willem J. van Asselt, William den Boer, Riemer A. Faber
April 2014

List of Abbreviations

AW	Athanasius Werke. Berlin: De Gruyter, 1996–.
BLGNP	D. Nauta, and others, eds. *Biografisch Lexicon voor de Geschiedenis van het Nederlands Protestantisme*. 6 vols. Kampen: Kok, 1978–2006.
CCCM	Corpus Christianorum Continuatio Medievalis. 267 vols. Turnhout: Brepols, 1966–.
CCSL	Corpus Christianorum Series Latina. 194 vols. Turnhout: Brepols, 1953–.
COGD	G. Alberigo and A. Melloni, eds. *Conciliorum Oecumenicorum Generaliumque Decreta*. Corpus Christianorum. Turnhout: Brepols, 2007–.
COR	Ioannis Calvini opera omnia denuo recognita et adnotatione critica instructa notisque illustrata. Geneva: Droz, 1992–.
CR	Karl Gottlieb Bretschneider, and others, eds. Corpus reformatorum. 101 vols. Halle: Schwetske, 1834-
CSEL	Corpus Scriptorum Ecclesiasticorum Latinorum. 95 vols. Wien: Verlag der Österreichischen Akademie der Wissenschaften, 1866–.
DLGTT	Richard A. Muller. *Dictionary of Latin and Greek Theological Terms: Drawn Principally from Protestant Scholastic Theology*. Grand Rapids: Baker, 1985.
DH	Heinrich Denzinger. (Edited by Peter Hünermann, based on the 32th edition by Adolf Schönmetzer, 1963.) *Enchiridion symbolorum definitionum et declarationum de rebus fidei et morum*. 43rd ed. Freiburg: Herder, 2010. English translation, edited by Robert Fastiggi and Anne Englund Nash: *Compendium of Creeds, Definitions, and Declarations on Matters of Faith and Morals*. San Francisco: Ignatius Press, 2012.
FC	Fontes Christiani. Freiburg: Herder / Turnhout: Brepols, 1990–.
GCS	Die griechischen Christlichen Schriftsteller der ersten Jahrhunderte. Leipzig: J.C. Hinrichs and Berlin: Akademie Verlag, 1897–.
GNO	Gregorii Nysseni Opera. Leiden: Brill, 1952–.
LCL	The Loeb Classical Library, at present edited by Jeffrey Henderson. 521 vols. Cambridge, MA: Harvard University Press, 1911–.
Mansi	Giovanni Domenico Mansi, ed. *Sacrorum conciliorum nova et amplissima collectio*. 60 vols. Paris: Hubert Welter, 1907–1927.
MPG	J.P. Migne, ed. Patrologiae Cursus Completus Series Graeca. 161 vols. Paris: Garnier, 1857–1866.
MPL	J.P. Migne, ed. Patrologiae Cursus Completus Series Latina. 221 vols. Paris: Sirou, 1844–1865.
NNBW	P.C. Molhuysen and P.J. Blok, eds. *Nieuw Nederlandsch Biografisch Woordenboek*. 10 vols. Leiden: A.W. Sijthoff, 1911–1937.

NPNF1	Philip Schaff and Henry Wace, eds. Nicene and Post-Nicene Fathers. First series. Reprint; Peabody: Hendrickson, 1995.
NPNF2	Philip Schaff and Henry Wace, eds. Nicene and Post-Nicene Fathers. Second series. Reprint; Peabody: Hendrickson, 1995.
OS	Petrus Barth and Wilhelm Niesel, eds. Ioannis Calvini Opera Selecta. 5 vols. Munich: Kaiser, 1926–1936.
PRRD	Richard A. Muller. *Post-Reformation Reformed Dogmatics: The Rise and Development of Reformed Orthodoxy, ca. 1520 to ca. 1725*. 4 vols. Grand Rapids: Baker Academic, 2003.
PTS	Patristische Texte und Studien. Berlin: De Gruyter, 1964–.
RC	Thomas Rees, trans. and ed., *The Racovian Catechism, with Notes and Illustrations, Translated from the Latin: To Which is Prefixed a Sketch of the History of Unitarianism in Poland and the Adjacent Countries*. London: Longman, Hurst, Rees, Orme, & Brown, 1818.
RTF	Willem J. van Asselt, J. Martin Bac, and Roelf T. te Velde, eds. *Reformed Thought on Freedom: The Concept of Free Choice in the History of Early-Modern Reformed Theology*. Texts and Studies in Reformation and Post-Reformation Thought. Grand Rapids: Baker Academic, 2010.
SC	Sources Chrétiennes. Paris: Cerf, 1942–.
SPT	*Synopsis Purioris Theologiae* [the present work].
USTC	Universal Short Title Catalogue. Hosted by the University of St Andrews. http://ustc.ac.uk/index.php.
VD16	Verzeichnis der im deutschen Sprachbereich erschienenen Drucke des 16. Jahrhunderts. www.vd16.de
VD17	Verzeichnis der im deutschen Sprachbereich erschienenen Drucke des 17. Jahrhunderts. www.vd17.de
WA	Ulrich Köpf, and others, eds. D. Martin Luthers Werke: Kritische Gesamtausgabe. 127 vols. Weimar: Böhlau, 1883–2009.
WCF	*Westminster Confession of Faith*. In Philip Schaff, ed., and David S. Schaff, rev., *The Creeds of Christendom: With a History and Critical Notes*, vol. 3, *The Evangelical Protestant Creeds*, 598–673. 6th ed., Grand Rapids: Baker, 1990.

Introduction

1 The Synopsis as Handbook of Scholastic Reformed Theology

This bilingual edition of the *Synopsis Purioris Theologiae* makes available for the first time to English readers a seminal treatise of Reformed Scholasticism. Composed by four professors of Leiden University, it gives an exhaustive yet concise presentation of Reformed theology as it was conceived in the first decades of the seventeenth century. During the remainder of the seventeenth century, the *Synopsis* had a prominent place as a theological handbook for use in training Reformed ministers in the Netherlands. The following Introduction gives a brief sketch of the historical and literary background of the *Synopsis*. (A more detailed account of the historical and theological contexts will be provided in Volume 3.) Next, an outline is given of the theological topics covered in the first 23 disputations of this volume, and important aspects of scholastic methodology and conceptuality are pointed out. The Introduction closes with some practical features of this edition.

Originally the *Synopsis Purioris Theologiae* consisted of a cycle of public disputations held in the Leiden theology faculty from 1620 to 1624.[1] In 1596 this faculty had started a cycle of disputations that covered all the topics of Reformed dogmatics, and during the next thirteen years the cycle was repeated five times. After the death of Jacobus Arminius (1609) and the departure of Franciscus Gomarus (1611), the theological faculty of Leiden had been shaken by the ecclesiastical difficulties that would be resolved by the Synod of Dort (1618/19). Following Dort's rejection of the Remonstrant teachings on grace and predestination, the Remonstrant spokesman Simon Episcopius (1583–1643) was removed from his teaching post, and new professors were appointed to join Johannes Polyander (1568–1646), who was then the only professor of theology. Toward the end of 1619, Antonius Walaeus (1572–1639) and Antonius Thysius (1565–1640) delivered their inaugural lectures at Leiden. The first disputation of a new cycle was defended on 6 February 1620, with Johannes Polyander presiding. For the first nine disputations Polyander, Walaeus and Thysius composed the theses and presided in turn, as was the custom in disputation cycles. In the fall of 1620, Andreas Rivetus (1573–1651) was added to the theological faculty, and

---

[1] For more details on the theological disputations at Leiden, see Donald Sinnema and Henk van den Belt, "The *Synopsis Purioris Theologiae* (1625) as a Disputation Cycle," *Church History and Religious Culture* 92.4 (2012): 506–513, 515–519.

immediately joined the cycle of public disputations started by his colleagues. From disputation ten on the four colleagues presided in this order: Polyander, Rivetus, Walaeus, Thysius.[2]

Reformed scholastic theology as presented in the *Synopsis* has a multifaceted character that is reflected in features of the text. It arises from an ecclesiastical background in the Reformed churches that were established in the Netherlands in the middle of the sixteenth century, and that had experienced a process of consolidation and conflict between 1570 and 1620. As the word "purer" in the title of the *Synopsis* points out, the authors position themselves explicitly in line with the orthodox Reformed teaching that had been articulated at the great Synod of Dort in 1618–1619. The newly appointed faculty at Leiden thought it important to display theological unity. For that reason the four professors mostly acted jointly, and so prevented the rise of disagreements within the theological faculty.[3] From their decidedly Reformed perspective they defined their Christian doctrine in contrast with alternative or opposite views.

At the same time, the *Synopsis* should be understood as a properly academic handbook of theology. The Leiden professors entered the arena of academic theology, and gave an account of the substantial and methodological presuppositions of their position. Familiar with discussions and opinions of their own time, well-versed in literatures ranging from classical antiquity and the early church to medieval theology and the Reformation, they argued their views in a concise but pointed way with clarity, precision, and logical reasoning.

Both on the academic level and on the ecclesiastical level, the *Synopsis* responds to challenges coming from the immediate context of the early seventeenth century. One century after the Reformation began, the Catholic church still posed enormous intellectual and practical challenges to the emerging Reformed churches. Groups that were labeled as Anabaptists, Spiritualists, or Libertines, presented alternative modes of belief and behavior from an entirely different perspective that could not be ignored by the Reformed theologians in the Netherlands. In addition to these more recognizable ecclesiastical frontiers,

---

2 See Sinnema and Van den Belt, "Disputation Cycle," 517–519. More information on the four professors and on the academic context in which they were teaching appears in Volume 3.

3 Walaeus's son reported later that the professors were concerned to avoid division within the theological faculty. They even decided not to pass their judgments on a controversy separately, but only together as colleagues; no theses were to be disputed publicly unless all colleagues had seen and approved them. See "Vita Antonii Walaei," in Antonius Walaeus, *Opera Omnia* (Leiden, 1647), 1:[27].

Reformed theology was confronted also with such movements of thought as Socinianism and other forms of anti-trinitarian thought that manifested themselves in the mid-sixteenth century.

As a compendium of Reformed theology, the *Synopsis Purioris Theologiae* engages the church fathers, various medieval *doctores*, and especially the Reformers and post-Reformation theologians. It provides a broad framework indispensable for all those who wish to understand the content of the Post-Reformation Reformed tradition, and to explore the wide range of viewpoints it embraces. Until the mid-twentieth century, Scholasticism (whether Catholic or Protestant) was considered an early-modern philosophical and theological *school of thought* consisting of certain precepts.[4] More recently, however, it is viewed that the term denotes not particular principles, but an educational approach. It is now held that Scholasticism refers to the teaching practices of the late-medieval universities, a *methodology* characterized by the use of a system of definitions, distinctions, argumentative techniques and styles of disputation. Appreciation of Scholasticism as a method of scholarly discourse has led to the realization that it is a feature not just of the Early Modern period, but also of the Renaissance. In fact, "… recent historical reappraisals of Protestant Scholasticism have concluded that the contrast so often drawn between Scholasticism, Reformation, and Humanism is outdated … these phenomena turn out to be closely related to each other."[5]

2 Genre and Form

Various genres of writing existed in early modern scholasticism. One of these is the disputation, which originated in the medieval university and which

---

[4] See, for example, Alexander Schweizer, *Die protestantischen Centraldogmen in ihrer Entwicklung innerhalb der Reformirten Kirche*, 2 vols. (Zurich: Orell, Fueslli & comp., 1854, 1856), esp. 1: 1–19.

[5] Richard A. Muller, "The Problem of Protestant Scholasticism—A Review and Definition," in: Willem J. van Asselt and Eef Dekker (eds.), *Reformation and Scholasticism: An Ecumenical Enterprise*, Texts and Studies in Reformation and Post-Reformation Thought (Grand Rapids: Baker Academic, 2001), 45–64, there 48; John Platt, *Reformed Thought and Scholasticism: The Arguments for the Existence of God in Dutch Theology, 1575–1650*, Studies in the History of Christian Thought, vol. 29 (Leiden: Brill, 1982), 239; Willem J. van Asselt, Michael D. Bell, Gert van den Brink, and Rein Ferwerda, *Scholastic Discourse: Johannes Maccovius (1588–1644) on Theological and Philosophical Distinctions and Rules* (Apeldoorn: Instituut voor Reformatieonderzoek, 2009), 3.

was re-introduced in the newly instituted academies of the sixteenth century. Other genres of scholastic writing are *Loci communes*, doctrinal digressions that arose from exegetical commentaries and that later were compiled in a more or less coherent order. There also were manuals based on catechetical or undergraduate instruction; these were called *Compendia, Medullae*, or *Systemata*; and treatises modeled on the great medieval examples of the method of the scholastic 'question' (*quaestio*).[6]

These genres share important features: a clear demarcation of the topic under discussion; a keen interest in definitions; a comprehensive treatment of relevant aspects by means of a topical structure; frequent usage of distinctions, partly to anticipate a treatment of the subject's various elements, partly to solve difficulties that are implied in the initial, undifferentiated statement; explicit statements of proofs and arguments supporting one's own position, and a corresponding refutation of counter-arguments. In fact, the 'question' structure, as the elementary tool of medieval scholastic inquiry, is recognizable in its application throughout the various genres of scholastic texts. Even when the 'question' structure is not followed explicitly, the techniques of definition, distinction, logical reasoning and refutation of objections are typical of scholastic discourse. The differences between the aforementioned genres consist in the degree of sophistication and detail and in the purpose of the work, which may be either didactic or polemical. Within the range of scholastic literature, the disputation tends to present a concise, lapidary discourse that encompasses the whole topic.

Along with lectures and practice sermons, disputations on theological topics formed an integral part of the education of theology students at Leiden. The common disputation, like its medieval predecessor, was intended to exercise the students' thinking power and skill in debate and discussion, and to help them digest what they learned. In the public disputation, one of the professors would preside, and a number of theses on the given topic would be defended by a student (called the 'respondent')[7] against the attacks of one or more fellow students (called 'opponents'). The set of theses, printed up beforehand by the

---

6 Cf. Muller, *PRRD* 1:202–203.

7 Brief biographical information of the respondents of the disputations included in the *Synopsis* is provided at the beginning of each disputation. For further information on disputations generally see Olga Weijers, "The Medieval *Disputatio*," and Joseph S. Freedman, "Disputations in Europe in the Early Modern Period," pp. 23–29 and 30–50 respectively, in Douwe D. Breimer and others, *Hora Est! On Dissertations*, Kleine Publicaties van de Leidse Universiteitsbibliotheek, vol. 71 (Leiden: Universiteitsbibliotheek Leiden, 2005).

university, was usually drafted by the presiding professor and given to the student to defend, but sometimes by the student himself and approved by the professor.

As indicated above, the cycle of disputations held from 1620 to 1624 was intended for publication as a handbook of theology. The complete work contains fifty-two disputations (chapters), and in the current edition these will be published in three volumes. Disputations 1–23, presented in this volume, consist of thirty to sixty 'theses' each; some of the later disputations are considerably longer. One thesis is a paragraph that contains a single stage in the overall argument. The structures, concepts, and arguments provided in the brief format of numbered theses point to more elaborate oral reasoning that probably was treated in the public disputations in which the 'respondents' participated.

In arranging the material, the authors of the *Synopsis* commonly follow this Aristotelian pattern of topical questions: What does the term mean? Does the object exist? What is it? What are its parts? What specific aspects can be discerned? What are the causes of the object? What effects or consequences follow from it? To what other entities is it related? What things are the opposite or contradictory to it?

In the more detailed arrangement, the authors of the *Synopsis* often proceed by distinguishing four so-called 'causes': the efficient cause; the formal cause or "form"; the material cause or "matter"; and the final cause or goal. Whereas this scheme originates from Aristotelian philosophy, it had been emptied of its (meta)physical connotations by medieval Christian philosophers. As the Reformed scholastic authors of the early seventeenth century use it, only the "efficient cause" and the "final cause" have true causal force. The "efficient cause" identifies the agent that brings a thing into existence. The "final cause" points to the reason or goal for which the "efficient cause" performs its function. Contrary to the original Aristotelian meaning, the "formal cause" and the "material" cause were no longer understood as active principles on the ontological level (form and matter that constitute individual existence) but as heuristic devices. The "form" indicates the essential (or formal) definition to which an entity should conform in order to be precisely that entity. "Matter" points to the object or material to which an act or event is directed.

One could consider Disputation 22, "On the Gospel," as an illustration of the structure of a disputation:

1	Basic statement of the topic	
2–6	Etymology of the term "Gospel"	
	2	General usage in secular authors
	3	Specific meaning in Holy Scripture

	4	In the general sense (the promise of salvation through Christ)
	5	In the specific sense (the account of the life of Christ)
	6	In the extended sense of the Gospel being preached
7		The principal, efficient cause: God Triune

In view of the decree (8) and the actual declaration (9) of the Gospel

- 10–11 The ascription of the Gospel to each of the three divine Persons
- 12–13 God's mercy as the impelling cause of the Gospel
- 14–18 The mediate and immediate declaration of the Gospel through different times and people
- 19 Christ incarnate as the proper subject of the Gospel

20–21 The object or address of the Gospel, indefinite (all people) and definite (God's children)

22 The 'form' of the Gospel: full proclamation of saving grace

23–31 Goal (*finis*) and effects of the Gospel
- 23 The ultimate goal: God's glory
- 24 The nearest goal: salvation for those who believe
- 25 The perdition of unbelievers as improper effect, arising from their own sin
- 26–29 The saving transfer of the faithful to God's kingdom
- 30 Names for the Gospel in view of these effects
- 31 Evil consequences are no proper effect of the Gospel

32–55 Gospel and Law
- 33–35 The 'mandates' of the Gospel: repentance and faith
- 36–37 Refutation of errors concerning the 'new mandates' of Christ
- 38–45 The 'mandates of Christ' in conformity with the commandments of the Decalogue
- 46–51 Specific refutation of the Socinian view of the 'mandates'

52 Agreement and different between Gospel and Law, as to promises (53–54) and threats (55)

56 Use of the Gospel

This basic structure is recognizeable in various applications according to different subject-matters. In what follows next, the structure of individual disputations will be elucidated only in sections that contain particularly complicated arguments, for example when two or more systematic questions are evoked simultaneously and they are answered in several subsequent theses.

3 Survey of the Contents of Volume One

The first twenty-three disputations of the *Synopsis* may be divided into five clusters that show the basic lines of scholastic Reformed theology:

1. Scripture as the Foundation of Theology (disputations 1–5);
2. The Triune God (6–9);
3. The Creation of the World (10–12);
4. Humanity as Creatures Fallen into Sin (13–17);
5. God's Address to Humanity in Law and Gospel (18–23).

The following sections give a summary account of these doctrines. A few points will be expounded in more detail in order to give a sense of the conceptual and argumentative strategies of Reformed scholastic theology.

3.1 *Scripture as the Foundation of Theology*

Theology is understood fundamentally as "the knowledge of God." The ultimate source of our knowledge of God lies in the intimate self-knowledge of God as Father, Son, and Holy Spirit. The authors of the *Synopsis* state that as humans we are limited in our understanding and access to the divine knowledge. Instead, we receive what God wills to make known to us by his revelation. Revelation, as the source of theology, consists mainly in the operation of the Holy Spirit in prophets, apostles, and other biblical writers, and it surpasses the natural abilities of mankind. The way in which theology receives and reflects God's self-communication can be described by two terms: 'knowledge' and 'wisdom.' Theology is knowledge, since it produces certain and definite knowledge of the divine truth; theology is wisdom, because it is concerned with a reality that exceeds regular knowledge, and because it gives guidance to a way of life that stands in service of God's glory.

Fundamentally speaking, theology is about God and it depends on God in every respect. The *means* by which we can know God is his self-revelation; the *quality* of theology is its conformity with God's own truth; its *goal* it is to know and to glorify God, and thereby to find man's own ultimate destiny of happiness. This consistent reference to God in every respect gives to theology an inner unity that is preserved through all ages and in all forms of expression.

This fundamental choice of God's revelation as source of our knowledge of God is elaborated in four disputations devoted to the doctrine of Scripture (disp. 2–5). At first glance, this appears as a typically Protestant feature, developed during the debates between Roman Catholicism and the Reformed

faith about the 'sola Scriptura' principle. Beneath the surface, however, lies a deeper continuity that connects the *Synopsis* with the theological tradition of the church fathers and medieval doctors. Throughout the ages, theology rested upon biblical exegesis, upon the reading of the 'sacred page' (*sacra pagina*). This continuing orientation on Scripture becomes more pointed in the debates about the necessity, the authority, and the perfection of Scripture with both Catholic theology and Anabaptist or Spiritualist movements.

At one end of the polemical spectrum stands the Catholic church—although the authors of the *Synopsis* are aware of the fact that the position of this church during the late fifteenth to early seventeenth century is certainly not representative of the whole tradition of Catholic theology, and therefore they often refer to the "papal theologians" (*Pontificii Doctores*). According to the authors of the *Synopsis*, these Catholic opponents posit unwritten tradition next to Scripture, and they claim a decisive role for the doctrinal authority of the church. It seems as though to them the church and Christians can do without Scripture; that the Bible needs the support of ecclesiastical authority, and that it is understood only by the authoritative interpretation of the church.

At the other end of the spectrum several Anabaptist groups appear. Also referred to as Libertines or Spiritualists, they are seen as making an appeal to the direct inspiration of the Holy Spirit apart from God's verbal revelation in Scripture. Originating in the 'Radical Reformation' of the sixteenth century, Anabaptist congregations were spread throughout Holland and the other provinces of the Netherlands.

Against both frontiers the *Synopsis* deploys its view that the Bible is God's self-given disclosure of his salvific will. As Holy Scripture is of divine origin, there can be no higher authority in the church (disp. 2). As the Bible is the complete and perfect source of our knowledge of God, nothing additional is needed, either in the form of ecclesiastical traditions or in the form of present-day 'prophetic' revelations (disp. 4). Scripture possesses inherent clarity and the intrinsic power of convicting people of its own truth. This does not exclude the necessity of explanation and interpretation, but these shall have to refer back to Scripture itself and should not be subjected to external norms such as human reason (disp. 5).

One finds numerous references to passages from Scripture itself in defense of these statements. Scripture's own witness has a leading and corrective function in the theological reasoning of the *Synopsis*. The practice of referring briefly to biblical texts in fact reflects a more extensive exegetical tradition.[8]

---

[8] Given the high view of Scripture as source and norm of theology, the considerable number

This appeal to Scripture may have one of the following functions in the arguments of the *Synopsis*:

- It may be the formal starting point of the exposition;
- It may be adduced as "proof" or "evidence" for a previously developed train of thought;
- It may be the material that adds more substance or detail to the initial statement of a doctrinal point;
- It may be used as an argument in refuting opposing views, for example, the views of Catholic theologians or Socinians.

In addition to the biblical evidence, the authors of the *Synopsis* do not hesitate to use general arguments. They adduce many historical, literary, and moral arguments to support the divine authority of Scripture. Antonius Walaeus also notes that only by the operation of the Holy Spirit is one convinced effectively of the divine origin of Scripture (2.12). In arguing against Catholic theologians, the appeal to church fathers and medieval doctors ("the more sound ones," *saniores*; 5.4, 15.29) plays an important role. When discussing the Anabaptist position, the *Synopsis* often points to inconsistencies and absurdities.

3.2 The Triune God

In the next clusters of disputations, the *Synopsis* introduces—so to speak—the antagonists in the history of salvation: God (6–9) and humanity (13), connected by God's act of creation (10). This connection is crucial for the theology of the *Synopsis*: humans owe their existence to the free and gracious decision of God to create a world that contains humans with whom He can share his goodness. Consequently, humans are not God's equals, and our world is not a necessary entity which God 'needs.'

A central tenet of the *Synopsis* is the doctrine of God, from which several other teachings flow forth. In fact, the way in which God acts as Creator and Redeemer is grounded in who he is. Moreover, the account the *Synopsis* gives of the created world and of the relationship between God and the world is governed by substantial insights from the doctrine of God.

---

of mistakes occurring in the biblical references is suprising. In the texts that follow, obvious mistakes or printing errors will be tacitly corrected. In other cases, the authors evoke an entire passage by citing only one text; then the reader will have to reconstruct the implicit argument from the entire context. Finally, quotations may be wrong because the authors cited by heart, and then confused related but different places.

Four disputations of the *Synopsis* jointly provide an answer to the question "Who is God?" Disputation 6 deals with the essence and attributes of God; the next three disputations are devoted to God's being in three Persons, to the unique relation between the Father and the Son, and to the divinity of the Holy Spirit.

When the *Synopsis* was written at the turn of the seventeenth century, the denial of the existence of God was not an option. Consequently, the *Synopsis* declares the fact of God's existence in a few words, and it appeals to the general sense of divinity that is common to all people. This general sense does not lead to any definite knowledge of who God is. In fact, God's essence surpasses our understanding and our concepts. The *Synopsis* emphasizes that for knowing God's essence we are entirely dependent on what he gives us to know, and for that reason the divine names by which God makes Himself known in the Old and New Testaments form the introduction (6.10–16). When it later provides a summary description of the divine essence, the *Synopsis* makes an emphatic statement about God as the Triune, Father, Son, and Holy Spirit (6.17–18).

As an elaboration of the statements about God's essence, two groups of divine 'attributes' are discussed. These should not be understood as qualities that can be conceived apart from God's essence, but they approach his one essence from various perspectives and in various relations. The first series of attributes shows the unique character of God, his being totally different from us and our world (6.23–29). He is simple and undivided, he does not change, he is infinite and eternal and omnipresent. An interesting aspect in the presentation of these 'negative' properties, defining the difference between God and us, is that they are constantly substantiated with 'positive' biblical statements of the greatness, patience and everlasting truth of the Lord. In this way, the first group of attributes is intrinsically connected to the second group of properties that indicate God's being related to and involved in reality outside himself: God's knowledge and wisdom, God's will with its qualities ("affects") of goodness, love, justice and anger, and the power by which God executes his will (6.30–43). In a concise way, the *Synopsis* presents a doctrine of God that had been developed more extensively in prior decades by authors such as Jerome Zanchi (1516–1590) and Amandus Polanus (1561–1610).[9]

---

9 Jerome Zanchi, *De natura Dei, sive de divinis attributis: Libri v, Ad illustrissimum principem Joannem Casimirum, comitem Palatinum ad Rhenum* (Heidelberg: Jakob Müller, 1577), also included as vol. 2 in *Omnium operum theologicorum tomi octo* (Geneva: Gamonet & Aubert, 1605; repr. Geneva: Samuel Crispin, 1617–1619); Amandus Polanus a Polansdorf, *Syntagma theologiae christianae juxta leges ordini methodici conformatum* (Hanau: Weichel / Aubry, 1615), 130–198.

The next three disputations are devoted to God the Triune God, and they deal with the internal relations that constitute God's essence. While consciously accepting the Trinitarian dogma of the early church, the authors of the *Synopsis* provide their own unique emphases. The decisive starting-point for this doctrine is the biblical testimony. The biblical narrative of God, Jesus, and the Spirit, and the mutual relations between Father, Son, and Spirit that become evident in it, as well as the actions and functions performed by each of the three, can only be adequately summarized in the confession that God is one essence in three persons. From the perspective of the twenty-first century the appeal to Scripture seems to be of no significance to the 'immanent' and the 'economic' aspects of the Trinitarian language of Scripture. The *Synopsis* implicitly understands the salvation-historical level on which the Bible speaks of Father, Son, and Spirit as an expression of the underlying, immanently Trinitarian existence of God.

The emphasis on the biblical substantiation of the doctrine of the Trinity is accompanied by a cautious attitude toward speculative reasoning about the inner-Trinitarian relationships. A similar wariness can also be found in John Calvin, in an earlier stage of Reformed theology. It seems plausible that the rise of anti-trinitarian movements in the sixteenth century played an important role in this respect. By raising acute rational objections to the traditional dogma, and by simplifying it into the question of whether God is one or three, radical spirits such as Michael Servet urged the Reformed to produce a cautious formulation of their belief in God as the Triune.[10] In the attempt to escape from the anti-trinitarian assaults, Calvin and his followers could be attacked from the other side by Catholic authors who uncritically maintained the whole traditional apparatus of terms and concepts. With obvious pleasure, Antonius Walaeus notes (8.18) that on this occasion Calvin is defended against Catholic opponents even by the great Catholic controversialist, Robert Cardinal Bellarmine.

The further investigation of the Trinitarian dogma presented in the Synopsis manifests some differences among the authors. Johannes Polyander (disp. 7) and Antonius Thysius (disp. 9) restrict themselves to explaining the traditional key terms *ousia* and *hypostasis* (7.3–9), the 'personal properties' that describe the mutual relations between the three Persons (7.10–14, 9.5–16), and the distinction of what should be said about God's operation toward the inside and

---

[10] On Calvin's debates with anti-trinitarian thinkers and the development of his own doctrine of the Trinity, see A. Baars, *Om Gods verhevenheid en Zijn nabijheid: De Drie-eenheid bij Calvijn* (Kampen: Kok, 2004).

toward the outside (*ad intra—ad extra*; 7.26, 9.8–13). After these basic explanations, they adduce biblical material as evidence for the doctrinal statements (7.16–20,40–49, 9.17–27). Disputation 8 by Antonius Walaeus on the relation between the Father and the Son is remarkable, as he addresses in a more penetrating way the questions concerning the eternal generation of the Son by the Father (8.6–17) and concerning the difference between the 'essential' and the 'personal' dimensions (8.18–22,31–33). In so doing, Walaeus touches upon themes and modes of argumentation that may be traced back via Anselm, the theologians of St. Victor (Richard and Hugh), and the Franciscan thinker Duns Scotus, to Augustine. An important motivation for this deeper investigation is the clarification that God's existence as Father, Son, and Spirit is not a 'loose' association depending on an accidental act of God's will. It seeks to clarify also that the triune existence cannot be reduced to a prior unity of essence; these three 'relations' have their own unique status and simultaneously constitute the essence of God.

Occasionally the authors of the *Synopsis* display an ecumenical attitude. In the well-known controversy between Eastern and Western Christianity over the *filioque*—whether the Holy Spirit proceeds from the Father alone or is spirated by Father and Son jointly—Antonius Thysius searches for formulations that combine both the Western and the Eastern interests (9.19). In conclusion, he states that "some have conveniently said, in keeping with the phraseology of some ancient authors, that the Father spirates the Holy Spirit through the Son, and that the Holy Spirit proceeds from the Father through the Son. For by that manner of speaking it is shown that He comes from both; and the mode of subsistence is shown, too; that is to say, He proceeds in a mediate and subordinate way from the Father through the Son." It seems plausible to associate this sensibility for Eastern theology with the actual contacts between the Greek-Orthodox church and Reformed, Calvinist theologians. It is remarkable that the 'solution' of the *filioque* problem presented in the *Synopsis* comes close to the outcome of ecumenical discussions of the last forty years.

3.3   *Creation*

The cluster of disputations (10–12) on the creation of the world addresses the fundamental question of the relationship between God and the world. Important insights from the doctrine of God are elaborated here, especially concerning the knowledge and the will of God. The *Synopsis* maneuvers between two extremes. On the one hand, there is the assumption that if God knows how things will happen, there is consequently no possibility of the opposite course of events, and thus everything is necessary. This necessity would eliminate any meaningful freedom on the creature's part, and God would have full moral

accountability for whatever evil that occurs in his world.[11] The other option is to cut the link between God and the world radically. Although God has brought the world into existence, he afterwards retreats and leaves the world to itself. Perhaps the divine foreknowledge can be upheld in this thought system, but there is no role for the divine will as an effective factor. Soon after the publication of the *Synopsis* in 1625, this latter view would gain great popularity under the name of 'Deism.'[12] The *Synopsis* uses the label "Epicureans" to indicate this position. The disputation on divine providence in particular reads as one continuous refutation of the Epicurean/deist assertion that God has no active involvement in the course of events in our world. As the *Synopsis* sees it, the biblical picture of God's interaction with the world and the creatures within it presupposes that in the created world everything depends on the will of God by which he gives effect and direction to the actions of creatures. Without God's continuous care and governance, the world couldn't even exist.

A striking element in the doctrine of creation is that the *Synopsis* pays attention to the Trinitarian aspect: while the work of creation is specifically ascribed ("appropriated") to the Father, the Son and the Spirit are fully involved in it as well (10.6–13). This articulation should not be understood in the sense that Arius and his followers take it, as if Christ (the Son) is a superior yet created intermediary agent or instrument by which God made the lower regions of creation. To the contrary, creation is a fully and uniquely divine work which he cannot and will not delegate to someone else. In his work of creation, God imparts his own goodness upon us.

Prominent among the specific concepts employed by the *Synopsis* to elucidate the relation between God and his creation is the notion of 'permission' (namely, of some evil things). Whereas John Calvin rejected this notion as placing God in the passive role of a mere spectator, subsequent Reformed thinkers continued to understand the idea of 'permission' as an indispensable element for describing the relation between God and a world where evil exists. If God's will is all-determining for our reality, how can this will include evil things? If God is infinitely good, isn't it impossible for him to will evil? On the other hand:

---

11   This 'determinist' assumption is mostly implicit in the discussions of the *Synopsis*. In other Reformed authors (e.g., John Calvin) one finds reference to the allegation of 'Stoic fate' as the utter consequence of the Reformed doctrine of divine providence. The discussion of the 'causes' of the first sin of Adam and Eve (14.21–23) shows that the authors of the *Synopsis* were aware of the possibility of a 'determinist' understanding of God's foreknowledge in relation to sin, and they explicitly rejected this understanding.

12   To be sure, in the *Dictionnaire* of Pierre Bayle (1697) the first occurrence of 'deisme' is in Pierre Viret's *Instruction chrétienne* of 1564.

if God is almighty, no evil can escape from his power and control. Three arguments help to illuminate the problem of evil in view of God's will:

a. First, it is denied that evil has an independent and foundational place in creation. Ontologically speaking, evil finds its basis in the good created by God, and it can only be the perversion of this good (11.20). In this respect, the *Synopsis* reiterates the classic notion, voiced by Augustine, of evil as a "deprivation of the good" (*privatio boni*). Evil takes a created entity, and then deprives it of the good in which it was created by God.
b. Next, the question is addressed of how evil is included in God's will and decree pertaining to this world (11.21–24). The *Synopsis* introduces the distinction between a direct act and an indirect act of God's will. Since God is essentially good, he cannot will evil in a straightforward sense. Neither is God's will the cause of the existence of evil and of its being evil. Evil origins on the level of creatures, as the direct expression of disobedience to God's good will, or as the indirect consequence of such disobedience. That being said, evil is still not withdrawn from the will of God. God lets evil happen, and when it happens, creatures endowed with freedom of choice are responsible for it. But this 'letting it happen,' as an indirect act of God's will, is in turn willed by God.
c. God's permission of evil may stand in service of a higher goal. Of itself, it is preferable to make a world in which mind-gifted creatures have freedom of choice—and if they can choose the good, they can by definition also choose the bad—than to make a world without genuine freedom. God can also make use of evil for attaining specific goals, such as imposing punishment for sin. When God makes his good use of evil, this does not remove its evil character (11.25). The indirect and permitting will of God preserves the respective responsibilities God and creature have, each on their own level.

3.4 *The Human Being as Creature and Sinner*

The components of the doctrine of creation anticipate the themes that dominate the treatment of humankind in disputations thirteen to seventeen. Man is a specific instance of creature: special, because together with the angels he belongs to the rational and morally sensitive beings, particularly because he is destined for interaction with God. The extensive treatment of man as a good creature that has fallen into sin is a prelude to the treatment of salvation-history.

The disputation on man as created in God's image (13) mingles exegetical arguments, psychological insights drawing from philosophical anthropology, and a sketch of the original moral and spiritual integrity of man as the basis

for God's communion with humanity. Unlike part of the patristic tradition, the *Synopsis* rejects the idea of a meaningful difference between the terms "image" and "likeness" in the narrative of man's creation (13.36). This rejection implies that there is no division between the nature of man and the actual direction of man toward God and his will. Man was designed for loving, honoring and serving God. Apart from loving God, man after the fall remains human, but he no longer shows God's image.

A large part of the anthropology in the *Synopsis* is devoted to "sin" and its various aspects. This seems to be occasioned by the fact that the biblical story of creation is immediately followed by the tale of the fall. Consequently, the first sin of our 'parents' Adam and Eve is discussed (14). This discussion reveals important insights: the first sin was caused neither by God, nor by the devil. Sin is an act of the human will (14.20–33). This voluntary aspect of sin is retained throughout the following disputations. A connection is established between the first sin, long ago, and our actual existence as sinners (15). The *Synopsis* does not spell out *how* we are involved in the transgression of our first 'parents,' but insists on the willful character of even this 'inherited sin' (15.12). The extensive description of 'actual sin' (16) as the actively willed, self-chosen transgression of God's commandment makes it clear that sin is defined insufficiently by more 'passive' terms such as "concupiscence" or "loss of original justice."

A separate disputation (17) on free choice (*liberum arbitrium*) makes explicit what was implied in all preceding disputations on man. It belongs to man's perennial properties to have a will that acts not by natural necessity but by deliberate choices of alternative options. This freedom of the will, or free choice, is exercised differently according to the various stages of the history of mankind. Just like other Reformed theologians, the *Synopsis* applies the distinction of four "states" or phases of man, a distinction that draws on Augustine and that was phrased in an influential way by Bernard of Clairvaux. In the first state, man could by his free will do what God demanded of him, but he could by the same freedom also turn away from the good and choose for sin (17.15–17). Once man has chosen to sin, the second state commences, in which humans are subjected to the power of evil (17.18–26). Although humans do not in practice have the ability to choose for the good anymore, still the possibility of the good belongs to their freedom of choice. For that reason, it is due to their own act of will that they choose to sin and continue sinning. In the third state, God's grace enters human life (17.27–42). People are born again and they receive a new life through God's Spirit. In this phase, the regenerate man suffers from a duality, a conflict between the good Spirit of God and his own "flesh" that contains the remains of evil. The final phase, the state of glory, sets in after this

life (17.43). By the constant operation of God's grace, the human will then is so trained and confirmed in choosing the good that by the final and definitive withdrawal from the power of sin, it no longer has the option of choosing for evil.

3.5 God's Address to Humanity: Law and Gospel

The final cluster of disputations (18–23) published in this volume returns to the subject matter with which the *Synopsis* started: God's revelation in Scripture. It is presented here from the perspective of God's twofold address to humans in law and gospel. The discussions of idolatry (19), the legitimacy of the oath (20), the observance of the Sabbath or Sunday (21) are clearly related to actual controversies with Catholic and Anabaptist opponents of the early seventeenth century. One can also recognize in these themes a number of commandments from the Decalogue, but not all ten commandments are discussed individually.

The *Synopsis* deals with issues that affect the structure of God's covenant with his people and of the history of salvation. The *Synopsis* does not develop a separate doctrine of the covenant, but some basic elements of this doctrine are present. For example, the duality of God's promise of eternal life and God's demand of obedience is central to the structure of the covenant. When the idea of covenant is discussed in terms of the Old and New Testaments (disputation 23), the emphasis is on the covenant of grace established by God with humankind after the fall. In this one covenant of grace, two administrations or dispensations are distinguished: the law that promises life on condition of complete obedience to the commandments, and the gospel that offers life on condition of faith in Jesus Christ.

The argument of disputation 23 on the unity and diversity of Old and New Testament as two administrations of God's covenant of grace displays a certain ambiguity. On the one hand, the difference between Old and New Testament is stated in strong terms (23.5–7): the Old Testament is a law that merely demands, a letter that kills (2 Corinthians 3:6–7), because no one is able to fulfill the required obedience. The New Testament is the gospel of unmerited forgiveness and eternal life through the alien righteousness of Christ that should be accepted in faith. The other line of reasoning locates the difference in non-essential aspects such as the times and circumstances and the material vs. spiritual character of salvation (23.14–21). Underneath these differences lies a substantial unity, which is ultimately the person of Christ as the substance of the covenant in both administrations.

INTRODUCTION

4   Features of this Edition

4.1   *The Latin Edition*
The *Synopsis* has been published, in Latin, in six editions. As the date that appears at the end of the Preface reveals, the four co-authors had completed their editorial collaboration for the first edition towards the end of December of 1624. This edition, entitled *Synopsis Purioris Theologiae, Disputationibus quinquaginta duabus comprehensa*, was printed by Elzevier in Leiden, and bears the date of 1625. A second edition, substantially identical to the first, was issued seven years later as the *Synopsis Purioris Theologiae, Disputationibus quinquaginta duabus comprehensa ... Editio secunda, priori emendatior* (Leiden: Elzevier, 1632). As the titles of the second, and third, editions show, some emendations were made: *Synopsis Purioris Theologiae, Disputationibus quinquaginta duabus comprehensa ... Editio tertia, prioribus emendatior* (Leiden: Elzevier, 1642). These changes concern mainly printer's errors and orthography; some alterations of a more substantial nature are discussed below.

The popularity of the *Synopsis* is evidenced by the publication of a fourth edition ten years later, namely *Synopsis Purioris Theologiae, Disputationibus quinquaginta duabus comprehensa ... Editio quarta, prioribus emendatior* (Leiden: Elzevier, 1652). Six years after that, the publishing house of Ravensteyn in Amsterdam collaborated with Elzevier in issuing the fifth edition. It bears the title, *Synopsis Purioris Theologiae, Disputationibus quinquaginta duabus comprehensa ... Editio quinta, prioribus emendatior* (Leiden: Elzevier, 1658 / Amsterdam: Johannes Ravensteyn, 1658). With this edition, the printing history of the Synopsis came to an end, until the late nineteenth century, when the neo-calvinist movement in the Netherlands led to a renewed appreciation of seventeenth-century orthodox theology. Herman Bavinck produced the sixth and final edition, the *Synopsis Purioris Theologiae, Disputationibus quinquaginta duabus comprehensa ... Editio sexta, curavit et praefatus est Dr. H. Bavinck* (Leiden: Donner, 1881). This has remained the standard modern edition of the *Synopsis* until now.

The current edition takes as its starting point the text of the 1625 edition. For the sake of consistency and readability, this text has been adapted slightly in aspects of orthography and interpunction. Abbreviations such as SS in 1625 are written out in full: *Spiritus Sanctus*. So too for the ligatures. In 1625 references to Old and New Testament passages in the Latin text appear both in long- and in short-form (e.g.: "Joh. 3,16" instead of "Johan. 3,16"; "Rom. 2,5" instead of "Rom. 2 vers. 5"); these are written consistently and with deletion of "vers." or "v." in the current edition. Punctuation, such as full stops, comma's or question marks, has been brought in line with the edition of 1652, which had clarified the syn-

tax. Occasionally, lower-case letters were changed into capitals to conform to the later editions and for the sake of consistency; for example: *Vetus Testamentum* instead of *vetus Testamentum* (26.47), *Dei Filio* instead of *Dei filio*, *Sacra Scriptura* instead of *sacra Scriptura*.

It should be noted that this edition does not aim at providing extensive annotations of a text-critical nature. The primary aim is to present a text that is most accessible to the present-day reader. A careful comparison of variants in the texts in the extant twenty-one disputations pamphlets, the five seventeenth-century editions from 1625 to 1658, and Bavinck's 1881 edition has yielded a very small number of significant textual variants, and these have been noted. Since the fourth edition of 1652 approximates modern standards of orthography and interpunction most closely, we have preferred it to the original version of 1625 in this respect. Most alterations are minor shifts of spelling such as *loquutus*: *locutus*, *caetera*: *cetera*, *eserit*: *exserit*, *tanquam*: *tamquam*, *nuncius* (*and derivatives*): *nuntius*, *adnotare*: *annotare*, *precium*: *pretium*, *solennis*: *solemnis*, *estet*: *exstet*. Furthermore, original printer's errors were changed in later editions, for instance *acti* for *actus* (16.10). Errors of this sort are corrected without mention, including references to the Bible which in the 1625 edition were incorrect. Lastly, in some cases the differences between the first edition and later ones are given in a footnote. In a few instances, a footnote is added to the text of the first edition referring to the version of 1652, while in other cases we print the later text referring in a footnote to the version of 1625.

Although the differences between the various editions generally are small and insignificant, there are a few passages in which the editors of later editions employed stronger language, especially when it concerns the refutation of opponents. Two examples will suffice: in the first edition of 1625 (9.29) heretics are said "to have opinions" (*sentiunt*), but in the 1642, 1652 and 1881 they "act like madmen" (*insaniunt*). When referring to the Pope (49.47), the authors of the 1642, 1652 and 1881 editions add the words *et superbia* ("and haugthiness") to *antichristiana usurpatione* ("by an anti-Christian appropriation"). In this way they seem to distance themselves from their opponents. In a few cases, later editions (from 1642 onward) contain additional quotations (e.g., from Plato's *Laws* in 11.8).

The six editions of the *Synopsis* are inconsistent in giving titles of books and names of ancient and contemporary authors. The current edition follows the modern practice of giving the names of authors in roman letters, and book titles in italics. Exact quotations are referenced in the footnotes to the Latin text, and point to current scholarly editions.

4.2 The English Translation

The purpose of the accompanying English translation is twofold: first, to make the text of the *Synopsis Purioris Theologiae* accessible to readers who have received little or no training in the Latin language, and second, to convey the scholastic argument in the original text through a close rendering of the concepts, ideas, and modes of thought. In order to produce a translation that is as close to the original text as possible and as free as is necessary for a smooth reading in English, we have relied on several widely-accepted resources. As the diction of the *Synopsis* ranges widely from classical and biblical antiquity to contemporary times, we have consulted the standard classical,[13] medieval,[14] and neo-Latin[15] dictionaries and lexicons. Hebrew and Greek texts cited in the *Synopsis* generally appear in English translation only; the text of the original language is preserved when the author wishes to make a specific point about the quoted word or term. So too for terms of grammar, rhetoric, philosophy, and theology. For the highly developed technical language that marks the *Synopsis* as a product of Protestant scholasticism we have adopted the translations of standard reference works and current scholarly publications.[16] As the combined product of four different authors, and composed over a period of time, the *Synopsis* displays a considerably varied style of writing. Whenever possible, we have sought to preserve the language, tone, and sentence structure employed by each of the four writers. At the same time, as it was also the intent of the writers, we have sought to preserve the sense of overall unity through the consistent rendering of recurring terms and modes of expression.

---

13 Esp. P.G.W. Glare, *Oxford Latin Dictionary* (Oxford, reprint 2006), and C.T. Lewis, C. Short, *A Latin Dictionary*. Founded on Andrews' Edition of Freund's Latin Dictionary (revised edition, Oxford, 1980).

14 J.F. Niermeyer, *Mediae Latinitatis Lexicon Minus*. A Medieval Latin-French/English Dictionary (Leiden, 1954–1976), and R.E. Latham, et al., *Dictionary of Medieval Latin from British Sources* (Oxford, 1976–).

15 R. Hoven, *Lexique de la prose latine de la Renaissance / Dictionary of Renaissance Latin from Prose Sources*, second, revised edition (Leiden, 2006), and the online Neulateinische Wortliste, edited by J. Ramminger (http://ramminger.userweb.mwn.de/, accessed February 27, 2014).

16 Especially R.A. Muller, *Dictionary of Latin and Greek Theological Terms Drawn Principally from Protestant Scholastic Theology* (Grand Rapids, 1985); Van Asselt and others, *Scholastic Discourse*; and R.A. Muller, *Post-Reformation Reformed Dogmatics*, 4 vols. (Grand Rapids: Baker Academic, 2003).

4.3   *Annotations and Glossary*

As a text almost four hundred years old, the *Synopsis* is not immediately accessible to the present-day reader. The religious, cultural, and socio-political contexts in which it originated are reflected in numerous references and allusions. The specific character of this scholastic text implies that concepts, definitions, arguments and testimonies are used that require knowledge of Scripture, patristic and medieval theological literature, and elementary philosophy as it was taught in the early modern universities. Without such knowledge, the reader will at best get a rough sense of the world of thought transmitted by the *Synopsis*.

The footnotes which accompany the English translation provide the literary sources to which the authors of the *Synopsis* allude, and historical information about persons and events mentioned in the text. They explain the structure of complicated arguments, and give cross-references to other theses. The footnotes also define and explain concepts, distinctions, and specific arguments. Lastly, they also analyze and interpret doctrinal positions, especially when these might be misunderstood in light of later discussions of them.

A more general explanation of the key terms and distinctions that occur in disputations 1 to 23 is provided in the Glossary. Concepts included in the Glossary are marked by an asterisk in both the Latin and the English text. Since the Glossary is based on the Latin terms, the reader is enabled to compare the English rendering with the Latin original.

Text and Translation

Praefatio Ad Illustrissimos, Potentissimosque Hollandiae Westfrisiaeque Ordines.

Illustrissimi ac Potentissimi Domini Ordines,

Duo sunt Reipublicae Christianae firmamenta, *Veritas et Pax*: quarum illa spiritualis nostra cum Deo communio, hac mutua cum hominibus societas in his terris stabilitur. Veritati Propheta Zacharias, ut duci et magistrae, principem; Paci, ut pedissequae, proximum locum merito assignat, cum nos admonet, ut veritatem et pacem diligamus. Veritas etenim natura sua perpetuo est justa, Deo grata, eamque profitenti salutaris; Pax vero si a veritatis tramite deflectat, fit injusta, Deo exosa, et cuilibet eam sectanti exitialis. Hinc Apostolus Paulus quoslibet Christianos adhortatur, ut cum omnibus hominibus in pace vivant, sub hac duplici conditione, *quantum in ipsis est*, et, *si fieri potest*: salva nempe veritatis professione. Quod ii recte perpendentes quibus vos in hac illustri dignitate successistis, pacem quidem omni ratione colere ubique studuerunt, sed veritati subnixam, seu, ut dici solet, usque ad aras, vel potius usque ad aram nostram Iesum Christum, qui ipsissima est veritas, prout de sese pronuntiat.

Quanta enim fide, fortitudine et constantia illi veram Christi doctrinam verbo ipsius revelatam adversus immanes Antichristi, praecipuorumque ejus

Preface addressed to the most honorable and all-powerful States of Holland and West-Friesland

Most honorable, all-powerful, highly respected sovereign lords of the States-General,[1]

The two foundations of the Christian Republic are Truth and Peace. The former provides the basis of our spiritual relationship with God, while the latter is the basis on which we associate with fellow-humans here on earth. The prophet Zechariah, when he exhorts us to "love truth and peace,"[2] gives pride of place to the Truth, as she is leader and mistress; and he rightly grants the next place to Peace, as she is her attendant. For by its very nature the Truth is always fair and just, acceptable to God, and salutary to all who profess her. But Peace, if she should deviate from the pathway of Truth, would become unfair, offensive to God, and destructive to everyone who walks in her ways. Hence when the apostle Paul exhorts each and every Christian to dwell in peace with all fellow-humans, he makes only two restrictions: "as much as it lies within you" and "if it is possible"[3]—that is, on the condition that the truth be professed. And because the men who preceded you in this distinguished and noble office have pondered all this carefully, they were eager to foster peace at every turn and in every way, so long as it was grounded in the truth. Or, as the saying goes, they fostered peace 'right up to the altar'[4]—no rather, as far as *our* altar, Jesus Christ, who is the very embodiment of Truth, as he himself declared.[5]

Our own history offers a splendid illustration of the loyalty, courage, and constancy with which your predecessors fought in defense of the true teachings of Christ as revealed in his Word, over against the frightful attacks of the

---

[1] The States-General formed the confederate government of the provinces in the Lowlands and exercised political power throughout the Dutch Republic after 1587.

[2] Zechariah 8:19.

[3] Romans 12:18, where the complete text is: "If it be possible, as much as in you lies, live peaceably with everyone."

[4] The Latin saying *usque ad aras* means being committed to something or someone up to the point at which death or religious conviction prevents it. The proverb *usque ad aras amicus*, 'a friend as far as the altars,' was popularized by Erasmus, who included it in his *Adages* (3.ii.10). For Erasmus' explanation of the saying and its Greek origins, see R.A.B. Mynors, ed., *Collected Works of Erasmus*, vol. 34: *Adages* 1 vii–3 iii 100 (Toronto: University of Toronto Press, 1982), 228–229.

[5] John 14:6, "I am the way and the truth and the life."

administrorum, persecutiones propugnaverint, historiae nostri aevi luculenter ostendunt. Capitale olim erat pro libertate vestrae Reipublicae ac Religionis dimicare, causamque eorum tueri, qui a Romani Pontificis idololatria, fictisque traditionibus, vel latum unguem recesserant. Illi nihilominus in patriae libertatis vindicias magno incumbentes animo, primis tyrannorum Ecclesias reformatas opprimentium armis feliciter restiterunt. Eodem animo ac successu fidos Evangelii praecones in templa a cultus divini profanationibus repurgata introduxerunt, ut in iis tanquam in publicis almae veritatis theatris, sacram Scripturam aliquot seculis ab Antichristo obscuratam et oppressam, in lucem proferrent, plebemque ab illo misere seductam, per viam veritatis ad metam portumque salutis per Christum partae adducerent.

Quibus hoc praeterea beneficium accessit, quod ad verae Religionis pomoeria latius proferenda, quantum operae ac subsidii ad Ecclesias nostras per totam hanc Provinciam instaurandas contulerant; tantum studii et industriae ad Academicum omnium scientiarum, sed inprimis divinae, promptuarium, in hac urbe erigendum, impendere voluerint. Qua in re *vos Illustrissimi Domini Ordines*, quemadmodum et in ceteris virtutibus heroicis, Decessores vestros imitati, nostram hanc Academiam annis porro succedentibus, omnigena virorum eruditorum ad eam exornandam undecumque vocatione florentem praestitistis: remotisque heterodoxarum opinionum zizaniis, quae nonnulli apud nos disseminaverant, Theologiam orthodoxam, non modo in integrum restituistis, sed ab iniquis contradicentium criminationibus vestro quoque suffragio in Synodo Dordracena nuperrime liberatam, aucto insuper, qui Theologiam profiterentur, numero, in exoptato dignitatis fastigio collocastis.

Antichrist and his foremost henchmen. For there was a time when it was a capital offense to contend for the freedom of your Republic and its Religion and to defend the cause of those who retracted only so much as the 'width of a finger-tip' from the idolatry and feigned traditions of the Romanist pope.[6] And they applied an equally great amount of courage in vindicating the freedom of our fatherland when they succeeded, fortunately, in resisting the leading armies of the tyrants who oppressed the reformed churches. And it was with the same courage, and success, that they introduced faithful preachers of the Gospel to the churches after they were swept clean of the desecrations done to the divine worship-service, so that they could expose to the light of day, as if in open theatres of wholesome truth, the Holy Scriptures that had been obscured and oppressed by the Antichrist for so many ages, so that they might guide the common folk whom he had wretchedly led astray back along the path of truth to the goal, the harbour of salvation that Christ had obtained.

No, what is more, there was the added benefit that they expended very much effort and support for the restoration of our churches throughout this entire province, in order to expand the boundaries of true religion further. And it was their determination to bestow as much dedication and industry in establishing an academic storehouse for all the sciences in this city, but especially for that of Religion. And you, most honorable and sovereign lords, just as you followed your predecessors in the other heroic and meritorious deeds, so also in this matter did you follow them. For in subsequent years it was you who caused this our Academy to flourish, when you endowed it with the appointments of learned men from every quarter. And when the 'weeds'[7] of heterodox fancies were plucked out—weeds which some in our midst had caused to be spread abroad—you not only granted restoration and complete recovery to orthodox Theology, but you also lent your support when she was being freed from the false accusations of gainsayers at the recently-held Synod of Dordrecht. It was you who additionally increased the number of professors of Theology, thus raising it to the required full complement.

---

6 The Latin phrase, *latum unguem recedere*, 'to withdraw even the width of a finger-tip,' may be traced back to Plautus, *Aulularia* 57; given its context in the Preface, it seems more likely that the phrase is alluding to a proverbial saying by Cicero, *a recta conscientia transversum unguem non discedere*, 'one should not depart even a finger's breadth from a clear conscience' (*Letters to Atticus* 13.20.4; cf. *Ep. ad Fam.* 7.25). These and similar expressions of smallest possible space were listed by Erasmus in his treatise on the abundant style of writing; see C.R. Thompson, ed., *Collected Works of Erasmus*, vol. 23–24: *De Copia* 191 (Toronto: University of Toronto Press, 1982), 557.

7 By using the Greek loanword *zizania*, the authors seem to allude to the parable of the "Weeds among the Seeds" (Matthew 13:24–29).

Hanc vestram curam ac vigilantiam, qua hoc Ecclesiarum nostrarum seminarium maximis superiorum tempestatum periculis ereptum in solido ac sereno posuistis, aeternis laudibus colendam, venerandam ac praedicandam censemus. Ad quod publice testandum, hoc nostrae gratitudinis debitaeque observantiae monumentum, vobis nuncupamus, SYNOPSIN, scilicet, PURIORIS THEOLOGIAE, quam in Academia vestra profitemur, omnibusque sub vestro nomine spectandam et ad Lydium sacrae Scripturae lapidem examinandam proponimus; tum ut totus terrarum orbis vos acerrimos et constantissimos illius esse defensores hinc cognoscat; tum, ut sacrarum litterarum candidati fidei nostrae commissi, in studiorum suorum cursu hanc Cynosuram oculis suis lustrent ac sequantur; tum denique, ut quibuslibet certo constet de fidei ac sententiae nostrae παναρμονίᾳ, mutuoque super omnibus sacrae Religionis capitibus consensu: minime dubitantes, quin Ecclesiarum nostrarum Pastores hoc nostrae concordis doctrinae specimen, toties a se desideratum, contemplati, vestrae Provinciae nobiscum hoc nomine sint gratulaturi, quod ex singulari Dei gratia, sopitis vestra auctoritate nostrorum dissidiorum intestinorum ignibus, non minus in nostrae Academiae pulpitis, quam in templorum cathedris, veritatem et pacem nunc iterum videant, ut Regii Prophetae Davidis utamur verbis, *sibi mutuo occurrere, seque invicem exosculari.*

Quod superest, Vos, *Illustrissimi Domini Ordines*, submisse rogamus, ut hoc exiguum devotissimae nostrae mentis signum sereno suscipiatis vultu, nosque benevolentia vestra complecti pergatis. Deus Optimus Maximus sub cujus praesidio sapientiae ipsius latifundia in hoc sacrario excolenda suscepimus, Vos quam diutissime sub umbra alarum suarum tegat servetque incolumes: Ac vestram Rempublicam omni benedictionum accessione cumulatissime locupletet, ad Nominis sui gloriam, et Ecclesiae suae incrementum.

And now it is our resolve to honour, venerate, and publish abroad with praise eternal the care and vigilance with which you have rescued this seminary of our churches from the gravest dangers of bygone tempests and placed it upon a firm and peaceable footing. And to make this testimony public, we announce the following as monument of the gratitude and esteem that we owe you: the *Synopsis*, namely, the *Synopsis of the Purer Theology* of which we are professors in your Academy. And it is in your name that we present it to everyone, to study it and to test it against the touchstone of Holy Scripture.[8] We do so in order that the entire globe may acknowledge that you are its most stalwart and steadfast defenders, but also in order that those candidates of the sacred letters who are entrusted to us may fix their gaze upon this North Star[9] and direct their way by it in the course of their studies. And finally we do this so that it may be clear to anyone and everyone that there is a total single-mindedness in what we believe and think, and that we share a consensus in all the headings of theology. We have no doubt whatsoever that the pastors of our churches, when they behold this work as the longed-for proof of the harmony in our teaching, will join with us in congratulating the Province that you command for the fact that by the special grace of God under your watch the flames of our internal dissentions have been quenched. And what is more, that they may now once again behold that on the lecterns in our Academy and on the pulpits in our church-buildings Truth and Peace "greet and kiss one another" (to use the words of king David the prophet).[10]

And finally we beseech you in all humility, O most highly respected and sovereign lords of the States, to accept this small token of our deepest devotion and commitment with friendly countenance, and to continue to surround us with your benevolence. And may the most high, almighty God, under whose protection we have undertaken, in this sanctuary, to cultivate the garden-estates of Wisdom herself, protect you under the shadow of his wings and keep you safe for as long as is possible. May he enrich your Republic with an over-abundant increase of every blessing, for the glory of his name and for the increase of his Church.

---

8   The Latin words, *lydius lapis*, 'Lydian stone,' refer to a flinty slate used by the ancients to assay the purity of gold and silver by the colour of the streak left when the metal (lydite or basanite) was rubbed against it.

9   The Latin word here used is *Cynosura*, which stands for the constellation of the Little Bear (*Ursa Minor*), by which the ancients plotted their naval journeys. Cicero notes that the wise man directs his thoughts by the Little Bear (*Academica* 2.66); cf. also Erasmus, *Adagia* 1.5.87 (487).

10 The quotation is of Psalm 85:10.

Datum Lugduni Batavorum, XXVIII. Decembris M.DC.XXIV.
Vestrarum Illustrissimarum Dominationum obsequio deditissimi
   Sacrosanctae Theologiae Doctores ac Professores,
Johannes Polyander
Andreas Rivetus
Antonius Walaeus
Antonius Thysius

Presented in Leiden, December 28, 1624
By the most devoted servants of your highly distinguished dominions
Doctors and Professors of most holy Theology,
Johannes Polyander
Andreas Rivetus
Antonius Walaeus
Antonius Thysius

DISPUTATIO I

De Sacrosancta Theologia

Praeside D. JOHANNE POLYANDRO
Respondente JOHANNE SWALMIO

Quandoquidem Scriptura divinitus inspirata, est SacrosanctaeTheologiae principium, argumentum et instrumentum, ab hac disputationes nostras ordiemur.

THESIS I THEOLOGIA est, juxta nominis notationem, ut quibusdam placet, sermo Dei, vel potius sermo de Deo, ut nos censemus.

II Nomen* hoc fuit primo usurpatum ab Ethnicis Graecis, teste Lactantio, Lib. 1, *de ira Dei*, cap. 11,ᵃ ac postea ab ipsis Christianis, ut colligi potest ex Apocalypsis ἐπιγραφῇ, in qua Johannes Evangelista et Apostolus, Theologi elogio insignitur: atque ex Basilii *epist.* 2. ad Greg. Nazianzenum,ᵇ ubi doctrinam Sacrae Scripturae Theologiam nuncupat.

ᵃ Lactantius, *De ira Dei* 11.8 (CSEL 27:96). ᵇ Basil the Great, *Epistulae* 7 (= 2nd letter to Gregory of Nyssa; Courtonne 1:21).

DISPUTATION 1

Concerning the Most Sacred Theology

President: Johannes Polyander
Respondent: Johannes Swalmius[1]

We shall commence our disputations with Scripture, since it, being divinely inspired, is the principle for the most sacred Theology, its source of proof, and its means of instruction.

According to the derivation of the noun, Theology is according to some 'the word of God'; or rather, as we think, 'the word about God.'

This noun* was first used by pagan Greeks (witness Lactantius, *On the Wrath of God*, book 1, chapter 11)[2] and thereafter by the Christians themselves, as can be gathered from the title of the book Revelation, in which John the evangelist and apostle is identified by the epithet, "the theologian"; and from the Second Letter of Basil[3] to Gregory of Nazianzus,[4] where he calls the doctrine of Holy Scripture "Theology."

---

1   Born in Westmaas in 1596, Joannes Arnoldi Swalmius matriculated on 22 May 1615 as an alumnus of the Leiden States College. He was ordained in Valkenburg (province of Holland) in 1621; he died in 1661. See W.M. du Rieu, ed., *Album studiosorum academia Lugduno-Batavae* MDLXXV–MDCCCLXXV (The Hague: Martinus Nijhoff, 1875), 120, and F.A. van Lieburg, *Repertorium van Nederlandse hervormde predikanten tot 1816*, 2 vols. (Dordrecht: Van Lieburg, 1996), 244; also BLGNP 1:166.

2   Lucius Caecilius (Caelius) Firmianus Lactantius (c. AD 250–c. 320) was a Christian author, rhetor and apologist. In 303 he left the imperial court, where he had been counselor to emperor Diocletian, as fierce persecutions against the Christians were unleashed. Later, he became tutor to the son of emperor Constantine. His major work is the *Divinae Institutiones* (*Divine Institutes*), a piece of Christian apologetics, and the first attempt of a systematic presentation of Christian doctrine in Latin. One of his shorter works is *De ira Dei* (*On the Wrath of God*), directed against Stoics and Epicureans; in it Lactantius attempts to show that God can express both anger and love.

3   One of the Cappadocian fathers, Basil "the Great" (c. AD 330–379) was born at Caesarea, "a metropolis of letters." He received his education in Constantinople, and thereafter in Athens, where he befriended Gregory of Nazianzus. He was ordained bishop of Cappadocian Caesarea in 370 and used his position to advance the cause of Nicea. Basil also promoted monasticism in Asia Minor.

4   Also one of the Cappadocian fathers, Gregory of Nazianzus (AD 329–389) took his name from the town in which he was born and where his father was bishop. His friend Basil appointed

III   Theologia, si rem* in se* spectemus, est una, si modum* rei diversis subjectis* inhaerentis, est diversa. Si enim in Deo consideretur, quatenus est scientia, qua se omniaque divina modo divino intelligit, est archetypa; ac proinde, ut ipsa Dei essentia,* ita haec scientia communis* est Filio cum Patre et Spiritu Sancto; et sicuti unius essentiae divinae tres sunt personae* mutua societate et communicatione conjunctissimae, sic eae intime et perfectissime se invicem norunt. Quo respiciens Christus ait, Joh. 7, 29. Ego novi Patrem, quia ab eo sum; et Joh. 10, 15. Prout me novit Pater, et ego novi Patrem.

IV   Si vero Theologia consideretur, quatenus est scientia a Deo cum creaturis intelligentia praeditis, aut in hoc seculo communicata, aut in futuro communicanda, illa est ectypa. Haecque a Deo tamquam ex archetypo variis communicationis modis ac gradibus exprimitur, nimirum in hominibus in hoc mundo versantibus per gratiam* revelationis, in Angelis vero et beatorum Spiritibus in coelum receptis per gratiam visionis, cujus beneficio nos quoque eum ipsum post hanc vitam de facie ad faciem, id est, coram ac proxime contemplabimur sicuti est, 1Joh. 3,2.

V   Cum Christo Θεανθρώπῳ haec Theologia fuit a Deo singulari et eximia ratione* communicata, per gratiam scilicet unionis, ex qua tanta in animam ipsius sapientiae plenitudo resultavit, quanta ad perfectissimam officii ipsius exsecutionem necessaria est, cujus plenitudinis respectu Deus ipsum unxisse dicitur oleo laetitiae prae ejus consortibus, Psalm 45, 8, eique Spiritum dedisse sine mensura, Joh. 3, 34, ut ex ejus plenitudine omnes in eum credentes certum

---

him bishop in the village of Sasima. Around 378 he went to Constantinople to oppose the Arianism popular there. With the support of the new emperor Theodosius he helped, through his preaching, to turn the city to Nicene orthodoxy. A few years later he quit his ecclesiastical post and retired to monastic life.

1. CONCERNING THE MOST SACRED THEOLOGY

Theology is of one kind if we consider the matter* in itself;* it is multiform 3
if we consider the way* in which the matter consists in its various subjects.*
For with respect to God, insofar as Theology is the knowledge whereby He
knows himself and all divine things in his divine way, it is archetypal theology.[5]
And hence, as it is the case with the very essence* of God, so this knowledge
is common* to the Son with the Father and the Holy Spirit. And just as the
divine essence has three persons* most closely joined together in fellowship
and communion with one another, so too those persons know one another
intimately and as perfectly as possible. With a view to this relationship Christ
states in John 7:29: "I know the Father, because I am from Him," and in John
10:15: "Just as the Father knows me so I know the Father."

And if Theology is viewed insofar as it is the knowledge that God either has 4
communicated to created beings endowed with understanding in this age, or
that He will share in the age to come, it is ectypal theology. And this knowledge
communicated by God has been, so to speak, reproduced from the original
in various ways and degrees of communication in people living on this earth,
obviously through the grace* of revelation. It was certainly received in angels
and the spirits of the saints in heaven through the grace of vision—through
which kindness we, too, shall see God himself face to face after this life, that is,
with our own eyes and in person (1John 3:2).

This theology has been communicated by God with Christ the 'God-and- 5
man' in a unique and exceptional manner,* that is, by the grace of the union,
which produced in Christ's soul as much fullness of wisdom as was necessary
for the most complete performance of his calling.[6] Regarding that fullness God
is said to have "anointed Him with the oil of gladness beyond his peers" (Psalm
45:7[8]) and "has given Him the Spirit without measure" (John 3:34), so that

---

5 An 'archetype' is an original pattern from which copies are made. *Theologia archetypa* is one of the branches of the epistemological distinction between *theologia archetypa* and *theologia ectypa* which is fundamental in Reformed Orthodoxy. *Theologia archetypa* signifies God's own knowledge of himself and his works; *theologia ectypa* signifies the creaturely knowledge of God and his works as God reveals it to his people. This distinction runs parallel to the traditional one between God's *theologia in se* and our *theologia viatorum*. See PRRD 1:225–238, and Willem J. van Asselt, "The Fundamental Meaning of Theology: Archetypal and Ectypal Theology in Seventeenth-Century Reformed Thought," *Westminster Theological Journal* 64 (2002): 319–335. Cf. footnote 7.

6 The knowledge Jesus Christ possesses is neither identical with God's own knowledge of himself (archetypal theology, thesis 3) nor with human theological knowledge (thesis 6). It is knowledge *sui generis*.

ejusdem Spiritus demensum acciperent, Joh. 1, 16. Unde et omnes sapientiae ac cognitionis thesauri in ipso absconditi dicuntur, Col. 2, 3.

VI   Nos Theologiam hoc loco ad solos homines in hoc stadio per fidem incedentes restringimus, quam, distinctionis gratia, *Theologiam revelationis* appellamus.

VII   Revelatio latius sumpta, in naturalem et supernaturalem distribui potest.

VIII Naturalem* vocamus, quae sit vel intrinsecus, per veritatem et legem naturae* omnium hominum cordibus inscriptam, de qua disserit Apostolus, Rom 1, 19, et 2, 15, vel extrinsecus, per rerum a Deo creatarum contemplationem, de qua idem disputat, Rom. 1, 20. Supernaturalem* nominamus, quam Prophetae et Apostoli immediate* a Spiritu veritatis sunt adepti, ut genuinam illius formam partim viva voce, partim scriptis suis Ecclesiae Dei explicarent et custodiendam traderent. Quocirca SacraeTheologiae revelatio a Deo Prophetis et Apostolis facta, est immediata; quae autem per hos Ecclesiae Dei manifestata est, mediata* est.

IX   Nos hoc loco de revelatione supernaturali disserentes, Theologiam definimus, scientiam vel sapientiam rerum divinarum, a Deo per verbi ipsius administros, Spiritu Prophetico afflatos, hominibus in hoc mundo revelatam, atque ad captum eorum attemperatam, ut eos in cognitionem introducat veritatis quae est secundum pietatem, ac sapientes reddat ad ipsorum salutem et gloriam suam aeternam.

1. CONCERNING THE MOST SACRED THEOLOGY

from his fullness all who believe in Him would receive a certain measure of that same Spirit (John 1:16). Therefore, it is said that all the treasures of wisdom and knowledge have been hidden in Him (Colossians 2:3).

In this *locus* we restrict Theology only to persons who are proceeding in faith in the current age, and in order to differentiate it, we call it 'the Theology of revelation.'[7]

Taken more broadly, revelation can be divided into natural and supernatural revelation.

We call natural* revelation what is either internal, written upon the hearts of all people through natural truth and natural law*[8] (which the apostle explains in Romans 1:19 and 2:15), or external, through the contemplation of the things God has created (which the same apostle discusses in Romans 1:20). We call supernatural* revelation what the prophets and apostles have obtained by the direct* agency of the Spirit of truth in order to unfold its genuine form to the Church of God, partly through the spoken word and partly through their writings, and to transmit it for safe-keeping. Hence the revelation of sacred theology which God gave the prophets and the apostles was direct and without intervention; however, the revelation that has been disclosed through them to the Church of God was via them as intermediaries.*

Because in this *locus* we are discussing supernatural revelation, we define Theology as the knowledge or wisdom of the divine matters that God has revealed to people in this world through ministers of his word inspired by the prophetic Spirit, and that He has adapted to their capability, to lead them to knowledge of the truth which accords with godliness and renders them wise unto their own salvation and God's eternal glory.

---

7 In prolegomena to Reformed scholastic theology distinctions are made between archetypal and ectypal theology; see, for example, Franciscus Junius, *De theologia vera* (1594), and cf. footnote 5 above. Ectypal theology is divided further into 1) a theology of union, 2) a theology of vision, and 3) a revealed theology. The third is mentioned here, and it refers to theology for believers today depicted as pilgrims on earth en route (*in via*) to heaven, as opposed to the second division, which refers to the saints who are in heaven and enjoy the beatific vision. And the first division of ectypal theology refers to all the wisdom of divine things communicated in the union of the theanthropic incarnate person of Christ.

8 "Natural truth" refers to theoretical knowledge, and "natural law" to practical or ethical knowledge common to all people by nature. Natural revelation delivers knowledge that is based on what is self-evident. Supernatural knowledge is due to God's specific revelation. On the epistemological meaning of 'natural' and 'supernatural' see Antonie Vos, *The Philosophy of John Duns Scotus* (Edinburgh: Edinburgh University Press, 2006), 337–340 and 527–528.

x   Genus* Theologiae, vel scientiam, vel sapientiam facimus. Scientiam quidem,
  1. Quia Sacra Scriptura epitheta et effecta scientiae ipsi attribuit, Es. 53, 11. Jer. 3, 15. Joh. 17, 3. 2 Cor. 8, 7.
  2. Quia est notitia* rerum necessariarum, vel absolute,* ut Dei et attributorum* ejus; vel ex hypothesi voluntatis* Dei, ut cultus et operum ipsius.
  3. Quia veritatis parit ἐπίγνωσιν, Tit. 1, 1, id est, certam mentique profundissime infixam agnitionem evidentissimis* suis demonstrationibus,* vel per priora et principia* constitutionis, ut Matth. 11, 26. Eph. 1, 5, vel per posteriora et principia cognitionis, ut Rom. 1, 20.

We classify the *genus**9 of Theology as knowledge or wisdom. It is knowledge,

1. Because Holy Scripture ascribes to it the epithets and effects of knowledge: Isaiah 53:11, Jeremiah 3:15, John 17:2[3], and 2 Corinthians 8:7.
2. Because it is the knowledge* of things that are necessary, either without relation to any other being,* as for example of God and his attributes,* or of things that are necessary on the presupposition of God's will,* such as knowledge of his worship and works.[10]
3. Because it brings forth the knowledge of the truth (Titus 1:1), that is, a definite recognition fixed very deeply within the mind by the clearest* shows of proof,* either through things that are prior and that are principles* of being[11] (as in Matthew 11:26, Ephesians 1:5), or through things that are posterior and that are principles of knowledge (as in Rom. 1:20).[12]

---

9   *Genus* is an overarching, general concept. In Aristotelian logic *genus* is a universal concept which answers the question "What is it?" ("animal," of man and beast). Thus *genus* or inclusive class is that part of the essence which the object has in common with other classes of things that resemble it. By way of contrast, *species* is the universal answer to the question "What is it?," of many that differ only in number ("man," of Plato and Socrates). See William A. Wallace, *The Elements of Philosophy: A Compendium for Philosophers and Theologians* (New York: Alba, 1977), 27–28.

10 Something can be necessary by itself ('absolutely'); e.g., that God exists or that He is just. Something can be necessary also if it is dependent on a condition ('hypothetically' or 'conditionally'): If x is the case, then it necessarily follows that y is the case, while y in itself is only contingent. In this context, the condition is God's will. For example, the obligation or necessity of Sunday rest or of baptism depends on God's free will. God could have chosen any other day of rest (or none) and any other sacramental means of salvation.

According to Aristotle, science can only be of what is necessary; it cannot be of contingent, particular things and events. By applying the hypothetical necessity of God's will to all of God's external works (in creation and in history), Polyander tries to maintain the Aristotelian condition for scientific knowledge, but in fact modifies it so that theology, as a science, can be of what in itself is contingent. See also RTF, 35–43.

11 *Principia constitutionis* corresponds to *principium essendi* (God as the essential foundation or source of theology) and *principium cognoscendi internum et externum* (the internal and external cognitive foundation whereby God reveals knowledge of himself to people by illumination of their spirit by his Spirit and by Scripture; Matt 11:26; Eph 1:5). *Principia cognitionis* corresponds to what can be clearly perceived in the book of nature (Rom 1:20). In the order of being, the divine causes or *principia constitutionis* are prior to the effects of which one gains knowledge; in the order of knowledge, however, one can start with the effects or *principia cognitionis*, and then reason back to the causes.

12 Medieval and early modern scholasticism commonly distinguishes between deductive knowledge from causes (*a priori*) and inductive knowledge on the basis of effects (*a posteriori*). The former was considered more certain and more perfect.

XI Sapientiam quoque genus Theologiae facimus, his moti rationibus:
1. Quoniam Salomon hoc nomine eam nuncupat, Prov. 1, cap. ac sequentibus, et Apostolus Paulus, 1 Cor. 1, 21. et 12, 8.
2. Quoniam principia sua reliquarum scientiarum principiis longe altiora, nempe, sacrosancta et augusta Dei ipsius mysteria humano ingenio inscrutabilia, hominibus methodo docendi exactissima atque excellentissima proponit.
3. Quoniam ejus contemplatio potissimum versatur circa subjecta aeterna, infinita, ineffabilia, immota, spiritualia, coelestia, nullique transmutationi aut corruptioni obnoxia, ut hac de re fuse scribit August. Lib. 12, *de Trin*. cap. 14.[a]
4. Quod haec veluti omnium disciplinarum norma architectonica, ac suprema omnium actionum rationumque arbitra ceteris scientiis praeluceat, iisque modum bene et beate vivendi, omniaque ad Dei gloriam referendi praescribat. Quidquid enim homo (ut ait Augustinus, lib. 12, *de Trin*. cap. 14.[b]) extra Theologiam didicerit, si noxium est, in Sacris Scripturis damnatur, si utile, ibi invenitur et approbatur.

XII Objectum Theologiae cum res* divinas esse asserimus, sub hac applicatione complectimur: 1. Deum ipsum. 2. Dogmata et beneficia divina ad salutarem Dei cognitionem, communionem, et fruitionem necessaria. 3. quaecumque sunt in rerum natura* a Deo creata et ordinata, quatenus ad Deum tamquam ad suum principium et finem sunt referenda. Quo postremo respectu Augustinus in epistola ad Volusianum[c] ipsam quoque Physicam, Ethicam, Politicam aliasque disciplinas terminis* Theologiae contineri ostendit.

XIII Theologiae causa* efficiens principalis est Deus, respectu triplicis effecti. Nam 1. illam Prophetis et Apostolis Spiritus sui afflatu suggessit, teste Paulo, 2 Tim. 3, 16. et Petro, 1 Pet. 1, 11. 12. et 2 Pet. 1, 21. 2. Veram illius tractandae

---

[a] Augustine, *De trinitate* 12.14.22–23 (CCSL 50:375–377).
[b] Erroneous reference; correct to Augustine, *De doctrina christiana* 2.42.63 (CCSL 32:76).
[c] Augustine, *Epistulae* 137.17 (CCSL 31B:272).

1. CONCERNING THE MOST SACRED THEOLOGY

We classify the *genus* of Theology also as wisdom, for the following reasons: 11
1. Because Solomon calls it by this name in Proverbs chapter 1 (and following); so too the apostle Paul in 1 Corinthians 1:21, and 12:8.
2. Because it presents to people, by way of teaching, its own most accurate and superior principles, which are loftier by far than the principles of the other sciences, namely, the most holy and majestic mysteries of God himself that cannot be fathomed by the human mind.
3. Because what it contemplates deals especially with subjects that are eternal, infinite, inexpressible, immovable, spiritual, heavenly, and not liable to any change or decay. Augustine writes extensively about this matter in *On the Trinity*, book 12, chapter 14.
4. Because it is, so to speak, like an architectonic standard that guides all the disciplines and as the final judge of all actions and thoughts outshines all other sciences and prescribes for them the standard for living well and happily, and for directing all things back to the glory of God. For whatever a man learns outside of Theology (as Augustine says in *On the Trinity*, book 12, chapter 14), if it is harmful, Holy Scripture discredits it; if it is useful, it is found and commended therein.

When we assert that matters* pertaining to God are the object of theology, 12 we include in the range of application: 1. God himself; 2. The doctrines and divine benefits required for a saving knowledge of God, for fellowship with and enjoyment of Him. 3. Everything that God has created and ordained in the nature* of things as they must be related to God as their origin and goal. Regarding this last point Augustine shows in the *Letter to Volusianus* that within the terms* of Theology are contained also Physics, Ethics, Politics, and the other disciplines.

God is the chief efficient cause* of Theology, regarding three ways in which 13 He brings it about.[13] For 1. his Spirit supplied it to the prophets and apostles by his inspiration, as Paul testifies in 2 Timothy 3:16, and Peter in 1 Peter 1:11,12 and 2 Peter 1:21. 2. He has appointed the true standard for treating Theology

---

13   Aristotle distinguishes four main categories of cause: efficient, material, formal, and final. An instrumental cause (thesis 14) is a secondary kind of efficient cause, the working of which depends on the principal efficient cause. A carpenter is the efficient cause of a bed and his saw is an instrumental cause. Wood and metal are the material cause, and a specific structure of wood and metal is the formal cause of the bed. Sleeping is the final cause, or goal, of the bed. The efficient and final causes are extrinsic, while matter and form are intrinsic causes. This fourfold causality is applied here to the concept of theology. Polyander mentions the efficient and instrumental cause of theology in theses 13 and 14, the final causes in theses 18–21. In thesis 21 he mentions also the form of theology. It is also applied to the doctrine of Scripture. See *SPT* 3.6 below.

formam praescripsit, quae falsis opponitur, 1 Tim. 1, 3. et 6, 4. 3. Efficaciam eidem tribuit mentes nostras salutaribus suis praeceptis imbuendi, Joh. 6, 45. 1 Cor. 3, 7. 1 Thess. 4, 9.

XIV   Theologiae causa instrumentalis est Dei Verbum,* hominum divinitus inspiratorum atque immediate a Deo vocatorum ore prolatum, ac sacris libris consignatum, 1 Pet. 1, 11. 2 Pet. 1, 21. Act. 20, 27. 1 Thess. 2, 13. et 4, 8.

XV   Modus,* quem Deus in Theologiae revelatione adhibere voluit, a quibusdam dividitur in ἐνδιάθετον seu internum, per solam Spiritus Sancti inspirationem, et προφορικόν seu externum, per organa et adminicula quaedam corporea a Deo cum hominibus communicatum.

XVI   Hic modus olim diverse a Deo Patre, Filio et Spiritu Sancto emanavit. Interdum enim clara voce, interdum somniis, visionibus, symbolis, imaginibus et similitudinibus adhibitis, interdum per Angelos assumpta specie* humana; interdum per Prophetas Spiritu Christi actos sub Veteri Testamento Patribus nostris est locutus, Genes. 15, 1. Num. 12, 6. 8. Genes. 18, 13. Exod. 23, 21. Act. 7, 30. 1 Cor. 10, 9. At tandem plenissime per Filium suum in carne manifestatum, Hebr. 1, 1.

XVII Quamvis hi diversi revelationum modi, ad omnium captum a Deo fuerint accommodati, alii tamen aliis pro diversa fidei mensura illam vel perfectius, vel imperfectius perceperunt.

XVIII Primus fructus ac finis* Theologiae est cognitio veritatis, quae est secundum pietatem, Tit. 1, 1. Qua descriptione veritas supernaturalis a naturali discernitur; quae in homine nondum regenito est insufficiens, et inefficax ad pietatem ac verum Dei cultum cordi ipsius instillandum, ut multis probatur* argumentis, Rom. 1. et 2.

and placed it over against false standards (1 Timothy 1:3, 6:4[3]). And 3. He has bestowed upon it the power to instill his wholesome teachings into our minds (John 6:45, 1 Corinthians 3:7, 1 Thessalonians 4:9).

The instrumental cause[14] of Theology is the Word* of God, spoken through the mouth of men divinely inspired and called directly by God, and recorded in the holy books (1 Peter 1:11, 2 Peter 1:21, Acts 20:27, 1 Thessalonians 2:13 and 4:8).

The manner* God chose to use for disclosing Theology is divided by some into *endiathetos*, or inward manner, solely through inspiration by the Holy Spirit, and *prophorikos*, or outward manner, conferred by God upon men through certain instruments and devices.[15]

This manner of revelation formerly flowed forth from God the Father, the Son, and the Holy Spirit in different ways. Sometimes He spoke by using clear speech, sometimes by means of dreams, visions, signs, appearances or likenesses. On other occasions He spoke through angels who had assumed human shape.* Sometimes He spoke to our fathers in the Old Testament through human prophets who were driven by the Spirit of Christ (Genesis 15:1; Numbers 12:6,8; Genesis 18:13; Exodus 23:21; Acts 7:30; 1 Corinthians 10:9). And at last He spoke most fully through his own Son as He was revealed in the flesh (Hebrews 1:1).

Although these different ways of revelation have been adapted by God to everyone's capacity for receiving them, some people have grasped them more fully and others less so, according to varying measures of faith.

The foremost fruit and goal* of Theology is knowledge of the truth that accords with godliness (Titus 1:1). By this description supernatural truth is distinguished from natural truth; the latter does not suffice in a man who is not yet reborn, and it does not have the power to infuse his heart with godliness and true service to God, as is evidenced* by many proofs in Romans 1 and 2.

---

14   For 'instrumental cause' see previous note and also *DLGTT*, s.v. *causa instrumentalis*.
15   This distinction goes back to the Stoic distinction between the *logos endiathetos* (inward or internal discourse, thought) and *prophorikos* (uttered or outward discourse, the spoken word) that became standard to Greek philosophy in the second century AD and was adopted by Justin, Tatian, and Theophilus of Antioch; see Claude Panaccio, *Le discours intérieur: De Platon à Guillaume d'Ockham* (Paris: Editions du Seuil, 1999), 53–93 (= chapter 2 "Logos endiathtetos"), and J.N.D. Kelly, *Early Christian Doctrine* (5th ed.; London: Continuum, 1985), 96–99. It was also used by Franciscus Junius, Johannes Scharpius, and Johann Heinrich Alstedt; see *PRRD* 1:243–244, and Henk van den Belt, *The Authority of Scripture in Reformed Theology: Truth and Trust*, Studies in Reformed Theology, vol. 17 (Leiden: Brill, 2008), 142–144.

XIX   Haec veritas est forma toti Theologiae ac singulis ejus partibus aequaliter infusa, ideoque Theologus eam passim in sacris literis uno semper eodemque modo considerat.

XX   Secundus Theologiae usus ac finis est, quod nos sapientes reddat ad salutem et omne bonum vitae praesentis et futurae, 2 Tim. 3, 15. 1 Tim. 4, 8.

XXI   Ultimus Theologiae finis est Dei gloria, qua hanc solam sibi proposuit, cum sibi soli sufficiens nulla re indigeat, nihilque ipsi per nos accedere possit.

XXII Ex his oritur quaestio: An Sacrosancta Theologia sit theoretica, an vero practica? Ad quam quaestionem, Theologorum alii, eam theoreticam, alii, eam practicam, alii, eam mixtam esse, respondent. Nos postremorum responsioni sic astipulamur, ut censeamus eam et theoreticam et practicam esse nuncupandam, tum propter duplicis illius finis, nimirum cognitionis et cultus Dei hac in vita aggregationem, tum propter unius sub altero ordinationem. Quemadmodum enim pietas nostrae beatitati ac gloriae Dei, sic cognitio pietati in sacris literis subordinatur, 1 Tim. 4, 8. Col. 3, 16. Tit. 1, 1.

XXIII Non ergo theoria et praxis sunt in Theologia differentiae oppositae: sed conditiones inter se ad vitam aeternam consequendam consociatae, suoque ordine collocatae.

XXIV Nec Theologia in nuda et inani consistit speculatione, sed in scientia practica, voluntatem omnesque cordis affectus efficaciter movente ad Deum colendum ac proximum* diligendum. Hinc Fides efficaciter agere dicitur per cari-

This truth is the form that pervades Theology in its entirety as well as its individual parts, and therefore the theologian always contemplates it in one and the same way throughout the sacred letters.[16]

The second use and goal of Theology is that it renders us wise unto salvation and to every good gift in this present life and the life that is to come (2 Timothy 3:15, 1 Timothy 4:8).

The glory of God is the highest goal of Theology, whereby He has prepared this glory only for himself, because He is all-sufficient unto himself and is in want of nothing, and because not a thing can be added to Him by our doing.

From this the question arises: Is the most holy Theology a theoretical or a practical discipline?[17] The reply of some theologians to this question is 'theoretical,' of others 'practical,' and of others yet again 'a mixture of the two.' We concur with the last reply in that we reckon Theology ought to be called both theoretical and practical both because of the combination of its two-fold goal, that is, the increase of knowledge and of the worship of God in this life, and because of the arrangement of the one below the other. For just as godliness is placed in the service of our blessedness and God's glory, so too knowledge is ranked in service to godliness in sacred literature (1 Timothy 4:[7–]8; Colossians 3:16; Titus 1:1).

Therefore in Theology theory and practice are not placed in opposition to one another, but they are conditions associated with each other for the purpose of obtaining everlasting life, and placed in their proper order.

And Theology consists not of bare and empty theory but of a practical science that powerfully stirs the human will and all the emotions of the heart to worship God and to cherish one's neighbor.* Hence it is said that faith works

---

16 The term 'form' or 'formal cause' indicates the normative quality of a given entity, that which makes it what it is to be. In the present context, conformity with the truth of God makes theology in its entirety and its parts to be what it should be. See further "formal cause" in the Glossary.

17 The question whether theology is speculative (theoretical) or practical is a conventional issue in medieval and Protestant scholasticism. This question comes after the one about the *genus* of theology as knowledge or wisdom (see theses 10 and 11 above). The adjectives 'theoretical' and 'practical,' like the nouns *theoria* and *praxis* from which they derive (used in describing the *genus* and object of theology) arise from the medieval theological tradition. They do not refer to metaphysical rationalization on the one hand and a pragmatic enterprise on the other, but to the question whether the goal of theology consists in knowledge or in action (namely, the worship of God). The authors of the *Synopsis* understood the discipline of theology as a mixture of 'theoretical' and 'practical' disciplines. Some theologians, like Bartholomaeus Keckermann, William Ames, and Gisbertus Voetius considered theology to be a purely 'practical' discipline. See *PRRD* 1:340–355.

tatem, Gal. 5, 6. 1 Thess. 1, 3. Hinc quoque se ipsos falsa ratiocinatione fallere dicuntur, qui Dei sermonem solum audiunt, non autem revera praestant, Jacobi 1, 22. et sequentibus.

xxv Huic verae Theologiae hactenus a nobis explicatae falsa repugnat; in qua bifariam peccatur:

1. Ἑτεροδιδασκαλίᾳ, id est, doctrina ab orthodoxa Prophetarum et Apostolorum institutione prorsus diversa, partim quoad res ipsas, partim quoad rerum tractationem, 1 Tim. 1, 3. et 4, 7. 2 Pet. 2, 1.

2. Ματαιολογίᾳ et λογομαχίᾳ, id est, vaniloquentia et verborum pugna, qua circa inanes quaestiones insanientes a vero immaculatae religionis* scopo aberrant, 1 Tim. 1, 6. et 6, 4.

xxvi Haec falsa Theologia ad tres praecipuas species* revocari potest; ad Theologiam scilicet,

1. Ethnicorum, qui Christum Salvatorem ignorant, quam Spiritus Sanctus damnat, Act. 17, 22. 23. 30. et 19, 34. et Rom. 1, 21.

2. Judaeorum, qui Christum (quem Hieronymus in cap. 12. et 13. Matth. vocat caput Sapientiae[a]) aspernantur, ac propterea aliquid sapienter intelligere nequeunt.

3. Haereticorum Pseudochristianorum, qui (ut idem loquitur Hieronymus in Cap. 23. Jer.[b]) Christi verba furantur, linguasque Prophetarum, Evangelistarum et Apostolorum assumunt, ut errores suos aut in doctrinae Christianae fundamento, aut circa hujus fundamentum,* sub fucosae veritatis specie incautioribus propinent.

xxvii Etsi dogmata Veteris et Novi Testamenti quibusdam inter se differant administrationis* adminiculis et circumstantiis, unica tamen quoad substantiam,*

---

[a] Jerome, *Commentaria in evangelium Matthaei* 2.13.12 (CCSL 77:103). [b] Jerome, *Commentaria in Jeremiam prophetam* 4.61.2 (CCSL 74:228).

powerfully through love (Galatians 5:6; 1 Thessalonians 1:3). Hence also they are said to deceive themselves by false reasoning who only hear the Word of God but in reality do not put it into practice (James 1:22 ff.).

The true Theology we have explained to this point is opposed by false theology, which errs in two ways:

1. By *heterodidaskalia*, that is, by utterly departing from the orthodox teaching of the prophets and the apostles, partly regarding the matters themselves, and partly insofar as it concerns the treatment of these matters (1 Timothy 1:3 and 4:7[6]; 2 Peter 2:1).
2. By *mataiologia* and *logomachia*, that is, empty chatter and disputes about words, whereby those who rage madly over foolish enquiries stray from the real goal of pure worship* (1 Timothy 1:6; 6:4).

This false Theology can be summarized in three particular types,* namely, the Theology:

1. Of the pagans, who do not know Christ as the Savior, which the Holy Spirit condemns (Acts 17:22, 23, 30, and 19:34; and Romans 1:21).
2. Of the Jews, who reject Christ (whom Jerome[18] in his commentary on chapter 12 and 13 of Matthew calls the source of Wisdom) and therefore who are not able to understand anything wisely.
3. Of the pseudo-Christian heretics, who (as the same Jerome states in his commentary on chapter 23 of Jeremiah) steal Christ's words and usurp the speech of the prophets, evangelists, and apostles in order to transmit their own deceptions under the semblance of a spurious truth, either on the foundation* of Christian doctrine or in matters concerning its foundation, to those who are rather careless.

Even though the Old and the New Testaments differ with respect to some of the tools whereby the teachings are administered* (and also their circumstances), yet they agree as far as the substance* is concerned.[19] And the same

---

18 Jerome (or Eusebius Sophronius Hieronymus, AD 347–420) was a prominent Latin church father. Born in the Dalmatian town of Stridon, he spent his teenage years in Rome, where he converted to Christianity. He served in different positions in Antioch, Rome, and Constantinople. Jerome also attended lectures by Didymus the Blind in the Catechetical School of Alexandria. He advocated and practised an ascetic way of life. Jerome is best known for his Latin Vulgate translation of the Bible and he was declared 'the greatest doctor in explaining the Scriptures' by the Council of Trent. Jerome reportedly died near Bethlehem in 420. For his *Commentary on Galatians*, see Thomas P. Scheck, *St. Jerome's Commentaries on Galatians, Titus, and Philemon* (Notre Dame: University of Notre Dame Press, 2010).

19 On the unity and difference between the Old and New Testaments see also *SPT* 23.14–20.

eademque Theologia in utroque Testamento proponitur, una voluntas Dei de genere humano redimendo, una fundamentalis promissio de salute per Christum conferenda, Gen. 3, 15. et 22, 18. Act. 15, 11. et 10, 43. etc.

XXVIII Illorum proinde sententia est explodenda, qui triplicem rationem adipiscendi salutem fingunt. Unam scilicet, iis qui ante legem scriptam vixerunt per legis naturae observationem; Secundam vero iis, qui sub lege scripta vixerunt per hujus praestationem; Tertiam denique iis, qui sub gratia Evangelii vivunt, per fidem in Jesum Christum.

XXIX Maxime vero sententia eorum est expugnanda, qui asserere non verentur, quamlibet Dei patefactionem hominibus qualicumque modo ac modulo factam, ad salutem adipiscendam ipsis etiamnum sufficere.

XXX Theologia non tantum est νοητική et σημαντική, sed etiam διανοητική. Plerumque enim argumentis utitur ad convincendos contradicentes: atque ex principiis suis ex prioribus per se indemonstrabilibus, aut conclusiones elicit ad veritatem comprobandam, aut solutiones ad captiosas Sophistarum objectiones refutandas, Matth. 22, 32. 33. 1 Cor. 15, 20. 21. 22.

Theology is advanced in both Testaments: God's single will to redeem the human race and the one basic promise that salvation must be obtained through Christ (Gen. 3:15 and 22:18; Acts 15:11, and 10:43, etc.).

Accordingly we must reject the opinion of those people who make up a three-fold way of obtaining salvation: the first for those who lived before the Law was recorded, by observing the law of nature; the second for those who lived under the written Law, by keeping it; and the third for those who live under the grace of the Gospel, through faith in Christ Jesus.

But we must battle especially the opinion[20] of those who are not afraid to claim that anything at all that has been disclosed by God, regardless of the manner and degree it has been made, is even now sufficient for them to obtain salvation.

Theology is not only noetic and semantic, but also dianoetic.[21] For often it employs arguments to refute those who oppose it, and it either draws logical conclusions to confirm the truth from its own principles that in and of themselves cannot be demonstrated from foregoing principles, or it produces solutions to refute the harmful objections of the Sophists (Matthew 22:32, 33; 1 Corinthians 15:20, 21, 22).

---

20   This is the opinion of the Socinians, who held (at least according to the Reformed theologians) that the remnant parts of natural revelation after the fall are still sufficient for salvation. See Faustus Socinus, *Praelectiones theologicae* (first edition: 1609) in: *Fausti Socini Senensis Opera omnia in duos tomos distincta* (Amsterdam 1656), 537–539.

21   The term 'noetic' refers to the primary and intuitive act of knowledge of the human intellect without any form of reflexivity and abstraction. By contrast, the term 'dianoetic' refers to discursive knowledge that proceeds by argument or reasoning. 'Semantic' is a term referring to the discipline developed by the *logica modernorum* in the Middle Ages which investigates the logical syntax of language, the meaning of terms in their specific contexts and their connotations. See L.M. de Rijk, *La philosophie au Moyen Age* (Leiden: Brill, 1985), 173–174.

DISPUTATIO II

De Sacrae Scripturae Necessitate et Auctoritate

Praeside D. ANTONIO WALAEO
Respondente JOHANNE CRUCIO

THESIS I   Quum de natura Theologiae antecedenti disputatione actum sit; sequitur jam, ut de revelationis ejus praecipuo instrumento, nempe SacraScriptura, agamus; quae est omnium Christianorum dogmatum principium* et fundamentum.*

II   Per Sacram Scripturam hic intelligimus, non ipsos characteres externos, sed verbum* iis characteribus ac literis significatum* et comprehensum. Scriptura enim omnis est symbolum et index verbi; verbum vero symbolum et index cogitationum ac conceptuum mentis.

III   Hanc autem Scripturam definimus, Instrumentum divinum, quo doctrina salutaris a Deo per Prophetas, Apostolos et Evangelistas, tamquam Dei actuarios, in libris Canonicis Veteris et Novi Testamenti est tradita.

IV   Etsi vero Deus ante exitum Israelitarum ex Aegypto, per solum verbum enuntiativum, πολυμερῶς καί πολυτρόπως patriarchis communicatum, et per

DISPUTATION 2

On the Necessity and Authority of Scripture

President: Antonius Walaeus[1]
Respondent: Johannes Crucius[2]

As the nature of Theology was treated in the preceding disputation, it now follows that we deal with the foremost means whereby it is revealed, namely, Holy Scripture, which is the principle* and foundation* for all Christian teaching.[3]

By Holy Scripture we here mean not the actual characters of the alphabet but the word* that is signified* and expressed in those characters and letters. For all scripture is a sign and indicator of the word; in fact, the word is a sign and indicator of the thoughts and concepts conceived in the mind.[4]

Moreover, we define this Scripture as the divine instrument whereby the doctrine of salvation was handed down by God through the prophets, apostles, and evangelists as God's secretaries, in the canonical books of the Old and New Testament.

Before the exodus of the Israelites from Egypt, God established his Church only through the spoken word, which He imparted to the patriarchs *polumerōs kai polutropōs*, "in many and various ways,"[5] and through *patroparadoton*, the

---

1   The same disputation is also published in *Antonii Walaei Opera omnia*, (Leiden, 1643) 2:319–322. Everard Bronchorst (1554–1627), professor of civil law in Leiden, reports that he had attended the disputation and posed some questions; see his *Diarium sive adversaria omnium quae gesta sunt in Academia Leydensi, 1591–1627*, ed. Jacob Cornelis van Slee (The Hague: Martinus Nijhoff, 1898), 147. Large sections of this disputation are also included in the more elaborate chapter "On Holy Scripture," Walaeus, *Loci Communes, Opera* 1:122–130.
2   Born in Haarlem in 1598, Johannes Crucius matriculated on 16 October 1615 as an alumnus of the Leiden States College. He defended this disputation on 22 February 1620. He dedicated his defense to his father Joh. Crucius (de la Croix), his uncle Jac. Crucius, to Polyander, Walaeus and Hommius and to his brother Nicolaus. He was ordained in Zaandam in 1620 and Haarlem 1628; he died in 1666. See Du Rieu, *Album studiosorum*, 122, Van Lieburg, *Repertorium*, 139, and *BLGNP* 2:150.
3   The terms *principium* and *fundamentum* have a background in logic: They indicate the starting point of a deductive reasoning. See De Rijk, *La philosophie au Moyen Age*, 87–96, and Vos, *Philosophy*, 530–539. On the function of Scripture as foundation or principle, see also *PRRD* 2:151–161.
4   The general principle that "everything written (*scriptura*) is a symbol and sign of a word" (thesis 2), is applied here to Scripture. This view on the relation between written symbols, (spoken) words, and concepts occurs in Aristotle, *De Interpretatione*, 16a4–5.
5   Hebrews 1:1.

traditionem πατροπαράδοτον, Ecclesiam suam instituit; cum tamen et longaevitas hominum jam minueretur, et corruptio quotidie augeretur, et Satanas oraculis suis atque apparitionibus deceptricibus, quibus Deum et ejus ὁράματα imitabatur, hominum generi jam passim illuderet; placuit Deo, quo divina veritas fidelius conservari, latius propagari, et collapsa facilius instaurari posset, etiam per Scripturas Ecclesiam suam deinceps usque ad finem mundi instituere.

v Quamobrem et ipse Deus exemplo suo Prophetis hic praeivit: cum legem, quam antea coram toto populo ex monte Sinai pronuntiaverat, lapideis tabulis inscripsit, Ex. 24, 12. et 34, 28. et Mosi ac reliquis Prophetis atque Apostolis, partim manifesto mandato, ut idem facerent, imperavit, ut Exod. 17, 14. et 34, 27. Jer. 36, 2. et 28. Apoc. 1, 19. partim quoque occulto instinctu, ut revelationes suas scripto Ecclesiae traderent, praecepit. Nam tota Scriptura divinitus est inspirata, 2 Tim. 3,16. et Petrus, 2 Epist. c. 1. agens de Scriptis Propheticis, testatur: Quod Prophetia olim libitu hominis allata non sit, sed acti a Spiritu Sancto locuti sint Sancti Dei homines.

vi Ex quo manifestum sit, quam falso Pontificii Doctores asseverent, verbum Dei scriptum Ecclesiae non esse necessarium, et non tam ad esse, quam ad

tradition of the elders.⁶ However, when length of life was shortened and the state of wickedness was increasing daily, and Satan by means of his misleading oracles and apparitions with which he imitated God and his appearance was deluding the human race throughout the world, it pleased God from then until the end of the world to establish his Church also by means of the Scriptures, to preserve the divine truth more reliably, to widen its extent, and to restore it more easily where it had fallen into ruin.

For this reason, too, at this point of time God Himself furnished the prophets with a precedent when onto stone tablets He wrote the law which He had announced previously from Mount Sinai in public to the entire people (Exodus 24:12, and 34:28). And He commanded Moses and the other prophets and apostles to do the same, partly by means of a direct command (as in Exodus 17:14, 34:27; Jeremiah 36:2, and 28; Revelation 1:19), and also partly by means of hidden instigation, He instructed them to record in writing what He revealed to the Church. "For all of Scripture is God-breathed" (2 Timothy 3:16); and Peter (2 Peter 1), in dealing with the prophetic writings testifies: "No prophecy was ever produced by the will of man, but holy men of God spoke as they were carried along by the Holy Spirit."

From this it is clear how false is the claim of papal teachers that the written Word of God is not necessary for the Church,⁷ and that it is less crucial to

---

6 Cf. 1 Peter 1:18, where this expression is used in a negative sense. A slightly variant expression is found in Matthew 15:2: *paradosis tōn presbuterōn*, "tradition of the elders."

7 The tenet that the written Word of God is dispensable for theology is not in keeping with medieval Roman Catholic doctrine. In the first half of the fourteenth century, in fact, *theologia* still meant: *Scriptura*. See Josef Finkenzeller, *Offenbarung und Theologie nach der Lehre des Johannes Duns Skotus* (Munster: Aschendorff, 1961). Heiko A. Oberman, *The Harvest of Medieval Theology: Gabriel Biel and Late Medieval Nominalism* (Cambridge: Harvard University Press, 1963), 361–412, describes the emergence of two different views on the relation of Scripture and tradition in late scholastic theology. The Council of Trent (1546) affirmed the existence of unwritten traditions besides the written Word of God (Session IV, Decree Concerning the Canonical Scriptures; DH 1501), but remained silent about the exact nature of their relation. Some earlier Catholic theologians, like John Driedo (d. 1535) and Martin Perez de Ayala (1504–1566), argued that Scripture is materially sufficient: It teaches all we need to know for our salvation, but the tradition of the Church is necessary for the correct reading of Scripture. Others, such as Thomas Stapleton (1535–1598), stated that Scripture by itself is not sufficient; its teachings have to be supplemented by ecclesial traditions. In reaction to the Protestant emphasis on the *sola Scriptura*, some Catholics went further and said that Scripture is not even necessary: e.g., Stanislaus Hosius (1504–1579) and the Jesuit Cardinal Robert Bellarmine (1542–1621; *Disputationes de controversiis christianae fidei adversus hujus temporis haereticos*, 1.iv.4: *Scripturas sine Traditionibus nec fuisse simpliciter necessarias, nec sufficientes.*). Melchior

bene esse Ecclesiae pertinere; imo et Ecclesiam Scriptura Sacra carere posse,* quemadmodum ea ante Legem latam caruit; et quemadmodum in suis Traditionibus non scriptis magnam divinae veritatis partem hodie conservari, inaniter contendunt.

VII Etsi enim fateamur, Deum etiam hodie sine Scriptura Ecclesiam suam colligere et tueri posse, quemadmodum olim fecit; tamen cum Verbum suum jam scripto consignari voluerit, et Sacra Scriptura testetur, id esse fundamentum fidei nostrae, Eph. 2, 20. imo et Christus ipse auditores suos ad Scripturam Veteris Testamenti ut salutem inde consequerentur, remiserit, Luc. 16. Joh. 5. et Apostolus Johannes, cap. 20,31. asserat: haec scripta esse, ut credamus quod Jesus sit Christus, et credentes vitam aeternam habeamus in nomine ejus; omnino Sacram Scripturam ex hac hypothesi jam esse necessariam, et Ecclesiam sine ea consistere non posse,* constanter asserimus.

VIII Hinc etiam apparet impietas sententiae Libertinorum nostri temporis, qui se Zelotas Spiritus appellant. Quorum aliqui Scripturae Sacrae grammaticum

---

Cano (1509–1560) and Peter Canisius (1521–1597) argued that the Church preceded the writing of Scripture and that faith and religion can exist without Scripture. For a rejoinder by a Reformed thinker, see William Whitaker, *Disputatio de Sacra Scriptura* (Cambridge: Thomasius, 1588), XI.vii. See also disputation 4 below. A survey, with bibliography, can be found in Anthony N.S. Lane, "Scripture, Tradition and Church: An Historical Survey," *Vox Evangelica* 9 (1975): 37–55.

2. ON THE NECESSITY AND AUTHORITY OF SCRIPTURE 53

the existence of the Church than to its well-being;[8] that to the contrary, even the Church can* do without Holy Scripture, in the same way that it managed without it before the law was given. They likewise foolishly assert that a great portion of the truth that proceeds from God is preserved nowadays in the Church's own unwritten traditions.

For we grant that God even today can gather and defend his Church without Scripture just as He did in former times. However, He did determine that his Word be recorded in writing, and Holy Scripture bears witness in Ephesians 2:20 that "it is the foundation of our faith." And indeed even Christ himself directed his listeners to the Scriptures of the Old Testament in order there to obtain salvation (Luke 16[:16–31], John 5[:39, 45–47]). And the apostle John in chapter 20:31 states that: "These things are written that we may believe that Jesus is the Christ, and that believing we may have eternal life in his name." On these grounds we steadfastly maintain that even today Holy Scripture is altogether necessary, and that the Church cannot* exist without it.

From this it becomes clear also what is the godless thinking of contemporary Libertines, who call themselves zealous followers of the Spirit.[9] Some of them

7

8

---

8 The distinction between 'essence' or 'being' and 'well-being' is common in scholastic discourse. The term *esse* refers to the essential make-up of an entity that cannot be changed without causing the entity to cease existing (for example: Man has a body), while *bene esse* indicates the additional qualities that can apply in different degrees (for example: John merely speaks his mother tongue, while Peter masters three foreign languages). In thesis 6 above, the distinction *esse—bene esse* is explained by the statement that follows it, namely that the Church can do without Scripture. This view was defended by the Bellarmine, *De Verbo Dei* 4.4.2 (Opera 1.200b–201a).

9 These Libertines must have been Enthusiasts of some kind. Here they are given a position opposite to the papal theologians of thesis 6. Reformed authors use the term 'Libertines' pejoratively, but the precise historical reference is unclear. A generation earlier, John Calvin had opposed Radical reformers who appealed to the Spirit over against the authority of Scripture (*Institutes*, 1.9.1–3). See M. van Veen, "Introduction," in John Calvin, *Contre la secte phantastique et furieuse des libertins qui se nomment spirituelz*, ed. M. van Veen [COR IV, vol. 1] (Geneva: Droz, 2005), 9–41, esp. 11. In the Dutch context, Walaeus probably has in mind free-thinking Anabaptists. S. Zijlstra, *Om de ware gemeente en de oude gronden: geschiedenis van de dopersen in de Nederlanden 1531–1675* (Hilversum: Fryske Akademy & Verloren, 2000), 320–326, describes groups of 'Libertines,' followers of Sebastian Franck and David Joris, that were active in the Netherlands around 1600. They believed that the power and supremacy of the Spirit surpassed Scripture. For a survey of Enthusiast, Spiritualist, and Anabaptist movements, see George Huntston Williams, *The Radical Reformation* (3rd rev. ed.; Kirksville: Truman State University Press, 2000) and John D. Roth and James M. Stayer, eds., *A Companion to Anabaptism and Spiritualism, 1521–1700*, Brill's Companions to the Christian

et genuinum sensum tamquam literam occidentem Ecclesiae Novi Testamenti inutilem contendunt, et nescio quae phanatica sui cerebri somnia sub Spiritus titulo hominibus conantur obtrudere. Alii vero usum quidem aliquem ejus in Ecclesia esse concedant, sed ad prima tantum Christianismi rudimenta; quum vero iidem jam adoleverunt, ac perfecti et regeniti sunt, tum, rudimentariis, Scriptura externa relicta, solius Spiritus instinctu esse proficiendum, et illius dictamen, tam in fide, quam in moribus, tantummodo sequendum.

IX Haec sententia falsa est et perniciosa, quia Sacrae Scriptura neglecta, nihil certi in Religione* Christiana constitui potest, quum nullum κριτήριον aut norma extra eam dari possit, quae a falsa persuasione et erroris efficacia, quam Deus Evangelii contemptoribus tamquam justus Judex saepe immittit, divinam veritatem distinguat; et quia SpiritusSanctus nonnisi per verbum externum et Sacram Scripturam in cordibus hominum ad salutem est efficax; unde et Paulus suum ministerium, ministerium Spiritus appellat, 2 Cor. 3.

X Nec minus falsa est, et Sacrae Scripturae contraria, opinio altera. Nam Sacra Scriptura usum sui et necessitatem, non tantum rudibus et Alphabetariis in Christianismo, sed et perfectioribus ac regenitis passim commendat, nec tantum in Veteri, sed etiam in Novo Testamento quemadmodum ex multis Scripturae locis et exemplis liquet; imprimis vero ex inscriptionibus omnium fere Epistolarum Apostolicarum. Paulus enim Rom. 1, 7. et 8. testatur, se scribere omnibus qui Romae erant, dilectis Dei, et vocatis Sanctis, quorum fides per totum mundum erat celebris, 1Cor. cap. 1, 2. Sanctificatis in Christo Jesu, et omnibus qui invocant nomen Christi in omni loco. Cap. 10, 15. Φρονίμοις, id est sapientibus. Ad Philip. 3, 15. τελείοις, id est perfectis. Timotheo, et Tito epistolas mittit, qui jamdiu Evangelistarum munere erant defuncti. Petrus 2. Epist. c. 1, 1. scribit iis, qui ἰσότιμον fidem cum ipso sortiti erant. Johannes 1. Epistola cap. 2, 12. Patribus, qui eum norant qui est a principio: item Adolescentibus, qui fortes

---

Tradition, vol. 6 (Leiden: Brill, 2006), 257–297 (on Spiritualists) and 299–345 (on Anabaptists in the Netherlands).

claim that the literal and genuine sense of Holy Scripture, like a letter that kills,[10] is of no use to the Church of the new testament, and they try to foist on people some fanatic dreams of their own, figments of the imagination in the name of Spirit. But others of them grant that there surely is some use for Scripture in the Church, but only for the first, initial lessons in the Christian faith. However, as soon as those converts have matured, been regenerated, and have reached perfection, then they should progress beyond the elementary principles solely by the instigation of the Spirit, leaving outward Scripture behind, and they must follow his order only, as much in matters of the faith as in conduct.

This thinking[11] is false and harmful. Because if Holy Scripture is neglected, then nothing in the Christian religion* can be established with certainty, for from outside of it no criterion or guidance could be given to distinguish the divine truth from false influences and erroneous forces, which God as just judge often sends on those who disdain the Gospel. This opinion is false also because the Holy Spirit works salvation in the hearts of people only through the outward Word and Holy Scripture. Whence also Paul calls his ministry the ministry of the Spirit (2 Corinthians 3, esp. 3:3).

9

The other opinion[12] is equally wrong, and contrary to Holy Scripture. For not only to those who are untrained in the Christian faith, and beginners, but also to those who are more accomplished and have been regenerated, Holy Scripture everywhere commends its own use and necessity, in the Old and the New Testament. This is clear from many passages and instances in Scripture, but especially from the introductions to almost all the apostolic letters. For Paul declares in Romans 1:7, 8 that he is writing to "all who are at Rome, who are loved by God and called to be Saints, whose faith is renowned throughout the world." In 1 Corinthians 1:2 he writes: "To the sanctified in Christ Jesus, and to all who call on the name of Christ in every place." In chapter 10:15 he writes *phronimois*, that is, "to sensible people"; in Philippians 3:15, *teleiois*, that is, "to those who are mature." He sent letters to Timothy and Titus, who had been discharging the office of evangelist for a long time already. Peter, in the second Epistle chapter 1:1, writes to those who "had received a faith *isotimos*, as precious as his own." John in the First Epistle chapter 2:12[-14] writes "to the fathers who have known Him who was from the beginning"; the same: "To the young men

10

---

10   'A letter that kills' refers to 2 Corinthians 3:6: *Litera enim occidit, Spiritus autem vivificat,* "the letter kills, but the Spirit makes alive."
11   Namely, the first thought mentioned in thesis 8.
12   Namely, the second thought mentioned in thesis 8.

sunt, in quibus Verbum Dei habitat, et qui malum illum vicerunt. Quemadmodum et Apostolus Judas inscribit Epistolam suam, vocatis, a Deo Patre sanctificatis, et a Jesu Christo servatis, versus 1.

XI   Necessitate* igitur Scripturae adversus Jesuitas et Libertinos evicta, deinceps nobis explicandum, unde ejus auctoritas pendeat, vel ut clarius loquamur, unde nobis constet, eam esse divinam, et αὐτόπιστον. Haec autem quaestio adversus duo hominum genera nobis examinanda est: primo, adversus homines profanos, qui cum Celso, Porphyrio, Juliano et similibus Ecclesiae Christi hostibus, Scripturae divinitatem in dubium vocant; deinde adversus Pontificios, qui auctoritatem ejus ex solo Ecclesiae suae testimonio suspendunt.

XII   Quod eos attinet, qui totius Sacrae Scripturae divinitatem in dubium vocant, cum illi Spiritu Christi adhuc sint vacui, ex Spiritus Sancti testimonio,* quod omnibus argumentis est validius, convinci non possunt: nam Spiritum illum mundus non novit, neque recipere potest, ut Christus Joh. 14, 17. testatur. Alia ergo arma adversus eos expedienda sunt, ut ipsorum animus sub obedientiam Christi paulatim redigatur, si forte per Spiritum suum illorum cordibus illucescat; aut ut ipsi contumaciae suae convicti, αὐτοκατάκριτοι maneant. Reducemus vero illa argumenta ad haec tria genera.

2. ON THE NECESSITY AND AUTHORITY OF SCRIPTURE   57

who are strong, in whom the word of God dwells, and who have overcome the evil one." In the same way also the apostle Jude addresses his letter "to the called, the ones sanctified by God the Father, and kept by Jesus Christ" (verse 1).

And so, now that the necessity* of Scripture has been proved over against the Jesuits and Libertines, we must explain next from where its authority derives, or to say it more clearly, from where we get the conviction that it proceeds from God and is *autopistos* [self-convincing]. We must consider this question, then, over against two kinds of people. First, against pagans, who along with Celsus,[13] Porphyry,[14] Julian,[15] and similar enemies of Christ's Church, call into question the divine origins of Scripture. And secondly, against the papal teachers who derive its authority from the affirmation of their Church alone.

As far as those are concerned who call into question the divinity of the entire Scripture, since they still are devoid of the Spirit of Christ, they cannot be refuted by the witness* of the Holy Spirit, which is more effective than all arguments. For, as Christ testifies in John 14:17: "The world does not know that Spirit, nor can it accept Him." Therefore we must procure other weapons against them, to restore their spirit little by little to submit to Christ[16] (if perhaps through his Spirit He will enlighten their hearts), or else so that they themselves, convicted in their own stubbornness, may remain *autokatakritoi* self-condemned.[17] We shall summarize those arguments according to the following three kinds.[18]

11

12

---

13   Celsus, a middle Platonist philosopher, was a fierce critic of Christianity and author of *Alēthēs Logos* (*True Doctrine*), c. AD 178. According to him, faith in incarnation is both irrational and immoral, because it is impossible. In AD 248 Origen composed his response, *Contra Celsum* (*Against Celsus*); see Henry Chadwick, *Origen: Contra Celsum* (2nd print, Cambridge: Cambridge University Press, 1965).

14   Porphyry (b. AD 232/3) was a student of Plotinus (AD 204/5–270). He defended traditional paganism in his *De Philosophia ex Oraculis Haurienda* (*Philosophy from Oracles*), written before the persecutions of Christians during the reigns of Diocletian and Galerius, in which he gave justifications for them.

15   Flavius Claudius Julianus, better known as Julian the Apostate (AD 331/32–363), was the last emperor of the Constantinian dynasty, and the last non-Christian Roman emperor, from 360–363. He sought to restore ancient Roman values in order to save the empire from dissolution. His rejection of Christianity implied support of Neoplatonic paganism.

16   This may be an allusion to 2 Corinthians 10:5.

17   Cf. Titus 3:11.

18   Thesis 12 announces that three kinds of arguments will be discussed against those who despise Scripture (theses 12–27). Here, external arguments are developed, in contrast with the internal witness of the Holy Spirit. Although medieval theology did present moral and rhetorical arguments in favor of the divine authority of Scripture (see *PRRD* 2:50), the

XIII   Primum argumenti genus* petimus ex illis notis et criteriis, quibus cujuscumque historiae fides et veritas solet et potest explorari. Nam si constet Historiam Sacram esse veram ac certam, eadem opera necessario constabit, eam esse divinam et θεόπνευστον; quia ipsa sibi ubique suae divinitatis testimonium amplissimum praebet.

XIV   Arrianus in praefatione, lib. 1. *de expeditione Alexandri*,[a] in historiis humanis certa veritatis κριτήρια esse asserit: Primo, si illi qui scribunt, sint personae fide dignae. Secundo, si actionibus quas scriptis mandant, ipsi interfuerint. Tertio, si neque necessitas, neque merces eis proposita fuerit, quare aliter, quam accidisset, scriberent. Quibus Josephus *contra App.* lib. 1.[b] et hanc addit, si de eisdem rebus eadem omnes scripserint.

XV   Haec, et quaecumque alia certitudinis historicae κριτήρια afferri possunt, multo ampliora et evidentiora in Historia Sacra exstant, quam in ullis scriptis humanis. Nam Scriptores Sacri, partim Reges et Principes fuerunt, partim in re ac statu tenuiori, sapientia plusquam humana celebres, omnes vero viri sancti et sinceri, qui nec suos nec suorum lapsus, si qui acciderint, dissimularunt; et qui sanctitatis ac justitiae testimonium, non tantum apud universos suos discipulos, sed ipsos quoque peregrinos et hostes meruerunt. Quemadmodum Flavius Josephus lib. *contra App.* 1,[c] Aegyptios ipsos hujus rei testes citat: qui Mosen ἄνδρα θαυμαστὸν καὶ θεῖον, admirandum et divinum, existimabant. Et Strabo, lib. 16. *Geographiae*,[d] Mosi et priscis Israelitis hoc testimonium praebet, quod fuerint δικαιοπραγοῦντες καὶ ἀληθῶς θεοσεβεῖς, justitiae cultores, et vere pii. Atque ipse Josephus, Johanni Baptistae, Jacobo fratri Domini, et Servatori

---

[a] Arrian, *Anabasis Alexandri*, preface.   [b] Flavius Josephus, *Contra Apionem* 1.3.15–18.   [c] Flavius Josephus, *Contra Apionem* 1.31.279.   [d] Strabo, *Geographica* 16.37.

increased prominence of these arguments as presented from thesis 13 onward reflects a humanist attitude that parallels the rise of rhetorical, moral and historical arguments for the existence of God; see John Platt, *Reformed Thought and Scholasticism: The Arguments for the Existence of God in Dutch Theology, 1575–1650*, Studies in the History of Christian Thought, vol. 29 (Leiden: Brill, 1982), 119–176.

2. ON THE NECESSITY AND AUTHORITY OF SCRIPTURE 59

We draw the first kind* of argument from those marks and criteria whereby the truth and reliability of any history whatsoever can be and normally is tested.[19] For if the statement holds that sacred history is true and reliable, then by the same token it unavoidably follows that it proceeds from God and is *theopneustos* [God-breathed], because history itself everywhere supplies the fullest evidence of its own divine character.

13

Arrian, in the preface of book 1 about Alexander's expedition,[20] states that in human history reliable criteria exist to establish the truth. First, if the writers are credible persons. Second, if they themselves participated in the events which they commit to writing. Third, if neither an obligation nor a financial reward was offered them, to cause them to write something different from what had happened. To these Josephus, in *Against Appius* book 1, adds this also: If all writers wrote the same things about the same subjects.[21]

14

These and whatever other criteria can be produced for historical certainty occur more abundantly and convincingly in sacred history than in any human writings. For some of the holy writers were kings and rulers, while others, of more modest wealth and standing, were renowned for surpassing human wisdom. But all were holy and honest men who did not hide their own failings or those of their people—if there were any—and who won a reputation for holiness and equity not only from among all of their own followers but also from foreigners and enemies. In the same way Flavius Josephus in book 1, *Against Apion*, mentions the Egyptians themselves as witnesses for this fact, as they considered Moses *andra thaumaston kai theion*, "a man worthy of their respect, and godly."[22] And Strabo in book 16 of the *Geography* provides this witness about Moses and the early Israelites: They were *dikaiopragountes kai alēthoos theosebeis*, "promoters of justice and truly devout."[23] And Josephus

15

---

19   Theses 13–16 deal with the first group of counter-arguments and concern the reliability of the biblical history and the quality of the biblical figures.

20   Arrian (or Lucius Flavius Arrianus) was a writer from Bithynia (c. AD 95–175). He enjoyed a successful career in the Roman army and acted as a public servant under the Emperor Hadrian. Walaeus is referring to Arrian's *Anabasis Alexandrou* (*The Anabasis of Alexander*), a source for the campaign of Alexander the Great.

21   Flavius Josephus (AD 37–c. 100), Jewish historian. His work *Contra Apionem* (*Against Apion*) defends the Jews against the Alexandrian scholar Apion by pointing out the antiquity of the Jewish writings and the lack of knowledge displayed by many Greek authors.

22   The characterization of Moses (traditionally considered the author of the Pentateuch) is taken from Josephus, *Contra Apionem* I 31.

23   Strabo (64/63 BC–c. AD 24) was a Greek geographer and historian. He finished his *Geography* in AD 23. It is the only extant work covering the whole spectrum of peoples and

nostro simile testimonium reddit, sicut et Plinius Junior, lib. 10 *epist.* 101. ad Trajanum Imperatorem,ᵃ de primis et Apostolorum aetati coaevis, aut proximis Christianis id ipsum testari fuit coactus.

XVI   Iidem quoque Scriptores Sacri, auditores et spectatores fuerunt eorum, quae scriptis consignarunt; idque sub conscientia multarum hominum myriadum, qui eadem viderunt, et audiverunt. Nullam quoque mundanam gloriam, aut opes, per scripta sua quaesiverunt; sed contra, non nisi persecutiones, cruces, et mortes illis in mundo fuerunt exspectandae; quum nulla ipsis, nisi adversum ipsos, arma essent parata, et plerique ipsorum suo sanguine veritatem a se propositam libenter obsignarint. Omnes denique uno consensu, diversis in locis, diversis temporibus, diversis conditionibus, eadem omnino docuerunt, et posteris suis reliquerunt. Aut nulla ergo humana scripta pro veris habenda sunt, aut Sacrae Historiae pro veris et certis ab omnibus sunt agnoscendae, ac proinde et pro divinis.

XVII   Haec ratio* hominis profani mentem convincere potest; quae sequuntur, etiam, per Dei gratiam,* fidem ingenerare.

Secundum ergo genus argumenti petitur a perfectione* et divinitate Religionis, quae libris illis continetur. Veram enim Religionem* a Deo solo profectam esse, nemo unquam negavit, quum illa foedus Dei cum homine comprehendat, atque ideo falsarum quoque Religionum Auctores divinitatem aliquam sint ementiti. Jam vero Religionem Christianam solam ex omnibus, quae hactenus in mundo publice receptae sunt, esse veram, inde demonstratur,* quod illa sola verae, ac proinde et divinae Religionis notas habeat.

ᵃ Pliny the Younger, *Epistulae* 10.96.7.

---

countries known during the reign of the emperor Augustus. See H.L. Jones, ed., *The Geography of Strabo*, Loeb Library (8 volumes), 1917–1932. Book XVI deals with Mesopotamia, Syria, Palestine and the Red Sea.

2. ON THE NECESSITY AND AUTHORITY OF SCRIPTURE 61

himself gives the same testimony about John the Baptist, James the brother of our Lord and Savior.[24] So too Pliny the Younger in the Epistle to the emperor Trajan (*Epistles*, book 10.101) was constrained to testify the same thing about the first Christians who were either contemporaries of the apostles or living shortly thereafter.[25]

Also the sacred writers witnessed with their own eyes and ears those things which they preserved in writing; and they recorded them with the awareness of many thousands of people who had seen and heard the same things. Furthermore, through their writings they sought no earthly glory or wealth; to the contrary, they could hope for nothing in this world except suffering, crucifixion, and death. Meanwhile, weapons were not rallied to support but oppose them, and very many of them freely sealed with their own blood the truth they promoted. In fact, all of them with one accord in different places, different times, and different circumstances taught entirely the same things and bequeathed these to those who came after them. Therefore either no human writings at all must be considered as true, or everyone must acknowledge that the sacred accounts are true and reliable—and hence, also divine.

This reasoning* can convince the mind of an unbeliever; the ones that come next are able even to instill faith, by God's grace.* Thus the second kind of argument is drawn from the perfect integrity and divine quality of the religion that these books comprise. For no-one has ever stated that true religion did not proceed from God alone, because it constitutes God's covenant with humanity; for that reason also the authors of false religions have feigned some divine character. Now as to the fact that the Christian religion alone is the true one of all the religions which till now have been commonly accepted in the world is demonstrated* in that it alone displays the marks of true religion, and so is the one that proceeds from God.

16

17

---

24   Josephus finished his *Jewish Antiquities* in AD 93. In *Jewish Antiquities, book* 18 § 63–64 the famous so-called *Testimonium Flavianum* about Jesus is found, but elsewhere he also writes on John the Baptist (*Jewish Antiquities, book* 18 § 116–119) and James, "the brother of Jesus, who is called Christ" (*Jewish Antiquities, book* 20 § 200).

25   Gaius Plinius Caecilius Secundus (AD 61–c. 112), better known as Pliny the Younger, was lawyer, author, and magistrate of Rome. Pliny is known for the letters he wrote to emperors or other notables such as the historian Tacitus. Especially noteworthy is a letter in which he asks the Emperor Trajan for instructions regarding official policy concerning Christians (*Epistulae* x.96–97).

XVIII Notae autem infallibiles Religionis verae, conscientia hominum id ipsis dictante, hae sunt. Primo, quod in illa verus Deus Creator, et Gubernator omnium rerum solus agnoscatur, et colatur; sicuti in sola Religione Christiana fit. Nam Ethnica, quae post Christianam est vetustissima, creaturas, imo et malos Genios pro Diis colit. Turcica vero, et Judaica hodierna, etsi de vero Deo glorietur, praeterquam quod ipsarum origo in mundo est recens, veri Dei atque operum ejus notitiam ineptissimis fabulis et commentis conspurcat.

XIX Secunda verae Religionis nota est: Quod in ea sola vera ratio explicetur, per quam homo peccator cum Deo reconciliari possit, quam in Christiana sola etiam reperire est; quia in illa sola sacrificium peccatis expiandis idoneum, et irae Dei placandae sufficiens invenitur. Quum contra in Ethnica per sacra nefanda, (qualia Saturni, Veneris, Cereris, Bacchi etc. fuerunt) in Turcica vero et Judaica hodierna, per inanes et superstitiosos ritus id frustra quaeratur, qui cutem et carnem a sordibus, non animum et conscientiam a peccatis purgare possunt.

XX Tertia Religionis verae nota est: Quod in ea vera et perfecta Officia erga Deum et proximum* praescribantur; quod in nulla quoque, quam Christiana Religione fit; in qua omnes tam internae, quam externae hominum actiones ad Deum colendum referuntur, omnia seria ac sancta praecipiuntur; in qua Deum supra omnia, proximos vero, imo et hostes nostros, sicut nos ipsos, jubemur diligere. Ethnici autem impiis ludis gladiatoriis et scenicis numina sua colunt. Judaei inanes ceremonias, et externum tantum legis corticem observant, et Sacrae Scripturae Veteris Testamenti manifestam vim inferunt. Ethnici vero, et Turcae, praeter superstitiosos cultus, quibus Deum venerari se profitentur, officia erga homines vel imperfecta praecipiunt, vel horrenda scelera in eos admittunt, religione ipsorum ea vel permittente, vel saltem impunita omnino relinquente.

XXI Tertium vero argumenti genus et praecipuum petitur a certis divinitatis notis, quas Deus in Sacra Scriptura peculiariter exstare voluit. Nam etsi Sacra Scriptura divinitatem suam omnibus in locis testetur, iis qui oculos a Spiritu Dei apertos habent; tamen quemadmodum quidam a sole radii procedunt, qui reliquis sunt illustriores et magis conspicui, ita etiam in divina illa Sacrae Scripturae luce, divinitatis quidam luculentiores radii diversis in locis se produnt, qui auctorem suum apertissime manifestant.

XXII Inter quos primo sunt miracula omnem creatam potentiam* longe excedentia; quibus verbum Dei initio fuit obsignatum, idque in conspectu totarum

Now the infallible marks of true religion, as the consciences of human beings prescribe, are these: First, that in it the true God, as creator and ruler of everything, is acknowledged and honoured, as is the case in the Christian religion alone. For paganism, which is the oldest religion after Christianity, worships created beings, indeed even evil spirits as though they were gods. In fact, the Turkish, and today the Jewish religion, besides the fact that their beginnings on earth are recent, even though it boasts about the true God, pollute the knowledge of the true God and his deeds with silly stories and inventions.

The second mark of true religion is that only it explains the true ground on which sinful man can be restored to God, and that is to be found in the Christian religion alone. For in it alone one finds the only sacrifice fitting for the atonement of sins, and one sufficient to appease God's anger. On the other hand, in pagan religion atonement is sought vainly in abominable rites (such as of Saturn, Venus, Ceres, Bacchus, etc.); and in the Turkish and Jewish religion nowadays it is sought in meaningless and superstitious rituals, which can clean dirt from the skin and body, but not the heart and conscience.

The third mark of the true religion is that in it are prescribed the right and complete duties towards God and the neighbor.* This, too, occurs in no religion except the Christian one, in which all of man's inner as well as outward deeds are directed to the honour of God, and all matters weighty and holy are taught. In it we are demanded to love God above all things, and our neighbors—no, even our enemies—as ourselves. But the pagans worship their deities with base gladiatorial games and theatrical plays. The Jews give heed to empty ceremonies and the outer shell of the law only, and inflict noticeable violence upon the Old Testament of Holy Scripture. But the heathens and the Turks, besides the superstitious forms of worship whereby they purport to revere God, either teach flawed duties towards other people or they permit horrible misdeeds against them, because their religion allows these, or at least lets these go entirely unpunished.

The third and foremost kind of argument is drawn from the specific marks of divinity which God has willed to stand out in Holy Scripture in a special way. For it is true that in every passage Holy Scripture bears witness to its own divinity to those who have their eyes opened by the Spirit of God. Yet, just as some rays coming from the sun are more brilliant and visible than others, so even in the divine light of Holy Scripture certain very bright rays of divinity come out in different passages that display their author most vividly.

First among these marks are the miracles that far surpass every created possibility* and first sealed the Word of God in the sight of all peoples, even

gentium, et sub oculis eorum, qui huic doctrinae totis viribus restiterunt; quorum multa quoque apud exteros historicos testimonia manifesta habent; quemadmodum Justinus Martyr, Tertullianus, et alii antiqui scriptores Christiani, in Apologeticis suis scriptis adversus gentiles demonstrant.

XXIII Deinde idem evidenter* ostendit Sacrae Scripturae materia: ad quam referimus tempus, et ordinem creationis mundi, propagationis hominum et gentium in mundo; dogmata de Deo uno et trino, Christo θεανθρώπῳ resurrectione carnis, extremo judicio, et similia; quae nulli sapientum hujus seculi unquam in mentem venerunt, ac proinde a solo Deo revelari potuerunt; item decem verbis Decalogi, omnem pietatem et justitiam; sex petitionibus precum Dominicarum, omnia ad salutem necessaria, divina plane methodo comprehensa. Huc quoque referimus prophetias et praedictiones sacras, aliquot annorum centurias, imo et chiliades, eventum ipsum antegressas. Quales praecipue sunt, praedictiones de venturo Messia, stante adhuc republ. Judaica; Prophetiae de vocatione gentium ad Ecclesiae communionem; Prophetiae de

before the very eyes of those who resisted this teaching with all their might. There are also many instances of miracles in the non-biblical historians, of the kind that Justin Martyr,[26] Tertullian,[27] and other ancient Christian writers demonstrate in their own apologetic writings against the gentiles.

Secondly, the content of Holy Scripture clearly* shows the same mark of its divine origin; for this we give as examples: the time and order of the creation of the world; the increase of human beings and peoples on earth; the teaching about God the three-in-one; Christ the *theanthrōpos*, God-and-man; the resurrection of the body; the final judgment; and similar doctrines, which have not ever entered the minds of any wise man of this age, and so could have been disclosed only by God. Likewise the ten words of the Decalogue, which contain all piety and justice; the six petitions in the Lord's Prayer— each of them necessary for salvation, clearly framed in a divine manner. For this we also cite as examples the sacred prophecies and predictions which preceded the actual events by several hundreds—even thousands—of years. Such pronouncements include especially the prophecies about the coming of the Messiah, while the Jewish state still existed; the prophecies about the

23

---

26 Justin Martyr (AD 100–165) was born in Shechem (present-day Nablus) and lived for some time in Ephesus. While studying the philosophies of his day he discovered the Hebrew prophets, and came to view their writings as the oldest, truest, and most divine of all philosophies. He moved to Rome where he wrote his *Apology*, addressed to the emperor Antoninus Pius, around 153. Afterwards, perhaps on a visit to Ephesus, he composed the text mentioned in the SPT 4.25, *Dialogus cum Tryphone* (*Dialogue with Trypho*). Justin represents a first attempt to bring together Christian thought and gentile philosophy and he is an important source for statements on the second-century status of the Gospels and the "Memoirs of the Apostles" (see *Dialogue* 99–107). For a nuanced view of Justin's theology see Craig D. Allert, *Revelation, Truth, Canon, and Interpretation: Studies in Justin Martyr's Dialogue With Trypho*, Supplements to Vigiliae Christianae, vol. 64 (Leiden: Brill, 2002).

27 Tertullian (c. AD 160–c. 225), living in North African Carthage, is the first of the fathers of the Western Church to write extensively in Latin. He was an apologist, writing against Marcion and Gnosticism. Later he became a follower of Montanus, adopting a life of strict asceticism. The reference is to his work *On Modesty*, in which he opposes the willingness of some to forgive penitent adulterers. In his view the *Shepherd of Hermas* is too lax on the issue and he therefore denies it a place in the canon. He approves of "an Epistle to the Hebrews under the name of Barnabas" that is "more generally received among the Churches than that apocryphal Shepherd of adulterers." He refers to the warning in Hebrew 6:4–6 that it is impossible to restore those who fall away after having been enlightened.

Idololatriae Ethnicae abolitione per adventum Christi, de liberatione gentis Judaicae ex servitute Aegyptiaca, et Babylonica; de eversione ultima urbis et gentis Judaicae; de haeresium multarum exortu; de erectione et eversione regni Antichristi, etc. Huc denique referimus promissiones spirituales credentibus in Christum factas, nempe remissionis peccatorum, pacis conscientiae, circumcisionis cordis, spiritus precum et adoptionis, tolerantiae in cruce, et similes; quarum effectum veri fideles sentiunt; increduli vero in aliis, velint nolint, coguntur obstupescere, et contrarias minas poenarum spiritualium in se ipsis frequenter experiri.

XXIV Sacrae Scripturae forma et finis* idem evincit: atque imprimis in eadem divina dogmata, summus ubique consensus, in maxima styli simplicitate* maxima majestas et efficacia, leges eaedem latae regibus et subditis, promissiones et poenae utrisque communes denuntiatae, idque non tantum externis actionibus, sed etiam consiliis et cogitationibus eorum secretissimis; finis ubique Dei gloria, et hominum salus, misericordiae erga humiles, et judiciorum adversus contumaces demonstratio.

XXV Adde huc effecta plane divina. Nam ubicumque verbum* Dei et Sacra Scriptura locum invenit, ibi Satanae ludibria, et spiritualis ejus potestas evanescunt; sicuti post Christi ascensum in orbe cognito factum videmus, stupentibus et mirantibus Ethnicis, cur daemonum oracula cessarent; et nostro aevo, ubi Sacra Scriptura in hominum manibus versari coepit, Satanae praestigiae, et vis omnis, qua in ignorantiae tenebris antea usus fuerat, fere disparuit. Eodem referenda est tot gentium in tenebris sedentium, sine armis, per solum hunc spiritualem gladium, et sanctorum patientiam, ad Christum conversio; tot hominum, qui antea sceleribus et mundi coeno involuti erant, in sanctitatis et justitiae exempla omnibus seculis et locis mutatio, quorum nihil simile ulla alia religio habuit.

XXVI Idem denique testantur horum librorum quaedam adjuncta. Inter quae est eorum antiquitas, omnium humanorum scriptorum vetustatem longe excedens; antiquissima autem religio a Deo, utpote origini suae proxima; item perpetua adversus eam Satanae odia et molitiones, tyrannorum persecutiones ac

calling of the gentiles into the fellowship of the Church; the prophecies about the removal of pagan idolatry through the coming of Christ, the release of the Jewish nation from slavery in Egypt and Babylon; about the final destruction of the city [Jerusalem] and of the Jewish people; about the rising of many heresies; about the formation and overturning of the kingdom of the Antichrist, and so on. And finally, we mention the spiritual promises that have been made to believers in Christ, specifically concerning the forgiveness of sins, the peace of the conscience, the circumcision of the heart, the spirit of prayer and sonship, of endurance in the cross; and the like. The true believers feel their impact; the unbelieving, however, are forced to be astounded by miraculous events of another sort, whether they like it or not, and are forced frequently to undergo the corollary threats of spiritual punishments in their own persons.

The form and the goal* of Holy Scripture prove the same divine origin. And foremost is the ubiquitous agreement regarding the same divine doctrine, the highest loftiness and effectiveness in the most plain* style, the same laws granted to kings and to subjects, the same promises and punishments announced to both groups equally, and that not only by outward deeds, but also by their most private plans and deliberations. And everywhere the goal is the glory of God, the salvation of humanity, mercy towards the meek, and the display of judgments against the obstinate. 24

Add to this the effects that are clearly of divine doing; for wherever the Word* of God and Holy Scripture find a place, there the mockeries and spiritual forces of the devil fade away—as we saw happen throughout the known world after Christ's ascension, while the gentiles marveled and wondered why the demonic oracles disappeared. In our times, too, when Holy Scripture is first taken up in the hands of people, the magic tricks of the devil and all the power he had wielded previously in the shadows of ignorance generally disappeared from sight. To this we should add that so many gentiles who were dwelling in darkness turned to Christ without the force of weapons, only through this spiritual sword and the endurance of the saints; the transformation of so many people who previously had been wrapped up in criminal activities and worldly filth, into models of holiness and justice in all ages and places. Not any other religion has produced any results such as these. 25

Finally there is the evidence of certain accompanying attributes in these books. Among these is the fact that they are from antiquity, by far surpassing the age of all writings of human origin; for the oldest religion is from God, as it must be close to its origin in time. So too for the continuous hostility and efforts of Satan against it, the persecutions and vain attempts by tyrants, indeed even 26

frustanei conatus, imo et Dei adversus eos horrenda judicia, qualia in Antiocho Epiphane, Juliano Apostata, et similibus orbis universus vidit.

XXVII   Hae sunt illae notae, ex quibus horum librorum divinitas luce clarius patescit; quam quivis re ipsa experietur, qui sese animo sincero, et salutis suae studioso, ad eorum lectionem et meditationem serio accingit.

XXVIII   Nec vero hic audiendus Socinus, atque alii nonnulli Christiani, qui Sacram Scripturam in rebus praecipui momenti divinam quidem esse concedunt, in circumstantiis tamen et rebus levioris momenti scriptores ejus a Spiritu Dei destitutos errare potuisse; quia haec sententia profanitati viam sternit, et Sacrae Scripturae diserte repugnat, quae testatur, quaecumque scripta sunt, ad nostram institutionem esse scripta, Rom. 15, 4. Et totam Scripturam esse divinitus inspiratam, 2 Tim 3, 16. Item esse interpretationis nullam Scripturam propriae 2 Pet. 1, 20. Imo ne jota quidem unum ex lege periturum, Matth. 5, 18. Nec cuiquam hominum licere ei quicquam addere vel demere, Deut. 4. Apoc. ult.

XXIX   Ex illis quae hactenus a nobis explicata et demonstrata sunt, jam perspicuum est, quam falso Pontificii multi contendant, Ecclesiae majorem auctori-

2. ON THE NECESSITY AND AUTHORITY OF SCRIPTURE

the terrible judgments of God against them, such as the whole world witnessed in the case of Antiochus Epiphanes,[28] Julian the Apostate,[29] and the like.

These are the marks whereby the divinity of these books is revealed more clearly than the light of day; which anyone whosoever will find out in fact, who with an honest heart and eager for his own salvation prepares to read and meditate upon them earnestly.[30]

And here one ought not to pay heed to Socinus[31] and several other Christians who grant that Holy Scripture is divinely-originated in issues of special importance, but that its authors in situations and circumstances of lesser importance were abandoned by the Holy Spirit and could have erred.[32] Because this opinion paves the way for contempt, and expressly contradicts Scripture which testifies that "everything that was written was written for our instruction" (Romans 15:4), and "all Scripture is God-breathed" (2 Timothy 3:16). Likewise "no Scripture is of one's own interpretation" (2 Peter 1:20); indeed, "not even one iota will disappear from the Law" (Matthew 5:18). "And it is not permitted for any man to add to or remove from it" (Deuteronomy 4[:2], Revelation 22[:18–19]).

From these arguments that we have explained and proved thus far it is now abundantly clear how wrong the contention of many papal teachers is, that greater authority rests with the Church than with Scripture;[33] and that

---

28   Antiochus IV Epiphanes (c. 215–164 BC) was Seleucid king of the Hellenistic Syrian kingdom from 175 to 164 BC. As ruler he was known for his promotion of Greek culture and institutions. His attempts to suppress the Jewish people and the desecration of the temple in Jerusalem brought on the Wars of the Maccabees, in which Antiochus was finally defeated.

29   See note at thesis 11.

30   Cf. Walaeus, *Opera* 1:126 for a fourth and fifth argument, the testimony of the Church and its martyrs, and the conviction by the Holy Spirit.

31   Faustus Socinus (1539–1604) was a lay theologian born in Siena and one of the leaders of the anti-trinitarian movements of the sixteenth century. His main work is *De Jesu Christo Servatore* (*The Savior Jesus Christ*, 1578). Socinus regarded Christ as fully human, though without sin. Christ showed the way of salvation, which is attained by imitating him. Socinus explained the person of Christ in terms of his work. Faustus Socinus is also mentioned in disputation 17 on "free choice," because of his optimism about man's ability to follow Christ.

32   Faustus Socinus, *De sacrae scripturae auctoritate libellus* (Racoviae: Sternacius, 1611). In his *Loci Communes* Walaeus mentions Erasmus as displaying the same pernicious view as Socinus, *Opera* 1:126.

33   In his *Loci Communes* Walaeus mentions the following Catholic authors: Wolfgang Hermann, Stanislaus Hosius and Jesuita Balacus, *Opera* 1:127.

tatem esse, quam Scripturae; alii vero, Scripturae auctoritatem a solo Ecclesiae testimonio, saltem quoad nos, pendere.

xxx Etsi enim libenter fateamur, ad Ecclesiae officium pertinere, ut Sacram Scripturam custodiat, cum omni religione ac cura ejus integritatem conservet, a corruptelis hominum vindicet, ejusque divinitatem aliis manifestet, ac probet, unde στῦλος καὶ ἑδραίωμα τῆς ἀληθείας a Paulo 1 Tim. 3. vocatur; nulla tamen hinc Ecclesiae in Scripturam auctoritas est colligenda, sed ministerium tantum et praeconium, quemadmodum principum et magistratuum edicta, a praeconibus et ministris auctoritatem suam non mutuantur, etsi per eos innotescant, et publicentur.

xxxi Sacrae Scripturae vero auctoritatem longe majorem esse quam Ecclesiae, inde nobis manifestum fit; quod Ecclesia errare possit, Scriptura non possit; deinde quod Ecclesiae autoritas (quaecumque tandem illa est) a Scriptura sit, sicut Pontificii ipsi agnoscunt, cum auctoritatem suam ex Scriptura probare* conantur; denique quia Spiritus Sancti testimonium, quod omnibus veris Christi ovibus commune est, Joh. 10. item notae illae divinae, quae in Sacra Scriptura se produnt, majoris multo sint auctoritatis et ponderis, etiam quoad nos, quam solum Ecclesiae testimonium, cum Ecclesiae hoc testimonium persuasionem non nisi humanam; Spiritus Sanctus autem, per Scripturae illas divinas notas, fidem salvificam et divinam animis nostris ingeneret.

xxxii Imo et testimonium Ecclesiae antiquae, quae Prophetis et Apostolis coaeva aut proxima fuit, nobis multo majoris est ponderis, quam hodiernae; quia Ecclesia illa antiqua, praeter illa argumenta quae cum hodierna habet communia,* externa quoque et singularia Propheticae et Apostolicae missionis signacula audivit et vidit. Nempe responsa per Urim et Tummim, miracula, Spiritus Sanctus singularia dona, prophetiam extraordinariam, et similia. Quare et Ecclesia hodierna antiquae illius testimonio, ad librorum divinorum auctoritatem agnoscendam, uti quoque debet et solet. Omne autem argumentum, quo aliquid probatur, evidentius et nobis notius esse debet, quam ipsa conclusio.

of others, too, who claim that the authority of Scripture derives from the testimony of the Church alone, at least insofar as it pertains to us.³⁴

For we admit freely that it is the Church's duty to guard Holy Scripture, to preserve its integrity with all reverence and care, to vindicate it from people's corrupting influence, to exhibit and prove its divine quality to others, whence it is called *stulos kai hedraiōma tēs alētheias*, "the pillar and bulwark of the truth," by Paul in 1 Timothy 3 [:15]. Be that as it may, from this no authority over Scripture should be drawn for the Church, but only service and proclamation, just as the edicts of leading civic officials do not get their authority from the heralds and servants, even though by these men they are made known and published.

It is made clear to us that the authority of Holy Scripture is much greater than that of the Church by the fact that the Church is capable of erring while Scripture cannot. Moreover, it is clear that the authority of the Church (whatsoever that may be) is derived from Scripture, just as the papal teachers themselves recognize, since they try to prove* their own authority from Scripture. And finally, because the testimony of the Holy Spirit, shared by all of Christ's true sheep (John 10), as well as those divine marks that present themselves in Holy Scripture, is of much greater authority and weight—even as far as we are concerned—than the mere testimony of the Church, since this testimony of the Church is nothing but human persuasion. But the Holy Spirit, by means of those divine marks in Scripture instills into our souls the divine faith that brings salvation.

To be sure, the testimony of the early Church, which was contemporary with or immediately after the prophets and apostles, is much greater and weightier to us than today's. For that Church of long ago, besides the proofs it shares* with the contemporary one, heard and saw also additional and unique wonders of the prophetic and apostolic mission. And those are: answers given by means of the Urim and Thummim, miracles, exceptional gifts of the Holy Spirit, extraordinary prophecy and similar acts. Therefore also the Church of today is and should be accustomed to use the affirmation of that early Church to acknowledge the authority of the divine books. For every instance of proof whereby anything is proved should be more evident and more accepted as valid to us than the conclusion itself.³⁵

---

34 In the *Loci Communes* Walaeus refers to Robert Bellarmine and Gregorius de Valencia, *Opera*, 1:127.

35 This sentence may be understood from the general theory of argumentation: In any discourse, the premises are more certain than the conclusion, as one might err in proceeding from premises to conclusion. When applied to Scripture, however, this insight

XXXIII Tantum vero abest, ut sacrorum librorum auctoritas ab Ecclesiae testimonio vel solum, vel praecipue apud fideles pendeat; ut contra nullo modo ab illo pendeat. Nam sicuti lex a Magistratu aliquo lata, a nullis pendet, nisi a quibus ipse Magistratus pendet; ita lex divina a nemine pendere potest, nisi ab ipso Deo: qui a nulla creatura pendet. Et sicuti principia* prima, ac normae immotae non pendent ab utentium auctoritate, sed ab eorum institutore solum, et a sua ipsarum luce atque evidentia;* ita quoque Sacra Scriptura, omnium sacrorum dogmatum supernaturale* principium, et morum ac fidei immota regula, non nisi a Deo, qui eam dedit, et a propria sua luce, quam ei indidit, pendere potest.

XXXIV Idcirco etiam Prophetae et Apostoli, auctoritatem verbi a se praedicati* et scripti, nunquam humanae, imo ne angelicae quidem, auctoritati subjecerunt, sed solius Dei: quemadmodum in Propheticis et Apostolicis prooemiis ac protestationibus passim est videre. Atque ideo denique Christus et Apostoli nunquam discipulos vel auditores suos ad Ecclesiae auctoritatem remittunt; sed vel ad Scripturam Veteris Testamenti vel ad notas illas, atque efficaciam vere divinam, quae se in eorum cordibus exserit, quibus Deus hujus seculi mentes non excaecavit. Gal. 3, 1. et 2. 2 Cor. 3, 3. 4. 2 Cor. 13, 5. 6. etc.

might make the case for the divinity of Scripture vulnerable, as it becomes dependent on contingent facts of historicity and morality. Paul Althaus, *Die Prinzipien der deutschen reformierten Dogmatik im Zeitalter der aristotelischen Scholastik* (Leipzig: Deichert, 1914), 235–256, makes this case against the orthodox Reformed doctrine of Scripture. However, a narrower interpretation within the direct context of thesis 32 seems more likely: The witness of the Early Church (seen as a premise) is weightier and more evident than later interpretations of the same witness (considered as a conclusion).

For believers the authority of the sacred books is so far from depending solely, or even mainly, on the testimony of the Church that it in fact does not depend on it at all. For just as a law given by some magistrate is dependent on no-one except those on whom the magistrate depends, so too the divine law can depend on no-one except God himself, who is dependent on no creature. And just as the first principles* and immovable norms do not depend on the authority of those who use them, but only on the one who has established them, and on its own light and evidence,* so too Holy Scripture, the supernatural* principle of all sacred teaching, and the unmoved rule of faith and moral conduct, can depend on nothing but God who has granted it, and on its own light, which He has put into it. 33

Therefore also the prophets and apostles never subjected the authority of the word they preached* and recorded to human, let alone angelic authority, but only to God's authority—as is evident everywhere in the prophetic and apostolic preambles and declarations. And for that reason, lastly, Christ and the apostles never pointed their disciples or listeners to the authority of the Church, but either to the Scripture of the Old Testament, or to those signs and truly divine results which are displayed in the hearts of those people whose minds have not been blinded by the god of this age (Galatians 3:1–2; 2 Corinthians 3:[2,]3, 4; 2 Corinthians 13:5, 6, etc.). 34

DISPUTATIO III

De Libris Canonicis et Apocryphis

Praeside D. ANTONIO THYSIO
Respondente THEODORO GISBERTI

THESIS I   Loco de Sacrae Scripturae Auctoritate universim proposito, subjicimus eum, qui est de libris Canonicis. Deus enim ex pluribus dictis, scriptisque (ut salvo aliorum judicio arbitramur) divinis, quae serviebant aliquando praesenti Ecclesiae usui, Num. 21, 14. Jos. 10, 13. 2 Chron. 33, 19. 1 Cor. 5,9. August. lib. *de Civ. Dei*, 18, c. 38.ᵃ Theod. *ad Jos.*ᵇ eos singulari providentia selegit, conservarique voluit, qui toti Ecclesiae ad veritatis et pietatis Canonem seu Regulam necessarii utilesque erant, Luc. 1, 1. 2. 3. Johan. 20, 30. 31, qui omnes simul, Sacra Scriptura seu libri Canonici dicuntur.

II   Est autem Sacra Scriptura, seu libri Canonici, Syntagma seu digestum sacrorum librorum, a Deo per servos suos divinitus afflatos, pro cujusque temporis et populi ratione, literis linguaque ab iis maxime intellectis, originaliter conscriptorum, totique Ecclesiae commissorum, ad communem* et perpetuam

---

ᵃ Augustine, *De civitate Dei* 18.38 (CCSL 48:633–634).   ᵇ Theodoret of Cyrus, *Quaestiones in Josuam* (MPG 80:473–476).

DISPUTATION 3

Concerning the Canonical and Apocryphal Books

President: Antonius Thysius
Respondent: Theodorus Gisberti[1]

Having related the *locus* concerning the authority of Holy Scripture generally, we add next to it the one about the Canonical books. For from the very many godly sayings and writings (regardless of the opinions of others[2]) which served as a benefit to the Church as it existed at that time (Numbers 21:14; Joshua 1:13; 2 Chronicles 33:19; 1 Corinthians 5:9; Augustine, *The City of God*, book 18, chapter 38; Theodoretus [of Cyrus][3] *On Joshua*), God in his special provision chose and determined to preserve those books which were necessary and useful to the entire Church as a canon or rule for truth and devotion (Luke 1:1, 2, 3; John 20:30, 31). Taken together, these are called Sacred Scripture or the canonical books.

Sacred Scripture (or the canonical books) is the arrangement or compendium of sacred books originally composed by God through his divinely inspired servants, with consideration for each era and people, in writing and language best understood by them. They have been entrusted to the entire Church for worldwide* and lasting instruction in the truth of salvation—that

---

1 Born in 1594 in Heicop (near Vianen), Theodorus Gysberti matriculated on 23 November 1619 in theology. He defended this disputation on 21 March 1620 and dedicated his defense to Thysius, to the Franeker professor of theology Maccovius (1588–1644), to the Leiden orientalist Erpenius (1584–1624), and to the Franeker professor of Hebrew Amama (1593–1629). He was ordained in Meerkerk in 1620, Heukelum (1638) and Polsbroek (1650); he died in 1661. See Du Rieu, *Album studiosorum*, 144, and Van Lieburg, *Repertorium*, 75; also *Classicale acta 1573–1620*, vol. 8, Classis Gorinchem 1579–1620, ed. A.J. Verschoor (Den Haag: Instituut voor Nederlandse Geschiedenis, 2008), 483 (6 April 1620, §12).

2 Protestant orthodox theologians disagreed on the issue whether some inspired writings were lost (see PRRD 2:387–395). Thysius says that God has chosen and preserved those books that were necessary out of a larger number of writings, thus implying that there were other inspired writings. He may be thinking of sources mentioned in the Old Testament, for example, the book of the wars of the Lord (Num. 21:14), and the book of Jasher (Jos. 10:13, 2 Sam. 1:18).

3 Theodoret (c. AD 393–c. 457) became bishop of Cyrus in 423. He played a role in the christological controversies, and defended the use of the term *theotokos* ("mother of God"; see also SPT 19.30). His extant writings include over 200 letters, commentaries, and the *Historia ecclesiastica* (*History of the Church*). The latter is cited several times by the authors of the *Synopsis*.

de salutari veritate, nempe de Deo, ejusque benevola et benefica voluntate,* institutionem; fidelioremque verbi et veritatis ejus conservationem; ulteriorem propagationem, et certiorem corrupti restaurationem.

III   Appellantur Scripta haec: *Scriptura Dei, Sancta,* Ex. 32, 16. *Sacra,* Rom. 1, 2. *Sacrae literae,* 2 Tim. 3, 15, et absolute* κατ' ἐξοχὴν *Scriptura,* Joh. 10, 35, seu *Scripturae,* Joh. 5, 39. Sancta quidem, quod a communi usu segregata; Sacra vero, quod Deo dicata; adeoque Sacrosancta, scilicet ab auctore Deo Sancto; rerum sanctarum et sacrarum argumento; scriptionis charactere divinae sanctitati congruo, sanctificationis fine effectuque. Quin etiam *Verbum,* Sermo, Eloquium, Oraculaque Dei; item Lex, Doctrina, Testimonium,* Foedus* et *Testamentum Dei,* etc. Psal. 19, 8. et 119. Esai. 2, 3. Rom. 3, 2. 2 Cor. 3, 14. 2 Pet. 3, 16. Atque his appellationibus, ut Vetus Testamentum fere insigniatur, comprehenditur tamen et Novum. Estque in his, excellentiae istorum, supra omnia humana qualiacumque scripta, declaratio; imo ab iisdem disjunctio.

IV   Quum *Syntagma* esse definitur, totum et corpus quoddam, pluribus partibus membrisque constans, seu digestum ac codex pluribus sacris libris constitutus, significatur,* 2 Tim. 3, 16. Ut porro singuli Scripturae libri, βίβλου et voluminis, Luc. 3,4. Act. 1, 20, ita plures simul partes, et totum, praeter Scripturae vocem* sylleptice sumptam, et Scripturarum appellationem, Bibliorum Sacrorum, et simpliciter Bibliorum κατ' ἐξοχὴν, nomenclatura venit, Deut. 29, 21. Act. 7, 42. 1 Cor. 15, 3. 4.

V   In hoc vero Syntagmate, consideramus singulorum librorum Scriptionem, et omnium simul Collectionem digestionemque.

VI   Scriptionis singulorum istorum librorum, causa* efficiens principalis, jussu instinctuque suo, Deus Pater est, in Filio, per Spiritum Sanctum, Exod. 17, 14. Jer. 36, 1. Apoc. 1, 1. et 2. cap. etc. Administri seu instrumenta, sancti Dei servi, Θεόκλητοι καὶ Θεόπνευστοι, divinitus vocati et afflati, et φερόμενοι, acti Sancti

3. CONCERNING THE CANONICAL AND APOCRYPHAL BOOKS

is, the truth about God and his bountiful and generous good pleasure*—and to preserve his Word and truth in a reliable way; further to proclaim them and surely to restore them in case of corruption.

These writings are called "the holy Writing of God" (Exodus 32:16), "sacred" (Romans 1:2), "sacred writing" (2 Timothy 3:15), and simply* "writing" (John 10:35) or "writings" (John 5:39). They are called "holy" because they have been set apart from every-day use; "sacred" because they have been dedicated to God. They are called "most holy" because the holy God is their author, because their subject matter is holy and devoted, because the nature of the writing accords with the divine holiness, and because their goal and aim is holiness of life. The Scripture is also called Word,* Speech, Utterance, Prophecy of God; also Law, Teaching, Testimony,* Covenant and Testament of God, etc. (Psalm 19:8, and Psalm 119; Isaiah 2:3; Romans 3:2; 2 Corinthians 3:14; 2 Peter 3:16). And just as these names generally apply to the Old Testament, so too do they cover the New Testament. And in these names is a declaration of their superiority over all human writings of any quality whatsoever, indeed, of their separation from them. 3

When Sacred Scripture is defined as an arrangement, it means* an entire unit, or sort of corpus, that consists of many parts and pieces, or a collection and volume formed by many sacred books (2 Timothy 3:16). Moreover, just as an individual book of Scripture is called *biblos* or "book" (Luke 3:4; Acts 1:20), so several books together, and also the book as a whole, are called* not only "Scripture" (with an improper use of the singular[4]), but above all "Scriptures," or "Sacred Books" or simply "Books" (Deuteronomy 29:21; Acts 7:42; 1 Corinthians 15:3, 4). 4

In this arrangement we give consideration to the writing of the individual books [6–11], and, taking them all together, we consider their arrangement and distribution [12–41]. 5

God the Father, in the Son and through the Holy Spirit, is the first efficient cause* of the writing of these individual books by his order and instigation (Exodus 17:14; Jeremiah 36:1[-4]; Revelation 1:1, chapter 2, etc.). The ministers or instruments are holy servants of the Lord, *theoklētoi kai theopneustoi,* 'called by God and breathed upon by Him,' and *pheromenoi,* 'driven' by the Holy 6

---

4 *Sylleptice*—rendered here as "with an improper use of the singular"—is a grammatical and rhetorical term of Greek origin that means "a figure by which a word, or a particular form or inflexion of a word, is made to refer to two or more words in the same sentence, while properly applying to or agreeing with only one of them, or applying to them different senses (e.g., literal and metaphorical)" (*Shorter Oxford English Dictionary*, Oxford: Clarendon, 1933).

Spiritus Unde Scriptura θεόπνευστος, divinitus inspirata, appellatur, 2 Timoth. 3, 16. Rom. 16, 26. 2 Pet. 1, 20. Veruntamen Decalogum Deus ipse suo digito exaravit, qui propterea singulariter Scriptura Dei dicitur Exod. 32, 15. Deut. 10, 4. et divinitus, humana manus, ad Balthazaris regis profanum epulum apparens, certa exitii praenuntia verba parieti inscripsit, Dan. 5, 5. 24, et Christus digito suo quaedam in terra scripsisse commemoratur, Joh. 8, 6. 8.

VII Modus* scriptionis hic fuit: modo Deus inspirantis et dictantis, Scriptores vero amanuensium, et ad certam formulam scribentium, Exod. 34, 27. 28. Apoc. 2, 1. etc.; modo assistentis et dirigentis, Matth. 22, 43. Hebr. 1, 1. ipsi vero, commentantium et auctorum rationem habuerunt, Luc. 1, 1. 3. Non enim semper mere παθητικῶς passive, sed et ἐνεργητικῶς, effective se habuerunt, ut qui et ingenium, mentisque agitationem et discursus, et memoriam, dispositionem et ordinem stylumque suum (unde scriptionum in iis diversitas) adhibuerunt, Amos. 7, 14. 15. 2 Cor. 10, 10. et 11, 6, praesidente tamen perpetuo Spiritu Sancto, qui ita eos egit et rexit, ut ab omni errore mentis, memoriae, linguae et calami, ubique praeservarentur, 2 Sam. 23, 1. 2. 1 Cor. 7, 25. 40.

VIII Quin et illi aliorum etiam interdum opera, ut scribarum, usi sunt, ut Jeremias Baruchi, Jer. 36, 4. Paulus Tertii, Rom. 16, 22; aut alienas scriptiones sua voce et auctoritate comprobarunt, ut Petrus Marci, Paulus Lucae Evangelium, ut volunt veteres Patres. Orig. apud Euseb. *Eccl. Hist.* Lib. 6. cap. 19.[a]

---

[a] Wrong reference; correct to Eusebius, *Historia ecclesiastica* 6.25.5 (SC 41:127).

Spirit. Hence Scripture is called *theopneustos*, "God-breathed" (2 Timothy 3:16; Romans 16:26; 2 Peter 1:20). But even so, God himself with his own finger inscribed the Ten Commandments, which in that special case are called the "Writing of God" (Exodus 32:15; Deuteronomy 10:4). And by divine action a hand in human form appeared at the impious banquet of King Balthazar and wrote upon the wall clear words foretelling his demise (Daniel 5:5, 24). And it is recorded that Christ with his own hand wrote something upon the ground (John 8:6, 8).

The manner* of writing was as follows: Sometimes God was the one who inspired and dictated, while the writers, like secretaries, were the ones who wrote according to a fixed formula (Exodus 34:27, 28; Revelation 2:1). At other times God assisted and directed (Matthew 22:43; Hebrews 1:1), while they had a task as interpreters and authors (Luke 1:1, 3). For they never conducted themselves purely *pathētikōs*, passively, but *energētikōs*, being involved in the process, as ones who applied their own intellect, mental activities and processes, recollection, order of the arguments, and their own style of writing (from where comes the variety of writing-styles among them) (Amos 7:14, 15; 2 Corinthians 10:10 and 11:6). But the Holy Spirit was constantly leading them, as He directed and guided them to such an extent that they were kept from every error in thought, memory, word and pen (2 Samuel 23:1, 2; 1 Corinthians 7:25, 40).

7

In fact, even those writers occasionally enjoyed the assistance of other men as their scribes, such as Jeremiah of Baruch (Jeremiah 36:4), Paul of Tertius (Romans 16:22); or they approved one another's writings with their own word of support and authority, such as Peter of the Gospel of Mark, and Paul of the Gospel of Luke, as the early church-fathers argued (Origen[5] in Eusebius,[6] *Ecclesiastical History*, book 6, chapter 19).

8

---

5   Origen (c. AD 184–254) was a teacher at the Catechetical School of Alexandria, and a prolific writer of exegetical works, practical treatises, dogmatic and apologetic studies. As a biblical scholar, Origen combined his knowledge of the languages and the history of Scripture with an allegorical exegesis of the Old Testament. In the doctrine of the Trinity, he defended a subordinationist view of the Son and the Spirit, which would influence later theologians. Some of his teachings, however, became controversial, especially his ideas of universal restoration and the pre-existence of the souls. See Ronald E. Heine, *Origen: Scholarship in the Service of the Church* (Oxford: Oxford University Press, 2010).

6   Eusebius (c. AD 263–339) was trained in his native city of Caesarea by the Origenist teacher Pamphilus († AD 309). He became bishop of Caesarea around 313. He was counselor to Constantine and wrote his biography. Eusebius played a role in the Council of Nicea in 325. As a proponent of Origen's subordinationism, he opposed Athanasius's strictly Nicene views. His most important work is *Ekklēsiastikē Historia* (*History of the Church*). He also wrote a *Universal History* (*Pantodapē historia*).

III. DE LIBRIS CANONICIS ET APOCRYPHIS

IX Materia scriptionis, est sermo, quo res, mens sententiaque divina, puta de natura* Dei, ejusque gratuita et benevola voluntate, enuntiatur; estque hic sermo, seu sermonis genus* et character plane divinus, 1 Cor. 2, 13. Forma autem est in veritatis et mentis divinae, sermone prolatae, divina expressione, scripto facta. Finis* denique, est omnium, et praesentium, maxime absentium, de rebus divinis institutio, 2 Cor. 10, 10. 11. Joh. 20, 31. Rom. 15, 4., quae, prout scriptio vel ad pauciores, vel plures primo dirigebatur et spectabat, ita vel particularior, vel communior fuit.

X Authentica porro Scripturae editio ea censenda est, quae αὐτογράφως, id est, primitus et originaliter, divina auctoritate est edita: quae est ἀρχέτυπον ipsum, Deut. 31, 9. 24. 26. 2 Reg. 22, 8. 13. 2 Paral. 34, 14., aut ejus ἀπόγραφον, id est, exemplar, Deut. 17, 18., nempe singuli libri Veteris Testamenti Hebraice, (nisi quod pauculae voces, sententiae et capita Chaldaice sint scripta) Novi vero Graece, praeter paucula Hebraice et Syriace inserta, ac Graece fere reddita; quod ea lingua tunc Orienti et Occidenti communissima esset, Cic. *pro Archia poeta*:[a] stylo tamen partim vulgari, partim Hebraeograeco, Hellenistis Judaeis usitato.

XI Expressa ex Authentica, est et ipsa Scriptura Sacra, quatenus ea in alias linguas religiosissime translata, presse et plene (quantum quidem ejus fieri potest) ei respondet; quod fieri non licitum modo et utile (secus quam quidam Pontificii volunt) sed omnino necessarium est, Act. 2, 4. 6. 11. Neh. 8, 8. 9. 14. 18, ut cujus usus est omnium, Deut. 31, 11. Col. 3, 16. ab omnibus et quibusvis, etiam Laicis, intelligi, legi, audirique possit, 1 Cor. 14, 9. 11. 19. 27. Ineptum tamen, aut Graecam 70 Interpretum, aut Latinam utriusque Testamenti versionem, cum iisdem Pontificiis, aut ullam aliam, non receptam usitatamque modo, sed Authenticam, facere. Concil. Trident. Sess. 4. c. 2.[b]

---

[a] Cicero, *Pro Archia poeta* 23.   [b] DH 1506.

3. CONCERNING THE CANONICAL AND APOCRYPHAL BOOKS 81

The subject-matter of the writing is the spoken word whereby something 9
is declared—in this case the intent and thought of God, namely, about his
nature* and his unmerited and bounteous good will. And this spoken word, or
the sort* and nature of this word, is derived completely from God (1 Corinthians
2:13). The form exists in the divine expression, turned into writing, of the
divine truth and intent brought forward by speech. And lastly, the goal* is
instruction in matters pertaining to God of all people, not only those present,
but especially those then absent (2 Corinthians 10:10, 11; John 20:31; Romans
15:4). This instruction is either more specific or more general, whether the
initial writing was directed and aimed at fewer or at more numerous people.

Furthermore, the edition of Scripture that should be considered authentic 10
is the one that was issued *autographōs*, that is, 'originally' and 'directly from
its source,' by the authority of God. This is the *archetypos* [archetype][7] itself
(Deuteronomy 31:9, 24, 26; 2 Kings 22:8, 13; 2 Chronicles 34:14), or its *apographos*,
that is, "the copy of it" (Deuteronomy 17:18). These certainly include the individual books of the Old Testament in Hebrew (with the exception of a very
few words, sentences, and chapters written in Aramaic), and those of the New
Testament in Greek, except for a few small insertions in Hebrew and Syrian—
nearly all translated into Greek, because that was the most common language
of the East as well as the West (Cicero, *In Defense of Archias the Poet*). As far
as the style is concerned, it was partly in the common language, partly in the
Hebraic-Greek style that the Hellenized Jews used.

Another rendering of the authentic version is itself also Sacred Scripture, 11
so long as it has been translated into other languages as devoutly as possible,
and corresponds to it precisely and completely—as much, at least, as this
can be done. Such translation is not only permitted and useful (contrary to
what certain papal teachers have determined), but also entirely necessary
(Acts 2:4, 6, 11; Nehemiah 8:8, 9, 14, 18), so that it may be of use to all people
(Deuteronomy 31:11; Colossians 3:16), and so that it may be understood, read,
and heard by all people and those of any kind—also lay-people. However, it
would be foolish (along with those same papal teachers) to declare either the
Septuagint, or the Latin translation of either Testament, or any other version,
not only the received and commonly employed version, but even the authentic
one. (Council of Trent, session 4, chapter 2).[8]

---

7   Note that *archetypos* is used here in the more general sense, and not in the specific sense of 'archetypal theology' discussed in *SPT* 1.3.
8   Against post-Tridentine Roman Catholic polemicists, who buttressed the Council's doctrine of the dogmatic superiority of the Vulgate by arguing a textual superiority of the Vulgate over the Masoretic Hebrew of the Old Testament (including its vowel points), the Reformed

XII Haec de scriptione sacrorum librorum. Συλλογὴ seu collectio et digestio eorum, facta est et ipsa divinitus, idque partim immediate,* partim mediate.* Immediate quidem librorum illorum, qui a Scriptoribus divinis, ut primo toti Ecclesiae exarati, ita et ei commissi et commendati sunt, Rom. 3, 2. Ut in Veteri Testamento libri Mosis, (qui in Sacrarium ab ipso illati, juxta Arcam, divino mandato, positi fuerunt, Deut. 31, 2.) et in Novo, Evangelia, quae, ut subjecto* communia, ita nullam, excepto Lucae, particularem inscriptionem prae se ferunt. Atque in his veritatis salvificae fundamentum* est.

XIII Mediate vero illorum, qui ab Auctoribus ipsis quidem ad particulares primum Gentes, Ecclesias, easque augustissimas et metropoles, vel earum Antistites (idque particulari saepe occasione, 1 Cor. 1, 11. et 5. 6. 7. 8. 9. capitibus) scripti, usum primum habuerunt particularem; atque ab his non temere seu fortuito, sed singulari Dei providentia (quae Ecclesiis de necessariis prospicit) sunt conservati, cumque aliis communicati, Col. 4, 16. 2 Thess. 3, 17. 2 Pet. 3, 15., tum mandato, tum pietatis sanctaeque communionis lege, divinoque instinctu, ab iis, imo omnibus, ut divini acceptati sunt; idque non libero aliquo Ecclesiae actu, sed necessaria susceptione. Atque in his salvificae illius veritatis uberior explicatio est.

XIV Haec autem communicatio et acceptatio, tum locum habuit, cum certum judicium de iis libris fieri et haberi potuit; nempe (praeter insitas et supra dictas notas) tum ordinarie seu ordinariis mediis, vel Scriptoris ipsius divini Testimon., Joh. 21, 24. Luc. 1, 1. 3. vel, αὐτῇ χειρί, id est, propriae manus scriptione, Gal. 6, 11, aut subscriptione, quae a fidelibus tunc temporis cognoscebatur, quo judicio Paulus ψευδεπιγράφας epistolas a germanis discerni voluit, 2 Thes. 2, 2. et 3, 17. vel fidis ejus rei Testibus, qui in inscriptione, vel salutationibus adhibentur, Rom. 16, 21. 22. 1 Cor. 1, 1. et 16. 19., tum extraordinarie, Prophetarum (quum Prophetiae donum in Ecclesia adhuc vigeret, 1 Cor. 12, 4. 7. et 14, 29. 32.) judicio. Atque hoc judicium tantum primae Ecclesiae fuit; posterioris, proprie* est ejus recognitio, et sibi commissi divini depositi apud posteros commendatio, et in manus traditio, Rom. 3, 2.

XV Unde factum est, ut de quibusdam libris (qui judicio Prophetarum et Apostolorum cessante, a succedente Ecclesia serius cum reliquis sunt communi-

---

defended the authenticity of the Hebrew text and the antiquity of the vowel points in the Hebrew text. See Richard A. Muller, "The Debate over the Vowel Points and the Crisis in Orthodox Hermeneutics," *After Calvin: Studies in the Development of a Theological Tradition* (Oxford: University Press, 2003), 146–155.

3. CONCERNING THE CANONICAL AND APOCRYPHAL BOOKS

Thus far about the writing of the sacred books. The *syllogē*, or accumulation, and collection of them itself was also divinely made, and that was partly non-mediated,* and partly mediated.* Immediately distributed books are those which from the start were entrusted and commended by the divine writers to the Church as a whole (Romans 3:2) just as they were written down for the first time. Such is the case for the Old Testament books of Moses (which he himself carried into the sanctuary and which by divine order were placed beside the ark, Deuteronomy 31:26) and for the New Testament Gospels, which, as they share the same subject* matter, have no individual dedication—with the exception of Luke. And these books comprise the foundation* of the truth that brings salvation.

Books that were distributed in a mediate way, however, are those that were written by the authors themselves for specific peoples or churches (these being the most venerable and metropolitan ones) or their leaders (and often on a particular occasion, 1 Corinthians 1:11, and chapters 5, 6, 7, 8, 9) and that first had a specific address. And these books were preserved by them not by chance or some rash decision, but by God's special providence (which looks out for the special needs of the Church), and they were communicated to others (Colossians 4:16; 2 Thessalonians 3:17; 2 Peter 3:15) and were received by them and indeed by all recipients as sent by God, both by command and by the law of piety and sacred fellowship, through the initiative of God. This happened not by some free act of the Church but as a necessary undertaking. And these books contain a more fulsome exposition of the truth that brings salvation.

This communication and reception took place at the time when a sure assessment of these books could be made and upheld (besides their previously mentioned obvious inherent qualities) in the ordinary fashion and by the usual means, either by the testimony of the divinely-inspired writer himself (John 21:24; Luke 1:1,3) or *autei cheiri*, that is, by writing "with his own hand" (Galatians 6:11). Or the testimony was in his signature, which was known to the believers at that time (by which test Paul determined that *pseudepigraphai*, falsely-authored letters, be distinguished from genuine ones, 2 Thessalonians 2:2, and 3:17). Or it was by faithful witnesses of the events, who are named in the opening greetings (Romans 16:21, 22; 1 Corinthians 1:1 and 16:19), in special fashion by the authority of the prophets (when the gift of prophecy in the Church still flourished, 1 Corinthians 12:4,7 and 14:29, 32). And this authority was only for the early Church; for the later Church it was proper* to acknowledge it and to recommend and transmit to future generations what had been entrusted by God to its safe-keeping (Romans 3:2).

Hence it happened that occasionally some people doubted and disclaimed the authority of certain books, which the succeeding Church later joined to the

cati) ab aliquibus aliquando dubitatum iisque contradictum sit. Certe omnes, post Zachariam et Malachiam postremos Prophetas, (a quibus deinceps Sapientes Synagoga Judaica enumerat) Jos. *contra App.* apud Eus. lib. 3. c. 9.[a] ut et post obitum Apostolorum et Apostolicorum virorum, cum extraordinariis donis Prophetia desinente, aut saltem interrupta, (a quo tempore *Patres* inchoat Ecclesia) scripti editique, pro utilibus quidem et Ecclesiasticis, at vero non pro sacris et divinis, sunt habiti.

XVI Finis istius collectionis, et conjunctionis librorum sacrorum est, ut haec Scriptura universae Ecclesiae Dei perfectus et perpetuus Canon esset, et Regula veritatis coelestis, id est, fidei et vitae, Ps. 102, 19. Rom. 15, 4. 2 Tim. 3, 16., utque Verbum Dei, et eo comprehensa veritas, conservaretur, ulterius propagaretur, et si quae corruptio incidisset, certius restauraretur, Luc. 1, 4. Mat. 22, 29.

XVII Quare haec Scriptura atque libri, Canonici, Ecclesiastica appellatione, in Syn. Laod.[b] Euseb. passim, Athan. in *Synopsi*,[c] e Scriptura deducta, 2 Cor. 10, 13. Gal. 6, 16. Phil. 3, 16. vocantur; nempe quod singuli eorum relati sint in Canonem et ad eum pertineant, simulque omnes perfectum omnibus modis Canonem constituant, id est, non tantum plenum numerum ac catalogum librorum sacrorum, sed et Regulam et Normam omnis sanae sanctaeque doctrinae, cultusque divini; qualiter dum simpliciter dicuntur, id ipsum non in parte, sed universim, et adaequate ad res, quarum sunt Canon, intelligendum est.

XVIII Proinde sola haec Scriptura, Principium* a quo; et Materia ex qua omnis salutaris veritas deducenda; Canon et Norma, ad quam exigenda omnis vera, adeoque et falsa de rebus divinis doctrina, Esai. 8, 20. Luc. 16, 29. Act. 17, 10. 11.

---

[a] Eusebius, *Historia ecclesiastica* 3.9–10 (SC 31:114–116).   [b] Mansi 2:589 (NPNF2 14:158).
[c] Athanasius, *Synopsis sacrae scripturae* (MPG 28:283–284). Most scholars assume that it is not written by Athanasius but by an unknown church writer from the sixth century.

others when authorization by the prophets and apostles ceased. At any rate, these are all the books written and published after the last prophets, Zechariah and Malachi (after whom the numbering of 'the Wise' by the Jewish Synagogue starts, Josephus, *Against Appian*, in Eusebius, book 3, chapter 9), and also those books written and published after the death of the apostles and the apostolic leaders, when the gift of prophecy, along with the exceptional gifts, came to an end or at least was interrupted (at which time the patristic era of the Church begins). While these books are useful and relevant to the Church, they have not been considered sacred or inspired by God.

The goal of the arrangement and combination of sacred books was for this Scripture to be the complete and everlasting Canon for the whole Church, and the rule of heavenly truth, that is, of faith and life (Psalm 102:19; Romans 15:4; 2 Timothy 3:16[, 17]), and that the Word of God and the truth it contains be preserved, further increased, and, if any corruption should come about, be restored more firmly (Luke 1:4; Matthew 22:29).

Therefore this Scripture and its books are called 'canonical' by ecclesiastical designation (in the Synod of Laodicea, Eusebius, *passim*; Athanasius[9] in *Synopsis*, drawn from Scripture, 2 Corinthians 10:[13–]16; Galatians 6:16; Philippians 3:16). And rightly so, because the individual books have been gathered into the canon and belong to it, and they together comprise the complete canon in every way, that is, not only as the full number and series of sacred books, but also as the rule and norm for every sound and sacred teaching, and of divine worship. And as each book individually is called canonical it must be understood not just for a portion of them but for the whole generally, and equally for the things of which they are the canon.

So then this Scripture alone is the fundamental principle* by which, and the material from which, every saving truth must be drawn. It is the rule and standard by which every true and also every false teaching about the things of God must be determined (Isaiah 8:20; Luke 16:29; Acts 17:10,11). In sum, it is

---

9 Athanasius (AD 296/298–373) was born to a Christian family near Alexandria. Athanasius served as deacon of the church of Alexandria and as the personal secretary of its bishop, Alexander, in which position he attended the Council of Nicea. After 328, Athanasius was the bishop of Alexandria for 45 years. During these years, he was involved in doctrinal controversies following the Nicene Council, and was sent into exile five times, totalling 17 years. Athanasius defended the Nicene doctrine of the Trinity against Arianism and semi-Arianism.

Testis denique et Judex αὐτόπιστος et irrefragabilis, sua scilicet evidentia,* a quo judicanda omnis, quae de rebus divinis. agitatur, controversia, Joh. 5, 39, 45.

XIX Κριτήριον autem, seu Norma judicii, hisce axiomatis comprehenditur. 1. Quicquid ea continetur, aut cum ea vel expresse, vel firma consequentia consentit, verum dogma est. 2. Quod dissentit, falsum esse necesse est. 3. Quicquid autem ea non continetur, quamvis simpliciter ab ea non dissentiat, non est necessarium ad salutem dogma.

XX Libri vero Canonici, ac proinde Canon, fuerunt initio libri Mosis, Deut. 4, 2. Rom. 2, 17. 18. 19. 20, quibus alii accesserunt, partim ad praxin et historiam Ecclesiae, ut succedentes Historici; partim ad interpretationem, applicationem et uberiorem praedictionem de Messia, ut Didactici, et Prophetici sic dicti; partim ad impletionem et complementum praedictionum de Messia ejusque regno, ut Novum Testamentum, etc. 2 Pet. 1, 19. Ita ut Vetus Testamentum sit fundamentum Novi, Novum Veteris complementum. Adeoque hisce libris Canon non est factus perfectior, quoad universalia salutis dogmata, sed quoad eorum singularitatem, claritatem et evidentiam.

XXI Divisio librorum in Vetus et Novum Testamentum, 2 Cor. 3, 14. non est intelligenda simpliciter respectu Legis et Evangelii, quatenus opponuntur, (nam Evangelium, quod idem est re cum promissione, etiam est in Vetere Foedere, et Lex pariter in Novo, Gal. 3, 8. Heb. 4, 2. Rom. 10, 4.) sed respectu totius

3. CONCERNING THE CANONICAL AND APOCRYPHAL BOOKS

a self-convincing[10] and irrefutable witness and Judge, namely by virtue of its own demonstrated proof* by which every controversy which arises over divine matters must be judged (John 5:39, 45).

Moreover, the criterion or norm for judging is comprised of these axioms: 1. Whatever Scripture contains, or whatever agrees with it either explicitly or by a necessary consequence from it, is true doctrine.[11] 2. That which disagrees with it must be false. 3. Whatever is not contained in it, although it may not be openly opposed to it, is a teaching not necessary for salvation.

The canonical books, and thus the canon, at first comprised the books of Moses (Deuteronomy 4:2; Romans 2:17, 18, 19, 20). To these others were added, partly regarding the practice and the history of the Church (such as the subsequent historical books), partly for the interpretation, application, and fuller proclamation about the Messiah (namely the so-called didactic and prophetic ones), and partly to complete and fill out the preaching about the Messiah and his kingdom (namely the New Testament, etc., 2 Peter 1:19). As the Old Testament is the foundation of the New, so the New Testament is the fulfillment of the Old. And so the canon was not made more complete by means of these books insofar as the universal doctrines of salvation are concerned, but insofar as their unique qualities, clarity, and evidence are concerned.

The division of the books into the Old and New Testament (2 Corinthians 3:14) should not be understood merely with respect to Law and Gospel, in that the one contrasts with the other (for the Gospel, which essentially is identical to the promise, is found also in the Old Covenant, and the Law equally in the New, Galatians 3:8, Hebrews 4:2, Romans 10:4), but with respect to the entire

---

10 The Greek word *autopistos* literally means credible of itself. It became influential in the Reformed concept of the authority of Scripture through Calvin (*Institutes* 1.7.5). The term originates from ancient Greek philosophy. In the original philosophical context the term refers to axioms that are convincing without further demonstration. See Van den Belt, *Authority of Scripture*, 148–153.

11 Here Thysius refers to the doctrine of good consequences (*bonae consequentiae*), i.e., the method of drawing necessary and valid inferences from the text of Scripture in order to establish Christian doctrine. See Willem J. van Asselt, "*Bonae Consequentiae*: Johannes Maccovius (1588–1644) and the Use of Reason in Explaining Scripture and Defending Christian Doctrine," in: Philippe Bütgen, and others, eds., *Vera Doctrina. Zur Begriffsgeschichte der Lehre von Augustin bis Descartes / L'idée de doctrine d'Augustin à Descartes* (Wiesbaden: Harrassowitz Verlag, 2009), 283–296. On the medieval backgrounds of this theory, see Norman Kretzmann, Antony Kenny, Jan Pinborg, eds., *The Cambridge History of Later Medieval Philosophy* (Cambridge: Cambridge University Press, 1992), 300–314. Some twenty-five years after the *Synopsis*, the idea of 'good and necessary consequence' was included in the Westminster Confession of Faith (*WCF* 1.6; Schaff, *Creeds*, 603).

dispensationis* salutis factae Veteri et Novo populo. Atque ut ibi est promissio, ita hic ejus exhibitio, seu Evangelium specialiter dictum, Rom. 1, 1. 2. Quamvis a potiore parte denominatio esse possit.

XXII Etiam distinctio in Propheticam et Apostolicam, Rom. 16, 26. 2 Pet. 1, 19. non ita accipienda est, quasi Veteris Testamenti libri omnes sint Prophetici proprie et singulariter, respectu subjecti, ita dicti, sed auctorum, quod a Prophetis scripti, vel saltem approbati fuerint; neque quod soli sint Prophetici, quum et Novi Testamenti tales sint, Eph. 2, 20. et 3, 5 et 4, 11, sed nomine* Prophetarum ad veteris populi Prophetas restricto, quique Christum ejusque regnum praedixerunt.

XXIII Utriusque Testamenti libri, si omnes sigillatim enumeres, sunt LXVI. Veteris quidem XXXIX, Novi vero XXVII. Atque illorum Catalogus et nomina haec sunt. Quinque libri Mosis, Josua, Judices, Ruth, duo Samuelis, duo Regum, duo Chronicorum, Esdras, Nehemias, Esther, (quem omittit Melito et eum secuti alii, Euseb. *Eccl. Hist.* lib. 4, c. 25.[a] Quidam vero eum dubitanter recensent, Nazianz. in *Metricis*,[b] sed errore manifesto, propter additamenta, totum apocryphum arbitrantes) Job, Psalmi, tres Salomonis, Proverbia scilicet, Ecclesiastes et Canticum Canticorum, Jesaias, Jeremias, Threni, Ezechiel, Daniel, Hoseas, Joel, Amos, Obadjas, Jonas, Micha, Nahum, Habacuk, Zephanjas, Haggaeus, Zacharjas, Malachias.

XXIV Veteres Judaei, pro numero Alphabeti Hebraeorum, ad XXII libros redigunt, Joseph. *cont. Appion*.[c] binos hos Judicum et Ruth, utrumque Samuelis, Regum, Chronicorum, itemque Esdrae et Nehemiae, Jeremiae Prophetiam et Threnos, XII item Prophetas Minores, sub uno singulos comprehendentes. Quod et Christiani veteres fere sequuntur, Hieronym. in *Prol. Gal*.[d] nisi quod, qui Esther omittunt, Ruth seorsim numerent, Melito apud Euseb. etc.[e] Orig. apud. Euseb. lib. *Hist.* 6, c. 19.[f] aliique. Atque pro duplicium literarum Hebraearum numero, quinque

---

[a] Melito in Eusebius, *Historia ecclesiastica* 4.26.14 (SC 31:211). [b] Gregory of Nazianzus, *Poemata theologica (dogmatica)* 1.1.12 (= *De veris scripturae libris*; MPG 37:472–474). [c] Flavius Josephus, *Contra Apionem* 1.8.38. [d] Jerome, *Prologus galeatus in libro Regum* (MPL 28²:593–600). [e] Melito in Eusebius, *Historia ecclesiastica* 4.26.14 (SC 31:211). [f] Wrong reference; correct to Origen in Eusebius, *Historia ecclesiastica* 6.25.2 (SC 41:126).

3. CONCERNING THE CANONICAL AND APOCRYPHAL BOOKS

dispensation* of salvation granted to the people of the Old and the New. And what appears as promise in the Old is a manifestation in the New, or the Gospel in the strict sense (Romans 1:1,2), for the name can come from the predominant part.[12]

Even the distinction between prophetic and apostolic (Romans 16:26; 2 Peter 1:19) should not be taken in such a way as though only and specifically the books of the Old Testament are prophetic regarding their stated subject, but with respect to their authors, because they have been written by prophets, or at any rate have been endorsed by them. Nor because they only are prophetic, since also the New Testament books are such (Ephesians 2:20, and 3:5, and 4:11), but the term* 'prophets' is limited to the prophets of the people of old, and to those who foretold the coming of Christ and his kingdom.

If you count all the books of the two testaments one by one, there are sixty-six; thirty-nine in the old, and twenty-seven in the new. The names in the list are as follows: the five books of Moses, Joshua, Judges, Ruth, 1 and 2 Samuel, 1 and 2 Kings, 1 and 2 Chronicles, Ezra, Nehemiah, Esther (which Melito[13] and the others following him omit [Eusebius, *Ecclesiastical History*, book 4, chapter 25]). And some deem the book Esther doubtful, like Nazianzus (in *On Metrics*)—but clearly erroneously, judging the entire work apocryphal on account of the added portions; Job, Psalms, three books by Solomon, namely Proverbs, Ecclesiastes, and the Song of Songs, Isaiah, Jeremiah, Lamentations, Ezekiel, Daniel, Hosea, Joel, Amos, Obadiah, Jonah, Micah, Nahum, Habakkuk, Zephaniah, Haggai, Zechariah, Malachi.

The Jews of antiquity reduce the number of books to twenty-two, in keeping with the number of letters in the Hebrew alphabet (Josephus, *Against Apion*), by combining each of the following: Judges and Ruth, 1 and 2 Samuel, Kings, Chronicles, and also Ezra and Nehemiah, the Prophecy of Jeremiah and Lamentations, as well as the twelve Minor Prophets. This arrangement most of the early Christians follow (Jerome, in his *Helmeted Preface*), except that those who leave out Esther, count Ruth apart (Melito in Eusebius, etc.; Origen in Eusebius, *Ecclesiastical History*, book 6, chapter 19 and others). However, in keeping

---

12 On the relation between Old and New Testament, see Disputation 23 below.
13 Melito († AD 180) was the first bishop of Sardes. He wrote several books, of which only a few remain. Melito conformed himself to many Jewish traditions, but he also blamed the Jews severely for Christ's death. He was a forerunner of the Alexandrian school. See Reidar Aasgaard, "Among Gentiles, Jews and Christians. Formation of Christian Identity in Melito of Sardis," in *Religious Rivalries and the Struggle for Success in Sardis and Smyrna*, ed. Richard S. Ascough, Studies in Christianity and Judaism, vol. 14 (Waterloo: Wilfrid Laurier University Press, 2005), 156–174.

duplices designari plerique volunt, scilicet, ut Hieronymus, in *Prol.* posteriores[a] illos quinque, ut Epiphanius priores, libro *de Pond. et mensuris.*[b] Nonnulli 24. supputant, historiam Ruth et Threnos sejungentes, Hier. in *Prol. Gal.*[c] Unde posteriores Judaei Scripturam Veteris Testamenti עשרים וארבע Esrim vearba appellant.

XXV Enumerationi distinctionem subjicimus. Eam porro missam facientes, quae est secundum Auctores et Tempus scriptionis, quod sit obscurior et accuratioris inquisitionis, distinguimus certis Classibus, quae Judaeis, Graecis, et Latinis non sunt ejusmodi. Atque secundum ordinem quem constituunt, in sacris Bibliis ab iis fere disponuntur et collocantur.

XXVI Antiquissima partitio ea est, quae ab Esdra putatur facta, qua usa est vetus Synagoga, quamque approbavit Christus et Apostoli, qui libros hos distribuunt vel in duos ordines, Legem Mosis (quae simpliciter Lex, et Moses dicitur) et in Prophetas, Act. 28, 23. Matt. 5, 17. Luc. 16, 29., vel interdum in tres, nempe et Psalmos, Luc. 24, 44, sub quibus tamquam praecipuo libro reliquos Hagiographos comprehendunt, quos Josephus hymnos et ὑποθήκας, id est, praeceptiones vitae appellat, Josephus *contra Appion.*,[d] Hieronymus Hagiographa, in *Prologo*,[e] voce* generaliore speciatim accepta.

XXVII Discrimen tantum est in numero. Josephus[f] secundi ordinis 13. Jobo et Daniele Prophetis annumerato; reliquos quatuor, tertii ordinis facit. Hieron.[g] ex Judaeorum sententia ait, quod post Legem, quam תורה Thora vocant, cujus libros singulos a prima voce denominant, nempe בראשית Bereschith, id est, in principio, etc, secundo ordini octo assignant, qui sunt: Josua, Judices et Ruth, Samuel, Reges, Esaias, Jeremias, Ezechiel, et תריעשר Tereasar, id est, duodecim

---

[a] Jerome, *Prologus galeatus in libro Regum* (MPL 28²:597).   [b] Epiphanius, *De mensuris et ponderibus* 4 (MPG 43:244).   [c] Jerome, *Prologus galeatus in libro Regum* (MPL 28²:600).   [d] Flavius Josephus, *Contra Apionem* 1.8.40.   [e] Jerome, *Prologus galeatus in libro Regum* (MPL 28²:599–600).   [f] Flavius Josephus, *Contra Apionem* 1.8.40.   [g] Jerome, *Prologus galeatus in libro Regum* (MPL 28²:598–600).

3. CONCERNING THE CANONICAL AND APOCRYPHAL BOOKS 91

with the number of Hebrew letters of double characters, a good many wish five to be counted together, as Jerome (in the *Preface*) does for the last five, or Epiphanius[14] (*On Measures and Weights*) for the first five. Some count twenty-four, separating the story of Ruth and Lamentations (Jerome, *Helmeted Preface*). Accordingly, the later Jews call the Scripture of the Old Testament *'Esrim v*^{e}*'arba*, 'the Twenty-Four.'

To the calculation of the number we add the division into groups. Leaving aside altogether the chronological divisions based on the authors and the time of writing, because it is somewhat unclear and in need of more precise investigation, we divide them into certain groups which are not the same for the Jews, Greeks, and Latins. And they are generally arranged and grouped by them in the sacred books following the order they made up.

The oldest division is the one thought to have been made by Ezra, which the early synagogue used,[15] and which Christ and the apostles endorsed, who sort these books either into two groups, the Law of Moses (which simply is called the Law, and Moses) and the prophets (Acts 28:23, Matthew 5:17, Luke 16:29), or sometimes into three, namely also the Psalms (Luke 24:44), among which as the foremost book they include the remaining hagiographical ones, which Josephus calls hymns and *hypothēkai*, that is, 'precepts of life' (Josephus, *Against Apion*), and Jerome 'hagiographies' in the *Preface*, applying the particular meaning of the general word.*

The difference is only in number. Josephus has thirteen in the second group, as he counts Job and Daniel among the prophets; he makes the remaining four belong to the third group. Jerome, following the thinking of the Jews, says that after the Law, which they call *Torah*, of which they call the individual books by the first word, namely *Bereshit*, that is, 'in the beginning, etc.,' they assign to the second group eight books, which are: Joshua, Judges and Ruth, Samuel, Kings, Isaiah, Jeremiah, Ezekiel, and *Tere'asar* ('twelve'), that is, the twelve

25

26

27

---

14   Epiphanius (AD 310/320–403) lived his early years in Palestine, became a monk and founded his own monastery. Later he was bishop of Salamis on Cyprus (since 365/367). His polemics were directed especially against the Arians; he also attacked Origen and his followers, whom he considered chiefly responsible for the errors of Arianism. His most important works include *De mensuris et ponderibus* (*On Measures and Weights*) and the *Panarion* (*Medicine Chest*) or *Adversus haereses* (*Against Heresies*), both of which are referred to in the *Synopsis*.

15   On the supposed role of Ezra in the formation of the Old Testament canon, see A. van der Kooij, "The Canonization of Ancient Books Kept in the Temple at Jerusalem," in *Canonization and Decanonization*, eds. A. van der Kooij, K. van der Toorn, Studies in the History of Religions, vol. 82 (Leiden: Brill, 1997), 17–40.

Prophetae, qui et liber Prophetarum dicitur, Actor. 7, 42. Reliquos vero ix. Hagiographis deputant, Job, David quem quinque incisionibus, et uno Psalmorum volumine comprehendunt, Salomonis Parabolae, Ecclesiastes, Daniel, Verba dierum seu Chronicon, Esdras, Esther; quibus addunt nonnulli Ruth et Threnos.

XXVIII Cum hac, eadem est hodierna Hebraeorum: quamvis quatuor ordines facere videantur. Nam post Legem, quam חמשה חומשי תורה Chamissa chomese thora, id est, πέντε πεντάδας νόμου id est, quinque quintas, scilicet partes, seu quiniones Legis appellant; subjiciunt seu conjungunt cum Lege, Sepher seu חמש מגלות Chames megilloth, id est, quinque volumina, puta Canticum Canticorum, Ruth, Echa, id est, quomodo, (ab initiali voce) Ecclesiasten, Estherem; non tamquam secundam Bibliorum partem, sed ob singularem Synagogae usum, anniversariam scilicet certis temporibus, juxta Legem eorum, lectionem, ab Hagiographis divulsa. Secundus itaque illis ordo, נביאים Nebiim, id est, Prophetarum, quos distinguunt in priores et posteriores; illi, qui a Josua usque ad Jesaiam ab Hieron.[a] numerati; hi reliqui, forte a tempore quo scripserunt, et eorum libri in Ecclesiae thesaurum sunt depositi, nominati sunt. Tertius denique כתובים Kethubim, quem γραφεῖα, alii ἁγιόγραφα vocitant.

XXIX Graeci, et ab iis Latini, Nomina, Numerum, Ordinem et Distinctionem fere eandem tenent. Quinque libros Mosis, Chald. Voce חומש Chomas expressa, πεντάτευχον; singulos vero a materia, γένεσιν, ἔξοδον, λευιτικόν, ἀριθμούς (numeros,) δευτερονόμιον, ut Judaei quidam משנה תורה Misne thora, id est, iterationem Legis, appellant. In Historicis ordinem temporis fere sequuntur, atque Octateuchum vocitant; ac sunt, Josua, Judicum, Ruth, libri Regum quatuor, (quibus Samuelis et Regum comprehendunt) παραλειπομένων, id est, Relictorum duo, (qualiter Chronicorum libr. indigitant) Esdras et Nehemias, Esther, in qua Historiam finiunt. Deinde subjiciunt Jobum, Psalmos, Salomonis παροιμίας seu Parabolas, Ecclesiasten, ᾆσμα (Canticum). Denique duodecim Prophetas, ac quatuor reliquos, (inter quos et Daniel, qui insignis fuit Propheta, Dan. 1, 17. Matth. 24, 15.) At Latini hos illis praemittunt.

---

[a] Jerome, *Prologus galeatus in libro Regum* (MPL 28²:598–599). It seems that the quotation was misread or misunderstood: Jerome counts the first group of prophets from Joshua up to "Jezeciel," not "Isaias."

prophets, who are also called the book of prophets (Acts 7:42). The remaining books they assign to the Nine Hagiographers: Job, David, whom they include in five sections within one volume of Psalms, and the Proverbs of Solomon, Ecclesiastes, Daniel, the Words of Days, or Chronicles, Ezra, Esther—to which some add Ruth and Lamentations.

The division into sections by the Jews of our day is similar, although it appears they make four groups. For after the Law, which they call *Chamisha Chumshei Torah*,[16] that is, *pente pentadai nomou* (that is, 'five fifths,' i.e., parts, or 'the quintet' of the Law)—to the Law they join or append *Sefer*, or *Chamesh megillot*, that is, these five volumes, namely: Song of Songs, Ruth, *'Echa*, that is 'how' (from the opening word [of Lamentations]), Ecclesiastes, Esther. They do this not as the second part of the Bible-books, but on account of its special use for the Synagogue, namely the annual reading at special times, according to their law, separate from the Hagiography. Thus the second group for them is *Nᵉvi'im*, that is, 'of the prophets,' whom they divide into former and latter; those of the first group are counted by Jerome from Joshua up to Isaiah; the rest perhaps received their names from the time in which they wrote and in which their books were placed into the treasury of the Church. Lastly, the third group is, *Kᵉtuvim*, which they call 'the writings,' others 'the sacred writings.'

28

The Greeks, and from them the Latins, keep nearly the same names, number, order, and division. They call the five books of Moses, pronounced by the Chaldean word *Chomas*, *pentateuchos* [pentateuch]; the individual books are called by the subject-matter: *genesis, exodos, leuitikos, arithmoi, deuteronomion*, as certain Jews call *Mishne thora*, that is 'the repetition of the Law.' In the historical writings they maintain generally a chronological order, and call it 'the Octateuch.' And these are Joshua, Judges, Ruth, the four books of Kings (in which they combine Samuel and Kings), *paraleipomena*, that is, 'the two remaining books' (as they denote the books of Chronicles), Ezra and Nehemiah, Esther, with which they end the History section. Thereupon they add Job, Psalms, the *paroimiai*, or Proverbs, of Solomon, Ecclesiastes, *asma* (Song of Solomon). Lastly, the twelve prophets, and the four remaining books (among which is also Daniel, who was a foremost prophet; Daniel 1:17, Matthew 24:15). But the Latins place them at the front of the prophets.

29

---

16 In rabbinic literature printed versions of the Torah as opposed to scrolls are often called Chamisha Chumshei Torah, the five fifths of the Torah. Hebrew versions in the sixteenth century had this title, e.g., Sebastian Münster and Marco Antonio Giustiniani, חמשה חומשי תודה *sive Hebraicus Pentateuchus Latinus planéque novus post omnes hactenus aeditiones evulgatus ac Hebraicae veritati quoad ejus fieri potuit, conformatus* (Venice: Justinianea, 1551).

XXX Distinctiones vero in Classes, aliae atque aliae. Inter Graecos quidem Greg. Nazianzenus, lib. suorum *Carm.*ª Historicos facit XII, Mose Historicis etiam annumerato; quinque Metricos seu Poëticos, Jobo iis accensito. Denique quinque Prophetarum: XII Prophetis uno volumine conjunctis. Epiph. nonnihil aliter, lib. *de Mens. et pond.*,ᵇ quem et sequitur Damasc.ᶜ Quatuor πεντατεύχους seu quinarios, et unum binarium facit. Primus est, νόμος seu νομοθεσία, Lex seu Legislatio. Secundus, γραφεῖα, seu ut alii, ἁγιόγραφα, ut sunt Josua, Judicum cum Ruth, Regnorum 1. et 2, (seu Regum potius), item tertius et quartus, Paralip. 1. et 2. qui praeter Judaeorum consuetudinem ita dicuntur. Tertius, στιχήρεις, ante recensiti. Quartus, προφητικός, scilicet δωδεκαπρόφητον, et singuli reliqui. Binarius denique, Esdras, et Esther.

XXXI Scholastici* vero similiter distinguunt in libros Legales, Historicos, Dogmaticos seu Sapientiales, ut vocant, et Propheticos, quos in Majores et Minores distinguunt.

XXXII Novi porro Testamenti libri, numero sunt XXVII. In eorum vero dispositione, non temporis, quo sunt scripti, sed materiae dignitatisque habita fere ratio* est.

XXXIII Distinguuntur vulgo in quatuor Classes. Prima, Evangelia, id est, dictorum factorumque Christi Historiam, Luc. 1, 1. 2. Actor. 1, 1. a quatuor Scriptoribus; duobus quidem Apostolis, Matthaeo et Johanne. Joh. 21, 20, 24. et duobus Apostolicis viris, Marco et Luca, quorum ille Petro et Paulo, hic vero singulariter Paulo συνεργός fuit, 2 Timoth. 4, 11. 1 Petr. 5, 13. descriptam continet. Secunda, Acta Apostolorum; quae initia et propagationem Ecclesiae per Apostolos, Luca similiter auctore, explicat, Actor. 1, 1. 2.

XXXIV Tertia autem Apostolorum Epistolas, pro re nata ad uberiorem veritatis Evangelicae declarationem scriptas, complectitur; puta tum Pauli XIV ad Ecclesias quidem nobilissimas, utpote ad Romanos, ad Corinthios binas, Galatas, Ephesios, Philippenses, Colossenses, Thessalonicenses binas; ad Ecclesiarum vero Antistites de earum regimine, ad Timotheum duas, et ad Titum; in re familiari ad Philemonem, datas; ac denique ad gentem integram, ad Hebraeos

---

ª Gregory of Nazianzus, *De veris Scripturae libris* (MPG 37:472–474). ᵇ Epiphanius, *De mensuris et ponderibus* 4 (MPG 43:244). ᶜ John of Damascus, *De fide orthodoxa* 90 (= 4.17; SC 540:246–248).

3. CONCERNING THE CANONICAL AND APOCRYPHAL BOOKS 95

As for the divisions of books into groups, some are different from others. Among the Greeks Gregory of Nazianzus in his *Poems* makes twelve historical books: Moses is counted among the historians; five Metrical or Poetic books, reckoning Job among them; and lastly, five of the prophets, by gathering the twelve prophets together into one volume. Not much different is Epiphanius (*Book on Measures and Weights*), whom also John of Damascus follows. He makes four *pentateuxoi* (or quintets) and one book of two's. The first is *nomos* or *nomothesia* (Law, or Legislation). The second, 'the writings,' or as with others, 'the holy writings,' which are Joshua, Judges with Ruth, 1 and 2 Kingdoms (or rather, Kings), likewise the third and fourth, 1 and 2 Chronicles, which are so named outside the Jewish tradition. The third 'rows,' enumerated previously.[17] The fourth, prophetic, namely the twelve prophets, and the remainders separately. Lastly, the twofold Ezra and Esther.   30

The Scholastics* make a similar division into Legal, Historical, Dogmatic or Wisdom Books, as they call them, and the Prophetic Books, which they split into Major and Minor.   31

Now for the New Testament there are twenty-seven books. In their arrangement consideration* was given not so much to the time when they were written but to their content and worth.   32

They are commonly divided into four groups. The first is the Gospel, that is, the history of the words and deeds of Christ (Luke 1:1,2; Acts 1:1) by four writers, of whom two were apostles, Matthew and John (John 21:20, 24), and two of apostolic status, Mark and Luke—the former of whom was co-worker of Peter and Paul, and the latter especially of Paul (a description found in 2 Timothy 4:11; 1 Peter 5:13). The second group is the Acts of the apostles, which sets forth the beginnings and expansion of the Church through the apostles, and of which Luke is also the author (Acts 1:1,2).   33

The third group includes the Letters of the apostles, written as the need arose, to divulge more fully the Gospel truth. These are the fourteen letters of Paul to the most prominent churches, namely to the Romans, two to the Corinthians, Galatians, Ephesians, Philippians, Colossians, two to the Thessalonians. And he wrote letters to those in charge of governing them, two were given to Timothy and [one] to Titus; one to Philemon about a domestic matter. And lastly, one letter to an entire race, namely to the Hebrews. Then there are   34

---

17   'Rows' refers to the literary form of the verses in these books. Here these books are called the 'five Metrical or Poetic books, reckoning Job among them,' in the previous thesis (29) they are summed up as 'Job, Psalms, the *paroimiai*, or Proverbs, of Solomon, Ecclesiastes, *asma* (Song of Solomon).'

scilicet; tum aliorum Apostolorum septem, Jacobi, Petri duas, Johannis tres, atque Judae; quae (exceptis duabus Johannis ad electam Dominam et Gajum) quod ad plures scriptae sint, Catholicae, quodque sub una formula ad plures mitterentur, Canonicae dicuntur, ut voce ea utitur Cassiod. Libr. 11 *Epist.* 33,[a] quas Suet. in *Domit.* c. 13.[b] Formales vocat. Postrema denique, Apocalypsin habet Johannis Apostoli, quae Prophetiam status Ecclesiae ad finem mundi exhibet.

xxxv   Ex his, de Epistola ad Hebraeos, ejusque auctore; Jacobi, item duabus posterioribus Johannis, Judae, atque Apocalypsi, ejusque auctore, dubitatum a quibusdam fuit; Eus. lib. 2. *Hist.* cap. 22.[c] Idem, Lib. 3. c. 18. et 19,[d] tum quod serius forte in Canonem illati, tum quod quidam ex illis viderentur aliqua continere reliquis non satis congruentia. Verum id privatum potius fuit quorundam judicium, neque satis attenta et recta inita fuit rerum* expensio. Contra, divinos esse hos libros, cum antiquae Ecclesiae judicio, Orig. *ad Psal.* 1, ut est apud Euseb. lib. 6,[e] tum rerum stylique divina majestate, evincitur. Illam ad Hebraeos Pauli esse, Timothei cooperarii Pauli mentio, valedictionis consueta formula, Heb. 13, 23. 24. et Petri, qui suam quoque Epistolam Hebraeis per Asiam dispersis inscripsit, 2 Petr. 3, 15, auctoritas arguit. Styli vero diversitatem ad Lucae

---

[a] Wrong reference; correct to Cassiodorus, *Variarum* 11.23 (CCSL 96:448).   [b] Suetonius, *Vita Domitiani* 13.   [c] Wrong reference; correct to Eusebius, *Historia ecclesiastica* 2.23.24–25 (SC 31:90).
[d] Wrong reference; correct to Eusebius, *Historia ecclesiastica* 3.24.18 and 3.25.4 (SC 31:133, 134).
[e] Eusebius, *Historia ecclesiastica* 6.25.1–2 (SC 41:125–126).

3. CONCERNING THE CANONICAL AND APOCRYPHAL BOOKS 97

seven from the other apostles, James, two of Peter, three of John, and one of Jude. These letters (with the exception of the two from John, to "the elect lady" and Gaius), because they were written for many people, are called Catholic, and because they were sent under one heading to many people, they are called canonical,[18] as Cassiodorus[19] uses that word (Book 11, Letter 23), which Suetonius[20] (*Life of Domitian*, chapter 13) calls 'formal letters.' And then the last group contains the Revelation to John the apostle, which contains a prophecy about the state of the Church to the end of the world.

Of these books some have expressed doubt about the Letter to the Hebrews and its authorship; about James as well as the two last letters of John, Jude; and about Revelation and its author (Eusebius, *Ecclesiastical History*, book 2, chapter 22; book 3, chapter 18 and 19). The reason is that perhaps they were introduced to the canon rather late, or because some of them seemed to contain things* that were not consistent enough with the others. But that was more the personal opinion of some individuals, nor has a sufficiently careful and sound assessment of the issues been undertaken. To the contrary, in light of the judgment of the early Church (Origen, on Psalm 1, in Eusebius, *Ecclesiastical History*, book 6), and of the godly worth of their subject matter and the style, it prevails that these books are of divine origin. The reference to Timothy the co-worker of Paul, the usual form of greeting (Hebrews 13:23, 24), and the authority of Peter, who addressed also his own letter to the Hebrews who were scattered throughout Asia (2 Peter 3:15), support the position that the one to the Hebrews is from Paul. The ancients attribute the difference in style to the

35

---

18   'Canonical' was an ordinary designation for the 'catholic' epistles. Thus John Calvin wrote a commentary on 1 Peter, 1 John, James, 2 Peter, and Jude, entitled *Commentarii in Epistolas canonicas* (1551).

19   Cassiodorus (c. AD 485–585), Roman statesman and writer, who also served the Ostro-Gothic rulers at Ravenna. His educational and literary efforts were devoted to bridging the cultural divides of the sixth century: the divide between East and West, between Greek and Latin culture, between Romans and Goths, and between a Catholic people and their Arian ruler. By establishing his own monastery, the *Vivarium*, Cassiodorus contributed significantly to the reproduction and transmission of documents from Antiquity to the early Middle Ages. See James Joseph O'Donnell, *Cassiodorus* (Berkeley: University of California Press, 1979).

20   Suetonius (c. AD 69–c. 122) was a Roman historian. He wrote biographies of twelve Roman rulers, *De vita Caesarum* (*The Lives of the Twelve Caesars*). The reference in the *Synopsis* is to the life of the twelfth one, Domitian.

aut Clementis, aut alterius interpretationem, referunt Veteres. Tertull. Barnabae tribuit.ᵃ Apocalypsin Johanni Phraseologia vindicat.

XXXVI   Atque hi Libri, Divini, Authentici atque Canonici sunt; qui vero extra hos, sive apud Graecos, sive Latinos, istis junguntur, ἀκανόνιστοι appellantur, quos in humanis, Ecclesiasticis, atque Apocryphis habemus, Orig. apud. Eus. lib. 6. cap. 19.ᵇ Hier. in *Praefat.*ᶜ Sunt vero Veteris Testamenti vel Supplementa et Appendices ad libros Sacros; ut Manassis oratio Latine edita, subjecta libr. Paralip. Appendix ad Estheram, a 10. cap. ad finem libri; ad Jobum, a versu 56, cap. 42. Ad Psalmos, Psalmus 151, qui in Graecis exemplaribus est; ad Jeremiae Prophetiam, Baruch et Epistula Jeremiae; praefatio ad Threnos: ad Danielem, Hymnus trium Puerorum, Historia de Dracone, Abacuco, et Susanna; quo etiam referimus omissa et addita, praeter contextum Hebraicum a Septuaginta Interpretibus. Vel sunt libri integri, ut liber 3. item et 4. Esdrae (qui tantum Latine exstat) Tobiae, Judith; utrumque hunc ex Chaldaico vertisse se Hieronymus dicit;ᵈ Macchabaeorum duo, et tertius, in Graecis; Sapientia, quae dicitur Solomonis, sed Philonis est sub Solomonis titulo; Ecclesiasticus Jesus Syrach, quem Hebraice quidem ab avo scriptum commemorat, sed conservatus non est.

XXXVII Ex quibus quaedam et Pontificii Apocryphis accensent, scilicet Precationem Manassis, appendicem Jobi, Psal. 151. Praefationem ad Jeremiam, et utrumque Esdrae, et postremum Macchabaeorum; reliquos in Sacris habent, Conc. Trid. sess. 4.ᵉ Sed nos omnia eodem ordine, quoad auctoritatem, habemus, ideoque

---

ᵃTertullian, *De pudicitia* 20.2 (CCSL 2:1324).   ᵇWrong reference; correct to Eusebius, *Historia ecclesiastica* 6.25.1–2 (SC 41:125–127), where Eusebius cites Origen's list of the 'canonical' books. Alternatively, Thysius—whose references to Eusebius in this disputation witness considerable confusion—could have had in mind the passage in which Eusebius himself uses the word 'apocryphal' in *Historia ecclesiastica* 3.25.4 (SC 31:134), to which he also refers in the preceding thesis.   ᶜJerome, *Prologus galeatus in libro Regum* (MPL 28²:601).   ᵈJerome, *Praefatio in librum Tobiae* (MPL 29:23–26).   ᵉDH 1502.

translation of Luke, or Clement,[21] or someone else.[22] Tertullian ascribes the work to Barnabas.[23] The manner of expression exonerates the Revelation to John.

Well then, these books are divine, authentic, and canonical; besides these the ones either the Greeks or Latins connected to them are called 'non-canonical,' which we consider as human, ecclesiastical, and apocryphal books (Origen, in Eusebius, *Ecclesiastical History*, book 6 chapter 19; Jerome, in the *Preface*). Those of the Old Testament may be additions and appendices to the sacred books, such as: the prayer of Manasseh, published in Latin, added to the book of Chronicles; the appendix to Esther, from chapter 10 to the end of the book; the addition to Job, from chapter 42:56; Psalm 151, added to the Psalms, which appears in the Greek edition. Also Baruch, and the letter of Jeremiah added to the prophecy of Jeremiah; the Preface to the book of Lamentations; the hymn of the three youths, added to Daniel; the history of the dragon, Habakkuk, and Suzanna. To this group we also assign the omissions and additions by the authors of the Septuagint, beyond the Hebrew text. There may also be entire books, such as book three and also book four of Ezra (which exists only in Latin), Tobias, Judith (Jerome states that he translated both of these books from Chaldean), two books of the Maccabees, and a third in Greek; Wisdom, which is reported to be from Solomon, but is actually Philo's under the name of Solomon,[24] the Ecclesiastic Jesus Sirach, which he claims was written in Hebrew by his grandfather, but which has not survived.

Also the papal teachers assign some of these to the apocrypha, namely the prayer of Manasseh, the Appendix to Job, Psalm 151, the Preface to Jeremiah, the two of Ezra, and the last book of the Maccabees; the rest they include among the sacred books (Council of Trent, Session 4). But we consider them all to be of the same rank as far as their authority is concerned, and we affirm that they

36

37

---

21 Clement of Rome († AD 99/101) was bishop of Rome and the first "apostolic father." Two letters are attributed to him, of which the second is probably not written by Clement. Cf. Bart D. Ehrman, ed. and trans., *The Writings of the Apostolic Fathers*, vol. 1 (Harvard: Harvard University Press, 2003).

22 Eusebius, *Ecclesiastical History* 3.38, suggested that Paul wrote the letter in Hebrew and that Luke or Clement of Alexandria translated it into Greek.

23 Barnabas is mentioned a few times in the New Testament, especially in the Acts of the Apostles. Traditionally, the *Letter of Barnabas* is ascribed to him, although it is probably written in Alexandria in the 130's.

24 William Whitaker, *Disputatio* I.i.12 (see note at *SPT* 2.6), states that "most of the ancients are of the opinion that Philo is the author of *Sapientia Salomonis*" and he refers to Bonaventura's commentary on the book.

neque cum Sacris miscenda, nec publice tamquam divina in Ecclesia legenda esse, asserimus, Laod. Syn. c. 59,[a] quamvis, ut utilia, privatim haberi et legi posse non diffiteamur.

XXXVIII   Causae quod nulla ex his scriptis in Sacris habeamus, sunt primo, Quod Prophetico Spiritu non sint edita, utpote, post tempora Artaxerxis scripta, quibus explorata amplius non fuit Prophetarum διαδοχή, Successio, Rom. 16,26. Joseph. *contra App.*[b] 2. Quod in Arca, ut tabulae Legis, neque juxta Arcam, ut libri Mosis, fuerunt reposita, Deuter. 31. Epiph. *de Mens. et pond.*[c] 3. Quod Lingua Hebraica non sint scripta, aut in ea conservata, neque ab Ecclesia Judaica, quibus divina Oracula concredita fuerant, unquam pro ejusmodi sint agnita, Joseph. ibid.[d] 4. Neque etiam a Christo, Apostolis et prisca Christiana Ecclesia; sed pro adulterinis habita, Amphilochius apud Balsam.[e] Nazianz. apud eundem,[f] et a postera Ecclesia, non sine magna varietate et disceptatione, aliquatenus admissa, puta, ut Ecclesiastica, Syn. Carthag 3.[g] Aug. *de doct. Christ.*[h] Rufinus *ad Symb.*[i] 5. Quod denique absurda, fabulosa complurima, et Sacris Literis non consentientia, contineant, quae nimis longum esset hoc loco recensere.

---

[a] Mansi 2:589 (NPNF2 14:158).   [b] Flavius Josephus, *Contra Apionem* 1.8.40.   [c] Epiphanius, *De mensuris et ponderibus* 4 (MPG 43:244).   [d] Flavius Josephus, *Contra Apionem* 1.8.42–43. [e] Amphilochius of Iconium in Theodore Balsamo, *Commentaria in Epistolas canonicas ss. Patrum* (MPG 138:925–927).   [f] Gregory of Nazianzus in Theodore Balsamo, *Commentaria in Epistolas canonicas ss. Patrum* (MPG 138:923–925).   [g] DH 186.   [h] Augustine, *De doctrina christiana* 2.8.13 (CCSL 32:39–40).   [i] Rufinus, *Commentarius in symbolum apostolorum* 38 (MPL 21:374).

should not be mixed with the sacred, nor read publicly in church as if they are divine (Synod of Laodicea, chapter 59), although we do not deny that they can be kept and read with benefit privately.

The reasons why we should consider none of these writings as sacred are: In the first place, that they were not produced by the Spirit of prophecy, since they were written after the time of Artaxerxes, in which no *diadochē*, or succession, of prophets was found (Romans 16:26, Josephus, *Against Appian*, 2). Second, because they were not placed in the ark, as the tables of the Law were, or beside the ark, as the books of Moses were (Deuteronomy 31, Epiphanius, *On Measures and Weights*). Third, because they were not written or preserved in the Hebrew language, nor did the Jewish church, to whom the divine oracles had been entrusted, ever acknowledge them as such (Josephus, *Against Appian* 4). Fourth, because neither Christ, nor the apostles, nor the early Church acknowledges them as such, but they considered them not genuine (Amphilochius[25] and Gregory of Nazianzus, both in Balsamon[26]), and were admitted by the later Church with considerable variance and dispute, and then only as ecclesiastical (Synod of Carthage, 3; Augustine, *On Christian Doctrine*; Rufinus,[27] *On the Creeds*, 5). Fifth, and finally, because they contain nonsensical, mainly fictitious things, and things that are not in harmony with the sacred writings—which it would take too long to review here.

38

---

25 Amphilochius of Iconium (AD 339/340–394/403; bishop of Iconium from 373–394) apparently was a cousin of Gregory of Nazianzus. He defended the Trinitarian teaching of the Cappadocians, and put emphasis on the truly human nature of Christ. He wrote several books, but only a few poems and fragments have been preserved. For his teaching on the canon, see *Iambi ad Seleucum* (*Iambics for Seleucus*), a didactic poetic work formerly attributed to Gregory of Nazianzus (MPG, vol. 37, col. 1593–1594; also in NPNF2, vol. 14).

26 Theodore Balsamon (c. 1130/40–c. 1195), a Byzantine scholar and canonist. As a deacon of the church of Constantinople, he led the ecclesiastical court. Starting in 1193, he was the official patriarch of Antioch but remained in Constantinople. His *Scholia in Nomocanon* (*Comments on Canon Law*) is one of the principal collections of Eastern Orthodox ecclesiastical and imperial laws.

27 Tyrranius Rufinus, or Rufinus of Aquileia (AD 340/345–410), was a Christian monk, historian, and theologian. Although he was on friendly terms with Jerome initially, a controversy over the thought of Origen pitted them against each other, with Rufinus defending the great Greek church father. Rufinus is known for his Latin translations of the Greek fathers, most notably Origen. These translations include Origen's *Peri archōn* (*De principiis*), and Eusebius's *Historica ecclesiastica*. His own writings include responses to Jerome, as well as *Commentarius in symbolum apostolorum* (*Commentary on the Symbol of the Apostles*), cited here and elsewhere in the SPT.

XXXIX   Qui praeterea libri Apostolorum aut eorum Discipulorum nomina prae se ferunt, eos ut ψευδωνύμους inter Apocryphos, habemus, quamvis non ejusdem sint ordinis. Antiquis multum celebrati sunt, *Liber Pastoris*, qui Hermeti inscribitur, tantae olim in quibusdam Orientis Ecclesiis auctoritatis, ut in iis publice legeretur, Eus. lib. 3, c. 3. etc. c. 32.[a] etc. Hier. in *Prol. Galeato*.[b] Item *Epistola Barnabae*, et Clementis duae Iren., lib. 3. c. 3.[c] aliique libri nonnulli. Reliqui plane abdicati fuerunt, ut τῆς ἀποκρυφῆς potius, quam αναγνώσεως ἄξιοι, occultatione potius, quam lectione digni, ut loquitur Athanasius in *Synopsi*.[d]

XL   Quantum vero Fidei ac Spei Symbolum attinet, a Veteribus etiam Fides, et Fides Catholica; Expositio, Confessio seu Professio; Regula Normaque, Articuli, atque Capita Fidei Veritatisque; Syn. Laod. c. 46.[e] et Iren. lib. 1. c. 1. et 2.[f] Tert. *de Praescript.* et *contra Praxeam*.[g] Hier. *Ad Paumach*.[h] August. *Serm. de Temp.* 19. et *de Fide et Symb*.[i] Amb. *ad epist.* 81.[j] et Apostolorum Symbolum, appellatum, quod, etiam ante Synodum Nicaenam, in Ecclesiis alibi (maxime ob Haereses obortas) non quidem re, sed verbis nonnihil variavit; in Occiduis autem intemeratum servatum fuit. Atque Symbolum quidem, id est, Collatio vel Nota dicitur; quia in eo, mira simplicitate* et brevitate, collatio collectioque Fidei Christianae facta sit; omnibusque Fidelibus pro nota, indicio, tesseraque esset, qua inter se unitatem testarentur, et ab infidelibus haereticisque disjungerentur; Clem. Rom. *ad Jac*.[k] Ruf. in *Symb. Apostolicum*[l] vero, vel quod ab Apostolis in orbem universum digredientibus, ut quidam (fide tamen non satis certa) scribunt, non singulatim singulis suum Articulum conferentibus, (unde duodenarium eorum numerum inepte sane, nisi forte memoriae ergo faciunt) sed communi consensu compositum est, Aug. *de Temp. Ser.* 115.[m] Vel potius, quod ab Apostolicis viris, aut prisca Ecclesia, ex Doctrina scriptisque Apostolorum ut ejus summarium, totidem fere verbis collectum conceptumque, in Ecclesiis,

---

[a] Eusebius, *Historia ecclesiastica* 3.3.6 (SC 31:99).   [b] Jerome, *Prologus galeatus in libro Regum* (MPL 28²:602).   [c] Irenaeus, *Adversus haereses* 3.3.3 (FC 8/3:32).   [d] Athanasius, *Synopsis sacrae scripturae* (MPG 28:432). This work is currently often attributed to an unknown church writer from the sixth century.   [e] Mansi 2:581 (NPNF2 14:154).   [f] Irenaeus, *Adversus haereses* 1.1, 2 (FC 8/1:128–140).   [g] E.g. Tertullian, *Liber de praescriptione haereticorum* 12.5, 13.1, 26.9 (CCSL 1:197, 208); idem, *Liber adversus Praxeam* 3.1 (CCSL 2:1161).   [h] Jerome, *Epistulae* 49.14 (CSEL 54²:371).   [i] Augustine, *Sermo* 186.2.2 (MPL 38:999); idem, *De fide et symbolo* 1.1.1 (CSEL 41:3).   [j] Ambrose, *Epistulae extra collectionem* 15.6 (= *Ep.* 81 in old numbering; CSEL 82/3:305).   [k] (Pseudo-) Clement of Rome, *Epistola Clementis ad Jacobum* (MPG 1:472–473); this passage from the letter is not included in Bernard Rehm and Georg Strecker, ed., *Die Pseudoklementinen I: Homilien*, 3rd rev. ed. (Berlin: Akademie-Verlag, 1992).   [l] Rufinus, *Commentarius in symbolum apostolorum* 2 (MPL 21:337–338).   [m] Augustine, *Sermo* 241.1 (MPL 39:2190); this sermon is no longer attributed to Augustine.

3. CONCERNING THE CANONICAL AND APOCRYPHAL BOOKS

Furthermore, we rank the books that are introduced under the names of the apostles or their disciples among the apocrypha as pseudonymous, although they are not of the same sort. Many were honoured highly among the ancients, such as the *Book of the Shepherd*, signed by Hermas, formerly of such authority in some churches of the East that it was read publicly in them (Eusebius, *Ecclesiastical History*, book 3, chapter 3, etc., chapter 32, etc.; Jerome in the *Helmeted Preface*). So too the Letter of Barnabas, two of Clement (Irenaeus,[28] book 3, chapter 3) and several other books. The rest were clearly rejected as more deserving of concealment, *tēs apokruphēs*, than of reading, *anagnoseōs axioi*, as Athanasius says in his *Synopsis*.

As far as the Symbol of faith and hope is concerned, the ancients have also called it the Faith, the Catholic Faith, the Explanation, the Confession or Profession, the Rule and Norm, the Articles, and the Headings of Faith and Truth, and the Symbol of the apostles (Synod of Laodicea, chapter 46, and Irenaeus, book 1, chapter 1 and 2, Tertullian, *The Prescription Against the Heretics*, and *Against Praxeas*; Jerome, *To Paumachius*, Augustine, *Sermons on the Liturgical Seasons* 19, *on Time*, and *On Faith and the Creed*, Ambrose in *Letter* 81). Even before the Synod of Nicea, in the churches at various places (especially in response to the rise of heresies) the symbol differed not at all in content but somewhat in wording. In the western churches, however, it was preserved unaltered. It is called a Symbol, that is, summary or sign because with wonderful candor* and conciseness it provides a collation and summary of the Christian faith. And [it is called a Symbol] so that it would be a sign, indication, or token, with which they could testify to their unity and distinguish themselves from unbelievers and heretics. [Ps.-]Clement of Rome (*Letter to James*) and Rufinus (*On the Apostolic Symbol*) call it 'Apostolic,' either because it was compiled by the apostles when they went separate ways throughout the whole world, as some writers explain (though not credibly enough). It is not as though each one individually contributed his own article (from where some derive their number of twelve, quite foolishly, except perhaps for the sake of remembering them), but it was compiled by mutual consent (Augustine, *Sermons on the Liturgical Seasons* 115, *on Time*). Or it is called 'Apostolic' because the apostolic fathers or the early Church gathered it from the teaching and writings of the apostles as a summary put together and devised in about so many words, and handed down by

---

28 Irenaeus of Lyons (c. AD 140–c. 202), born in Asia Minor to a Christian family. He became acquainted with Polycarp, the bishop of Smyrna. After the martyrdom of Polycarp, he moved to Lyons and became bishop there around 155. Irenaeus wrote against Gnosticism and is especially known for his work *Adversus Haereses* (*Against Heresies*, c. 180).

saltem Occidentis, a Catechistis, Catechumenis memoriae mandandum, viva voce* traditum, a Baptizandis autem Diabolum solemniter renuntiantibus, et Deum profitentibus, redditum sit, August. lib. 1. *de Symb. ad Catechum*.[a] Laod. Syn. c. 46.[b] Matth. 28, 19. Id, inquam, si non auctore, re tamen, ac fere verbis, plane divinum est.

XLI   Ecclesiasticis denique scriptis, puta Synodis, et imprimis Synodorum Universalium symbolis, ut Nicaeno, Constantinopolitano, Ephesino, Chalcedonensi, (quibus et Athanasii adjungimus) tamquam totius Ecclesiae judicio, ex verbo Dei instituto; Sanctis quoque Patribus, eorumque consensui, non parum deferimus. Haec tamen omnia ad primam Veritatem, Scripturam scilicet Sacram, referenda et exigenda esse censemus, a qua, ut luna a sole, lumen suum et fidem accipiunt, August. lib. 3. *contra Maxim*. cap. 14.[c]

---

[a] Augustine, *De symbolo sermo ad catechumenos* 1.1 (CCSL 46:185).   [b] NPNF2 14:154.   [c] Augustine, *Contra Maximum haereticum* 2.14.3 (MPL 42:772).

word* of mouth in the churches (at least in the western ones) to be entrusted by the instructors in the catechism for memorization by the catechumens, and then recited by those who were baptized as they solemnly renounced the devil and professed God (Augustine, *On the Creed to the Catechumens*, book 1; Synod of Laodicea, chapter 46; Matthew 28:19). This summary, I declare, if not divine with respect to its authorship, is clearly divine in its substance, and nearly so in words.

And finally, we value highly the writings of the Church, that is, of the synods, and especially on the symbols of the universal synods such as that of Nicea, Constantinople, Ephesus, Chalcedon (to which we join also the Athanasian one)—as much as upon the judgment of the entire Church that is based upon the Word of God; and so too upon the saints and church-fathers, and of their unanimous consent. However, we reckon that all of these must be judged and tested against the foremost truth, namely Holy Scripture, from which, like the moon from the sun, they receive their own light and trustworthiness (Augustine, *Against Maximus*, book 3, chapter 14).

DISPUTATIO IV

De Sacrae Scripturae perfectione, et inutili traditionum non scriptarum ad eam adjectione

Praeside D. JOHANNE POLYANDRO
Respondente ABRAHAMO SWALMIO

THESIS I Expositis quaestionibus praecedentibus de Sacrae Scripturae necessitate, auctoritate, et numero librorum Canonicorum ab Apocryphis distinguendorum, nunc quarta, de illius perfectione, est excutienda.

II Sacrae Scripturae perfectio* a quibusdam dupliciter consideratur, aut ratione* materiae, seu ipsarum rerum in hac vita ad salutem simpliciter cognitu necessariarum, aut respectu formae externae, seu vocum, atque enuntiationum genuinum illarum rerum* sensum plane exprimentium, quam alio nomine perspicuitatem appellamus. Nos de priore Sacrae Scripturae perfectione hoc tantum loco disputabimus; tum absolute* in se, tum relate ad traditiones non scriptas et opposite consideratas.

III Bellarminus, in sua disputatione *de Verbo Dei non scripto*, statum quaestionis sic describit, lib. 4. c. 3.[a] Nostros Theologos docere, in Scripturis omnia

---

[a] Bellarmine, *De verbo Dei* 4.3 (*Opera* 1:197a).

DISPUTATION 4

On the Perfection of Scripture, and the Futility of Adding Unwritten Traditions to it

President: Johannes Polyander
Respondent: Abraham Swalmius[1]

While in the preceding investigations we explained the necessity and authority of Holy Scripture, and the number of canonical books that we must keep separate from apocryphal ones, in this fourth one we shall investigate its perfection.

Some look at the perfection* of Holy Scripture in two ways: either with respect* to its content (the very things that one simply must know in this life in order to be saved), or with respect to its outward form (the words and phrases that lend clear expression to the true meaning of those things*), which by another name we call 'perspicuity.' At this point we shall debate the perfection of Holy Scripture only in the former sense, both absolutely *or in itself[2] and in relation and opposition to the unwritten traditions.[3]

Bellarmine,[4] in his treatise on the unwritten Word of God, depicts the state of the question as follows (Book 4, chapter 3), that our theologians teach

---

1   Born in Westmaas in 1597, Abrahamus Arnoldi Swalmius matriculated on 19 May 1615 in philosophy. He defended this disputation on 9 May 1620 and dedicated his defense to Coymannes, G. Timmermannus, G. van der Putten, who supported and sponsored him, to Jac. Trigland and A. Smoutius, Amsterdam pastors, to Polyander, Amesius and Goetiaerus (= Hugh Goodyear, pastor of the English church at Leiden), and to his friend C. Kerstemannus. He was ordained in Kethel (north of Schiedam) in 1622; emeritus in 1667. See Du Rieu, *Album studiosorum*, 120, and Van Lieburg, *Repertorium*, 244; also BLGNP 1:166.
2   See theses 3–25.
3   See theses 26–39.
4   Robert Bellarmine (1542–1621) was one of the most influential Roman Catholic theologians of his time. The authors of the *Synopsis* refer mostly to his works when taking issue with Catholic viewpoints. Born in Montepulciano (Italy), he joined the Jesuits in 1560, and taught in Louvain from 1570 to 1576. He was appointed to the chair of controversial theology at the Roman College, becoming Rector of the College in 1592. Bellarmine was created Cardinal in 1598. In this capacity he acted as one of the judges at the trial of Giordano Bruno, and concurred in the decision which condemned Bruno to be burned at the stake as a heretic. In 1616, Galileo Galilei was summoned before Bellarmine's Congregation of the Index, and ordered to abandon his Copernican, heliocentric views. As archbishop of Capua, Bellarmine was also largely responsible for implementing the decrees of the Council of Trent (1545–1563)

contineri ad fidem et mores necessaria, ac proinde non esse opus Verbo non scripto: Pontificios vero Doctores asserere, in Scripturis non contineri expresse totam doctrinam necessariam, sive de fide, sive de moribus, ideoque praeter Verbum* Dei scriptum, requiri verbum Dei non scriptum, id est, divinas, Apostolicas et Ecclesiasticas traditiones.

IV In qua status controversiae descriptione, tria ab ipso omissa desiderantur; quorum 1. est, omnia dogmata tam de fide, quam de moribus, quae ad integram et salutarem Dei cognitionem summamque beatitatis consecutionem necessario requiruntur, sufficienter Verbo Dei scripto comprehendi, vel expresse, seu totidem verbis disertis, vel analogice,* seu verbis aequipollentibus atque ex ipso Sacrae Scripturae fonte per proximam,* necessariam, perspicuam, atque indubitatam consequentiam deductis. Quod nos asseveramus.

V Alterum est, traditiones illas non scriptas, tamquam vel ore tenus a Christo, vel a Spiritu Sancto dictatas, et continua successione in Ecclesia Catholica conservatas, pari pietatis affectu, eademque reverentia esse suscipiendas, qua omnes libros tam Veteris quam Novi Testamenti suscepimus. Quod statuit Concilium Tridentinum. 1. Decreto Sess. 4.ª

VI Tertium est, Sacras Scripturas sine traditionibus nec fuisse simpliciter necessarias, nec sufficientes. Quod disserit Bellarminus *de Verbo Dei non scripto*, lib. 4. c. 4ᵇ etc. Stanislaus Hosius *adversus Brentium*, lib. 4. *de Traditionibus*.ᶜ

VII Probationes,* quibus asseverationis nostrae Thesi quarta expositae veritatem adversus Pontificios astruimus, sunt partim divinae, partim ecclesiasticae, quarum priores ex ipso Verbo Dei scripto, posteriores ex scriptis patrum Orthodoxorum haurimus.

ª DH 1501. ᵇ Bellarmine, *De verbo Dei* 4.4 (*Opera* 1:200b). ᶜ Stanislaus Hosius, *Confutatio prolegomenoon Brentii* ... (first published 1557; Paris: Guillaume Desboys, 1560), 180.

aiming at the reformation of the Catholic Church. His main work is the *Disputationes de controversiis christianae fidei adversus hujus temporis haereticos* (*Disputations about the Controversies over the Christian Faith against the Heretics of our Time*), first published in three volumes in 1586–1593. During the next decades, several Reformed theologians (e.g., William Whitaker, William Ames, Sibrandus Lubbertus, and Amandus Polanus) felt obliged to react to Bellarmine's statements.

"that all things necessary to the faith and moral behavior are contained in the Scriptures, and hence that there is no need for the unwritten Word"; but the papal teachers contend that "the Scriptures do not explicitly contain all the necessary teaching, either about faith or about moral behavior, and therefore that in addition to the recorded Word* of God the unwritten Word of God is required, that is, the traditions from God, the apostolic traditions, and the traditions of the church."

In this portrayal of the dispute as it stands currently three things are missing that he left out; the first is that all the doctrines about the faith and moral conduct necessarily required for a comprehensive and saving knowledge of God and for the pursuit of supreme blessedness are contained sufficiently in the written Word of God, either explicitly in so many clear wordings, or by analogy* in words of equal significance, and deduced from the very source of Holy Scripture through an immediate,* necessary, transparent and indubitable logical inference. That is what we affirm.

The second is that "those unwritten traditions, as if either proceeding straight from the mouth of Christ or dictated by the Holy Spirit and preserved by an unbroken sequence in the Catholic Church, must be accepted with the same amount of awe and reverence with which we accept all the books of the Old and New Testaments." This the Council of Trent has decided (Decree 1, session 4).

The third is that "without the traditions the Holy Scriptures were neither simply necessary nor sufficient." This is what Bellarmine argues about the unwritten Word of God (Book 4, chapter 4, etc.; cf. Stanislaus Hosius,[5] *Against [Johannes] Brenz*, Book 4, *On the Traditions*).

Some of the proofs* we used to demonstrate the truth of our assertion against the papal theologians in thesis number 4 above have their origins in God, and others in the church. We draw the former kind of proofs from the written Word of God itself,[6] and the latter from the writings of the orthodox church fathers.[7]

---

5 Stanislaus Hosius (1504–1579), Polish theologian, diplomat, preacher and strong defender of the Catholic Church against Protestant rulers. He was prince-bishop of Warmia, promoted to cardinal in 1561, and partipated in the final sessions of the Council of Trent. His most popular work is the *Confessio catholicae fidei christianae* (*Confession of the Catholic Christian Faith*, 1552/53). He argues that traditions are a necessary supplement to Scripture.
6 See theses 9–24.
7 See thesis 25.

VIII Priorum probationum prima sumitur a Verbi scripti encomiis, quibus summa ejus perfectio, tum ab auctore, tum a virtute et efficacia, ipsi ab auctore suo ad finem,* quem is intendit, infallibiliter consequendum communicata, denotatur. Ab auctore enim suo, nempe Deo causa* omnium suprema, cujus omnia opera sunt perfecta, Deut. 32, 4. interdum Verbum Dei, ut 2 Petr. 1, 21. interdum Lex Dei, ut Psal. 1, 2. et 19, 8 et 119. interdum Scriptura divinitus inspirata vocatur, ut 2 Tim. 3, 16. A virtute et efficacia sibi a Deo immediate* communicata, dicitur posse* hominem sapientem reddere ad salutem, 2 Tim. 3, 15.

IX Secunda petitur ab epitheto perfectionis ac sufficientiae, quod ipsi expresse attribuitur Ps. 19, 8. 9. Lex (id est, doctrina) Dei est integra. Integrum autem est cui nihil deest, et extra quod nihil eorum quae sunt ejus, accipi potest, ut recte observavit Arist. lib. 2. *de coelo* c. 4.[a] Nihil ergo quod lex Dei est, extra legem Dei scriptum reperitur.

X Hinc Deus olim prohibuit, ne quid legi suae adjiceretur, aut detraheretur, Deuter. 4, 2. Quod interdictum de lege ab ipso Mose conscripta esse intelligendum, tum ex Mosis, tum ex Pauli patet interpretatione. Moses enim totam Dei legem vocat verba in libro suo conscripta, Deut. 28, 58. Et Paulus, Galat. 3, 13. Propterea quod nihil a Mose Dei nomine Israëlitis viva voce* traditum fuerit, quod literis non consignarit; teste ipso Mose, Exod. 24, 4. Deut. 31, 9.

XI Ex illa legis integritate hoc porro argumentum a comparatis elicitur: Si lex Veteris Testamenti est integra, nihilque in ea desideratum fuit ad salutem populi Israëlitici necessarium: multo magis tota doctrina Veteris ac Novi Testamenti est integra, nihilque in ea desiderari potest, quod necessarium sit ad salutem populi Christiani. Illud verum esse, David eodem Psal. 19. probat ab his legis adjunctis, et effectis, quod sit recta, justa, auro pretiosior, melle dulcior, parvulis veram sapientiam suppeditans, et beatos reddens quotquot ex animo in ea meditantur.

XII Tertia probatio nititur titulo *Testamenti*, quo Sacra Scriptura insignitur, Hebr. 9, 15. 16. 17. Testamenti autem haec est prima proprietas, ut perfectam Testatoris voluntatem* declaret, et plus satis idoneum sit ad omnia et singula haeredi significanda* quae ad adeundam haereditatem requiruntur. Secunda, ut

---

[a] Aristotle, *De coelo* 2.4.286b17–19; idem, *Physica* 3.207a8.

4. ON THE PERFECTION OF SCRIPTURE

The first of the former kind of proofs is taken from the passages that heap high praise upon the written Word, and which indicate its surpassing perfection, whether by the author or by the power and efficacy that the author communicates to it to reach the goal* which he has planned for it flawlessly. For by its author, namely God, who is the supreme cause* of everything and perfect in all his works (Deuteronomy 32:4), the written Word is sometimes called "the Word of God" (as in 2 Peter 1:21), sometimes "the Law of God" (Psalm 1:2; 19:8; 119), sometimes "Scripture that is God-breathed" (as in 2 Timothy 3:16). And by the power and efficacy that God has bestowed on it directly,* it is stated that the Word "is able* to render a person wise unto salvation" (2 Timothy 3:15).

The second proof comes from the qualities of perfection and sufficiency that are attributed explicitly to it (Psalm 19:8, 9): "the Law (i.e., teaching) of God is whole." For something is whole when it lacks nothing, and when it can receive nothing beyond what it possesses, as Aristotle rightly noted (*On the Heavens*, Book 2, ch. 4). Therefore nothing that belongs to the Law of God is found over and above the written Law of God.

Hence formerly God commanded that nothing be added to his Law or taken away from it (Deuteronomy 4:2). We must realize that the prohibition is about the Law as it was recorded by Moses himself, as both Moses' and Paul's explanation shows. For Moses calls God's Law in its entirety the words that have been written in his book (Deuteronomy 28:58), and so too Paul (Galatians 3:[10–]13). It is for this reason that everything Moses on behalf of God communicated to the Israelites by word* of mouth was also delivered in writing, as Moses himself testifies (Exodus 24:4; Deuteronomy 31:9).

From this integrity of the Law a further argument is drawn through comparison: if the Law of the Old Testament is whole and lacked nothing that was necessary for the salvation of the Israelite people, then how much more is the entire doctrine of the Old and New Testaments complete, and can lack nothing that is necessary for the salvation of the Christian people. In that same Psalm 19 David proves this to be the case by pointing to the traits and effects of the Law, that it is right, just, more precious than gold and sweeter than honey, making the simple truly wise, and causing all who ponder it sincerely to be blessed.

The third proof rests upon the title "Testament," which identifies Holy Scripture (Hebrews 9:15–17). Now the chief property of a testament is that it makes known the complete will* of the testator, and is very well suited to identify* for the heir each and every requirement he must meet in order to take possession of the inheritance. The second property is that once a will has been ratified,

eo confirmato, nullus illud abroget, aut aliquid ei superaddat, sicuti ex ipso Gentium jure, atque exemplo, ostendit Apostolus, Galat. 3, 15. Quod etiam citat Basilius de fide[a] disserens, et Augustinus *in Psal.* 21.[b]

XIII Quarta probatio inde eruitur, quod sit regula fidei et vitae, ut videre est Galat. 6, 16. Quicumque secundum hanc regulam incedunt, pax erit super eos, et misericordia. Et Phil. 3, 16. Omnis autem regula adeo est perfecta, ut nullam diminutionem, aut adjectionem admittat: alioqui non esset regula. Quod Gerson ad Sacrae Scripturae normam convenienter applicat in tract. de exam. doct. Tom. 1. parte 2.[c]

XIV Propterea Apostolus Johannes Sacrae Scripturae canonem hac postrema sua praemonitione sic obsignat, ut illa ad universum quoque Scripturae corpus extendi debeat, Apoc. 22, 18. 19. Si quis adjecerit ad haec, imponet ei Deus plagas scriptas in libro isto. Et si quis abstulerit ex verbis libri Prophetiae hujus, auferet Deus partem ejus ex libro vitae, ex urbe sanctorum, atque ex iis quae scripta sunt in libro isto.

XV Quinta deducitur ex verbi pronuntiati et scripti, tamquam duorum adminiculorum ἀντιστρεφομένων atque aequipollentium, exaequatione. Nam et Scriptura, verbi divini, et hoc vicissim, illius nomine insignitur. Unde sicuti Christus et Apostoli nihil extra Scripturas Veteris Testamenti dicere voluerunt, teste Evangelista, Luc. 24, 27. Actor. 17, 2. et 26, 22. ut innuerent, quicquid olim a Mose et Prophetis viva voce fuit prolatum, idem ab ipsis, quoad rei summam ac substantiam,* scripto fuisse comprehensum: sic etiam Apostoli et Evangelistae eodem, quo Moses et Prophetae, Spiritu pariter afflati, ex pari officio sibi a Spiritu Christi injuncto, totum de Christo Evangelium a se annuntiatum, literis mandarunt, ut colligi potest ex variis locis, ac nominatim ex Phil. 3, 1. Librum confeci de omnibus quae coepit Jesus facere et docere. Non piget me eadem vobis scribere, quae scilicet ex me audistis. 2 Thes. 2, 15. Retinete traditam doctrinam quam edocti estis, sive per sermonem, sive per Epistolam nostram. 1 Johan. 1, 3. 4. Quod vidimus et audivimus, id etiam annuntiamus, ut vos communionem habeatis nobiscum; et communio nostra sit cum Patre et Filio ejus

---

[a] Basil the Great, *De fide* 2 (MPG 31:680). *Ennarrationes in Psalmos* 54.21 (CSEL 94/1:169).
[b] Erroneous reference; correct to Augustine,
[c] Jean Gerson, *De examinatione doctrinarum* 2.1 (*Œuvres complètes* 9:465).

4. ON THE PERFECTION OF SCRIPTURE

no-one annuls it or adds anything to it, as the apostle shows with the example of the Gentiles' law (Galatians 3:15). Basil also cites this passage when he discusses faith, and so too Augustine on Psalm [54:]21.

The fourth proof is derived from the fact that it is the "rule" of faith and life, as can be seen in Galatians 6:16: "And peace and mercy shall come upon whoever walks by this rule" (and Philippians 3:16). For every rule is so complete that it allows nothing to be removed or added to it; otherwise it would not be a rule. Gerson has applied this proof suitably to the rule of Holy Scripture, in his treatise *On the Examination of Doctrine*, Tome 1, part 2.[8]

Therefore the apostle John seals the canon of Holy Scripture with the following word of final warning in such a manner that it should be extended to the whole corpus of Scripture (Revelation 22:18, 19): "If anyone adds to these words God will inflict on him the plagues described in this book. And if anyone takes away from the words of the book of this prophecy, God will take away his share from the book[9] of life and from the city of the saints, and from what is described in this book."

The fifth proof is derived from the equation that is made between the spoken word and the written one, like two complementary and equally strong supports. For even Scripture is called "the Word of God," and vice versa. For this reason Christ and the apostles resolved to say nothing beyond the Scriptures of the Old Testament (witness the evangelist, Luke 24:27; Acts 17:2, and 26:22), in order to signal that everything Moses and the prophets long ago had delivered orally is the same as what they had expressed in writing, as far as the main points and the content* are concerned. For the same reason also the apostles and the evangelists, inspired by the same Spirit just as much as Moses and the prophets were, and out of the same sense of duty which the Spirit of Christ had laid upon them, entrusted to writing the entire Gospel concerning Christ which they had proclaimed, as one can conclude from various places, and particularly Philippians 3:1: "It is not irksome to me to write the same things to you" that is to say, the things you had heard from me. And 2 Thessalonians 2:15: "Hold to the doctrinal tradition you were taught by us, either by preaching or by our letter." 1 John 1:3,4: "That which we have seen and heard we proclaim also to you, so that you may have fellowship with us; and our fellowship may be with

---

8 Jean Gerson (1363–1429) was an influential nominalist theologian and chancellor of the University of Paris. His *De examinatione doctrinarum* (*The Examination of Doctrines*) was published in 1423. See Brian Patrick McGuire, *Jean Gerson and the Last Medieval Reformation* (University Park: Pennsylvania State University Press, 2005).
9 Modern editions read "tree" instead of "book."

Jesu Christo. Et haec scribimus, ut gaudium vestrum sit plenum. Luc. 1, 3. 4. Visum est mihi omnia ad te scribere, ut agnoscas earum rerum veritatem quas auditione accepisti. Et Act. 1, 1. Librum confeci de omnibus quae coepit Iesus facere et docere.

XVI Sexta probatio petitur ab enumeratione partium* essentialium, materiae scilicet, et formae. Materia Scripturae consistit in rerum amplitudine, quas Deo placuit electis suis revelare. Forma in infallibili rerum illarum certitudine, et genuina secundum Dei praescriptum repraesentatione. Ex quibus haec duo eruimus:

XVII Primum, respectu materiae, omne quod ad hominis salutem est necessarium, aut mediorum, aut finis analogi* rationem habet. Utraque in sacris literis reperiuntur. Media etenim fini analoga, sub fidei in Jesum Christum, et finis mediis illi analogis, sub vitae aeternae nomine synecdochice comprehenduntur: Joh. 17, 3. Haec est vita aeterna, ut te cognoscant solum verum Deum, et quem misisti Jesum Christum, et 20. 31. Haec scripta sunt, ut credentes vitam habeatis per nomen ejus.

XVIII Secundo, formae ratione, quae ex admirabili Dei οἰκονομία, toti sacro volumini ac singulis ejus paginis sic est indita, ut ipsum Deum veritatis salutaris archetypum nobis passim ob oculos proponat; ideoque a Mose κατ' ἐξοχὴν vocatur sapientia et scientia perfectissima coram omnibus populis, Deut. 4, 6.

4. ON THE PERFECTION OF SCRIPTURE

the Father and his Son Jesus Christ. And we are writing this that your joy may be complete." Luke 1:3,4: "It seemed good to me to write all these things to you, so that you may recognize the truth of those things which you have received by hearing." And Acts 1:1: "I have completed a book about all the things which Jesus began to do and teach."

16 The sixth proof derives from an account of the parts* that make up the essence, namely matter and form.[10] The matter of Scripture exists in the scope of the things God was pleased to reveal to his elect. The form exists in the unerring certainty of those things and the true representation of them following God's prescription. Of these we draw forth the following two:

17 First, with respect to the matter: everything that is necessary for a person's salvation has the character either of the means or of the goal that corresponds* to them. And both are found in the sacred writings. For the means that correspond to the goal are included in the faith in Jesus Christ, and the goal with its corresponding means is included in the name "eternal life" by synecdoche, or as part for the whole;[11] John 17:3: "And this is eternal life, that they know you the only true God, and Jesus Christ whom you have sent"; John 20:31: "These things are written that believing you may have life through his name."

18 Secondly, concerning the form, which thanks to God's remarkable economy pervades the entire sacred book and each individual page to such an extent that it presents God himself everywhere before our eyes as the archetype[12] of the truth that saves. For that reason Moses in the presence of all the people calls it above all "wisdom" and the most complete knowledge [Deuteronomy

---

10 In Aristotle's philosophy matter and form are the two inherent principles that constitute the essence or substance of material beings. For example, a human being is composed of body and soul. 'Essential parts' are distinguished from 'integral parts,' mentioned in thesis 19: see: Andrew Arlig, "Medieval Mereology," *The Stanford Encyclopedia of Philosophy* (Winter 2008 Edition), Edward N. Zalta (ed.), accessed February 27, 2014, http://plato.stanford.edu/archives/win2008/entries/mereology-medieval/.

Richard A. Muller writes: "These two primary perfections, the material and the formal, can be considered as an 'essential perfection' in doctrine and as an integral or 'systematic' perfection in the books themselves, their succession, and their inclusion in the canon. Thus, even as Scripture is perfect as a whole, so also does it have a perfection in its parts, of quantity as well as essence," *PRRD* 2:313.

11 Synecdoche is a figure of speech whereby a more comprehensive term is employed to refer to a less comprehensive one, as a whole for part, or vice versa. In the case of John 17:3, "eternal life" is the 'goal' and the wider meaning employed in place of the 'means' and narrower meaning of "knowing God and Jesus Christ."

12 Cf. *SPT* 1.13 above.

a Christo ipsa veritas, Joh. 17, 17. a Paulo veritas secundum pietatem, Tit. 1, 1. Nec non, sermo fidelis, sanus, irreprehensibilis et dignus qui omnibus modis recipiatur.

XIX Septima probatio exstruitur ex partibus ejus integralibus,* Lege scilicet, et Evangelio, id est, caritatis ac fidei praeceptis, in quibus tota religio* Deo grata nobisque salutaris continetur. Quod autem constat omnibus partibus integrantibus, est integrum et totum, et quod totum est, perfectum est, et vice versa. Haec enim invicem convertuntur.

XX Octava ratio est a perfectis ejus effectis, quod hominem, scilicet, sua institutione reddat perfectum, et perfecte instructum ad omne opus bonum, eumque pleno gaudio perfundat, 2 Tim. 3, 17. 1 Joh. 4. Effectorum perfectorum causam quoque perfectam esse necesse est.

XXI Nona petitur a gravissima Esaiae commonefactione, quoslibet ab humanis commentis ad solam Scripturae Mosaicae ac Propheticae normam revocantis, cap. 8, 20. Ad legem et ad testimonium; si non dixerint juxta hoc verbum, nulla ipsis est lucis scintilla. Si autem prisca Ecclesia Judaica ab Esaia ad solam Scripturam sub lege conscriptam reducitur, pari ergo ratione, imo majori, ad solum Veteris simul et Novi Testamenti testimonium* Ecclesia Christiana remittitur.

XXII Decima est a communi* et confesso Judaeorum testimonio, ab ipso etiam Christo approbato, Joh. 5, 39. Scrutamini Scripturas, nam existimatis vos in ipsis vitam habere. Si Judaei hoc recte, ex Christi sententia, de Scripturis Veteris Testamenti existimarunt, nos idem ergo majori jure de toto utriusque Testamenti volumine censemus.

XXIII Undecima est a responso Abrahami, Luc. 16, 29. quo testatur, fratres divitis epulonis, si audiant Mosem et Prophetas, eam posse ex scriptis eorum haurire cognitionem, quae sola ad cruciatus inferorum evitandos sufficiat.

XXIV Duodecima est ab usu Sacrae Scripturae, ad hominem Dei, id est, Ecclesiae Doctorem, adeoque et auditorem, secundum omnes partes sacrosancti Ministerii plene informandum. Utilis enim esse dicitur ad doctrinam, redargutionem, correctionem, institutionem in justitia, 2 Tim. 3, 16, et ad consolationem, Rom. 15, 4.

4. ON THE PERFECTION OF SCRIPTURE

4:6], Christ "the truth itself" (John 17:17), and Paul "the truth that accords with godliness" (Titus 1:1). And also "the faithful, sound, irreproachable word that is worthy to be received in every way."

The seventh proof arises from its integral* parts,[13] namely the Law and the Gospel, that is, the commands of love and faith that comprise the whole of religion* pleasing to God and for us means salvation. For whatever consists of all the parts that combine to make up the whole is whole and entire, and whatever is entire is perfect, and vice versa. For these two things are interchangeable.

The eighth reason comes from its perfect results, the fact that it renders a person perfect through its instruction and perfectly equipped for every good work, and showers him with perfect joy (2 Timothy 3:17; 1 John 4). It is necessary that the cause of these perfect effects itself must be perfect also.

The ninth reason is sought from the very stern admonition of Isaiah who calls everyone away from human inventions to the only rule of Mosaic and prophetic Scripture (Isaiah 8:20): "To the Law and to the testimony; if they would not speak according to this word, then there is no spark of light for them." Moreover, if the ancient Jewish church is led back by Isaiah to the only Scripture that was recorded in writing under the Law, then by the same reasoning—no, by greater reasoning—is the Christian Church sent back to the single testimony* of the Old together with the New Testament.

The tenth reason comes from the commonly* professed testimony of the Jews, one that was approved even by Christ himself, in John 5:39: "You search the Scriptures, because you think that in them you have life." If this estimation of the Old Testament Scriptures by the Jews is right, as can be taken from Christ's statement, then we more rightfully hold the same with regard to the entire book of the two testaments.

The eleventh comes from Abraham's reply, in Luke 16:29, where he testifies that if the brothers of the rich banqueter heed Moses and the prophets, they are able to draw from their writings the only knowledge sufficient to avoid torment in the realm of the dead.

The twelfth reason is from the usefulness of Holy Scripture for the "man of God" (that is, to the teacher of the church) and therefore also for the hearer who must be fully instructed according to all the parts of the most holy ministry. For it says that Scripture is "profitable for teaching, for reproof, for correction, and for training in righteousness" (2 Timothy 3:16), and "for encouragement" (Romans 15:4).

---

13 'Integral parts' are quantitative parts that make up a whole. For example, arms and legs are integral parts of a human body. See also footnote 11.

xxv His probationibus divinis, ad retundendos Pontificios Patrum auctoritate adversus nos plerumque abutentes, addi possunt testimonia Irenaei, lib. 3. cap. 1.ᵃ Basilii, *Epistola* 1. et 80.ᵇ Chrysostomi, *Homil. 1. in Acta*,ᶜ Tertulliani *adversus Hermogenem*,ᵈ Ambrosii, lib. 1. *Hexaem.* cap. 6.ᵉ Hieronymi *ad Demetriadem Virginem*, et *in Mich.* lib. 1, cap. 1.ᶠ Justini Martyris *in Tryph.*ᵍ Origenis *in Jer. Homil.* 1.ʰ Augustini, lib. 2. *de Doctr. Christ.* cap. 9.ⁱ et lib. 7. *Confess.* c. 7.ʲ atque aliorum Patrum, asserentium, Scripturas esse fidei columnam et scaturiginem, tantamque earum esse plenitudinem, ut in iis omnia sufficienter inveniantur, quae continent fidem, moresque bene beateque vivendi, spem scilicet, et caritatem; quae testimonia hic, brevitatis gratia, non reponimus.

xxvi Hactenus Sacram Scripturam absolute,* atque in se* consideratam, perfectam esse demonstravimus; eandem relate ad traditiones non scriptas et opposite consideratam, duplici respectu perfectam esse asserimus. Aliae enim generaliori et impropria* significatione* sumptae, utiles sunt ac necessariae ad salutem; aliae speciaiori, ac propria significatione acceptae, inutiles et non necessariae. Illae per ἰσοδυναμίαν seu aequipollentiam, tamquam ὁμογενεῖς, ac Sacrae Scripturae consentaneae, Sacrae Scripturae finibus includuntur; hae tamquam

---

ᵃ Irenaeus, *Adversus haereses* 3.1.1 (FC 8/3:22).   ᵇ Basil the Great, *Epistulae* 2.3 (= *Ep.* 1 in old numbering; Courtonne 1:8) and 189.3 (= old *Ep.* 80; Courtonne 2:134).   ᶜ John Chrysostom, *Homilia in Acta* 1 (MPG 60:13–26).   ᵈ Tertullian, *Liber adversus Hermogenem, passim* (CCSL 1:397–435). ᵉ Ambrose, *Hexameron* 1.6.20–24 (CSEL 32/1:16–23).   ᶠ Jerome, *Epistulae* 130.9 (CSEL 56/1²:188); idem, prb. *Comm. in Michaeam* 1.1.10/15 or 16 (CCSL 76:435 or 437).   ᵍ Probably Justin Martyr, *Dialogus cum Tryphone* 7.1–3 (Philippe Bobichon, *Justin Martyr: Dialogue avec Tryphon*, 2 vols., Paradosis 47/1–2 (Fribourg: Academic Press Fribourg, 2003), 1:202–204).   ʰ Probably Origen, *In Jeremiam homiliae* 1.4 (SC 232:202).   ⁱ Augustine, *De doctrina christiana* 2.9.14 (CCSL 32:40–41). ʲ Augustine, *Confessiones* 7.7 (CCSL 27:99–100)

4. ON THE PERFECTION OF SCRIPTURE

In order to restrain the papal theologians who commonly abuse the authority of the Fathers against us, one can add to these proofs from the divine sources the statements of proof by Irenaeus in book 3, chapter 1; Basil, *Letter* 1 and 80; Chrysostom,[14] *Sermon* 1 on Acts; Tertullian, *Against Hermogenes*; Ambrose,[15] *Hexameron* book 1, chapter 6; Jerome, *To Demetriades on Virginity*; and *Commentary on Micah* book 1, chapter 1; Justin Martyr, *Dialogue with Trypho*; Origen, *Sermon* 1 on Jeremiah; Augustine, *On Christian Doctrine*, book 2, chapter 9, and *Confessions*, book 7, chapter 7; and of other Fathers, who affirm that the Scriptures are the pillar and source of faith,[16] and that their fullness is so great that in them one will discover sufficiently everything that contains faith and the habits for living a good and blessed life, namely hope and charity. For the sake of brevity we do not record these testimonies here.

Up to this point we have demonstrated that Holy Scripture, examined absolutely* and by itself,* is perfect; when we examine it in relation and in opposition to the unwritten traditions, we assert that it is perfect in two respects. For some [traditions], taken in a broader and improper* sense,* are beneficial and necessary for salvation; others, taken in a more specific and proper sense, are not useful or necessary. The former, by virtue of *isodunamia* or equivalence, being of the same kind, and in harmony with Holy Scripture, are included

---

14 John Chrysostom (c. AD 347–407) was born in Antioch to noble parents. He pursued studies under Diodorus of Tarsus. After entering the priesthood around 386, he became preacher at Antioch for twelve years, exercising exegetical skills and delivering practical sermons, holding to a simple, grammatical understanding of Scripture, and drawing a large following. When the See of Constantinople became vacant in 398, Chrysostom was appointed archbishop of the capital. Following political intrigues led by Theophilus, the patriarch of Alexandria, Chrysostom was condemned and deposed in 403. He died in exile in Pityus.

15 Ambrose (c. AD 337–397) was born in Trier, son of a praetorian prefect of Gaul, and educated in Rome for a civilian post to which he was appointed around 374 in Milan. After the death of the Arian bishop Auxentius, a theological struggle ensued and it is reported that when the young governor entered the church, the cry "Ambrose, bishop!" went up. Accepting this as a call of God, Ambrose studied theology, and in performing his office as a bishop he acted as both a preacher and an administrator. As defender of the Nicene faith, author of ethical writings, and developer of Christian hymnology, Ambrose was considered a 'doctor' of the church.

16 This is an allusion to Irenaeus, who writes that Scriptures are the "foundation and pillar of our faith" (*fundamentum et columna nostrae fidei*) (*Adversus Haereses* book 3, chapter 1.1), which in turn alludes to 1 Tim. 3:15.

ἑτερογενεῖς, ac dissentaneae, iis excluduntur. De illis recte docet Nazianzenus, lib. 5. *Theologiae*,[a] quod quidem sint, tamen non expresse dicantur in Scripturis; de his, quod nec in iis sint, nec in iis dicantur.

xxvii Utraeque aut sunt dogmata aut rituales. Illae tantummodo divinae, Propheticae et Apostolicae; hae vero humanae traditiones sunt appellandae.

xxviii Quicquid enim est divinum, illud vel tacite, vel expresse, aut κατὰ γένος aut καθ' ἕν, a Prophetis et Apostolis est conscriptum. Male ergo divinae traditiones a Bellarmino distinguuntur ab Apostolicis, lib. 4. *de Verbo Dei non scripto*, c. 2.[b] Nullae etenim traditiones, extra sacras literas Apostolorum manu consignatas, pro divinis sunt habendae; nullae ad Apostolicarum album referendae, tamquam ab Apostolis Spiritus Sancti assistentia, ut loquamur verbis Bellarmini, institutas, quarum summa capita nusquam in Scripturis inveniuntur.

xxix In censu traditionum, quae in sacris literis inveniuntur, iisque insunt per aequipollentiam analogicam, contra quam Pontificii arbitrantur, praeter articulos Symboli Apostolici, haec axiomata collocanda censemus. Infantes Christianorum esse baptizandos; Coenam Domini mulieribus quoque esse impertiendam; Jesum Christum esse Deo Patri suo ὁμοούσιον seu coessentialem; Duo esse, nimirum, Baptismum et Coenam Domini, novi foederis sacramenta;* Baptismum non esse iterandum; Apostolos ex inspiratione Spiritus Sancti diem Dominicum selegisse in locum diei Sabbati a Judaeis usque ad ipsorum tempora sanctificati, et similia quae καταχρηστικῶς traditiones Apostolicae a quibusdam Patribus nuncupantur, nimirum, ab Origene, in c. 6. *ad Rom*.[c] Augustino, lib. 4. *de Baptismo contra Donatistas* c. 23.[d] Theodoreto, lib. 1. c. 8. *Histor. Eccles*.[e] Epiphanio, *haeres*. 69. *adversus Arrianos*,[f] et aliis.

xxx In catalogo traditionum, quarum aliae nullo modo exstant in Sacris Scripturis, aliae iis repugnant, haec sequentia ponimus: Paschatis sub Novo Testamento celebrationem die Dominico decimumquartum diem Lunae Martii proxime sequente; Superstitiosum quadragesimae jejunium; Adorationem imaginum et reliquiarum; Invocationem Sanctorum; Signi crucis adorationem; Missae sacrificium; Transubstantiationem panis in S. Coena; Abrogationem usus calicis in eadem; Circumgestationem panis per vicos et compita, ut adoretur; Chrisma, Aquae lustralis benedictionem, Vota Monastica, Peregrinationes,

---

[a] Gregory of Nazianzus, *Oratio* 31.22–23 (= *Oratio theologica* 5; SC 250:316–320).   [b] Bellarmine, *De verbo Dei* 4.2 (*Opera* 1:196a–b).   [c] Origen, *Ad Romanos* 5.9.13 (on Rom 6:6; SC 539:498). [d] Augustine, *De baptismo contra Donatistas* 4.23.30 (CSEL 51:258).   [e] Theodoret of Cyrus, *Historia ecclesiastica* 1.8 (SC 501:210–216).   [f] Epiphanius, *Panarion* or *Adversus Haereses* 69 *adversus Arrianos* (MPG 42:201–335).

4. ON THE PERFECTION OF SCRIPTURE 121

within the boundaries of Holy Scripture; the latter, by being of a different kind and divergent, are excluded by the boundaries. Concerning the former Gregory of Nazianzus (*Theological Orations*, Book 5) correctly teaches that they do indeed occur, but are not mentioned explicitly in Scriptures; concerning the latter, that they neither occur nor are mentioned in them.

Both are either doctrines or rituals. Only the former are divine, prophetic and apostolic; the latter should be called human traditions.

For everything that originated with God was recorded by the prophets and the apostles, either tacitly or expressly, either generally or singularly. Therefore Bellarmine wrongly distinguishes divine from apostolic traditions (*On the Unwritten Word of God*, Book 4, ch. 2). For no traditions should be viewed as divine, except the sacred writings recorded by the hand of the apostles. No traditions should be put in the list of apostolic ones as if coming "from the apostles with the assistance of the Holy Spirit," to quote the words of Bellarmine, of which their main points are found nowhere in Scriptures.

In the list of traditions that are found in the sacred writings, or that occur there by having the same force by analogy, we think (contrary to what the papal teachers think) that, besides the articles of the Apostles' Creed, the following axiomatic statements may be assembled: That the children of Christians ought to be baptized; that the Lord's Supper ought to be given also to women; that Jesus Christ is *homoousios* or of the same essence with his Father; that there are two sacraments* of the new covenant, namely Baptism and the Lord's Supper; that Baptism is not to be repeated; that the apostles, inspired by the Holy Spirit, chose the day of the Lord [Sunday] instead of the Sabbath-day that had been sanctified by the Jews until their times; and similar things which are loosely called apostolic traditions by some of the church-fathers; namely, by Origen (in the commentary on Romans ch. 6.); Augustine (*On Baptism, Against the Donatists*, ch. 23); by Theodoretus (*History of the Church*, Book 1, ch. 8); Epiphanius (*Against the Arians*, Heresy 69); and by others.

In the catalogue of traditions which do not appear at all in Holy Scriptures, or which are incompatible with them, we place the following: the celebration of Easter under the new testament on the Sunday following the fourteenth day of the [new] moon of March; the superstitious keeping of the forty-day fast; the worship of images and relics; the invocation of saints; the worship of the sign of the cross; the offering of the mass; the transubstantiation of the bread in the Lord's Supper; the discontinued use of the cup in the same; the carrying about of the bread through neighborhoods and at crossroads for the purpose of adoration; blessing of lustral water; monastic vows; pilgrimages; the repeated

Recitationes salutationis Angelicae ad Virginem Mariam. Nec non *Canones*, qui (sicuti et praecedentium traditionum pleraeque) Apostolis a Pontificiis falso ascribuntur.

XXXI   Alii enim ex Patribus *Canones* illos in totum tamquam adulterinos rejecerunt, alii aliquot dumtaxat ex iis admiserunt, ut videre est apud Zephyrinum, et Gratianum in 1. part. *decret.* dist. 16.[a] Alii eos immutarunt, ut patet ex c. 6. Sextae Synodi; qualis est inter ceteros Canon 68.[b] quo jubetur, Clericum quadragesimam non jejunantem, deponendum, laicum vero communione privandum.

XXXII   Ceteras quoque traditiones supra numeratas esse adulterinas et supposititias, vel ex eo constat, quod pleraeque earum (ut supra indicavimus) scriptis Apostolicis ex diametro adversentur. Quaecumque autem ab Apostolis, vel ore, vel scripto sunt tradita, sibi invicem utrobique sunt consona, utpote ab uno eodemque Spiritu veritatis dictata, qui sibi nunquam contradicit, neque, *ita et non*, nullam repugnantiae speciem, in Apostolorum doctrina inveniri voluit, 2 Cor. 1, 19.

XXXIII   Nec praetereundum est, quod Pontificii in ista traditionum non scriptarum enumeratione sibi contradicunt. Nam, ut reliquas nunc praetereamus, Cajetanus Missae sacrificium traditionibus Apostolicis non scriptis ascribit, in cap.

---

[a] See the note on the facing page.   [b] Erroneous reference; the sixth ecumenical council (Third Council of Constantinople) of 680–681 speaks about a 40-day fast in canon 56 (Mansi 11:970).

chanting of the angel's greeting to the virgin Mary. So also the Canons,[17] which like most of the other forementioned traditions the papal teachers wrongly attribute to the apostles.

For some of the church-fathers have rejected these Canons altogether for being forged, while others have accepted at least a few of them, as can be seen in Zephyrinus, and Gratian (1 Part Decret. Dist. 16).[18] Others have made changes to them, as is clear from Chapter 6 of the Sixth Synod: such as Canon 68, among others, which commands that "the cleric who does not fast for the forty days [of Lent] must be removed from office, while the laic must abstain from communion."[19]

The fact that very many of the traditions (as we have indicated above) are diametrically opposed to the apostolic writings proves that also the other traditions listed above are forged and spurious. For all the things that the apostles have handed down, either by word of mouth or in writing, are in harmony with one another from both sides, since they were pronounced by one and the same Spirit of truth, who never contradicts himself and who wanted that no contradiction or any kind of contrariety be found in the teaching of the apostles (2 Corinthians 1:19).

Nor should we overlook the fact that the papal teachers are at odds with each other regarding that list of unwritten traditions. For (leaving aside all the other traditions), Cajetan[20] ascribes the sacrifice of the Mass to the unwritten

---

17 The *Canons of the Apostles* is a collection of fifty (in the West) or eighty-five (in the East) ecclesiastical rules from the early Church attributed to pope Clement. For an English translation see NPNF2, 14: 594–600.

18 The *Decretum*, compiled by the twelfth-century jurist Gratian, was the most important collection of canon law in the Middle Ages. Gratian discusses the authenticity of the *Canons of the Apostles* in Distinction 16, where he also mentions a letter by Pope Zephyrinus (199–217), stating that the *Canons* are to be received: Gratian (Augustine Thompson, James Gordley, and Katherine Christensen, trans. and eds.), *The Treatise on Laws (Decretum DD. 1–20), With the Ordinary Gloss*, Studies in Medieval and Early Modern Canon Law, vol. 3 (Washington: Catholic University of America Press, 1993), 60–61.

19 Polyander is referring to a canon that was actually drawn up by the Council in Trullo (also called Quinisext Council) of 692, whose disciplinary canons were intended to complete the fifth and sixth ecumenical councils held in 553 and 680–681 (i.e., the Second and Third Council of Constantinople). The *Concilia generalia ecclesiae catholicae Pauli V pont. max. auctoritate edita* (4 vols.; Rome: Vatican, 1608–1612), which Polyander likely used as the standard edition of his time, includes the canons of the Trullan Council under the Sixth Ecumenical Council (see 3:300–342). The preface attributes the canons to the Second Council of Constantinople.

20 Thomas de Vio (1469–1541) was also known as Cajetan, after his hometown Gaeta in Spain. Cajetan was a Dominican cardinal, an advocate of Thomistic theology. As imperial delegate,

2 Thess. 2, 2.ᵃ Bellarminus vero illud in Sacra Scriptura praecipi, ex variis hujus locis probare satagit, lib. 1. *de Missa* c. 6. et seqq.ᵇ

XXXIV Notandum praeterea, quod Pontificii asserant, Apostolos non omnia sibi a Deo revelata cum omnibus suis auditoribus communicasse, sed quaedam palam et universis, quaedam secreto et paucis demandasse. Quam assertionem Tertullianus, lib. *de praescriptione adversus haereticos*,ᶜ non immerito ipsam *dementiam* nuncupat.

XXXV Ista enim assertione Apostoli non obscure, perfidae atque inexcusabilis inoboedientiae insimulantur, quasi aliquam partem mysteriorum sibi a Deo revelatorum, ut ea omnibus a se instituendis pro muneris sibi injuncti necessitate* patefacerent, Matth. 10, 27. et 28, 19. tum in contionibus, tum in scriptis suis praetermiserint. Quod ut negat Apostolus Paulus, Act. 20, 27, sic contrarium asseverat, 1 Cor. 1, 5. 6. et 15,1.2. 1 Thess. 1, 5. 2 Thess. 2, 13. 14. 15.

XXXVI Ex eadem assertione sequitur, neminem posse certo scire, quaenam sint arcanae illae traditiones, et quibus regulis vel notis verae a falsis distinguantur.

XXXVII Nam regulae ac notae, quae extra Sacram Scripturam, certissimum sui et obliqui in omnibus credendis et observandis indicem, a Bellarmino proferuntur, lib. 4. *de Verbo Dei non scripto* c. 9.ᵈ incertae sunt, obscurae et fallaces. Non

---

ᵃ Tommaso de Vio Cajetan, *In s. Scripturam commentarii*, 5 vols. (Lugduni: sumptibus Jacobi & Petri Prost, 1639), 5:286.   ᵇ Bellarmine, *De Eucharistia* 5.6–14 (= *De sacrificio Missae*; *Opera* 4:309b–343a).   ᶜ Tertullian, *Liber de praescriptione haereticorum* 22.2, 25.1 (CCSL 1:203, 206). ᵈ Bellarmine, *De verbo Dei* 4.9 (*Opera* 1:216b–218a).

---

he took part in the Diet of Augsburg (1518) and negotiated with Luther to convince him to revoke his statements.

4. ON THE PERFECTION OF SCRIPTURE

traditions of the apostles (at 2 Thessalonians 2:2). But Bellarmine spends much effort to prove from various passages that it is taught in Holy Scripture (*On the Mass*, Book 1, ch. 6 and following).[21]

34 We should observe further that the papal teachers claim the apostles did not share with their listeners everything God had revealed to them, but that they entrusted some things to everyone and publicly and other things to only a few and privately.[22] Tertullian in his book *Against the Heretics*, rightly calls that claim insane.

35 For by that claim the apostles are obviously charged with faithless and unpardonable disobedience, as if in their sermons as well as in their writings they had left out some part of the mysteries that God had revealed to them, for the purpose of making them known to everyone whom they were to instruct, according to the necessity* of the task imposed on them (Matthew 10:27, and 28:19). The apostle Paul denies this (Acts 20:27), and actually states the opposite (1 Corinthians 1:5,6, and 15:1,2; 1 Thessalonians 1:5; 2 Thessalonians 2:13, 14, 15).

36 From the same claim it follows that no-one can know for sure what those hidden traditions are, and by what rules and marks the true ones are to be distinguished from the false ones.

37 For the rules and marks Bellarmine puts forward outside Holy Scripture are doubtful, as Scripture alone is the most reliable indicator of right and wrong[23] in all the things one must believe and keep (*On the Unwritten Word of God*, Book 4, ch. 9). His rules are not clearly spelled out, and misleading.[24] For then

---

21 The biblical 'proofs' adduced by Bellarmine for the sacrificial character of the Mass include Christ's own words of institution, the connection with the Paschal Lamb, several prophetic passages, and the comparison made by Paul in 1 Corinthians 10 between the time of Moses and the truth of Christ.

22 This view is especially expressed by Melchior Cano, *De locis theologicis* III.3 (Salamanca: Mathias Gastius, 1563), 103–107. See further George H. Tavard, "Tradition in Early Post-Tridentine Theology," *Theological Studies* 23 (1962): 377–405.

23 Cf. Aristotle, *On the Soul*, I, 4, 411a5–6: "A straight line is the judge [*iudex*] of both itself and the curved."

24 Bellarmine, *De Verbo Dei* (*Disputationes*, Ingolstadt: D. Sartorius, 1587, vol. 1, book 4, chapter 9, pp. 292–296) lists the following rules. Something should be accepted and believed as apostolic tradition: (1) when the universal church embraces it as a dogma of faith, even if it is not found in Scripture; (2) when the universal church preserves something that only God could have instituted, but that nevertheless is not found in Scripture; (3) when it is preserved in the universal church from ancient times as being instituted by the apostles, even if it could have been instituted by the church itself; (4) when all doctors of the church—whether they are gathered in a general Council or are writing separately in their books—teach with common consent

enim omnia dogmata, quae universa Ecclesia circa Scripturam amplectitur, ac servat a proximo ab Apostolis aevo, communique Doctorum ejus consensu approbantur, ab ipsis Apostolis prodiisse, necessario credendum est; sed e contrario, propterea quod ab ea ejusque Doctoribus, sine Scripturae auctoritate recipiantur, ac retineantur, pro traditionibus non Apostolicis sunt habenda.

XXXVIII   Quicumque enim in eo errant cum Ecclesia Romana, quae continuatam ab Apostolis successionem sibi arrogat, ut existiment non omnia in Sacra Scriptura contineri ad salutem necessaria; in hoc altero facile decipi possunt, ut putent, aliquam doctrinam esse Apostolicam, quae tamen non profluxerit ab Apostolis.

XXXIX   Cui rei testimonio est Ecclesia primitiva Apostolicae proxima. Papias enim errorem Chiliastarum sub titulo traditionis Apostolicae in eam invexit, teste Eusebio, lib. 3. cap. 39.[a] et Irenaeus, velut ex traditione Apostoli Johannis, docuit Christum passum fuisse anno fere aetatis suae 50. lib. 2. c. 39. 40.[b] In quibus illam Ecclesiam a suis Doctoribus deceptam fuisse, ipsi quoque Pontificii confitentur.

---

[a] Eusebius, *Historia ecclesiastica* 3.39.11–13 (SC 31:156).   [b] Erroneous reference; correct to Irenaeus, *Adversus haereses* 2.22.5 (FC 8/2:188).

---

that it descends from apostolic tradition; and (5) when it is accepted by those churches that are within the integral, continuous apostolic succession.

4. ON THE PERFECTION OF SCRIPTURE

we must of necessity believe that not all the teachings which the universal church embraces about Scripture (which it preserves from the age immediately following the apostolic one, and which are endorsed by the common consensus of its teachers), proceeded from the apostles; but, to the contrary, on account of the fact that they have been received and retained by the church and its teachers without the sanction of Scripture, they must be deemed as non-apostolic traditions.

For everyone who together with the Roman church, which claims for itself an unbroken succession from the apostles, errs in thinking that Holy Scripture does not contain everything that is necessary for salvation, can be deceived easily in the following aspect also: that some other doctrine which actually did not emanate from the apostles is apostolic. 38

A demonstration of this point is the early church, immediately following the apostolic one. For under the guise of apostolic tradition Papias imported the error of the Chiliasts into the church (witness Eusebius, Book 3, ch. 39); and Irenaeus (Book 2, ch. 39, 40) taught that, according to the tradition of the apostle John, Christ's suffering took place around his fiftieth year of age. Even the papal teachers admit that the church of that time was misled by its own teachers in these matters. 39

DISPUTATIO V

De Sacrae Scripturae Perspicuitate et Interpretatione

Praeside D. ANTONIO WALAEO
Respondente ROMBERTO STELLINGWERF

THESIS I   Quae hactenus de Sacra Scriptura disputata sunt, eo pertinent, ut ei divina sua majestas et dignitas constet; quae vero sequuntur, ejus usum et fructum in Ecclesia Christi proprie commendant; nam cognitio divinitatis, auctoritatis, et perfectionis ejus parum nobis prodesset, nisi ea et a fidelibus intelligi, et ad dogmata fidei ac morum constituenda, in Christi Ecclesia explicari, atque applicari recte posset.

II   Ut igitur hic Sacrae Scripturae usus et fructus, Ecclesiae Christi integer maneat, de ejus Perspicuitate, atque Interpretatione deinceps nobis est agendum.

III   Sacrae Scripturae lux, seu Perspicuitas, duobus modis considerari potest: vel absolute* et in se, vel relate ad nos et intellectum nostrum.

IV   Absolutam et in se* consideratam Sacrae Scripturae lucem, nobiscum agnoscunt etiam saniores Pontificii. Cum enim Sacra Scriptura a Patre luminum profecta sit, non potest non in se continere veritatem et lucem purissimam, qua mentes eorum, qui eam cognoscunt, illustrentur, et ab errorum tenebris

DISPUTATION 5

About the Perspicuity and the Interpretation of Holy Scripture

President: Antonius Walaeus
Respondent: Rombert Stellingwerf[1]

The matters concerning Holy Scripture that have been debated up to this point aim to confirm its divine majesty and dignity; in what follows we shall commend especially its use and benefit in the Church of Christ. For the recognition of its divinity, authority, and perfection would be of no advantage to us at all, unless we believers can understand Scripture correctly and explain and apply it in the Church of Christ in order to establish the doctrines of faith and moral conduct.

Therefore in order for this use and benefit of Holy Scripture to remain intact for the Church of Christ, we must now treat the perspicuity[2] and interpretation of it.

The lucid quality or perspicuity of Holy Scripture can be considered in two ways: either absolutely* and by itself, or in relation to us and our intellect.

Considered apart and by itself,* the light of Holy Scripture is recognized by the most sensible papal theologians, along with us. For since Holy Scripture proceeded from the Father of lights,[3] it is impossible that it should not possess in itself the truth and the purest light, whereby the minds of those who come to

---

1 There is no record of his matriculation in Leiden in the *Album studiosorum*; nor is there any information about his life in *Repertorium* or *Album studiosorum academiae Franekerensis*. He defended this disputation on 23 May 1620 and dedicated his defense to representatives of the States of the province of Holland and West-Friesland and of Amsterdam: J. Witsius, Joh. de Vries, and Jac. Hoochkamer, to Jac. Trigland (Amsterdam pastor), G. Timmermannus, P. van Geel, R. de Vries and Joh. Noyen who supported and sponsored him, to Walaeus, Hommius and Amesius, and to P. ab Opmeer and R. Kempius and "all who were helpful to him in his studies in many ways."
2 A traditional attribute of Scripture, perspicuity refers to the clarity, lucid quality, and transparency of Scripture (*DLGTT*, s.v. "perspicuitas"). In being used as one of the 'properties' of Scripture in the emergent Protestant doctrine of Scripture, perspicuity has a recognizable origin in medieval theology, yet the context in which the term is applied shifts from the 'fourfold meaning of Scripture' (*quadriga*) to the prominently literal-grammatical reading of the text. See *PRRD* 2:324–340, where 'perspicuity' and 'clarity' are treated as synonyms.
3 Cf. James 1:17.

liberentur. Quamobrem et sapientia, et Thesaurus scientiae Scriptura vocatur, et puritas ejus auro septies recocto, ac carbunculis pretiosior esse affirmatur, Prov. 3, 13. etc.

V   Tota ergo controversia in ejus perspicuitate ad nos relata* consistit; quia perspicuum hic proprie* dicitur, quod claritate sua aliis conspicuum est, et ab iis cognosci, et intelligi potest, qui intelligendi facultate* sunt praediti.

VI   Haec perspicuitatis ratio* ad duo hominum genera referri potest; vel ad captum, seu facultatem hominis naturalis,* id est, (ut Chrysostomus recte explicat[a]) cujus intellectus nulla alia luce est donatus, nisi quam Deus, per propagationem naturalem, omnium hominum animis, diverso licet demenso, inserit, ut et ipsa Scriptura loquitur, Johann. 1, 9, vel ad captum et facultatem hominis spiritualis, id est, cujus mens supernaturali* luce insuper, varia quoque mensura, est illustrata: quemadmodum haec distinctio exprimitur 1 Cor. 2, 14. et alibi.

VII   Quod primum hominum genus* attinet, fatemur quidem multa in Sacris literis narrari ac doceri, quae naturali modo ab homine naturali intelliguntur, si diligentiam aliquam adhibeat, et linguarum aliarumque artium instrumentalium adminiculo sit instructus, quum Deus per Prophetas et Apostolos suos, lingua inter homines usitata, et loquendi modis ex medio sumptis, plurimum sit locutus, etiam cum de rebus agit humanum intellectum longe excedentibus. Unde quoque videmus, quosdam gentiles Philosophos in suos usus nonnulla ex Sacra Scriptura esse mutuatos; alios vero in scriptis suis conatos fuisse se iis opponere, quod ab iis fieri nequivisset, nisi verborum sententiam et grammaticum sensum naturali saltem modo percepissent.

VIII   Negamus tamen, hominem naturalem seu animalem, quicumque is sit, eo quo decet modo, id est, spirituali evidentia,* promptitudine, animique reverentia et sanctimonia, multo minus certa mentis πληροφορία et assensu, ea comprehendere, dijudicare, aut salutariter sibi applicare posse, nisi Spiritu Sancto sit illustratus. Quemadmodum de confessione Petri loquitur Christus, Matth. 16, 17. Caro et sanguis haec non revelavit tibi, sed Pater meus qui est in coelis. Et 1 Cor. 1, 23. Praedicamus Christum crucifixum, Judaeis scandalum, et Graecis stultitiam, iis vero qui vocati sunt, praedicamus Christum, qui est potentia et sapientia Dei. Et 1 Corinth. 2, 14. Naturalis homo non percipit ea quae sunt Spiritus Dei, nec potest ea percipere, quia spiritualiter dijudicantur.

---

[a] The precise source for this reference could not be determined. In any event, it does not appear to be an actual quotation, but a paraphrase or summary. The closest match appears to be John Chrysostom's discussion of 1 Cor 2:14—the same text is cited by Walaeus at the end of this thesis—in *Homilia in Epistulam primam ad Corinthios* 7.4–6 (MPG 61:60–63). Some of the themes occur also in *Homilia in Genesin* 27 in Gen 8:20 (MPG 53:242).

know it are illumined, and are freed from the darkness of error. For this reason Scripture is also called "Wisdom," and "the storehouse of knowledge," and its purity is affirmed to be like gold seven times refined, and more precious than jewels (Proverbs 3:13[14–15]), etc.

Therefore the entire point of discussion is about the perspicuity of Scripture in its relation* to us, for properly* speaking in this context 'perspicuous' is said to be what by its clarity is transparent to others, and can be learned and understood by those who have been endowed* with intelligence. 5

This definition* of perspicuity can be related to two kinds of people: Either to the understanding and faculty of natural* man, that is (as Chrysostom rightly explains) people "whose intellects have been endowed with no other light than the one God has implanted in the souls of all people through natural reproduction," albeit in various degrees, as Scripture itself also states (John 1:9). Or the definition can be related to the understanding and faculties of the spiritual man, that is, whose mind has been enlightened additionally by a supernatural* light from above (also in varying degrees). The distinction is articulated in this way in 1 Corinthians 2:14, and elsewhere. 6

As far as the first kind* of people is concerned, we acknowledge that the sacred books narrate and teach many things which a person in the natural state understands in a natural manner, if he applies some thoughtful attention, and if he is trained in employing the languages and other useful disciplines, since most of the time God spoke through his Prophets and Apostles in everyday popular language and in modes of speech drawn from the general public—even when He deals with matters that far surpass the human intellect. From here we see also that some pagan philosophers borrow some things from Holy Scripture for their own purposes, whereas others have attempted in their own writings to contradict them, which they could not have done if they had not understood the meaning of the words and the grammatical sense, at least in a natural way. 7

However, we declare that a natural or unspiritual man, whoever he may be, is not able, in the way that is fitting (that is, with spiritual lucidity,* acuteness, heartfelt respect and holiness, much less with certainty of thought and agreement), to understand those things, to discern between them, and to apply them to himself for salutary effect, unless he has been enlightened by the Holy Spirit. As for instance Christ says about Peter's confession in Matthew 16:17: "Flesh and blood has not revealed these things to you, but my Father who is in heaven." And 1 Corinthians 1:23[-24]: "We preach Christ crucified, a stumbling block to the Jews and folly to the Greeks, but to those who have been called, we preach Christ, who is the power and wisdom of God." And 1 Corinthians 2:14: "The natural man does not perceive the things of the Spirit of God, nor is he able to perceive them, because they have been discerned in a spiritual manner." 8

IX   Praecipua vero controversia est inter nos et Pontificios de homine per Spiritum Christi, diversa mensura et in diversos fines illustrato; et adversus eosdem cum Augustino asserimus,ª Deum ita attemperasse stylum et phrasin Scripturae Sacrae ut quaecumque continent fidem et mores vivendi, spem scilicet et caritatem, aperte in Scripturis posita inveniantur, atque ab omnibus pro vocatione et fidei mensura, dijudicari et salutariter sibi applicari possint.

X   Nec tamen interea negamus, quin nonnulla quoque difficiliora in iis exstent, ut Petrus 2. Epistola cap. ult. testatur; et quae stylo magis recondito sunt tradita, tum ut contemptus et fastidium ab ejus continua lectione removeatur; tum ut arrogantia dometur, et omnium diligentia excitetur; tum denique, ut non nisi cum reverentia, nostri sanctificatione, et precibus ad ejus lectionem ac scrutationem accedamus, exemplo Davidis Psal. 119. Sed rursus cum eodem Augustino *de doctr. Christ.* lib. 2, c. 6.ᵇ affirmamus: nihil fere de difficultatibus illis erui, quod non alibi planissime dictum reperiatur, adeo ut Spiritus Sanctus locis apertioribus fami occurrat, obscurioribus vero fastidia detergat.

XI   Haec Sacrae Scripturae in rebus ad fidem moresque vivendi necessariis perspicuitas, multis invictis argumentis et disertis Sacrae Scripturae locis demonstratur.*

XII   Primo ex eo, quod Deus alioquin frustra jussisset in Veteri Testamento ut ad instructionem fidei et morum suorum non tantum Sacerdotes et Levitae, sed quivis etiam fideles Sacram Scripturam legerent, aut legi audirent. Regi expresse mandatur Deut. 17, 19. ut legat in ea omnibus diebus vitae suae, ut discat timere Jehovam Deum suum, observare omnia verba hujus legis, et statuta ista, faciendo ea. Deuter. 31, 11. praecipitur, ut legatur haec lex coram toto Israele in auribus eorum etc, ut audiant et discant, timeantque Jehovam etc, et Isai. 8, 20. ad legem et testimonium consulendum totus populus remittitur.

ª Augustine, *De doctrina christiana* 2.9.14 (CCSL 32:40–41).   ᵇ Augustine, *De doctrina christiana* 2.6.8 (CCSL 32:36).

5. ABOUT THE PERSPICUITY OF HOLY SCRIPTURE

But the difference in understanding between us and the papal teachers concerns especially the man who, in different degrees and to different ends, has been illumined by the Spirit of Christ; and over against them we assert, together with Augustine, that God has so accommodated the style and wording of Holy Scripture, that: "Whatever things contain faith and moral conduct, namely hope and love, are stated plainly in the Scriptures," and in accordance with the calling and the measure of faith, everyone can discern and apply them for their own wellbeing.

And yet we do not deny, meanwhile, that in the Scriptures also some matters that are more difficult to understand appear, as the final chapter of the Second Letter of Peter shows. And there are things that have been transmitted in a more abstruse style, sometimes to eliminate contempt and aversion from continually reading it; sometimes to break pride, and to stimulate everyone's attentiveness; and finally, at other times so that we do not undertake reading and searching it except with a sense of awe, with sanctification of ourselves, and with prayer, as in the case of David (Psalm 119). Yet, again with the same Augustine (*On Christian Doctrine*, Book 2, ch. 6), we state: "That almost nothing is dug up from those difficult passages, which is not found elsewhere set forth most plainly, precisely so that the Holy Spirit meets our hunger by means of readily-grasped passages, but drives away boredom with the more obscure passages."

This perspicuity of Holy Scripture in matters that are indispensible for faith and moral conduct is demonstrated* by many irrefutable arguments and eloquent passages of Holy Scripture.[4]

First is the argument from the fact that if this were not the case, it would have been in vain that God in the Old Testament commanded, for instruction in the faith and morals of his people, that not only the priests and Levites but also every believer whosoever should read Holy Scripture (or hear it read). Deuteronomy 17:19 expressly commands the king: "That he shall read in it all the days of his life, that he may learn to fear the Lord his God, to keep all the words of this Law, and its statutes, by doing them." Deuteronomy 31:11–12 teaches that: "This Law shall be read before all Israel in their hearing, etc., so that they may hear it and learn, and may fear the Lord, etc." And in Isaiah 8:20 the entire people is sent "back to consult the Law and the testimony."

---

4 These arguments are grouped as follows: theses 12–15 expound the commands throughout Scripture to the people of God to hear and read the Word in order to be instructed in matters of faith and morals; thesis 16 provides explicit Scriptural evidence for its own clarity; thesis 17 mentions the effects that the written Word of God has on the hearts and lives of those who read it; and thesis 18 argues that the term "testament" implies the clarity of the expression of God's will as contained in Scripture.

XIII Sic etiam in Novo Testamento Joh. 5, 39. jubet Christus ut scrutentur Scripturas, quia existimabant se vitam aeternam in iis inventuros. Luc 16. Abraham remittit fratres divitis ad Mosem et Prophetas, ut inferni poenas vitare possint. Joh. 20, 31. dicit, haec scripta esse, ut credatis (quosvis alloquitur) Jesum esse Christum, et credentes vitam aeternam habeatis in nomine ejus. Petrus 2. epist. c 1. dicit, quod recte faciant (fideles ad quos scribit) quod attendant sermoni prophetico, id est, Scripturis, donec lucifer in ipsorum cordibus oriatur.

XIV Imo vero beati praedicantur* a Davide Ps. 1, 2. qui interdiu ac noctu in lege Dei meditantur. Et Act. 17, 11. laudantur prae ceteris Judaei Berrhoeenses quod Scripturas quotidie examinarent, an eae sic se haberent. Et Apoc. 1, 3. beati fore dicuntur, qui legunt et audiunt sermones prophetiae ejus, et servant quae in illa erant scripta. Quae omnia mandari ac commendari fidelibus nullo modo possent,* nisi Scriptura ita esset attemperata, ut ea quae salutem spectant in fide et moribus, ab iisdem pro vocatione cujusque intelligi possent.

XV Demonstrant illud etiam inscriptiones plerorumque librorum sacrorum, imprimis epistolarum Apostolicarum, quae ad omnes fideles et nomen Dei invocantes diriguntur; quod sane ab omni ratione* esset alienum, nisi ab ipsis legi et pro vocatione intelligi possent, cum eo quo decet modo et reverentia ad earum lectionem accedunt.

XVI Quinimo Sacra Scriptura multis disertis locis suae perspicuitatis et evidentiae sibi testimonium* praebet. Deuter. 29, 29. dicit Moses: Haec nobis et filiis nostris sunt revelata, ut faciamus omnia verba hujus legis. Cap. 30, 11. dicitur praeceptum hoc non esse occultum a nobis nec longinquum. Ps. 119, 105. vocatur lucerna pedi nostro, et lux itineri nostro. Prov. 6, 23. dicitur lex lux. 2 Petr. 1. appellatur fax splendens in obscuro loco. 2 Cor. 3, 14. testatur Apostolus, velamen quod in lectione Veteris Testamenti Judaeorum induratorum cordibus erat impositum, per Christum aboleri et ab eorum cordibus ablatum iri, cum ad Dominum conversi fuerint. Cap. 4, 2. scribit, se declaratione seu evidentia veritatis, commendare se ipsum apud omnem conscientiam hominum in conspectu Dei; imo si Evangelium suum tectum est, iis tectum esse qui pereunt, in quibus Deus hujus seculi excaecavit mentes, ne irradiet eos lumen Evangelii.

XVII Idem demonstrant effecta, quae verbo scripto passim in Scriptura attribuuntur, erga omnium hominum genera, etiam maxime imperitorum et simplicium.

So also in the New Testament, in John 5:39, Christ bids: "That they search the Scriptures, because they suppose that they will find eternal life in them." In Luke 16, Abraham sends the brothers of the wealthy man back to "Moses and the Prophets," so as to be able to avoid the punishments of the world below. John 20:31 states: "These are written that you may believe (he is speaking to anyone and everyone) that Jesus is the Christ, and that believing you may have eternal life in his name." 2 Peter 1:19 states: "That they (the believers to whom he is writing) will do well to pay attention to the prophetic Word, that is the Scriptures, until the Morningstar rises in their hearts."

Indeed David calls* them "blessed" who "day and night meditate on the law of God" (Psalm 1:2). And in Acts 17:11 the Jews in Beroea are praised beyond the others "because they were examining the Scriptures daily to see whether these things were true." And in Revelation 1:3 they are said to be blessed "who read and hear the words of this prophecy, and keep what is written therein." All of these things in no way could* be commanded and entrusted to believers unless Scripture had been adjusted in such a way that they could understand, according to the calling of each, the things which concern their salvation, in matters of both faith and moral conduct.

Even the introductory greetings of numerous sacred books demonstrate this point, especially the letters of the Apostles, which are directed "to all who believe and who call upon the name of the Lord." This would make no sense* at all, unless people could read and understand them in accordance with their calling, when they come to a reading of them with the appropriate manner and reverence.

In fact, in many eloquent passages Holy Scripture bears witness* to its own perspicuity and transparency. In Deuteronomy 29:29 Moses states: "These things have been revealed to us and our sons, that we may perform all the words of this law." Chapter 30:11 states that: "This commandment is not obscured from us, nor is it far away." In Psalm 119:105 it is called a "lamp to our feet and a light to our path." In Proverbs 6:23 the Law is called light. In 2 Peter 1[:19] it is called a "lamp shining in a dark place." In 2 Corinthians 3:14 the Apostle testifies that the "veil which had been placed over the hearts of the hardened Jews has been done away with through Christ and would be lifted from their hearts when they should turn to the Lord." In chapter 4:2 he writes that "by the open statement or evidence of the truth, he commends himself to the conscience of all men in the sight of God; but that even if the Gospel is veiled, it is veiled only for those who are perishing, in whom the god of this world has blinded their minds, lest the light of the Gospel should cast its rays on them."

The same point is demonstrated by the effects upon all kinds of people, which throughout Scripture are attributed to the written word—indeed even

Ps. 19, 8. Doctrina Jehovae integra est, restituens animum, testimonium verax sapientiam afferens imperito; mandata Jehovae sunt recta, laetificantia animum, praeceptum Jehovae purum, illustrans oculos. Ps. 119, 130. Aditus verborum illuminat, prudentia instruit simplices. Prov. 1, 1. Proverbia Salomonis, etc. ad dandam fatuis astutiam, puero scientiam et solertiam. Rom. 15, 4. Quaecumque antea scripta sunt ad nostram doctrinam scripta sunt, ut per patientiam et consolationem Scripturarum spem habeamus. 2. Tim. 3, 15. s. literas a puero nosti, quae te possunt sapientem reddere ad salutem. 1Joh. 2, 13. Scribo vobis, patres, quoniam nostis eum qui est a principio; scribo vobis, adolescentes, quoniam malum illum vicistis; scribo vobis, pueruli, quoniam nostis Patrem, etc.

XVIII   Denique id demonstrat nomen* Testamenti, quod Sacrae Scripturae Veteris et Novi foederis passim tribuitur. Quis enim verus pater unquam testamentum suum dedita opera ita scripsit, ut ab haeredibus suis, cum opus est, aut legi aut intelligi, saltem in necessariis, non posset? Aut cur Concilia, Patres, et Pastores doctrinam suam ex Sacra Scriptura probare* apud populum solent et debent in omnibus, quae fidem necessariam et mores spectant, si fideles pro vocatione sua eas intelligere non possint? Intellectus enim verborum et sententiae, fidem, quae ex verbo Dei. non hominum, concipitur, necessario antecedit: nec ulla aedificatio aut consolatio ex verbo non intellecto capi potest, ut Paulus ex professo demonstrat, 1 Cor. 14.

XIX   Nec hinc tamen sequitur, supervacuam esse Sacrae Scripturae explicationem, aut verbi praedicationem, quia subordinata non pugnant, et verbi praedicatio,* inter cetera quoque, est medium a Deo in Ecclesia ordinatum, quo fideles reliqui Scripturam Sacram, et facilius intelligere, et rectius sibi applicare

5. ABOUT THE PERSPICUITY OF HOLY SCRIPTURE

upon unskilled and the unsophisticated people. Psalm 19:8: "The Law of Jehovah is whole, reviving the soul; the testimony is sure, bringing wisdom to the ignorant; the precepts of Jehovah are right, rejoicing the heart, the precept of Jehovah is pure, enlightening the eyes." Psalm 119:130: "The unfolding of the words gives light, it teaches prudence to the simple." Proverbs 1:1: "The proverbs of Solomon, etc., for giving wisdom to the foolish, knowledge and learning to the youth." Romans 15:4: "For whatever was written in former days was written for our instruction, that by steadfastness and encouragement of the Scriptures we might have hope." 2 Timothy 3:15: "from your childhood up, you know the sacred writings, which are able to make you wise unto salvation." 1 John 2:13: "I write to you, fathers, because you know Him who is from the beginning; I write to you, young men, because you have overcome the evil one; I write to you, children, because you know the Father, etc."

Finally, the very word* "Testament" demonstrates this, which is applied everywhere to the sacred writing of the old and new covenant. For what true father has ever intentionally written his own will in such a way that when it was needed, it could not be read nor understood by his heirs, at least in the things that really mattered? Or why is it that Councils, church-fathers, or pastors are used to proving* their own teaching to the people from Holy Scripture—and so they ought to do in everything that pertains to the necessary faith and moral conduct—if the faithful could not, according to their calling, understand them? For understanding the words and sentences necessarily[5] comes before faith, which is born of the Word of God, not of men. Nor can any upbuilding or consolation be taken from a word if it has not been understood, as Paul openly demonstrates in 1 Corinthians 14.[6]

However, from this it does not follow that the explanation of Holy Scripture, or the preaching of the Word, is superfluous; because matters that have been subordinated to one another do not conflict,[7] and the preaching* of the Word is, among other things, a means ordained in the Church by God, whereby the other believers learn both to understand Holy Scripture more easily and to apply it to

---

5 The "necessity" mentioned here resides in the order of mental operations: one cannot assent to a proposition unless the meaning of its constituent words and sentences is understood.
6 Further reference to this chapter is found in thesis 34 below. In 1 Corinthians 14, Paul uses the edification of the community as a criterion for ranking the gifts of the Spirit: prophesying edifies many, while speaking in a tongue edifies merely oneself.
7 Here the general rule, "matters that are subordinated to one another do not conflict," is applied to public preaching, viewed as a means directed toward the goal of understanding Scripture. As the means is subordinated to the goal, it can never be in direct conflict with the goal.

discant. Utraque ergo haec in vera Christi Ecclesia sunt conjungenda, non separanda: sicuti Christus utrumque in Ecclesia sua instituit. Nam Judaeos monet, ut scrutentur Scripturas, quas tamen passim, in contionibus suis explicavit, et ad electorum salutem applicavit, quemadmodum Act. 8. Philippum Evangelistam ad Eunuchum Reginae Candaces misit, ut explicaret ei textum illum Prophetae Esaiae quem legebat et ex se non satis intelligebat, sed explicatum agnoscebat, et vera fide jam agnitum amplectebatur; et c. 17. Berrhoeenses laudantur, quod doctrinam a Paulo praedicatam cum Sacrae Scripturae lectione conjungebant.

xx Hoc fundamento* jam strato ac supposito, quaestio secunda, de qua hic agendum, nempe qui sit Sacrae Scripturae legitimus Interpres, adversus Pontificios a nobis facilius solvetur.

xxi Pontificii contendunt, Ecclesiam esse summum et infallibilem Sacrae Scripturae Interpretem; sed rogati quid per Ecclesiam intelligant, fatentur se non intelligere Ecclesiam ovium, sed pastorum; rogati rursum an intelligant quosvis pastores, recurrere solent ad Ecclesiam suam repraesentativam, id est, Episcopos et Praelatos, in concilio congregatos; denique rogati quid per concilia intelligant, respondere coguntur, omnia concilia errare posse, ac proinde esse incertos Scripturae Interpretes, nisi a Pontifice probentur; quem volunt in conciliis et de conciliis judicare, sicut Rex aliquis in suo senatu judicare solet; ac proinde totam decernendi ac judicandi potestatem esse penes ipsum, tamquam qui solus in interpretatione Scripturae errare non possit, adeo ut illustre illud Ecclesiae nomen, de quo gloriari tantopere solent, in solius Pontificis Romani nomen et personam tandem resolvatur et terminetur.

5. ABOUT THE PERSPICUITY OF HOLY SCRIPTURE

themselves more accurately. Therefore both of these[8] must be joined together, not separated, in the true Church of Christ: just as Christ has instituted both of them in his Church. For He warns the Jews to search the Scriptures, which He explained everywhere in their assemblies and applied to the salvation of the elect. So in Acts 8 He sends Philip the evangelist to the eunuch of Queen Candace, to explain to him that text from the prophet Isaiah which he was reading and which he could not understand sufficiently on his own, but which he came to understand when it was explained; and as soon as he understood it, he embraced it in true faith. And in Chapter 17, the people of Beroea are praised because they connected the teaching of Paul with the reading of Holy Scripture.

Now that this foundation* has been laid as a premise, the second question which we must deal with here over against the papal teachers will be solved more easily, namely: Who is the lawful interpreter of Holy Scripture? 20

The papal teachers maintain that the Church is the highest, infallible interpreter of Holy Scripture; but when asked what they understand by "church," they admit that they do not mean the Church of the sheep, but of the shepherds. When asked again whether they mean any shepherds whatsoever, they usually take recourse in their "representative" Church, that is the bishops and prelates when these meet in council. And finally, when asked what they understand by "councils," they are compelled to reply that all councils are capable of erring, and therefore that they are unreliable interpreters of Scripture, unless they are approved by the pope. They hold the view that the pope passes a judgment in the councils and about the councils, like some king is used to judging in his own senate. Accordingly, all the power of deciding and judging rests with him, as if he alone is not able to make a mistake in the interpretation of Scripture— with the result that the distinguished name of Church, about which they tend to boast so much, in the end comes down to and ends in the name and person of the Roman Pontiff alone [*Pontifex Romanus*].[9] 21

---

8   The remainder of this thesis suggests that the expression, "both of these," means both the personal, private reading of Scripture, and the public preaching of the Word in explication and application.

9   One statement by Bellarmine, *De verbo Dei*, 3.3 (Opera 1:176a), moves into the direction indicated in thesis 21: "Tota igitur quaestio in eo posita est, *ubi sit iste Spiritus*. Nos enim existimamus hunc Spiritum, etsi multis privatis hominibus saepe conceditur, tamen certo inveniri in Ecclesia, id est, in *Concilio Episcoporum* confirmato a summo Ecclesiae totius Pastore, sive *in summo Pastore* cum Concilio aliorum Pastorum. (…) hic in genere dicimus, iudicem veri sensus Scripturae, et omnium controversiarum, esse *Ecclesiam*, id est, *Pontificem cum Concilio*, in quo omnes Catholici conveniunt: et habetur expresse in *Concilio Tridentino* sess. 4." (Translation: "Therefore the entire question is put thus, 'Where is that Holy Spirit

XXII Sed Pontificem Romanum non esse legitimum et certum Sacrae Scripturae Interpretem, probatur primo, quia multi Pontifices Romani, ipso jure canonico et ipsorum historicis fatentibus, fuerunt haeretici; deinde, quia multi Pontifices contraria decreta ediderunt, atque alii aliorum Institutiones abrogarunt; tertio, quia multi Pontifices fuerunt homines impii, profani, scelerati et magicis artibus dediti; denique, quia multi inter Pontifices fuerunt Sacrae Scripturae plane imperiti, et eam in decretis suis valde absurde et contra directam Sacrae Scripturae mentem interpretati sunt; quod adeo est evidens, ut Bellarminus et alii Pontificii Doctores propterea cogantur statuere, Pontificem in argumentis et praemissis errare posse, sed in conclusionibus, licet ex falsis praemissis, semper tamen vera decreta colligere.

XXIII Ut ergo haec quaestio secundum verbi Dei normam recte explicetur, dicimus: Scripturam esse sui ipsius Interpretem, vel potius Deum in Scripturis et per Scripturas loquentem, qui in locis clarioribus et necessariis voluntatem* suam fidelibus aperte indicat, ut antea est demonstratum, in locis vero obscurioribus per comparationem eorum cum clarioribus eandem voluntatem suam iis magis ac magis confirmat.

XXIV Quemadmodum enim Imperator aliquis aut Rex, non tantum controversiarum civilium est Judex aut voluntatis suae Interpres, quando praesens cum praesentibus loquitur, sed etiam cum per rescripta aut libellos hoc facit: sic etiam Deus non tantum summus controversiarum Judex et voluntatis suae Interpres est, quando cum Mose, Prophetis et Apostolis, et per eos ad Ecclesiam est locutus, sed etiam cum per rescripta sua et verbum* literis mandatum, voluntatem suam Ecclesiis exponit.

XXV Etenim Scriptura Sacra non est res* muta, aut mortua, aut quae sententiam suam ab hominum corruptelis vindicare non possit, sed sermo Dei est vivus et efficax, et penetrantrior quovis gladio ancipiti, pertingensque usque ad divisionem animae simul ac spiritus, compagumque ac medullarum, et dijudicat cogitationes et conceptiones cordis, ut Paulus testatur, Hebr. 4, 12. et propterea etiam ministerium justitiae et Spiritus appellatur, 2 Cor. 3, 8. 9. quia Spiritus Sanctus per illud in cordibus hominum ad veritatem et justitiam est efficax.

---

at work?' For we are of the opinion that this Spirit, although he is often granted to many individual people, is certainly found in the Church, that is in the Council of Bishops that is confirmed by the greatest shepherd of the entire church, or in the greatest shepherd together with the council of other shepherds ... in general we say that the judge of the true sense of Scripture and of all controversies is the church, i.e., the Pope with the council, in whom all Catholics find their unity. And it is expressed in this way in the Council of Trent, session 4.")

5. ABOUT THE PERSPICUITY OF HOLY SCRIPTURE

But that the Roman Pontiff is not the lawful and definitive interpreter of Holy Scripture is proved firstly by the fact that many Roman popes—as the canonical law itself and their own historians admit—were heretics; secondly, because many popes have published conflicting decrees, and because some have repealed the Instructions of others; thirdly, because many popes were wicked, unholy, criminal, and devoted to magic arts; and finally, because from among the popes many were patently unfamiliar with Holy Scripture, and in their decrees interpreted it most non-sensically and contrary to the straightforward meaning of Scripture. This is so obvious, that Bellarmine and other papist teachers are forced for that reason to take the position that the Pontiff is able to err in argumentations and presuppositions, but that in the conclusions—even though these are based on false premises!—they nevertheless always draw up true decrees.

Therefore in order to explain this question correctly according to the norm of God's Word, we say that Scripture is its own Interpreter, or rather, God, speaking in and through the Scriptures, who openly indicates his own will* to the believers in the more transparent and indispensible passages, as was demonstrated earlier, while in the more obscure passages He increasingly confirms his same will through a comparison of them with the more clear ones.

For just as some emperor or king is the judge and interpreter of his own will in civil disputes (not only whenever he is present and speaks to those who are present, but also when he does this through his written decrees or letters), so too God is not only the highest Judge of disputes and the Interpreter of his will, when He spoke with Moses, the Prophets and the Apostles, and through them to the Church, but also when through his written decrees and word* entrusted to writings, He expounds his own will to the churches.

For Holy Scripture is not a speechless or dead thing,* or one which cannot vindicate its meaning from people's spoiling influences, but: "The Word of God is living and effective, sharper than any two-edged sword, piercing to the division of soul and spirit, of joints and marrow, and discerns the thoughts and intentions of the heart" (as Paul testifies, Hebrews 4:12[10]). And accordingly it is called the ministry of righteousness and of the Spirit (2 Corinthians 3:8,9), because by means of it the Holy Spirit has the power to effect truth and justice in people's hearts.

---

10   For the ascription of the letter to the Hebrews to the apostle Paul, see *SPT* 3.34–35.

XXVI Hinc est quod Ps. 50, 4. Deus inclamat coelos superne et terram, Jus populo suo dicturus: et Esaias cap. 8. populum Israëliticum ad legem et testimonium remittit ad consulendum Deum suum. Hinc Ps. 25. aperit Jehova arcanum reverentibus ipsum, et foedus suum, ut experimento testetur iis. Hinc omnes qui ad Christum veniunt, sunt a Deo edocti, Joh. 6. et si quis aliud sentiat, Deus id illi quoque revelabit, Phil. 3, 13., in quibus omnibus et multis aliis locis, Deus ipse agere dicitur, quae per verbum efficiuntur; quia per verbum et cum verbo suo Ecclesiis suis semper praesens, haec omnia in fidelium animis et coetibus operatur.

XXVII Quia vero Deus, etsi ab eo solo sit incrementum, hominum tamen ministerio, et judicio quoque utitur, ac proinde et Paulo plantandum sit, et Apollo rigandum, idcirco fatemur libenter, in vera Christi Ecclesia esse aliud quoque interpretum genus, nempe ministeriale, et sub Deo et verbo ipsius constitutum; cui et judicandi potestas, in Sacra Scriptura tribuitur, 2 Chron. 19, 8. Ezech. 44, 24. Zach. 3, 7. 1Cor. 2, 15. 1Cor. 10, 15. et cap. 14, 29. etc.

XXVIII Est autem ea Interpretandi vel Judicandi potestas duplex, vel publica, vel privata; utraque nititur vocatione et dono singulari.

XXIX Potestas privatim Judicandi de Sacrae Scripturae vero vel falso sensu in rebus ad salutem necessariis, competit omnibus vere fidelibus, ad confirmationem fidei propriae et aedificationem alienae, secundum caritatis legem, doni accepti mensuram, et vocationis diversae rationem. Hoc diserte monet Joh. cap. 10, 3. ac deinceps, Oves veri pastoris vocem audiunt, et eum sequuntur, quia vocem ejus norunt; alienum autem nequaquam sequentur, sed fugient ab eo, quia non norunt vocem alienorum, et Matth. 7, 15. Cavete vobis a pseudoprophetis. Sic loquitur Paulus 1Cor. 10. Tamquam intelligentibus loquor, judicate vos quae dico. 1Joh. 4, 1. Dilecti, ne credite cuivis spiritui, sed probate spiritus, an ex Deo sint.

XXX Hoc Judicandi genus nititur dono quod διακρίσεως seu discretionis appellatur a Paulo, 1Cor. 2, 15. Spiritualis homo διακρίνει, dijudicat omnia, et Hebr. 5, 14. dicit, quosdam esse pueros, qui lacte opus habent, quosdam perfectos seu adultos, qui propter habitum, sensus habent exercitatos εἰς διάκρισιν ad discretionem boni et mali, atque ab eodem Apostolo vocatur δοκιμασία τῶν

5. ABOUT THE PERSPICUITY OF HOLY SCRIPTURE

For this reason in Psalm 50:4 "God calls upon the heavens above and the earth, to pronounce judgment upon his people," and in Isaiah chapter 8[:20] He sends the Israelite people "to the Law and the testimony" to seek counsel of their God. And therefore in Psalm 25[:12, 14?] Jehovah discloses "the sacred mystery to those who fear Him, and his covenant, so that he gives witness to them by experience."[11] Therefore all who come to Christ are "taught by God" (John 6:[45]), and "if anyone is minded otherwise, God will reveal that to him also" (Philippians 3:13[= 15]). In all these and many other passages it is stated that God himself performs what is brought to pass by the Word; because He, being present always to his churches through the Word and with his Word, works all these things in the hearts and gatherings of believers.

But because God, even if the growth comes from Him alone, still uses the ministry of men, and also their power of judgment—and accordingly Paul must plant while Apollos must water—therefore we freely confess that in the true Church of Christ there is also another kind of interpreter, namely "ministerial," and established under God and under his Word; and Holy Scripture ascribes the power to judge to this kind of interpreter: 2 Chronicles 19:8; Ezekiel 44:24; Zechariah 3:7; 1 Corinthians 2:15; 1 Corinthians 10:15; and chapter 14:29, etc.

Moreover that power of interpretation or passing judgment is twofold: either public, or private; and both of them rest upon a special calling and gift.

The power of judging the right or wrong meaning of Holy Scripture in a private capacity in matters indispensible to one's salvation applies to all the true believers; for the strengthening of their personal faith and the upbuilding of another's, according to the law of love, the measure of the grace received, and the reason for a different calling. John chapter 10:3 and following clearly teaches this: "The sheep hear the voice of the true shepherd, and they follow Him, because they know his voice; but by no means do they follow a stranger, instead they flee from him, because they do not know the voice of strangers." And Matthew 7:15: "Guard yourselves from false prophets." Paul speaks in this way in 1 Corinthians 10:15: "I speak as to sensible people; you yourselves judge what I am saying." 1 John 4:1: "Beloved, do not believe every spirit, but test the spirits, whether they come from God."

This type of judging rests on the gift that Paul calls discernment [*diakrisis*] (1 Corinthians 2:15): "The spiritual man discerns all things," and Hebrews 5:[13–]14 says: "Some are children who have need of milk; others are complete or mature, who through practice have their senses exercised for discerning good and evil," and by the same Apostle it is called "the testing of things that differ"

---

11   This phrase is unclear; the Latin quoted by Walaeus differs from the text of the Vulgate.

διαφερόντων, Phil. 1, 10. Et hoc precor, ut caritas vestra magis et magis redundet in cognitione et omni sensu, ut probetis vel dignoscatis ea, quae discrepant.

XXXI Etsi vero hoc donum omnibus fidelibus non communicetur eadem mensura, sed quibusdam ut adultis, quibusdam ut pueris, sicut Paulus Hebr. 5. loco jam adducto testatur; tamen necessarium est, ut in omnibus Christi ovibus et vere fidelibus hoc aliqua saltem mensura agnoscamus, quia alioquin eorum fides non niteretur verbo Dei, sed solo testimonio humano, contra dictum Apostoli Rom. 10, 17., et omnes oves aliquam vocis pastoris proprii notitiam habent, ut Christus Joh. 10. testatur; et pueri quoque in Ecclesia Dei lac verum ac salubre ab insalubri et venenoso possunt discernere, saltem in dogmatis ad salutem absolute necessariis.

XXXII Potestas publice interpretandi Scripturam et de veritate interpretationis publice judicandi, non competit omnibus, sed quibusdam tantum, qui et dono et vocatione ad hoc instructi sunt. De vocationis diversis gradibus agit Paulus Eph. 4, 11. 12. 13. Christus, inquit, dedit alios quidem Apostolos, alios autem Evangelistas, alios autem Pastores et Doctores, ad coagmentationem sanctorum, ad opus ministerii, ad aedificationem corporis Christi etc, ut ne simus amplius pueri qui fluctuemus et circumferamur quovis vento doctrinae, etc, et alibi passim.

XXXIII Donum ad hoc necessarium vocat Apostolus donum prophetandi ac docendi. Atque antecedens illud, nempe διακρίσεως et δοκιμασίας, discretionis et probationis spirituum, includit.

XXXIV De hoc loquitur Paulus Rom. 12, 6. Habentes autem diversa dona pro gratia quae nobis data est, sive prophetiam, prophetet pro proportione fidei; sive ministerium, in ministrando; sive doctrinam, in docendo, sic quoque 1 Cor. 14, 3. et deinceps. Qui prophetat, hominibus loquitur ad aedificationem, et exhortationem, et consolationem; qui loquitur lingua, se ipsum aedificat; qui vero prophetat, Ecclesiam aediticat, etc. Et versus 29. Prophetae autem duo aut tres loquantur, et alii dijudicent, etc.

XXXV Etsi vero non negemus, quin inter alios quoque Christianos omnibus seculis exstiterint, qui per diligentem Sacrae Scripturae lectionem et meditationem, donum Sacram Scripturam ad usus publicos interpretandi, et spiritus probandi, ampliori mensura quam nonnulli pastores, acceperint; tamen donum illud inter eos praecipue quaerendum esse, quos Deus ad Ecclesiam suam publice instituendam peculiariter vocavit, Sacra Scriptura multis locis, et ipsa quoque experientia testatur; nam labia Sacerdotis custodient scientiam, et lex petetur ex ore ejus, quia est angelus Jehovae exercituum, ut Deus ipse Malach. 2. docet,

5. ABOUT THE PERSPICUITY OF HOLY SCRIPTURE

[*dokimasia tōn diapherontōn*] (Philippians 1:10): "And I pray this, that your love may abound more and more in knowledge and all feeling, that you may approve or distinguish the things that are a matter of dispute."

Yet this gift is not imparted to all believers in the same measure, but to some as adults and to others as children, as Paul testifies in Hebrews 5 (in the passage just quoted); nevertheless it is necessary that we acknowledge that there is at least some measure in all Christ's sheep and in all true believers. For otherwise their faith would not rest upon the Word of God, but on human testimony alone, contrary to the statement in Romans 10:17. And all sheep have some familiarity with the voice of their own shepherd, as Christ testifies in John 10[:4]; and also the children in the Church of Christ are able to discern true and nourishing milk from unhealthy and poisonous milk, at least in doctrines that are absolutely necessary for salvation.

The power to expound Scripture in public, and of publicly deciding upon the truth of interpretation, does not apply to everyone, but only to those who by their gifts and their calling have been trained for this task. Paul deals with the varying degrees of calling in Ephesians 4:11, 12, and 13. "Christ," he says, "has given some as Apostles, some as evangelists, and others as pastors and teachers, for equipping the saints, for the work of ministry, for the edification of the body of Christ, etc., so that we may no longer be children who float away and are carried about by every wind of doctrine, etc.," and in many other places.

The Apostle calls the gift that is necessary for this task "the gift of prophesying and instructing." And this gift includes the preceding one, namely, the gift of discerning and testing the spirits [*diakrisis* and *dokimasia*, thesis 30 above].

Paul speaks about this in Romans 12:6: "Having gifts that differ according to the grace that has been given to us: if prophecy, let one prophesy in proportion to his faith; if service, in serving; if teaching, in teaching." So too 1 Corinthians 14:3 and following: "He who prophesies speaks to men for their upbuilding and encouragement and comfort; he who speaks in a tongue edifies himself; he who prophesies, edifies the church, etc." And verse 29: "Let two or three prophets speak, and let the others judge," etc.

And yet we should not deny that among other Christians also throughout the ages there were people who through diligent reading and meditation upon the Holy Scripture, received the gift to interpret Holy Scripture for public benefit, and of testing the spirits, in greater measure than some pastors. And yet Holy Scripture in many passages (and also experience itself) witnesses to the fact that this gift must be sought among those especially whom God has called specifically to establish his Church publicly; for: "The lips of the Priest should guard knowledge, and the Law should be sought from his mouth, because he is a messenger of the Lord of hosts," as God himself teaches in Malachi

et Tit. 1, 9. exigitur a pastoribus omnibus ut sint tenaces fidelis illius sermonis, qui ad doctrinam facit, ut possint et exhortari doctrina sua, et contradicentes convincere.

XXXVI Utrumque tamen hoc donum, et interpretandi facultas, subest Dei verbo, et Spiritui Sancto in Scriptura loquenti; nam qui publico interpretandi et prophetandi dono ornati sunt, judicium suum ex Sacra Scriptura efformant, et aliis fidelibus fundamenta ex Sacra Scriptura ostendunt, ac proferunt, quae a singulis fidelibus pro certis et veris per donum illud διακρίσεως et δοκιμασίας deinde agnoscuntur; vel si a falsis Doctoribus non satis fideliter ex Sacra Scriptura deprompta sint, aut in alienum sensum detorta, rejiciuntur et reprobantur, ut Thesi 29 a nobis est probatum.

XXXVII Nec tamen ideo cujusque privatum spiritum facimus, singulorum fidei, multo minus totius Ecclesiae, summum judicem, sed solum Dei verbum et Spiritum Sanctum, qui ex Sacra Scriptura eandem fidem, saltem in dogmatis necessariis, toti verae Ecclesiae, et singulis veris ejus membris, ex iisdem fundamentis obsignat.

XXXVIII Quo pacto vero controversiae, quae de ipsis dogmatis fidei nonnumquam in Ecclesia Christi oriuntur, ex eadem Scriptura, per eundem Spiritus Sancti ductum componendae sint, non est hujus loci proprie tractare, sed per Dei gratiam* tractabitur, cum ad locum de Consiliis et Magistratu erit deventum.

XXXIX Hoc tantum hic conclusionis loco monemus: Deum per Spiritum et verbum suum, ita perpetuo adesse verae Ecclesiae suae, quae est domus ejus, ut nec ipsa, nec viva ejus membra in fundamentis saltem fidei et morum necessariis, ad perniciem suam errent; alias enim Ecclesia vera Christi esse desineret, contra promissionem Christi Matth. 16, 18. Portae inferorum adversus eam non praevalebunt. Et Johan. 10, 5. Oves Christi alienum nequaquam sequentur.

2[:7]. And Titus 1:9 demands from all pastors that they should: "Hold fast to that trustworthy word, which makes for instruction in doctrine, that they will be able both to give instruction in its doctrine, and to confute those who contradict it."

However, both these gifts,[12] and the competency to interpret, are subject to the Word of God, and to the Holy Spirit who is speaking in Scripture; for those who have been adorned with the gift of explanation and prophesying in public, develop their own judgment from Holy Scripture, and show to the other believers its underlying support from Holy Scripture, and bring forward those teachings which subsequently the believers individually recognize as certain and true, through that gift of discernment and testing. Alternatively, if false teachers have not produced these conclusions with enough credibility from Holy Scriptures, or twist them into a strange meaning, then they reject and condemn them, as we have proved in thesis 29.

And yet we do not for that reason make anyone's personal thinking the highest judge of the faith of other individuals, much less of the entire Church, but only the Word of God and the Holy Spirit, who from out of Holy Scripture seals the same faith—at least in the necessary doctrines—upon the whole true Church and its individual true members, out of those same fundamental elements.

It is not fitting in this chapter to deal with the way in which controversies should be settled that sometimes arise in the Church of Christ about the teachings themselves of the faith from the same Scripture, and through the same guidance of the Holy Spirit. By God's grace* this topic will be treated when we reach the chapter on church councils and governance.[13]

In lieu of a conclusion we offer the following: That God through the Spirit and his Word is present to help his true Church (which is his house[14]) so constantly that neither it, nor any living members of it should wander to their own destruction in at least the necessary elements of faith and morals. For otherwise the true Church of Christ would cease to be, contrary to Christ's promise in Matthew 16:18: "The gates of hell shall not prevail against it," and in John 10:5: "In no way shall Christ's sheep follow another."

---

12 Namely, the gift of personal understanding and the gift of public explanation of Scripture.
13 See *SPT* 49.
14 Cf. 1 Timothy 3:15 and Titus 1:7.

COROLLARIUM.

I   Etsi Sacra Scriptura per Anagogen, Tropologiam, Analogiam,* similesque explicandi modos, ad Ecclesiae usus, in multis locis applicari possit, unicus tamen immediatus* et certus ejus sensus est, sensus grammaticus seu historicus.

II Allegorias ex Scripturis struere non licet, nisi ubi Sacra Scriptura ipsa nobis praeit, aut necessaria ratio* ex Sacris Scripturis petita id facere cogit.

III Etsi ex Allegoriis et Parabolis Scripturae, firma argumenta ad fidem et mores confirmandos peti non possint, si Allegoriarum et Parabolarum circumstantias spectes, tamen si praecipuum ipsarum finem* et scopum consideres, non minus firma ex iis petuntur quam ex aliis locis; ac proinde dicimus, illud Scholasticorum* axioma, Theologia parabolica non est argumentativa, vel de allegoricis interpretationibus, ex humano ingenio profectis, vel de circumstantiis tantum Allegoriarum et Parabolarum intelligendum.

Corollary.¹⁵

Although Holy Scripture can be applied in many places for the use of the church anagogically, tropologically, analogically,* and by similar modes of explanation, yet the only immediate* and certain meaning of it is the grammatical or historical sense.¹⁶

We are not permitted to build allegories on Scripture, unless where Scripture itself leads the way, or where a necessary reason* taken from Scripture urges us to do so.

From the allegories and parables of Scripture no definitive arguments can be taken to confirm faith and morals if one looks at the circumstances of these allegories and parables. Nevertheless, if their primary objective* and scope is considered, no less definitive arguments are taken than those from other places. And for this reason we say that this maxim of the Scholastics,* "Parabolic theology provides no arguments," should be understood either in view of allegorical interpretations advanced by the human mind, or merely with respect to the circumstances of the allegories and parables.¹⁷

---

15 A corollary, literally "a proposition that follows with little or no proof required from one already proven; inference or deduction," is an addition to the proper argument of the disputation. It discusses related issues, provides extra documentation, or contains a more detailed discussion of a specific question. It is probable that the few corollaries in the *Synopsis* were attached to the main text of the disputation as a result of the oral defense.

16 On the 'fourfold sense' of Scripture, see the brief discussion by PRRD 2:35–37. A definition of the different layers of meaning is provided from the *Glossa ordinaria*: "*historia*, which tells what happened (*res gestae*); *allegoria*, in which one thing is understood through another; *tropologia*, which is moral declaration, and which deals with the ordering of behaviour; *anagoge*, through which we are led to higher things that we might be drawn to the highest and heavenly" (translation by Muller). See also Beryl Smalley, *The Study of the Bible in the Middle Ages*, (3rd. rev. ed.; Oxford: Blackwell, 1983); Henri de Lubac, *Exégèse medieval: les quatre sens de l'Écriture*, 4 vols. (Paris: Aubier, 1959–1964) [English translation: *Medieval Exegesis: The Four Senses of Scripture* 4 vols. (Grand Rapids: Eerdmans, 2009)].

17 For the application of the maxim *theologia parabolica non est argumentativa* in Reformed orthodox hermeneutics, see PRRD 2:474–475. A fundamental distinction occurs between symbolic or allegorical exegesis that fit to the words and scope of the text itself—and thus fall under the 'literal sense' of Scripture—and freely invented figures and allegories. The latter, it is argued, do not have the force of proving any point of faith; the former can be included in a doctrinal or ethical demonstration. The statement above denies the argumentative function not only of freely invented parables, but also of the accidental or circumstantial aspects of biblical allegories and parables.

DISPUTATIO VI

De natura Dei et divinis attributis

Praeside D. ANTONIO THYSIO
Respondente LUDOVICO RENESSE

THESIS I   De Deo in SacrosanctaTheologia tractatur, non tantum, qua principium* constitutionis ejus, aut etiam cognitionis nostrae est, sed qua subjectum, et primus ac primarius Theologiae est locus, a quo reliqui fluunt, sub quo continentur, et ad quem referri debent. Unde et hinc ipsa Theologia nomen* habet.

II   Non tamen simpliciter est subjectum* contemplationis, qualiter Metaphysicus de Deo agere instituit, qualiterque Deus se ipsum vere cognoscit, et nos in altera vita Deum plenius cognoscemus, 1 Cor. 13, 9. etc. 2 Cor. 12, 4. Sed qua ejus scientia in hac vita est debitum officii nostri, ut eum vere cognoscentes, vitam aeternam adipiscamur, Joh. 17, 3.

III   Quamvis autem quaerendum in Theologia non sit, *An Deus sit*: cum ut scientia suum subjectum, ita hoc ipsum Theologia praesupponat, quodque id, ut sua luce clarum, a piis disputari fas non sit; tamen propter insanam et plus quam Diabolicam Atheorum quorundam blasphemiam Deum negantium, Jac.

DISPUTATION 6

About the Nature of God and his Divine Attributes

President: Antonius Thysius
Respondent: Ludwig Renesse[1]

In most-sacred Theology God is treated not only as the principle* upon which it is constructed and the source of our knowledge of it but also as the subject* and the foremost, primary *locus* of theology from which all the others flow forth, by which they are held together, and to which they should be directed. Hence Theology derives its very name* from this starting-point.

God is not simply the subject* of contemplation in the sense that a metaphysical philosopher undertakes to reflect upon God and in the way God truly knows himself, and as we in the next life shall come to know God more fully (1 Corinthians 13:9, etc.; 2 Corinthians 12:4); but in the sense that to know Him in this life is what we have to do in order to obtain eternal life by truly knowing Him (John 17:3).

Furthermore, in Theology one should not ask "whether God exists," since Theology takes for granted that He does exist (as any science assumes of its subject), and since it is as clear as day that believers have no right to debate that question.[2] Nevertheless, because of the foolish and devil-surpassing blasphemy

---

1 Born in Utrecht in 1599, Lodovicus a Renesse matriculated on 28 April 1616 in theology. He defended this disputation on 20 June 1620 and dedicated his defense to the States of the province of Utrecht, to his relative Johannes van Renesse, to Polyander and Erpenius (see Disputation 3, footnote 1), and to his friends G. Masius and G. Magirius. He was ordained in Maarssen (1620) and Breda (1638), where he was also professor at the *collegium illustre* there from 1646 to 1669; he died in 1671. See Du Rieu, *Album studiosorum*, 124, Van Lieburg, *Repertorium*, 203, and BLGNP 2:372–374.

2 The question "whether something exists" (*an sit?*) and the question "what something is?" (*quid sit?*) have their origin in the Aristotelian theory of science. In the Christian doctrine of God a third question was added: "who is it?" (*quis sit?*). These three questions were used as a framework to discuss (1) the existence of God and the proofs of his existence; (2) the "whatness" (*quidditas*) of God or his names, essence and essential attributes; and (3) the doctrine of the divine Persons of the Trinity. This framework was already present in the work of John of Damascus (c. 675–749) and was used by Thomas Aquinas and many Reformed authors such as Musculus, Zanchius, Danaeus, and Ursinus, Cocceius, Voetius and Turretin. Although not explicitly mentioned, this scheme also shapes the exposition of the doctrine of God in the *Synopsis*. SPT 6.3–17 discusses the existence of God, theses 18–45 the essence of God. In disputations 7 to 9, the doctrine of the Trinity is discussed. According

2, 19. Ps. 10, 4. 14, 1. et 53, 2. (quamvis conatu potius, quam sensu) duplici indicio, *Naturae et Rationis*, id demonstrabimus.

IV *Naturae hominis* quidem, quod haec notio, ut prima veritas, et primum principium humanae menti sit inscripta, Rom. 2, 15. et ad eam, inclinationem et propensionem habeat talem et tantam, ut indicasse sit evicisse, Rom. 1, 19. Act. 17, 27. 28. Atque ita sensus, et consensus communis* omnium, Deum esse arguit.

V Quin *natura* ipsa* ratioque, id est, universus mundus, fabrica, ordine, dispositione, ornatu suo ac vario usu, maxime homo μικρόκοσμος, imo imago Dei, qua pressius Deum exprimit, sapientissimum, beneficentissimum et potentissimum artificem et architectum nobis exhibet, Job 12, 7. 8. 9. etc. Ps. 19. Rom. 1, 20. Act. 17, 26.

VI Cui accedunt et aliae rationes, eaeque graves et variae; nempe a mundi, et maxime constanti, et ordinato coelestium motu, ad primum motorem, motusque auctorem, qui actu* sit, Arist. lib. *Metaphys.* 12. c. 6.[a] ab ordine causarum* efficientium ad primam efficientem, in qua consistatur, et a qua reliquae dependeant; a finibus ad extremum finem* et finitorem; ab esse, bono et perfectione,* ad primam essentiam, summum bonum et perfectissimam naturam; a conscientiae metu post admissa peccata, tamquam metuentis supremum judicem; a poenis atrocibus, quibus Deus contemptum sui, et atrocia peccata punit, etc. Cic. *de Natur. Deor.*[b]

VII Sed multo firmius id tenetur a fidelibus testimonio Dei et fidei lumine, secundum illud Apostoli, Accedentem ad Deum oportet credere, quod sit, etc. Heb. 11, 6.

VIII *Testimonia* autem sunt in apertis oraculis, operibus variis, tum creationis, tum sustentationis et gubernationis universi; variis apparitionibus, quibus se saepissime, ut sub formis aspectabilibus aliisque modis exhibuit, Exod. 19, 16.

---

[a] Aristotle, *Metaphysica* XII.6 1071b2–1072a18. [b] Cicero, *De natura deorum* 3.35.85.

> to Andreas J. Beck, it would be incorrect to draw the conclusion that this arrangement of the doctrine of God implies a kind of rationalistic 'natural theology' or that the doctrine of the Trinity is supposed to be overshadowed by the doctrine of divine attributes. Both doctrines are inextricably connected. The principle of division is simply that the properties common to the three Persons are discussed before their personal properties. Thus from the very beginning the triune God is envisaged. See Andreas J. Beck, *Gisbertus Voetius (1589–1676): Sein Theologieverständnis und seine Gotteslehre* (Göttingen: Vandenhoeck & Ruprecht, 2007), 227–232. For modern misrepresentations of the order and arrangement of the *locus de Deo*, see PRRD 3:154–159.

6. ABOUT THE NATURE OF GOD AND HIS DIVINE ATTRIBUTES

of certain atheists who deny (although more as an attempt than as a result of experience) the existence of God (James 2:19; Psalm 10:4; Psalm 14:1; and Psalm 53:2)—, we shall demonstrate his existence by two kinds of evidence: nature* and reason*.[3]

The first evidence comes from our human nature, because the notion of God has been inscribed on the human soul as a first truth and a first principle (Romans 2:15), and since humanity is thus and so strongly inclined, and so disposed that to have observed this fact is to have proved the point (Romans 1:19; Acts 17:27, 28). And so experience and the common* consent of all humanity prove that God exists.

In fact, nature* and its order, that is, the whole world, display to us the wisest, most generous, and most powerful master-mind and designer, by its craftsmanship, order, disposition, by its adornment and its diverse uses; and especially the human being as a microcosm, who as the image of God displays God very closely (Job 12:7,8,9, etc.; Psalm 19; Romans 1:20; Acts 17:26).

To this other arguments can be added, weighty and diverse ones. That is to say, one can reason from the movement of the universe (and especially the constant and regulated motion of the heavens) to the prime mover and the author of motion (who exists in actuality*) (Aristotle, *Metaphysics*, book 12, chapter 6). One can argue from the sequence of efficient causes* to the first efficient cause where the sequence stops, and on which the other causes depend. Or one argues from the goals to the final goal* and the force that determines the goal; from being, from the good, from perfection,* up to the prime essence, the highest good and the most perfect nature. Or one can use the argument from the dread of the conscience as it fears the highest judge if sins have been committed, or from the terrible punishments whereby God punishes those scorning Him, and their heinous sins (Cicero, *On the Nature of the Gods*).

But this conviction of God's existence is maintained much more firmly by believers through the testimony of God and the light of faith, in keeping with the Apostle's statement: "For whoever draws near to God must believe that He exists" (Hebrews 11:6).

There are, however, also testimonies* of God's existence in the manifest oracles, in the various works of creation and in the maintenance and ruling of the universe; the various appearances whereby He has revealed himself so frequently, as in visible shapes and in other modes (Exodus 19:16; 20:19,

---

3 For a summary of the development of this point in the Reformation and early Reformed Orthodoxy, see Michael Sudduth, *The Reformed Objection to Natural Theology*, Ashgate Philosophy of Religion Series (Farnham: Ashgate, 2009), 9–28.

et 20, 19. etc. miraculis illustribus, Ps. 72, 18., Propheticis vaticiniis et eorum eventis, Esai. 41, 23., maxime promissionis et exhibitionis Messiae. Denique in interna, viva et efficaci Spiritus Sancti per haec ipsa revelatione, quae in nobis fidem testimonio Divino respondentem gignit et efficit.

IX   Est igitur Deus, ejusque notitia habetur, quare et γνωστὸν τοῦ θεοῦ, Apostolo dicitur Rom. 1, 19. Habetur autem patefactione cum Naturali,* Ps. 19, 12. Act. 14, 15. 17. et 17, 24. 1 Corint. 1, 21. quae in natura corrupta ex parte, inconstans, et ad salutem inefficax est, Rom. 1, 20. tum Supernaturali,* quae integra, certa, atque in electis cum effectu salutari est, Ps. 19, 8. 1 Cor. 1, 21.

X   Pro diversitate porro linguarum, propter nos (Deus enim alias ἀνώνυμος, Gen. 32, 29.) summa haec essentia,* aliis nominibus appellatur, quae licet in diversis linguis a diversis ejus proprietatibus desumpta sint, tamen notione conveniunt. Hebraeis quidem אלה Eloah (quod rarum in sacris) et ab eo Elohim plurali numero, notione saepe singulari, idque non ab אלה Ala, id est, dejeravit, sed ab inusitata radice Alah cum He mappik, Arabibus vero usitata, pro *colere*, quasi *colendum* dicas, qualiter et Graecis σέβασμα dicitur, 2 Thess. 2, 4. Unde quidam decurtatum volunt אל El, quod loco singularis illius Eloah frequenter usurpatur, quamvis alii a fortitudine dictum velint.

XI   Graecis vero Θεός, Deus, sive a θεῖναι, cum Herodoto, Herod. in *Euterpe*,[a] quod omnes res* regionesque ordine disponat, sive a θεῖν, currere, ut post Platonem Eusebius, Plato in *Cratylo*,[b] Eus. lib. 1. *Evang. praeparat.*,[c] non quod antiquis primum Dii sidera, ut ille; sed ut hic, quod omnia virtute et providentiae actibus percurrat; sive a θεᾶσται, cernere, ut Basilius, *ep. 141 ad Caes.*[d] quod omnia cernat et decernat; vel a δέος, timor, non quod, ut ille haud pie, *Primus in orbe Deos fecit timor*,[e] sed quod timendus Deus sit. Alii his Graecis Hebraeam

---

[a] Herodotus, *Histories* 2.52.4.   [b] Plato, *Cratylus* 397d.   [c] Eusebius, *Praeparatio Evangelica* 1.9.12 (SC 206:172).   [d] Basil the Great, *Epistulae* 8.11 (= *Ep.* 141 in old numbering; Courtonne 1:35).   [e] Statius, *Thebais* 3,661.

6. ABOUT THE NATURE OF GOD AND HIS DIVINE ATTRIBUTES 155

etc.), the well-known miracles (Psalm 72:18), prophetic predictions and their outcomes (Isaiah 41:23)—especially those of the promise of the Messiah and his appearing. And finally, in the inner, vivid and effective revelation of the Holy Spirit by means of these things. This revelation implants and produces a faith in us that responds to the divine testimony.

Thus God does exist, and we have knowledge of Him, wherefore the Apostle calls it "what may be known of God" (Romans 1:19). However, revelation can be viewed either as natural* (Psalm 19:2; Acts 14:15, 17, and 17:24; 1 Corinthians 1:21), which in the corrupt nature is only a partial, fickle knowledge, ineffective unto salvation (Romans 1:20); or as supernatural,* which is unimpaired, reliable, and effective unto salvation in the elect (Psalm 19:8; 1 Corinthians 1:21).[4]

Reflecting the variety of different languages, this highest Being* is called by different names for the sake of us humans (for otherwise God would be nameless, *anōnumos*, Genesis 32:29)—although they have been drawn in the various languages from his different personal qualities, they conceptually agree. In Hebrew He is called *'Eloah* (rare in sacred Scripture), and from that *'Elohim* in the plural (often with the force of the singular). And that word is not derived from *'Ala*, that is, "He has sworn," but from the unusual root *'Alah* (with *mappiq he*[5]), as it is employed by the Arabians to mean "to worship," as if to say, "to be worshiped," like the Greek *sebasma* [an object of worship] (2 Thessalonians 2:4). From that some want to make the abbreviation, *'El*, that is frequently used instead of the singular *'Eloah*, although others think that it is derived from the word for might.[6]

In Greek He is *theos*, "God," which comes either from *theinai*, "to establish," as in Herodotus (*Histories* book 2, *Euterpe*), because He ordains all places and things,* or from *thein*, "to run," as in Eusebius following Plato (Plato, *Cratylus*, Eusebius, *Preparation for the Gospel*, book 1), not because according to the ancients the gods are stars (as Plato maintains), but, as Eusebius has it, because He imbues everything with his strength and deeds of providence. Or it comes from *theasthai*, "to behold," as Basil has it (*Letter 141, To the Caesareans*), because He beholds and discerns all things; or from *deos*, "fear," not because—as he says irreverently—"Fear was the first to bring about the gods in the world," but because He is worthy of fear. Others add to these Greek terms a Hebrew sense,

---

4 See also the earlier discussion of natural and supernatural knowledge of God, SPT 1.8.
5 *Mappiq he*: In Hebrew, the point inserted in the final *he* indicates that it should be vocalized as aspirate, and so expressed as a consonant.
6 John Calvin, for instance, in his explanation of the law, says that *El* as a name for God is derived from might (*fortitudo*). Calvin, *Institutes* 2.8.18.

notationem addunt, a די *Dai*, id est, *sufficit*, unde *Saddai*, Dei nomen sit. Latini a Graeco, aspirata in tenuem mutata, Deus efformarunt.

XII Usurpatur autem nomen hoc Dei in Scripturis dupliciter, vel ὄντως, vere et usitate, vel καταχρηστικῶς, abusive, illudque rursus vel οὐσιωδῶς,* cum communiter* sine determinatione* personarum Divinarum accipitur, ut Deus est spiritus, Joh. 4, 24., vel ὑποστατικῶς,* cum Dei nomen certae personae* subjective tribuitur, ut Patri, Rom. 7, 25. et 8, 3., Filio, ut 1 Tim. 3, 16. Act. 20,28., et Spiritui Sancto, Act. 5,4. Maxime autem Patri appropriatur, Rom. 1, 1. tum propter ordinem, qui est in Personis, tum oeconomiam* et dispositionem, ad mysterium salutis nostrae procurandum, factam.

XIII Καταχρηστικῶς καὶ ἀκύρως abusive et improprie,* creaturis tribuitur, vel κοινωνικῶς, id est, communicatione, cum Angelis vel hominibus, propter excellentem dignitatem, potentiam et gubernationem, in qua a Deo constituti, quamque erga alios exercent; vel δοξαστικῶς, ex opinione et errore, falsis Diis, Joh. 10, 34. Exod. 22, 28. Ps. 82, 6. 1 Cor. 8, 4. 5. Quo fit ut nomen Dei, quod individuae ejus essentiae significandae* proprium est, commune et appellativum factum sit.

XIV Quare ut se ab omnibus, qui Dei nomine veniunt, disjungeret, nomen hoc suum quibusdam proprietatibus circumscribit, dum se Deum Abrahami, Isaaci et Jacobi seu Israëlis dicit, Exod. 3, 6. Deum exercituum, Esai. 1, 24. Deum Deorum, Deut. 10, 17. Deum verum et vivum. Quinimo, אל שדי El Saddai, Exod. 6. et simpliciter Saddai, omnipotentem, a שדד vastavit, forma plurali Chaldaica; et אדן Adon, Dominum, אדנים Adonim, et Adonai. Domini, plurali similiter forma; et עליון Eljon, excelsum, etc. vocat.

6. ABOUT THE NATURE OF GOD AND HIS DIVINE ATTRIBUTES

from *day*, that is, "it is enough," from where comes God's name *Shadday*. The Latins formed the words *deus* from the Greek by turning the aspirate ["th"] into the corresponding medial ["d"].

12 Now this name for God is exercised in two ways in the Scriptures, either essentially in the proper and usual way, or in an improper way. In the proper way, the word "God" is used either of the essence* of the Godhead, when the word is taken generally* without specifying* the divine persons, as in "God is Spirit" (John 4:24), or personally,*[7] when the name of God is attributed to a certain person* as subject, as of the Father (Romans 7:25, and 8:3), of the Son (1Timothy 3:16, Acts 20:28), and of the Holy Spirit (Acts 5:4). However, it is appropriated to the Father especially (Romans 1:1), both because of the relation between the persons, as well as because of the economy* and plan that was established in order to maintain the mystery of our salvation.

13 In the improper* and wrong sense the name "God" is bestowed on created beings, either by making it common with angels or people, on account of the surpassing dignity, power and management in which God has placed them, and which they carry out towards others. Or, when misapplied to false gods, out of misconception and error (John 10:34; Exodus 22:28; Psalm 82:6; 1Corinthians 8:4,5); wherefore it happens that the name of God, which is the proper name for signifying his individual essence, has become a common appellative noun.[8]

14 Therefore, in order to set himself apart from all who come by the name "God," He has defined his own name by means of certain personal properties, as when He calls himself "the God of Abraham, Isaac, and Jacob (or Israel)" (Exodus 3:6); "the God of hosts" (Isaiah 1:24); "God of Gods" (Deuteronomy 10:17); "the true and living God." So too He calls himself *'El Shadday* (Exodus 6), and simply *Shadday*, "all-powerful," from *shadad*, "he has laid waste," in the Chaldean plural form; and *'Adon*, "lord," *'Adonim*, and *'Adonai*, "lords," again in the plural form; and *'Eljon*, "the exalted."

---

7 The Greek adverbs *ousiōdōs* and *hupostatikōs* were used in the debate concerning the Trinity in the Early Church, when the divine essence was called *ousia* and the three Persons *hupostases*. In Scripture the word "God" can refer to both.

8 The *nomen appellativum* is the appellative noun, which names the species to which someone belongs. The opposite is *nomen proprium*, the proper name.

xv Inprimis singulari nomine, puta Tetragrammato, id est, quatuor consonantibus constante, ut Veteres vocarunt, יהוה IHVH, et contracte יה Iah, se ab omnibus separavit, quod ut proprium Dei nomen, ita et incommunicabile* est, Esai. 42, 8. Atque id a Deo sibi impositum, Dei populo expositum, Exod. 3, 15. notum et cum reverentia ex Dei praecepto usurpandum, Exod. 20, 2. 7. et olim publice, et privatim prolatum, lectum et auditum, imo et gentibus vicinis non ignotum, 1 Reg. 17,12. 2. Chron. 6, 32. tandem post Prophetarum tempora superstitiose a Judaeis in arcanis haberi et coli coepit, adeo ut non nisi in sacris, et quidem a sacerdotibus efferretur, et demum omnino pronuntiari desierit. Unde et ἀνεκφώνητον, ineffabile vocatum, et vocibus, Adonai, cum chametz et Elohim, vicariis, punctisque horum illis substratis, prolatum est, a 70 Interpr. et Lat. Vulgat. Exod. 3, 6., ubi exprimit Adonai. Si tamen ad analogiam aliorum nominum exprimere licet, Jeheve vel Jheve seu Jave sive Jihve sonabit. Maxime cum Ehie et Jihie idem sit nomen; prima persona, utpote Dei loquentis, in tertiam, Mose jusso, de Deo ad populum loqui, commutata, Exod. 3, 14. et 15. Quamvis non diffiteamur, etiam Jehova analogice scribi posse; at Jehovi non item, quod id analogia linguae non patiatur.

xvi Deducitur a voce* quidem Hava, esse, sed ratio* nominis singularis est, Exod. 3, 14. Septuaginta interpretantur ὁ ὤν absolute,* plenius Johan. in Apoc. ὁ ὤν, ὁ ἦν καὶ ὁ ἐρχόμενος Apocal. 1, 4. 8. et 4, 8. et 11, 17. et 16, 5., ita ut aeternitatem notet. Est autem ratio nominis, quod ipse vere et in aeternum sit, (ita ut nomen* sit essentiale*) quodque omnibus essentiam tribuat; atque singulariter, quod promissa faciat esse, et in praestandis iis se fidelem et veracem praebeat: qualem sese exhibuit populo suo in praestando promisso de terra Canaan

6. ABOUT THE NATURE OF GOD AND HIS DIVINE ATTRIBUTES

God has set himself apart from everything particularly by his special name, 15
that is, the *Tetragrammaton*⁹—as the ancients called it—the word made up
of four consonants *YHVH*, and in shortened form *Yah*, because as it is the
proper name of God, it is incommunicable* (Isaiah 42:8). And God gave this
name to himself and introduced it to the people of God (Exodus 3:15); it is
well-known and it is to be used with reverence according to God's command
(Exodus 20:2,7), and once it was uttered both in public and privately, read
out loud and so heard, and was familiar even to the neighboring peoples
(1 Kings 17:12; 2 Chronicles 6:32). At length, after the times of the Prophets,
the Jews superstitiously started to reckon that the name belongs to the secret
things, and they treated it that way to such an extent that it was mentioned
solely on sacred occasions and then only by the priests, and in the end it
ceased being spoken altogether. From where it is also called *anekphōnētos*,
"inexpressible," and it was uttered by means of the substitute words *Adonai*
(with qamets¹⁰) and *Elohim* (with their vowel marks placed underneath it), by
the Septuagint and the Latin Vulgate (Exodus 3:6) where it says *'Adonai*. But if
one may express it by analogy with the other names, it would sound *Yeheve* or
Yheve or *Yave* or *Yihve*. Especially so because *'Ehye* and *Yihye* are one and the
same name, with change from the first person (when God is speaking) into the
third (as when Moses is commanded by God to speak to the people; Exodus
3:14, 15). And yet we do not deny that by analogy his name can be written also
Yᵉhova; but not so *Yᵉhovi*, because the analogy of the language does not allow
that.

The name is derived from the word* *Haja*, "to be," but the meaning* of the 16
name is unique (Exodus 3:14). The Septuagint interpret "the one who is" [*ho
ōn*] in an absolute* sense; John in Revelation more fully: "The one who is, and
who was, and who is to come" [*ho ōn, ho ēn kai ho erchomenos*] Revelation
1:4,8; and 4:8 and 11:17 and 16:5), so that it conveys the aspect of eternity. For
the meaning of the name is that He exists truly and in eternity (so that it is a
name* for his very essence*), and that He grants to every thing its essence. And
in particular, its meaning is that He makes his promises to come about, and
He reveals himself as faithful and true by fulfilling them. He displayed himself
as such to his people when He caused the promise He had made to Abraham

---

9 *Tetragrammaton* in Greek literally means a word consisting of four letters. The 'ancients' referred to are the older Jewish writers. Philo coined the use of this Greek term for the Hebrew name of God, *On the Life of Moses* 2.114.
10 *Qamets*: A Hebrew vowel point represented by two perpendicular lines underneath a letter, usually indicating the phoneme "a."

Abrahamo facto, et demum de Messia mittendo, etc, quum illa liberatio ex Aegypto hujus fuerit typus, Exod. 6, 3. R. Moses, lib. 1. c. 60. Jer. 16, 14.

XVII   Deum ergo propria significatione acceptum, qui (utpote ὑπερούσιος καὶ ἀκατάληπτος, omnem essentiam excedens et incomprehensibilis) definiri non potest,* ex variis ejus descriptionibus passim obviis, Exod. 34, 6. etc. Deuter. 10, 17. Apocal. 4, 8. Actor. 17, 24. etc. 1 Corinth. 8, 4. 5. 6. 1 Timoth. 1, 17. et 6, 15. 16. et simul collectis, ita describimus. Quod sit essentia spiritualis simplicissima et infinita, aeterna scilicet, immensaque atque immutabilis; vivens et immortalis, intelligens, sapiens et omniscia; ipsa bonitas, caritas, beneficentia, misericordia, longanimitas, justitia, sanctitas, etc. Unus essentia, trinus personis, Pater qui Filium ab aeterno genuit, Filius qui a Patre nascitur, Spiritus Sanctus qui a Patre et Filio, et quidem a Patre per Filium procedit: Creator, conservator et gubernator universi, Redemptor, servator et glorificator Electorum.

XVIII   Haec Dei descriptio tribus membris constat, unius Essentiae per varia attributa declaratione, Personarum divinarum enumeratione, et Operum patefactione. Sed duobus postremis omissis, in praesentia de primo agemus.

XIX   Essentiae* Divinae nomine intelligimus id quod Deus est; dicitur enim esse, Heb. 11, 6. et ὁ ὢν καὶ ὁ ἦν, Apoc. 4, 8. tribuitur ei φύσις, natura, Gal. 4, 8. et Divina natura, 2 Pet. 1, 4. (quamvis id ad Divinas proprietates restringatur) atque

6. ABOUT THE NATURE OF GOD AND HIS DIVINE ATTRIBUTES

about the land of Canaan to be fulfilled, and about sending the Messiah at last, etc.; while the deliverance from Egypt was a prefigurement of this (Exodus 6:3, Maimonides[11] book 1, chapter 60, Jeremiah 16:14).[12]

17 Taking the word in the proper sense of denoting Him, we shall describe God—who cannot* be defined, inasmuch as He "surpasses every essence and is incomprehensible"—from the various descriptions of Him apparent throughout Scripture and collected together (Exodus 34:6, etc.; Deuteronomy 10:17; Revelation 4:8; Acts 17:24, etc.; 1 Corinthians 8:4,5,6; 1 Timothy 1:17, and 6:15,16): He is a spiritual essence, entirely simple and infinite,[13] that is eternal and immeasurable, and immutable; living and immortal, understanding, wise and all-knowing. He is goodness itself, love, kindness, mercy, forbearance, righteousness, and holiness, etc. He is one in essence, but three in persons: the Father who has brought forth the Son from eternity; the Son who is born of the Father; the Holy Spirit, who proceeds from the Father and the Son, who even proceeds from the Father through the Son.[14] He is the Creator, the Preserver, and the Ruler of the universe, the Redeemer, Savior and the Glorifier of his elect.

18 This description of God comprises three parts: the revelation of the one Essence by means of various attributes; the enumeration of the divine Persons; and the revelation of his deeds. Leaving aside these latter two, for the present we shall treat the first part.

19 In using the phrase "divine Essence"* we mean that what God is; for "to be" is said of Him (Hebrews 11:6, and *ho ōn kai ho ēn*, Revelation 4:8). To Him are attributed "nature," *phusis* (Galatians 4:8), and "divine nature" (2 Peter 1:4;

---

11 Mosheh ben Maimon, or Moses Maimonides (1135–1204; also known with the Hebrew acronym RaMBaM), was a medieval Jewish philosopher, physician, and rabbi, who took a leading role in the Jewish communities in Morocco and Egypt. As one of the most prolific and influential scholars of the Torah in the Middle Ages, he is known today for his works *Mishneh Torah* (*Complete Statement of the Oral Law*) and *Moreh Nevukhim* (*Guide for the Perplexed*).

12 Maimonides (trans. M. Friedländer), *Moreh Nebuchim. The Guide for the Perplexed* (2nd ed.; New York: Dover, 1956). 1: 87–95 deals with the *tetragrammaton*. See especially page 95: "It is, therefore, clear that all these names of God are appellatives, or are applied to God by homonymy, the only exception being the *tetragrammaton*, the Shem ha-meforash (the *nomen proprium* of God), which is not an appellative; it does not denote any attribute of God, nor does it imply anything except his existence."

13 God's simplicity is the absence of any composition and division in God. Cf. PRRD 3:271–298; DLGTT, s.v. "simplicitas." God's infinity means that He is not limited, neither by time nor space, as the *Synopsis* explains. Cf. PRRD 3:325–338; DLGTT, s.v. "infinitas." Both simplicity and infinity can be used as a way of describing all of the divine attributes.

14 On "through the Son" see SPT 9.19.

θεότης, deitas, Colos. 2, 9. Et θειότης, Divinitas, Rom. 1, 20. Et τo θεῖον, Divinum seu numen, Act. 17, 29. Et μορφὴ Θεοῦ, forma Dei, Phil. 2, 6. Et Θεὸς, Deus appellatur, Act. 17, 24. 29. Ab hac vero, et in hac, sunt et exsistunt omnia suo participationis modulo.*

xx   Est autem ea Spiritualis. Dicitur enim Deus Spiritus in Scriptura Sacra Joh. 4, 24. quatenus ab ea corpus, atque omne quod corporeum, ejusque vis et actus removetur, Luc. 24, 39. Esai. 31, 3. Et quidem sicuti non corpus, sed Spiritus est, ita et coloris, formae figuraeque expers est, Deut. 4, 12. ac proinde sensibus corporeis non est perceptibilis, adeoque neque visibilis, tactilis, imaginabilis, sed invisibilis, Rom. 1, 20. 23. Esai. 40, 18. Joh. 1, 18. Colos. 1, 15. 1 Tim. 1, 17. et pura mente animoque apprehendenda. Quamvis secundum gradus gloriae externae sibi appropriatae, Exod. 24, 16. et 33, 18. 19. 20. 23. (quae remissa, dorsum, et intenta facies dicitur, Num. 12, 8. 1 Timoth. 6, 16.) videndum se praebuerit, sed qua est intentissima, non item. Est autem omnis spiritualis naturae auctor, unde et Pater et Deus Spirituum dicitur, Num. 16, 22. et 27, 16. Atque hinc quis et quid sit Deus, cognoscimus.

xxi   Quamvis porro essentia haec Deo absolute* competat, ita ut non sit aliud et aliud in Deo, sed quicquid est, ipsius essentia sit; attamen varias proprietates seu attributa,* quae θεότητες nomine veniunt, Rom. 1, 20. tamquam ab ea, et inter se differentia, ei vere assignamus; non tamen realiter, sed σχέσει et

6. ABOUT THE NATURE OF GOD AND HIS DIVINE ATTRIBUTES

although it is restricted to the divine properties), *theotēs*, "deity" (Colossians 2:9) and *theiotēs*, "divinity" (Romans 1:20), and *to theion*, "the divine" or "the godhead" (Acts 17:29), and *morphē theou*, "the form of God" (Philippians 2:6); and He is called *theos*, "God" (Acts 17:24, 29). From and in this divine nature all things are and exist, everything by means of its own way* of participation.[15]

Moreover, the divine Essence is spiritual. For God is called Spirit in Scripture (John 4:24) in that body and anything corporeal, including its strength and movement is excluded from it (Luke 24:39; Isaiah 31:3). And moreover, just as He is not a body but a Spirit, so too He has no appearance, form or shape (Deuteronomy 4:12); and hence God cannot be perceived by the bodily senses. And indeed He cannot be seen, touched, or imagined, but He is invisible (Romans 1:20, 23; Isaiah 40:18; John 1:18; Colossians 1:15; 1 Timothy 1:17) and can be grasped only by a pure mind and the soul. Yet according to the degrees of external glory that are appropriate to Him (Exodus 24:16; 33:18, 19, 20, and 23, where this glory is called the hindmost side, the back, and by facial features, Num. 12:8, 1 Tim. 6:16), He has allowed himself to be seen, but not in his highest glory. However, He is the author of all spiritual nature, wherefore He is called Father and God of the spirits (Numbers 16:22, and 27:16). And so we know who and what God is.

Furthermore, although this essence applies to God in an absolute* way so that there is not one thing and another thing in God, but all what He is, is his essence, we nevertheless rightly assign to Him various properties or attributes,* which are classified under the title of divinity (Rom. 1:20), suggesting that there is a difference between essence and properties and between the properties themselves. Yet this is not a real distinction,[16] but a relational or rational

---

15 Everything that exists derives its existence from the divine essence. The concept of the communicable attributes rests on this relationship, here explained by the notion of participation (on the connection of these two concepts, see also thesis 30 below). This participation must not be misunderstood as divinization, but interpreted in line with the statement of Thomas Aquinas regarding God as the efficient cause of creation (see also *SPT* 10.5, 22 on creation "out of nothing"). 'All beings apart from God are not their own being, but are beings by participation.' Aquinas, *Summa theologiae*, 1.44.1.

16 A *distinctio realis* distinguishes two things (*res*). See *PRRD* 3:286: "There are, in the first place, what the scholastics called 'real distinctions'—distinctions *between* one *res* and another *res*, one thing and another thing. These real distinctions can obtain between different things of different essences (e.g., between a flower and a table), or between two things of the same essence (e.g., between two tables), or between the separable parts of a composite thing (e.g., between the tabletop and the legs of the table). Since there is only one God and since God is one and non-composite or simple, this kind or level of distinction does not apply to God." On the other hand, there is a relational or

ratione, prout in creaturis et nostra perceptione diversa sunt. Atque hinc, quis qualisque sit Deus, se nobis cognoscendum praebet, hisque verum Deum a falsis, rebusque omnibus disjungimus.

XXII Sunt autem illa attributa duorum generum, alia primi generis seu ἀκοινώνητα, incommunicabilia; alia secundi seu κοινωνητὰ, communicabilia.*

XXIII Illa dicuntur, quae re ipsa secundum propriam et integram vocum* notionem, creaturis non communicantur, sed aliqua tantum parte et comparate, ut sunt vera simplicitas (unde dependet unitas, immutabilitas) et infinitas, id est, aeternitas et immensitas. Quae ita distinguere licet ut quaedam sint generaliora, ut quae plures categorias respiciunt, earum scilicet negationem indicantia, ut simplicitas et immutabilitas; quaedam specialiora, ut infinitas, (quae solam quantitatem) et sub se continet aeternitatem et immensitatem. Atque hae infallibiles Deitatis notae sunt.

XXIV *Simplicitas** est attributum essentiae Dei primi generis, et quidem generalius, qua illa omnis omnino compositionis expers significatur,* sive ea sit ex partibus* materialibus et integrantibus,* sive essentialibus,* materia et forma, genere* et differentia, subjecto* et accidente,* actu* et potentia,* esse denique et essentia atque existentia; ac proinde vere simplicissima est. Quod quidem ex eo constat, quoniam praeterquam quod Spiritus, Joh. 4, 24. et Jehova dicitur, Exod. 3, 14. et absolute ac sine ulla adjectione, ὁ ὢν seu ens nominatur, Esai. 43, 13. et abstractis vocibus, vita, lux, caritas et veritas, Joh. 14, 6. 1Joh. 1,

---

rational distinction when some aspect is indicated following an act of the intellect but that nevertheless is grounded in the thing itself (*in re*). It must be distinguished from the purely conceptual distinction that applies when one thing following the act of the intellect has no grounding *in re*. See DLGTT, s.v. "distinctio."

distinction, in so far as they differ in creatures and in our perception. With these properties God himself grants to us the knowledge of who God is and what He is like, and through these attributes we can distinguish the true God from the false ones and from all other things.

These attributes, then, are of two sorts: those of the first type are incommunicable,* those of the second sort are communicable*.¹⁷

Those are called incommunicable which according to the proper and true sense of the words* are not really imparted to created beings, but only partially and in a comparative sense—such as true simplicity (on which unity and immutability depend) and infinity, that is, eternity and immeasurability. One may distinguish these features in such a way that some are more general, since they concern more categories (namely, as indicating the negation of them) such as simplicity and immutability. Certain other ones are more specific, such as infinity (pertaining only to quantity) which comprises eternity and immeasurability. And these are infallible marks of the Deity.

Simplicity* is an attribute of God's essence of the first type, and certainly one of the more general attributes, indicating* that the divine essence is altogether without any composition, whether that composition be from material and integral parts,* or from the essential parts* of matter and form, from genus* and difference, subject* and accident,* act* and potency,* and finally, essence and existence. Accordingly it truly is a very simple essence. This is evident from the fact that besides being called Spirit (John 4:24) and Yᵉhova (Exodus 3:14), He is called absolutely (without any adjective) *ho ōn*, or "the being" (Isaiah 43:14[13]), and by the abstract¹⁸ names "life," "light," "love," "truth" (John 14:6;

---

17   The classification into communicable and incommunicable attributes was well known but not universally followed by the Reformed orthodox. Cf. PRRD 3:223–226. The distinction does not necessarily imply that properties attributed to both God and creatures have a common, ontological ground in their respective essences (*analogia entis*). The terms 'communicable' and 'incommunicable' function within a theory of predication: Some terms can be predicated of both God and creatures and then transmit a common thought content (e.g., goodness, wisdom, power); other terms apply to God alone, while the opposite is true of creatures (e.g., infinity, eternity, independence). The 'incommunicable' attributes of God, though differing from our created reality, can still be known by us because God reveals his being so.

18   The term 'abstract names' refers to a distinction between 'abstract' and 'concrete' attribution of properties to God. For example, Girolamo Zanchi explains that abstract, substantive terms such as 'life,' 'wisdom,' 'light,' etc., are used to indicate that God has these qualities in and by himself, and that he does not derive them from a source that would then be superior to God (*De natura Dei* book I, chapter 1). On the other hand, the same qualities can be predicated in a concrete, adjective sense by calling God 'living,' 'wise,' 'full

5. 1 Joh. 4, 8. Jac. 1, 17. etc. appellatur. A qua omnes simplicitatis in natura gradus fluunt.

xxv   Ut porro essentia nullam compositionem admittit, ita neque divisionem in partes, species* et numerum; adeoque unus est Deus, Deut. 6, 4. Marc. 12, 29. 32. unitatis voce non accepta, qua principium numeri est, sed numero opposita, ita ut non sint neque esse possint plures, non sit alius, nullus praeterea, et ultra, et praeter ipsum, neque ullus secum, seu coram ipso, aut uspiam in coelo et terra sit Deus, sed ipse tantum, solus, et solum sit Deus. 1 Cor. 8, 4. Deut. 4, 35. Esai. 45, 5. 21. Deut. 32, 39. Exod. 20, 3. 2 Reg. 19, 15. Ps. 86, 10. Joh. 17, 3.

xxvi   *Immutabilitas** Dei est attributum essentiae Dei generalius; quo ab illa omnis omnino mutatio et motus, Malach. 3, 6. Num. 23, 19. puta generatio* seu ortus, et corruptio seu interitus, incrementum et decrementum, successio atque translatio seu loci mutatio, alteratio seu variatio, et passio removetur, ac Divina essentia eadem manere significatur, Ps. 102, 13. 25. etc. Heb. 1, 11. Unde Deus, Ehie, Ero, nominatur, et immutabilis et incorruptibilis et idem dicitur, 1 Tim. 1, 17.

xxvii   *Infinitas** Dei est attributum essentiae Dei specialius, utpote quod quantitatem specialiter respicit, qua Divina essentia omnis omnino finis* et termini* expers est, id est, nullis terminis, nempe essentiae seu magnitudinis, loci, ac denique temporis continetur, sed omnes excedit. Atque secundum quam nihil Deo par aut aequale est, Jer. 10, 6. Phil. 2, 6. Distinguitur vero in aeternitatem et immensitatem.

xxviii   *Aeternitas* est attributum durationis essentiae Dei infiniti, juxta quam illa terminorum temporis, et a quo, principii* scilicet, et ad quem, finis; vel successionis, prioris et posterioris, praeteriti et futuri, expers est: ac proinde ita jam est, ut et ante fuerit, et post futura sit, idque utrimque in infinitum; adeo ut omnes partes temporis simul comprehendat; imo omne tempus excedat, quinimo ab eo immunis sit. Unde in Scriptura dicitur, antiquus dierum, Dan. 7, 9. 13. annos ejus non deficere, Ps. 102, 13. 28. annorum ejus numerum impervestigabilem, Job. 36, 26. Gen. 21, 33. a seculo fuisse, et in secula esse, imo ante secula, et permanere in seculum, Rex esse seculi et seculorum, esse in generationem et generationem, in secula usque et semper, esse et fuisse et futurum esse, ante

---

of light,' etc., in order to point out that God possesses these qualities in a real, actual manner. In this connection, Zanchi refers to Bernard of Clairvaux, *De diligendo Deo*, XII.35 (MPL 182, 996B). See also *DLGTT*, s.v. "in abstracto," where the distinction is explained specifically in the context of the Reformed-Lutheran debate on the *communicatio idiomatum* of the divine and human natures of Christ.

1 John 1:5; 1 John 4:8; James 1:17), etc. From this all the degrees of simplicity in nature flow forth.

And again, just as his essence does not allow any composition, so too it does not allow any division in parts, species* and number. And thus God is one (Deuteronomy 6:4; Mark 12:29, 32)—using the word "one" not in the sense of the first number but as the exact opposite of number. Thus there are not many gods, nor could there be many gods; and there is not any other god, let alone one beside or beyond Him, nor any with or before Him or anywhere else in heaven or on earth. But He alone is God, the one and only (1 Corinthians 8:4; Deuteronomy 4:35; Isaiah 45:5, 21; Deuteronomy 32:39; Exodus 20:3; 2 Kings 19:15; Psalm 86:10; John 17:3).

The immutability* of God is one of the more general attributes of God's essence. It entirely excludes alteration and change (Malachi 3:6; Numbers 23:19), such as begetting* or coming into existence, decay and death, growth and decrease, succession and transference (or change of place), alteration or variation, and passions.[19] And it indicates that the essence of God stays the same (Psalm 102:13,25, etc.; Hebrews 1:11). Hence God is called *'Ehye*, "I shall be," and He is called unchanging, incorruptible, and the same (1 Timothy 1:17).

The infinity* of God is a more particular attribute of God, since it concerns quantity in particular, whereby the divine essence is altogether free from any ending* or boundary.* That is, the essence is enclosed by no boundaries at all, namely of essence or size, of place, and lastly of time, but it surpasses every one of them. And according to this attribute nothing is equal to or on a par with God (Jeremiah 10:6; Philippians 2:6). It is divided into eternity and immensity.

Eternity is an attribute of the duration assigned to the essence of the infinite God, whereby his being is exempt from a temporal *terminus a quo*, a beginning,* and a *terminus ad quem*, an ending; it is also free of any succession (i.e., former and latter), of bygone and future time. Accordingly the essence of God is now, and has been before now and shall be hereafter, and each of these infinitely, to such an extent that it embraces all parts of time at once, indeed that it surpasses all time—no rather, that it is unaffected by time. Therefore in Scripture He is called "the Ancient of Days" (Daniel 7:9, 13); "His years have no end" (Psalm 102:13, 27[28]) and "the number of his years is unsearchable" (Job 36:26; Genesis 21:33). He has been from eternity, and He is in eternity, even before the ages, and He will remain in eternity. The King of the age and of all ages is from generation to generation; for ages and always He is and was and will be, from before the

---

19 See PRRD 3:553–557. God cannot undergo (Latin: *pati*) any influence of external factors or agents.

mundum et omnia, habitare aeternitatem, et simpliciter ὁ ὤν, ὁ ἦν καὶ ὁ ἐρχόμενος vocatur, et ἀΐδιος et αἰώνιος, aeternus et sempiternus, primus et novissimus dicitur, Ps. 29,10. et 90. 2. Apoc. 4, 8. 1Tim. 1, 17. Rom. 16, 26. Ergo primum ens est et a nemine dependet.

XXIX *Immensitas* est attributum essentiae Dei infiniti, secundum quod omnes essentiae terminos excedens, magnitudinis proprie, et dimensionis, longi, lati et profundi, et partium, ac definitionis loci, seu inferioris et superioris, anterioris et posterioris expers est; ac proinde ita hic, ut et ibi, et alibi, et ubique, adeoque omnipraesens, omnia simul loca complens, eaque excedens; imo illocalis sit, atque in se consistens com plectatur et contineat omnia. Unde in Scriptura עליון Eljon, Excelsus, Genes. 14, 19. 20, 22. nominatur, et ita magnus et amplus, Job. 36, 26. Deut, 10, 17. dicitur, ut simul sit in coelo, inferno, et extremo maris, coelum et terram impleat, imo excelsior sit coelo, profundior inferno, longior terra, latior mari, coelum ei sit sedes, terra vero scabellum pedum ejus, et coelum coelorum illum non capiat, Ps. 139, 7. Jer. 23, 24. Job. 11, 8. 9. Esa. 66, 1. 1Chron. 16, 18. Act. 19, 28.

XXX Attributa secundi generis, quae ad qualitatem* respectum habent, ita sunt Dei ut et creaturis quodammodo communicentur, et ab iis revera participentur, ideoque de Deo et creaturis propter ordinem quem ad Deum habent, ἀναλόγως* praedicantur,* ut sunt praecipue, vita, sapientia, voluntas et potentia;* quae per

world and everything in it. He dwells in eternity, and is simply called "the one who is, who was, and who shall be" (*ho ōn, ho ēn kai ho erchomenos*), "eternal and everlasting" (*aïdios, aiōnios*). He is called "the first and the last" (Psalm 29:10, and 90:2; Revelation 4:8; 1 Timothy 1:17; Romans 16:26). Therefore He is the first being and is dependent on no-one.

Immensity is the attribute of the essence of the infinite God, whereby He surpasses all boundaries of essence. Properly speaking He is devoid of any size, and of measurement, of length, width and depth, and of parts and of a specific position in space—whether below or above, in front or behind. Accordingly his essence is here, and there, and elsewhere, and everywhere, and consequently omnipresent, embracing all places at the same time and surpassing them. In fact it is not spatial, and existing in and of itself, it embraces and contains everything. From this He is called in Scripture "exalted," *'Eljon* (Genesis 14:19, 20, 22), and He is called so great and so ample (Job 36:26; Deuteronomy 10:17[14]) that simultaneously He is in heaven above and on earth below, and in the depth of the sea; that He fills heaven and earth, in fact He is higher than the heavens, lower than the world below, and wider than the earth, broader than the sea. Heaven is his seat and the earth his footstool, and the highest heaven cannot hold Him (Psalm 139:7; Jeremiah 23:24; Job 11:8,9; Isaiah 66:1; 1 Chronicles 16:18;[20] Acts 19:28).

Attributes of the second sort, which pertain to quality,* belong to God in such a way that they are communicated also to created beings to some degree, who thus actually participate in them. And therefore, because of the relation creatures have to God, these attributes are predicated* of both God and creatures by way of analogy*.[21] Foremost of these are life, wisdom, will, and power;* and

---

20   More adequately: 1 Chronicles 16:14, 25 or 2 Chronicles 6:18.
21   Analogical predication rests on the idea of structural similarity that renders it legitimate to draw an analogy between a representation and what it represents. As Thomas Aquinas says: "... the names said of God and creatures are predicated neither univocally nor equivocally but analogically ..." (*Summa Contra Gentiles*, I, 34). "And in this way some things are said of God and creatures analogically, and not in a purely equivocal nor in a purely univocal sense. For we can name God only from creatures. Thus whatever is said of God and creatures is said according to the relation of a creature to God as its principle and cause, wherein all perfections of things pre-exist excellently" (*Summa theologiae*, 1.13.5). See Daniel Bonevac, "Two Theories of Analogical Predication," in *Oxford Studies in Philosophy of Religion*, vol. 4, ed. Jonathan L. Kvanvig (Oxford: University Press, 2012), chapter 2.

attributa primi generis traducta Deo propria sunt. Atque ita nullus Deo similis intelligitur, 1 Chron. 17, 20. 2 Chron. 6, 14. Act. 17, 29.

XXXI Attributa haec distingui possunt in ea quae facultatem, vim, actumque Dei immanentem, significant. Immanens* vita est; quae est attributum essentiae Dei, perfectionem* per se indicans, quo essentia Dei in se actuosa esse, id est, vivere declaratur; idque simplicissime, seu essentialiter, et per se, immutabiliter, seu constanter et infinite, id est, ab aeterno, et sine incremento et decremento, atque ubique. Unde Deus non modo vivens, et vivere, Deut. 5, 26. Act. 14, 15. Num. 14, 21. sed et in se ipso vitam habere, et vita ipsa, et aeternum vivere, solus immortalitatem habere, atque ἄφθαρτος, incorruptibilis, seu immortalis, Joh. 5, 26. 1 Joh. 5, 20. Deut. 32, 40. omnisque vitae in creaturis auctor et fons, et vivificus dicitur, omniaque in eo vivere, Ps. 36, 10. Act. 17, 25. 28.

XXXII Vita haec Dei in intellectu et voluntate est. Intellectus, cognitio, scientia,* sapientiaque divina, est vitae Dei facultas* seu actus,* natura et ordine primus, quo Deus vivus omnia, se ipsum scilicet, et extra se universa et singula, quae esse possunt, quaeque esse vult et ipse facit, aut a creaturis fieri vult vel permittit, et sunt, earumque causas, modos et circumstantias, praesentia, praeterita et futura, magna et parva, (quibus divina scientia non vilescit) et rationalis creaturae cogitata, animi recessus, dicta, conatus, facta, initia, progressus et exitus, distincte, ut rebus intimus, infinita sua essentia intelligit, scit et novit, Ps. 139,

because they are qualified by the attributes of the first sort they belong to God in the proper sense.²² And so no-one is considered similar to God (1 Chronicles 17:20; 2 Chronicles 6:14; Acts 17:29).

These attributes can be divided into those which point out God's immanent potency, strength, and activity.²³ Life is immanent;* it is an attribute of God's essence, displaying perfection* in itself, whereby the essence of God is declared as full of activity in itself, that is, living—and that in the most simple or essential way; and by itself, unchangeably, or constantly and unendingly, that is, from eternity and without increase or decrease, and everywhere.²⁴ From this it is said that God not only is living and alive (Deuteronomy 5:26; Acts 14:15; Numbers 14:21), but also that He has life in himself, and is life itself, and lives eternally, that He alone has immortality, and is incorruptible [*aphthartos*] or immortal (John 5:26; 1 John 5:20; Deuteronomy 32:40), and that He is the author and source of all life in created beings, and life-giving, and that everything lives in Him (Psalm 36:10; Acts 17:25, 28).

This life of God exists in intellect and will. The intellect, knowing, knowledge,* and divine wisdom are a faculty* or activity* of God's life, and is first²⁵ in nature and order. By this faculty the living God in his infinite essence understands, perceives and knows all things, namely himself, and all universal and individual things outside himself which can possibly exist and which He wills to exist. And these things which He performs or which He wills or permits to be done by his creatures and which do exist, including their causes, ways and circumstances, present, past and future things, great and small (through which the divine knowledge is not made worthless), and the thoughts of the rational creature, the recesses of the heart, the statements, attempts, deeds, beginnings, advancements, and endings (Psalm 139:1, etc.; Job 34:21; Psalm 44:22)—all these

---

22 The act of predication implies that the subject and the predicate are not convertible: The predications such as "God is life, wisdom, will and power" etc., do not allow the inference that life, wisdom etc. "is God." It means that the language of God's communicable attributes presumes not only an identity but also a (formal) difference between the divine subject and its communicable predicates, and between the predicates themselves as well. See PRRD 3:195–199.

23 The emanating activities are dealt with in thesis 36 and onwards.

24 On the *vita Dei*, see Dolf te Velde "Eloquent Silence: The Doctrine of God in the *Synopsis of Purer Theology*," *Church History and Religious Culture*, 92.4 (2012): 581–608, esp. 603–605.

25 The 'first' faculty of the intellect is related to 'the other' of the will, in thesis 34. The third faculty is that of power, thesis 36.

1. etc. Job. 34, 21. Ps. 44, 22., se quidem per sese et directe; cetera extra se, bona (ut quae ejus simulacrum habent) indirecte; mala, per contraria.

xxxiii   Scit autem simplici et uno, immutabili, infinito et aeterno actu: id est, omnia, semper, simul et semel, atque necessario, Act. 15, 18. Heb. 4, 13. lta ut nihil ignoret, discat, non proficiat, fallatur, opinetur, obliviscatur, reminiscatur, imo ne praesciat quidem proprie, Ps. 90, 4. 2 Petr. 3, 8. Esai. 40, 14. licet respectu rerum futurarum praescire, praeteritarum meminisse, praesentium scire, vere dicatur; non successive unum post alterum, aut unum ex altero per discursum, sed unum cum altero intelligat et videat. Unde non modo sapientia et intelligentia ei attribuitur, Rom. 11, 33. et sapiens vocatur, sed apud eum, et ejus esse sapientia, solus sapiens, 1 Tim.1, 17. omniscius, καρδιογνώστης, noscens corda, dicitur, omnisque sapientiae fons et origo est, Ps. 147, 4. etc. Dan.2, 20. 21. 22. Prov. 2, 6. Act. 15, 8.

xxxiv   Voluntas* Dei est altera vitae Dei facultas seu actus illi succedens, quo Deus intelligens se, et omnia bona, ut naturae et ordini mentis suae consentientia, vult et probat, contraria improbat necessario, quae *voluntas Approbans* dicitur; et ex iis quae extra se facere potest, quaedam praevia sapientia libere vult, eligit, et decernit, et facit, quae voluntas *Efficiens*; et a creaturis bona a se praecepta fieri vult, et exigit, quae voluntas *Praecipiens*; mala vero quae prohibet, et tamen a creaturis fiunt, certo consilio vult permittere, quae *voluntas Permissiva* vocatur.

things He knows with a distinct knowledge, as most intimately familiar with things. Himself He knows directly and through himself; as regards the other things outside of himself, He knows indirectly what is good (since they bear his image) and what is evil He knows by their opposite.

Moreover, God exercises knowledge in a simple, single, immutable, infinite and eternal act; that is, He knows all things, always, immediately and at once, and necessarily (Acts 15:18; Hebrews 4:13). He knows everything in such a way that He is unaware of nothing, has to learn nothing, does not advance in knowing anything; He does not err, He supposes nothing, forgets nothing, and He does not remind himself of anything. Indeed, properly speaking He even does not have foreknowledge (Psalm 90:4; 2 Peter 3:8; Isaiah 40:14), although in respect of future things it is rightly said that He does have foreknowledge, as well as that He remembers bygone events, knows the current ones—not successively (one after the other), or one thing by reasoning it from another, but He understands and sees one thing simultaneously with another.[26] Therefore wisdom and understanding are accorded to Him (Romans 11:33)—and He is called "wise"—but wisdom also is with Him and from Him, and He is called "the only wise one" (1 Timothy 1:17), "all-knowing," "knowing the hearts" (*kardiognōstēs*), and the source and fountain of all wisdom (Psalm 147:4[-5], etc.; Daniel 2:20, 21, 22; Proverbs 2:6; Acts 15:8).

God's will* is the other faculty of God's life; it is the act that follows upon God's knowledge, whereby the knowing God wills and approves himself and all good things, as they accord with his nature and the structure of his mind, and whereby He necessarily disapproves of the things that are opposite to them. This is called the "approving will." And from the things He can do outside himself, He freely wills by his prior wisdom certain things, chooses them, decides to do them and actually does them which is called his "efficient will." And the will with which He wills and requires the good things He has commanded to be done by his creatures, is called "the commanding will." But the will according to a particular counsel to permit bad things which He forbids and which are yet done by his creatures, is called "the permitting will."[27]

33

34

---

26 As God's knowledge is understood as one undivided eternal act, it follows that God's knowledge of things or events in created reality is itself not successive; in that case, God would have separate, successive acts of knowing. The eternal character of God's knowledge does not imply, however, that the temporal succession in created reality itself is denied. God does not know events one after another, but He does know them as coming one after another.

27 The distinction between the approving, efficient, commanding, and permitting will makes it possible to discern between the good things God approves of and the bad things he

xxxv Quae porro vult, ut liberrime vult, ita ab aeterno, et immutabiliter vult, Es. 46, 10. Mal. 3, 6. adeo non coactus seu invitus vult quod vult, Matth. 20, 15. neque ab ullo principio, seu causa priore impellitur ac movetur ad volendum, sed ejus voluntas est et prima et suprema causa, Eph. 1, 11. ut qui quae vult, a se, et propter se vult, neque contraria seu contradictoria vult, seu idem vult, et non vult, Ps. 89, 35. neque jam vult, aut non vult quod ante simpliciter noluit, aut voluit, nec plura aut pauciora jam vult, quam antea voluit, nec denique ejus voluntas impediri potest, quo minus id quod absolute voluit, fiat ac impleatur, Esai. 14, 27. Rom. 9, 19. et 11, 29.

xxxvi Tantum de illo attributo quod facultatem et actum immanentem habet. Sequitur quod emanantem* declarat, puta potentia, quae circa res externas versatur et exercetur, qua fieri possunt. Est autem *Potentia** Dei attributum,

---

disapproves of, but still wills to be actualized. Although it is not very clear how Thysius relates the four to each other, the first two seem to refer to the will of God himself and the second two to the will of God with respect to the will and acts of creatures. For a detailed discussion of the distinctions in the will of God see *PRRD* 3: 472.

6. ABOUT THE NATURE OF GOD AND HIS DIVINE ATTRIBUTES

Moreover, what He wills, He freely wills, and He also wills it from eternity and immutably (Isaiah 46:10; Malachi 3:6), and thus whatever He wills is not by compulsion or involuntarily (Matthew 20:15); nor does any other initiative or prior cause force or drive God to will, but his will is the prime and highest cause (Ephesians 1:11). For what He wills He wills from himself and on account of himself; nor does He will contrary or contradictory things;[28] nor does He will and not will the very same thing (Psalm 89:35), nor does He now will or not will what He simply did not will (or did will) previously; nor does He will more or less things now than He willed before. And finally, his will cannot be hindered from being performed and completed regarding what He willed absolutely (Isaiah 14:27; Romans 9:19, and 11:29).

Thus far about the attribute that pertains to his immanent faculty and action. What follows explains the emanating* potency, that is, the power that concerns and is practiced upon things that are outside of Him—whereby things can happen.[29] Well then, the power* of God is the attribute whereby

---

28   Freedom of contrariety indicates the possibility of the will to choose this or that object (a or b); freedom of contradiction is the possibility of the will to either choose or reject the same object (choosing a or not-choosing a). For the distinction between contrariety and contradiction see *RTF*, 45–46.

29   In the first instance, the distinction of 'immanent' and 'emanating' faculties points to the sphere of operation of God's knowledge and will on the one hand, and his power on the other hand. Knowing and willing are internal, mental acts of God that can be completed without external operations. God's power, on the other, is precisely that faculty which executes God's will in or upon external objects, and therefore is called an 'emanating' potency. Viewed in a wider context, the *ad intra-ad extra* pattern is a fundamental architectonic device in the Reformed doctrine of God in the SPT, and was already hinted at by the distinction archetypal and ectypal theology in *SPT* 1.3. The *ad intra-ad extra* language intends to differentiate between the absolute and necessary knowledge, will and power of God *ad intra* and the *ad extra* and, and therefore, free and contingent knowledge, will and power of God. Thus God is said to have both a necessary and voluntary knowledge (thesis 32), both an immanent and a transient will (thesis 34–35), and both an absolute and ordained power (thesis 36–37). All three of these attributes (knowledge, will, and power) are classed as the attributes of the divine life (*vita Dei*, thesis 32), which is itself a category of attributes that bears out the *ad intra-ad extra* pattern. These distinctions were not new to the Reformed orthodox: They derive from the medieval scholastic background. But the *ad intra-ad extra* language was explicitly used by the Reformed orthodox to underline their major concern that the absoluteness (or the simplicity and immutability) of God serves not to exclude but rather to define the nature of divine relationality and to undergird its radical freedom and contingency. See Van Asselt, "Fundamental Meaning," 319–353, and note especially Beck, *Gisbertus Voetius*, 264–277, 344–351, 382–395.

quo Deus vivus, intelligens, ac volens, vi et facultate valet ad exterius agendum. Quae quidem simpliciter, et seorsim a voluntate considerata, *Absoluta** est, et ad omnia possibilia refertur, non item ad simpliciter impossibilia, Mat. 3, 9. et 19, 26. Luc. 1, 37. conjuncta vero cum voluntate *Actualis** est, Ps. 115, 3. Eph. 1, 11. quae immediate* vel mediate* (unde appellatur Deus Sebaoth, exercituum) exercetur.

xxxvii   Est vero ea potentia Dei, in Deo simpliciter, im mutabiliter et infinite, ita ut non per qualitatem,* sed per se, non ab alio, sed a se potens sit Deus, non potentia passiva, sed ἐνεργουμένη, Eph. 3, 20. non incipiat aliquid posse* quod ante non potuerit, sed quod potest, ab aeterno potuerit, Rom. 1, 20. nec plura, nec pauciora possit, sed omnia possit quae velle facere potest, potentiamque exerceat in iis quae vult esse, idque sine labore, aut difficultate. Atque in hoc potentiae suae exercitio, et alia, et aliter, plura, majora et excellentiora, vel minora et pauciora potest. Unde etiam Scriptura impotentiam a Deo removet, potentiam, robur, fortitudinem, efficacitatem tribuit, 1 Cor. 1, 25. Eph. 1, 19. 1 Tim. 6, 15. 16. et potens, et solus potens, et *El Saddai*, seu omnipotens dicitur, Gen. 17. Apoc. 1, 8.

xxxviii   Cum istis, tum vita Dei intelligentis et volentis, tum potentia, cohaeret *Dominium Dei*, vis, potestas et auctoritas in omnia quae extra se potest et vult facere, et facit; quod item est aeternum et immutabile. Unde etiam Dominus dicitur, et Dominus Dominorum, Deus Deorum, Rex regum, 1 Tim. 6, 15. et habere potestatem liberrimam et absolutam in omnia, Rom. 9, 21. Mat. 20, 15. quod est ἀδέσποτον et αὐτεξούσιον esse. Atque ab eo fluit et est omne Dominium, Rom. 13, 1.

xxxix   *Affectus boni* (qui in hominibus passiones sunt) et Virtutes, tum Intellectus, tum Voluntatis, quae in illis ethici et morales habitus sunt, affectuumque moderationem designant; quales sunt, veritas, amor, bonitas, benignitas, caritas, beneficentia, misericordia, longanimitas; ira, odium, justitia, et denique sanctitas, etc. de Deo vere et proprie, submota scilicet omni imperfectione, dicuntur; ac nihil aliud sunt quam ardens erga nos Dei voluntas, ejus in

the living, knowing, and willing God through his strength and potency has the power to perform deeds that are external to Him. This potency, when treated simply by itself and separate from the will, is *absolute*,* and relates to all possibilities, and similarly does not relate to all that is simply impossible (Matthew 3:9, and 19:26; Luke 1:37). However, when joined to the will it is *actual** (Psalm 115:3; Ephesians 1:11), and it is exercised either without* or with an intervening agent* (for which reason He is called Lord Sabaoth, the God of hosts).

That power of God, then, resides in God in a simple, unchanging and infinite way, so that it is not on account of some quality* that God is powerful, but by himself. He does not obtain his power from another but from himself; it is not a passive power, but as "working within," *energoumenē* (Ephesians 3:20). He does not start to be capable* of something that He had not been capable of previously, but what He is able He has been able from eternity (Romans 1:20). He also could not be capable of more, or less, but He can do all things which He can to do, and He performs his power upon whatever He wills to be, and that without labor or effort. But in this exercise of his power, He can do other things and in another way, more, greater and more excellent things or minor or less things. Therefore Scripture even deprives God of inability, but ascribes to Him power, strength, firmness and efficacy (1 Corinthians 1:25; Ephesians 1:19; 1 Timothy 6:15,16) and He is called powerful, only-powerful, and *'El Shadday*, or all-mighty (Genesis 17; Revelation 1:8).

Closely linked to these two attributes (namely, the life of the knowing and willing God, and his power) is God's dominion: his strength, rule, and authority over everything outside of himself that He is able and willing to do, and does. This dominion, too, is everlasting and unchangeable. Therefore He is called Lord, and Lord of Lords, God of gods, King of kings (1 Timothy 6:15), and He is said to have the most free and absolute power towards everything (Romans 9:21; Matthew 20:15) which is to be without master and in one's own power (*adespoton* and *autexousion*). And every dominion issues from Him and is established by Him (Romans 13:1).

God's good affections (which in human beings are the passions), and the virtues of his intellect and will (which in mortals are the ethical and moral qualities which designate regulation of the affections), are: truth, love, goodness, gentleness, charity, generosity, mercy, and long-suffering, anger, hatred, justice, and also holiness, etc., and are truly and properly said of God (of course with the removal of every imperfection from them); and they are nothing other than God's ardent will towards us, and its power and effect in creatures. These are classified by different names, according to the variety of things that are their

creaturis potentia et effectus, quae pro rerum objectarum diversitate, et agendi modis, effectisque variis, diversa nomina sortiuntur.

XL *Veritas* itaque seu veracitas est, qua Deus tum in verbis tum signis, tum operibus et factis, veritatem amat et adhibet, maxime vero in promissis fidem vult et potest praestare, Ps. 145, 13. Rom. 3, 3. 4. *Bonitas*, qua creaturis, bene velle ac bene facere, et potest, et vult, et facit, Exod. 33, 19. Rom. 2, 4. *Amor*, quo vult et approbat bonum in creaturis, in eoque acquiescit, ac sese indebite benignum et gratiosum praestare vult, potest, et praestat, quae relata* ad hominem φιλαντρωπία dicitur, Mal. 1, 2. 3. Tit. 3, 4. *Miseratio* et *Misericordia*, qua miseris succurrere vult, potest, et facit, Ps. 136, 1. etc. Exod. 34, 5. 6. 7. *Justitia*, qua juste omnia disponit, et justis praemia, injustis poenas decernit, et retribuere vult, et potenter facit, Ps. 11, 7. et 119, 137. et 145, 17. *Ira*, qua ad puniendum peccatorem propensus est, et peccatum ulcisci vult, potest et facit, Odium, quo peccatum et peccatorem aversatur, et malos constanter potest et vult a se rejicere. *Sanctitas* denique, qua in se purissimus omnem munditiem probat, et abhorret a contrario. Unde Deus dicitur in Scriptura verax, bonus, benignus, judex universi mundi, et justus judex, etc. imo solus verax, bonus, sanctus, Apoc. 4, 7. Rom. 3, 4. Mat. 19, 17. etc, et ita de reliquis, omnisque veritatis, bonitatis, justitiae ac sanctitatis fons est.

XLI Ut porro haec Deo vere attribuuntur, ita et vitia virtutibus hisce contraria a Deo removentur, ut mendacium, injustitia, reliquaque, Num. 23, 19. 2 Chr. 19, 7. Rom. 9, 14. Unde et ἀψευδὴς, mentiri nescius, ἀπείραστος κακῶν, qui malis tentari nequit, dicitur, et injustus esse negatur, Tit. 1, 2. Jac. 1, 13. Rom. 3, 5. Etiam

6. ABOUT THE NATURE OF GOD AND HIS DIVINE ATTRIBUTES

object, and according to the ways in which they are performed, and their various effects.[30]

Truth, or veracity, is the virtue whereby God both in words and signs, in works and deeds, loves and exercises the truth—but most of all the virtue whereby He is willing and able to show his trustworthiness in his promises (Psalm 145:13[17]; Romans 3:3,4).

Goodness is the virtue whereby He is able, willing and performing unto his creatures, both the acts of willing the good and doing the good (Exodus 33:19; Romans 2:4).

Love is whereby He wills and approves the good in created beings and He abides in it; He wills, is able to present, and actually presents himself kind and gracious (though He does not have to do so). When applied* to human being it is called philanthropy (Malachi 1:2,3; Titus 3:4).

Compassion and mercy are whereby He wills, is able to provide, and actually does provide help to those who are wretched (Psalm 136:1, etc.; Exodus 34:5,6,7).

Justice is the virtue whereby He deals with everything fairly, and whereby He decrees rewards for the upright, and punishment for the unjust, and whereby He wills to work retribution, and He does so powerfully (Psalm 11:7, 119:137, and 145:17).

Anger is whereby He is disposed to punish the sinner and wills, is able to avenge and actually does avenge the sin.

Hatred is whereby He abhors the sin as well as the sinner, and whereby He is able and willing consistently to cast the wicked away from himself.

Holiness, finally, is the virtue whereby He, being most pure, approves everything that is pure, and whereby He is repulsed by its opposite. For this reason in Scripture God is called truthful, good, kind, the judge of the whole world, and the just judge, etc.; in fact, the only one who is truthful, good, holy (Revelation 4:7; Romans 3:4; Matthew 19:17), etc. And so concerning all that remains, He is the source of all truth, good, justice, and holiness.

Moreover, just as these qualities rightly are attributed to God, so too the vices opposite to these virtues are far from God: falsehood, injustice, and the rest (Number 23:19; 2 Chronicles 19:7; Romans 9:14). Therefore He is also called: "The one who does not know how to lie" [*apseudēs*], "He who does not know how to be tempted by evils" [*apeirastos kakōn*], and the One "of whom is denied that He is unjust" (Titus 1:2; James 1:13; Romans 3:5). Even regret, fear, grief, hope

---

30   In their relation to creation, God's will and intellect are described as affections and virtues; these descriptions function as dispositions or conditions of the divine will and intellect. See *DLGTT*, s.v. "affectus voluntatis Dei."

poenitentia, metus, dolor, spes et desperatio, ceteraque ejusmodi in perfectam Dei naturam proprie non cadunt, Num. 23, 19.

XLII Quae denique de Deo dicuntur, atque perfectionem quidem in creaturis designant, non absolute,* sed cum modo creaturis proprio, ea Deo proprie* non competunt, sed propter similitudinem aliquam cum Deo, tropice et metaphorice dicuntur, ut sunt rerum inanimatarum, animatarum et maxime hominis nomina, partes, membra, proprietates et actiones, Ps. 94, 7. Quibus jungenda sunt quae Deus oeconomice* sibi propria facit, ut est corpus pro tempore assumptum, sermo, vox,* verbum* in aëre a se efformatum. Quae omnia ἀνθρωποπαθῶς de Deo dicuntur, et θεοπρεπῶς sunt intelligenda, et ad proprietates efficientiamque divinam significandam referenda sunt.

XLIII In istis porro omnibus divinis Attributis consistit Dei *Perfectio*, ut in quo nullus est defectus; *Excellentia* et *praestantia* super omnia, ut cui nihil est par vel simile; *Gloria* vel *Majestas*, cum interna, in proprietatibus suis, qua in se gloriosus est, Esai. 48, 11. tum externa in luce inaccessibili, Exod, 33, 18. 22. 1 Tim. 6, 16. atque *Beatitudo*, qua nullius indigus, et omnium bonorum complementum se ipso fruitur, et in se acquiescit, 1 Tim. 6, 15. Act. 17, 25. ideoque unice suscipiendus, benedicendus, honorandus, colendus, eique soli serviendum, adorandus, laudandus, invocandus et verbis factisque glorificandus est, Rom. 1, 21. Tit. 1, 16. Atque is divinae cognitionis finis et usus est.

XLIV Repugnant huic doctrinae, *Atheismus*, id est, negatio omnis Dei; πολυθεΐα, multitudo Deorum, sive plures Dei prorsus factitii statuantur, ut gentes faciebant, quas Paulus ἀθέους vocat, Eph. 2, 12. sive vero Deo falsi adjungantur, ut Israelitae; *Idolomania* gentium, et Judaeorum, qui idola in Deos efformabant, vel in iis colebant Deos, aut etiam Deum verum; *Phantasia de Deo*, id est, veri Dei quidem aliqua cognitio, at non talis, qualis ipse est et se verbo manifestavit, sed qualem quis imaginatur, ut olim Samaritani, (quorum cognitio ignorantia Dei dicitur, Joh. 4, 22.) ut et hodie Judaei et Mahumetani; denique

6. ABOUT THE NATURE OF GOD AND HIS DIVINE ATTRIBUTES

and desperation, and the likes are not found as befitting God's perfect nature (Numbers 23:19).

Finally, there are things predicated of God that actually denote perfection in created beings also (though not absolutely,* but in some fashion appropriate to creatures), which do not apply to God properly,* but because of some similarity to God they are expressed through figures of speech and metaphorically. Such are the names, parts, limbs, properties and actions of inanimate and animate things, and especially of man (Psalm 94:7[-9]). We may add to them the qualities which God in his dispensation* makes his own, like a physical body that He assumes for the occasion, or speech, a voice,* a word* He formed in the air. All of these are said of God in an anthropopathic way [*anthrōpopathōs*], but they must be understood in a way that is appropriate to God [*theoprepōs*] and taken as indicating the properties and workings of God.[31]

What is more, the perfection of God consists in all those divine attributes, as of one in whom there are no shortcomings. There is excellence and pre-eminence above all things, for nothing is similar or equal to Him. There is glory or majesty, whether inwardly in his personal properties, whereby He enjoys glory in himself (Isaiah 48:11), or outwardly, in unapproachable light (Exodus 33:18, 22; 1 Timothy 6:16). And there is blessedness in which He lacks nothing and enjoys in himself the fullness of all good things and abides in himself (1 Timothy 6:15; Acts 17:25). And we must acknowledge only Him, and we must bless, honour, worship, and serve only Him, and adore, praise, invoke, and glorify Him in words and deeds (Romans 1:21; Titus 1:16). This is actually the goal and purpose of knowing God.

Opposed to this teaching are the following:
- Atheism, that is the total denial of God.
- Polytheism [*polutheia*]), or the completely fabricated construction of many Gods, as was done by the gentiles, whom Paul calls "without God; godless" [*atheous*] (Ephesians 2:12), or by those who add false gods to the true God, as the Israelites did.
- The idol-worship of the gentiles, and the Jews, who used to shape idols into gods, or by means of them worshiped gods, or even the true God.
- Fantasizing about God, that is, although with some knowledge of the true God, yet not such as He really is and has revealed himself in his Word, but as someone imagines Him to be. Such the Samaritans once did (whose understanding is called ignorance of God, John 4:22), and nowadays the Jews and Mohammedans.

---

31   In Reformed scholastic doctrine, human-like qualities or passions, when ascribed to God, are understood in ways that are appropriate to God. See *PRRD* 3:555–559.

Epicureismus, id est, divinae praescientiae et providentiae negatio, quae et Dei re ipsa inficiatio est.

XLV Item inter Christianos quondam *haeresis Manichaea* de duobus principiis, bono et malo. *Anthropomorphitarum*, qui Deo corpoream figuram attribuerunt. *Pontificia* ἀποθέωσις sanctorum, *Idolomania* in imaginando et in imaginibus colendo Deo sanctisque. Eorum qui alium nobis Deum fingunt, quam suo verbo revelavit. Omnes denique de Deo *blasphemiae* et opiniones falsae vitaeque improbitas; quae et ipsa Dei negatio dicitur, Tit. 1, 16.

6. ABOUT THE NATURE OF GOD AND HIS DIVINE ATTRIBUTES

– And finally, Epicureanism, that is, the denial of God's foreknowledge and providence, which essentially is the denial of God.[32]

Likewise among Christians in former times there was the Manichaeans' heresy of the two principles: good and bad. The heresy of the Anthropomorphists, who ascribed to God a physical body; the papist *apotheōsis* of the saints. The worship of idols by the making of images and by worshiping God and the saints by means of images. And the heresy of those who make up a god different from the one He has revealed in his Word. Lastly, all blasphemies and false claims about God; and a crooked lifestyle—which itself is also called the denial of God (Titus 1:16).

---

32 See also *SPT* 11.4 for the claim that the denial of God's providence entails the denial of God as such.

DISPUTATIO VII

De Sacrosancta Trinitate

Praeside D. JOHANNE POLYANDRO
Respondente TOBIA DAMMANNO

THESIS I   Quemadmodum fides Christiana Deum unum in Trinitate, sic personarum Trinitatem in essentiae divinae unitate veneratur.

II   De hac personarum divinarum Trinitate disputaturi, primum voces, deinde rem* ipsam examinabimus.

III   Vox* personae* apud Latinos, ut τοῦ προσώπου apud Graecos, est aequivoca.* Interdum enim larvam et qualitatem* hominis, seu conditionem externam denotat, ut Act. 10, 34. interdum subsistentiam* ratione* praeditam, ut 2 Cor. 1, 11. Nos hanc vocem analogice* ad personas Trinitatis accommodantes, eam posteriori significatu* usurpamus.

IV   Quamvis vox Graeca, πρόσωπον, cui nomen* personae correspondet, non αὐτολεξεὶ, vel totidem syllabis in sacris literis inveniatur personis divinis attributa,* utrique tamen aequipollens exstat in Epistola ad Hebraeos, cap. 1, 3. ubi Christus vocatur ὁ χαρακτὴρ τῆς ὑποστάσεως τοῦ πατρὸς, id est, expressa imago subsistentiae Patris.

V   Idem de vocabulo Trinitatis asserimus. Hujus enim synonymum, ex lege conjugatorum, est tres. Numerus enim numerans in concreto et numerus numeratus in abstracto, sunt idem re ac significatione. Illum autem numerum Patri,

DISPUTATION 7

On the Holy Trinity

President: Johannes Polyander
Respondent: Tobias Dammanus[1]

Just as the Christian faith worships one God in Trinity, so too does it worship the Trinity of Persons in the unity of the divine essence.[2] 1

In setting out to present the argument about this Trinity of divine persons, we shall consider first the words and then the actual subject-matter.* 2

In Latin the word* "person,"* like *to prosōpon* in Greek, has a two-fold* meaning. For sometimes it stands for facial mask; a person's distinguishing features;* or countenance, as in Acts 10:34. At other times it means subsistence*[3] endowed with reason,* as in 2 Corinthians 1:11. Adjusting this word by means of analogy to the persons of the Trinity, it is with the latter meaning* that we employ it. 3

Although the Greek word *prosōpon*, to which the noun* "person" corresponds, when attributed* to the divine persons does not occur in the sacred writings in precisely these letters or with as many syllables, there is a word which is equivalent to each in the Epistle to the Hebrews, in chapter 1:3, where Christ is called "the expressed image of the subsistence of the Father." 4

We make the same claim for the term "Trinity." For its synonym, according to the linguistic rule for cognates, is "three." For the number that counts in a concrete sense and the number that is counted as an abstraction are exactly the same in fact and meaning. The apostle John allots that number to the Father, 5

---

1 Born in Ovezande (province of Zeeland) ca. 1599, Tobias Dammannus matriculated on 11 October 1619 in theology. He defended this disputation on 4 July 1620 and dedicated his defense to the authorities and the church at Zierikzee, to all who supported and sponsored him, to E. Maenius (Harderwijk pastor) and Joh. Pontanus and J. Hoeingius (both professor at Harderwijk university). He was ordained in Zonnemaire in 1621, Oosterland (province of Zeeland) in 1624, and Zierikzee in 1638; he died in 1640. See Du Rieu, *Album studiosorum*, 143, and Van Lieburg, *Repertorium*, 46.
2 This thesis alludes to Article Three of the Athanasian Creed. See Philip Schaff and David S. Schaff, eds., *The Greek and Latin Creeds*, vol. 2 of *The Creeds of Christendom* (reprint; Grand Rapids: Baker, 1996), 66.
3 "Subsistence" is a technical term used for the persons of the Trinity to indicate an individual instance of the divine essence. It is the "Latin equivalent of *hupostasis*" and a more "philosophically adequate term than *persona* for indicating the Father, Son, and Spirit in the Trinity." See "modus subsistendi" and "subsistentia" in DLGTT.

Sermoni seu Filio, et Spiritui Sancto Apostolus Johannes assignat. 1 Epist. 5, 7. cum ait: hos tres in coelo testificari.

VI Quocirca sicut iis, qui sunt decem, decas, sic tribus, Trinitas ascribi potest: et sicuti Apostolus ex voce Deus, Deitatem, Col. 2, 2. sic Patres Orthodoxi ex dictione tres, Trinitatem recte deduxerunt.

VII Etsi Patres Graeci posteriores οὐσίαν* et ὑπόστασιν* accurate distinxerint, illam absolutam* et communem, hanc singularem et relatam naturam nuncupantes: Latini tamen personae vocabulo propterea uti maluerunt, quod hypostasis proprie* sumpta, aequivoce substantiae primae et secundae, rationali et irrationali, persona vero, substantiae tantum primae ac rationali attribui possit.

VIII Persona in genere* definitur, quod sit substantia,* vel natura* individua, intelligens, per se subsistens, ac proprietate sua incommunicabili, ab aliis vere ac realiter distincta.

IX Haec definitio ad quamlibet Sacrosanctae Trinitatis personam adaptata, sic restringitur, quod sit substantia divina intelligens, per se subsistens, proprietate sua incommunicabili,* a ceteris, ad quas refertur, realiter distincta, eandem ac totam essentiam* divinam in se habens ab aeterno.

X In qua definitione quinque ponderanda sunt. Quorum primum est, quod sit substantia, peculiari quodam subsistendi modo, quem Graeci τρόπον ὑπάρξεως vocant. insignita ac circumscripta.

7. ON THE HOLY TRINITY

to the Word or the Son, and to the Holy Spirit (1 John 5:7), when he says: "These three bear witness in heaven."

For this reason, just as "decade" can be assigned to ten things, so "Trinity" may be assigned to three; and just as the Apostle construes the word "Deity" from "Deus" (Colossians 2:9),[4] so the orthodox church-fathers rightly construed "Trinity" from the word "three."

Although the later Greek church-fathers made a careful distinction between *ousia** [essence] and *hupostasis** [person] by using the former term for absolute* and shared nature, and the latter for a singular and relational nature, the Latins preferred to employ the term "person" on the grounds that *hupostasis*—understood in the strict* sense[5]—can be attributed equivocally to the first and to the second substance (both the rational and the irrational), while "person" can be attributed only to the first and rational substance.[6]

In general,* "person" is defined as a substance,* or individual nature,* endowed with intelligence, subsisting by itself, really and truly distinguished from others by its own incommunicable property.[7]

This definition, adjusted to any one person of the holy Trinity, is restricted in sense so that it is a divine substance endowed with intelligence, subsisting by itself, in reality distinguished by its own incommunicable* property from the others to which it relates, and possessing in itself the same and entire divine essence* from eternity.

In this definition there are five points which we should ponder. The first of them is that it is an [independent] substance, distinguished and circumscribed by some peculiar mode of subsisting, which the Greeks call "manner of existence."

---

4 The Greek word in Colossians 2:9 is θεότης, cognate with θεός.
5 Translated literally from Greek into Latin *hupo-stasis* becomes *sub-stantia*.
6 'Man' may signify a concrete, individual human being like John or Mary (first substance), or man in general, as a species (second substance). The distinction is made by Aristotle in *Categories* 5, 2a11–18.
7 Polyander combines the classic definitions of 'person' by Boethius, "individual substance of a rational nature," and by Richard of St. Victor, "an incommunicable existence of a nature." As applied to the divine persons, "incommunicable property" refers to the intra-trinitarian sense that contrasts the divine attributes, such as eternity, power, and wisdom, which the three Persons have in common, with the personal, exclusive characteristics of each of the three Persons of the Trinity, which by definition they do not have in common. For further explanation of these personal characteristics, see theses 21–25 below. For Richard of St. Victor's contribution to the doctrine of the Trinity, see Nico den Bok, *Communicating the Most High: A Systematic Study of Person and Trinity in the Theology of Richard of St. Victor* († 1173), Bibliotheca Victoriana, vol. 7 (Paris: Brepols, 1996), esp. 203–242.

XI Differt ergo persona seu subsistentia divina, a Dei essentia, tamquam angustius et determinatum,* ab eo quod latius patet atque indeterminatum est.

XII Nequaquam tamen arbitramur, personam seu subsistentiam in hoc mysterio esse instar substantiae primae, essentiam instar substantiae secundae. Ipsa etenim Dei essentia est maxime unica, individua ac singularis, ideoque de tribus personis tamquam species* de individuis nullo modo dici potest.*

XIII Neque asserendum putamus, essentiam Dei tribus personis divinis, tamquam totum quoddam, communicari, aut personas in ea, tamquam partes in toto sibi communicato, subsistere. Nam cum essentia Dei sit infinita, ac prorsus impartibilis, non potest illa de personis divinis, ut totum de suis partibus, praedicari.*

XIV Modus* ergo hujus mysterii, ut rationi humanae inexplicabilis, humili potius fide adorandus, quam periculosis locutionibus definiendus est.

XV Porro subsistentiam, tam Filio et Spiritui Sancto, quam Patri esse ascribendam, ex eo colligi potest, quod et nomina, et actiones, quae sunt suppositorum,* illis attribuantur.

XVI Nam Domini epitheto, quod est personae subsistentis, non tantum Pater et Filius, sed et Spiritus Sanctus in Sacris Bibliis insignitur, ut patet ex horum duorum locorum parallelorum collatione, Esai. 6, 8. et Act. 28, 25. Nomina vero Patris, Filii et Spiritus Sancti non nisi personarum subsistentium sunt, Matth. 28, 19.

XVII Actiones personales* sunt, alicui apparere, suoque mandato certum munus injungere, semen Abrahae assumere, speciem columbae induere; quorum primum Esai. 6, 8. descriptum, et Filio, Joh. 12, 14. et Spiritui Sancto Act. 28, 25. alterum soli Filio, Heb. 2, 16. tertium soli Spiritui Sancto assignatur, Matth. 3, 16.

7. ON THE HOLY TRINITY

A divine person or subsistence differs from the essence of God as something narrower and determinate* than that which stretches out more broadly and is indeterminate.

However, it is not at all our view that a person or subsistence in this mystery amounts to the same as the first substance, or that the essence amounts to the same as the second substance. For the very essence of God is, in the highest possible degree, unique, individual, and singular, and therefore it can* in no way be said of the three persons as a species* is said of individuals.⁸

And we think that one cannot state that the essence of God is imparted as something whole to the three divine persons, or that the persons exist in that essence like parts in a whole that they share. For since God's essence is infinite, and utterly incapable of being parted, it cannot be predicated* of the divine persons as a whole is of its parts.

Therefore, as it cannot be explained by human reason, the mode* of this mystery should be adored in humble faith, rather than be defined by risky statements.

Next, that subsistence must be ascribed to the Son and to the Holy Spirit as well as to the Father may be gathered from the fact that nouns as well as actions, which belong to self-subsistent individuals,* are attributed to them.⁹

For by means of the title, "Lord," which is appropriate to a subsistent person, Holy Scripture designates not only the Father and the Son, but also the Holy Spirit; this is evident from the comparison of these two parallel texts: Isaiah 6:8 and Acts 28:25. But the names of Father, Son, and Holy Spirit are only appropriate to subsistent persons (Matthew 28:19).

Personal* actions are: to appear before someone, to charge a certain duty by one's command, to assume the seed of Abraham, to take on the appearance of a dove. The first of these—depicted in Isaiah 6:8—is assigned both to the Son (John 12:14) and to the Holy Spirit (Acts 28:25); the second is assigned only to the Son (Hebrews 2:16); the third only to the Holy Spirit (Matthew 3:16).

---

8 In thesis 7 the strict analogy of the twofold sense of 'man' as individual in the first substance and as species in the second substance breaks down when applied to the persons and essence of God, since the divine essence, when considered as a whole, is itself individual and singular.

9 It is a classic dictum of scholasticism to state that "actions belong to supposits or self-subsistent individuals." Only first substances act, not second substances.

XVIII   Secundum, quod in personae divinae descriptione posuimus, est, eam esse intelligentem ac proinde volentem. Id Patri, Filio et Spiritui Sancto aequaliter convenire, hinc liquet, quod Filius et Spiritus Sanctus iisdem sapientiae, scientiae, veritatis, consilii ac beneplaciti elogiis, quibus Pater, in sacro codice passim ornentur, ut Prov. 8. Es. 12, 2. Joh. 14, 17. 1 Cor. 12, 11. etc.

XIX   Tertium in personae divinae definitione notandum est, eam proprietate incommunicabili ab aliis personis, ad quas refertur, realiter esse distinctam. Quod de qualibet Trinitatis persona vere dici, relativa nomina Patris, Filii et Spiritus Sancti declarant.

XX   Quamquam enim divinae personae ab humanis in eo differunt, quod harum una non sit in altera, illae vero sint ἐνυπόστατοι, id est, in se invicem exsistentes, teste Christo, Joh. 14, 11. Credite mihi, me in Patre et Patrem in me esse, non sola tamen ratione, sed re ipsa inter se sunt distinctae, ut una earum non sit altera, nec esse possit.

XXI   Notae quibus hae personae divinae inter se distinguuntur, aut sunt internae, aut externae. Illae ex tribus diversis proprietatibus characteristicis, opera earum ad intra* connotantibus, cognoscuntur.

XXII   Harum proprietatum prima est, quod Pater ingenitus, Filium ejusdem essentiae communicatione ab aeterno genuerit. Quam Patris proprietatem, Graeci ἀγεννησίαν, nos minus apte innascibilitatem appellamus.

XXIII   Secunda est, quod Filius a Patre genitus, eandem cum Patre essentiam participaverit. Quam secundae personae proprietatem, Graeci γενέσεως, nos nativitatis nomine exprimimus.

7. ON THE HOLY TRINITY

18   The second point we make in a description of the divine person is that it possesses intelligence and, consequently, volition. It is evident that this applies equally to the Father, the Son, and the Holy Spirit from the fact that everywhere in the holy Book the Son and the Holy Spirit are awarded the same descriptions of wisdom, knowledge, truth, counsel and goodwill as the Father is, as in Proverbs 8; Isaiah 12:2; John 14:17; 1 Corinthians 12:11, etc.

19   The third thing that should be noted in the definition of the divine person is that the person is in reality, by his incommunicable property, distinct from the other persons to whom he relates. The relative names "Father," "Son," and "Holy Spirit" affirm that this is correctly said of any person of the Trinity.

20   For although the divine persons differ from human ones in that in the latter sort, one person does not exist within another, the former persons are enhypostatic;[10] that is, they exist mutually in one another, as Christ testifies (John 14:11): "Believe me, that I am in the Father and the Father is in me." They are, however, distinct from each other not only conceptually but also in reality, so that one of them is not the other, nor can he be.

21   The marks whereby these divine persons are distinguished from each other are either internal or external ones.[11] The internal* ones are recognized on the basis of three different characteristic properties, which connote their inward workings.

22   The first of these properties is that the unbegotten Father has generated the Son by the imparting of his own essence from eternity. The Greeks call this property of the Father "unbegottenness," and we, less fittingly, "incapable of being born."

23   The second is that the Son, begotten of the Father, participates in the same essence with the Father. The Greeks express this property of the second person with the word "birth," and we with "nativity."[12]

---

10   Enhypostatic: having one's subsistence in that of another; literally "personality within." The unity of essence is effected by the co-inherence of the persons. This is usually applied to the union of the dependent human nature with the independent divine nature in the person of Christ. In this case, it is applied to Father, Son, and Holy Spirit, subsisting in one another, in *circumincessio*. See *DLGTT*, s.v. "enhypostasis."

11   On the scholastic distinctions between *opera ad intra* 'the internal works' and *opera ad extra* 'the external works,' see *DLGTT* s.v. "opera Dei ad extra" and "opera Dei ad intra." Cf. *PRRD* 4: 255–274.

12   The statements of theses 22 and 23 are elaborated in disputation 8 "Concerning the Person of the Father and of the Son."

XXIV   Tertia est, quod Spiritus Sanctus a Patre et Filio emanet. Quam Spiritus Sanctus proprietatem, Graeci ἐκπόρευσιν, nos processionem* nominamus.

XXV   His tribus proprietatibus characteristicis, internas actiones personales connotantibus, tres personae Trinitatis non tantum inter se interno discrimine distinguuntur, sed etiam mutua relatione* quasi invicem opponuntur, nimirum, Pater gignens, Filio genito, et uterque spirans, uni spirato,* ac vice versa.

XXVI   Notae externae ex quibus earundem personarum distinctio animadvertitur, sunt operationes ad extra; quae partim sunt essentiales,* quatenus a totius essentiae,* tribus personis aequaliter communis,* principio* proficiscuntur; partim personales, aut quatenus ordo personarum agentium in iis consideratur, ut creatio, quae ordinis respectu Patri, tamquam primae personae, κατ' ἐξοχὴν attribuitur, aut quatenus sapientiae divinae οἰκονομία seu dispensatio* singularis in iis spectatur: cujus respectu missio Filii ad Redemptionem Patri, Redemptio Filio incarnato, ac Sanctificatio Spiritui Sancto peculiariter ascribitur.

XXVII   Quartum quod in personae divinae delineatione observavimus, est, quod eandem ac totam essentiam in se habeat. Quod divinae personae quarto modo proprium est; quo differt ab humana persona, quae totam quidem specie,* sed separatam individuo, humanam naturam occupat.

The third is that the Holy Spirit flows forth from the Father and the Son. The Greeks call this property of the Holy Spirit "the proceeding," and we "procession."*¹³

With these three characteristic properties, which connote internal personal actions, the three persons of the Trinity are distinguished from each other not only by an internal distinction, but also by a mutual relation* as if they are opposed to one another, namely the Father who generates, over against the Son who is generated, and both of them spirate*,¹⁴ as distinct from the one who is spirated, and vice versa.

The outward marks whereby the distinction between these persons is noted are their outward workings; in part these workings belong to the essence,* insofar as they go out from the principle* of the whole essence,* which is equally common* to the three persons. In part they are personal, either insofar as one considers in them the order of the acting persons—like creation, which, regarding the order, is attributed pre-eminently to the Father (as the first person) or insofar as one sees in them the particular administration or dispensation* of divine wisdom, regarding which the sending of the Son for the work of redemption is ascribed in particular to the Father, the redemption to the incarnate Son, and sanctification to the Holy Spirit.

The fourth observation we make in delineating the divine person is that He possesses the same and entire essence in himself. This is proper to the divine person in the fourth mode;¹⁵ and hereby He differs from a human person, who possesses the entire human nature with regard to the species,* but a separate human nature with regard to the individual.

---

13   See also Disputation 9 "On the Person of the Holy Spirit."
14   Spirating is the internal, eternal activity of the Father and the Son by which they bring forth the Holy Spirit. See *SPT* 9.3,4, 9–13.
15   The expression *proprium quarto modo* stems from William of Ockham's textbook on logic *Summa Logicae* (1.24), written around 1323. He distinguishes four senses or modes of the word *proprium* (property). In the first sense it is a property that belongs only to the members of one species but not to all, e.g., 'being a grammarian' is said only of humans but not of all of them. In the second sense a property belongs to all members of a species, but not only to them, e.g., 'biped' as a property of all humans, but also of other animals. In the third sense, it belongs to all the members of a species and only to them, but not always, e.g., 'turning grey' belongs only to old humans. The strictest, fourth sense of the word refers to a property that always and only belongs to all members of one species, e.g., 'being able to laugh' is a universal and exclusive human property. *Ockham's Theory of Terms: Part I of the Summa Logicae*, trans. and intro. Michael J. Loux (Notre Dame: University of Notre Dame Press, 1974), 100–101.

xxviii Non ergo essentia est aliquid re ipsa a persona abstractum, aut separatum, sed τῷ λόγῳ seu ratione* tantum ab ea distinctum. Modus* enim subsistendi, non realiter personam ab essentia dividit, sed ratione ac notione tantum discernit.

xxix Hinc quaelibet persona divina totus ac perfectus Deus, tam in Vetere, quam in Novo Testamento, tum subjective, tum attributive, vocatur, Gen. 1, 1. Rom. 9, 5. Act. 5, 4. et 20, 28.

xxx Ultimum quod personae divinae tribuimus, est quod tota essentia divina in ea sit ab aeterno.

xxxi Non igitur una persona divina certo aliquo tempore ab alia orta est, ut quaelibet humana, sed per sempiternam unius ejusdemque essentiae aeternae communionem cum altera semper exsistit.

xxxii Unde essentia unius personae est alterius essentia, et quicquid de Deo communiter dicitur, de qualibet etiam Trinitatis persona singulariter pronuntiatur, quod nimirum sit simplicissima, infinita, aeterna, immutabilis,* intelligens, misericors, justa, bona, sancta, omnipotens, etc.

xxxiii Haec divinarum personarum Trinitas, non ut essentiae Dei unitas, ex naturae, sed ex solius Scripturae documentis demonstrari* potest.

xxxiv Liber enim naturae viam ostendit rationi humanae a creaturis ad Deum creatorem, tamquam ab effectis ad causam* entium primam atque universalem assurgendi, Rom. 1, 19. 20.

xxxv Liber autem Scripturae, sola Spiritus Sancti revelatione supernaturali,* fidem Christianam ad magnum illud pietatis arcanum de uno Deo, personis Trino, deducit, quod nec ratione comprehendi, nec sensu percipi, nec lingua exprimi, nec experientia doceri, nec exemplo declarari potest.

7. ON THE HOLY TRINITY

28 Therefore the essence is not something that in reality is abstracted or separated from the person, but it is distinguished from it only conceptually.* For the mode* of subsistence does not in reality divide the person from the essence, but it differentiates them only conceptually and notionally.[16]

29 Hence each one of the divine persons is called the entire, complete God, in the Old Testament as well as in the New Testament, in terms of being a subject and its attributes (Genesis 1:1; Acts 5:4 and 20:28).

30 The last thing we attribute to the divine persons is that the entire divine essence exists in it from eternity.

31 Therefore, one divine person has not arisen from another person at some specific point in time, as is the case with each and every human person, but He has always been in existence through an eternal sharing of the one and the same eternal essence with the other person.

32 Hence the essence of the one person is the essence of the other, and whatever is said about God collectively is declared also about any person of the Trinity individually, namely that He is most simple, infinite, eternal, immutable,* endowed with intelligence, tenderhearted, just, good, holy, omnipotent, etc.[17]

33 This Trinity of divine persons cannot, unlike the unity of the essence of God, be demonstrated* from documented proofs in nature, but from what we can learn from Scripture alone.

34 For the book of nature shows to our human reason how the route rises up from created beings to God the Creator, as from effects to the prime and universal cause* of beings (Romans 1:19, 20).

35 The book of Scripture, however, by the supernatural* revelation of the Holy Spirit alone, conducts the Christian faith to that profound secret of piety about the one God who is threefold in persons—which cannot be comprehended by reasoning, nor be perceived by senses, nor be expressed in words, nor be taught by experience, nor be explained by an example.

---

16 The scholastics distinguish five so-called 'notions' in Trinitarian theology. These are innascibility (the condition of not being born), paternity, sonship, active and passive spiration. See, for example, Bonaventure, *Breviloquium*, I.3.5, and Thomas Aquinas, *Summa theologiae*, 1.28.4. These notions, applied to the respective persons of the Trinity, describe the individual subsistence of each, and mark the only 'difference' between the three. Cf. *PRRD* 4:187, and see note 16 at *SPT* 6.21 for an explanation of the different types of distinctions.

17 The statement that what is predicated of God collectively is also predicated of each person of the Trinity connects this thesis to disputation 6, "About the Nature of God and his Divine Attributes." Cf. *SPT* 6.12.

XXXVI Quae a Mercurio Trismegisto in libro qui inscribitur *Pimander*, Dial. 4.[a] dicuntur Monadem genuisse Monadem, et suum in se ardorem reflexisse, adeo sunt obscura et ambigua, ut in diversos sensus trahi possint, ac potius de alia ab uno Deo propter sui ipsius amorem productione, intelligenda videantur, quam de ea, quam nos credimus, unius Filii ab uno Patre generatione* et Spiritus Sanctus ab utroque processione.

XXXVII Quamvis enim nonnullae purioris Religionis* reliquiae, vel ex Hebraeorum traditione, vel ex Bibliorum lectione collectae, apud Mercurium illum Trismegistum,[b] Platonem[c] ipsorumque discipulos exstare videantur, non tamen ex iis ostendi potest, quod tres distinctas personas in una Deitate agnoverint, sed tres potius οὐσίας atque essentias diversas constituerint.

XXXVIII Hoc mysterium Trinitatis in Novo Testamento multo clarius, distinctius ac frequentius, quam in Vetere, traditur, quoniam scilicet Deo plenam ac perfectam hujus abstrusi mysterii patefactionem in Messiae adventum differre placuit.

XXXIX Interim loca nonnulla Veteris Testamenti producemus, ex quibus pluralitas atque adeo Trinitas personarum numero plurium adumbrata colligi potest. Quae ad 6 potissimum classes revocari possunt.

XL Prima classis est eorum locorum, in quibus Elohim cum Jehova conjungitur. In illis enim, Jehova unam essentiam, Elohim plures personas in ea distinctas indicat, maxime quod voci plurali Elohim adjectiva et verba singularia saepius adjungantur.

---

[a] Hermes Trismegistus, *Pimander* 4.10/11. [b] Hermes Trismegistus, *Pimander* 4.10/11. [c] Polyander most likely has in mind the Demiourgos of Plato's *Timaeus*. In Neoplatonism, especially Plotinus, there is indeed one god: the One. See Plotinus, *Enneads* 6.9 *passim*.

7. ON THE HOLY TRINITY

36 The things that are said by Hermes Trismegistus[18] in the Fourth Dialogue of the book entitled *Pimander* [IV.10.11], "that a Monad[19] begot a Monad, and reflected his own ardour in himself," are so vague and ambiguous, that they can be dragged into having various meanings. They appear to have to be understood, as being about a production from an only god on account of his love for himself, rather than about what we believe: the production of the one and only Son from the one Father by generation,* and of the Holy Spirit by procession from them both.

37 For although it appears that there are a few remnants of the purer Religion* (either gathered from the Jewish tradition or from a reading of the Bible-books) in the works of the aforementioned Hermes Trismegistus, and in Plato, and in their followers, it cannot be shown from them that they acknowledged three distinct persons in one Deity; rather they made up three *ousia's*, that is, different essences.

38 This mystery of the Trinity is handed down much more clearly, elegantly and frequently in the New Testament than in the Old, because surely God was pleased to delay the full and complete revelation of this profound mystery until the coming of the Messiah.

39 Meanwhile we shall bring out several passages of the Old Testament from which the plurality and even the Trinity of persons can be gathered as foreshadowed by a plural number. These passages can be gathered together into six groups.

40 The first group is of those passages in which *'Elohim* is joined with *Y^ehovah*. For in them *Y^ehovah* stands for a single essence, while *'Elohim* stands for many persons distinguished within the essence, especially because adjectives and verbs in the singular are very often connected to the plural noun *'Elohim*.

---

18   This thesis refers to the Fourth Dialogue of the book entitled *Pimander* (*Poimandres*) by Hermes Trismegistus. Hermes (*Trismegistos* means "the thrice greatest") is a fictitious, legendary figure, the Greek incarnation of his Egyptian counterpart, the god Thoth. According to Willis Barnstone, a modern translator of *Poimandres*, the dialogues belonging to the 'Hermetic Literature' describe the Greco-Roman system of gnosis. The *Corpus Hermeticum* dates to the first through the end of the third centuries. Poimandres is the speaker in a 'Socratic' dialogue proposing a dualistic view of life. See Willis Barnstone and Marvin Meyer, eds., *The Gnostic Bible* (London: Shambhala, 2003), and Anna Van den Kerchove, *La Voie d'Hermè: Pratiques, rituelles et traités hermétiques*, Nag Hammadi and Manichaean, vol. 77 (Leiden: Brill, 2012).

19   'Monad' is derived from the Greek word 'monas,' which means 'unity.' As a philosophical concept, it has its origin in the thought of Pythagoras and his school.

XLI Etsi vero *Elohim* interdum de una tantum Trinitatis persona enuntietur, ut Ps. 45, 7. non tamen id fit exclusive, sed inclusive per locutionem synecdochicam, qua, tum ob essentiae unitatem tribus personis communem,* tum ob personarum ἐμπεριχώρησιν, seu mutuam inexistentiam, sub unius personae denominatione, ceterae comprehenduntur.

XLII Secunda classis est locorum, in quibus Deus in plurali numero de semetipso proprie* loquitur, ut Gen. 1, 26. Faciamus hominem ad imaginem nostram, et Gen. 3, 22. Ecce Adam quasi unus ex nobis, et c. 2, 7. Dixit Deus, descendamus et confundamus linguam eorum, etc.

XLIII Cui simile exemplum ne in Regibus quidem ambitiosissimis ex Sacra Scriptura produci potest, sed e contrario ostendi, eos de se locutos fuisse in numero singulari, nimirum, ex Gen. c. 14. et 20. et 41. Dan. c. 2. et seqq. 2 Chron. 36. Esd. c. 1. 6. et 7.

XLIV Ceteros quod attinet, qui nobis a Judaeis objiciuntur, ex 2 Sam. 16, 20. Job. 15, 3. Dan. 2, 36. Cant. 1, 4. illos non de se solis proprie, sed etiam figurate de aliis, quorum personas repraesentabant, in plurali numero fuisse locutos, ex eorundem locorum circumstantiis probari* potest.

XLV Tertia classis est eorum, in quibus nomen Jehovae et Dei tribus distinctis vicibus in una sententia repetitur, ut Num. 6, 23. 24. 25. 26. Sic benedicetis filiis Israël: Benedicat tibi Jehova, et custodiat te; lucere faciat Jehova faciem suam ad te, et misereatur tui: et tollat Jehova faciem suam ad te, et donet tibi pacem.

XLVI Quarta est eorum, in quibus Deus tribus appellationibus sibi propriis ornatur, ut Es. 6, 3. Seraphim clamabant alter ad alterum: Sanctus, Sanctus, Sanctus Dominus Deus exercituum.

7. ON THE HOLY TRINITY

Yet although *'Elohim* occasionally is expressed for only one person of the Trinity (as in Psalm 45:7), nevertheless the title does not function exclusively, but inclusively through a synecdochical expression, whereby the other persons are included within the name of one person by metonymy[20]—sometimes on account of the unity of essence that is common* to the three persons, sometimes on account of the mutual interexistence of the persons [*emperichoresis*].[21]

41

The second group is of those passages in which God speaks specifically* about himself in the plural number, as in Genesis 1:26: "Let us make man in our own image," and Genesis 3:22: "Behold, Adam is like one of us," and chapter 11:7: "God said, 'let us go down and confuse their speech'," etc.

42

No example like this can be found in Holy Scripture even for those overly pretentious kings, but to the contrary, it can be shown that they spoke about themselves in the singular number, as is evident in Genesis chapter 14, 20, and 41; Daniel chapter 2 and following, 2 Chronicles 36; Ezra chapter 1, 6, and 7.[22]

43

As for the other kings whom the Jews cite in objection to us (2 Samuel 16:20, Job 15:3,[23] Daniel 2:36, Song of Solomon 1:4), it can be proven* from the circumstances in those passages that these kings were speaking not specifically about themselves only, but also figuratively about other people whose persons they were representing.

44

The third group is of those passages in which the name *Yᵉhovah* and "God" is repeated on three separate occasions in one sentence, as in Numbers 6:23, 24, 25, and 26: "Thus you shall bless the sons of Israel: *Yᵉhovah* bless you, and guard you; *Yᵉhovah* make his face to shine upon you, and be gracious towards you; *Yᵉhovah* lift up his countenance upon you, and give you peace."

45

The fourth group is of those in which God is adorned by three invocations appropriate to him, as in Isaiah 6:3: "And the Serafim were calling to one another: 'holy, holy, holy, the Lord God of hosts.'"

46

---

20 *Denominatio*: the Latin rhetorical term for metonymy, a figure of speech in which an attribute of something is used to stand for the thing itself. See Heinrich Lausberg, *Handbook of Literary Rhetoric: A Foundation for Literary Study*, ed. David E. Orton and R. Dean Anderson (Leiden: Brill, 1998), s.v. "denominatio," § 565.

21 *Emperichoresis*: the interrelation of the persons in their very subsistence. See DLGTT, s.v. "emperichoresis."

22 In other words: The plural forms do not indicate merely a 'royal we.'

23 Reference unclear; perhaps Job 15:18.

XLVII   Quinta est, in quibus Dominus de Domino loquitur, ut Ps. 110, 1. Dixit Dominus Domino meo: sede a dexteris meis. Ose. 1, 7. Sic dicit Dominus: Miserebor domus Judae, et salvabo eos in Domino Deo suo, etc.

XLVIII   Postrema classis est eorum, in quibus plures personae distincte et variis nominibus appellantur, utpote Jehova et Angelus Jehovae ac faciei Jehovae, Sapientia, Filius, Verbum* Jehovae ac Spiritus Jehovae, Genes. 48, 16. Exod. 14, 19 et 23. Ps. 2. Prov. 8. Esai. 63, 9. Agg. 2, 6, 8. etc.

XLIX   Novi Testamenti testimonia* legi possunt, Matt. 3, 16. 17. et 28, 19. Joh. 14, 16. et 15, 26. 2 Cor. 13, 13. 1 Joh 5, 7. Apoc. 1, 4. 5. et similia quam plurima Christiano ac pio lectori non ignota.

L   Ex superioribus assertionibus verbo divino consentaneis sequitur, falsam ac blasphemam esse omnium cum veterum, tum recentiorum Antitrinitariorum, ac hodie Socinianorum sententiam, qua statuunt, unam tantum esse personam divinam, Deum nempe, Patrem Domini nostri Jesu Christi; ad hujus confirmationem abutentes Sacrae Scripturae testimoniis prave intellectis, ut Joh. 17, 3. 1 Cor. 8, 6. Eph. 4, 6. et similibus, quibus Deus qui invocatur a Christianis, a falsis quos colunt Ethnici, hoc epitheto atque elogio tribus personis divinis communi discernitur, quod is sit solus verus Deus: ac proinde Pater, nec Filio, nec Spiritui Sancto, sed idolis exclusive opponitur.

The fifth is of those in which the Lord is talking about the Lord, as in Psalm 110:1: "The Lord said to my Lord: 'sit at my right hand'"; Hosea 1:7: "Thus says the Lord: 'I shall pity the house of Judah, and I shall save them by the Lord their God.'"

The last group is of those passages in which more persons are addressed separately and by different names, such as Y^{e}hovah and the Angel of Y^{e}hovah and of the face of Y^{e}hovah, Wisdom, the Son, the Word* of Y^{e}hovah, and the Spirit of Y^{e}hovah (Genesis 48:16; Exodus 14:19, and 23; Psalm 2; Proverbs 8 [:1, 12, 14]; Isaiah 63:9; Haggai 2:6, 8, etc.).

The proofs* from the New Testament can be read in Matthew 3:16, 17, and 28:19; John 14:16, and 15:26; 2 Corinthians 13:13; 1 John 5:7; Revelation 1:4,5, and very many similar passages that are not unfamiliar to the devout Christian reader.

From the above-mentioned assertions consistent with the divine Word it follows that the idea of all the Antitrinitarians (both the ancient as well as the more recent ones) is false and blasphemous, along with the opinion of the Socinians nowadays,[24] who hold that there is only one divine person, namely, God the Father of our Lord Jesus Christ. They abuse the testimonies of Holy Scripture (wrongly understood) in order to prove this, such as John 17:3, 1 Corinthians 8:6, Ephesians 4:6, and similar ones, wherein the God upon whom Christians call is separated from the false gods whom the gentiles worship by this epithet and expression that is common to the three divine persons: That He alone is true God. And it is for this reason that the Father is placed exclusively over against the idols, and not over against the Son or the Holy Spirit.

---

24 Socinianism dates to the sixteenth century and is named after Lelio and Fausto Sozzini (Laelius and Faustus Socinus). A statement begun at the end of Faustus's life later became the basis of the *Racovian Catechism*, first published in Polish in 1605, in German in 1608, with a first Latin edition in 1609, and in English in 1652. When interpreting Scripture, whatever is contrary to 'right reason' or involves a contradiction is to be rejected. The notion of the Trinity is therefore considered unscriptural and irrational since God is most emphatically one. See "Socinianism" in *The Dictionary of Historical Theology*, eds. Trevor A. Hart and Richard Bauckham (Grand Rapids: Eerdmans, 2000), 522–524. Cf. PRRD 4:78–79, 91–94.

DISPUTATIO VIII

De Persona Patris et Filii

Praeside D. ANTONIO WALAEO
Respondente ANTONIO SCRIVERIO

THESIS I Quum antecedenti disputatione de Sacrosancto Trinitatis mysterio generatim actum fuerit, ordo a nobis antea propositus postulat, ut de persona* Patris et Filii sigillatim agamus.

II Quando primam in Sacrosancta Trinitate personam Patrem nominamus, non referimus id ad creaturas, quae ex nihilo a Deo productae sunt; nec ad fideles, qui filii Dei adoptivi sunt, quorum respectu in Scripturis Deus etiam Pater nonnunquam vocatur; sed referimus ad Filium qui ab aeterno ab eo est genitus, et vocem* Patris ὑποστατικῶς seu personaliter usurpamus.

III Personam Patris vere personam esse, et a nulla persona originem habere, apud omnes Christianos in confesso est. Quum ergo a se ipso esse, et αὐτοφυὴς καὶ αυτογέννητος a nonnullis orthodoxis dicitur, id negative, non affirmative* est intelligendum; quia nempe a nullo est, sed a se ipso et per se ipsum ab omni aeternitate subsistit.

DISPUTATION 8

Concerning the Person of the Father and of the Son

President: Antonius Walaeus
Respondent: Antonius Scriverius[1]

As we treated the mystery of the holy Trinity in the preceding disputation, the previously established order requires that we deal now with the person* of the Father and the Son, separately.

When we call the first person in the most holy Trinity "Father," we do not refer to created beings, which have been produced by God out of nothing.[2] Nor do we use it as referring to believers whom God has adopted as his children, and whose God the Sriptures sometimes indeed do call "Father." But we use it in relation to the Son who was begotten by Him from eternity, and we employ the term* "Father" in a hypostatical[3] or personal way.

It is generally acknowledged by all Christians that the person of the Father truly is a person, and that his origin comes from no other person. Therefore when it is stated that He comes from himself, and He is called "self-grown and self-generated" by some orthodox teachers, it must be taken in a negative sense, and not as a positive affirmation.*[4] For without a doubt He comes from no-one, but He is in subsistence from himself and through himself from all eternity.

---

1 Born ca. 1593, Antonius Scriverius matriculated on 26 July 1616 in theology. He defended this disputation on 26 September 1620 and dedicated his defense to Polyander, Hommius and to D. Castellanus, pastor of the Leiden Walloon church. He was ordained in Hilversum in 1622; he died in 1667. See Du Rieu, *Album studiosorum*, 126, and Van Lieburg, *Repertorium*, 125.
2 This sentence reveals that the key terms of the doctrine of the Trinity do not focus on what is true in the natural world, and they are not related to God's work of creation. The classic doctrine of the Trinity moves on the level of what is essential for God, as ontologically distinct from created reality.
3 On the meaning and use of "hypostatic," see note at *SPT* 7.7.
4 The distinction between a 'negative' and a 'positive' or 'affirmative' sense in which a term can be used belongs to standard scholastic language. A term can be fully, positively affirmed; for example, an 'autodidact' has literally taught himself. Or a term can be used not to affirm a positive quality but to deny that the opposite is the case. The latter applies to the terms *a se ipso*, *autophuēs*, and *autogennētos*: they do not indicate that the Father originates or grows or is generated from himself (which would bring a duality of cause and effect in God), but merely in a negative sense that there is no source or cause of his existence at all.

IV Deitatem quoque ejus veram et aeternam nemo Christianorum in dubium vocavit; nisi quod Marcionitae et similes, alium Deum creatorem et Veteris Testamenti auctorem; alium vero Patrem Jesu Christi et Novi Testamenti conditorem, blaspheme, contra universae Sacrae Scripturae consensum, imaginati sunt; quae unum Deum Patrem nobis ubique proponit, et eundem quoque Patrem esse Jesu Christi et Novi Testamenti conditorem, constanter testatur, nominatim vero Christus ipse, Matt. 11, 25. et Joh. 8, 54. item Apostoli, Act. 8, 14. Gal. 3, 17. Hebr. 8, 8. etc.

V Patrem autem primam personam esse dicimus; tum respectu subsistentiae* ejus, quae a nulla alia persona est, et a qua reliquae suam originem habent; tum respectu operationum divinarum quae ad extra sunt, et ab eo tamquam a primo fonte per Filium et Spiritum Sanctum derivantur; tum denique respectu ordinis quem Sacra Scriptura passim usurpat, imprimis vero in formula Baptismi nostri, Matt. 28.

VI Proprietas vero characteristica et interna Patris, qua a Filio et Spiritu Sancto ὑποστατικῶς distinguitur, est *generatio activa*. Etsi enim et *Spiratio* * *activa* Patri conveniat, ea tamen ejus characteristica proprietas non est, quia ei cum Filio est communis.

VII Est vero haec *activa generatio*,* interna et personalis* Dei Patris actio, qua spirituali et ineffabili modo Filium suum, ut imaginem suam, ab aeterno ex sese in eadem essentia* genuit, et eandem infinitam essentiam totam, per eandem generationem, ei communicavit. Cujus definitionis singula membra nobis diligentius explicanda sunt et probanda.*

8. CONCERNING THE PERSON OF THE FATHER AND OF THE SON

4 And no Christian has called into question his true and eternal Deity, except that the Marcionites[5] and those like them have sacrilegiously fantasized that one God is the creator, and the author of the Old Testament, but another God is the Father of Jesus Christ and the originator of the New Testament. This is contrary to the consensus of the entire Holy Scripture, which everywhere presents one God the Father to us, and consistently provides evidence that the same person is also the Father of Jesus Christ and author of the New Testament, in particular Christ himself (Matthew 11:25; John 8:54) and also the apostles (Acts 8:14; Galatians 3:17; Hebrews 8:8, etc.).

5 Moreover, we say that the Father is the first person; firstly regarding his subsistence,* which comes from no other person, and from which the other persons have their own origin. We say this secondly regarding the divine operations that are outwardly directed, and that derive from Him as if from a fountain-head through the Son and the Holy Spirit. And we say this thirdly regarding the order which the Holy Scripture employs it everywhere, most notably in the formula for our baptism (Matthew 28:[19]).

6 And the property characteristic and internal to the Father, whereby He is distinguished from the Son and the Holy Spirit hypostatically, is active generation.[6] For though active spiration* also applies to the Father, nevertheless that property is not a characteristic of Him, because He shares it with the Son.

7 Well then, this active generation* is the internal and personal* action of God the Father, whereby in a spiritual and indescribable manner He has, from eternity and from himself, begotten his own Son in the same essence,* as his own image, and through that generation He made Him share the same infinite essence entirely. We should explain and prove* the individual elements of this definition more carefully.

---

5   Marcion (c. AD 85–160) was born in Sinope of Pontus in northeast Asia. His work is only known through citation by the early church fathers, most notably Tertullian. Marcion's thought was based on three principles: the good as the supreme God, the just Demiurge or creator God, and matter as the evil principle. Marcion rejected the Old Testament as merely the scripture of the Demiurge, and retained only the Gospel of Luke and the Pauline Epistles as testimony of the good Father of Jesus Christ. His thought presented a challenge for the early church. The Marcionite movement can be seen as a radical spiritualization of the Christian faith.

6   The term 'active generation' is used in contrast with 'passive generation' in order to indicate the correlative personal characteristics of the Father and the Son respectively. The Father generates or begets the Son (actively), whereas the Son is generated or begotten by the Father (passively). The same correlative structure is found in the relation of the Spirit to the Father and the Son: the Spirit is (passively) 'spirated'; the Father and the Son together (actively) 'spirate' the Spirit. The 'personal properties' are defined exclusively in terms of the personal relations of origin between the three divine Persons. See also *SPT* 7.21–25.

VIII Generationem hanc internam et personalem, Dei Patris actionem cum dicimus, opponimus eam creationi et gubernationi rerum, quae extra Deum et ejus essentiam occupantur; opponimus quoque internis et immanentibus Dei actionibus essentialibus,* qualis est praescientia rerum omnium aeterna, Act. 15, 18. aeterna nostri electio, Eph. 1, 4. πρόγνωσις seu praeordinatio aeterna agni illius pro nobis offerendi ultimis temporibus, 1 Pet. 1, 20. etc, quae actiones quidem immanentes* sunt et aeternae, sed essentiales et personis communes,* quia in creaturas vel earum saltem respectu exercentur; etsi agendi modus* peculiaris et proprius in eis quoque assignari possit.

IX Hujus generationis testimonia* plurima nobis suppeditantur a Scriptura, ut Ps. 2, 7. Filius meus es tu, ego hodie genui te. Prov. 8, 22. Jehova possidebat me in principio viae suae, et 24. Quum nullae essent abyssi, edita vel concepta eram. Mich. 5, 1. Ejus exortus inde a principio, a diebus seculi. Ideo vocatur Filius Dei unigenitus, et quidem unigenitus a Patre, Joh. 1, 14. item Filius Dei proprius, Rom. 8, 32. et πρωτότοκος πάσης κτίσεως, genitus ante omnem creaturam, Col. 1, 15. et Pater illius proprius Pater, Joh. 5, 18. Idem quoque indicant etsi figurate nomina Sapientiae, Verbi, Imaginis, χαρακτῆρος et ἀπαυγάσματος, quae ei Prov. 8. Joh. 1. Col. 1. et Heb. 1. tribuuntur, et ortum ejus ac genituram hanc perspicue indicant.

X Eadem testimonia aeternitatem quoque hujus generationis demonstrant, et multa praeterea alia, quae pro aeternitate subsistentiae ejus proferuntur; imo et ipsa hujus generationis natura id postulat. Nam cum ipsa non minus, quam ipse Deus Pater, omnis mutationis et vicissitudinis expers necessario statuenda sit, eam etiam omni temporis principio* carere omnino consequitur. Pater enim absque Filio cogitari non potest.*

XI Quemadmodum vero haec generatio omni temporis initio caret, ita etiam omni fine eam carere necessario fatendum est; cum aeternitatis vel praecipua proprietas sit, quod tota simul est et omnis finis* expers. Actu* ergo, quemad-

When we call this internal and personal generation the action of God the Father, we distinguish it from the creation and governance of things that are performed outside of God and his essence. We distinguish it also from the internal and immanent essential* actions of God, such as the eternal foreknowledge of all things (Acts 15:18), our election from eternity (Ephesians 1:4), the *prognōsis* or eternal pre-ordination of the Lamb that would be slain for us in the fullness of time (1 Peter 1:20, etc.). These actions, while immanent* and eternal, belong to the essence and are shared* by the persons, because they are carried out upon created beings, or at least with respect to them. Even so, in them one is able to assign a peculiar and proper mode* of action.[7]

We supply very many proof-texts*[8] of this generation from Scripture, such as Psalm 2:7: "You are my Son, today I have begotten you." Proverbs 8:22: "The Lord possessed me at the beginning of his way," and verse 24: "When there were no depths, I was brought forth" or conceived. Micah 5:1[= 2]: "His origin is from the beginning, from the days of eternity." For that reason the Son of God is called "only-begotten" and also "only-begotten of the Father" (John 1:14), and likewise "God's own Son" (Romans 8:32) and "begotten before all creation" (Colossians 1:15) and the Father is called "his own Father" (John 5:18). The same is shown, albeit figuratively—by the names that are given to Him: "Wisdom," "Word," "Image," "character," and "radiance" (Proverbs 8, John 1, Colossians 1, and Hebrews 1). These clearly show his origin and this offspring.

The same proof-texts show also the eternal nature of this generation, besides the many others that are produced to support the eternity of its subsistence. In fact, even the very nature of this generation requires it. For since we must posit that this generation, no less than God the Father himself, is necessarily devoid of all change and variation, it follows that it is wholly free from any beginning* in time. For it is impossible* to think of the Father apart from the Son.

But just as this generation lacks any starting-point in time, so too we must necessarily grant that it lacks any ending,* since the foremost property of eternity is that it is "all at once" and "free from any limit."[9] Therefore in the

---

7 See *SPT* 7.26. Both disputations 7 and 8 touch upon the distinction between the *ad intra* and *ad extra* dimensions of the doctrine of the Trinity, but they do not explicitly employ the classic notion of *appropriatio* (cf. *SPT* 10.12). For a more detailed discussion, see *SPT* 9.8–13, and cf. *PRRD* 4:257–274.

8 On the function of the so-called proof-texts and their rootedness in a detailed exegetical tradition, see *PRRD* 2:509–520.

9 This description of eternity combines the definition by Boethius, "eternity is the complete and simultaneously perfect possession of unending life" (*aeternitas est interminabilis vitae tota simul et perfecta possessio*), with an emphasis on the absence of limits. See also *SPT* 6.28, where the latter predominates.

modum omnis spiritualis generatio, perpetua est et effectu semper perfecta; sicuti sol perpetuo et indeficienter lucem suam producit, sine ullo ejus defectu vel augmento. Alioquin enim daretur Dei Patris generare incipientis, generantis, et generare desinentis mutatio. Unde et veteres non absurde locum illum, Ps. 2. Hodie genui te, de hoc aeterno et semper eodem generationis actu intellexerunt.

XII   Eandem generationem cum internam et spiritualem esse dicimus, opponimus geniturae corporum, in quibus res genita extra gignentem procedit; opponimus etiam opinionibus variorum haereticorum, qui effluxum, vel defluxum, vel partitionem aliquam divinae essentiae hic sunt imaginati. Demonstrat* hoc essentiae divinae in Patre et Filio identitas, quam paulo post invictis argumentis astruemus; item similitudines quae in hac materia a Sacra Scriptura proponuntur, quae Thesi 9. expressae sunt. Demonstrant denique clara Sacrae Scripturae loca, imprimis dicta Christi, Joh. 10, 30. ubi eandem suam et Patris potentiam* esse asserit, et versus 38. testatur, quod Pater sit in ipso, et ipse in Patre; et quod Pater in ipso μένων, manens haec opera faciat, Joh. 14, 10. quam ἐμπεριχώρησιν Graeci, Scholastici* vero mutuam circumincessionem nominarunt.

XIII   Ex his quae dicta sunt, facile solvitur illa Arrianorum Stropha, qua Patres antiquos olim intricare conati sunt; nempe an Pater suum Filium volens genuerit, an nolens. Nolentem genuisse dici non posse,* nec etiam volentem, quia voluntatis* actiones sunt liberae, ac proinde et non esse possunt. Responsio

act,* just as in all spiritual generation, it is continuous and in its outworking it is always perfect. In a similar fashion the sun produces its light constantly and unfailingly, without any weakening or strengthening. For otherwise there would be a change in God the Father when He begins to generate, is in the process of generating, and stops generating. Therefore also the ancients wisely understood the passage, Psalm 2 [:7]: "Today I have begotten you," as about this act of generation that is eternal and always the same.

When we say that this generation is internal and spiritual, we mean something different than the offspring of corporeal entities in which what is born issues forth outside the body of the one that is giving birth. We also mean something different from the opinions of various heretics who on this point have dreamt up some "flowing forth," "flowing down," or "some partitioning" of divine essence. This point is proved* by the identity of the divine essence in the Father and the Son, which we shall provide with irrefutable arguments a little farther below. Similar proof is in the comparisons supplied by Holy Scripture on this subject-matter; these are presented in thesis 9 above. And lastly, the point is proved by clear passages of Holy Scripture, especially the words of Christ in John 10:30, where He asserts that his power* is the same as that of the Father. And in verse 38 He testifies that the Father is in Him, and He in the Father; and "that the Father dwelling in Him does these works" (John 14:10), which the Greeks call *emperichōrēsis* [mutual interexistence],[10] and the Schoolmen, "mutual circumincession" [co-inherence].[11]

What has been stated here easily pulls apart the twisted ploy whereby the Arians once tried to entangle the ancient fathers. That is: Whether the Father begot his Son by willing so or by not willing so. And also that it cannot* be said that He who did not so will it, begot Him, and not even by so willing it, because the acts of the will* are free, and consequently it is possible that they are not.[12]

12

13

---

10   "Emperichoresis": mutual interexistence, or inexistence. "A term applied to the interpenetration of persons or hypostases of the Godhead, indicating the interrelation of the persons in their very subsistence" (*DLGTT*, s.v. "emperichoresis"; see also *PRRD* 4:185–186).

11   "Circumincession": coinherence. The term refers to the "coinherence of the persons of the Trinity in the divine essence and in each other" (*DLGTT*, s.v. "circumincessio").

12   The assumption of the dilemma in which the Arians attempted to force the 'ancient fathers' is that acts of the will are always free, in the sense that also the opposite is possible ("it is also possible that they are not the case"). In stating it in these terms, some decisive implications of the theory of will are brought forward. First, *willing* implies *being free*. However, Walaeus also states that *being free* implies the possibility that it is *not* the case, and precisely this is contingency. Therefore, second, *being free* implies *being contingent*. When applied to the relation of the Father to the Son it means that if the Son

enim vera et certa haec est, quod Deus Pater genuerit Filium suum natura; quemadmodum bonus, justus et sapiens est natura* sua, voluntate scilicet generationem hanc, sicut et bonitatem, justitiam, sapientiam ejus, semper comitante ac probante, non eam antecedente nec producente, unde et Filius εὐδοκίας, et ἀγάπης αὐτοῦ, Matth. 17, 5. et Col. 1, 13. appellatur.

XIV Quod vero Pater per generationem hanc aeternam Filio suo totam suam essentiam communicaverit, evincit aequalitas ejus cum Patre, Joh. 5, 18. ubi dicitur, quod se ipsum aequalem, nempe sermone suo, fecerit Deo, et Phil. 2, 6. quod non duxerit rapinam, aequalem vel parem esse cum Deo. Joh. 5, 20. Pater amat Filium, et omnia ostendit ipsi quae ipse facit, etc. sicut enim Pater suscitat mortuos et vivificat, sic et Filius quos vult, vivificat, etc, ut omnes honorent Filium, sicut honorant Patrem. Evincunt id etiam diserti alii loquendi modi, quos alibi usurpat Scriptura, ut Joh. 5, 26. Sicut Pater vitam habet in se ipso, sic Filio quoque dedit habere vitam in se ipso, et Joh. 10, 30. Ego et Pater unum sumus, nempe potentia, ac proinde et essentia divina, ut versus 33. ab ipsis Judaeis recte colligitur, et Joh. 16, 14. Ipse, nempe Spiritus Sanctus, me glorificabit, quia de meo accipiet, et renuntiabit vobis; omnia quae habet Pater, mea sunt; propterea dixi quod de meo accipiet, et renuntiabit vobis.

XV De modo seu forma hujus generationis veteres Patres adversus Arrianos et Samosatenianos olim quoque disputare sunt ausi, et plurimi inter eos, quos et Scholastici sunt secuti, statuerunt, Patrem genuisse Filium suum in eadem essentia, dum se ipsum in aeternitate atque infinitate* sua, ineffabili modo

---

is generated by the Father's willing it, the (free) will of God constitutes the generation, and the generation is thus a free act. If an act is free, it is *possible* that it is *not* the case: it is conceivable that the Father does *not* generate the Son (the opposite of what he in fact does). This contingency of the generation is rejected by Walaeus, because in the latter case the Father is possibly without the Son, and thus possibly not the Father, which would destroy the whole concept of the Trinity, because for Walaeus an eternal generation is a necessary generation. The second horn of the dilemma—the Father generates the Son *not willing so*—reduces the generation to a natural, necessitarian process of emanation, and renders the notions of 'generation' and 'action' obsolete. The "true and certain answer" provided by Walaeus rests on the insight that God is *willing* in all that he is and does. In connection with this other scholastics speak of God's *natural* will as distinct from his *free* will.

8. CONCERNING THE PERSON OF THE FATHER AND OF THE SON

For the true and certain answer is this: That God the Father begot his own Son by nature,* even as He is good, just, and wise by his nature. To be sure, his will always accompanied and approved this generation, as it does also his goodness, justice, and wisdom—but it did not precede or produce it. Hence also the Son is called the Son "of his pleasure" and "of his love" (Matthew 17:5; Colossians 1:13).

The equality of the Son with the Father proves definitively that the Father shared his entire essence with his Son through this eternal generation. In John 5:18 it says that "He had made himself equal"—that is, by what he himself said—"to God"; and Philippians 2:6: "He did not consider being equal or on par with God something to be grasped." John 5:20[-23]: "The Father loves the Son and shows Him all that He himself is doing, etc., for just as the Father raises the dead and gives them life, so also the Son grants life to whom He wishes, etc., that all may honour the Son, even as they honour the Father." Other clear manners of expression, which Scripture employs elsewhere, prove this too, such as John 5:26: "Even as the Father has life in himself, so also He has granted the Son to have life in himself." And John 10:30: "I and the Father are one," namely, in power, and therefore also in divine essence, since in verse 33 it is rightly inferred by the Jews themselves. And John 16:14: "He himself"—namely the Holy Spirit—"will glorify me, for He will take what is mine, and He will declare it to you. All that the Father has is mine; therefore I said that He will take from what is mine and declare it to you."

14

Concerning the manner or shape of this generation the ancient church-fathers long ago ventured to debate the Arians and Samosatenians,[13] and many among them (whom also the Schoolmen followed), stated that the Father had begotten his Son in the same essence, since He knows and beholds himself fully and perfectly in his eternity and infinity* in a way that cannot be explained. And in the same manner as our soul ponders and knows itself through

15

---

13   See also *SPT* 19.30. The Samosatenians were followers of Paul of Samosata (AD 200–275), bishop of Antioch from 260–272 who denied that Jesus was eternal God. Through his pupil Lucian he influenced Arius considerably. The name 'new Samosatenians' was given to a sixteenth century group of Anabaptists who followed the unitarian Giovanni Valentino Gentile (1520–1566). He was tried at Geneva in 1566 and sentenced to beheading, but he recanted. He was executed in 1566 at Bern, on the insistence of Heinrich Bullinger and Theodore Beza. The heresy of the 'new Samosatenians' was rejected by Josias Simmler of Zürich in chapter v of his *De aeterno Dei Filio Domino et Servatore Nostro Iesu Christo* (...) (Zürich: Christoph Froschauer, 1568). Rivetus, who may have learned the views of this sect during his study at Bern, accuses them in this disputation of giving divine honour to Christ despite the fact that they denied he is God.

perfecte ac plene cognoscit atque intuetur; et sicuti mens nostra, quum se ipsam per reflexionem cogitat atque intelligit, imaginem aliquam sui ipsius, etsi nec perfectam nec distincte subsistentem, in sese efformat: sic Deum Patrem, quum se ipsum eminentissimo ac divino, eoque ineffabili modo intelligit, perfectissimam et distincte subsistentem sui imaginem in se produxisse, et aeternum producere; quemadmodum per reciprocum Patris ac Filii amorem, Spiritum Sanctum ab utroque procedere senserunt.

xvi Unde quoque duplex discrimen, inter generationem Filii et Spiritus Sancti productionem, observarunt: 1. quod in vera generatione unum activum principium* tantum requiratur, in productione vero Spiritus Sancti duae personae inter se conspirent; 2. quod ad veram generationem requiratur similitudo seu imago ejus qui producit, in eo qui producitur; imago autem haec in actione illa intellectus, non in actione naturali* voluntatis reperitur.

xvii Hunc productionis modum collegerunt ex analogia* humanae mentis, quae imaginem Dei prae ceteris omnibus creaturis refert, et ex epithetis ac nominibus, quibus Sacra Scriptura Filium Dei peculiariter insignit: quando nempe eum appellat Dei sapientiam, Prov. 8. 1 Cor. 1, 24. λόγον seu verbum* Dei, Joh. 1, 1. ἀπαύγασμα gloriae ejus et characterem substantiae* ejus, Hebr. 1, 3. item imaginem Dei inconspicui, Col. 1, 15. etc, quae omnia mentem fidelem huc videntur tamquam manu ducere; etsi de Spiritu Sancto nomen* δυνάμεως potius, quam ἀγάπης usurpetur, Luc. 1, 35. Quia vero Sacra Scriptura illud tam perspicue ac distincte non asserit, nos fidelem ignorantiae professionem, temerariae assertioni praeferendam judicamus; et diem illum exspectare malumus, in quo de

reflection, and fashions in itself some image of itself (even though it is neither complete nor has a distinct existence), so too God the Father, since He knows himself in the most lofty and divine—and thus inexplicable—manner, has eternally produced and produces an image of himself that is most perfect, one that exists distinctly. They [the church-fathers] likewise perceived that the Holy Spirit, through the mutual love of the Father and the Son, proceeds from them both.[14]

From there they also noted the two-fold distinction between the generation of the Son and the production of the Holy Spirit. 1) That for a true generation only one active principle* is required, but in the production of the Holy Spirit two persons act in unison together.[15] 2) That for a true generation a likeness or image of him who is producing is required in him who is produced. This image, however, is found in the action of the intellect, not in the natural* action of the will.[16]

They gathered this manner of production from an analogy* to the mind of humans, who more so than all other creatures bear the image of God; and from the epithets and names whereby Holy Scripture denotes the Son of God in particular. Namely, when it calls Him the wisdom of God (Proverbs 8:1; 1 Corinthians 1:24), the Word, or the Word* of God (John 1:1), the brilliance of his glory and the stamp of his nature* (Hebrews 1:3), the image of the invisible God (Colossians 1:15). All of these texts seem, so to speak, to lead the believer's mind by the hand to this conclusion. Moreover, the word* "power" rather than "love" is used for the Holy Spirit (Luke 1:35). But because Holy Scripture does not make this claim so transparently and distinctly, we judge that an honest admission of ignorance is to be preferred to an all too daring assertion. And we

---

14 An influential explanation of the inner-trinitarian relations in terms of 'self-knowledge' and 'mutual self-love' occurs in Augustine, *De Trinitate* IX and XV.

15 The expression *inter se conspirent* ("act in unison") contains a pun upon *Spiritus* ("Spirit") in *conspiro* ("breathe together").

16 The argument stated in thesis 16 draws implicitly on John Duns Scotus's analysis of the Trinity in terms of two different 'principles of production' (*principia productionis*) in God: knowing (which generates the Son) and willing (from which the Spirit proceeds). The decisive structural difference between these two principles is that knowledge has a one-way, necessary relation to its object (cf. the term 'image' in the final clause of thesis 16), while the will is structurally free in relation to its objects. See further F. Wetter, *Die Trinitätslehre des Johannes Duns Scotus* (Münster: Aschendorff, 1967); Henri Veldhuis, "God is liefde: Over de voortbrenging van de Heilige Geest (*Lectura* I 10, q.1)," in *Geloof geeft te denken: Opstellen over de theologie van Johannes Duns Scotus*, eds. Andreas J. Beck and Henri Veldhuis, Scripta franciscana vol. 8 (Assen: Van Gorcum, 2005), 173–182.

facie ad faciem Deum sumus intuituri, atque illud quod hic ex parte cognoscimus, perfecte ac plene sumus cognituri.

XVIII   Ex fundamentis* antea propositis liquet, utrum Filius Dei recte dicatur αὐτόθεος, necne; quod in Calvino post maledicum illum Genebrardum[a] malitiose calumniantur quidam Jesuitae, excusante tamen ipsum Bellarmino.[b] Asserimus enim, Filium Dei, si Deitatem seu essentiam ejus absolute* spectes, et esse et recte vocari αὐτόθεον, quemadmodum a quibusdam Patribus eo respectu sic vocatur. Sin vero eandem essentiam consideres ut in Filio sub certo et distincto ὑπάρξεως τρόπῳ subsistentem, tum Deum esse de Deo et lumen de lumine, quemadmodum in Symbolo Niceno definitum est.

---

[a] Gilbert Génébrard, *De sancta trinitate libri tres contra huius aevi Trinitarios, Antitrinitarios, & Autotheanos* (Paris: Paris: Jean Bienné, 1569), 43–81.   [b] Bellarmine, *De Christo* 2.2.19 ("An Filius Dei sit autotheos"; *Opera* 1:333b–336a).

8. CONCERNING THE PERSON OF THE FATHER AND OF THE SON

prefer to await eagerly that day when we shall see God face to face, and when we shall know perfectly and fully what we know only in part here.

From the fundamental* observations that were put forth previously it is clear whether or not the Son of God is rightly called "God of himself."[17] Certain Jesuits, in line with that scurrilous Génébrard,[18] maliciously accused Calvin of holding the latter view, even though Bellarmine pleaded in his defense.[19] For we assert that, if one considers his deity or essence as absolute,* the Son of God rightly is and is called *autotheos*, as some of the church-fathers also called him in this regard. Yet, if you consider the same essence as existing in the Son under a certain and distinct mode of subsistence, then He is God of God, light of light, as defined in the Nicene Creed.

---

17   The question whether the term *autotheos* ("God of himself") applies to the Son of God caused an intricate debate. A brief exposition is given by PRRD 4:324–332. Of special interest to the *Synopsis* is Muller's reference to a debate in Leiden beginning in 1606 involving Jacob Arminius and Lucas Trelcatius Jr. (328–329).

18   Gilbert Génébrard (1535–1597), French Benedictine exegete and Orientalist, was Archbishop of Aix en Provence from 1592–1597. While most of his works are exegetical, including translations of rabbinic writings on the Old Testament, he also edited the works of Origen, and wrote a treatise *De Sancta Trinitate* (*On Holy Trinity*, Paris: Jean Bienné, 1569), which contains an attack on Calvin. After having discussed the 'Trinitarians' (tritheists) and 'anti-trinitarians' (unitarists), he identifies the *autotheani* as proponents of a new heresy, which he attempts to refute in a lengthy section, pages 43–81. His main target is Calvin (*Institutes*, 1.13.23–24; Preface to *Impietas Valentini Gentilis* [*The Godlessness of Valentino Gentile*]; *Brevis admonitio* [*Brief Warning*] addressed to the 'Polish brethren'), but also Theodore Beza and Nicolaus Gallasius. Génébrard argues that the assumption of a separate principle of deity for the Son and the Spirit amounts to accepting that there are "three Gods." He criticizes Calvin's reservations against the Nicene terms *Deum de Deo, Lumen de Lumine* ("God of God, light of light"). Génébrard's own position involves a strong emphasis on the unity of God, the virtual extinction of the distinction between *ousia* and *hypostasis*, and allows a merely rational distinction between the divine essence and the personal modes of subsistence.

19   In response to Génébrard (see previous footnote) and some other Catholic authors, Bellarmine holds that Calvin erred in his formulations by denying the terms "God of God, light of light," etc., of the Nicene Creed, and by suggesting that the Son has his own "principle of divinity." Considered substantially, however, we should acknowledge, according to Bellarmine, that Calvin called the Son *autotheos* "with respect to the essence" (*respectu essentiae*), not "with respect to person" (*respectu personae*). Moreover, Calvin developed his terminology in the context of the debate with Valentinus Gentilis, who denied the true divinity of the Son. Against this renewed Arianism, Calvin emphasized the Son being "God himself" by using a term (*autotheos*) that has the risk of overstating the personal distinction between the Father and the Son.

XIX Quae hactenus de Persona Patris dicta sunt, Filii Dei notitiam nobis quoque manifestant, quia relatorum haec natura est, ut simul sint et cognoscantur; ut tamen orthodoxa haec doctrina adversus veteres et hodiernos Haereticos tanto firmius stabiliatur, quaedam praeterea de eo nobis sunt explicanda.

XX Est ergo Filius Dei secunda Trinitatis persona,* ab aeterno a Patre genita, ejusdem cum Patre divinitatis ac essentiae, et tamen a Patre ac Spiritu Sancto per proprietates suas characteristicas realiter distincta. Cujus definitionis nonnulla membra ex antecedentibus satis liquent, quae vero ulteriore demonstratione opus habent, sequentibus proponentur.

XXI Ea autem ad haec duo capita a nobis ordinis causa revocabuntur. Primo demonstrabimus adversus Samosatenianos, Arrianos et Socinianos, Filium Dei esse Patri vere ὁμοούσιον, id est, ejusdem cum Patre essentiae ac divinitatis. Deinde adversus Sabellianos et Servetianos, eum tamen esse veram et distinctam a Patre personam.

8. CONCERNING THE PERSON OF THE FATHER AND OF THE SON

19 The things said thus far about the person of the Father also make plain to us what is to be known about the Son of God, because it belongs to the nature of related persons that they exist and are known at one and the same time. However, in order that this orthodox doctrine may be established much more firmly against ancient as well as contemporary heretics, we must explain some additional points about Him.

20 Well then, the Son of God is the second person* of the Trinity, begotten of the Father from eternity, of the same divinity and essence with the Father, and yet in reality distinguished from the Father and the Holy Spirit through his own characteristic properties.[20] Several elements of this definition are clear enough from what has preceded, but the ones that are in need of further proof will be put forward in what follows.

21 For the sake of good order, we shall summarize these elements under the two following headings. First we shall prove over against the Samosatenians, Arians and Socinians, that the Son of God is truly "of the same substance" [*homoousios*],[21] that is, of the same essence and divinity as the Father. Next, contrary to the Sabellians and Servetians, that He is still a true person, and distinct from the Father.[22]

---

20 "In reality distinguished" means that the Son does not only differ nominally or rationally from the Father, as various sorts of modalism would have it. The emphasis on the *homoousios* in thesis 21 below also excludes an interpretation that makes the Father and the Son into two different, separate 'substances.' The "real distinction" stated here should be understood with help of the notion *modus subsistentiae*: the Son has his own personal, relatively independent way of existing, while still being of the same substance or essence with the Father.

21 *Homoousios* is the central term of the Nicene Creed, intended to refute the teaching of Arius that the Son of God is not himself God, but the first creature of God. On the different meanings attached to *homoousios* by theologians prior to and following the Nicene Council, see J.N.D. Kelly, *Early Christian Creeds* (3rd edition; London: Longman, 1972), 231–254. Ironically, the orthodox key term *homoousios* was rejected by the synod of Antioch (268) in the sense in which Paul of Samosata, one of the proponents of a modalist view of Trinity, employed it (see Johannes Quasten, *Patrology*, vol. 2: *The Ante-Nicene Literature After Irenaeus* (reprint Notre Dame: Christian Classics), 140–142). On the Socinians and the challenge they posed to the orthodox doctrine of the Trinity, see PRRD 4:78–79, 91–99.

22 While in the first half of thesis 21, the "Samosatenians, Arians and Socinians" are mentioned as denying the Son as being "of the same substance" with the Father, the second half identifies "Sabellians and Servetians" as eliminating the distinct personality of the Son. Sabellius (c. AD 215) believed that God was one and indivisible. His solution for the trinitarian problem was to see the Father, the Son and the Spirit as three modes of the

XXII Filium Dei esse Deo Patri vere et absolute ὁμοούσιον, demonstratur sequentibus duobus immotis fundamentis. Primum petitur ex diversis locis Veteris Testamenti in quibus, quae de vero atque aeterno Deo ac Patre intelliguntur et praedicantur,* eadem quoque in Novo Testamento de Jesu Christo Dei Filio intellecta et praedicata esse asseruntur; quod nisi eadem utriusque esset essentia ac divinitas, fieri nulla ratione* posset.

XXIII E multis locis ejusmodi, haec tria tantum proferimus. Num. 14, 22. Ps. 95, 8. Es. 63, 10. et alibi passim verus Jehova et Deus Israëlis tentatus dicitur in deserto ab Israelitis, Paulus vero 1 Cor. 10, 9. Christum ab iis fuisse in deserto tentatum, disertis verbis ait. Ps. 102, 26. de vero Jehova et Deo Davidis dicitur: Tu ab initio, Domine, terram fundasti, et opera manuum tuarum sunt coeli; illa peritura sunt, tu autem permanes, etc. quae verba de Filio Dei enuntiata esse, idem Apostolus ad Heb. 1, 10. clare testatur. Esai. 6. Prophetae apparet Dominus insidens solio gloriae, et Cherubinorum stipatu cinctus, qui eundem mittit ad populum Israëlis, ut pronuntiet adversus ipsorum contumaciam divina judicia. Johannes vero cap. 12, 41 asserit, *haec* dixisse Esaiam cum gloriam ejus, nempe Christi, videret et testaretur de ipso.

XXIV Alterum fundamentum petitur ex communione nominum, proprietatum, operum et cultus divini, quae est inter Filium et Patrem tamquam verum et aeternum Deum.

---

one God. The Logos cannot be anything else than a particular appearance of the Father. This view was challenged by the church-father Tertullian in *Adversus Praxeam (Against Praxeas)*, in 217. Perhaps Tertullian is writing specifically against Sabellius and uses the pseudonym Praxeas for Sabellius. The Sabellians believed that the Son and the Spirit were different modes of the divine Father. They therefore believed that God the Father himself had suffered on the cross (Patripassianism). This view made it impossible to think of the Son as a divine person. See Alfred Adam, *Lehrbuch der Dogmengeschichte* (2 vols.; Darmstadt: Gerd Mohn, 1965, 1968), 1:165–171. Michael Servet (1509/1511–1553) was born in Villanueva de Sijena in the Spanish Province of Huesc. As a Renaissance humanist, he was versed in many sciences. Servet was one of John Calvin's adversaries in Geneva, where ultimately Servet was sentenced to death by the Genevan council due to his anti-trinitarian writings. His most important work was *Christianismi Restitutio (Restoration of Christianity*, 1553). For an analysis of Servet's anti-trinitarian ideas and his conflict with Calvin, see A. Baars, *Om Gods verhevenheid en Zijn nabijheid: De Drie-eenheid bij Calvijn* (Kampen: Kok, 2004), 146–229; cf. PRRD 4:74–81. On the place of Servet in the history of the Reformation, see Andrew Pettegree, "Michael Servetus and the Limits of Tolerance," *History Today* 40 (1990): 40–45, and Robert M. Kingdon, "Social Control and Political Control in Calvin's Geneva," in *Die Reformation in Deutschland und Europa: Interpretationen und Debatten*, ed. Hans R. Guggisberg (Gütersloh: Gütersloher Verlagshaus, 1993), 521–532.

8. CONCERNING THE PERSON OF THE FATHER AND OF THE SON

That the Son of God is truly and absolutely of the same substance as God the Father is proved by the following two unshakable fundamental arguments. The first comes from the various places in the Old Testament where the very same things that are known and predicated about the true and eternal God and Father are asserted in the New Testament as known and preached* about Jesus Christ the Son of God. This fact could not occur upon any grounds* unless both have the same essence and divinity.

From the many places of this sort we furnish only these three: Numbers 14:22, Psalm 95:8, Isaiah 63:10; and in many places elsewhere it is stated that the true *Yᵉhovah* and God of Israel is tested by the Israelites in the desert, but Paul in 1 Corinthians 10:9 says with clear words that it was Christ whom they had tested in the desert. In Psalm 102:26 [25] this is stated about the true *Yᵉhovah* and God of David: "From the beginning you, Lord, have laid the foundation of the earth, and the heavens are the works of your hands. They will perish, but you remain, etc." These words are spoken about the Son of God, as the same apostle clearly testifies in Hebrews 1:10. In Isaiah 6 the Lord appears to the prophet seated upon the throne of glory, and surrounded by a throng of Cherubim, and He sends him to the people of Israel to pronounce divine judgments against their hardness of heart. But John in chapter 12:41 states that "Isaiah said these things because he saw his—that is, Christ's—glory and testifies concerning Him."

The second foundation is taken from the names, properties, works and divine veneration that are shared in common by the Son and the Father as true and eternal God.

xxv   Nam cuicumque absolute* et simpliciter tribuuntur nomina Deo propria, proprietates Dei essentiales, opera vere divina et cultus soli Deo conveniens, is est verus, aeternus et coessentialis cum Patre Deus. At haec omnia Filio Dei absolute et simpliciter tribuuntur. Ergo Filius Dei est verus, aeternus et coessentialis Patri Deus.

xxvi Major hujus Syllogismi est αὐτόπιστος. Nam cum unus tantum sit Deus, qui gloriam suam alteri non dat et cum per haec γνωρίσματα se ipsum a creaturis et diis imaginariis passim distinguat, necessario atque irrefutabiliter sequitur, eum, cui eadem quae Patri tribuuntur, esse ejusdem essentiae ac divinitatis cum Patre. Minor vero multis perspicuis ac solidis Sacrae Scripturae locis nititur, e quibus sequentia sufficiunt.

xxvii Nomina, quae Deo propria sunt, et Filio vel absolute communicantur, vel cum ejusmodi epithetis quae nulli alii competunt, inter cetera sunt haec: Nomen Jehovae, Jer. 23, 6. et vocabitur Jehova justitia nostra. Nomen Dei, tum attributive, Joh. 1, 1. Verbum erat Deus, tum subjective, Act. 20, 28. Deus redemit Ecclesiam suo sanguine, vide et Ps. 45, 7. et 1 Tim. 3, 16. Dominus, Ps. 110, 1. Dixit Jehova Domino meo, item conjunctim, Deus mi et Domine mi, Joh. 20. 28. Vocatur quoque scrutator renum et cordium, Apoc. 2, 23. Rex Regum et Dominus dominantium, Apoc. 17, 14. etc. 19, 16. Principium et finis, Alpha et Omega, primus et ultimus, Apoc. 22, 13. Item a Paulo Deus super omnia laudandus in

8. CONCERNING THE PERSON OF THE FATHER AND OF THE SON

For to whomever the names that suit God are attributed absolutely* and simply—as well as the essential properties of God, the truly divine works and the veneration that befits God alone—He is true, eternal and coessential[23] God with the Father. And all these are indeed attributed to the Son of God as one, and without reference to another. Therefore the Son of God is true, eternal, and coessential God with the Father.

The major proposition of this syllogism is self-convincing.[24] For since there can be only one God who does not bestow his own glory upon another,[25] and since through these signs of recognition He sets himself apart everywhere from created beings and from imaginary gods, it follows necessarily and without question that He to whom the same things are attributed as to the Father, is of the same essence and divinity as the Father. And the minor proposition rests upon the many clear and reliable places in Holy Scripture, from which the following ones are enough.

The names which are proper to God, and which are shared with the Son either absolutely or with the sort of epithets that apply to no one else, are, among others, these: The name of Y^{e}hovah (Jeremiah 23:6): "and He will be called Y^{e}hovah our righteousness." The name of God, either as an attribute, as in John 1:1: "The Word was God," or as a subject, in Acts 20:28: "God redeemed the Church with his own blood." See also Psalm 45:7 and 1 Timothy 3:16. The name Lord, in Psalm 110:1: "The Lord said to my Lord," and in combination: "My God and my Lord" (John 20:28). And He is also called "He who searches the kidneys and hearts" (Revelation 2:23). "King of kings and Lord of lords" (Revelation 17:14, etc.; 19:6). "The beginning and the end, Alpha and Omega, the first and the last" (Revelation 22:13). Likewise, by Paul: "God to be praised above all"[26]

---

23 *Coessentialis*: standard Latin rendering of *homoousios*.
24 In SPT 2.11 the term *autopistos* is used in a specific sense to indicate the self-convincing quality of Scripture. Here, it stands in a more general sense of a syllogistic argument that is evident: it is affirmed as soon as it is understood. A syllogism, first developed by Aristotle in his *Analytics*, is the basic form of scholastic reasoning. It typically consists of a general statement (the *maior*: "all human beings are mortal"), a specific or individual instance (the *minor*: "Socrates is a human being"), and the conclusion that follows from joining the *maior* and the *minor* ("Socrates is mortal"). Following Aristotle, medieval and early modern scholastics recognized different types or modes varying on the basic form. The analysis of arguments in the syllogistic structure also facilitates the detection of logical errors (fallacies).
25 Implicit quotation of Isaiah 42:8, 48:11.
26 The omission of "is" (compared to modern translations that insert "is") is crucial to the argument here. Without "is," Paul's exclamation is directly connected to Christ; the insertion of "is" shifts Paul's exclamation from Christ to God the Father. For a discussion of

secula, Rom. 9, 5. Dominus gloriae, 1 Cor. 2, 8. Deus ille magnus, Tit. 2, 13. ac denique a Johanne verus Deus et vita aeterna, 1 Joh. 5, 20. etc.

XXVIII   Proprietates Dei essentiales, Filio quoque passim in Scripturis communicantur, quales sunt: Aeternitas, Joh. 17, 5. Glorifica me tu, Pater, apud temetipsum, ea gloria, quam habui apud te, priusquam mundus esset, et Col. 1, 17. Ipse est ante omnia. Plura de hoc attributo Thesi 9. Infinitas* et omnipraesentia, Mat. 18, 20. Ubi duo aut tres congregati sunt in nomine meo, ibi sum in medio eorum, et cap. 28, 20. Ego vobiscum sum omnibus diebus usque ad consummationem seculi. Sic Joh. 3, 13. loquebatur in terra cum Nicodemo, et tamen erat in coelo. Omniscientia, etiam cogitationum hominis, Joh. 2, 24. Christus se eis non credebat, quia ipse omnes noverat, et 21, 17. Domine, tu nosti omnia, tu nosti quod amem te. Omnipotentia, Joh. 10, 29. Pater est major, vel potentior, omnibus, etc. Ego et Pater unum sumus. Sic Phil. 3, 21. tribuitur ei efficacia qua sibi potest omnia subjicere. Talis etiam proprietas est immutabilitas,* Hebr. 1, 12. Tu idem es, et anni tui non deficiunt, et Heb. 13, 8. Christus Jesus heri, et hodie idem, et in secula.

XXIX   Opera Deo propria, Filio quoque ubique tribuuntur. Quale est, mundi creatio, Joh. 1, 3. Omnia per eum facta sunt, etc, Col. 1, 16. Per eum condita sunt omnia, quae in coelis sunt et quae in terra sunt, visibilia et invisibilia. Omnium rerum creatarum sustentatio, Coloss. 1, 17. Omnia per eum consistunt. Heb. 1, 3. Omnia sustentat verbo potentiae suae. Tale opus est resuscitatio mortuorum, Joh. 5, 21. Quemadmodum Pater suscitat mortuos et vivificat, sic et Filius quos vult, vivificat, et Joh. 6, 40. Ego illos suscitabo ultimo die. Item missio Spiritus Sancti Joh. 16, 7. et multorum aliorum miraculorum divinorum patratio, Marc. 16, 20. etc. Talia quoque sunt sanctificatio et glorificatio nostri, quae Christo passim in Scripturis ascribuntur, et alibi tamen Deo propria vindicantur.

XXX   Denique cultus Deo proprius et singularis, Filio quoque non minus quam Patri passim defertur. Qualis est adoratio et invocatio, Act. 7, 59. Lapidaverunt igitur Stephanum invocantem et dicentem: Domine Jesu, suscipe spiritum meum, et Act. 9, 14. inquit Ananias de Saulo: Accepit potestatem vinciendi omnes, qui invocant nomen tuum. Sic Paulus passim in principio et fine Epistolarum suarum eum invocat, et gratiarum actionem et laudem eandem cum

this text-critical problem, see B.M. Metzger, "The Punctuation of Rom. 9:5," *New Testament Studies: Philological, Versional, and Patristic*, New Testament Tools and Studies, vol. 10 (Leiden: Brill, 1980), 57–74.

8. CONCERNING THE PERSON OF THE FATHER AND OF THE SON

(Romans 9:5). "Lord of glory" (1 Corinthians 2:8); "God the great" (Titus 2:13), and lastly by John he is called: "The true God and life eternal" (1 John 5:20), etc.

28 Throughout the Scriptures the essential properties of God are also shared with the Son; they are of the following sort. Eternity (John 17:5): "Father, glorify me in your own presence with that glory which I had with you before the world existed." And Colossians 1:17: "He is before all things." (More about this attribute in thesis 9 above). Infinity* and omnipresence, Matthew 18:20: "Where two or three are gathered in my name, there I am in their midst," and chapter 28:20: "I am with you every day until the closing of the age." Thus in John 3:13 He was speaking upon this earth with Nicodemus and yet "He was in heaven."[27] Omniscience, even of a person's thoughts, John 2:24: "Christ did not trust himself to them, because He himself knew them all." And 21:17: "Lord, you know everything; you know that I love you." Omnipotence, John 10:29: "The Father is greater, or more powerful, than all, etc." "I and the Father are one." In Philippians 3:21 capability is attributed to Him, "whereby He is able to subject all things unto himself." Such a property is also his immutability:* "You are the same and your years do not fade away" (Hebrews 1:12). And Hebrews 13:8: "Christ Jesus is the same yesterday, and today, and for ever."

29 The works proper to God are also everywhere attributed to the Son. Such work is the creation of the world, John 1:3: "All things were made through Him." Colossians 1:16: "Through Him all things were created that are in heaven and on earth, visible and invisible." The maintenance of all created things, in Colossians 1:17: "All things hold together in Him." Hebrews 1:3: "He upholds all things by the word of his power." Such work is the revival of the dead, John 5:21: "For as the Father raises the dead and gives them life, so also the Son grants life to whomever He wills." And John 6:40: "I shall raise him up on the last day." So too the sending of the Spirit, John 16:7, and the performing of many other divine miracles, Mark 16:20, etc. Such works also include our sanctification and glorification, which everywhere in the Scriptures are ascribed to Christ, and yet in other places they are claimed as proper to God.

30 And finally the veneration that is appropriate and peculiar to God, is also conferred upon the Son no less than upon the Father. Such veneration includes adoration and prayer, Acts 7:59: "And they stoned Stephen as he was praying, saying: 'Lord Jesus, receive my spirit.'" And in Acts 9:14, Ananias says about Saul: "He has received the power to bind everyone who calls upon his name." And so Paul everywhere calls upon Him at the beginning and end of his letters, and he

---

27 Modern translations of John 3:13 would no longer allow for this argument, as the element of the "Son [presently] in heaven" is omitted there.

Patre ei offert, quod et Sancti in coelis faciunt, Apoc. 5, 9. imo et Angeli Dei omnes, Hebr. 1, 6. et Apoc. 5, 12. etc. Ita etiam baptizamur in nomine Filii, sicut in nomine Patris et Spiritus Sancti, Mat. 28. Credimus in ipsum, Joh. 14, 1. Creditis in Deum, et in me credite. Speramus in ipsum, 1 Cor. 15, 19. Si in hac vita tantum in Christo speramus, miserrimi sumus omnium hominum. Imo vero omnes tenentur honorare Filium, sicut honorant Patrem, Joh. 5, 23.

XXXI Quae hactenus a nobis proposita sunt, coram conscientiis omnium eorum, qui fidem suam Dei verbo sincere subjicere cupiunt, invicte demonstrant, hunc fidei nostrae fundamentalem articulum esse certum et firmum. Restat ut jam breviter adversus Sabellianos et Servetianos probemus, Filium Dei esse veram et distinctam a Patre personam.

XXXII Veram esse personam, ostendunt conditiones illae, quae in vera persona requiruntur. Est enim individuum per se subsistens, quia antequam Abraham esset, ipse est, Joh. 8, 58. vivit, nam Pater dedit ei vitam habere in se ipso, Joh. 5, 26. intelligit, nam novit omnia, Joh. 21, 17. vult, nam Filius quos vult, vivificat, Joh. 5, 21. facultatem* agendi habet, nam habet potestatem ponendi animam suam et eam rursus sumendi, Joh. 10, 18. operatur, nam quae Pater facit, ea Filius similiter facit, Joh. 5, 19.

XXXIII Distinctam vero a Patre personam esse, omnia illa loca, quae supra a nobis allata sunt, manifesto quoque evincunt; et praeter ea, quae testantur, eum esse apud Deum, in sinu Patris, Filium Dei, missum a Patre, alium testem a Patre, mittere Spiritum Sanctum a Patre, imaginem expressam Patris; item in quibus Pater dicitur per Filium creasse omnia, in ipso et per ipsum nos elegisse, nos in ipso reconciliasse, et similia infinita, quae ubique Sacras Scripturas legenti occurrunt, et expressam distinctionem notant.

gives the same thanks and praise to Him as to the Father, which also the saints in heaven do (Revelation 5:9), as well as all the angels of God (Hebrews 1:6, and Revelation 5:12), etc. Thus we are also "baptized into the name of the Son," just as into the name of the Father and the Holy Spirit (Matthew 28). In Him we believe, John 14:1: "You believe in God, believe also in me." In Him we hope, 1 Corinthians 15:19: "If in this life only we hope in Christ, we are of all men most wretched." No indeed, all are bound "to honour the Son, even as they honour the Father" (John 5:23).

What we have brought forward thus far proves irrefutably before the consciences of all people who desire sincerely to subject their own faith to the Word of God that this basic article of our faith is firm and sure. It remains for us now briefly to prove against the Sabellians and the followers of Servetus that the Son of God is a true person and distinct from the Father. 31

The conditions[28] that are required in a real person show that He is a true person. For He is an individual, who exists through himself, "because before Abraham was, I am" (John 8:58). He is alive, "for the Father has granted Him to have life in himself" (John 5:26). He has understanding, "for He knows everything" (John 21:17). He has a will, "for the Son grants life to whomever He wills" (John 5:21). He possesses the power* of doing, "for He has the power of laying down his own life and of taking it up again" (John 10:18). He performs action, "for whatever the Father does, that the Son does likewise" (John 5:19). 32

All of the passages adduced above also prove clearly and without a doubt that He is a person distinct from the Father. And besides these there are the passages which testify that He is in the presence of the Father, in the bosom of the Father, the Son of God, sent by the Father, another witness from the Father, sending the Holy Spirit from the Father, the expressed image of the Father. Likewise the places in which the Father is said to have created all things through the Son, that in Him and through Him He has chosen us, that He has reconciled us in Him, and similar countless places which occur everywhere to the reader of the Holy Scriptures, and indicate an explicit distinction. 33

---

28 In the next sentence, these 'conditions' are derived from the definition of a person as "an individual that exists through himself" (*individuum per se subsistens*), itself a qualification of the definition by Boethius: "A person is an individual substance of a rational nature" (*persona est individua substantia rationalis naturae*). By replacing 'substance' with 'subsistence,' the definition is corrected from the point of view of the doctrine of the Trinity. See PRRD 4:33–35 (Richard of St. Victor), 47 (Thomas Aquinas). Cf. the definition of 'person' as applied to the persons of the Trinity in SPT 7.8–9.

xxxiv   Concludimus ergo adversus omnis generis Haereticos recentes et antiquos, qui impegerunt in hunc angularem lapidem, in quo tota domus fundata et firmata est, Jesum Christum Dei unigenitum Filium, esse unum et aeternum cum Patre Deum, in eadem divina essentia distincto ὑπάρξεως τρόπῳ subsistentem, cui cum Patre et Spiritu Sancto sit honor et gloria in secula, Amen.

Therefore we conclude contrary to both all the recent and the ancient 34 heretics of every kind, who have stumbled over this corner-stone upon which the entire house has been founded and built up, that Jesus Christ the only-begotten Son of God, is the one and eternal God with the Father, who in the same divine essence exists in a distinct mode of subsistence, to whom with the Father the Holy Spirit be the honour and glory for ever and ever, Amen.

DISPUTATIO IX

De Persona Spiritus Sancti

Praeside D. ANTONIO THYSIO
Respondente FRANCISCO JOSIO

THESIS I Quum de tribus Divinitatis Personis, primum conjunctim, inde sigillatim de Patre Filioque sit actum, consequens est ut hac συζητήσει de Spiritu Sancto similiter agamus.

II Quamvis *Spiritus* hic vox,* a creaturae notione plane submovenda sit, tamen propter analogiam* aliquam quam habet creatura ad Deum, communiter* explicari non abs re erit. Significat* ergo רוח πνεῦμα, spiritus, proprie* flatum, adeoque essentiam subtilem et potentem, sive is sit ventus, Gen. 8, 1. Joh. 3, 8. sive animantis halitus, Es. 2, 22. atque inde metaphorice hominis animum, Eccles. 12, 7. Luc. 23, 46. 1 Cor. 2, 11. et angelum, Heb. 1, 7. 14. quin et creaturae vim, affectionem, motumque vehementem, Agg. 1, 14.

III Deinde commoda analogia ad Deum translata, vel divinam essentiam absolute* et communiter acceptam, Joh. 4, 24. essentiaeque proprietatem, virtutem et potentiam* in Deo residentem, aut ad creaturas exsertam, denotat, vel relate personam in divinis tertiam; qui Spiritus Dei, Gen. 1, 2. 1 Cor. 2, 11. et Domini, Es. 61, 1. et Spiraculum omnipotentis, Job. 33, 4. nempe relatione* habita ad spirantem Deum, Spiritus, scil. a Deo spiratus; qui et *Spiritus Sanctus*, Es. 63, 10. et *Spiritus Sanctus Dei*, Eph. 4, 30. natura, officio, effectuque appellatur; indeque novus ac renatus homo, novi ac sancti motus etiam spiritus nomine veniunt, Joh. 3, 6. Atque illa relata in divinis notione hic accipimus.

DISPUTATION 9

On the Person of the Holy Spirit

President: Antonius Thysius
Respondent: Franciscus Josius[1]

Since we have treated the three persons of the Godhead (first jointly and then separately about the Father and the Son), it follows that in this disputation we treat the Holy Spirit in a similar fashion.

Although it is obvious that the word* "Spirit" must be kept detached from any notion of a created being, nevertheless because some kind of analogy* exists between a created being and God it will not be unreasonable to explain them generally.* Well then, the proper* sense* of the word *ruaḥ, pneuma, spiritus*, is "a blowing," and thus a fine and powerful essence—whether it be the wind (Genesis 8:1, John 3:8) or the breath of a living being (Isaiah 2:22). And from there it comes to mean figuratively the soul of a person (Ecclesiastes 12:7; Luke 23:46; 1 Corinthians 2:11) or of an angel (Hebrews 1:7, 14); but also the zeal of a creature, a state of mind, and a lively stirring (Haggai 1:14).

From there transferred via a suitable analogy to God, the word signifies the divine essence taken in an absolute* and general way (John 4:24), the characteristic of his essence, the power* and strength that resides in God or that is disclosed to creatures.[2] Or, taken in a relative way, it signifies the third person of the divinity: the Spirit of God (Genesis 1:2; 1 Corinthians 2:11) and of the Lord (Isaiah 61:1), and the breath of the Almighty (Job 33:4)—namely with a relation* to the God who breathes, "the Spirit," that is, breathed by God. He is called also Holy Spirit (Isaiah 63:10) and Holy Spirit of God (Ephesians 4:30) because of his nature, office, and effect. For that reason also the new man who is reborn, and even the renewed and sanctified activities come by the name "spirit" (John 3:6). And it is according to this relative sense in God that we take it here.

---

1   Born ca. 1600 and coming from Middelburg, Franciscus Josius does not appear in the *Album studiosorum* of Leiden. Among those who were promoted in 1620 a certain "Franciscus Josius, Medioburgo-Zelandus" is listed as a student in Geneva; thus Suzanne Stelling-Michaud, *Le livre du recteur de l'Académie de Genève: (1559–1878)*, vol. 1: *Le texte* (Geneva: Droz, 1959), 164. He was ordained in Terneuzen in 1626; he died in 1635. The stone of his grave is still in the Terneuzen church. It is probable that "Franciscus Jodoci from Middelburg," who matriculated in Leiden on 16 March 1618 in philosophy aged 17, is the same person. See Du Rieu, *Album studiosorum*, 135, Van Lieburg, *Repertorium*, 115, and www.terneuzen.com/historie/geschiedenis/hervormdekerkterneuzen (accessed February 27, 2014).
2   On the essential 'spirituality' of God, see SPT 6.20.

IV   Est autem Spiritus Dei sive Sanctus, tertia Deitatis seu Sacrosanctae individuae Trinitatis hypostasis, id est, persona,* a Deo Patre Filioque ineffabili spiratione,* sine ulla perpessione ab aeterno procedens: adeoque ab utriusque persona singulari distincta, et essentiae unione et communione conjuncta.

V   *Hypostasin** seu personam, et quidem *divinam* esse, arguunt et evincunt personae definitio, ac personalia* omnia. Utpote substantia* et vita, ut qui essentiae et vitae omnis auctor, Emitte Spiritum tuum, et creabuntur, Ps. 104, 30. Intelligentia, Scrutatur, et novit profunda Dei, 1 Cor. 2, 10. Voluntas,* Distribuit singulis prout vult, 1 Cor. 12, 11. Potentia, Actiones, effectaque, ut est creatio, regeneratio, sanctificatio, etc. 1 Cor. 12, 11. Item, quod de Christo testatur, Christum glorificat, Apostolos docet, et ducit in omnem veritatem, consolatur, futura eis annuntiat, mundum arguit, etc. Joh. 14. 15. 16. cap. Quin quae circa eum usu veniunt, ut quod sub specie columbae, venti, et ignearum linguarum apparuerit, Matt. 3, 16. Act. 2, 4, quod ad iram provocetur, Es. 63, 10. contristetur, Eph. 4, 30. peccatum et blasphemia in illum committatur, Matt. 12. aliaque quae personae proprie competunt, adjungantur.

VI   Quinimo distincta a Patre et Filio persona est. Non enim Pater aut Filius, sed alius a Patre et Filio, Joh. 14, 16. Rogabo Patrem, et alium Paracletum dabit vobis. Illi mittunt, hic venit, Joh. 15, 26. Cum autem venerit advocatus ille, quem ego mittam a Patre. Certe qui mittit Pater et Filius, et qui venit, diversae personae sunt. Quotiescumque etiam Sacra Scriptura totam Trinitatem exprimit, Spiritum Sanctum, ut distinctam personam a Patre et Filio, proponit, Matt. 3, 16. et 28, 19.

VII   Tertia persona est in divinis. Matt. 28, 19, non naturae diversitate, aut majestatis inaequalitate, sed subsistendi ordine: unde etiam Tertia persona vocatur.

VIII   *Modus** ὑπάρξεως Spiritus Sancti ei cum Filio communis, est in communicatione divinae essentiae,* ejusque participatione: non in parte, per quandam decisionem (non enim dividua est divina natura) sed unius ac totius communione, neque illa in tempore, (ἄχρονος enim, et extra tempus, auctor temporis) sed

9. ON THE PERSON OF THE HOLY SPIRIT

The Spirit of God, then, or the Holy Spirit, is the third hypostasis,* that is, person,* of the Godhead or the most holy undivided Trinity, who proceeds by means of inexpressible spiration* from God the Father and the Son effortlessly and from eternity. And so He is distinct from the particular person of them both, and joined to them through a unity and sharing of essence.

The definition of a person,* and everything belonging to a person, demonstrate and prove that He is a hypostasis,* or person, and a divine one at that.³ Such things include: substance* and life, as He is the author of all being and life—"Send forth your Spirit, and they will be created" (Psalm 104:30). Understanding: "He searches and knows the deep things of God" (1 Corinthians 2:10). Will:* "He distributes to each one individually as He wills" (1 Corinthians 12:11). Power, actions, and effects, such as creation, regeneration, sanctification, etc. (1 Corinthians 12:11). Similarly, that He testifies about Christ, glorifies Christ, teaches the Apostles, and shows the way to all truth, brings consolation, declares to them the future, convicts the world, etc. (John, chapters 14, 15, 16). And also whatever happens concerning Him, the fact that He appeared in the guise of a dove, of the wind, and of tongues of fire (Matthew 3:16, Acts 2:[2–]4), that He is aroused to anger (Isaiah 63:10), that He is grieved (Ephesians 4:30), that sin and blasphemy are committed against Him (Matthew 12:31–32), and other things which properly belong to a person are applied to Him.

In fact He is a person distinct from the Father and the Son. For He is not the Father or the Son, but one other than the Father and the Son, John 14:16: "I shall ask the Father, and He will give you another Paraclete." The Father and the Son send Him; He comes, John 15:26: "But when the Counselor comes, whom I shall send from the Father." Surely the Father and the Son who send and He who comes are different persons. And also, whenever Holy Scripture speaks about the entire Trinity, it presents the Holy Spirit as a person distinct from the Father and the Son (Matthew 3:16, and 28:19).

Among the divine persons He is the third (Matthew 28:19), not by a difference in nature or a disparity in majesty, but by the order of subsistence—wherefore He is also called the third person.

The Holy Spirit's mode* of existence, held by Him in common with the Son, consists in the communication of the divine essence* and in participating in it; not partly, through some division (for the divine nature is not divisible) but through a sharing of the single and entire essence. And that sharing is not time-bound (for the author of time is a-temporal, and outside of time) but

---

3 For a similar argument, and the underlying definition of 'person' applied to the Son, see *SPT* 8.32.

ab aeterno, ac proinde ignorat temporis partes, ac sic neque futura, neque fieri, neque facta dici potest. Unde sive hic actus* in praesenti, ut cum dicitur a Patre procedere, sive in praeterito, ut cum dicitur spiratus, explicetur, sine partium temporis relatione intelligendum est.

IX *Modus singularis* qui subsistentiam* ejus constituit, et quo a Patre Filioque distinguitur, est in spiratione Dei ac ei respondente processione. Ut enim spirando producitur, ita emanando subsistit; quod vel vox Spiritus, qui proprie procedere, scilicet a spirante, dicitur, comprobat.

X Processionis* porro vox non accipienda est secundum virtutis et efficaciae a Deo emanationem, quatenus opera Dei procedunt ab operante; vel secundum interiorem et immanentem* in essentia Dei actionem, quae tamen tendit in objectum extra Deum, qualiter decreta Dei sunt et procedunt a Deo; sed juxta actionem Dei ad intra* (ut loquuntur scholae), id est, qua ita agit Deus in essentia sua, ut reflexus in se ipsum, divinae essentiae communione relationem* realem constituat.

XI Neque tamen intelligenda est quatenus communiter quoque Filio competere potest,* cui ratione* personalis exsistentiae a Patre, etiam ἔξοδος, egressio a diebus aeternitatis, et respectu missionis, et adventus in carnem ἐξέλευσις, exitus a Patre tribuitur, Mich. 5, 1. Joh. 16, 27. 28., sed qua singulariter Spiritui Sancto ἐκπόρευσις, processio, ut personalis characteristica proprietas, in sacris literis assignatur, Joh. 15, 26.

from eternity, and accordingly it does not know of periods of time; therefore the person cannot be spoken of as going to be made, or becoming, or having been made. And so, whether explained in the present tense, as when it is said that He is proceeding from the Father, or in the past tense, as when it is said that He was breathed—this act* should be understood without reference to periods of time.

The particular mode which comprises his subsistence,* and whereby He is distinguished from the Father and the Son, is in God's spiration* and in the procession that corresponds to it. For as He is brought forth by spiration, so He has subsistence by emanating*—which the word "Spirit" bears out, as He is said to go forth in a proper sense, namely from someone who does the breathing.

Moreover, the word "procession"* should not be taken in the sense of the flowing forth of God's power and efficacy, insofar as the works of God proceed from Him who performs the works; nor in the sense of an interior and immanent* act residing within God's essence but aiming at an object outside of God, such as the decrees that are of God and that proceed from Him. But it should be taken according to God's act directed toward the inside* (as the schoolmen say), that is, whereby God so acts within his own essence, that the reflection upon himself constitutes a real relationship* by a communion of the divine essence.[4]

And "procession" also should not be understood in the sense that it can* apply commonly to the Son as well, to whom, by reason* of his personal existence from the Father, even "exodus"—the going forth from the days of eternity—is attributed, and in reference to his sending and to his coming into the flesh, a "going out," or issuing, from the Father is attributed (Micah 5:1; John 16:27, 28). But rather it should be understood in the way that "the proceeding," or going forth, is ascribed in the sacred writings uniquely to the Holy Spirit, as his personal characteristic property (John 15:26).

---

4 For the distinction between *ad intra* and *ad extra* see SPT 6.36. God's eternal acts are 'immanent,' whereas his acts in time and history are 'extrinsic.' More precisely, some authors distinguish between *personal* works (the immanent and economical operations of the Trinity) and *essential* works (performed by the Trinity as a whole) of God, and in the category of *essential* works between *internal* works (the eternal decree) and *external* works (creation, providence, and so on); see, e.g., Amandus Polanus, *Syntagma theologiae christianae*, IV.1–6 (ed. Hanau: Weichel / Aubry, 1615), fol. 236–238. Like paternity, filiation, spiration, the procession is one of the four personal relations in the *opus ad intra* of the Trinity. Thysius seems to argue here that these personal relations are not purely mental distinctions only distinguished by reason. They refer to a real relation between the persons of the Trinity. The unique divine essence subsists in three distinctive persons without either blurring the distinction of persons or dividing the divine essence.

XII Locum vero illum illustrem quo dicitur, Spiritus ille veritatis qui a Patre procedit, Joh. 15, 26. veteres quidem omnes de processione aeterna Spiritus Sancti, at vero recentiorum nonnulli de ea quae in tempore fit, ἐνεργείας et operationis, intelligunt; nos vero utrumque actum* comprehendimus, illum quidemprimario, hunc vero secundario.

XIII Distinctio inter generationem* et spirationem,* nativitatem et processionem, ex nomenclatura et re ipsa, ab humanis (unde fluxere vocabula et notiones) ad res* divinas relata, aliquo modo innotescit. Illa Patris Filiique est, haec oris, in quo quidem potentia interna animae sese profert. Unde et Spiritus oris et labiorum Dei dicitur, Ps. 33, 6. Es. 11, 4.

XIV Sed quoniam haec, figurate* scilicet et ἀνθρωποπαθῶς; dicta, θεοπρεπῶς; sunt intelligenda, complures inter veteres et recentiores, ut Filium natum per modum intellectus, (dicitur enim Sapientia et λόγος Dei, Prov. 8. et Joh. 1.) ita Spiritum Sanctum processisse per modum voluntatis,* amoris, imo potentiae, statuunt. Unde sane Spiritus Sanctus et virtus altissimi inter se commutantur, Luc. 1, 35. Matt. 12, 28. collato cum Lucae 11, 20. Nobis sufficit, quod diversis illis vocibus et notionibus distinctio productionis personarum divinarum utcumque indicetur; neque ineffabilia temere definire praesumimus.

9. ON THE PERSON OF THE HOLY SPIRIT

But all the ancient interpreters understand the well-known passage which states, "The Spirit of truth who proceeds from the Father" (John 15:26), as being about the eternal procession of the Holy Spirit, whereas some of the more recent ones take it to concern what occurs within time—of his activity and operation. We, however, keep the two acts* together, though the one is primary and the other secondary.[5]

12

The distinction between the generation* [of the Son] and the spiration* [of the Spirit], between being born and proceeding, becomes clear in some way from the terminology and the thing itself, when it is transferred from human reality to the divine things* (that is why the terms as well as the concepts fluctuate). The former term applies to a father and to a son, the latter refers to a mouth by which the interior strength of a soul presents itself. Accordingly He is also called "the Spirit of the mouth and lips of God" (Psalm 33:6; Isaiah 11:4).

13

But since these things, being stated figuratively* and in an anthropopathic way, must be understood in a way that befits God,[6] many ancient authors as well as more recent ones have posited that just as the Son was born by means of the intellect (for He is called the Wisdom and Word of God, Proverbs 8 and John 1), so too the Holy Spirit proceeded by means of the will,* of love, nay rather, of power.[7] For this reason the terms "Holy Spirit" and "the power of the most high" are rightly used interchangeably (Luke 1:35; Matthew 12:28, compared with Luke 11:20). For us it suffices that somehow by means of these different words and concepts the difference is indicated in the production of the divine persons; and we do not presume to give definitions recklessly to matters that cannot be expressed in words.[8]

14

---

5   It is not clear to which 'recent interpreters' Thysius is referring here. John Calvin refuted the Greek orthodox conclusion from the text that the Spirit does not proceed from the Son and thus implies that the text refers to the eternal procession. For various interpretations of John 15:26, see *PRRD 4*, 374–376.

6   The same rule is stated in *SPT* 6.42.

7   The mention of 'power' as characteristic of the mode of procession of the Spirit might refer to Calvin's predilection for this denotation of the Spirit; cf. Baars, *Om Gods verhevenheid*, 669 note 121.

8   See *SPT*. 8.15–17. Some Reformed theologians used elements of patristic and medieval vocabulary to indicate the *ad intra* relations of the Godhead. William Ames, for example, reflected this language of the Son and the Spirit as processions of intellect and will or love, respectively. See *Medulla*, I.v.16. Voetius, however, criticized these formulations as speculative, identifying them as learned ignorance (*docta ignorantia*) or a speculative question (*quaestio curiosa*). According to Voetius, the Word does not proceed as divine cognition or as generation through the intellect; the Spirit is not produced *per modum amoris* and *amor* is not the proper name of the Holy Spirit. See *Syllabus problematum*, II, iv (fol. 11, 12).

xv Quin Spiritus Sanctus a Filio sigillatim distinguitur, quod Filius sit solummodo a Patre, Spiritus autem Sanctus conjunctim a Patre et Filio. De quo gravis et diutina inter Ecclesiam orientalem et occiduam fuit controversia, illa asserente, a Patre tantum procedere, hac, ab utroque, Patre scilicet et Filio.

xvi Ab utroque vero procedere, requirit essentiae in duabus istis personis prius considerandae unitas, quae alias everteretur. Nam si spiratio Patris consideretur sine spiratione Filii, separatam Filii a Patre essentiam statuere necesse erit. Quin et personalis in personis ordo, qui alias tolletur, ac Spiritus Sanctus non tertia persona jam erit, sed in pari ordine ac serie cum Filio collocabitur, eique quasi opponetur. Denique relatio et respectus cum intrinsecus id exigit, qui alioquin inter Filium et Spiritum Sanctum nullus erit.

xvii Idque contra sacrarum literarum definitionem. Non enim tantum Patris, Matt. 10, 20. et Spiritus Dei Patris, sed et Filii, Ad Gal. 4, 6. et Filii Dei, et Christi, Rom. 8, 9. et Jesu Christi, et Domini, Phil. 1, 19. 1 Pet. 1, 11. diserte dicitur. Quin accipit non a Patre tantum, sed et a Filio quae alios doceat, Joh. 16, 14. 15. nempe per aeternam communicationem et temporalem manifestationem.

xviii Ad haec ipsum mittendi jus et missio et datio et effusio et quae cum ea cohaerent, etiam Filio tribuuntur. Imo vero Apostolis cum afflandi actu Spiritum Sanctum contulit, Joh. 20, 22. Etsi autem temporalis Spiritus Sancti missio, non sit eadem cum processione illa aeterna, fundamenta* tamen habet in origine et ordine personarum. Ideo enim Pater a nemine mittitur, quia a nemine est, sed a sese; Filius a Patre mittitur, quia a Patre; et similiter Spiritus Sanctus ab utroque, quod ab utroque sit. Quod vero alibi et Filius a Spiritu Sancto mitti dicatur, Es. 61, 1. Luc. 4, 18. id non qua Filius, sed humanae naturae respectu, ut et unctio, intelligendum est.

xix Attamen ad controversiam hanc inter Graecos Latinosque moderandam et componendam, non incommode, juxta antiquorum quorundam phraseologiam, dixerunt quidam, Patrem per Filium Spiritum Sanctum spirare, et Spiritum Sanctum a Patre per Filium procedere. Isto enim loquendi modo ab

In fact, the Holy Spirit is singly distinguished from the Son, because the 15 Son is only from the Father, but the Holy Spirit is from the Father and the Son jointly. Concerning this point a serious and long-lasting debate arose between the eastern and western Church, the former claiming that He proceeds from the Father only, the later from both, namely, from the Father and the Son.

In fact, the unity of essence in these two persons—which should be given 16 prior consideration—demands that He proceeds from them both—or else the unity would be destroyed. For if the spiration* of the Father is considered without the spiration of the Son, it will be necessary to place the Son's essence apart from the Father's. Thus also the personal order among the divine persons would be destroyed, and the Holy Spirit would no longer be the third person, but He would be positioned in an order and ranking equal to the Son, and, as it were, placed over against Him. And lastly, because the relation and relatedness demands this, for otherwise there would be no relatedness at all between the Son and the Holy Spirit.

And this would be contrary to the definition in Holy Scriptures. For He is 17 called not only of the Father (Matthew 10:20), and the Spirit of God the Father, but clearly also of the Son (in Galatians 4:6) and of the Son of God and of Christ (Romans 8:9), and of Jesus Christ and of the Lord (Philippians 1:19; 1 Peter 1:11). Indeed, the things He is to teach to others He receives not only from the Father but also from the Son (John 16:14, 15), and that through eternal communication and through temporal manifestation.

Thereby the right of sending Him, and the sending, and the giving, and 18 the outpouring, and whatever belongs with it are attributed also to the Son. Indeed Christ bestowed the Holy Spirit upon the Apostles by the act of breathing (John 20:22). For even the sending of the Holy Spirit within time, although it is not the same as the eternal procession, nevertheless has its groundings* in the origin and order of persons. For this reason the Father is sent by no-one, because He is from no-one except himself; the Son is sent by the Father, because He is from the Father. And in the same way the Holy Spirit is sent by both of them, because He is from both of them. But as to the fact that it is stated elsewhere that also the Son is sent by the Holy Spirit (Isaiah 61:1; Luke 4:18), it must be understood not in so far as He is the Son, but with reference to his human nature, like also his anointing.

But in order to put the controversy between the Greeks and Latins in its 19 proper place and settle it, some have conveniently said, in keeping with the phraseology of some ancient authors, that the Father spirates the Holy Spirit through the Son, and that the Holy Spirit proceeds from the Father through the

utroque esse significatur;* et modus subsistendi assignificatur; nempe mediate* et subordinate a Patre per Filium procedere, quo et Graecorum ab uno principio,* etiam personali Patris, propter originis ordinisque in Patre antecessionem, non tollitur spiratio et Spiritus Sancti processio; atque relatio et subordinatio Spiritus ad Filium stabilitur, Joh. 15, 26. et 16, 14. 15.

xx   Ex originis autem ratione, relationis modo ordineque quem Spiritus Sanctus ad Patrem et Filium habet, haec proprietas exsurgit, ut quemadmodum Spiritus Sanctus omnia habet a Patre et Filio, seu a Patre per Filium, ac proinde similiter agit et operatur, ita omnia refert per Filium ad Patrem. Atque eo respectu quaedam ἐξοχὴ et ἀξίωσις est ipsius Patris et Filii ad Spiritum Sanctum, quae tota originis et ordinis tantum est.

xxi Quin sicuti oriter hinc, taciti illius consilii divini in opere redemptionis sapientissima, et personarum origini ordinique convenientissima, et admirabilis dulcedinis oeconomia,* seu dispositio, ita et Spiritus Sancti opus atque officium; adeo ut, quemadmodum Pater Dei irati et conciliandi, fontisque

Son.⁹ For by that manner of speaking it is shown* that He comes from both; and the mode of subsistence is shown, too; that is to say, He proceeds in a mediate* and subordinate way from the Father through the Son. Thereby the Greeks' position is not destroyed, namely that the one and even personal principle* of the spiration and procession of the Holy Spirit is the Father—because the Father precedes in origin and order. To be precise: their position of the personal starting point is the Father on account of the Father's antecedence* in origin and rank. And hereby both the relationship and subordination of the Spirit to the Son is established (John 15:16 and 16:14, 15).¹⁰

Moreover, by reason of the origin, the mode of relation, and the order which the Holy Spirit has towards the Father and Son, the following property arises: Just as the Holy Spirit has everything from the Father and the Son (or from the Father through the Son) and therefore acts and operates in a similar way, so too does He render everything to the Father through the Son. And in this regard there is a certain eminence and worthiness from the Father himself and the Son towards the Holy Spirit, which is entirely a matter of origin and order alone.

Well then, just as from this point the wonderfully charming economy* (or disposition) of that unspoken divine counsel arises, which in the work of redemption is most wise and corresponds very closely to the origin and order of the persons, so too does the work and office of the Holy Spirit. And it does so to such an extent that just as the Father assumes and accomplishes the role and office of God who has been angered and who must be appeased and who is the

---

9   The procession of the Spirit *per filium* (through the Son) instead of *filioque* (from the Son) was proposed as a consensus formula between the Eastern and Western Churches at the Council of Florence in 1439. The council maintained that it was from one *principium* by a single spiration. Cf. DH 1301, and also see H. Bavinck, *Reformed Dogmatics*, vol. 2: *God and Creation*, ed. John Bolt (Grand Rapids: Baker Academic 2006), 316–317. For a systematic theological discussion see David Coffey, *Deus Trinitas: The Doctrine of the Triune God* (Oxford: Oxford University Press, 1999), 48, 53–54, 165.

10 In connection with the intention to do justice to "the Greeks' position," it is worth noting that at the Dutch embassy at Constantinople there was an exchange of learning between Reformed and Greek Orthodox theologians who visited each other's worship services. Andreas Rivetus was acquainted with Cyrillus Loukaris (1572–1638), a Greek Orthodox theologian, who became patriarch of Alexandria. He wrote a *Confessio Fidei* (published in 1629 at Geneva, followed by a Greek edition in 1633) that bore a decidedly Calvinistic stamp. It caused a great uproar in the Eastern Church, and, as a result, in 1638 Loukaris was sent into exile, strangled at sea, and his body thrown overboard. See H.J. Honders, *Andreas Rivetus als invloedrijk theoloog in Hollands bloeitijd* (The Hague: Martinus Nijhoff, 1930), 77–79; E. Benz, *Die Ost-Kirche im Lichte der protestantischen Geschichtsschreibung bis zur Gegenwart* (Freiburg/Munich: Alber, 1952), 47–54.

redemptionis nostrae, Filius redemptoris et conciliatoris, ita Spiritus Sanctus meriti et beneficii impetrati a Filio, applicatoris, illuminatoris et sanctificatoris nostri conditionem, partes et munus sustineat et exsequatur. Utroque autem et illo agendi ordine, et nos salvandi opere Spiritus Sanctus insuper a Patre Filioque distinguitur.

XXII   Ut ergo ex his apparet distinctio Spiritus Sancti a Patre Filioque, nempe operibus tum ad intra,* tum ad extra, quae maxime conspicua sunt in gratioso illo opere redemptionis nostrae: ita etiam ex iisdem ὁμοούσιος Patri Filioque evincitur. Sed propter πνευματομάχους, divinitatem ejus negantes, uberiorem ejus demonstrationem* hanc instituimus. Cui Dei nomen, attributa, opera, dominium, cultus atque honor, ut Deo propria, conveniunt; ille est verus Deus. At vero haec Spiritui Sancto omnia conveniunt. Ergo, etc.

XXIII   Ac nomen* quidem Dei: Sic Spiritus Domini qui per Davidem locutus est, exegetice mox Deus Israëlis dicitur, 2 Sam. 23, 1. 2. Ananias, qui Spiritui Sancto, mox Deo dicitur mentitus, Act. 5, 3. 4. Vocamur templum Dei et Spiritus Sancti, 1 Cor. 3, 16. et 6, 19. 20. Quin proprio illo nomine Dei, quod voce Domini redditur, appellatur Es. 6, 9. collato cum Act. 28, 25. 26. Nam Dominus Zebaoth illic loquens, hic Spiritus Sanctus declaratur.

XXIV   *Attributa** vero; ut Aeternitas, secundum illud, obtulit se Deo per Spiritum aeternum, Ebr. 9, 14. Omnipraesentia, Quo ibo a Spiritu tuo, Ps. 139, 7. Quin inhabitat fideles, 1 Cor. 3, 16. 1 Cor. 6, 19. Omniscientia, Nobis Deus revelavit per Spiritum suum; Spiritus enim omnia perscrutatur, etiam profunditates Dei, 1 Cor. 2, 10. Unde et futura annuntiat, Joh. 16, 13. Per eum prophetae locuti sunt, 1 Pet. 1, 11. 2 Pet. 1, 21.

XXV   Liberrima item voluntas, et omnipotentia. Sic Apostolus, postquam varia et magnifica Dei dona commemorasset, quae nemo dare potest quam solus Deus, ut sunt gratia* sanitatum, prophetiae, sapientiae, etc. Haec omnia, inquit operatur idem Spiritus distribuens singulis sicut vult, 1 Cor. 12, 8. 9. 11. Ubi enim

source of our redemption, and just as the Son assumes and accomplishes the role and office of redeemer and mediator, so too the Holy Spirit assumes and accomplishes the role and office of the one who applies the merit and benefits obtained by Christ; who illuminates and sanctifies our life. By the offices and that order of working, as well as by his work of saving us, the Holy Spirit is once more distinguished from the Father and the Son.

Therefore, as the distinction of the Holy Spirit from the Father and the Son becomes clear from these things—namely their operations directed both toward the inside* and toward the outside, which are evident especially in that most gracious work of our redemption—so from these same things is demonstrated his sharing of one essence *homoousios** with the Father and the Son. But for the sake of the pneumatomachians[11] who deny his deity, we undertake the following, more abundant demonstration* of it. Someone to whom the name, attributes, works, dominion, worship and honour that are appropriate to God apply, is true God. Surely all these do apply to the Holy Spirit. Therefore, etc.:[12]

As for the name* of God: it is in this way that "the Spirit of the Lord" who spoke through David is shortly thereafter called, exegetically, "God of Israel" (2 Samuel 23:1, 2[2, 3]). The Holy Spirit, to whom Ananias lied, is shortly thereafter called God (Acts 5:3, 4). We are called the temple of God and of the Holy Spirit (1 Corinthians 3:16, and 6:19, 20). And in fact He is addressed by the proper name of God, which is rendered by the name Lord (Isaiah 6:9, compared with Acts 28:25, 26). For the "Lord Sabaoth" who is speaking in that passage, is revealed in this passage as the Holy Spirit.

And considering his attributes,* these are: eternity, as in the text, "He offered himself to God through the eternal Spirit" (Hebrews 9:14). Omnipresence: "Whither shall I go from your Spirit" (Psalm 139:7). And "He dwells within the believers" (1 Corinthians 3:16; 6:19). Omniscience: "God has revealed to us through his Spirit; for the Spirit searches everything, even the depths of God" (1 Corinthians 2:10). Wherefore He also announces the future (John 16:13). Through him the prophets spoke (1 Peter 1:11; 2 Peter 1:21).

Likewise his most free will and his almighty power. Thus the Apostle, after he recalled the various and splendid gifts of God, which no-one is able to grant except God himself (such as the gift* of sound health, prophecy, wisdom, etc.) says: "All these things, the one and same Spirit works, apportioning to each one individually as He wills" (1 Corinthians 12:8,9,11). For when he sets the Holy

---

11 For the *pneumatomachians* see note 13.
12 The same pattern of argumentation is displayed in *SPT* 8.24–30.

distinxit Spiritum Sanctum collatorem, a donis collatis, collationem in liberrima ejus voluntate et potestate ponit, atque ab ejus potentia* fluere declarat.

xxvi *Opera* autem; ut Creationis et Sustentationis, juxta illud, Spiritus Dei fecit me, et spiraculum omnipotentis vivificavit me, Job. 33, 4. Redemptionis, Ille enim Christi conceptum efficit, Luc. 1, 35. Mat. 1, 18. 20. eum ungit, requiescit super eo, eum mittit, Es. 61, 1. 2. Luc. 4, 18. Christus per eum miracula edit, Mat. 12, 28. Ille homines in tenebris sedentes illuminat, regenerat, renovat, recreat, sanctificat, spirituales reddit, salvat, resuscitat a mortuis, Joh. 3, 5. 8. Tit. 3, 5. 2 Cor. 3, 18. Rom. 8, 11.

xxvii Cultus et honor denique soli Deo debitus; ut cum fides et invocationis cultus ei tribuitur, Mat. 28. 19. 2 Cor. 13, 13. Apoc. 1, 4. et e contrario, de peccato in eum commisso pronuntiatur, Omne peccatum et blasphemia remittetur hominibus, Spiritus vero Sancti blasphemia non remittetur hic aut in futuro seculo, Mat. 12, 32. quo peccatum in Spiritum Sanctum, non tam aequatur in Patrem Filiumque perpetrato, quam, certo respectu ad nos habito, etiam gravius censetur, ac irremissibile pronuntiatur; quod neutiquam fieri posset,* nisi aequali natura* et majestate cum Patre Filioque esset.

xxviii Ex his omnibus liquido apparet, et concludimus, Spiritum Sanctum Patri Filioque ὁμοούσιον esse. Certe ita in Deo, ex Deo, et Dei est, ut Deus sit.

xxix Atque haec Orthodoxa de Spiritu Sancto est doctrina, cui adversantur haereses: 1. Macedonii, qui Spiritum Sanctum creaturam, et Filii ministrum statuebat, atque hoc nostro aevo Campani, ejusque asseclarum. Item Antitrini-

Spirit, as the one who bestows, apart from the gifts that are bestowed, he places the bestowal in his completely free will and rule, and he declares that they flow forth from his power.*

Then the works: such as of creation and its maintenance, according to that text, "The Spirit of God has made me, and the breath of the Almighty has given me life" (Job 33:4). Of redemption, for He brought about the conception of Christ (Luke 1:35; Matthew 1:18,20); He anoints Him, He rested above Him, and He sent Him (Isaiah 61:1,2; Luke 4:18); and Christ performed miracles through Him (Matthew 12:28). He enlightens people who are sitting in darkness; He regenerates, renews, recreates, sanctifies, renders spiritual, saves, and revives from the dead (John 3:5,8; Titus 3:5; 2 Corinthians 3:18; Romans 8:11).

And finally there is the worship* and honour that is owed to God alone, as when faith and worship in prayer are ascribed to Him (Matthew 28:19; 2 Corinthians 13:13; Revelation 1:4). And, on the opposite side, when pronouncement is made concerning sin committed against Him: "Every sin and every blasphemy will be forgiven men, but the blasphemy against the Holy Spirit will not be forgiven, either in this age or in the future one" (Matthew 12:32). In this the sin against the Holy Spirit is not so much equated with one perpetrated against the Father and the Son; rather, with a view to us, it is deemed even more serious, and is declared unforgiveable—which is in no way possible* unless He is equal with the Father and the Son in his nature* and majesty.

From all these passages it is obviously clear and we conclude that the Holy Spirit is of the same essence as the Father and the Son. Certainly, He is to such an extent in God, from God, and of God, that He is God.

And this is the orthodox doctrine about the Holy Spirit, against which these heresies are opposed: First, those of Macedonius,[13] who held that the Holy Spirit is a creature, and a minister of the Son; and, in this, our own age, those of Campanus[14] and his followers. And so too the heresies of all the

---

13   Macedonius was bishop of Constantinople from AD 341–360. He was blamed for denying the divinity of the Holy Spirit. The *pneumatomachians*, or 'Spirit-fighters' were thought to be his followers, but the historical connection is not clear. Since the Synod of Alexandria (362) and the Council of Constantinople (381–382) the idea that the Spirit was a creature was rejected. On Macedonius cf. R.P.C. Hanson, *The Search for the Christian Doctrine of God: The Arian Controversy 318–381* (Edinburgh: T. & T. Clark, 1988), 280–282. On the *pneumatomachians*, see Michael A.G. Haykin, *The Spirit of God: The Exegesis of 1 and 2 Corinthians in the Pneumatomachian Controversy of the Fourth Century* (Leiden: Brill, 1994).

14   Johannes Campanus (c. 1500–1575) was one of the leaders of the Radical Reformation. He was imprisoned in Jülich for twenty years until shortly before his death. He denied that the Spirit was a Person in the Godhead: "With no Scripture may it be adduced that the Holy

tariorum omnium, qui ipsi πνευματομάχοι sunt, ac Spiritus Sancti personam distinctam in Deo negant, eoque vel Patrem vel ejus virtutem, donum motusque sanctos, ac vim hominis regeniti tantum significari insaniunt.[a] Denique eorum impietas, qui singularem patefactionis modum eo denotari blasphemant, ut omnes fere Libertini.

---

[a] The 1625 edition has 'are of the opinion' (*sentiunt*) instead of 'madly assert' (*insaniunt*).

Spirit is the third person, for Holy Scripture is concerned with only two persons—him who bore and him who was born." On this statement, see Chalmers MacCormick, "The 'Antitrinitarianism' of John Campanus," *Church History* 32/3 (1963): 278–297, esp. 283. According to MacCormick this was only a terminological error. He also finds it difficult to tell how far his influence extended but that it is possible—though not certain—that he influenced Socinianism. This might be the reason why Thysius speaks of his followers.

9. ON THE PERSON OF THE HOLY SPIRIT 245

Anti-Trinitarians, real opponents of the Spirit, who deny the distinct person of the Holy Spirit in God, and who, therefore, madly assert that it indicates merely the Father or his power, a gift and holy affection, or the capability of a regenerated man. And finally, the godlessness of those who blasphemously state that it denotes a particular way of revelation, as nearly all the Libertines do.[15]

---

15   Though the term 'Libertines' is not very precise, Walaeus probably has in mind the radical wing of the Reformation, the Anabaptists or Spiritualists like David Joris (c. 1501–1556), Sebastian Franck (1499–c. 1543) and Hendrik Niclaes (c. 1501–c. 1580). See Walaeus, *Loci Communes*, in *Opera Omnia* I, 120b (*De Theologia*): "In our own time, the opinion of the Libertines is represented by David Georgius, Francius, Henricus Nicolas, and men of similar ilk, who appropriately call themselves Zealots of the Spirit." ("Sententia Libertinorum nostri temporis est ut Davidis Georgii, Francii, Henrici Nicolai et similis farinae hominum, qui se ideo Zelotas Spiritus appellant.")

According to the *Synopsis* the Libertines have many errors. They deny the necessity of Scripture (2.8 and 2.11), they do not regard the Holy Spirit as a person but only as a way of divine revelation (9.29 and 25 antitheses 2.3.). They also make God to the author of evil (16.31) and contend that Jesus had no real body (28.3). In ecclesiology, they deny that the believers who have passed away are now in heaven (40.9 and 40.24), and state that an external and visible church is redundant. Angels are, in their view, not distinct persons (12.8).

DISPUTATIO X

De Mundi Creatione

Praeside D. JOHANNE POLYANDRO
Respondente HENRICO HAMERS

THESIS I Dei Optimi Maximi, quo hactenus disseruimus, tum essentiae, tum personarum respectu, opus ordine primum est mundi creatio.

II Mundum hic proprie* accipimus pro universa hac machina, quam Sacra Scriptura ab ejus partibus describens, vocat coelum, terram, mare et quae sunt in eis, Exod. 20, 11.

III Per mundi creationem, ejus ex nihilo productionem sola Dei virtute omnipotente factam intelligimus. Unde et in Sacra Scriptura et in Symbolo Apostolico, Creator coeli et terrae epitheto Dei omnipotentis insignitur.

IV Hanc suam omnipotentiam Deus in rebus a se creatis duplici ratione* demonstravit: aut immediate,* quatenus rerum nonnullarum naturam prorsus ex nihilo produxit, ut terram, aquam, Angelos et primorum nostrorum parentum animas, aut mediate,* quatenus res aliquas ex rudi materia praeexsistente efformavit, ut plantas terrae, corpus Adami et bruta animalia.

V Hinc mundi creationem definimus actionem externam Dei omnipotentis, creaturis incommunicabilem, qua per se, ac pro liberrima sua voluntate,* a nullo alio permotus, coelum et terram in principio* temporis ex nihilo condi-

DISPUTATION 10

Concerning the Creation of the World

President: Johannes Polyander
Respondent: Henricus Hamers[1]

1 Up to this point we have discussed the essence and persons of the greatest and most high God. As for his work, the first one (in order) is the creation of the world.

2 Here we take 'world' in the strict* sense of this universal framework, which Holy Scripture portrays by its parts, calling it heaven, earth, sea and all that is in them (Exodus 20:11).

3 We understand 'creation of the world' to mean its production from nothing, achieved by the almighty power of God alone. Therefore also in Holy Scripture and in the Apostles' Creed, the Creator of heaven and earth is designated with the epithet 'God almighty.'

4 God has shown his omnipotence in the things He has created in two respects:* Either immediately*,[2] since He has produced the nature of many things entirely out of nothing (such as the earth, water, angels, and the souls of our first parents). Or mediately*,[3] since He shaped some things from raw, pre-existing matter[4] (such as the plants of the earth, the body of Adam, and non-rational animals).

5 Hence we define the creation of the world as an external action of the almighty God that cannot be shared with human creatures, whereby through himself and by his own most free will* (and influenced by no-one else), He founded the heavens and the earth out of nothing, at the beginning* of time.

---

1 Born in 1594 in Frankfurt a.M. (Germany), Henricus Hamers matriculated on 12 November 1619 in theology. He defended this disputation on 14 November 1620 and dedicated his defense to G. Martinus, P. van Borre, A. Meusenhol (pastor in Breda), D. de Reuter and H. Misson. He was ordained in 's-Gravendeel in 1621; he died in 1653. See Du Rieu, *Album studiosorum*, 144, and Van Lieburg, *Repertorium*, 84.
2 'Immediately' is the literal translation of *immediate* and means 'without any means; without an intervening agent; non-mediated.'
3 'Mediately' is the literal translation of *mediate* and means 'with the use of means; with an intervening agent.' In this case, the means used concerns raw pre-existing matter.
4 Given that the creation of the world is out of nothing (see thesis 3), also the raw pre-existing matter was created by God God used this matter for the creation of many things (such as the body of Adam) by giving it shape or form. Although creation in this sense is not immediate, it still is the work of divine omnipotence.

dit, et res* singulas quas ex prima illa materia effingere voluit, suo ordine, sex dierum spatio disposuit, ut gloriam immensae suae sapientiae, potentiae* ac bonitatis creaturis suis, praesertim rationalibus, patefaceret, easque ad nominis sui celebrationem invitaret.

VI   Hac nostra definitione Deum omnipotentem essentia unum, personis trinum, mundi causam* efficientem facimus, nitentes his Sacrae Scripturae testimoniis,* Gen. 1. Ps. 33, 6. Job. 33, 4. et consimilibus.

VII   Quocirca Arriani et Duliani olim merito damnati fuerunt, quod statuerent mundum a Christo factum esse tamquam a Patris instrumento. In communi enim operatione ab omnipotentia Dei tantummodo profluente, altera personarum est alteri coaequalis.

VIII Hoc opus creationis Deo Patri, Filio et Spiritui Sancto communiter ascribimus, quoniam omnia Dei opera, quae ad extra* vocantur, sunt indivisa, tametsi, ut in ceteris, sic in opere creationis diversus operandi modus* atque ordo sit observandus.

10. CONCERNING THE CREATION OF THE WORLD

And in the space of six days He arranged in their proper order all the individual things* which He willed to mold from that prime matter, in order to reveal the glory of his own immeasurable wisdom, power,* and goodness to his creatures—especially to the ones endowed with reason—and to summon them to the praise of his name.

With this definition of ours we make the almighty God, who is one in essence but three-fold in persons, the efficient cause*5 of the world, relying as we do on these proof-texts* of Holy Scripture: Genesis 1, Psalm 33:6, Job 33:4, and texts like them.

It was on account of this that the Arians and Dulians of former times were deservedly condemned, because they held that the world had been made by Christ as if He were an instrument of the Father. In fact, in the collective working that issues only from God's omnipotence, each person is co-equal to the others.⁶

We assign this work of creation jointly to God the Father, the Son, and the Holy Spirit, because all the workings of God that are called 'outward* workings' are indivisible—although, as in other works, so too in the work of creation a different mode* and order of operation may be noted.⁷

6

7

8

---

5   Disputation 10 is structured according the Aristotelian scheme of the four causes: theses 6–21 discuss the efficient cause of creation (including instrumental, impelling and directive causation); theses 22–23 the material cause, or rather the lack thereof; thesis 28 the formal cause; and theses 29–30 the final cause. When God is called the "efficient cause of the world," this should not be understood as if he were a cause *within* the world; rather, God is the one who brings the world into existence out of nothing (see thesis 22 below).

6   The doctrine that Christ was merely an instrument of God when He created the world was a consequence of the Arius's teaching that the Son was not consubstantial and coeternal with the Father, as there was a time when the Son did not exist (as condemned during the First Ecumenical Council in Nicea, 325). Theodoret of Cyrrhus, *Compendium of Heretical Accounts*, IV.4, refers to a group of (semi-)Arians which he called Dulians because they taught that the Son was a servant of the Father who created the world (MPG 83, 421: Δουλειανοὶ γὰρ ὠνομάσθησαν, τὸν μονογενῆ τοῦ Θεοῦ Υἱὸν δοῦλον τοῦ Πατρὸς τολμήσαντες καλέσαι).

7   Polyander refers here to the classical Augustinian rule according to which the workings of the Trinity towards the outside world are indivisible (*opera trinitatis ad externa indivisa sunt*); cf. e.g., Augustine, *Epistulae* 164,6 (CSEL 44,537,11–12); *Enchiridion* 12 (CCSL 46,71,19–22). 'Creation' is an outward work of this sort and thus common to all Persons of the Trinity, although the mode and order of operation can differ (see *SPT* 9 and 7.26).

IX Nam Pater a se per Filium et Spiritum Sanctum mundum creavit, Filius a Patre per Spiritum, et hic a Patre et Filio, ut patet ex his Sacrae Scripturae locis, Gen. 1. Job. 33, 4. Joh. 1, 2. 3. 1 Cor. 8, 6. Col. 1, 15. etc.

X Hinc mundi creatio, tum sigillatim Deo Patri, 1 Cor. 8, 6. Filio, Joh. 1, 3. Col. 1, 16. Heb. 1, 2. 10. Spiritui Sancto, Job. 33, 4. tum conjunctim, aut Patri et Filio, ut 1 Cor. 8, 6. aut tribus simul personis tribuitur, ut Gen. 1. Ps. 33, 6.

XI Ceterum, ut Deus Pater singulari quadam ratione se in mundi creatione patefecisse dicitur, Gen. 1, 26. nimirum hoc suo sermone ad Filium et Spiritum Sanctum, Faciamus hominem ad imaginem nostram: sic in plerisque Sacrae Scripturae locis, quemadmodum in Symbolo Apostolico, creatio coeli et terrae ipsi κατ' ἐξοχὴν ac peculiariter attribuitur.

XII Neque hoc aliis officit sacri Codicis testimoniis, in quibus creatio tribus personis divinis communiter ascribitur. Nusquam enim solus Deus Pater, Filio et Spiritu Sancto exclusis, Creator nuncupatur. Et quamvis Dei actiones externae Trinitati sint communes,* ad unam tamen personam* singulariter referri possunt, vel ob primarium ordinem causae agentis, ut creatio ad Patrem, vel ob singularem praeterea οἰκονομίαν, seu dispositionem divinam, ut redemptio ad Filium, vel ob proximum* in nobis immediatumque agendi principium,* ut sanctificatio ad Spiritum Sanctum.

XIII Hanc mundi creationem solius Dei opus esse asserimus, propterea quod solo verbo potentiae suae, nullis aliorum ministeriis, nulloque exemplari aliunde adhibito condiderit, teste Mose, Gen. 1, 3. Dixit Deus, sit lux, et fuit lux. Et Davide, Ps. 33, 9. Dixit Deus, et facta sunt, mandavit Deus, et creata sunt omnia. Quo respiciens Esaias cap. 40, 13. Quis (inquit) adjuvit Spiritum Domini? aut quis fuit consiliarius ejus?

10. CONCERNING THE CREATION OF THE WORLD

For the Father created the world by himself through the Son and the Holy Spirit, the Son created the world by the Father through the Spirit, and the Spirit created the world by the Father and the Son, as is well known from these passages of Holy Scripture: Genesis 1, Job 33:4, John 1:2,3, 1 Corinthians 8:6, Colossians 1:15, etc.[8]

Hence this creation of the world is attributed sometimes separately to God the Father (1 Corinthians 8:6), to the Son (John 1:3; Colossians 1:16; Hebrews 1:2,10), and to the Holy Spirit (Job 33:4); sometimes jointly, either to the Father and the Son (as 1 Corinthians 8:6) or to the three persons together (as Genesis 1; Psalm 33:6).

Moreover, as God the Father is said to have manifested himself in a singular way in the creation of the world (Genesis 1:26)—evidenced in his speech to the Son and the Holy Spirit: "Let us make man in our own image"—so in many places of Holy Scripture (as well as in the Apostles' Creed), the creation of heaven and earth is pre-eminently and particularly attributed to Him.

And yet this does not conflict with the other witnesses in the sacred Book, in which creation is ascribed jointly to the three persons. For nowhere is God the Father alone called the Creator, to the exclusion of the Son and the Holy Spirit. And even though the external actions of God are common* to the Trinity, they nevertheless can be referred to one person* in particular, either because of the foremost position of the acting cause (like creation to the Father), or on account of the special divine economy or arrangement (like redemption to the Son), or on account of the closest* and immediate principle* of action in us (like sanctification to the Holy Spirit).[9]

We assert that this creation of the world is the work of God alone, because He founded it merely by the word of his power, without assistance from any others, and without applying any model from elsewhere. Witness Moses, in Genesis 1:3: "God said, 'let there be light,' and there was light." And David, Psalm 33:9: "He spoke, and they came to be; God commanded, and all things were created." With respect to this, Isaiah 40:13 says: "Who has assisted the Spirit of the Lord? Or who was his counselor?"

---

8 This order reflects the Western *filioque*-doctrine according to which the Holy Spirit proceeds from both the Father and the Son; see SPT 9.19–20.

9 On the notion of personal *appropriation* of the commons works of the Triune God, see SPT 8.8.

xiv Ad hoc problema, An creatio mundi sit creaturis prorsus incommunicabilis,* non dubitanter, ut plerique faciunt Scholasticorum,* sed asseveranter respondemus, mundi creationem prorsus creaturis esse incommunicabilem; cujus nostrae asseverationis tres causas praecipuas proferemus.

xv Earum prima est, quod creatio mundi sit actio potentiae* infinitae, ac proinde non magis cum creaturis finitis, quam infinita Dei potentia, communicari potuerit.

xvi Secunda est, quod in hac actione nulla creatura cum suo Creatore concurrere potuerit, nec ut causa principalis, nec ut instrumentalis. Non ut principalis, quia nulla creatura cum suo Creatore aequaliter potest* operari. Nec ut instrumentalis, quoniam in creatione ex nihilo, nihil est in quo instrumentum occupetur.

xvii Tertia est, quod Sacra Scriptura plerumque ex mundi creatione, Patrem, Filium et Spiritum Sanctum, unum illum ac verum Deum a fictitiis distinctum esse demonstrat, ut Es. 40. Jer. 10. Joh. 1. Heb. 1, 2.

xviii Creationis mundi causa impellens προηγουμένη est summa Dei bonitas, qua ad se tamquam summum bonum rebus a se creandis communicandum ac patefaciendum affectus fuit. De qua sic loquitur Augustinus, in suo *Enchiridio*, cap. 9.[a] Satis est Christiano, rerum creatarum causam, non nisi bonitatem credere Creatoris.

xix Hanc Dei bonitatem Psaltes variis in Psalmis celebrat, atque imprimis Ps. 8. 104. et 136. ubi haec clausula aliquoties reperitur, Celebrate Dominum, quia bonus est.

xx Ejusdem creationis causa directrix est Dei sapientia; exsecutrix potentia ejus infinita. Haec ex nova rerum origine, illa ex accurata formarum diversarum dispositione ac serie percipitur.

xxi Tanta est enim rerum creatarum varietas, tam exacta et admirabilis earum constitutio, ut cuilibet homini, eas consideranti, divinam Creatoris sui sapientiam et potentiam quasi aperto ore annuntient, atque exserto digito commonstrent, Ps. 19, 2. 3. Rom. 1, 20.

---

[a] Augustine, *Enchiridion* 3.9 (CCSL 46:53).

As to the question: "Whether creating the world can in any way be common* with creatures," we reply without hesitation (as many of the Schoolmen* do)¹⁰ and emphatically that creating the world cannot be common with creatures. In support of our assertion we shall produce three major reasons.

The first of them is that the creation of the world is an act of infinite power,* and consequently could have been communicated to finite creatures no more than the infinite power of God.¹¹

The second is that in this action no created being was able to collaborate with his Creator, neither as principal cause nor as instrumental cause. Not as principal cause, since no creature is able* to work on equal terms with his Creator. Nor as instrumental cause, since in the creation out of nothing there is nothing in which an instrument is used.

The third is that Holy Scripture frequently demonstrates from the creation of the world that the one true God, Father, Son, and Holy Spirit, is set apart from phony gods (Isaiah 40; Jeremiah 10; John 1; Hebrews 1:2).

The impelling cause¹² of the creation of the world is God's highest goodness, whereby He was moved to communicate and reveal himself as the highest good to the things He would create. In his *Enchiridion*, chapter 9, Augustine speaks about it as follows: "It is enough for the Christian to believe that the only cause for the creation of things is the goodness of the Creator."¹³

The Psalmist praises this goodness of God in various Psalms, and especially in Psalm 8, 104, and 136, where this phrase is repeated several times: "Praise the Lord, because He is good."

The directive cause of this creation is God's wisdom; the executive cause is his infinite power. The latter is seen in the new coming-about of things; the former is seen in the meticulous arrangement and sequence of the various forms.

For the variety of created things is so great, their makeup so precise and wonderful, that to every person who beholds them they proclaim their Creator's divine wisdom and power with mouth wide-open, so to speak, and they point to it with outstretched finger (Psalm 19:2,3; Romans 1:20).

---

10 Peter Lombard, who wrote the *Sentences*, a major theological textbook of the Middle Ages, allowed for the possibility that God delegated the power to create to angels: *Sent.* 4, 5. 1. 3. 3 *ad* 4–5.7 and *Sent.* 2. 1. 1. 3. In his early work, Thomas Aquinas follows the Lombard, but rejects it later (*Summa theologiae*, 1.45.5).

11 The power of God is the divine attribute according to which He can carry out the decisions of his will; see SPT 6.36.

12 The impelling cause (*causa impellens*, in Greek *proegoumene*) is that by which the agent is motivated to act. See also DLGTT, s.v. "causa impulsiva."

13 Augustine, *Enchiridion* 9 (MPL 40, 235–236).

XXII Haec rerum universitas producta est ex nihilo, non privative* sed negative sumpto, ideoque per ἀφαίρεσιν et negationem omnis entitatis, a nostro intellectu concipitur; quod a quibusdam καταχρηστικῶς ac valde ἀκυρολόγως materia ex qua nominatur; ubi enim nihil est, ibi improprie* materia esse dicitur.

XXIII Materia vero ex nihilo producta, in principio fuit indisposita et inhabilis ad omnia ea, quae Deus postea suo loco disponere, suaque forma singulari exornari voluit.

XXIV Quaestionem Scholasticorum nimis curiosam, An mundus non potuerit creari ab aeterno? Christianorum responsione indignam censemus, haud ignorantium, quod sacrae literae ipsa voce* creationis, mundum in tempore a Deo fuisse conditum, Deumque solum sine principio ac per se aeternum esse, passim doceant. Quod Augustinus ad Angelos applicans, l. 12. *De Civitate Dei*, c. 15.[a] Quomodo, inquit, Angeli creati dicendi sunt, si semper fuisse intelliguntur?

XXV Quemadmodum autem Deum in tempore, sic libere eum ac secundum voluntatis suae beneplacitum, tempore a se definito,* mundum hunc condidisse asserimus, quem, si ita ipsi fuisset visum, aut prius aut serius creare potuisset.

XXVI Ad hanc otiosorum hominum quaestionem, Cur Deus mundum non prius condiderit? respondemus, non ipsorum esse tam curiose de temporibus atque opportunitatibus inquirere, quas Deus solus in sua habet potestate, Deumque non minus secula, quam universam hanc machinam pro suo arbitratu fecisse, Act. 1, 7. Hebr. 1, 2.

---

[a] Augustine, *De civitate Dei* 12.16 (= 12.15 in old numbering; CCSL 48:371).

This whole of things was brought forth out of nothing (taken in the negative, not privative* sense), and so our minds conceive of what is brought forth by means of the removal and negation of all entity.¹⁴ By some this idea is loosely—and quite inaccurately—called 'the matter from which'; but where nothing exists, there it is incorrect* to speak of matter.

But as for the matter that was brought forth out of nothing, in the beginning it was without order and unsuitable for all those things which God willed to put in their proper places later, and to be adorned with their own unique forms.

We deem the overly-inquisitive question of the Schoolmen, "Whether the world could not have been created from eternity," not worthy of a reply by Christians, who very well know that the sacred writings everywhere teach by the very word* 'creation' that the world was established by God within time, and that only God is without beginning and eternal in himself. Augustine, in applying this to the angels, states in Book 12, chapter 15 of *the City of God*: "How can it be said that angels were created, if it is understood that they have always existed?"¹⁵

But as we assert that God founded this world within time, He did so freely, too, and according to the good pleasure of his own will at a time determined* by himself—which He could have created earlier or later in time, whenever it pleased Him to do so.

To this question of idle men, "Why did God not establish the world earlier?," we reply that it is not for them to make such meddlesome enquiries about times or opportunities, which only God in his power possesses, and that by his own choice God has created the ages no less than this universal framework (Acts 1:7; Hebrews 1:2).¹⁶

---

14 'Nothing' in the negative sense means the mere negation of something, whereas 'nothing' in the privative sense means that in fact nothing is there, although something ought to be there. For example, 'not-seeing' is a negation, but 'blind' is a privation. As God did not need anything in order to create, the creation out of nothing is related to 'nothing' in a negative rather than a privative sense.

15 During the Middle Ages, the question was not so much whether God actually created a non-eternal world, but whether He could have created a world without a beginning in time. See, e.g., J.B.M. Wissink, ed., *The Eternity of the World in the Thought of Thomas Aquinas and His Contemporaries* (Leiden: Brill, 1990). See, similarly, SPT 12.5 on the creation of the angels as temporal beings.

16 The question why did God not create the world earlier, was already raised by Parmenides in the sixth century BC. It was discussed by Aristotle, Gregory of Nyssa, Augustine, throughout the Middle Ages, up to Leibniz and Kant. See: Richard Sorabji, *Time, Creation and the Continuum: Theories in Antiquity and the Early Middle Ages* (Ithaca: Cornell University Press, 1983), 232–240.

XXVII   Ad illam eorundem quaestionem, An ergo Deus antequam mundum creaverit, otiosus fuerit? summae vanitatis esse respondemus, de Deo quaerere an unquam fuerit otiosus, qui praeter semetipsum omnia a se creanda ab aeterno contemplatus est, nosque in Christo Filio suo dilecto ante jacta mundi fundamenta cognovisse atque eligisse dicitur, Rom. 8, 28. Eph. 1, 4.

XXVIII   Forma mundi a Deo creati spectatur in artificiosissima omnium ejus partium dispositione, aptissima earum in se εὐταξίᾳ summaque inter se παναρμονίᾳ.

XXIX   Finis* est, bonitatis, sapientiae ac potentiae Dei patefactio, harumque virtutum per omnes creaturas, ac praesertim per rationales, perpetua celebratio.

XXX   Hunc finem viri Dei, tum in Psalmis, tum in aliis Sacrae Scripturae locis, ad Dei gloriam, animarum suarum recreationem, ac communem omnium piorum institutionem variis rationibus accommodarunt.

COROLLARIA.

I   Cum Sacra Scriptura et unicum mundum, et unicum illius Servatorem Jesum Christum esse doceat, Origenis[a] sententia ab Hieronymo aliisque Patribus orthodoxis merito fuit repudiata, qua statuebat, unum quidem uno tempore mundum esse, sed ante hunc tamen alios fuisse, et post hunc alterum fore, et illi semper successurum alium atque alium; ideoque et Christum saepius passurum, ut quod profuit semel, semper prosit assumptum.

---

[a] Origen, *De principiis* 2.3.5 (SC 252:260–262); 3.5.7 (SC 268:230–232).

And as to their question, "Whether God was idle before He created the world," we reply that it is uttermost folly to ask of God whether He was ever idle, who besides himself has carefully contemplated from eternity all the things that would be created by Him. And it is said that He knew and chose us in Christ, his beloved Son, before the foundations of the world were laid (Romans 8:28; Ephesians 1:4).[17]

The form of the world created by God is discerned in the most skillful assembly of all its parts, the very functional arrangement within them, and the greatest harmony among them.

The goal* is the revelation of the goodness, wisdom, and power of God; and the everlasting praise of these virtues through all creatures, especially those endowed with reason.

The men of God, in the Psalms as well as in the other passages of Holy Scripture, have pursued this goal for the glory of God, for the recreation of their own souls, and for the common instruction of all devout people in various ways.

Corollary.

Since Holy Scripture teaches both that there is only one world and that its only Savior is Jesus Christ, Jerome and the other orthodox church-fathers rightly refuted the opinion of Origen, whereby he posited that while there is only one world at one time, yet before this one there were others, and after this one there will be another (and thereupon another, and another will always follow); and for that reason Christ, too, will suffer more often, on the ground that what was beneficial once will be beneficial always.[18]

---

17 The question what God was doing before he created heaven and earth occurs in Augustine's *Confessions*, book 11, chapter 12. Augustine first gives the ironical answer (chapter 14): "Then he prepared the hell for those who pry into mysteries." Moreover, he develops a sophisticated theory of time to make it clear that there can be no time before the creation of the universe, since time is the measurement of things that come into existence and pass away (chapters 15 to 40).

18 Quoted from Jerome's attack against Origen, *Apology against Rufinus* (*Apologia contra Rufinum*, ed. P. Lardet, CCSL 79, Turnhout: Brepols 1982, pp. 19–20). It seems that Jerome does not do justice to Origen. Origen was known for holding the theory of an endless succession of worlds, yet he also maintained the uniqueness of the incarnation: P. Tzamalikos, *Origen: Philosophy of History and Eschatology*, Supplements to Vigiliae Christianae, vol. 85 (Leiden, Brill, 2007), 71–81. For an historical overview of the notion of a plurality of worlds, see Steven Dick, *Plurality of Worlds: The Origins of the Extraterrestrial Life Debate From Democritus to Kant* (Cambridge, Cambridge University Press, 1982).

II Cum Sacra Scriptura asseverat, Deum coelum et terram creasse in principio, Gen. 1. Prov. 8, 22. et seqq. Joh. 17, 5. Eph. 1, 4. non est hoc axioma, Mundum in tempore a Deo creatum esse, inter problemata Dialectica referendum: ac si de eo in utramque partem disputari posset.*

III Cum eadem Scriptura omnem Dei creaturam bonam esse attestetur, Gen. 1, 31. et 1 Tim. 4, 4. merito olim damnati sunt Manichaei, qui aliquas naturas simpliciter malas, et a Deo malo creatas esse opinabantur.

10. CONCERNING THE CREATION OF THE WORLD

Since Holy Scripture declares that "in the beginning God created heaven and earth" (Genesis 1; Proverbs 8:22, ff.; John 17:5; Ephesians 1:4), the axiomatic statement that "the world was created by God in time" should not be considered among debatable issues, as though one could* argue about it in either way.

Since the same Scripture testifies that every creature of God is good (Genesis 1:31; 1 Timothy 4:4), the Manicheans of former times were rightly condemned, who were of the opinion that some natures simply are evil, and were created by an evil God.

DISPUTATIO XI

De Providentia Dei

Praeside D. ANDREA RIVETO
Respondente CAROLO BECIO

THESIS I   Creationis omnium rerum, visibilium et invisibilium considerationem, divinae providentiae inquisitio ordine commodo, sequi debet. Nec enim in principio creaturarum, haec omnia sunt a Deo ita constituta et disposita, ut postea, patrata rerum universitate, atque perfecta, cunctam a se curam illius ablegaverit; quin potius asserimus cum Salviano, Deum nostrum ab universitate omnium rerum, nec munus dignantissimae visionis avertere, nec regimen suae providentiae tollere, nec indulgentiam benignissimae pietatis auferre, *De gub. Dei*, liber 2.[a]

II   De providentia igitur acturi, notationem nominis* satis alias notam omittemus, ut ad rem* rectam veniamus. Consideratur secundum duplicem actum:* unum aeternum, alterum in tempore; quos una definitione complecti possu-

---

[a] Erroneous reference; correct to Salvian, *De gubernatione Dei* 1.1.3 (CSEL 8:4).

DISPUTATION 11

On the Providence of God

President: Andreas Rivetus
Respondent: Carolus Becius[1]

An inquiry into divine providence must, in good order, follow the investigation into the creation of all things visible and invisible. For it is not true that in the beginning of creation God established and arranged all this in such a way that when He had accomplished and finished everything completely, He put away from himself every care for it.[2] Rather, we assert with Salvian "that our God neither withdraws the benefit of his most generous observance nor entirely removes the rule of his providence from everything; He also does not withdraw the favor of his most benevolent faithfulness" (*On the Government of God*, 50.2).[3]

And so, as we set out to treat providence, we shall leave aside the definition of the word,* which is sufficiently known from other sources,[4] so that we make our way straight to the subject* proper. The subject is considered as a two-fold act:* The one is eternal, the other is within time. We can combine the two

---

1   Born in 1597 in Dordrecht, Carolus Becius matriculated on 8 September 1615 as an alumnus of the Leiden States College. He defended this disputation on 28 November 1620 and dedicated his defense to his father Johannes (pastor in Dordrecht), to Polyander, Rivetus, Walaeus and Hommius. He was ordained in Rijsoord (near Ridderkerk) in 1622 and Nieuwpoort in 1637; emeritus in 1653. See Du Rieu, *Album studiosorum*, 121, and Van Lieburg, *Repertorium*, 16; also BLGNP, 2, 50–51.

2   In his first disputation (see the Introduction) Rivetus treats the doctrine of providence on the basis on the doctrine of creation. The God who creates is the God who cares (*pro*videt—in contradistinction to *prae*videt = He fore-sees). This point is the basic positive one. Negatively, the deistic neutrality of God is repeatedly rejected in this disputation.

3   Salvian of Marseille (c. AD 400–c. 480) was born to a distinguished Christian family and dedicated himself from an early age to religious life. In 425 he went to Lerinum, and he lived in Marseille from 439. His main work, *De gubernatione Dei* (*On the Government of God*) recalls Augustine's *De civitate Dei* (*The City of God*) in its historical setting and its religious scope. See Jan Badewien, *Geschichtstheologie und Sozialkritik im Werk Salvians von Marseille*, Forschungen zur Kirchen- und Dogmengeschichte, vol. 32 (Göttingen: Vandenhoeck & Ruprecht, 1980).

4   On the meaning and use of the concept of providence in Christian thought, see Johannes Altenstaig, *Lexicon theologicum*, and Rudolph Goclenius, *Lexicon philosophicum*, s.v. "providentia." For a survey of fifteenth century discussions on providence see Antonino Poppi, "Fate, Fortune, Providence and Human Freedom," in Charles B. Schmitt, Quentin Skinner and Eckhard Kessler (eds.), *The Cambridge History of Renaissance Philosophy* (Cambridge: Cambridge University Press, 1988), 641–667.

mus, si dicamus, esse praeexsistentem in mente divina rationem ordinis rerum in finem,* id est, notitiam* Dei practicam, qua ab aeterno praeordinavit, et in tempore dirigit unamquamque rem* in finem suum, ad gloriam suam. Unde constat, Providentiam partim ad intellectum, partim ad voluntatem pertinere; cum enim sit in intellectu, praesupponit voluntatem* finis.

III Hic cum habeamus duo: rationem ordinis aeternam, quae proprie* est providentia, et ejusdem exsecutionem in tempore, quae dicitur gubernatio, et creationis quaedam velut συνοχή, de qua in praesentiarum nobis praesertim agendum est; eam describimus, Actualem et temporalem omnium et singularum rerum quae sunt et fiunt, juxta decretum Dei aeternum, immutabile* et liberrimum, conservationem, directionem et deductionem ad finem ab ipso determinatum,* sapientissime et justissime factam ad ipsius gloriam.

IV Esse in Deo Providentiam, nemo nisi prorsus ἄθεος negare potest,* quia ratio* ejus ita cum divinitate conjuncta est, ut nullo pacto possit separari;

11. ON THE PROVIDENCE OF GOD   263

into one definition if we say that it is "the pre-existent structural ordaining, in God's mind, of things towards a goal;* that is, the practical knowledge* of God whereby He pre-ordained each and every single thing* from eternity and directs them in time to their proper goal—for his own glory." From this it is plain that providence pertains partly to the intellect and partly to the will. For as it is situated in the intellect, it presupposes the will* of the goal.[5]

Since we have two things here, the eternal structural order, which properly* speaking is providence and its execution within time (which is called government), and also a kind of maintenance of creation in the present, which we must treat in particular, we shall define it as: "The actual and temporal preservation, direction, and guidance that God has achieved very wisely and justly, according to his eternal unchangeable* and entirely free decree, of all individual things which exist and come into being, to the end that He has determined* for them, and to the praise of his glory."[6]

3

No-one, unless he is an utter atheist, can* deny that providence exists in God, because the reason* for its existence is bound up with the divinity to such a degree that it cannot be separated from it in any way.[7] Indeed, so much so

4

---

5   In providence, God's intellect and will operate jointly; the conceptual nexus between them is the 'practical knowledge' (*notitia practica*) by which God *knows* the *things* that are about to happen with a view to the *goal* He establishes for them by his *will*. The notion of God's *practical knowledge* presupposes the notion of *theoretical knowledge*. God's *practical knowledge* is God's knowledge of what He does himself and of what He will actualize outside himself, and God's *theoretical* knowledge is the knowledge of what is possible (see also *SPT* 14.20–23). Cf. *PRRD* 3:408 for a concise treatment of the distinction between practical and theoretical knowledge, and for a fuller account of it in the context of human free choice see *RTF*, 190–192. The definition of providence given by Rivetus is built on the *knowledge-will* model. The *knowledge-will* model implies the rejection of both a model based purely on God's *knowledge* (Thomism, Molinism) and of a model based purely on God's *will* (nominalism, Cartesianism).

6   Here Rivetus makes an interesting connection between providence viewed as God's eternal decree of what has to come about, and the actual, temporal execution of this decree. He starts by stating that the eternal decree is 'providence' properly speaking, but he then shifts attention to the temporal component of preservation, direction and guidance of all things. The 'unchangeable' character of God's decree does not make it 'necessary' in an absolute sense; the unchangeable decree is 'most free.' The typically Reformed line of thought that follows the Scotian disconnection of 'eternity' and 'necessity' is evident here. See Antonie Vos and others, *Contingency and Freedom: John Duns Scotus Lectura I 39* (Dordrecht: Kluwer Academic: 1994) 164–167; Vos, *Philosophy*, 494–496 and 580–583. The elements mentioned in the execution of providence are discussed separately in theses 12 (preservation) and 13 (direction or guidance).

7   In early seventeenth century Europe, atheism occurred only as a marginal position and was treated mostly as rationally impossible by Reformed writers (cf. *SPT* 6.5–6 above). In a prac-

adeo ut omnes alioqui verae religionis* expertes, vi ipsa et quadam necessitate* compulsi, pendere omnia a Deo, et moveri, ac regi agnoverint. Videbant enim, cum Deus sit omnium rerum causa, et omne agens agat propter finem, inde sequi, Deum, qui Deus esse, et sapientia carere non potest, res* omnes ad suum finem ordinare. Nec potuerunt ordinem illum contemplari, in tam apta rerum omnium in mundo concatenatione; aptissima et convenientissima partium omnium dispositione; motuum actionumque certis legibus constantium successione, in rebus etiam sensu et ratione* carentibus; quin inferrent, esse mentem quandam sapientem ordinis illius effectricem, directricem et conservatricem. Quoniam id quod de Deo cognosci potest, manifestum est in ipsis, Deus enim eis manifestum fecit, Rom. 1, 19. 20.

V   Christianis sufficere debent apertissima Scripturae testimonia,* in qua nulla pars doctrinae coelestis frequentius et diligentius inculcatur; cum docet, Deum dare omnibus vitam, et halitum, et omnia, Omnia Dei verbo sustineri, in ipso nos vivere, moveri et esse, passerculum non cadere humi sine Patre nostro, capillos omnes capitis nostri esse numeratos, et Deum efficere omnia secundum beneplacitum voluntatis suae, Act. 17, 25. 28. Hebr. 1, 3. Mat. 10, 29. Eph. 1, 11.

VI His et similibus testimoniis evincitur, materiam sive objectum providentiae, non esse tantum coelestia et incorruptibilia, ut voluerunt, qui densas nubes latibulum Deo esse, existimantes, inferiora haec eum aspicere non judicabant, sed ambitum coelorum obambulare, Job. 22, 14. Sed nullam rem sive superioris sive inferioris naturae excipiendam esse; quin potius statuendum et certa fide tenendum, esse in Deo providentiam omnium omnino rerum, tam singularium quam universalium; tam corruptibilium et contingentium, seu fortuitarum, quas vocant, quam incorruptibilium et necessariarum; tam vilium atque infimarum,[a] quam earum quae praestantiorem sortitae sunt naturam.

VII Cum Scriptura Deo, omnium rerum, actionum et motuum efficientiam tribuat, ut quod operetur omnia in omnibus, quod ex ipso, per ipsum, et in ipso

---

[a] 1625 has "infirmarum."

tical sense, an 'atheist' is someone who lives in a godless way. See PRRD 3:110–113, 122–125, 177–181, and the literature mentioned there; cf. also Beck, *Gisbertus Voetius*, 61–64. The statement that the concept of 'providence' cannot be separated from the concept of 'God' itself can be connected to the explanation of the Greek word *theos* given by (Pseudo-)Dionysius (*De divinis nominibus*, 12.2, MPG 3:969 C) and John of Damascus (*De fide orthodoxa* chapter 12, MPG 94:835), who derive the word from the verb *theein*, 'to run,' or *theasthai*, 'to see.'

that all who otherwise lack true religion* are compelled by its power and by a certain necessity* to realize that everything depends upon God and is moved and ruled by Him. For they saw that since God is the cause of everything, and since every agent acts for the sake of a goal, it follows thereupon that God, who cannot be God and lack wisdom, ordains everything* towards its own goal. And they could not consider that order—that most fitting linkage of everything in the universe, that most apt and suitable arrangement of all the parts, that succession of constant motions and actions by definite laws, even in things that lack feeling and reason*—without coming to the conclusion that there is some wise mind that effects, directs and preserves that order. "For what can be known about God is plain to them, for God has shown it to them" (Romans 1:19,20).

For Christians the very clear witnesses* of Scripture ought to be enough, which inculcates this divine teaching more frequently and carefully than any other part, since it teaches that God grants life to all, and breath, and everything (Acts 17:25). It teaches that all things are sustained by the Word of God (Hebrews 1:3); that in Him we live and move and have our being (Acts 17:28); that the sparrow does not fall to the ground without our heavenly Father; that all the hairs on our head are numbered (Matthew 10:29, 30); and that God accomplishes everything according to the good pleasure of his will (Ephesians 1:11).

These and similar witnesses prove that the subject-matter of providence is not just the heavenly and incorruptible things—as those people suggested who thought that "thick clouds form a concealing curtain for God" and who reckoned that He did not look down on things below but that "He traversed the pathway of the heavens" (Job 22:14). The witnesses prove that no thing, whether it be of a higher or lower nature, should be excepted; but rather, with an unwavering faith one must hold and maintain the position that in God resides the providence for all things, both singly as well as together; things that are subject to decay and contingent (or fortuitous, as they call them) as well as things incorruptible and necessary; things that are humble and lowly, as well as of those which have received a more lofty nature.

Scripture attributes to God the power to effect[8] all things, actions, and movements—such as the fact that He works all things in everyone (1 Corinthi-

---

8 A fundamental component of the Christian view of God is his 'efficiency' (*efficientia*), his power to effect. God is the primary 'efficient cause' of all created beings, as nothing can exist or act independent of him. The interconnected doctrines of creation and providence express this belief. See also theses 13–14 below, where God's efficient causality is related to secondary causes in the created world. The model of first and second causes implies that God's *efficientia* should not be understood as exclusive all-causality.

sint omnia, quod det omnibus vitam et inspirationem, 1Cor. 12, 6. Rom. 11, 36. Act. 17, 25. cum ea quae sunt, et quae fecit, pro eodem habeantur, et Deus in tempore nihil agat, quod non ab aeterno decreverit, et sic agendum decreverit, sicut agit: plane consequens est, omnium quae sunt et fiunt in mundo, esse ab aeterno rationem in Deo, qua in suos fines in tempore ordinantur.

VIII Nec alienum est a Dei majestate, ut quidam putant, si etiam minutissima quaeque regat, et in numerato habeat, cum omnium sit creator et dominus. Cui probrum non est ea fecisse, multo minus facta dirigere; nec fit humilis, qui ad humilia attendit, aut altissime habitare cessat, qui demississime prospicit, Ps. 103, 19. ut dicendum sit, curam boum a Deo removere Apostolum, 1Cor. 9, 9. non absolute,* sed per comparationem ad homines, maxime fideles: ἐπειδὴ οἱ μὲν κοινῆς προνοίας, οἱ δὲ καὶ εἰδικῆς καὶ ἐξαιρέτου προστασίας ἀπήλαυσαν.[a] Alioqui enim Deus noster dat jumentis cibum, et pullis corvorum qui crocitant, Ps. 147, 7. 9. Lapides magnos sine parvis bene strui negant architecti, ait Plato;[b] cavendum ergo ne quis Deum viliorem putet mortalibus opificibus.[c]

IX Cum autem in toto mundo nihil sit a divinae providentiae legibus exemptum, fatendum est etiam, quanto major cura est Deo de homine, quam de aliis rebus intellectu carentibus; tanto magis actiones ejus subjici providentiae Dei, quam actiones seu mores rerum aliarum intellectu carentium; E loco habitationis suae prospicit omnes habitatores terrae: formator pariter cordis eorum respicit ad omnia opera eorum, Ps. 33, 14. 15. Hinc Scriptura corda, voluntates et actiones hominum, in Dei manu, potestate ac dispositione esse

---

[a] The source for this quotation could not be identified.   [b] Plato, *Leges* 902e8.   [c] "Lapides ... opificibus" is absent from the original 1620 disputation pamphlet, and was inserted to the 1625 edition of the *Synopsis*.

ans 12:6); that from Him, through Him, and to Him are all things (Romans 11:36); and that He gives life and breath to all (Acts 17:25). And since the things that exist and the things He has done are considered one and the same, and since God does nothing within time which He had not decreed from eternity, and since He so conducts things as He once had decreed they would be done, it follows clearly that the ground of all the things which are and which come about in the world is in God from eternity, and they are ordained for their own goals in time.[9]

Nor is it foreign to the majesty of God, as some think it is, for him to rule and keep account of even the most minute things, since He is the Creator and Lord of everything. It is not a source of shame for Him to have created them, and much less to govern that which He has made. And He who cares for humble things does not himself become humble; and He who looks down upon the lowliest does not cease dwelling in the highest places (Psalm 103:19). Thus it must be said that the Apostle deprives the oxen of God's care (1 Corinthians 9:9) not in an absolute* sense, but in comparison with people, especially believers, since the former enjoy the benefit of his general providence, and the latter his specific and exalted protection. For in any case our God gives food to the hungry, and to the young ravens that cry (Psalm 147:9). Architects state that large stones cannot be laid well without small ones (so says Plato). Therefore we should guard ourselves from thinking that God is a less worthy craftsman than mortal ones. 8

However, since nothing in the whole world is exempt from the laws of divine providence, we must profess that by how much more God cares for humans than for other things (that lack intellect), by so much more are the actions of humans subjected to the providence of God than the actions or behaviors of things that lack intellect. "From his dwelling-place He looks upon all the inhabitants of the earth; He who formed their hearts observes all their deeds" (Psalm 33:14,15). Hence Scripture shows* that the hearts, wills and actions of men are in God's hand, power, and control.[10] Accordingly it accredits all the 9

---

9   See thesis 3 above for the combination of the eternal and temporal dimensions of providence.

10 Implicitly, a distinction between 'free' and 'natural' causes is employed here. Natural causes operate without understanding and will, following the laws of nature, and thus operate 'by necessity.' Free causes, by contrast, act on the basis of prior deliberation and choice and thus can act otherwise than they actually do (contingently). 'Free causes' denote the class of personal agents. The subsumption of free causes under God's providence leads to a strong but nuanced view of God's involvement in human actions, and so avoids determinism. See theses 12–13 and 21–22 below.

significat;* omnia bona hominum opera Deo, ac proinde gubernationi ejus ascribit et eventus et successus omnium nostrarum actionum ab ipso pendere docet, Prov. 21, 1. Gen. 45, 8. Exod. 4, 11. Jac. 4, 17. Phil. 2, 13. Jer. 10, 23. Prov. 20, 24. etc.

x Neque enim in actionibus liberi arbitrii* creatura intellectualis exempta est ab ordine primae causae; quia omnino necesse est, ut in Deum, tamquam in primam, perfectissimam ac proinde efficacissimam causam,* omnis creatura, omnisque ejus actio, atque ipsius cujuslibet actionis modus omnis ac perfectio* reducatur. Sequitur ergo, nullam esse in creaturis libertatem voluntatis, quae non sit ex participatione libertatis summae increatae, quae sit causa prima, propria atque intima omnis creatae libertatis, omniumque liberarum actionum, quatenus hujusmodi sunt.

xi Tantum igitur abest, ut operatio divinae providentiae destruat libertatem voluntatis creatae, ut haec absque illa prorsus consistere nequeat. Nam cum ab efficacia voluntatis divinae pendeat, non solum actio quaelibet creaturae, sed etiam actionis ipsius modus;* consequens est, per Dei providentiam non destrui, sed statui, humanorum actuum libertatem. Quod etiam de contingentia* rerum in genere,* dicendum est. Divina enim providentia non corrumpit naturam, sed perficit; non tollit, sed tuetur; Et omnia quae creavit, sic administrat, ut ipsa suos etiam exercere et agere proprios motus sinat, August. *De Civit. Dei*, lib. 7, c. 30.[a]

xii Ad hanc Dei gubernationem pertinet ἡ διαμονὴ, permansio, quae etiam opus est divinae συνεκτικῆς δυνάμεως, quae omnes res creatas conservat, ut supersint, et persistant et in suae naturae et proprietatum naturalium* statu permaneant, ne in nihilum creatura recidat impediens, quod fieret si Deus

---

[a] Augustine, *De civitate Dei* 7:30 (CCSL 47:212).

11. ON THE PROVIDENCE OF GOD

good works of men to God, and to his governance; and it teaches that the events, good things, and outcomes depend upon Him (Proverbs 21:1; Genesis 45:8; Exodus 4:11; James 1:17; Philippians 2:13; Jeremiah 10:23; Proverbs 20:24, etc.).

For also in actions of the free will* a creature endowed with intellect is not exempt from the ordering of the first cause;* because it is altogether necessary that every creature and its every action, and even the manner and completion* of whatever action it takes are traced back to God, as to the first, most perfect and accordingly most efficient cause. Therefore it follows that in creatures there is no freedom of the will which does not arise from sharing in the highest, uncreated freedom, which is the first, proper and innermost cause of the created freedom, and of all free actions (insofar as they are of that sort).[11]

The notion that the functioning of divine providence destroys the freedom of the created will is so far from the truth, that the will cannot exist at all without it. For since not only each and every action of the creature but also the manner* of his action depends upon the effective working of the divine will, it follows that the freedom of human actions is established, and not destroyed, through God's providence. This must be said even of the contingency* of things in general.* For divine providence does not corrupt nature, but perfects it; it does not take it away, but guards it.[12] And everything which He created He administers in such a way that He allows each one even to carry out and perform its own particular motions (Augustine, *On the City of God*, book 7, chapter 30).

Also continuance or maintenance belongs to this government of God, as it too is a work of the divine power of preservation and sustains and upholds all created things so that they survive and continue to exist and remain in the state of their own nature and natural* properties. This power also prevents created things from falling back into nothing, which would happen if God

---

11 Precisely in being free, creatures share in the divine freedom. Because God's creative will is most free, the created world produced by this will displays structural freedom as well. An early expression of this relation between God's providential will and creaturely freedom was given by Jerome Zanchi (*De natura Dei*, book 5, chapter 1, question 4); cf. RTF, 86–89.

12 This sentence is a variation of the famous dictum by Thomas Aquinas: Grace does not destroy nature, but perfects it (*gratia non tollit naturam, sed perficit*), *Summa theologiae*, 1.1.8. The crucial insight presented in thesis 11 is that a created free will cannot exist at all without the divine providential will. The reason for this is that the whole of creation depends on God granting existence to it and providing the conditions for all acts and events. Providence does not 'corrupt' nature, that is, it does not take away but rather preserves the contingent nature of created reality.

subtraheret virtutem suam. Neque tantum arcana inspiratione vegetantur in genere omnes mundi partes; sed omnes ac singulae, simulatque faciem averterit Deus, consternantur; ubi spiritum reduxerit, intereunt; quo rursus emisso creantur, et facies terrae renovatur, Ps. 104, 28. 29. 30.

XIII Quas creaturas Deus conservat in natura* et proprietatibus suis, easdem etiam pro ratione* naturae uniuscujusque, ad agendum movet et applicat, eisdem concursum suum praebet, et ita cum eis concurrit, ut actione sua immediate* in actionem creaturae influat, ut una et eadem actio a prima et secunda causa dicatur proficisci, quatenus unum opus seu ἀποτέλεσμα hinc exsistit; in quo si quid est inordinati, est ab actione, non quatenus est creatoris, sed creaturae; ut in sectione accidunt quaedam ab objecti aut instrumenti vitio, quae fabro per securim agenti, non sunt imputanda.

XIV Ex his quae diximus, apparet, Deum saepe non sine medio inferiora per superiora gubernare, instituere causas secundas, quibus utitur ad ulteriores effectus producendos, non propter defectum suae virtutis, sed propter abundantiam suae bonitatis, dignitatem suae causalitatis creaturis communicando; ut per eas facilius Deum nobis auxiliantem sensu percipiamus, Dominum universorum agnoscamus, qui ad suam gloriam et salutem nostram, pro sua

were to withdraw his strength. For all the elements of the world do not receive growth generally by secret inspiration merely, but each and every one of them "is terrified as soon as God hides his face; when He takes away his Spirit, they die, and when He sends it forth, they are created, and the face of the earth is renewed" (Psalm 104:28, 29, 30).[13]

The creatures whose nature* and peculiar properties God sustains are moved and driven by Him to conduct themselves according* to their own nature; and He gives them his concurrence.[14] And He so concurs with them that through his working He directly* influences the action of the created being, so that one and the same action is said to proceed from the first and the second cause, inasmuch as one work, or the completed work, results from this source.[15] If there is anything in it that is not in order, it comes from the action of the creatures and not of the Creator; just as in wood-carving some things happen through the fault of the object or the instrument—things which should not be imputed to the artisan via the axe he wields.

From what we have stated it is clear that often God governs the inferior matters through the superior ones not without any means; that He establishes secondary causes which He uses in order to effect ulterior results—not because he lacks the power, but because of the abundance of his goodness, by communicating the worthiness of his own causality to creatures. He does this so that through the secondary causes we may more easily perceive with the senses that God is supplying his aid to us, that we may acknowledge as Lord of all things Him who employs created beings as much as He wills for his own glory and our

---

13   The century after the publication of the *Synopsis* saw the rapid rise of the natural sciences that discovered and formulated the 'laws of nature.' These discoveries led to the philosophical idea of immanent causality as governing all processes in the natural world and to the denial of any meaningful divine involvement in the 'natural' courses of events. Thesis 12 presents the position that the immanent processes of nature can occur only through God's active and continuous maintenance, without which they would fall back into nothing.

14   God gives creatures his concurrence. God conserves and serves his reality. He acts and makes it possible that human persons act too. The underlying assumption is that every good has to be ascribed to God, and every evil to ourselves. By giving concurrence, God is not morally (nor causally) responsible if man acts wrongly by deviating from God's will. See also thesis 20 below.

15   On the concept of influx or influence (*influxus*) see RTF, 30–33, 225 (scheme 11). The point of this notion is that God not only provides the circumstances as prerequisites for human action, but also has a direct ("immediate") influence that gives power and determination to the human will in the specific act.

voluntate creaturis utitur; nec abutamur mediis, aut a Deo ordinata negligamus, cum non solum actionum fines, sed etiam media ad finem, decreverit, providentiae suae subjecta et subalternata.

xv Unde id tenendum, etiam cum media adhibet, rebus omnibus nihilominus immediate providere, intime et absque dependentia a causis mediis per quas agit, quia immediate in omnibus illis operatur, illis semper praesens adest, in iisque specialem suam vim exserit, juxta illud, Non ex solo pane vivit homo, sed ex omni verbo quod procedit ex ore Dei, Deut. 8, 3.

xvi Non igitur dicendum est, Deum tantum produxisse causas secundas, iisque vim agendi tribuisse, et tam causas quam virtutes iis inditas conservare, eas autem intima virtute ad motum et actionem non impellere. Item liberi arbitrii actiones a Deo non procedere, nisi secundum indifferentiam ad bonum et malum. Itaque Deum non esse causam* actionum ejus, nisi quatenus liberum arbitrium a Deo est et conservatur. Ex qua opinione id praeter alia absurdi sequitur, quod causa secunda respectu singularum actionum, rationem habebit causae primae et primi moventis, quia movebit non mota; et ita erunt plura prima principia,* et Deus qui est primum ens, non erit proprie causa universalis

salvation.¹⁶ Nor do we abuse the means, or neglect what has been ordained by God, since He has decided not only the goals of the actions but also the means to the goals, subject to and subsumed under his providence.

For this reason we must maintain that even when He employs means He nonetheless provides for all things directly, deeply within and without depending on the middle causes through which He operates, since He is directly at work in all of them, is always present to them,¹⁷ and reveals his own special power through them, according to these words: "Man does not live by bread alone, but by every word which proceeds from the mouth of God" (Deuteronomy 8:3).

One therefore ought not to state that God produced only the secondary causes, and attributed to them the power to act (and that He preserves both the causes and the powers He conferred on them), but that He does not incite them on to motion and action through an inner force. Similarly: One therefore ought not to state that the actions of the free will do proceed from God, in as much as they are indifferent in good and evil. And therefore that God is not the cause* of the free will's actions, except insofar as the free will comes from God and is preserved by Him. From this belief it follows, in addition to other absurd beliefs, that the second cause regarding individual actions will take over the essential role of the first cause and of the first mover, because it moves without having been moved. And so there are many principles,* and God—who is the first being—is not properly the universal cause of all beings.¹⁸

---

16   Thesis 14 makes it clear that the so-called secondary causes are far from unimportant. The fact that God, as the first cause, exerts a universal force of sustenance and governance does not entail that God 'takes over' the activity of his creatures; rather, God often pursues his own goals by including instrumental causes that have their own power of producing effects and their own freedom of choice.

17   Here one may observe a connection between the notions of divine omnipresence, omnipotence and providence. Because God is essentially present to all things, He can work powerfully in all of them, and exercise his providence over all things. One is reminded of the hexameter that sums up the scholastic understanding of God's omnipresence: *Enter, praesenter, Deus hic et ubique potenter* ("by his essence, by his presence, and by his power, God is here and everywhere").

18   For an explication of the scholastic Reformed usage of the causality language, see the Glossary. The theory of the first cause indicates that God enjoys a proper kind of causality, which is characteristic of Him as Creator. The distinction between the *causa prima* and the *causae secundae* functions differently in different models. In necessitarian thought, the first cause is the only proper cause, while the second causes work only as instruments or tools. In contingency thought it implies that there are also other agents, acting in their own ways under the universal influence of God. The argument in thesis 16 denies that created agents can act apart from God's overarching causality.

omnium entium. Addimus hoc etiam quoad fidem et bona opera, Pelagianismum induci hac opinione.

XVII   Ordinem rerum ad finem, praecipue ultimum, providentiae Dei etiam subjecimus; neque enim tantum ad eam pertinet mediorum ad finem ordinatio, sed finis quoque consecutio. Nam etsi providentia, ut in homine consideratur, defectui obnoxia, et quae frustrari possit, saepe consistat sine consecutione finis a providente intenti; id tamen de providentia Dei dici non debet, quia semper illud evenit quod Deus, tamquam universalis omnium προνοητής eventurum ordinavit, atque sibi proposuit. Quae enim inter res creatas particularis alicujus causae ordinem egrediuntur, per aliam causam particularem, in primae et universalis ordinem incurrunt.

XVIII   Rectius igitur dicemus, ad providentiam non pertinere ut per eam res unaquaeque ad finem particularem sibi convenientem dirigatur, sed absolute* in finem qui toti operi congruit; quomodo qui ligna comburit in familia, non ea ordinat in finem lignis convenientem, sed familiae unius curam gerit; quam si cum nonnullis σκληρῶς, ne quid gravius dicam, pronuntiemus providentiam Dei aliquando frustrari assecutione finis, quocumque sensu intelligatur. Est enim providentia Dei qua res gubernat, similis providentiae qua paterfamilias gubernat domum, et rex civitatem, quibus bonum commune eminentius est singulari, quae causa est cur plus attendant quid communitati conveniat, quam quid uni tantum.

XIX   Inter res gubernationi Dei subjectas* id etiam animadvertendum, esse quasdam, quibus Deus providet propter se ipsas; alias autem, quibus propter aliud, ut in domo propter se providentur ea in quibus bonum domus consistit, sicuti filii, possessiones et hujusmodi; alia vero ad horum utilitatem, ut vasa et similia. Sic in universo, propter se ea quae essentialiter* pertinent ad perfectionem universi, quae propterea non corrumpuntur, propter illa autem, particularia quaedam corruptioni obnoxia; quae manent tantum, quamdiu necessarium est in his propter quae providentur.

We add that, with respect to faith and good works, Pelagianism is introduced by this belief.

17 We place under God's providence also the direction of things to their goal— especially their final goal. Indeed, to his providence belongs not only directing the means towards the goal, but also achieving the goal. When considered in the case of human beings, providence is subject to failure and can be thwarted and it often exists without the pursuit of the goal intended by the one who exercised the foresight. However, the same should not be said concerning God's providence, because what God as the universal supervisor has ordained and proposed to himself to happen always does happen. For what among the created things goes beyond the direction of some particular cause, through some other particular cause meets the direction of the first and universal cause.

18 Therefore we shall say more correctly that the concern of providence is not to direct each and every thing to a particular goal suitable for it; rather, it is in itself* a goal that agrees with the operation as a whole. It is as when someone in the family burns wood and so uses the wood for a goal that is not particularly suited for it, but he does execute his responsibility for one family. This is a better way of speaking than if we make the harsh statement made by some (not to say anything more offensive), that the providence of God sometimes is prevented from pursuing its goal (in whatever way that is understood). For the providence whereby God governs things is similar to the providence whereby the head of the household governs the home, and the king his state, for whom the common good takes priority over an individual one. This is the reason why they pay attention more to what is beneficial to the community than to only one individual.

19 Among the things subject* to God's government we ought to note also the fact that He exercises his providence over some things for the sake of the things themselves, but that there are other things in which He shows providence for the sake of something else, as in a home those things are provided for in which the very well-being of the home consists—such as the children, possessions and similar things. But other things are provided for the benefit of the prior ones, such as dishes and the like. So too in the universe: For its sake provisions are made of things which pertain essentially* to the perfect condition of the universe; on account of that these things are not destroyed. However, for its sake there are also certain particular things which are liable to destruction, and they remain only so long as it is necessary in these matters because of which they are provided for.[19]

---

19 Theses 18 and 19 differentiate between the individual things that God wills to come about through his providence and the goal for which He wills them. By this distinction,

xx	Hic videndum, an peccata etiam cadant sub divinam providentiam? Providere Deum peccata, quo sensu providere est procurare, dictu nefas asserimus. At de peccatis Deum providere, dici non solum posse, sed etiam debere, non dubitamus. Praevidet enim peccata, et permittere vult, et praevisa ordinat ad bonum aliquod vel universale, vel particulare, sive ad ostensionem misericordiae suae, sive justitiae, vel ad quodcumque aliud, atque ita, dum de illis bene facere disponit, de iisdem providere, recte dicitur. Quodsi in peccato solum consideretur id quod est reale et, ut loquuntur, positivum, quod alii materiam dicunt, scilicet ens aliquod vel actio; hac ratione, etiam dici possunt peccata a Deo provisa, sed tantum secundum quid,* non absolute;* eo quod peccati ratio* formalis consistit in privatione* entis et boni, in deformitate quadam et ἀταξίᾳ, quae non est a Deo, ac proinde ab eo provisa esse non potest.

xxi	Distinctio actionis Dei providentis ἑκάστῳ, ἢ συγχωρούσης ἢ ἀπονεμούσης, in efficientem et permittentem, hic locum habet. Prima est qua Deus efficaciter operatur et perficit in omnibus et singulis quod operis sui est; nempe bona omnia in communi* et singulari natura, tam bona naturae, ut substantias,* motus, actiones et perfectiones rerum, quam bona moralia, ut virtutes omnes tam civiles quam spirituales; quia, ut summum bonum, ita etiam omnis boni auctor est et origo.

---

conceptual space is kept open in two directions: (a) in view of partial courses of events that seem to run aground, one should look at the higher goal God has in mind and that is never frustrated even when parts of the way toward the goal break up; and (b) the insight that God takes inferior things in service for a higher good anticipates the discussion, in theses 20–24, of God's providence in relation to evil and sin.

At this point we should see whether sins, too, fall under divine providence. We assert that it is wrong to say God provides sins in the sense that to provide means to attend and to care for. But we do not doubt that it may, and indeed should be said that God exercises providence concerning sins.[20] For He foresees sins in advance, and wills to permit them; and as they are seen beforehand, He destines them to some universal or particular good, whether for a display of his mercy or justice, or for some other good. And so it is rightly said that He exercises providence regarding them, since He disposes to do well regarding them. But if one considers only that which is real in sin and 'positive,' as they say, what others call 'the matter' of sin, namely, as an entity or as an action, in this sense sins can be said even to be provided by God,[21] but only in a relative* sense and not in itself.* That is because the formal structure* of sin exists in the absence* of being and of good, in a certain deformity and disorderliness, which does not come from God and so cannot have been provided for by Him.[22]

Here is a place for a distinction in the ways God handles providence when He implements it—it is either effective, or permitting. The first is the one whereby God works effectually, and in all things generally and individually perfects his work (namely all things both general* and specific in nature), not only the essential good—the substances,* motions, actions and completions of things—but also the moral good, such as all civic and spiritual virtues. Because, as the highest good, He is also the author and source of all good.

---

20   Namely, in an indirect relation.
21   Namely, in the sense of a direct object.
22   The argument of thesis 20 maneuvers between attributing evil directly to God's providence which compromises God's essential goodness and justice and detracting a significant part of what occurs in our world from God's providential control, which robs God of his essential omnipotence. The solution to this dilemma is found in two distinctions. First, evil is not the *direct, absolute object* of God's providential will (as if He wills it for its own sake), but only the *indirect, relative object* inasmuch as God includes it in a course of events leading to a higher goal (this distinction anticipates on the notion of 'permission' treated in theses 21–24). The second distinction is made between the different ontological aspects of an evil act (assuming that evil is primarily something acted out by someone). Viewed apart from its moral quality, it has the status of an entity that exists in reality, and can as such be willed by God. For example: The actual taking of a knife, raising one's hand and stabbing the knife into a human body are 'positive' actions and can be attributed to God. However, insofar as these actions constitute murder (and are morally defective) they cannot be attributed to God's activity. In terms reminiscent of the Aristotelian duality of matter and form, the act itself is the 'matter' of sin, while the sinful character is the 'form' that makes it sin. This 'form,' furthermore, consists of an active deviation (*privatio* has the connotation of 'robbery' or 'deprivation') from the good intended by God.

XXII   Secunda, Deo etiam in Scriptura tribuitur, in qua saepe dicitur aliquid permittere; non solum dum concedit ut consequi possimus quod optamus in actionibus et rebus bonis, vel mediis aut indifferentibus, quae permissio cum approbatione et efficientia Dei conjuncta est, ut Heb. 6, 3. et 1 Cor. 16, 7. Sed etiam dum mala et peccata quae alioqui vetat, non impedit cum posset,* qui legem de impediendis non habet; quae permissio, etsi ipsa approbetur, non continuo tamen approbantur quae per ipsam permittuntur. Sic accipitur Jes. 2, 6. Jer. 16, 13. Act. 14, 16. Rom. 1, 24. et 28. Ps. 81, 13.

XXIII   Hanc omnium peccatorum permissionem Deum providere fatemur. Nam etsi peccata mala sint, ideoque provideri a Deo non possint, bona tamen est eorum permissio. Quam proinde et vult Deus, et directe decernit, et ordinat ad bonum aliquod majus, quam sit illud, cujus privatio est malum quod permittitur. Nam Deus cum summe bonus sit, nullo modo sineret mali aliquid esse in operibus suis, nisi adeo esset omnipotens, ut de malo etiam bene faceret, ut recte August. *Ench.* c. 11.[a]

XXIV   Sic permissionem illam Dei, non esse otiosam, statuimus, aut Deo invito aliquid accidere, aut non curante, aut quod agitur negligente; ac proinde voluntati ejus et consilio non debet opponi. Permittit enim Deus volens, et consulto;

---

[a] Augustine, *Enchiridion* 3.11 (CCSL 46:53–54).

The second is attributed to God also in Scripture, in which it is often said that He permits something; not only when He allows us to obtain what we wish in actions and affairs that are good, or middling actions that make no difference, for which the permission is linked to God's approval and effective operation (Hebrews 6:3 and 1 Corinthians 16:7). But even when He does not prevent the evils and the sins which He forbids (though He is able* to), as He does not have a law about hindering things. For this permission is granted; nevertheless, the things that are permitted by it are not approved continuously.[23] In this way the following texts are interpreted: Isaiah 2:6, Jeremiah 16:13, Acts 14:16; Romans 1:24 and 28; Psalm 81:13.

We acknowledge that this permission for all sins belongs to God's providence. For although sins are evil, and accordingly cannot be provided by God, nevertheless the permission of them is good. So then, God both wills and directly decrees the permission, and ordains it for some good purpose that is greater than that of which the absence is the evil that is permitted. For since God is good to the highest degree, He would in no way permit there to be anything evil in his workings, unless He were not so almighty that even concerning evil He would still do good, as Augustine justly states (*Enchiridion* chapter 11).

And so we think that God's permission is not idle, or that something happens without the will of God, or without his care, or that He is neglecting anything that happens.[24] And accordingly his permission should not be understood as opposed to his will and counsel. For it is in accordance with his will and after

---

23 The fact that the permission of some (evil) thing is affirmed by the divine will, does not imply that the thing permitted itself is approved of. Expressed in a brief formula: gW(PaWp) ≠ gWaWp ≠ gWp (in words: "God wills to permit subject a to will act p" is not equal to "God wills subject a to will act p" nor equal to "God wills act p"). God's will is involved in the permission of evil acts, but in an indirect way, not related to the evil act itself, but to the permission of a separate act of the created will that performs the evil act. Because of this indirect relation, God cannot be held morally responsible for the evil act permitted by him. For Voetius' theory of permission (also with reference to Maccovius) see Beck, *Gisbertus Voetius*, 334–344.

24 For John Calvin, the notion of 'permission' suggests that God merely acquiesces in an act performed by creatures, without being decisively involved, "as if God sat in a watchtower awaiting chance events, and his judgments thus depended upon human will" (*Institutes*, 1.18.1). Calvin argues instead that even the evil acts of Satan and of the wicked fall under the direct command of God's will. Through the acts of men and devils, God exercises his own judgments and performs his own work. For details see Dolf te Velde, *The Doctrine of God in Reformed Orthodoxy, Karl Barth, and the Utrecht School: A Study in Method and Content*, Studies in Reformed Theology, vol. 25 (Leiden: Brill, 2013), 779–780.

ac potenter dirigit peccata, nec raro eam permissionem ad judicia sua exercenda adhibet, quandoque etiam ut ἀντιμισθίαν praecedentium peccatorum. Quo sensu agnoscunt Scholastici,* Deum habere scientiam* practicam peccatorum, quatenus ea permittit, vel impedit, vel facta ordinat ad finem, Thom. 1. p. q. 14. art. 13.ᵃ

xxv   Addimus etiam, antequam fiant, et cum fiunt, Deum sapientissime sanctissimeque administrare argumenta et occasiones, quae velut incitamenta sunt, ad actum* qui a creatura sine peccato non fit, etiamsi per se mala non sint, concursum suum etiam ad actum qua talis, non qua peccatum non denegare; *praesidere*, ut ipse agnoscit Bellarm., ipsis voluntatibus malis easque regere et gubernare, in eis invisibiliter operari, ut a divina providentia, suo vitio malae, ad unum potius quam ad aliud ferantur. Addit, Deum impiorum voluntates flectere et torquere, *De amiss. grat. et stat. peccat.* cap. 13.ᵇ ab iis loquendi formulis non abhorrens, imo duriores usurpans iis quas ab aliis prolatas ad calumniam detorquet.

xxvi   Hujus doctrinae finis est idem qui omnium rerum a Deo creatarum: Gloria nempe Dei, cui juncta est electorum salus, qui ex ea multiplicem usum referunt: Deum ex omnium rerum gubernatione agnoscentes, summe sapientem, bonum, potentem, omnium rerum Dominum, a quo pendent omnes creaturae; fiduciam in eum conjicere edocti, tamquam Patrem, de omnibus ipsis prospicientem, et in ejus protectione, cujus judicio subjacent, secure quiescentes; in adversis patientes, ad primam causam oculos attollentes, agnoscentes et emendantes peccata sua, in prosperis grati, nomen ejus celebrantes; Deum in cujus manu sunt omnes creaturae, timentes et reverentes, summo amore prosequentes, quem norunt peculiarem suorum curam gerere, et haereditatem coelestem eis parasse.

ᵃThomas Aquinas, *Summa theologiae* 1.14.13.   ᵇBellarmine, *De amissione gratia et statu peccati* 2.13 (*Opera* 5:278a).

taking counsel that God grants permission. And He powerfully controls direction over sins, and it is not unusual for Him to apply his permission to carry out his judgements, occasionally even as a recompense for previously committed sins. In this sense the Schoolmen* acknowledge that God "possesses a practical knowledge* of sins, insofar as He permits, or prevents, them, or—once committed—appoints a goal for them" (Thomas Aquinas 1.14. art. 16).²⁵

In addition to this we state that before they occur, and while they are occurring, God in his great and most holy wisdom directs the arguments and opportunities that are like incentives to an act* that does not happen without sin on the creatures' part, yet these opportunities are not evil in and of themselves, so that He does not refuse his concurrence to the act as such (though not as sin).²⁶ We state "that He presides (as Bellarmine himself admits) over wrongful wills, and rules and governs them, is invisibly at work in them, so that from his divine providence, though evil by their own vice, they are led more to the one than to the other." Likewise he adds that God "bends and twists the wills" of the ungodly (*On the Loss of Grace and the State of Sin*, chapter 13), not shunning those types of expressions, instead using even harsher ones than those he adopts from others and distorts into a false accusation.²⁷

The goal of this teaching is the same as that of teaching that God has created everything: the glory of God, to which is joined the salvation of the elect, who derive manifold benefits from it. By his government of everything the elect come to acknowledge God as most wise, good, and powerful, the Lord of all things, upon whom all creatures depend. They learn to place their trust in Him like a Father who in all things provides for their best interests, as they rest securely in the protection of the one to whose judgement they subject themselves. They are patient in times of adversity, as they raise their eyes up to the prime cause, acknowledging and correcting their own sinful ways. They are grateful in prosperous times, bringing praise to his name; they fear and honour God in whose hand are all creatures, and with the utmost love they follow after Him whom they know exercises his particular care for those who are his own, and who has prepared for them an inheritance in heaven.

---

25 On God's 'practical knowledge,' see the explanation in thesis 2 above. Here, God's practical knowledge, joined to his will, is considered in its relation to evil things. While the *scientia Dei* is good itself, still evil things and sins do fall under his knowledge and are known as evil. But the evil character of these objects of knowledge does not affect the perfection of God's knowledge.

26 For the way in which God grants concurrence (*concursus*) to acts of creatures, see the explanation in thesis 13 above. On the distinction between the "act as such" and the "sinful character" of the act, see thesis 20 above.

27 The specific target of Bellarmine's accusation are Zwingli, Calvin, and Beza.

XXVII Si quis plura desideret, et ad omnes humanae rationis quaestiunculas responsum exspectet, audiat eumdem quem initio laudavimus, Salvianum: Possum quidem rationabiliter et satis constanter dicere, nescio secretum, et consilium divinitatis ignoro. Sufficit mihi ad causae hujus probationem* dicti coelestis oraculum. Deus a se omnia dicit aspici, omnia regi, omnia judicari. Si scire vis quid tenendum sit, habes literas sacras: perfecta ratio est hoc tenere, quod legeris. Qua causa autem Deus haec de quibus loquimur, ita faciat, nolo a me requiras. Homo sum, non intelligo secreta Dei; investigare non audeo, et ideo etiam attentare formido, quia et hoc ipsum genus sacrilegae temeritatis est, si plus scire cupias quam sinaris. Sufficiat tibi, quod Deus a se agi ac dispensari cuncta testatur, *De gub. Dei*, lib. 3.[a]

XXVIII Quae cum ita sint, eorum vecordiam et amentiam perhorrescimus (sunt verba Isidori Pelusiotae, lib. 3, *epist*. 154.[b]) qui aut Deum non esse statuunt: aut esse quidem, mundum autem haudquaquam condidisse; aut si condiderit, minime gubernare; aut si gubernet, iis qui vitium amplexantur, oblectari; aut si non delectetur, imperium aliis concessisse; aut si non concesserit, invito ei ereptum fuisse; aut si non ereptum sit, improbos ulcisci nolle; aut si velit, non posse; aut si possit, otium antiquius habere; aut si carius non habet, ab astrorum motu superari; aut si non superetur, inertem ac desidem esse velle: et si quas similes blasphemias impiorum evomant ora, qui sentient tandem, quod

> Ἔστι μέγας ἐν οὐρανῷ
> Θεὸς ὃς ἐφορᾷ πάντα καὶ κρατύνει
> Ὧι δόξα εἰς τοὺς αἰῶνας.[c]

---

[a] Salvian, *De gubernatione Dei* 3.1.2–3 (CSEL 8:42).   [b] Isidore of Pelusium, *Epistulae* 3.154 (MPG 78.846).   [c] Based on Sophocles, *Electra* 174–175; for the last line, cf. Galatians 1:5 and 2 Timothy 4:18. For a discussion of the use of this unattributed classical text in the *Synopsis* see Riemer A. Faber, "Scholastic Continuities in the Reproduction of Classical Sources in the *Synopsis Purioris Theologiae*," *Church History and Religious Culture* 92.4 (2012), 563.

11. ON THE PROVIDENCE OF GOD

If anyone desires more and expects answers to all the minor questions arising from human reason, let him listen to the same person whom we praised at the outset of this disputation, Salvian: "I can say with sufficient reason and confidence: I do not know what is hidden, and I am ignorant of the counsel of the divine. In support* of this position the revelation of the heavenly statement is sufficient for me: God says that by Him all things are observed, by Him all things are governed, and by Him all things are judged. If you wish to know what it is you must hold on to, you have the sacred writings. There is a perfect reason to hold on to what you have read. However, I do not wish that you ask me for what reason God so performs the things about which we are speaking. I am only a man; I do not understand the secret things of God. I do not make bold to search into them and therefore I am afraid even to attempt it, because if you desire to know more than is permitted to you, that too is a kind of irreverent impudence. Let it be sufficient for you that God bears witness that all things are performed and managed by Him" (*On God's Government* book 3).

Since these things are so, "we recoil in terror from the madness and folly [the words are those of Isidore of Pelusium,[28] book 3 Epistle 154] of those who posit either that there is no God, or that there is one, yet who by no means whatsoever founded the world. Or that if He had founded it, does not govern it at all; or that if He governs it, He takes delight in those who embrace vice. Or that if He does not enjoy it, that He forfeits rule over it to others; or that if He has not forfeited the rule, that it was snatched away from Him against his will. Or that if the rule was not snatched away, that He is unwilling to avenge evil-doers; or that if He did wish to avenge, that He is not able to. Or that if He is able to, He has been idle for a very long time. Or that if He has nothing more valuable to do, that He is being over-ruled by the motion of the stars; or if He is not being over-ruled, that He wishes to be idle and lazy." And if the mouths of the wicked spew forth any other blasphemies like this, they will in the end realize that:

Great in Heaven
Is God who beholds and rules over every thing,
To whom belongs the glory for ever and ever.

---

28 Isidore of Pelusium († before AD 450) was born in Alexandria and became a priest and abbot in the monastery of Lychnos near Pelusium. He wrote an estimated ten thousand letters of which some two thousand remain. He wrote to Cyril of Alexandria in order to render full justice to the memory of John Chrysostom, who was venerated by Isidore. Isidore opposed the heresies of Nestorianism and Eutychianism, but in a moderate manner.

DISPUTATIO XII

De Angelis Bonis ac Malis

Praeside D. ANTONIO WALAEO
Respondente ADRIANO HASIO

THESIS I   Quandoquidem de rerum omnium creatione et gubernatione praecedentibus thesibus est actum, sequitur jam ut de speciali quarundam creaturarum statu deinceps agamus. Quia vero Angeli inter illas praecipuae sunt, ab iis hac disputatione exordium sumemus.

II   Angelorum nomen* Sacrae Scripturae peculiare (quod profani scriptores Graeci per vocem* δαιμόνων, Latini, geniorum, fere exprimunt) significat* creaturas spirituales, per se subsistentes,* intellectu et voluntate* libera instructas, potentia* vero ac virtute eximia, ad opera sua naturae convenientia extra se obeunda, prae ceteris creaturis pollentes.

III   Angelos esse Dei creaturas, ex ipsorum quo Deo serviunt ministerio, abunde liquet, et praeterea multis perspicuis Sacrae Scripturae locis demonstratur. Praeterquam enim, quod ex eo, et per eum et in ipsum sunt omnia, Rom. 11, 36. etiam verbo Jehovae coeli facti sunt, et spiritu oris ejus totus exercitus eorum, Ps. 33, 6. Imo, per eum condita sunt omnia, quae in coelis sunt et in terra, visibilia et invisibilia, sive throni, sive dominia, sive principatus, sive potestates; omnia per eum et in eum sunt condita, et ipse est ante omnia, et omnia per eum consistunt, Col. 1, 16. 17.

DISPUTATION 12

Concerning the Good and Bad Angels

President: Antonius Walaeus
Respondent: Adrianus Hasius[1]

Since we have treated the creation and the government of all things in the preceding theses, it follows now that we deal next with the special state of some created beings. Since the angels indeed are the foremost of these, we shall start with them in this disputation.

The name* 'angels' is peculiar to Holy Scripture (the pagan Greek writers express it roughly by the word* *daimones*, and the Latin ones by *genii*) and signifies* spiritual creatures which subsist* on their own, are equipped with intellect and a free will,* and have exceptional power* and ability to perform tasks suitable to their nature outside of themselves, being more powerful than other creatures.

It is abundantly clear from the service they render to their God and also from the many clear passages of Scripture that angels have been created by God. For besides the fact that "from Him and through Him and to Him are all things" (Romans 11:36), there is also: "By the Word of the Lord the heavens were made, and all their hosts by the breath of his mouth" (Psalm 33:6). Indeed, "for in Him all things were created, in heaven and on earth, visible and invisible, whether thrones or dominions or principalities or authorities—all things were created through Him and unto Him. He is before all things and by Him all things consist" (Colossians 1:16,17).[2]

---

1 Born in 1601 in Rotterdam, Adrianus Gerardi Hasius matriculated on 6 December 1616 in medicine. He defended this disputation on 27 January 1621. He was ordained in Kralingen in 1623, Poortugaal and Hoogvliet (1627), Brielle (1636) and Leeuwarden (1644). In 1650 he accepted a call to Rotterdam, but died before his installation and was buried there. See Du Rieu, *Album studiosorum*, 128, Van Lieburg, *Repertorium*, 88, and Bronchorst, *Diarium*, 161.

2 In the exegetical tradition, the words 'thrones,' 'dominions,' 'principalities' and 'authorities' were regarded as referring to angels. Walaeus follows this tradition; the annotations on this text in the *Statenvertaling*, the Dutch translation of the Bible, also give this interpretation, which Walaeus, being one of the translators of the New Testament, might have written. However, Walaeus does not follow the exegetical tradition of using this text to establish a ranking of angels; see thesis 50 below.

IV   De tempore autem creationis eorum, olim inter Christianos disceptatum fuit. Origenes[a] cum multis Graecis Patribus et nonnullis Latinis, eorum creationem longe ante hunc mundum visibilem conditum arcessit, sed illi validissime ex eo refutantur, quod per phrasin hanc, antequam hic mundus esset, item ante jacta mundi fundamenta, ipsa aeternitas in Scriptura Sacra passim indicatur, ut videre est Joh. 17, 5. Eph. 1, 4. 1 Petr. 1, 20. etc.

V   Imo vero Moses Dei ipsius aeternitatem ex eo celebrat, Ps. 90, 2. quod fuerit, quum nondum essent montes, antequam formasset terram, orbemque habitabilem. Et Sapientia illa increata hoc privilegio adversus omnem creatam sapientiam gloriatur, quod inuncta fuerit ante primordia terrae, et quod edita sit cum nullae essent abyssi, Prov. 8, 22. et Johannes Evangelista inde Deitatis Filii Dei demonstrationem orditur, quod in principio erat verbum,* quae omnia omnino essent inefficacia, si Angeli aut ullae aliae creaturae ante hunc mundum conditum, vel ante hoc temporis initium jam exstitissent.

VI   Etsi vero de ipso die creationis eorum nimis anxie disputandum non sit, illorum tamen sententiam veritati magis convenientem judicamus, qui primo die cum ipso supremo coelo eos creatos statuunt. Quemadmodum enim homo mundo huic jam perfecto statim fuit impositus, ita et ipsorum domicilio constructo, illos tamquam incolas statim fuisse ei adjunctos, omnino consentaneum est; adde quod a simplicissimis essentiis in toto hoc Dei opere ad magis composita progressus est factus, et Deus ipse, Hiob. 38, 4. et deinceps testatur, hosce Dei filios creatori suo laudes cecinisse, quum fundaret terram, quum disponeret mensuras ejus, quum bases ejus firmaret, etc.

VII   Creatos ergo initio temporis ex nihilo, et quidem bonos omnes et ad imaginem Dei, adversus Manichaeos et Priscillianistas asserimus. Nam Deus inspexit

---

[a] See Origen, *De principiis* 2.3, 3.5 (SC 252:248–274, 268:218–234).

Concerning the time of their creation, however, there was a debate among Christians in the past. Origen, along with many Greek church-fathers and several Latin ones, contended that they were created long before this visible world was established. But they are refuted very strongly by the fact that throughout Scripture the phrases "before this world existed" and "before the foundations of the world were laid" mean eternity itself, as can be seen also from John 17:5, Ephesians 1:4, 1 Peter 1:20, etc.

In fact Moses glorifies the eternity of God on the grounds that "He existed before the mountains came to be, before He formed the earth and the habitable world" (Psalm 90:2). And because of this excellence, uncreated wisdom is glorified over and above every created wisdom: "For before the beginning of the earth [divine Wisdom] was anointed, and it was brought forth when there were no depths" (Proverbs 8:22, etc.). And John the evangelist commences his demonstration of the deity of God's Son with the fact that "in the beginning was the Word*." Now all these statements would be entirely devoid of force if the angels or any other creatures existed before this world was founded, or before this beginning of time.[3]

Whereas the precise day of their creation should not be debated too fretfully, we nevertheless judge that the opinion coming closest to the truth is of those who posit that they were created on the first day, along with the highest heaven itself. For just as mankind was instantly placed upon this world after it had been completely made, so too is it altogether consistent that once their dwelling-place was constructed, the angels came into existence and were placed in it as residents. Add to this the fact that in this whole work of God there was a progression from the most simple essences to the more composite ones. And God himself (in Job 38:7 and following) states that these sons of God "sang the praises of their creator, when He laid the foundations of the earth, when He determined its measurements, when He established its foundations etc."[4]

Therefore contrary to the Manichaeans and the followers of Priscillian[5] we assert that they were created out of nothing at the beginning of time, and also that they all were good and in God's image. "For God saw everything that He

---

3 See, similarly, *SPT* 10.24 on the creation of the world within time.
4 Like many of his contemporaries, Walaeus understood the term 'sons of God' in Job 38:7 (cf. Gen. 6:2; Job 1:6) as a reference to the angels.
5 Priscillian of Avila († AD 386), a charismatic teacher in Galicia, promoted idiosyncratic ascetic practices and was accused of being a 'Crypto-Manichee.' He was put to death in 386 for heresy which included alleged magical practices and illicit relations with women. Against him and his followers Augustine wrote his *Contra Priscillianistas* (415). See Henry Chadwick, *Priscillian of Avila: The Occult and the Charismatic in the Early Church* (Oxford: Clarendon, 1976), esp. 132–138.

quidquid fecerat, et ecce erat valde bonum, Gen. 1, 31. ac propterea filii Dei, servi Dei, Angeli Dei, Potestates ac Principatus, imo et Dii in Sacra Scriptura appellantur. Et ipsi quoque qui ex illis defecerunt, dicuntur in veritate non perstitisse, Joh. 8, 44. et originem suam non servasse, Jud. versus 6. unde et in veritate fuisse, et originem sanctam habuisse, necessario consequitur.

VIII Ex hac peculiari ipsorum creatione evincimus contra Saducaeos antiquos, Act. 23, 8. et nostri aevi Libertinos, Angelos veras esse hypostases,* seu substantias* separatim et per se subsistentes. Deus enim nulla accidentia* separatim creasse legitur. Evincunt hoc quoque eorum actiones et opera quae ipsis passim tribuuntur. Evincunt apparitiones eorundem etiam in corporibus assumptis. Evincunt praemia quae assignantur bonis, et poenae quae reservantur malis; et alia plurima de quibus postea agemus.

IX Etsi vero non pauci ex antiquis et recentibus scriptoribus, sua quoque corpora, vel coelestia, vel ignea, vel aërea Angelis attribuant, nos tamen esse meros spiritus et omni omnino corpore proprie* dicto carere, constanter asserimus. Tum quia Scriptura eos diserte Spiritus vocat, Mat. 8, 16. Hebr. 1, 14. qui carnem et ossa non habent, nec sensibus externis comprehendi possunt, Luc. 24, 39.

had made, and behold it was very good" (Genesis 1:31), and therefore in Holy Scripture they are called sons of God, servants of God, angels of God, powers and principalities, indeed, even 'gods.' And it is said of those who have fallen away from them that they did "not stand firm in the truth" (John 8:44) and "did not keep their original state" (Jude 6)—from where it necessarily follows that they had been in the truth and that they had a holy beginning.

From this peculiar creation of them we succeed in demonstrating against the Sadducees of long ago (Acts 23:8) and the Libertines of our age[6] that angels are true *hypostases*,* or substances* that subsist separately and on their own. For we do not read that God created any accidental* properties separately.[7] This is proved also by their actions and works, which are ascribed to them everywhere.[8] Appearances of them, also through the bodies they have assumed, demonstrate this. The rewards that are bestowed on the good angels and the punishments that are kept in store for the bad ones prove this, too; and there are many other proofs, which we shall treat later on.

But whereas not a few of the ancient as well as recent writers attribute to angels also their own bodies, whether heavenly, fiery, or airy ones, we firmly assert that they are mere spirits, and that they are entirely devoid of all body in the proper* sense of the word.[9] Not only because Scripture clearly calls them spirits (Matthew 8:16; Hebrews 1:14) which do not have flesh and bones, and are not able to be grasped by the outward senses (Luke 24:39). But also because

---

6 According to John Calvin the contemporary Libertines taught that angels and devils do not really exist. J. Calvin, *Contre la secte phantastique et furieuse des libertins qui se nomment spirituelz*, ed. M. van Veen [COR IV, vol. 1], (Geneva: Droz, 2005), 86. According to the Libertine David Joris, man is a devil to himself (86 note 1). For the Libertines see *SPT* 9.29 n. 15.

7 Walaeus's argument involves an implicit syllogism that depends on 1) the basic Aristotelian understanding of reality as consisting in accidents (what exists in another and can be said of it) and substances (what subsists separately and on its own). Since 2) Scripture does not present God as ever creating accidents 'separately,' it follows 3) that the angels must be substances (as Walaeus had posited in the first sentence of this thesis).

8 The argument rests on the classic scholastic dictum that actions belong only to self-subsistent individuals. This also applies to the Persons in the Trinity. Cf. *SPT* 7.7, n. 5 and 7.15.

9 The reason for ascribing some kind of body to angels was that they would be infinite if they did not have bodies. The idea that angels have 'airy bodies' goes back to Augustine who cites Lucius Apuleius (c. AD 125–175) who states that demons are airy regarding their body (*quod corpore aeria*); see Augustine, *De Civitate Dei* VIII, 16. Although the Fourth Lateran Council (1215) called the nature of the angels *spiritualis* (DH 800), many later theologians still taught that angels have a kind of body. The Reformed Girolamo Zanchi (1516–1590) preferred the patristic view that angels have a heavenly or ethereal body to later scholastic theories. Zanchi, *Opera* 3, 69. Cf. Bavinck, *Reformed Dogmatics* 2, 455, who also refers to Gerardus Joannes Vossius (1577–1649) as an proponent of this position.

Tum quia corporalia, iisdem immotis aut illaesis penetrant, quemadmodum ex ἐνεργουμένοις apparet, item ex Angelorum per coelos descensu atque ascensu, et ex eorum comparitione in aedibus aut carceribus occlusis, Mat. 2, 13. Act. 12, 7. etc. Tum denique quia multa daemonia unum hominem saepe ingrediuntur, Mat. 12, 45. imo et integra legio, Luc, 8, 30.

x   Nec vero huic sententiae contrarium est, quod nonnunquam in corporibus humanis apparuerunt. Nam et Filius Dei ante incarnationem suam, et Spiritus Sanctus corporea specie quandoque apparuit, nec tamen inde essentiam ejus corpoream esse evincitur; et Moses, Mat. 17. externa specie discipulis visus fuit, nec ideo tamen animas corporeas esse concedendum. Quia vel corpora illa in speciem talia esse potuerunt, sicuti in somniis aut visionibus ecstaticis contigit, vel si vera corpora fuerunt, quod de nonnullis apparitionibus omnino statuendum est, ea ad tempus divina virtute iis adjuncta sunt, ac postea denuo in sua principia* resoluta, quemadmodum et vestimenta, quae in hac sua oeconomica* cum hominibus conversatione gesserunt.

xi   Ex hac eorum spirituali natura* sequitur etiam eorundem immortalitas. Nam etsi eadem potentia, qua ex nihilo producti sunt, in nihilum quoque redigi possint, cum tamen eorum essentia* ex diversis principiis internis composita non sit, per sese ipsi in alia principia resolvi non possunt, nec ex Dei voluntate unquam resolventur, propterea Christus, Luc. 20, 35. 36. eos qui digni habiti fuerint futuro seculo, mori amplius non posse* asserit, quia ἰσάγγελοι, id est, angelis pares sunt futuri; mali vero Angeli, etsi spirituali morte puniantur, aeternis tamen vinculis sub caligine custodiuntur in diem judicii, Jud. versus 6. et post extremum judicium iisdem aeternus quoque ignis paratus est, ut Christus loquitur, Mat. 25, 41.

xii   Haec de Angelorum substantia ex Sacra Scriptura dicta sumpto; jam de eorum attributis* et adjunctis nonnullis quaedam breviter sunt annotanda.

they penetrate corporeal things without being moved or wounded by them, as is evident from the people whom they affect, as well as from the fact that they ascend and descend through the heavens, and from the manifestation of them in buildings or locked prisons (Matthew 2:13, Acts 12:7, etc.). And finally, also because many spirits (Matthew 12:45), indeed even an entire legion (Luke 8:30), often enter into one man.

Nor is it contrary to this viewpoint that they often appear in human bodies. For also the Son of God before his incarnation, and the Holy Spirit sometimes, appeared in bodily form, yet it is not thereby proved that his essence was corporeal; and Moses (in Matthew 17) was seen by the disciples in outward form, and yet it must not be granted therefore that souls are corporeal. Because either those corporeal bodies were able to be such in appearance (as happens in dreams or ecstatic visions), or if they were truly bodies—which in the case of some apparitions must be acknowledged as fact—these bodies were attached temporarily to the spirits by divine power, and thereupon were resolved into their original elements* once again, like the clothing they wore during their occasional* interaction with human beings.

From the fact that their nature* is spiritual it follows that they are also immortal. For even if the same power which brought them forth out of nothing is able also to render them into nothing, nevertheless because their essence* is not composed of diverse internal elements, they cannot of their own accord ever be resolved into other principal elements, nor will they ever be resolved out of God's will.[10] Wherefore Christ asserts that "those who will be worthy of the future age can* no longer die" (Luke 20:36) because they will be *isaggeloi*, that is, they will be on a par with angels. But the wicked angels, although they will be punished with spiritual death, are being kept in eternal chains in darkness until the day of judgment (Jude 6), and an eternal fire has been prepared for them also after the final judgment, as Christ says (Matthew 25:41).

This much must be said from Holy Scripture, then, about the substance of angels; now a few observations should be made briefly about some of their attributes* and qualities.[11]

---

10 The immortality of the angels flows from their simple or non-composite nature, because death is the separation of soul and body or form and matter. Only composite beings can die. The point is that angels will not be annihilated; God can do this, but it is against his will.

11 In theses 14–25 Walaeus discusses the angels' knowledge (*cognitio*), in theses 25–35 their will (*voluntas*), and in theses 36–46 their power (*potentia*). Because angels are not eternal and do not emanate from God's essence but are created by God out of nothing, their knowledge, will and power are finite and limited. But like their knowledge, their will and power far transcend any human capacity.

XIII   Angelos intellectu, voluntate et potentia eximia esse praeditos, omnes ipsorum actiones satis demonstrant, et expresse sapientia illis tribuitur, 2 Sam. 14, 20. Dominus meus Rex sapiens est, tamquam sapientia Angeli Dei. Voluntatis interni et proprii actus* illis tribuuntur, Dan. 4, 17. Ex decreto Vigilum verbum hoc, et 1 Pet. 1, 12. in quae cupiunt Angeli introspicere. Robur vero et potentia singularis, Ps. 103, 20. Benedicite Jehovae Angeli ejus valentissimi robore, et passim alibi.

XIV   De intellectu Angelico multa valde curiose a Scholasticis* disputantur; nos μὴ ἐμβατεύοντες ἃ μὴ ἑωράκαμεν, quantum vel ex Scriptura, vel ratione* firma possumus colligere, paucis indicabimus.

XV   Omnem intellectum per aliquam conjunctionem rei* cognitae cum facultate* cognoscente fieri, inter Philosophos fere constat; conjunctio autem haec fit, vel per essentiam ipsam rerum, vel per earum ideas seu species,* quae species vel nascuntur cum intellectu, vel per sensus et ratiocinationem a rebus abstrahuntur, vel per revelationem divinam animis inseruntur.

XVI   Quod primum cognitionis modum* attinet, ipsum Deum ab Angelis per ipsam ejus essentiam cognosci, statuendum est, quemadmodum lux ab oculo conspicitur. Nam Sacra Scriptura testatur eos semper videre faciem Patris, Mat. 18, 10. et hoc illis cum beatis omnibus commune* est, quod eum videant sicuti est, 1 Joh. 3, 2. eumque cognoscant sicuti cogniti sunt, 1 Cor. 13, 12. Se

12. CONCERNING THE GOOD AND BAD ANGELS

13 All their actions sufficiently demonstrate that angels are endowed with the gifts of intellect, will and outstanding power; wisdom also is attributed explicitly to them (2 Samuel 14:20): "My lord, the king possesses wisdom, like the wisdom of an angel of God." Internal and proper actions* of the will are attributed to them—Daniel 4:17: "This word comes from the decision of the angels that keep watch." And 1 Peter 1:12: "Things into which even angels long to look." They possess strength and singular power (Psalm 103:20): "Praise the Lord, you his angels, most powerful in strength," and elsewhere in other passages.

14 Concerning the intellect of angels the Scholastics* hold many wildly inquisitive debates. As for us, not entering upon what has not been revealed to us,[12] we shall indicate briefly as much as we can gather from Scripture or sound reason.*

15 Philosophers are generally agreed that every understanding arises through some coming together of the thing* that is known and the faculty* that knows.[13] However, this coming together occurs either through the essence of things themselves, or through the ideas or concepts[14] of them. These concepts* are innate to the intellect, or are abstracted from things through the senses and logical reasoning, or they are implanted in our souls through divine revelation.[15]

16 As far as the first mode* of cognition is concerned, we must hold that God himself is understood by the angels by means of his own very essence in the same way as light is seen by the eye. For Holy Scripture bears witness that "they always behold the face of the Father" (Matthew 18:10), and with all the blessed they share* the fact that "they see Him as He is" (1 John 3:2), and "they know Him just as they themselves are known" (1 Corinthians 13:12). And in this same

---

12   Cf. Colossians 2:18 "... worshipping of angels, intruding into those things which he has not seen."

13   According to Aristotle, the conjunction consists even in an identity of knower and thing known. See *On the Soul* 3.4 (430a4): "What thinks and what is thought are identical; for speculative knowledge and its object are identical."

14   In medieval epistemology *species* refers to ideas or concepts that humans are able to frame. Knowledge is described as a discursive step-by-step process in which the human intellect abstracts from sensory experience through images (*phantasmata*) to intelligible species or universals that can be combined subsequently in order to form judgments. See Anthony Kenny, *A New History of Western Philosophy*, vol. 2: *Medieval Philosophy* (Oxford: Clarendon Press, 2005), 236–237.

15   Walaeus distinguishes four ways in which angels know. The first is cognition by means of the essence of the object known (thesis 16). Next, angelic knowledge by means of species is subdivided by the origin of the species. They are either innate, implanted in the angels' intellects at their creation (thesis 17), acquired by the angel himself through abstraction (thesis 18), or given in a special divine revelation (thesis 19).

ipsos quoque hoc pacto norunt; nam si Spiritus hominis qui est in ipso, novit quae sunt in homine, 1Cor. 2, 11. multo magis de Angelico intellectu hoc est sentiendum.

XVII   Per species* vero ipsis naturaliter* a prima creatione insitas, plurima quoque nosse, non est dubium; nam si prima principia in animis hominum a primo ortu nascantur, ut saniores Philosophi agnoscunt; et si primi hominis intellectui tanta fuerit congenita vis, ut omnium animantium naturas perspicere potuerit, fatendum nobis multo magis, omnium creatarum rerum saltem universales ideas a Deo ipsorum intellectui a primo ortu fuisse insertas, ex quarum ad res* singulares applicatione, individuorum quoque notitia, quanta ad muneris cui adhibentur, exsecutionem est necessaria, in iis exsistit.

XVIII   De cognitione quae per sensus aut ratiocinationem fit, difficilior est quaestio. Etsi vero nec sensus externi nec ratiocinatio proprie dicta illis conveniat, cum organis externis et internis careant, non est tamen negandum, quin species rerum multarum extrinsecus ab illis recipiantur, qua scientiam experimentalem acquirant, et ex signis et effectis causas, aut ex causis et signis eventa, quae antea ipsis fuerant ignota, eminentiori licet modo, colligant; quemadmodum Paulus Eph. 3, 10. testatur, nunc innotescere Principatibus ac Potestatibus in coelo per Ecclesiam πολυποίκιλον illam Dei sapientiam; quod idem ex Angelorum colloquiis et actionibus aliis, quae nobis in Sacra Scriptura repraesentantur, abunde quoque liquet.

XIX   De modo illo ultimo, qui per extraordinariam revelationem fit, res clara est in prophetiis sacris. Nam nemo nec in coelo, nec in terra, nec subter terram, librum illum divinae providentiae septem sigillis ad illud usque tempus

12. CONCERNING THE GOOD AND BAD ANGELS

way they know also themselves, for if the spirit of a man which is in him knows what is in a man (1 Corinthians 2:11), we should all the more view the intellect of angels in this way.

It is beyond doubt that they also know very many things through the concepts* naturally* planted in them when they were first created. For if the first principles are innate in the souls of men at the moment they come into being (as the sounder philosophers have acknowledged[16]), and if so much ability had been produced along with the intellect of the first man as to make him capable of perceiving the natures of all living beings, we must confess all the more that, at the moment angels came into being, God implanted in their intellects at least universal concepts of all created things. And on the basis of the application of these universals to individual things* also the knowledge of individual things exists in them, insofar as this knowledge is necessary to carry out the task for which they are summoned.

A harder question concerns the knowledge that arises through the senses or logical reasoning. For although 'external senses' or 'logical reasoning' properly speaking does not apply to angels, since they lack internal and external organs, we should not deny that they do receive the concepts of very many things from without. And thus, they obtain knowledge from experience, albeit in a more eminent way, and they gather both the causes (from the signs and their effects) and the effects (from the causes and the signs) that were previously unknown to them. Paul testifies to this effect in Ephesians 3:10: "Now to the rulers and authorities in the heavenly realms, through the church the manifold wisdom of God should be made known." The same fact is abundantly clear from the conversations and other actions of the angels, which Holy Scripture presents to us.

Regarding the final mode of cognition, which occurs through extraordinary revelation, the issue is clear in the sacred prophecies. For "no-one, either in heaven, or on earth, or under the earth, could open the book of God's

---

16   The epistemological idea that the first principles of knowledge, such as the law of non-contradiction, are innate, was common among philosophers. The Reformed orthodox held that the human mind had a structure that enabled it to recognize the truth of the first principles of knowledge. Zanchi rejects both the Platonic theory of recollection of forms and the Aristotelian axiom that all knowledge stems from sense perception. Like the Stoics and Cicero, he holds that the first principles proceed together with the intellect and thus "the ideas common to us all are inborn, not furnished by experience." Zanchi, *Opera* 3, 636–637. Cf. Herman Bavinck, *Reformed Dogmatics*, vol. 1: *The Prolegomena* (Grand Rapids: Baker, 2003), 67; Beck, *Gisbertus Voetius*, 160–165.

obsignatum, aperire aut inspicere potuit, nisi Leo ille ex tribu Judae; a quo deinde Angelus illa accepit et Dei servis revelavit, Apoc. 1, 1. et 5, 5.

xx An autem omnia quae norunt, semper actu* illis sint praesentia, an vero eorum intellectus in nonnullis quoque sit in potentia,* curiosa potius est quam utilis quaestio. Nos soli Deo hoc privilegium ascribimus, quod purus sit actus; Angelorum intellectui tamen semper ea actu praesentia credimus, in quibus ipsorum beatitudo per se consistit, aut quae muneris a Deo ipsis impositi rationem spectant.

xxi Ex quibus omnibus liquet, magnam quidem esse Angelorum sapientiam, non tamen infinitam, quia finita natura infiniti* capax non est; nec quoque omnium rerum et actionum quae in mundo contingunt, quum hoc de Deo tamquam illi proprium praedicet* Scriptura, quod nulla res creata sit occulta in conspectu ejus, sed omnia nuda sint et aperta coram oculis ejus, Hebr. 4, 13.

xxii Multo minus illis tribuimus notitiam cogitationum humanarum, nisi quando per signa se produnt, nam Deus novit solus corda omnium filiorum hominis, 1 Reg. 8, 39. aut cognitionem certam rerum futurarum contingentium, et ex arbitrio hominum vel Dei singulari providentia pendentium, nisi quando ab eo ipsis revelantur; quemadmodum de die judicii ipsis ignoto Christus loquitur, Marc. 13, 32. et in genere Deus apud Prophetam Esaiam, 44, 7. testatur: Quis ut ego praedicit et indicat istud? aut ordinat istud mihi ex quo disposui populum aeternum, ut quae futura sint aut eventura, indicentur?

providence, sealed with seven seals until that very time, except the Lion from the tribe of Judah," from whom the angel thereupon received and revealed it to the servants of God (Revelation 1:1; 5:5).

However, it is a curious rather than useful question whether everything the angels know is always present to them in actuality* or whether their understanding in some instances is also in potency.* We ascribe only to God the special right of being 'pure act.'[17] Nevertheless, we do believe that those things in which the angels' blessedness exists as such, or which relate to the nature of the task God has imposed upon them, are always present in actuality to the angels' understanding.

From all this it is clear that the angels' wisdom is very great, though not infinite, because finite nature is not capable of infinity;* and they also do not have knowledge of all the things and actions which occur in the world, since Scripture declares* this as belonging to God alone, "because nothing in creation is hidden from God's sight, but everything is laid bare and revealed before his eyes" (Hebrews 4:13).

Much less do we attribute to them a knowledge of the thoughts of human beings, except when these reveal themselves through signs, "for only God knows the hearts of all the sons of man" (1 Kings 8:39). Nor do we assign to them a definitive knowledge of future contingencies dependent upon the choice of men or upon God's singular providence,[18] except when these have been revealed to them by Him. In this way Christ speaks of the day of judgment that is unknown to them (Mark 13:32), and God testifies in general to the prophet Isaiah (44:7): "Who proclaims to be as I am? Then let him declare it. Or let him lay out before me what has happened from the time when I established my ancient people. Or let him reveal what the future is or what is yet to happen."

---

17 The Aristotelian distinction between potency (*potentia*) and act (*actus*) was very important in the scholastic tradition. These two concepts indicate that the end of each thing is, as it were, found in it as a possibility or potency, and that this end must be realized, or actualized, or become act. In God, however, there is no such transition from potency to actuality. God is *actus purus*, that is pure or perfect actuality, the only being not in potency. See DLGTT, s.v. "actus purus." With respect to the specific question whether the angelic intellect is sometimes 'in act' and sometimes 'in potency,' see Thomas Aquinas, *Summa theologiae*, 1.58.1.

18 On God's knowledge and providence concerning future contingencies, see SPT 6.32–33 and 11.11.

XXIII   Ex quo evidenter consequitur, Angelos non esse a nobis invocandos, quia solus ille invocandus est, qui gemitus cordis et cogitationes nostras novit, Rom. 8, 27. et in quo tamquam omnium rerum sciente et potente plene possumus confidere, Rom. 10, 14., ut jam taceamus Angelorum cultum et adorationem expresse condemnari ab Apostolo Paulo, Coloss. 2, 18. et ab ipso Angelo, Apoc. 19, 10. et 22, 9.

XXIV   Interim tamen ad fidelium consolationem et praemunitionem discimus, Angelos in genere* omnium omnino hominum singularium habere notitiam. Mali enim Angeli operantur in filiis contumaciae, Eph. 2, 2., et pios instar leonum rugientium circumeunt, 1 Pet. 5, 8. Boni vero Angeli praeterquam quod omnium piorum custodia illis sit commissa, Hebr. 1. versus ult. in poenis a Deo infligendis impios a piis secernunt, Ezech. 9, 4. et Apoc. 7, 3. Et ultimo die a Christo mittentur, ut congregent electos ex quatuor ventis coeli, ab extremo terrae ad extremum coeli, Marc, 13, 27. et omnia scandala et facientes iniquitatem colligant ex regno ejus, et abjiciant in caminum ignis, Mat. 13, 41.

XXV   Secunda facultas, omni naturae intelligenti, ac proinde et Angelis competens, est voluntas,* de qua non minus quoque curiose disputant, quam temerarie extra Scripturas multa definiunt Scholastici.

XXVI   Nos vero, ut intra eosdem, quos antea nobis praefiximus limites, maneamus, agnoscimus, Angelos a prima sui creatione non minus libera voluntate fuisse praeditos, quam homines, imo vero eo quoque liberiore, quo intellectus et sanctitatis praestantia eisdem antecellunt.

XXVII   Hanc libertatem fatemur etiam hac in re sitam fuisse, quod potestatem habuerint perseverandi in illo naturae bono, in quo a Deo per creationem fuerant constituti; quemadmodum ex eo demonstratur, quod Deus eis non pepercisse dicatur, qui peccaverunt, sed ad judicium in Tartaro servandos tradiderit, 2 Pet. 2, 4. et Joh. 8, 44., quod Diabolus pater sit mendacii, et cum mendacium

From this it clearly follows that we should not call upon angels, because 23
we should call upon Him only who knows the groanings of the heart and our
thoughts (Romans 8:27) and in whom we can fully confide (Romans 10:14),
since He knows, and has power over, all things. Not to mention the fact that
the worship and adoration of angels is condemned expressly by the apostle Paul (Colossians 2:18), and also by the angel himself (Revelation 19:10,
22:9).

Meanwhile, however, for the comfort and preservation of believers we learn 24
that the angels in general* do have a knowledge of every individual person. For
the bad angels are at work in the sons of disobedience (Ephesians 2:2), and
they surround the pious like roaring lions (1 Peter 5:8). But the good angels,
besides the fact that they have been entrusted with guarding all pious believers (Hebrews 1:14), distinguish the impious from the pious in imposing God's
punishments (Ezekiel 9:4[-6]; Revelation 7:3). And on the last day "they will be
sent by Christ to gather his elect from the four winds of heaven, from the ends
of earth to the ends of heaven" (Mark 13:27), and they "will gather out of his
kingdom everything that causes sin and all who do evil, and throw them into
the fiery furnace" (Matthew 13:41).

The will* is the second faculty which all intelligent nature, and consequently 25
also the angels, possess. About it the Scholastics debate no less speculatively
than they rashly come up with many definitions from outside the Scriptures.[19]

But, to stay within the same boundaries which we previously established 26
for ourselves, we acknowledge that angels have been endowed with a free
will from the beginning of their creation, no less than men—indeed, a will
as much more free as they surpass them in the pre-eminence of intellect and
holiness.

We confess that this freedom had been bestowed even in this point: That 27
they had the power to persevere in that natural good in which God had first
placed them through creation; for instance, this is demonstrated by the fact
that God is said "not to have spared the angels who sinned but handed them
over to hell to be kept for judgment" (2 Peter 2:4), and that "the devil is the father

---

19 The complaint about scholastic speculation regarding the subject of 'angels' is common in Reformed orthodoxy. This disputation also claims that 'the Scholastics' speculate about their will (*SPT* 12.25, 34), perseverance (*SPT* 12.30) and ranking (*SPT* 12.50). It is difficult to find precise references for these opinions. For a survey of later medieval theories about the free will of angels, see: Tobias Hoffmann, "Theories of Angelic Sin from Aquinas to Ockham," in *A Companion to Angels in Medieval Philosophy*, ed. Tobias Hoffmann (Leiden: Brill, 2012), 283–316.

loquitur, ἐκ τῶν ἰδίων, ex propriis loquatur. Non ergo ex aliquo naturae defectu aut impotentia, sed ex mera contumacia peccarunt, qui defecerunt.

xxviii Quodnam autem fuerit hoc primum eorum peccatum, in quod ex libero voluntatis abusu inciderunt, tam clare in Scripturis non exprimitur. Valde tamen probabile est, id in divinitatis aliqua affectatione, atque in Dei Filium peculiari contumacia constitisse. Quod ex tentatione qua Satan primos nostros parentes seduxit, colligitur, et ex perpetuo conatu quo Dei gloriam in se transferre studet. Speciatim vero ex odio quo Christum et ejus ecclesiam persequitur, cujus viva imago nobis Apoc. 12. describitur.

xxix Quaenam vero causa fuerit, quod illis libero suo arbitrio* abutentibus, reliqui in veritate perstiterint, et originem suam servarint, quaestio est, non minus utilis, quam ardua.

xxx Scholasticorum plerique inde perseverantiam ipsorum ortam volunt, quod actus* beatificus in voluntate creaturae omnem actum contrarium excludat, beatificum vero hunc in voluntatem influxum eos meruisse primo liberi sui arbitrii actu.

xxxi Haec assertio praeterquam quod temeraria est et extra Scripturam, etiam Sacrae Scripturae locis refutatur. Quis enim prior dedit ei, quod illi retribuatur? nam ex ipso, per ipsum et in ipsum sunt omnia, Rom. 11, 35. Et quaenam, obsecro, analogia est inter actum aliquem obedientiae, eumque ex jure creationis debitum, et inter aeternum hoc atque indebitum praemium?

xxxii Nos ergo contra asserimus, etiam beatis Angelis non nisi in Domino gloriandum, cum Sacra Scriptura manifesto ex Dei peculiari gratia* eorum beatitudinem arcessat, quando passim filii Dei, et Angeli electi, ab ea vocantur, 1 Tim. 5, 21. Filiorum vero haereditas sub meritum non cadit, nec electio ulla ad hanc filiationem nisi ex gratia est. Unde et Paulus, propositum Dei quod est secundum electionem, manere, ait, non ex operibus sed ex vocante, Rom. 9, 11.

12. CONCERNING THE GOOD AND BAD ANGELS

of lies, and when he speaks lies he speaks out of himself" (John 8:44). Therefore those who fell did not sin out of some defect or weakness in their nature but out of pure obstinacy.[20]

28 The Scriptures do not so clearly express what the very first sin was into which the angels fell by the free abuse of their will. However, it is very likely that it consisted of some desire to be like God, and in a particular obstinacy against the Son of God. For this can be gathered from the temptation whereby Satan seduced our first parents, and from the constant attempt whereby he strives to draw the glory of God unto himself. This can be gathered especially, however, from the hatred with which he pursues Christ and his church; a vivid picture of this is portrayed to us in Revelation 12.

29 But it is a useful and equally difficult question to ask for the reason why some angels stood firm in the truth and kept their origin while other angels abused their own free choice.*

30 A majority of the Scholastics argues that the angels' perseverance arose from the fact that [God's] act* by which He made the angels beatific, excludes in the creature's will every contrary action, and that they merited this beatific influence upon their will by virtue of the first act of their free choice.

31 This claim, besides the fact that it is rash and beyond Scripture, is refuted also by passages of Holy Scripture. For "who has ever given to God that God should repay him? For from Him and through Him and to Him are all things" (Romans 11:35–36). And what comparison is there, I ask, between one act of obedience which by virtue of creation is owed, and this eternal reward that is not indebted?

32 We therefore make the contrary assertion that even the blessed angels must boast in nothing except in the Lord, since Holy Scripture evidently derives their blessedness from God's individual grace,*[21] when it everywhere calls them sons of God and elect angels (1 Timothy 5:21). But the inheritance of sons does not come as a result of merit, nor is there any election to this sonship except by grace. Whence also Paul says that "God's purpose according to election stands not by works but by the one who calls" (Romans 9:11).

---

20   The volitional character of angelic disobedience is emphasized here, as it is for human sin; cf. *SPT* 14.30–31.

21   Angels are substances that subsist separately and on their own (*SPT* 12.8). Hence, the reason why some angels stood firm in the truth (*SPT* 12.29) does not lie in any merit of those angels (*SPT* 12.31) but in the individual or peculiar grace which they received thanks to Christ's mediation (*SPT* 12.33). Angels, like humans, are subject to God's predestination (*SPT* 24.7, cf. 12.34).

XXXIII   An vero ad conservationem originis suae opus habuerint Mediatore, disputatur inter scriptores orthodoxos tam veteres quam recentes. Nos affirmativae sententiae, quae gravissimos auctores habet, libentius accedimus; tum quia Christus solus in Scriptura vocatur Filius ille in quo Patri, nempe per se, complacuit; tum quia Christus peculiariter Angelorum princeps et caput appellatur; tum denique, quia etsi nullum peccatum in iis fuerit a quo redimendi fuerunt, tamen etiam in iis divina justitia inveniret quod requireret in assignando illis aeterno praemio, si secum eos compararet, atque ex se et in se solis eos respiceret, sicuti ex Hiob. 4, 18. et c. 15, 15. apparet; ut jam de locis illis Eph. 1, 10. et Col. 1, 20. nihil dicamus, qui quidem ab aliis de solis animabus tempore mortis Christi in coelo degentibus, sed tamen sine similis phraseos exemplo, exponuntur.

XXXIV   Ex quibus omnibus firmiter concludimus, Angelos jam beatos, atque electionis et perseverantiae suae omnino esse certos. Quae vero praeterea de libertate exercitii et specificationis in voluntate Angelica, respectu reliquorum obedientiae actuum, qui ipsorum essentialem* beatitudinem non spectant, a Scholasticis dicuntur, nos ut temere disputata et sine ratione definita, praeterimus,

There is a debate among ancient and recent orthodox writers whether 33
the angels were in need of a Mediator for the preservation of their original
state.[22] We readily concur with the affirmative position (which has very weighty
authors), because, on the one hand, in Scripture Christ alone is called the Son
in whom the Father, namely by himself, was well pleased; and because, on the
other hand, Christ specifically is called the prince and head of angels. And
finally, we concur because although the angels had no sin from which they
needed to be redeemed, nevertheless, even in them would God's justice find
something lacking for granting the reward of eternal life to them, if He would
compare them with himself, and would take notice of them as they are in and
of themselves alone, as appears from Job 4:18 and 15:15. To say nothing now
about those passages in Ephesians 1:10 and Colossians 1:20, which admittedly
are explained by others (but without providing a parallel of similar wording
elsewhere) as referring only to the souls that were dwelling in heaven at the
time of Christ's death.[23]

From all these points we firmly conclude that angels are already in the state 34
of blessedness[24] and altogether certain of their own election and perseverance.
But the things the Scholastics additionally state about the freedom of exercise
and the freedom of specification in the will of angels (in respect of the other acts
of obedience that do not pertain to their essential* blessedness), we pass over
on the grounds that they are debated rashly and defined without argument.[25]

---

22   In his *Loci Communes* (*Opera* I, 194–195) Walaeus mentions Augustine, Chrysostom, Calvin, Bucer and Junius as theologians who answer the question whether angels need a Mediator in the affirmative, whereas Beza responds in the negative. Walaeus dinstinguishes between a Mediator of reconciliation and one of preservation. Angels need the latter but not the former.

23   Walaeus is probably thinking of Beza, who did not follow the common understanding of the words "all in heaven" in Eph. 1:10 and Col. 1:20 as a reference to the angels, but argued that Paul referred to the fathers under the old covenant who had died in faith and were already in heaven at the time of Christ's incarnation. See his *Annotationes majores in Novum Dn. Nostri Jesu Christi Testamentum* ([Geneva]: [Jérémie des Planches], 1594), part II, 352b–353a and 405a–b. The slight hesitancy expressed by Walaeus in appealing to these verses, which in their common interpretation support his argument, may reflect the authority of Beza and his New Testament annotations.

24   Cf. *DLGTT*, s.v. "beatus": Those who are in heaven in a purified state and no longer tainted with concupiscence.

25   Freedom of exercise (*libertas exercitii*) and freedom of specification (*libertas specificationis*) are ramifications of the concept of freedom of the will in (Reformed) scholastic anthropology. Freedom of exercise is the equivalent of freedom of contradiction (*libertas contradictionis*) whereas freedom of specification is the equivalent of freedom of contra-

hoc unum ex Scripturis certi, quod perpetuo et in omnibus, Dei et Christi ejus voluntati obediant, idque maximo cum studio, et summa cum alacritate, sicuti eorum exemplum nobis propterea in Scripturis saepe proponitur.

xxxv   Intellectum et voluntatem creaturae rationalis necessario sequitur potentia, qua extra sese efficax est, et actiones naturae suae convenientes producit. Eam vero valde insignem esse in Angelis, ex ipsorum admirandis operibus liquet, unde et Ps. 103, 20. valentissimi robore, et 2 Thess. 1, 7. Angeli potentiae Dei dicuntur; Satan vero Mat. 12, 29. ὁ ἰσχυρός, et 2 Cor. 4, 4. Deus hujus seculi appellatur.

xxxvi   Potentia autem haec eorum ex objectis, circa quae in hoc mundo versatur, optime explicabitur. Quae sunt vel animae vel corpora, illa rursum vel viva vel vitae expertia, et haec denique vel elementaria vel aetherea.

xxxvii Quod aetherea corpora attinet, etsi plurimi inter philosophos Intelligentias coelestibus orbibus praeficiant, quae[a] eis assistant, eosque perpetuo in orbem agant, aut quae stellas etiam sigillatim circumferant; nos tamen id tamquam figmentum nulla solida ratione* nixum rejicimus, quia Sacra Scriptura quae nobis Angelorum officia amplissime passim describit, nullam ejus rei mentionem facit, sed contra eorum domicilium in supremo coelo seu Paradiso collocat, atque omnes propter salutem fidelium mitti asserit, Heb. 1, 14. Et virtutem illam qua coeli ac stellae in orbem feruntur, a prima creatione eis divinitus fuisse insitam, ac per Dei singularem providentiam in iisdem conservari, non obscure indicat, sicuti videre est Job. 38, 31. Ps. 19, 5. et 104, 19–23. Eccl. 1, 5. etc.

---

[a] All texts have *qui*.

riety (*libertas contrarietatis*). For the meaning of these distinctions, see *SPT* 6.35 (note 28). Walaeus declares this distinction irrelevant with respect to the will of angels.

12. CONCERNING THE GOOD AND BAD ANGELS

For we are certain of this one thing from Scriptures, that they obey the will of God and of his Christ constantly and in everything, and that they do so with utmost dedication and the highest eagerness—as it is for this reason that the Scriptures often present them to us as exemplary.

35 A reasonable creature's intellect and will are necessarily followed by power, whereby the creature is effectual outside itself, and whereby it produces actions befitting its own nature. It is clear from their marvelous deeds that this power is exceedingly strong in angels, wherefore they are said to excel in strength (Psalm 103:20) and are called angels of God's power (2 Thessalonians 1:7). But Satan, in Matthew 12:29, is called "the strong one," and in 2 Corinthians 4:4 "the god of this world."

36 This power of the angels will be explained best from the objects around which it operates in this world. And these objects are either souls or bodies, the former being either alive or dead, and the latter being either elementary or ethereal.

37 As far as the ethereal bodies are concerned, very many philosophers assign to the heavenly spheres powers of intelligence[26] that are to support them and propel them constantly in their orbit, or to conduct individual stars in their circle. We reject this, however, as an invention not based on any solid argument.* For Holy Scripture, which everywhere describes the duties of the angels most fully to us, makes no mention of this matter, but to the contrary places the angels' dwelling-place in the highest heaven or Paradise, and asserts that they all are being sent for the salvation of believers (Hebrews 1:14). And the Bible clearly indicates that the force by which the heavens and the stars are carried in their orbit had been grafted in them by divine providence from the first creation onwards, and is preserved by God's singular providence—as can be seen from Job 38:31, Psalm 19:5[-6] and 104:22[19–23], Ecclesiastes 1:5, etc.

---

26 According to medieval cosmology the luminaries consist of ether, a fifth, non-earthly element. Augustine had left the possibility open: "I am not even certain upon this point: whether the sun, and the moon, and all the stars, do not form part of this same society, though many consider them merely luminous bodies, without either sensation or intelligence," *Enchiridion*, 58 (MPL 40, 259–260). Platonists thought that celestial bodies were animate and moved themselves. Aristotelians, e.g., Thomas Aquinas, held that celestial bodies were moved externally by separate intelligent substances, identified with the angels. The Platonic position is not mentioned in thesis 37. Walaeus rejects the idea that the heavenly bodies are moved by independent intellects and does not see the heavenly bodies as animate, nor these supposed souls as angels.

XXXVIII Falsum etiam est, et illusionibus daemonum omnino ascribendum, quod incantatores carminibus suis, solis ac lunae cursum se sistere, aut sidera vertere retro, olim gloriati sunt, cum Sacra Scriptura hoc inter Dei extraordinaria et ei maxime propria miracula recenseat, Jos. 10, 13. Es. 38, 7.

XXXIX In elementaria vero corpora majorem vim eos obtinere, Sacra Scriptura docet, nempe ad ea agitanda, alteranda, sistenda, dissipanda, etc. Nam Angelorum sanctorum ministerio Sodoma et Gomorra eversa sunt, Gen. 19. Vis ignis ab iis inhibita, Dan. 3. Venti ne flarent, cohibiti, Apoc. 7. Carceres et catenae ferreae sine strepitu effractae, Act. 5. et 12. atque a Satana ignis de coelo, ac venti tempestuosi in greges ac domum filiorum Hiobi praecipitati sunt, Hiob. 1, 16. 19. item in terram, Apoc. 13, 13. unde et potestas aeris illi peculiariter tribuitur, Eph. 2, 2.

XL In hominum atque animantium reliquorum corpora non minori efficacia pollent. Transferunt ea per aërem celerrime, ut ex Christi ipsius, Matth. 4. et Philippi exemplo, Act. 10. liquet; motus ipsorum animales impediunt; mutos, surdos et caecos, organis tamen integris, reddunt, et eorum nervis ac linguis pro libitu suo utuntur, ut ex obsessorum et a Christo in Evangelio curatorum exemplis constat. Boni etiam non minus quam mali, morborum infligendorum potestatem habent, ut 2 Sam. 24, 16. Hiob. 2, 7. Act. 12, 23. et alibi videre est; et una nocte multas hominum myriadas unus ex iis conficit, Exod. 12, 23. 2 Reg. 19. etc.

XLI An vero morbos eadem potentia curare valeant, difficilior quaestio. Nos multorum morborum genera, ab iis sanari posse, non diffitemur, sed per causas* secundas, aut per occulta remedia ab iis occulte et solerter adhibita, aut per exemptionem aut translationem materiae morbificae. Morbos vero plane letales, aut in quibus alicujus partis forma plane periit, ab iis curari posse, omnino

Also false and altogether worthy of being assigned to devilish illusions is what the magicians once claimed that by their chanting they could stop the course of the sun and the moon, or turn back the stars,[27] since Holy Scripture reckons this among the extraordinary miracles that are restricted to God himself in particular (Josiah 10:13; Isaiah 38:7).

But Holy Scripture does teach that angels possess a greater power over the elementary bodies, namely to excite them, or change, stop, scatter them, etc. For Sodom and Gomorrah where overturned by the work of holy angels (Genesis 19). The force of fire was checked by them (Daniel 3); they stopped winds from blowing (Revelation 7); and prisons and iron chains were smashed without a sound (Acts 5 and 12). And by Satan fire from heaven and stormy winds were hurled down upon the herds and home of Job's sons (Job 1:16, 19), and similarly upon the earth (Revelation 13:13)—from where also the power of the air is assigned to him specifically (Ephesians 2:2).

Upon the bodies of human beings and the other living creatures they exert powers that are equally effective. They very quickly transport them through the air, as is evidenced in the case of the body of Christ himself (Matthew 4), and of Philip's (Acts 10[8:39]); they impede their natural movements. They render bodies dumb deaf, and blind, while the organs remain intact, and they use their muscles and tongues at will, as is clear from the instances of the possessed and those healed by Christ in the Gospel. The good angels, no less than the evil ones, have the power to inflict diseases, as is seen from 2 Samuel 24:16, Job 2:7, Acts 12:23 and elsewhere. And in one night one of them slew many myriads of human beings (Exodus 12:23; 2 Kings 19 [:35], etc.).

A more difficult question is whether they possess the same power to cure the sick. We do not deny that they are able to cure many types of diseases, but they do so through the secondary causes,* or by hidden remedies that they apply secretly and cleverly; or they do so by the removal or transference of matter that brings disease.[28] But we flatly deny that they are able to cure diseases that

---

27 The expression "magicians ... claimed that by their chanting they could ... turn back the stars" (*incantatores carminibus suis ... sidera vertere retro gloriati sunt*) contains a verbal echo of Vergil, *Aeneid* 4.487–489, where Dido's sister Anna tells of a Numidian witch who promises to turn back the course of the stars with her chanting (*carminibus promittit /... / vertere sidera retro*). For a discussion of this and other classical texts cited in the *Synopsis* see Faber, "Scholastic Continuities," 561–579.

28 In the seventeenth century it was a common idea that illness was caused by some pathogenic matter (*materia morbidica*). When a patient's health deteriorated, the decline was believed to be caused by this pathogenic matter migrating to the chest or the head and this could lead to the death of the patient. Through bloodletting by venesection they

negamus; quia hoc divinae plane virtutis est, et divinae vocationis aut missionis extraordinarium signum.

XLII   Multo minus iis tribuimus potestatem homines mortuos in vitam reducendi, aut eorum animas ex inferis excitandi, sicuti Gentilitas olim credidit, et inter Pontificios non pauci. Exemplum vero Samuelis excitati per incantationem Sagae, cujus mentio 1 Sam. 28. fit, imposturam fuisse Satanae, se ipsum pro Samuele venditantis, omnino statuimus.

XLIII   Unde quoque evidenter concludimus, vera miracula ab iis fieri non posse. Nam et boni Angeli haec nunquam sibi vendicarunt, cum Scriptura illa inter opera Deo propria recenseat, Ps. 72, 18. et 136, 4. cujus gloriam ad se nunquam rapiunt. Malorum vero Angelorum prodigia, quae ab iis venditantur, vel praestigiis et illusionibus constant, vel operibus quidem humanum captum excedentibus, ita tamen ut causae aliquae a sapientioribus ex ipsa natura dari possint, unde et signa ac prodigia mendacii a Spiritu Sancto vocantur, 2 Thess. 2, 9.

XLIV   Difficillima vero, et tamen explicatu necessaria quaestio est, quam vim in animas humanas obtineant. Fatemur, tam bonos quam malos Angelos, sensus externos et internos hominum miris modis afficere posse, sicuti scotomate ab iis percussi sunt Sodomitarum oculi, Gen. 19, 11. Sui ipsorum et aliarum personarum* ac rerum species* repraesentare solent, coram animis hominum vigilantium aut dormientium, citra externorum sensuum opem, quod ex propheticis somniis et visionibus liquet. Sic Angelus Satanae Spiritus mendax fuit in prophetis Achabi, 1 Reg. ult. et homines obsessi varias illorum illusiones patiuntur, ut experientia testatur.

XLV   Sicuti autem boni Angeli potestatem habent, cogitationes bonas et sanctas suggerendi, sic contra mali potestatem habent suggerendi cogitationes malas, 1 Chron. 21, 1. item affectus hominum perturbandi atque irritandi, ut exemplo Saulis 1 Sam. 16, 15. demonstratur.

XLVI   Negamus tamen, eos immediatam habere potestatem in judicia hominum practica, aut in ipsorum voluntatem, quia Scriptura id Prov. 21, 1. et alibi soli Deo ascribit. Imperium ergo, quod Sacra Scriptura in homines impios malis Angelis ascribit, morale tantum est, et tamen ex justo Dei judicio ita efficax, ut eos tamquam mancipia quocumque volunt, agant. Nam cum a Deo deseruntur,

---

sought to remove the *materia morbidica* from the body. In his inaugural speech at the Athenaeum Illustre in Amsterdam entitled *The Oration on the Dignity and the Usefulness of the Mathematical Sciences* (1634), Martin van den Hove (1605–1639) stated that a doctor should not only take heed of the agitation of the *materia morbifica* but he should also consider the motion of the moon and examine the state of the year from the stars. See Mordechai Feingold, *History of Universities* XXI/1, (Oxford: Oxford University Press, 2006), 112–113.

12. CONCERNING THE GOOD AND BAD ANGELS

are obviously fatal, or diseases by which some body-part completely loses its form—because this belongs clearly to the jurisdiction of God's power, and is an extraordinary sign of a divine calling or mission.

42 Much less do we ascribe to them the power of restoring dead men to life, or of arousing their souls from the underworld, as the ancient heathens and not a few of the papal teachers believed. We are altogether certain that the case of Samuel summoned by the incantation of the medium (mentioned in 1 Samuel 28) was a deception of Satan, who put himself forward in the guise of Samuel.

43 From this we also draw the clear conclusion that angels are not able to perform true miracles. For even the good angels never claim these for themselves, since Scripture counts them among the works that belong to God (Psalm 72:18; 136:4), whose glory they never seize for themselves. But the signs which are put forward by the bad angels consist either of tricks and illusions, or of works which surpass human understanding—in such a way though that wiser persons can give some of their causes out of nature itself, whence they are also called "counterfeit signs and wonders" by the Spirit of God (2 Thessalonians 2:9).

44 A much more difficult question, though one which must be answered, is what power they possess over human souls. We hold that both good and bad angels are able to influence the external and internal senses of men in amazing ways, as when they struck the eyes of the men of Sodom with blindness (Genesis 19:11). Without needing the outward senses, they habitually portray their own likenesses,* or those of other persons* and things, to the minds of people when they are awake or asleep, which is evident from the prophetic dreams and visions. Thus an angel of Satan was a lying spirit among the prophets of Ahab (1 Kings 22[:21–24]), and people who are possessed experience various apparitions of them, as experience reveals.

45 Moreover, just as good angels have the power to prompt good and holy thoughts, so too on the other hand do the evil ones have the power to suggest evil thoughts (1 Chronicles 21:1), also in order to confuse and upset people's feelings, as the case of Saul (1 Samuel 16:15) shows.

46 However we deny that they exert direct control over people's practical judgments, or over their will, because Scripture ascribes that to God alone, in Proverbs 21:1 and elsewhere. Therefore the influence which Holy Scripture attributes to bad angels over wicked people is only a moral one; yet by God's just judgment it is so effective that they are able to drive them wherever they wish, like slaves. For when they are abandoned by God, or when He implants

aut efficacia erroris ab eodem immittitur, ad ingratitudinem aut contumaciam antecedentem puniendam, instar pecudum affectibus abripi, et instar caecorum etiam in manifestis errare solent, sicuti videre licet Rom. 1, 28. Eph. 1, 2. 2 Cor. 4, 4. 2 Thess. 2, 11. etc.

XLVII Idcirco piis diligenter vigilandum est et orandum ne unquam in tentationem ducantur, sed a malo illo liberentur; semper quoque certi esse debent, nec Angelos bonos pro iis quicquam, nisi ex Dei imperio; nec Angelos malos, nisi ex Dei judicio et concessione, adversus eos posse. Imo vero et sanctorum Angelorum praesentia per eos quoque a Deo postulari potest; quorum potentia et auxilio Satanae vis et efficacia impediri, et Satanas ipse ligari in Scripturis asseritur, Apoc. 12, 8. item 20. etc.

XLVIII Consideratis Angelorum essentialibus facultatibus, restant explicanda nonnulla adjuncta, quae breviter annotabimus, nempe numerus, motus, locus, ordo et officia ipsorum.

XLIX Angelorum numerum esse maximum, ex Scripturae multis locis patet; nam millies centena millia, et decies centena millia Dei solium circumstant, Apoc. 5, 11., et integra daemonum legio unum hominem occupavit, Luc. 8, 30. Motus eorum celerrimus est et instar fulguris, Luc. 10, 18. unde et cum ventis et igni comparantur, Ps. 104. Locus vero eorum non est quidem instar corporum circumscriptivus, sed definitivus, qui non est tantum operationis sed et essentiae ipsorum ad certum *ubi* applicatio.

L Ordinem aliquem esse inter Angelos, non diffitemur. De Angelis malis res clara est ex Mat. 25, 41. et Apoc. 12, 7. De bonis vero Angelis ex nonnullis cir-

a 'strong delusion' in them [2 Thess. 2:11] in order to punish them for their lack of gratitude or for prior obstinacy, like dumb animals they are carried away by their passions, and like blind people they get lost even where the way is clear, as can be seen in Romans 1:28, Ephesians 2:2, 2 Corinthians 4:4, 2 Thessalonians 2:11, etc.

Therefore the devout must guard diligently and pray that they may never be led into temptation, but be delivered from the evil one. And they should be certain always that good angels are not able to do anything for them without God's command, nor are bad angels able to do anything against them except by God's judgment and permission. In fact, people may even beseech God for the support of the holy angels; through their power and help even Satan's power and influence can be hindered, and Satan himself can be bound up, as is attested in Scripture (Revelation 12:8, 20[:2], etc.).

Now that we have considered the essential characteristics of angels, it remains to explain some attendant circumstances (which we shall note briefly), namely their number, movement, place, rank, and duties.

It is clear from many passages in Scripture that the number of the angels is very great; for thousands upon thousands, and ten thousand times ten thousand stand around God's throne (Revelation 5:11); and an entire legion of demons possessed one man (Luke 8:30). Their movement is extremely swift, and as fast as lightning (Luke 10:18), for which they are compared to wind and fire (Psalm 104[:4]). Though not confined (as bodies are), their place is determined—which is the apposition of a certain 'somewhere' not only in their activity, but also in their essence.[29]

We do not deny that a ranking of some sort exists among angels. Concerning bad angels the matter is clear from Matthew 25:41 and Revelation 12:7. Also concerning good angels the same may be gathered from some situations, even

---

29   In the Latin text a distinction is made between *locus circumscriptivus* and *definitivus*. Because angels are not mere thoughts but substantial beings who exist and move in space, they may be said to be in one place and not in another (*definitive*); but not that they are bounded locally by a place or spatially extended in it (*circumscriptive*). Aquinas held that angels became localized only by working on material objects in space, but that by their essence they were not localized or spatially determined. This position was condemned in 1277. See Richard Cross, "The Condemnations of 1277 and Henry of Ghent on Angelic Location," in *Angels in Medieval Philosophical Inquiry: Their Function and Significance*, eds. Isabel Iribarren and Martin Lenz (Aldershot: Ashgate, 2008), 73–88.

cumstantiis idem colligi potest, etsi quis ille sit, a Dionysio[a] Pseud. Areopagita, atque ex illo a Scholasticis temere sit definitum.

LI Officia ipsorum passim nobis in sacris literis explicantur. Dei enim solio semper assistunt, eum et Christum ejus celebrant, atque ab eodem mandata accipiunt, tum ad eos qui heredes salutis erunt, docendos, consolandos, defendendos, tum ad ejus judicia adversus impios exercenda. Malorum vero opera Deus quoque utitur ad suos exercendos, et ad infideles et impoenitentes agitandos et puniendos.

LII An vero singulis hominibus unus aliquis Angelus sit attributus non ita perspicue ex Scripturis colligi potest. Hoc nobis sufficit, quod saepe integer eorum exercitus uni sancto tuendo sit praefectus, ut ex Jacobi Patriarchae et Elisaei exemplo liquet, saepe multi certo fidelium generi, ut Mat. 18, 10. et saepe unus integrae provinciae, aut populo, ut ex Es. 37, 36. et Dan. Prophetia apparet.

---

[a] Dionysius the Areopagite, *De coelesti hierarchia* 4–5 *passim* (PTS 33:143–190).

though Dionysius the Pseudo-Areopagite[30] and following him the Scholastics have rashly determined precisely what that order is.[31]

51 Their offices are set forth for us everywhere in the sacred books. For they stand before the throne of God constantly, they praise Him and his Christ, and they receive orders from Him, not only to teach, comfort, and guard those who are heirs of salvation, but also to carry out his judgments against the ungodly. But God also uses the work of bad angels to test his own people, and to punish and trouble the faithless and unrepentant.

52 It cannot be gathered so clearly from Scriptures whether a single angel is assigned to each individual person. For us it is enough to know that often an entire army of them has been put in charge of guarding one saint, as is clear from the case of the patriarch Jacob, and Elisha.[32] Often many angels are put in charge of a certain type of believers, as in Matthew 18:10; and often one is put in charge of an entire region, or people, as appears from Isaiah 37:36 and the prophecy of Daniel.[33]

---

30 The late fifth- and early sixth-century Christian mystic theologian and philosopher who identified himself as "Dionysius" was identified (erroneously) as Dionysius the Areopagite, member of the Athenian judicial council (*areopagus*) and, more importantly, as a first-century convert (cf. Acts 17:34). This status, which was not challenged in a sustained way until the late fifteenth century (by, e.g., Lorenzo Valla and Desiderius Erasmus), helped boost the authority of his writings, which were influential throughout the Middle Ages and Renaissance. His extant works display a distinct Neoplatonic influence and include the *De divinis nominibus* (*Divine Names*), *De ecclesiastica hierarchia* (*Ecclesiastical Hierarchy*), and his angelology, cited here, *De coelesti hierachia* (*Heavenly Hierarchy*).

31 The different words for angel in Scripture (e.g., Col. 1:16,17; cf. the note with thesis 3 above) were thought to refer to different kinds of angels. Building on the previous work of Pseudo-Dionysius (*De coelesti hierachia*) and Pope Gregory the Great (*XL homiliarum in Evangelia*, homily 34.7, 10), Thomas Aquinas divided the angels into three hierarchies, each containing three orders: 1) Seraphim, Cherubim, and Thrones; 2) Dominations, Virtues, and Powers; and 3) Principalities, Archangels, and Angels (*Summa theologiae*, 1.108). Walaeus is inclined to accept that there are different kinds of angels, but he does not adopt the order in which they had been arranged.

32 See Genesis 28:12 and 2 Kings 6:16–17.

33 The view that there are special guardian angels for individual persons, places or callings is contested by almost all Reformed theologians, following the precedent set by Calvin (*Institutes*, 1.14.7), who rejects it as a papal heresy. Voetius, however, relates that sometimes belief in guardian angels was represented in the Reformed Church. See his *Disputationes Selectae* vol. 1 (Utrecht: Joannes à Waesberge, 1648), 900, in which he refers not only to Zanchius, Alsted, Chamier, but also to G. Vossius and Grotius: "It seems that both of them were influenced to some extent by the authority of the church-fathers. We, however, embrace Calvin's view, found in his *Institutes* (book I, chapter 14, 7) and his commentaries (on Psalm 91 and Matthew 18) … and we surmise that on this point something of Plato's philosophy and the pagans' mythical theology had attached itself to the thinking of the early fathers."

DISPUTATIO XIII

De Homine ad imaginem Dei creato

Praeside D. ANTONIO THYSIO
Respondente JOHANNE OLIVARIO

THESIS I Actum est universim de opere Creationis, et in specie ex creaturis rationalibus, de Angelis tum persistentibus in prima origine et veritate, tum ex ea prolapsis; consequens est, ut porro de homine ad imaginem Dei creato agamus.

II Et sane homo est inferioris naturae consummatio et finis,* superioris congener, totius compendium et vinculum, quo coelestia terrenis conjunguntur.

III Intelligimus autem eo non corpus aut animam seorsim, sed ex utroque, anima videlicet rationali et corpore, vinculo quodam amicissimo et arctissimo inter se colligatis, in unam naturam compositum, atque hypostasi unitum.

IV Hujus creationem duplicem consideramus: primam et immediatam, Gen. 1, 27., secundam et mediatam, Gen. 6, 7. Ps. 102, 19; illa, primorum parentum, haec, reliquorum hominum ex iis progenitorum.

V Primi homines immediate* a Deo sunt conditi, tum respectu efficientiae, tum materiae. Efficientiae quidem, quod a Deo conditi sine ulla Angelorum

DISPUTATION 13

About Man Created in the Image of God

President: Antonius Thysius
Respondent: Johannes Olivarius[1]

We have given a general treatment of the work of creation and a particular one of the creatures endowed with reason, the angels—both the ones who keep the state and the truth they had at first, and those who have fallen from it. It follows that we now deal with man as created in the image of God.

Man is clearly the high point and goal* of nature's lower order, yet he also belongs to a higher order, he is the 'sum' of everything and the bond that links earthly and heavenly things.[2]

However, by that we do not mean the body and the soul separately but something that is composed from both, that is from the rational soul and the body which a very tight and close bond binds together into one nature, united in one person.

We view the creation of man as two-fold: a first and immediate one (Genesis 1:27) and a second, mediated one (Genesis 6:7; Psalm 102:19). The former is of the first parents, the latter of the other people they brought forth.

The first people were made by God without mediation,* both with respect to efficiency and with respect to the physical matter.[3] With respect to efficiency, because they were made by God without the collaboration of any angel. With

---

1   Born in 1600 in Vlissingen, Johannes Olivarius matriculated on 11 September 1617 in theology. He was ordained in Ovezande and Driewegen in 1622, Biezelinge and Kapelle (1627); he died in 1630. See Du Rieu, *Album studiosorum*, 128, Van Lieburg, *Repertorium*, 88, and Bronchorst, *Diarium*, 161.

2   Here Thysius seems to be alluding to the idea of man as 'microcosm,' a unity of body and intellectual soul which combines the lower, corporeal and the higher, spiritual realms of reality. Originating with Aristotle, the idea was elaborated by Philo and the Neoplatonists and made its way into Christian theology, including the writings of Luther and Calvin. For references see Richard C. Gamble, "The Sources of Calvin's Genesis Commentary: A Preliminary Report," *Archiv für Reformationsgeschichte* 84 (1993): 206–221, esp. 209–210.

3   The distinction between 'efficiency' and 'physical matter' is reminiscent of the distinction between the efficient cause (*causa efficiens*), "which is the agent productive of the motion or mutation in any sequences of causes and effects" and the material cause (*causa materialis*), "which is the substantial basis of the motion or mutation, the *material* on which the *causa efficiens* operates" (*DLGTT* s.v. "causa").

cooperatione. Materiae vero, quod vel nulla, ut animae; vel non habilis, apta et idonea, ut corpori, si proximam* ejus materiam spectes, iis efficiendis subfuit materia.

VI   Condidit vero Deus hominem postremum post reliqua omnia, ut a minus perfectis ad perfectius fieret progressio; quodque, cum omnia propter hominem sint, omnia praeexsistere necesse fuerit, quae ad eum ut finem diriguntur et ad ejus bonum et felicem statum faciunt; quod sane singularis divinae providentiae est actus,* et humanae dignitatis demonstratio.*

VII Ad cujus insuper amplitudinem et magnitudinem dignitatis facit, quod illum creaturus, non ad modum reliquarum creaturarum solo verbo produxit, sed de eo creando consultavit, decrevit, vel potius accinxit sese operi, ut singulare et eximium opus operose moliturus. Quinimo neque Deus sub communi* appellatione hic venit, sed tres Personae* Divinae simul id agere inducuntur, dum ait Deus, Faciamus hominem in imagine nostra, secundum similitudinem nostram. Quo Personarum Divinarum hic pluralitas evidenter indicatur, Prov. 8, 22. usque ad versum 30. Joh. 1, 3. Job. 33, 4. Ps. 104, 30.

VIII Quin summa ejus dignitas eo aperitur, quod ad imaginem suam eum creare instituit. Reliqua enim vestigium, umbram et similitudinem aliquam Dei gerunt, solus homo ad imaginem Dei factus est, qua pressior ejus expressio declaratur.

IX   Duabus autem partibus constantem creavit, corpore et anima, Gen. 2, 7., quamvis alibi Scriptura in tres deducat, corpus, animam et spiritum, 1 Thess. 5, 23. voce* animae strictius accepta. Haec principalis est, illa administra.

respect to matter, because for fashioning them either no physical matter existed (as in the case of the soul), or there was no physical matter that was proper, suitable, and apt (in the case of the body), if you look at the proximate* matter.⁴

But God made man last, after everything else, so that there would be a progression from less to more perfected things. And since everything exists for the sake of mankind, all things that are directed to him as their goal had to be in existence beforehand, things that make his condition a good and happy one. This sequence of creation is a unique feat* of divine providence, and also an illustration* of the dignity of humanity.

To enhance the scope and greatness of dignity of mankind further, God saw to it that when He was going to create him, He did not produce man in the same way as the other creatures, by his word alone, but He took council concerning his creation, and made a plan. Better yet, He girded himself for the task, like someone about to fashion a unique and exceptional work with great effort. In fact, in this matter God does not go by his collective* name, but the three persons* of the Godhead are brought on to act together, since God says, "Let us make man in our own image, according to our likeness." This obviously indicates the plurality of the divine persons (Proverbs 8:22–30; John 1:3; Job 33:4; Psalm 104:30).

Indeed, the fact that God "decided to create him in his own image" shows the superior dignity of mankind. For other things created do bear some vestige, shade, and likeness of God, but only mankind was made "according to the image of God"—which declares that he is a rather close copy.

God also created man to consist of two parts, "a body and a soul" (Genesis 2:7), although elsewhere Scripture divides it into three parts, body, soul, and spirit (1 Thessalonians 5:23), taking the word* soul in a stricter sense. The first distinction is the main one, the second is useful.⁵

---

4 'Proximate matter' signifies the organic body apart from its final form, i.e., with the soul. As such it is contrasted with completely formless prime matter.
5 On the historical background of the distinction between dichotomous and trichotomous anthropological views in the first century AD, in particular in the apostle Paul and Philo of Alexandria, see G.H. van Kooten, "The Two Types of Man in Philo and Paul: The Anthropological Trichotomy of Spirit, Soul and Body," in *Paul's Anthropology in Context: The Image of God, Assimilation to God, and Tripartite Man in Ancient Judaism, Ancient Philosophy and Early Christianity*, Wissenschaftliche Untersuchungen zum Neuen Testament, vol. 232 (Tübingen: Mohr Siebeck, 2008), 269–312. Trichotomous views had become suspect by the seventeenth century, because some Anabaptists, like Balthasar Hubmaier (c. 1485–1528), used a tripartite theory to exclude the human spirit from original sin. Hence, they were accused of Pelagianism: Thomas N. Finger, *A Contemporary Anabaptist Theology: Biblical, Historical, Constructive*

x   Corpus quidem primi hominis essentia* omnibusque suis partibus Deus primo creavit, et instar figuli ex pulvere terrae, seu pulverem e terra plasmavit. An vero ex aliis quoque elementis, Scriptura non dicit, attamen id si ita est, praesertim ex terra aqua macerata, a praedominante parte, reliqua intelligenda fuerint. In materia vero nulla fuit potentia* et aptitudo ad corpus, et quidem tale efformandum, sed totum illud a potentia Dei accepit.

xi   Per plasmationem hanc quae et manibus Dei tribuitur, Joh. 10, 8. Ps. 119, 73. intelligimus non proprie* corpoream et manuariam, assumpto a Deo corpore, ut quidam volunt, Dei actionem; sed diligentem, singularem, et respectu materiae non idoneae immediatam ejus creationem. Reliqua animantia aqua et terra, simul, et tota produxit; at hominis corpus primum et singulariter quasi manu sua effinxit. Unde et ipse Adam Hebraice ab Adama, ut homo ab humo, omnesque ab eo homines denominationem accipiunt, Gen. 3, 19. et 5, 2.

xii Ut autem in materia terra est admonitio nostrae infirmitatis et humilioris naturae argumentum, Gen. 3, 19. ita in immediata hac excellenti plasmatione, dignitatis est commendatio.

xiii Corpus vero ita a Deo efformatum δεκτικὸν fuit animae humanae, atque ita comparatum, ut idoneum instrumentum foret talis animae actionumque ejus, ac nullius praeterea spiritualis naturae per se.

(Downers Grove: IVP Academic, 2004), 469–473. A trichotomous anthropology was also associated with the fourth-century heresy of Apollinarius.

In the beginning, God created the body of the first man in its essence* 10
and with all of its parts; and like a potter He fashioned him "from the dust
of the earth" or "the dust from the earth." Yet Scripture does not say whether
God fashioned him also from other elements; if that were so (from earth
softened with water especially), then we could infer the other elements from
that predominant one.[6] But in itself the material was not capable* or fit for
forming a body (especially such a body), but it received that entire body by
God's power.[7]

By this 'fashioning,' which also is accorded to the hands of God (John 11
10:8[28–29?]; Psalm 119:73), we do not literally* mean a physical, manual action
by God after He had assumed bodily form, as some would have it.[8] We mean a
careful, unique, and, as far as the unfit material is concerned, a direct creation
by Him. The other living creatures He produced through water and earth, all at
once and fully formed; but He molded the body of man first and uniquely, as if
by his own hand. Hence also Adam derives his name from the Hebrew 'adama,
like [the Latin] *homo* (man) from *humus* (ground), and so all men after him
(Genesis 3:19; 5:2).[9]

Moreover, just as the earthly material is a reminder of our weakness and 12
proof of our humbler nature (Genesis 3:19), so too the immediate and exceptional fashioning is a testimony to our dignity.

The body, then, was thus formed by God to be fit for a human soul, and 13
it was made ready so as to be a suitable instrument for such a soul and its
actions—and for no other spiritual nature by itself.[10]

---

6   Cf. thesis 19 below.
7   Cf. William Ames, (th. 64), "the body was made of elementary matter, but the soul was produced not out of matter existing before, but rather by the immediate power of God," and (th. 79) "the body of the male was made out of the earth mixed with other elements," in William Ames, *The Marrow of Theology*, Based on 3rd Latin edition 1629, ed. and trans. John D. Eusden (Grand Rapids: Baker Books, 1968), 105, 106.
8   Cf. the rejection of the ascription, by the Anthropomorphists, of a physical body to God, SPT 6.45.
9   This derivation may be traced to the *Etymologies* of Isidore of Seville, the late-seventh century author of miscellanies and compendia: "Man (*homo*) is so called because he was made from earth ... for strictly speaking *homo* comes from *humus*. Humble (*humilis*): As if bending down to the earth (*Etymologies* 11.4; cf. 10.115)." The derivation occurs also in Donatus, *Ars Grammatica* 29 (*de nomine*; CCCM 40D:66), and may be traced further to Cassiodorus, *Expositio Psalmorum* (CCSL 97:4), Peter Abelard, *Expositio in Hexameron* (CCCM 15.86), and ultimately to Varro, *De Lingua Latina* v.34. For a discussion of the origins of this and other etymological derivations in the *Synopsis* see Faber, "Scholastic Continuities," 566–567.
10 The human body is not an instrument suitable for other beings that are spiritual in and of themselves, such as angels. See footnote on thesis 17 below.

XIV Corpori hujusmodi addidit deinde et indidit Deus animam seu spiraculum vitae, quae generali voce Hebraica dicitur רוח, ruach, spiritus, specialiore נפש, nephesch, anima, quae animantis tantum est, ac specialissima נשמה, neschema, id est, spiraculum seu halitus, quae homini fere accommodatur. Qualis distinctio Latinis inter Spiritum, Animam et Animum, non quod ipsa flatus quidam seu ventus, aut halitus ac evanidus spiritus sit, sed quod similitudine rerum illarum, naturae hujus subtilitas et potentia significetur,* spiritualis scilicet natura, corporeae opposita.

XV Est itaque non accidens* aut qualitas,* sed substantia;* et quidem non corporalis, tactui visuique subjecta, sed omnino spiritualis. Quamvis inter veteres Graecos patres quidam, etiam inter Latinos Arnobius et Tertullianus etc. subtile corpus statuere videantur. Nos vero illam a natura corporis plane sejungimus.

XVI Imo vero talis spiritus est, qui separatim a corpore subsistere potest,* quod comprobant haec Sacrae Scripturae testimonia,* Gen. 2, 7. Eccl. 12, 7. Mat. 10, 28. Luc. 23, 43. 46. Act. 7, 59. etc.

XVII Differt ab Angelica natura, (qui et ipsi spiritus sunt) quod Angeli ita separatae sint a corpore essentiae, ut nullam ad corpus affectionem naturalem* habeant, anima vero contra.

XVIII Est autem *ex Deo*, non ut ex materia et ex traduce Dei, ceu ejus quaedam particula; sed ut e causa* efficiente, et accessu quodam naturae propiore ad essentiam Dei divinarumque proprietatum assimilatione, Act. 17, 28. 29.

God added to this sort of body by putting the soul or the breath of life into it, which goes by the general Hebrew word *ruaḥ*, 'spirit.' More precise is *nefesh*, 'soul,' which applies only to a living creature; and most precise is *neshama*, that is 'breath' or 'exhaling,' which is usually applied to mankind. In Latin a similar distinction exists between spirit, soul, and mind [literally: 'wind'], not because the spirit is some sort of blowing, or wind, or an exhaling or something fleeting, but because the subtlety and the power of its nature is portrayed* by its similarity to them, namely its spiritual as opposed to bodily nature.

And so the soul is not an accident,* or a quality,* but a substance.* But it is actually not corporeal, subject to the senses of touch and sight; it is completely spiritual. Yet there are some among the ancient Greek church-fathers, and also among the Latin ones (Arnobius,[11] Tertullian, etc.), who seem to hold that it is a very delicate corporeal body. But we separate the soul clearly from the nature of the body.

Indeed the soul is a spirit of such kind that it can* exist apart from the body, as the following witnesses* from Holy Scripture bear out: Genesis 2:7, Ecclesiastes 12:7, Matthew 10:28, Luke 23:43, 46; Acts 7:59, etc.

But the nature of the human soul is not like the angels (who are also spirits), because angels are essences that are distinguished from body to such a degree that they do not tend by nature* to have a body; but the soul, on the other hand, does have that tendency.[12]

Yet the soul does come from God, though not from God's material being or as an offshoot from him, nor as some particle from him. It comes from Him as the efficient cause,* and from some very close approximation of its nature to the essence of God, and from its being made similar to the divine properties (Acts 17:28, 29).

And the soul also was not created or made from any one essence whatsoever, whether celestial or elementary;[13] but for that first man the soul was blown "out of nothing" into his face, mouth, and especially his nostrils, and it was created by means of the blowing, as Augustine puts it.

---

11 Arnobius of Sicca (died c. AD 330) was a Christian convert and apologist. Biographical details are known to us only via Jerome. Arnobius wrote seven books entitled *Adversus Gentes* (*Against the Heathens*, according to Jerome) or *Adversus Nationes* (*Against the Nations*, more commonly) in which he defends the Christian faith against pagan opponents. In his view, the soul is created not by God, but by an intermediate being, and it is corporeal and of itself not immortal.

12 Whereas the human soul is 'incomplete' without the human body, angels are spirits that are complete in themselves. See *DLGTT* s.v. "spiritus completus."

13 According to classical Greek cosmology the matter of all sublunar bodies consisted of

XIX   Neque ex ulla omnino essentia, sive coelesti sive elementari, creata factaque; verum *ex nihilo* primo homini in faciem, os et singulariter nares insufflata, et insufflando creata, ut ait Augustinus.ᵃ

XX   Afflatum seu inhalationem quidam proprie, ut plasmationem intelligunt, pro corporea oris actione assumpto corpore facta; symbolumque externum fuisse volunt ipsius animae creatae, hominem animantis; alii improprie* pro singulari et simpliciter immediata Dei vi et actione in condenda hominis anima. Huic sententiae et nos accedimus. Et sane duo hic consideranda, quod anima exterius advenerit, et analogice* divinae essentiae respondeat.

XXI   De sede ejus et speciatim mentis, varie disputatum est. Sunt qui inexplicabilem hanc quaestionem fecerunt. Alii per totum corpus aequaliter diffusam volunt, totam in toto et in qualibet parte totam, sed in certa quadam parte magis videri inesse, quod ibi sit ejus facultatis praecipuum instrumentum, ut post Ambrosium et Augustinumᵇ Scholastici.* Alii specialem illi sedem attribuunt, et Academici quidem caput seu cerebrum, Peripatetici ac Stoici pectus seu cor.

XXII   Nos postremam sententiam, Scripturam Sacram et Veteres fere Patres secuti, amplectimur, ac in corde ut in centro ac recessu animam esse secundum essentiam (unde et cor pro omnibus animae facultatibus,* nempe sapientia, voluntate et affectu ponitur) statuimus; exercere autem suas potentias in corpore, et quidem per propria ejus instrumenta, utpote per cerebrum intelligere. Ita ut essentialiter* in certa hac parte sit, virtualiter in toto corpore, Deut. 29, 4. Rom. 1, 21. Mat. 15, 19. et 22, 37.

XXIII   Quod vero alibi anima omnis carnis, adeoque et hominis, in sanguine dicatur, imo ipse sanguis anima, Gen. 9. et Lev. 17., quod et Empedoclesᶜ aliique affirmarunt, intelligendum est non de anima ratiocinante, sed vitali ejus facultate et vita ipsa.

XXIV   Habet ea naturalem et immotam affectionem et sympathiam ad corpus, ut ad alteram compositi partem, organumque ejus accommodatum et proprium; ipsaque corpori sensum, vitam ac motum tribuit, et in eo principatum exercet, illud regit ac moderatur. Non tamen ab eo simpliciter dependet, aut organica

---

ᵃ See, e.g., Augustine, *De civitate Dei* 12.24 (CCSL 48:381) and *De Genesi ad litteram* 10.1 (CSEL 28/1:295).   ᵇ For Augustine, see e.g. *Epistulae* 166.2.4 (CSEL 44:550–553), and the discussion in Allan D. Fitzgerald (ed.), *Augustine through the Ages: An Encyclopedia* (Grand Rapids / Cambridge UK: Eerdmans, 1999), 808 s.v. "soul."   ᶜ Empedocles Fr. B105 Diels-Kranz. The word 'soul' does not appear in the fragments of Empedocles; 'thought' (noêma), however, does and is said to swim in one's blood. The 'others' could refer to the *medici* from the school of Hippocrates.

(a mixture of) the four elements, earth, water, air and fire. Celestial bodies were thought to be made of a fifth, incorruptible element, also called 'quintessence.'

Some understand 'inblowing' or 'inbreathing' literally (like 'fashioning'), for the physical action of the mouth that was performed after a corporeal body was assumed, and they argue that it was an outward symbol of the created spirit which causes man to live. Others understand it figuratively* for God's special and simply direct and powerful action in making the human soul. And we agree with this way of thinking. To be clear, two facts must be observed here: That the soul came from without, and, that it corresponds to the divine essence by analogy.*

There have been various debates about the seat of the soul, and in particular that of the mind. There are those who consider this question unanswerable. Some argue that the soul has been spread out evenly throughout the whole body (completely throughout the whole body, and completely in any given part of it), but that it is evidenced more in one specific part because the main instrument of its abilities is there (as the scholastics* hold, following Ambrose and Augustine). Others assign a specific seat to the mind: The Academics the head, or the brain; the Peripatetics and Stoics the chest or heart.[14]

We embrace this last way of thinking, in line with Sacred Scripture and nearly all the ancient fathers, and we hold that with regard to its essence, the soul has the heart as its central place of retreat (wherefore the heart stands also for all of the soul's faculties,* namely, wisdom, the will, and feeling). However, we are of the view that the soul exercises its powers within the body, and in fact by means of its appropriate instruments, just as understanding is conducted through the brain. In essence,* then, it is located in this specific part, but its workings are throughout the entire body (Deuteronomy 29:4, Romans 1:21, Matthew 15:19, and 22:37).

As to the fact that other passages state that the soul of all flesh—and so of man, too—is in its blood, indeed, that the blood itself is the soul (Genesis 9, Leviticus 17, which also Empedocles and others asserted), we must understand this not about the soul as it exercises reason, but in its function of sustaining life, and as life itself.

The soul has a natural, constant feeling for and leaning towards the body as towards the other half of a composition, and to its aptly suited and proper instrument. And it is the soul that grants feeling, life, and movement to the body. In the body the soul exercises its authority, control, and government. However, the soul does not depend entirely upon the body; nor is it organic,

---

14   The 'Academics' are the Platonists, and the 'Peripatetics' the Aristotelians. For discussions about the location of the soul, see G. Santoro and others, "The Anatomic Location of the Soul from the Heart, through the Brain, to the Whole Body, and Beyond: A Journey through Western History, Science, and Philosophy," *Neurosurgery* 65 (2009): 633–643.

est, ut quae ab eo separari, per se subsistere, privata munia obire sine ejus adminiculo possit, corporique superstes maneat. Nihilominus sine eo plene beata non est, sed tum demum plene felix, cum corpori conjuncta est. Unde corporis necessaria ad beatitatem hominis resurrectio evincitur.

xxv Non tantum autem separabilis a corpore, et superstes corpori, sed et natura* immortalis est, quod Scripturae testimoniis, et evidentibus* argumentis probatur.* Testimoniis quidem e Vetere Testamento, Ps. 49, 16. Eccl. 12, 7. 1 Sam. 28, 11. 1 Reg. 17, 21., e Novo Testamento, Mat. 10, 28. Phil. 1, 22. 23. 1 Pet. 3, 19. Apoc. 6, 9. et 7, 9. et passim.

xxvi *Argumentis*: primo ex *creationis forma*, inspiratione enim Dei creata est, sine ulla omnino materia praejacente, imo ex Deo ipso, assimilatione essentiae, adeoque ad Dei imaginem. Nihil autem mortale immortalis Dei imago est.

xxvii Deinde ex ipsius *natura*, quod essentia simplex sit, nihil admixtum, concretum, copulatum aut coagmentatum habens, unde neque secerni, dividi atque discerpi potest, ac proinde interitus expers. Est enim interitus, quasi discessus, secretio et diremptio earum partium, quae ante interitum junctione aliqua tenebantur.

xxviii Quin ex praeclaris *animi dotibus, effectis, divinisque functionibus*. Miranda enim solertia ingenii, cogitationis celeritas, facilitas perceptionis, judicii acrimonia, discursus et ratiocinatio de rebus omnibus, memoria rerum praeteritarum, praesentium contemplatio, futurarum praevisio, et maxime in se ipsam conversio et reflexio, suique contemplatio, quae omnia a nulla elementorum compositione, sed diviniore natura sunt, atque immortalem eam arguunt.

xxix Imprimis ex ipsa animae indita *Dei cognitione religioneque*, veri et falsi, aequi et iniqui, juris et injustitiae, pulchri et turpis, honesti et inhonesti differentia et perceptione, artium innumerabilium excogitatione et scientia. Evanidus enim vigor non posset* ad Deum immortalem et fontem vitae assurgere, atque coelestia et divina, admiranda ingenii vi perscrutari.

xxx Ex *conscientiae testimonio*, quae ex reatu peccatorum horribiles terrores concipit. Nisi sane hominum animae post mortem superstites essent, nihil causae haberent impii cur de futuris poenis tantillum formidarent.

since it can be separated from the body, can subsist by itself, and can attend to its own duties without the support of the body, and since it continues to outlive the body. Nevertheless, without the body the soul is not entirely blessed, but it is fully happy only when it is united with the body. This is proof that the resurrection of the body is necessary for mankind's blessedness.

However, the soul is not only separable from the body and outlives it, it is also immortal by nature,* as the witnesses of Scripture and evident* arguments* prove. The witnesses from the Old Testament are Psalm 49:16; Ecclesiastes 12:7; 1 Samuel 28:11; 1 Kings 17:21. Witnesses from the New Testament are: Matthew 10:28; Philippians 1:22, 23; 1 Peter 3:19; Revelation 6:9 and 7:9, and throughout. 25

The evident arguments are these. The first argument is from the form of its creation, for it was created by the inbreathing of God, not with any precast matter whatsoever, but rather from God himself, through an assimilation to his essence, and thus in the image of God. However, nothing that is mortal can be the image of the immortal God. 26

Secondly, the argument from its own nature, for it is a simple essence that has nothing mingled, added, joined or fastened to it; wherefore it also cannot be separated, divided, or dispersed, and hence it is immune to death. For death is like a separation, breaking-up, or splitting-apart of those parts which before death were held together by some union. 27

And then there is the argument arising from the marvelous gifts, effects, and godlike functions of the soul. For its clever genius is awe-inspiring, as is its swift thinking, its ease of perception, its sharp discernment, its discourse and reasoning about all things, its recollection of past events, its consideration of current events, its ability to foresee future events, and especially its ability to turn towards itself and reflect upon itself, and its self-awareness. All of these abilities come not from a combination of (physical) elements, but from a more divine nature, and they prove that the soul is immortal. 28

The foremost argument comes from the soul's knowledge and worship of God that has been implanted in the soul, by the discernment and perception of true and false, fair and unfair, just and unjust, beautiful and base, honest and dishonest, and by the discovery and knowledge of countless arts. For a strength that passes away would not be able* to rise up to the immortal God and the source of life, or to contemplate the heavenly and divine realms with such admirable power of intellect. 29

There is the argument from the witness borne by our conscience, which devises horrible fears from the guilt of our sins. Surely if people's souls did not remain alive after death, the godless would have no reason to fear even the tiniest future punishment. 30

xxxi   Sed et cibus animae humanae est immortalis, ut est Deus ejusque fruitio. Et ni anima esset immortalis, vana esset fides et spes nostra, omnisque religio,* 1 Cor. 15, 14. Accedit denique communis omnium fere gentium etiam barbarissimarum consensus.

xxxii   Ad *facultates animae* quod attinet, nos Philosophorum subtilioribus disputationibus posthabitis, eas distinguimus in intellectum seu mentem, et voluntatem; seu cum Apostolo in spiritum et animam; restrictiore significatione nomine* spiritus superiorem facultatem, mentem scilicet; animae vero, inferiorem, sensitivam et vegetativam intelligentes. Quod Latini per animum et animam efferunt.

xxxiii   *Intellectu* objecta vel approbanda vel improbanda apprehendimus et discernimus; estque duplex: theoreticus, quo verum a falso; practicus, quo bonum a malo, aequum ab iniquo. In quo consideramus συντήρησιν et συνείδησιν, scientiam et conscientiam, quae simul juncta practicum syllogismum constituunt.

xxxiv   *Voluntate** autem, cujus natura* est non cogi, et secundum naturae primae facultatem nulla necessitate* ad extrema restringi, objecta eligimus et repu-

Yet the food for the human soul is also immortal, as that is God and the enjoyment of Him. And if the soul were not immortal, then our faith and hope would be futile along with our whole worship* (1 Corinthians 15:14). And lastly, the consensus [about the soul's immortality] that is common to nearly all races, even the most uncivilized ones, provides additional support for this fact.

As far as the faculties of the soul are concerned, leaving aside the more subtle debates of the Philosophers, we divide them into the intellect (or the mind) and the will; or, with the apostle, into the spirit and the soul. In a more restricted sense we mean by the word* 'spirit' the higher faculty, that is the mind; whereas with the word 'soul' we mean the lower one, the one of the senses and of (vegetative) growth. The Latins express these by means of *animus* (spirit) and *anima* (soul).¹⁵

With the intellect we grasp objects and decide whether they should be approved or condemned. And this process is two-fold: Theoretical, whereby true is distinguished from false, and practical, whereby good is distinguished from evil, and fair from unfair. In this process we regard *synthērēsis* and *syneidēsis*, science and conscience, which, when joined together, constitute a practical syllogism.¹⁶

But by the will,* whose nature* it is not to be forced, and in keeping with the first nature's¹⁷ ability is not restricted by any necessity* towards things beyond

---

15 Aristotle discerned three parts of the soul: the vegetative, sensitive and rational parts. Plants have only a vegetative soul, which accounts for growth, nutrition and reproduction. Non-rational animals have a soul that is also sensitive, enabling them to have sensory perception and emotions. The human soul includes the third, rational part, consisting of intellect and will. Thysius alludes to 1 Thessalonians 5:23, where Paul distinguishes between soul and spirit (see also thesis 9 above). Finally, the philosophical distinction between *animus* and *anima* goes back to Lucretius' *De Rerum Natura* (first century BC). Cf. Paul McDonald, *History of the Concept of Mind: Speculations about Soul, Mind and Spirit from Homer to Hume* (Aldershot: Ashgate, 2003), 80–88.

16 'Syntheresis' and 'conscience' are two key concepts in scholastic ethical theory. 'Syntheresis' (also spelled 'synderesis') signifies innate knowledge of the principles of right behavior, 'conscience' signifies the application of these general principles to concrete situations. The application leads to a conclusion about what should be done. This is the so-called practical syllogism. For example: applying the general principle 'Murder is to be avoided' (syntheresis), to the concrete situation 'This act is murder,' leads to the conclusion 'I should not perform this act' (conscience). Cf. Douglas Langston, "Medieval Theories of Conscience," in: Edward N. Zalta (ed.), *The Stanford Encyclopedia of Philosophy* (Fall 2010 Edition), accessed February 27, 2014, http://plato.stanford.edu/archives/fall2008/entries/conscience-medieval/.

17 'First nature' could refer to the original state of the will before the Fall or to an abstract status of the will as such, apart from someone's personal dispositions.

diamus, prout ea bona vel mala esse intellectus judicat. Saepe etiam est electio inter aequalia et inaequalia, quin voluntas quoque actionem suam suspendit.

xxxv Atque ita homo factus est in animam viventem, corpore et animo hypostatice* inter se unitus, quo homo integer constituitur.

xxxvi Totus autem homo et anima et corpore in imagine Dei et secundum similitudinem ejus creatus est, quorum hoc ad exegesin illius facit. Imo vero et epitheti rationem ad illius amplificationem habet, quasi dicat imaginem simillimam, Gen. 1, 27. et 5, 1. Secus quam Patres quidem arbitrantur, qui imaginem ad naturam, similitudinem ad actiones Deo conformes referunt.

xxxvii Ea intelligimus bonitatem, rectitudinem et perfectionem* seu statum ejus optimum, supra reliqua animantia excellentiam et excessum, et propiorem ad Deum accessum.

xxxviii Integritas interna est in anima, corpore, affectibus et actionibus, totiusque hominis immortalitate. Ratione* mentis homo scientia fuit insigni, Gen. 2, 19. etc. Voluntatis vero ea libertate, ut non modo a coactione, sed et peccati necessitate* esset liber, menti et rectae rationi ac divinae voluntati consentiens. Affectuum seu inclinationum et appetituum ea εὐταξία, ut menti voluntatique obsecundarent. Corporis ac membrorum sancta compositio, ex quibus omnibus rectae sanctaeque actiones oriebantur.

itself, we choose objects or reject them, as the intellect judges them to be good or evil. Often the choice is between equal and between unequal things; then, in fact, the will halts its own operation.¹⁸

And so man was made into a living soul, personally* united in body and spirit together, which constitutes the whole man.

Moreover, the whole man in both soul and body "is created in the image of God and according to his likeness," in which the latter phrase serves to expound the former. It even bears the force of an epithet which 'amplifies' the former, as if to say a "similar image" (Genesis 1:27, 5:1). This is different from the understanding of some of the church-fathers who take "image" as referring to the nature, and "likeness" as referring to the actions conforming to God.¹⁹

By this expression we mean the goodness of man, his uprightness and perfection* (or ideal state), his surpassing excellence over all other living creatures, and his closer approximation to God.

An inner integrity is found in the soul, the body, the affections and actions, and in the immortality of the whole man. Regarding* intellect, man was of outstanding knowledge (Genesis 2:19, etc.). He had such freedom concerning his will that he was not only free from coercion but even from the necessity* of sinning; he was in harmony with the mind, the good reason, and the will of God. The affections (or inclinations and appetites) were so composed that they complied with the intellect and the will. His body and limbs formed a constitution that was holy; upright and wholesome actions were to arise from them all.

---

18 In scholastic discourse, whereas human beings can be coerced with regard to their motion in space, they cannot be coerced with regard to their will, which can be guided, inclined, or persuaded, yet remains free from the necessity of coercion. See Van Asselt and others, *Scholastic Discourse*, 32, 356–357, and RTF, *passim*. Disputation 17 below is completely devoted to a discussion of 'free choice.' William Ames (1576–1633), a near-contemporary of the authors of the *Synopsis*, asks whether the will can do anything against its conscience and he says, "Yes. The will can suspend its act at pleasure ... the will can turn away the understanding from an object ... the will can move itself ... because whatever good the understanding presents to the will ... it does so with a kind of indifference of judgement." The reason he gives is that otherwise the problem lies with the understanding and not the will. And that would mean the first sin was already in the understanding before the will willed anything. And it would mean that the will does not need to be renewed in regeneration, but only the understanding. See Ames, *Cases of conscience*, 1:22–25.

19 Irenaeus of Lyons and Tertullian introduced the difference in meaning between 'image,' as referring to human nature, and 'likeness,' as a superadded perfection that was lost by the fall into sin. See Tertullian, *De Baptismo*, 5.7 (CCSL 1:282), Irenaeus, *Adversus Haereses*, 5.6.1 and 5.16.2 (FC 8/5:58, and FC 8/5:134–136). Calvin comments that the distinction is superfluous, since 'likeness' was added to 'image' simply for purposes of clarification and he refers to the Hebrew use of parallelism (*Institutes*, 1.15.3).

XXXIX Quibus accessit non animae modo, sed et corporis seu totius hominis immortalitas, Rom. 5, 12. et 6, 23. Utraque naturalis: illa, quod mori anima ut simplex neutiquam possit; haec, quod moriturum corpus non fuisset, tum propter εὐκρασίαν, tum conservationem animae, quae perpetuo et vitaliter illud fovisset et conservasset.

XL Hanc partium omnium in homine creato harmoniam et consensum, *justitiae originali* ut matri et magistrae acceptam referimus: quae naturalis dici potest, quod ea collata fuerit et eam acceperit homo, non ratione individui, sed totius speciei,* quodque ejus contrarium peccatum originale, naturae corruptae sit. Non tamen propterea omnem ulterius Dei gratiam excludit, sed infert, ut ita natura gratia* foveretur.

XLI Excessum illum hominis super omnia animantia, imo terram ipsam (cui et reliqua subserviunt) Scriptura explicat Dominio, dum ait: Qui dominentur in pisces maris, etc. Et, Dominamini, etc. quo et posteri comprehenduntur. Eo autem dominio majestateque, imago Dei a Mose describi videtur, ut ab ejus proprietate effectuque. Equidem ut dominium quis exerceat, anima ratiocinante praeditum esse oportet; ut vero aequum ac placidum, certe sapientem, sanctum et justum; ut quoque actu exerceat, corpus bene comparatum ad animae integrae consentaneas actiones; ut denique sit perpetuum, immortalem hominem esse necesse est.

XLII Atque Apostolus consentienter Dei imaginem ab anteriori collocat in sapientia, sanctitate et justitia; ut etiam ex ejus contrario, amissa Dei imagine, et restauratione intelligi potest, 2 Cor. 3, 18. Eph. 4, 22. 23. 24. Col. 3, 9. 10.

XLIII Atque hinc consequitur et accessus ad Deum propior, dum homo Deo conformis, Deo unitur et adhaeret, quem actum etiam imago Dei infert et comprehendit.

XLIV Status ergo hominis fuit beatissimus; ad quem accessit externa dignitas, collocatio ejus in horto seu Paradiso a Deo consito, qui graphice a Mose loco situque, aliisque circumstantiis describitur. Nos omissis quae de ejus fluminibus,

13. ABOUT MAN CREATED IN THE IMAGE OF GOD

In addition to these there was "immortality," not only of the soul, but also of the body, or, "of the whole man" (Romans 5:12 and 6:23). And each of these was naturally immortal, because the soul, being non-composite, could die in no way whatsoever. And the body was immortal, because it was not going to die, both because of its good constitution and by being preserved by the soul, which would have nurtured and preserved it constantly and vitally.

We attribute this harmony and consensual action of all the parts of the created man to original righteousness, as to a mother or a mistress.[20] This may be called natural, because it was bestowed and man received it, in the sense not of the individual but the whole species,* and because its opposite, original sin, is of a corrupt nature. However, this does not therefore preclude every further grace of God, but it includes it, so that in this way grace* may foster nature.

With the word "dominion" Scripture expresses this surpassing prominence of man over all living things, indeed, over the whole earth (which the other creatures serve), when it says: "That they may have dominion over the fish of the sea, etc.," and "have dominion over," etc.—in which phrase also man's descendants are implied. Furthermore, by means of those words for dominion and majesty, Moses seems to be representing God's own image via its properties and effects. Indeed, for someone to exercise dominion, he must be endowed with the gift of a soul that reasons; but to do so fairly and peaceably, he must certainly be wise, holy, and just. And if he would also put his dominion into practice, he must have a body well-prepared for actions that accord with a soul that is sound. And finally, for the dominion to be perpetual, the man must be immortal.

Consistent with this the apostle places the image of God, viewed from its beginning, in wisdom, holiness, and justice; this can be gathered also from its opposite, after the image of God had been lost, and from its restoration (2 Corinthians 3:18, Ephesians 4:22–24; Colossians 3:9,10).

And from here comes the closer access to God, since man conforms to God, and is united with and clings to Him. This act, too, is expressed and embraced by the image of God.

Therefore the condition of mankind was a very blessed one. And in addition to it there was the external dignity, as he was placed in the garden, or Paradise planted by God, which Moses exquisitely portrays in its location, setting, and environs. Leaving aside the debates about its rivers, the size, and how long

---

20 'Original righteousness' was the pristine state Adam and Eve enjoyed before the Fall. It was lost by 'original sin.' Opinions differed as to what exactly it implied. Usually, 'original righteousness' is associated with rectitude of the will and extra gifts like immortality. See also Muller *DGLTT*, s.v. "iustitia originalis."

XLV latifundo, et duratione disceptantur, eum in, vel juxta Mesopotamiam, versus Tigridem et Euphratem collocandum censemus.

XLV   Illum porro exornavit omni genere pulcherrimarum herbarum et arborum, quae ad esum et voluptatis usum facerent. Inter quas Arbor vitae et scientiae boni et mali. Illa quidem ita dicta, non quod vitam insitam haberet, aut corpori aut animo per se, ut panacea quaedam, praestaret, ut Scholastici* post Patres quosdam arbitrantur, sed potius Sacramentali* ratione: quod obsignaret utramque, quin imo spiritualem subsecuturam adumbraret, Apoc. 2, 7.

XLVI   Haec autem, scientiae scilicet boni et mali, nuncupata, non quod ei inesset scientia (quod absurdum) vel occultam vim insitam haberet efficiendi eam, seu acuendi ingenii, ut Josephus[a] voluit; sed quod esset arbor, ex divino instituto, Sacramentalis, qua jubebatur homo non ultra velle sapere quam vellet Deus, aut bonum malumque suo ingenio metiri; quaque explorans Deus ejus obedientiam fructus comestione, sensurus esset atque experturus bonum quo privandus, et malum in quod casurus.

XLVII   Horto huic Deus hominem imposuit, tamquam Dominum in Basilica sua ad eum colendum et custodiendum, Gen. 2, 15. Colendum quidem jucundo et sancto opere, sine fatigatione et taedio; custodiendum autem in eo statu quo erat, et ab animalium incursu et eversione. Atque haec in personis protoplastorum in Paradiso collocatio, suo modo quoque ad progenitos spectat.

XLVIII   Ceterum Deus hominem (hominis voce communiter accepta) duplici sexu condidit, secundum illud, Masculum et feminam creavit eos, natura et dignitate tamen inaequales, hanc infirmiorem et inferiorem, unde singulariter mulier, imago et gloria viri dicitur, ut vir Dei, 1 Cor. 11, 7. ad propagandum videlicet in mundo humanum genus, Gen. 1, 27.

---

[a] The reference appears to be erroneous; perhaps it is to Philo, *De allegoriis legum* 1.90 3 and following.

Paradise existed, we are of the opinion that it should be placed in or near Mesopotamia, near the Tigris and the Euphrates.[21]

Moreover God furnished the garden with every kind of very beautiful plants and trees which would serve for food and enjoyment. Among these trees was the "tree of life and [the tree] of the knowledge of good and evil." The first one is so called not because it possesses life within itself or because it has the power—like some panacea—to grant life to the body or the soul (as the Schoolmen* following some church-fathers think), but rather in virtue of the sacraments,* since the tree would seal each sacrament—indeed, would foreshadow the spiritual life that is to come (Revelation 2:7).

The other tree, however, is called the tree "of the knowledge of good and evil" not because it possessed knowledge (that is silly) or that implanted in it was some secret power to bring about knowledge or to sharpen the mind, as Josephus thought. But it is so called because it is a sacramental* tree by God's decision, which bids man not to wish to know more than what God wills, or to measure good and evil by his own ways of thinking.[22] And by this tree also God would test man's obedience in the eating of the fruit, so that he was going to sense and experience the good from which he would be deprived and the evil into which he would fall.

Into this garden "the Lord put the man" like a master in his kingly court, "to work it and to maintain it" (Genesis 2:15). Indeed, "to work it" as a pleasant and sacred task, without tiring or wearying. And "to maintain it" in the condition in which he received it, and to guard it from the incursion and destruction of wild animals. And as our ancestors were placed in Paradise in person, in the same manner would their descendants be included there.

And God created humans (using the word 'man' in a general sense) of two sexes, as it says, "male and female He created them," namely, for the propagation of the human race in the world (Genesis 1:27). Yet they were unequal in nature and dignity, as she was more feeble and lower—whence especially the woman is called the image and glory of the man, as man is the image of God (1 Corinthians 11:7).

---

21   On sixteenth and seventeenth century speculations about the location of Paradise, see J. Delumeau (trans. M. O'Connell), *History of Paradise: The Garden of Eden in Myth and Tradition* (reprint; Champaign: University of Illinois Press, 2000), 155–174.

22   Augustine calls the tree of life a 'sacrament' or 'sign' in his *Literal Commentary on Genesis*, book 8, chapter 4, section 8 (MPL 34, 375). The idea was adopted by, among others, John Calvin (*Commentary on Genesis* 2.9 in: *Calvini Opera Omnia* vol. 23(= CR vol. 51) (Brunsvig: Wilhelm Baum, 1882), 38–39. Cf. Ames, *Marrow*, 113: "In this covenant there were two

XLIX Nec simul et eodem modo utrumque. Prius enim virum exstruxit, deinde feminam, ut viri dignitas supra feminam esset commendata, 1 Cor. 11, 8. Atque sicut Deus unum est principium* creationis rerum, sic primus homo unum esset principium generationis* omnium hominum, ut dum cognoscerent se ab uno esse omnes, se quasi unum amarent et communi quodam sanguinis nexu inter se devincirentur, Act. 17,26.

L Tum etiam virum e pulvere, feminam vero ex viri soporati costa, eaque carne investita, et e lateribus ejus exempta, non autem de capite, nec de pedibus, efformavit: nempe quod viro nec domina, nec ancilla parabatur, sed socia, ut juxta se ponendam cognosceret, quam de latere suo sumptam didicisset. Factique sunt in carnem unam, et origine, et conjugali consortio, eorumque communi fructu, ad mutuam necessitudinem inter conjugatos firmandam, Eph. 5, 28. etc.

LI Tantum de prima hominis creatione, sequitur *secunda et mediata,* quae est naturae humanae constitutae, et vasis ad generationem aptis instructae, qua Deus benedictione sua, et vim prolificam addidit, eamque fecundavit, ut ita homo ex homine, mare scilicet et femina, generaretur, ad terram hominibus implendam, secundum illud: Benedixit eis, ac dixit, Crescite et multiplicamini, et replete terram.

LII Agitatum hic fuit inter Patres olim problema, utrum animae reliquorum hominum per traducem parentum deriventur, an vero creentur et infundantur a Deo. Nonnulli, Tertullianus[a] aliique senserunt, totum hominem ex toto homine propagari, nempe corpus ex corpore, animam ex anima, ut lumen de lumine accenditur, vel ut alii, totum ex vi genitalis seminis.

LIII Communis autem opinio huic contraria est, nempe non esse ex traduce, sed a Deo, non quidem quasi ante ab initio mundi praeexistentes, ut Origenes[b]

---

[a] Tertullian, *Liber de anima* 27.1–9 (CCSL 2:822–824).   [b] Origen, *De principiis* 1.7.4 and 3.4 (SC 252:214–216 and 268:198–216).

> symbols or sacraments. (…) The reward for obedience was marked by the tree of life and punishment was marked by the other tree, that of the knowledge of good and evil. (…) The one was the sacrament of life and the other the sacrament of death."

Nor did God create both of them at the same time or in the same manner. For first He constructed the man, and then the woman, so that the dignity of man would be set above the woman's (1 Corinthians 11:8). And just as God is the one starting point* of creation of things, so the first man was to be the one starting point for the generation* of all men, so that that while they would know that they are all from one man, they would love one another as one and be united with each other in a common bond of blood (Acts 17:26).

And then God also formed man "from dust," but woman from "the rib of the man as he slept," and He clothed her with flesh, and took her from his side and not from his head or his feet. She was made ready not as his sovereign, nor as his handmaid, but as his companion, so he would learn that she, whom he knew was taken from his side, should take her place at his side. And they were made into one flesh, in order that their origin, conjugal relationship, and their common offspring would strengthen the bond of mutual affection in marriage (Ephesians 5:28).

Thus far concerning the first creation of man; what follows next is the second, mediated* creation, which is of the human nature that had been made and equipped with organs suitable for reproduction, whereto God through his blessing also granted the power to reproduce. And He made it fruitful in such a way that man may be generated from man (namely male and female) in order to fill the earth with people, according to that word: "He blessed them, and said, 'grow and multiply, and fill the earth.'"

On this point there once arose a discussion among the church-fathers, 'whether the souls of people stem as offshoots from their parents, or are in fact created and infused by God.'[23] Some fathers, including Tertullian and others, were of the opinion that the entire man is propagated from the whole man, namely, body from body, soul from soul, in the same way that light is kindled from light, or as others thought, from the power of the reproductive seed.

The common consensus, however, counters this view, namely, that it is not from an off-shoot, but from God (not, to be sure, as though already in existence from before the beginning of the world, as Origen thinks), as created

---

23 'Traducianism' and 'creatianism' present two different opinions about the origin of the soul. Traducianism holds that the soul is derived from the parents; creatianism holds that God creates each soul individually at or after conception. According to Herman Bavinck the issue remains unsettled. In the Early Church traducianism had many advocates (e.g., Tertullian, Rufinus, Apollinaris, Gregory of Nyssa), but later it was embraced only by Lutherans (Luther, Melanchthon). Creatianism was adopted by most Roman Catholic and Reformed theologians. For a helpful overview, see Bavinck, *Reformed Dogmatics* 2:580–588. See also Heinrich Heppe (2nd edition by Ernst Bizer), *Die Dogmatik der evangelisch-reformierte Kirche* (Neukirchen: Neukirchener Verlag, 1958), 182–185, and *SPT* 15.24 below.

voluit, verum immediate creari, corporibusque ubi jam in utero matris corpus ad talem animam suscipiendam comparatum et dispositum fuerit, coelitus infundi, aut potius, ut alii volunt, increari. Augustinus in medio quaestionem relinquit.[a] Nos vulgatam sententiam veritati magis consentaneam arbitramur.

LIV   *Finis et usus creationis* et creati hominis est, ut ipse ex tam admirando sui opificio, excellentia et statu, eximiam Dei sapientiam, potentiam et benignitatem, quam in ortu nostro declarat, cognoscat, agnitam tum interne, tum externe colat, ad omnimodam ejus beatitatem, Deique gloriam.

---

[a] For Augustine's position, see Fitzgerald, *Augustine*, 843 s.v. "Traducianism."

immediately and in bodies—when in the mother's womb a body has been put together and arranged in order to receive such a soul—, infused, or rather, as others prefer, created within the body, from heaven above. Augustine leaves the matter undecided. We think that the conventional thinking accords better with the truth.

The goal and profit of creation and of the created man is that he himself, from such a marvelous workmanship that he is, and from such pre-eminent status, should come to know God's exceeding wisdom, power, and benevolence, which He reveals in our origin. And once man has come to discern these things, to worship God inwardly as well as outwardly, for every sort of bliss for himself, and for the glory of God.

DISPUTATIO XIV

De Lapsu Adami

Praeside D. JOHANNE POLYANDRO
Respondente D. JOHANNE ZELIO

THESIS I Peccatum est ἀνομία, seu vitium legi Dei repugnans, 1Joh. 3, 4.

II Subjectum* illius est creatura rationalis ad imaginem Dei creata a bono declinans, quod lege Dei praescribitur, et ad malum inclinans quod illa prohibetur.

III Illud, aut in malis Angelis, aut in primis nostris parentibus, Adamo et Eva, aut in horum posteris consideratur.

IV Nos de primorum nostrorum parentum peccato disserere constituimus, quod in genere* inobedientia, transgressio, ac lapsus ab Apostolo appellatur, Rom. 5, 12. et seqq.

V Quamvis hoc peccatum ab Adamo et Eva commissum fuerit, ad solum tamen Adamum ab Apostolo refertur, Rom. 5,12. tamquam ad caput ac principium* universale totius generis humani, ex quo ipsa quoque Eva fuerit condita, 1Cor. 11, 8. et in quo Deus omnes homines, tamquam in primario parente, pro ratione* pacti cum ipso initi, censuerit.

VI Edictum divinum quod Adamus sua inobedientia directe violavit, ab ipso Deo fuit immediate* promulgatum in Paradiso: Ex omni arbore horti come-

DISPUTATION 14

On the Fall of Adam

President: Johannes Polyander
Respondent: Johannes Zelius[1]

Sin is lawlessness or a vice that conflicts with the law of God (1 John 3:4).   1

The subject* of sin is the rational creature made in God's image who falls   2
away from the good that the law of God prescribes and who falls into the evil it
forbids.

Sin may be examined in wicked angels, in our first parents Adam and Eve, or   3
in their descendants.

We undertake to give a treatment of the sin of our first parents, which the   4
apostle (as to its generic character*) calls disobedience, transgression, or fall
(Romans 5:12 ff.).[2]

Although this sin was committed by Adam and Eve, the apostle assigns it   5
only to Adam (Romans 5:12) as the head and universal beginning* of the whole
human race, from whom Eve, too, had been created (1 Corinthians 11:8). In him
God includes all people, as he is the chief parent by virtue* of the covenant God
established with him.[3]

The divine commandment which Adam straight out violated by his disobe-   6
dience was stated directly* by God in Paradise: "You may eat from every tree of

---

1 No information about Johannes Zelius, the respondent of this disputation, appears in in Du Rieu, *Album studiosorum* or other *Alba*, in Van Lieburg, *Repertorium*, or in BLGNP.
2 The common distinction of *genus* and *species* is evoked here (see the Glossary). The second part of this pair occurs in thesis 9 below ("the specific character").
3 The development of covenantal theology is characteristic of the Reformed tradition, in contrast to Lutheran orthodoxy. An early statement of the concept of covenant was provided by Caspar Olevianus and Heinrich Bullinger, and John Calvin also included it in his *Institutes*. Covenant theology distinguishes two fundamental forms of God's covenant in salvation history: the covenant of works *ante lapsum* and the covenant of grace *post lapsum*. The former was a description of the situation of man in Paradise before the Fall; the second was promulgated immediately after the Fall, when the covenant of works had been violated by the disobedience of Adam. The role of Adam as the representative head of God's covenant with humanity, mentioned in thesis 5, refers to the 'covenant of nature' (*foedus naturae*) that regulated man's relationship with God in the world before the Fall. See DLGTT, s.v. "foedus" and "foedus naturae," and Willem J. van Asselt and others, *Introduction to Reformed Scholasticism* (Grand Rapids: Reformation Heritage Books, 2011), 148–149. Further discussion of the concept of covenant occurs in SPT 23.3–4,10–21.

dendo comedes, at ex arbore scientiae boni et mali non comedes, Gen. 2, 27. Quo posthabito edicto, experiri voluit an arbori illi vis inesset majorem ipsi scientiam conferendi.

VII   Eadem inobedientia legem moralem, expressam legis naturalis* ipsi a Deo inditae ὑποτύπωσιν, consequenter transgressus est.

VIII   Nam primam ejus tabulam sua incredulitate ac numinis divini profanatione; secundam, sua ingratitudine in Patrem suum coelestem, sui ac posterorum suorum homicidio, intemperantia, furto ac contrectatione rei alienae, assensu falsi testimonii,* pravaque altioris scientiae ac status cupiditate violavit.

IX   De specie* illius peccati discrepantes sunt Doctorum sententiae.

X   Pontificiorum alii statuunt, fuisse superbiam, alii gulam, qua parentes nostri esum pomi, tamquam non in perpetuum vetiti; alii intemperantiam, qua usum conjugii anticipaverint.

XI   Brentius[a] existimat, fuisse defectionem a Christo Dei Filio, qua imperium ipsius detrectaverint.

---

[a] See the note on the facing page.

the garden that is for eating, but from the tree of the knowledge of good and evil you shall not eat" (Genesis 2:16-17). In ignoring that decree, man willed to test whether the tree possessed the power to bestow greater knowledge on him.

By the same disobedience he consequently transgressed the moral law, the stated sum of the natural law* implanted in him by God.[4]

For he violated the first table of the law through his unbelief and his godless behavior; he violated the second table by his ungratefulness toward his heavenly Father, by the murder of himself and his descendants, by his lack of self-control, by the theft and seizure of another's possessions, by complying with a false witness,* and by the wrong desire for a higher knowledge and status.

The opinions of the scholars are divided about the specific character* of this sin.

Some of the papal theologians hold that it was pride, others gluttony whereby our parents ate the apple before it was right to do so (as though this was not a permanent prohibition). Others hold that it was lack of self-control whereby they had intercourse while not yet being married.[5]

Brenz is of the opinion that it was by a desertion from Christ, the Son of God, that they snubbed his rule.[6]

---

4 On moral law and natural law see *DLGTT*, s.v. "lex moralis" and "lex naturae": "In substance, the *lex moralis* is identical with the *lex naturalis* (...), but, unlike the natural law, it is given by revelation in a form which is clearer and fuller than that otherwise known to the reason." Muller also mentions a "law of paradise" (*lex paradisiaca*) given long before the Mosaic form of the Decalogue, but substantially identical to it. The connection with the Decalogue is visible in thesis 8 that lists several examples from both 'tables' of the law of God. Polyander argues that the single act of disobeying God's commandment regarding the tree of knowledge implies the transgression of the whole law of God. A fuller treatment of the law of God is given in *SPT* 18 (also presided by Polyander)—see especially *SPT* 18.12-13 and *SPT* 18.20-24 on natural law, and *SPT* 18.34-39 on the moral law revealed by God.

5 The positions mentioned here are not readily identified. Robert Bellarmine defended the position that pride (*superbia*) is the character of the first of sin (*On the Loss of Grace and the State of Sin*, 3.4; *Opera* 5:308-311). Cf. Marcia L. Colish, *Peter Lombard*, Brill's Studies in Intellectual History, vol. 41 (Leiden: Brill, 1993), 372-373, where she lists some patristic and early scholastic authors who provide various specifications of the initial sin of Adam and Eve: disobedience (*Summa sententiarum*), doubt (Hugh of St. Victor), pride (Roland of Bologna, Peter Lombard) or vainglory (Honorius), concupiscence (Robert of Melun), avarice (Anselm of Laon, Hugh of St. Victor), and gluttony (*Sententie Anselmi*, Hugh of St. Victor). It is plausible that these different views were transmitted to Roman Catholic theology up to the early seventeenth century.

6 Johannes Brenz (1499-1570) received his theological education in Heidelberg. As the preacher of Schwabisch Hall, he played an important role in implementing the Reformation in the

XII Nostrorum plerique infidelitatem fuisse asserunt, qua fidem huic comminationi divinae abrogarunt: In qua die comedes ex arbore scientiae boni et mali, morte morieris, Gen, 2, 17.

XIII Quae sententia admitti potest, si potius quid parentes nostri primum fecerint, quam quo primum respexerint atque animum suum intenderint, recte perpendamus.

XIV Initium enim, seu primus motus gradusque illius peccati, fuit dubitatio de veritate interminationis, qua Deus suum interdictum sancire voluit; ut ex ordine tentationis qua Diabolus Evam seduxit, evidenter demonstrari* potest.

XV Hanc enim primum ad dubitationem de verbo Dei, dubia sua interrogatione sollicitavit: Etiamne dixit Deus, Non comedetis ex omni arbore horti? Gen. 3, 1.

XVI Deinde ex nutantis feminae ad Dei interdictum aliquid adjicientis responso audacior factus, sanctionem Dei hac manifesta contradictione elevavit: Non moriemini; sed novit Deus, quod in die qua comedetis ex ea, aperientur oculi vestri, et eritis sicut Dii, scientes bonum et malum.

XVII Cui mendacio diabolico Eva potius credens, quam divinae veritati, similitudinem illam ac scientiam divinam per esum fructus illius vetiti affectavit.

XVIII Plures iterum motus affectusque inordinati, cum primo illo infidelitatis actu concurrerunt. Nam sicuti parentum nostrorum infidelitas ambitioni januam aperuit, sic huic annexae fuerunt ingratitudo, impietas in Deum, et contumacia mater defectionis, qua, Deo spreto ac derelicto, se in castra Diaboli contulerunt.

XIX Causa* hujus peccati, aut externa est, aut interna.

XX Causa illius externa non fuit Dei praescientia, nec ejus permissio, nec impulsio, sed Diaboli instigatio.

Duchy of Wurttemberg. In several debates with Zwinglian and Calvinist theologians, he defended the Lutheran position on the unity of the body of Christ and the bread in the Lord's Supper, advocating the omnipresence of Christ's body. It is difficult to identify the opinion mentioned in thesis 11. Brenz's commentary on John 8:37–47 elaborates the contrast between believing in Christ as staying in the truth, and following Satan as leaving the truth in favor of lies: *In divi Joannis Evangelion Exegesis* (second edition, Hagenau: Johannes Secerius, 1532), 164–168.

14. ON THE FALL OF ADAM

12 Most of our teachers state that it was unbelief whereby they withheld their faith in that divine threat, "on the day on which you eat from the tree of the knowledge of good and evil, your will die" (Genesis 2:17).

13 We can admit this interpretation if we give the right weight to what our parents first did, rather than what they first saw or directed their attention to.

14 For the beginning of that sin, its first move or step, was doubting the truth of the threat whereby God willed to sanction his command;[7] this can be demonstrated* clearly from the order in which the devil led Eve into temptation.[8]

15 For he first solicited her to doubt God's word by his doubtful question: "Did God really state, 'you shall not eat of every tree in the garden'?" (Genesis 3:1).

16 Then, being more emboldened by the reply of the wavering woman as she added something to God's command, he removed God's sanction through this obvious contradiction: "You will not die, but God knows that on the day you eat of it your eyes will be opened, and you will be like God, knowing good and evil" [Genesis 3:5].

17 Eve, placing her trust in the devil's lie rather than in the divine truth, endeavoured passionately to have that likeness and divine knowledge by eating of the forbidden fruit.

18 And after that first act of unbelief many inordinate emotions and feelings came rushing along. For as the unbelief of our parents opened the door to ambition, so linked with it were ingratitude, thanklessness, impiety towards God, and willful disobedience (the 'mother' of defection), by which Adam and Eve spurned God and abandoned Him and took refuge in devil's camp.

19 The cause* of this sin is either external or internal.[9]

20 The external cause of it was not God's foreknowledge, nor his permission or impulse, but the instigation of the devil.

---

7 A distinction is made here between the command of God, "you shall not eat," and the sanction or threat attached to it, "you will die." As theses 16 and 17 explain, Eve started to disbelieve the sanction, and thereby was led to break the command.

8 The structure of the detailed exposition of the first sin in theses 14 to 40 can be sketched as follows: First, a brief narrative account of this event is given, closely following the text of Genesis 3. Next, a more structural analysis is provided in terms of different causes: external (20–28), internal (30–33), formal and final (34), and the effects (35–40).

9 The distinction between external and internal causes appears to be crucial for a right understanding of sin. External causes are factors outside man that contribute to the act of sinning. The internal cause is located inside man himself. As the subsequent discussion shows, the identification of external causes cannot serve as an excuse for man's own disobedience.

xxi Non Dei praescientia, sive illa seorsim absque actu* voluntatis* determinantis,* sive conjunctim cum illo consideretur.

xxii Nulla enim Dei praescientia* theoretica, seu indeterminata, rerum praescitarum causa esse potest,* cum illa non in alio, sed in se tantum agat, nec propterea res* sint futurae, quod Deus eas nuda cognitione praesciverit, sed ideo futuras praesciverit, quod eas fieri, vel, ut ab aliis fierent, permittere decreverit.

xxiii Praescientia autem practica, quae adjunctam sibi habet Dei voluntatem, non ex se sola, sed ex suo cum actu voluntatis consortio, foris agit: nec res futuras tantummodo sub ratione entitatis ac veritatis, sed etiam sub ratione boni et tamquam justissimae suae voluntatis objecta intuetur.

xxiv Quocirca, cum peccatum non sit bonum, sed deflexio a bono, tum naturali,* quod Deus in omnibus suis creaturis efficit, tum morali, quod lege sua praecipit, tum finali, quod in sapientissima rerum omnium gubernatione ac directione sibi proponit, nequaquam causa peccati ab Adamo et Eva commissi, ipsi absque manifesta blasphemia attribui potest.

xxv Nec Dei permissio causa istius peccati statui potest, cum illius interventu Deus peccatum istud non effecerit, sed a nostris parentibus, quorum illicitum appetitum cohibere non tenebatur, committi siverit, ut summum ex eo bonum eliceret.

xxvi Nec Dei impulsio, cum nec malo ullo Deus possit tentari, nec ad malum, quod expressa sua lege se odisse, mortisque supplicio ulturum pronuntiat, alios tentare.

xxvii Diaboli vero instigatio est peccati nostrorum parentum causa externa principalis. Nam sicuti Evam serpentis adminiculo, sic Adamum Evae suggestione seduxit.

It was not God's foreknowledge, whether that knowledge is seen separately from the act* of the deciding* will,* or jointly with it.¹⁰

21

For the cause of things that are known beforehand cannot* be a theoretical or indeterminate foreknowledge* of God, since this knowledge does not act in anything other than itself, nor do events* occur because God foreknew them with a bare cognition. Instead, He foreknew things that were going to happen precisely because He decreed them to happen or to permit them so that they would be done by others.

22

Moreover, practical foreknowledge, which has God's will joined with it, does not act externally from itself, but in its partnership with the act of the will. Nor does it have future events in view only for their existence and truth, but also in the aspect of being good and as the objects of its own very just will.

23

For this reason, since sin is not a good but a turning away from the good (the natural* good God effects in all his creatures, the moral good He teaches in the law, and the final good He proposes to himself as He governs and directs everything most wisely), the cause of the sin committed by Adam and Eve in no way whatsoever can be attributed to Him without manifest blasphemy.

24

Nor can God's permission be stated as the cause of that sin, since by its intervention God did not bring about sin, but He let our parents, whose unlawful desire He was not bound to restrain, to commit the sin—in order that He might draw the highest good from it.

25

Nor can an impulse¹¹ of God be the cause, for God cannot be tempted by any evil, nor can He tempt anyone else to evil,¹² as He declares in his explicit law that He hates it and will punish it with the penalty of death.

26

In fact the principal external cause for the sin of our parents is the instigation of the devil. For just as he led Eve astray through the agency of the snake, so he seduced Adam through the prompting of Eve.

27

---

10   For an explanation of the different aspects of God's foreknowledge (theoretical—practical, separated from or joined to the divine will) see *SPT* 11.2,24. The final clause of thesis 24 below reveals an important motivation for this statement: It would be blasphemous to attribute evil to God. On the conceptual level, a direct causal nexus between knowledge and actualization is denied here: Whatever happens is decided not by God's foreknowledge but by his decree; and in relation to sin, the decree is further specified as "permission" (thesis 25 below).

11   See *DLGTT*, s.v. "causa impulsiva": "A cause external to the traditional Aristotelian model of first or efficient, material, formal, and final causes (...); it moves or provides opportunity for the efficient cause, though not in an absolute or necessary sense, not as a prior efficient cause." Even with these restrictions, no 'impulse' towards evil can be ascribed to God. See also the footnote on *causa impellens* in *SPT* 10.18.

12   Cf. James 1:13.

XXVIII   In qua seductione quadruplex Diaboli actus* est observandus:
1. Quod ad suam fallaciam aptius occultandam, Evae sub forma serpentis apparuerit.
2. Quod animalis, reliqua calliditate atque in hortum irrependi facilitate superantis, corpus assumpserit.
3. Quod mulierem imbecillioris consilii, priusquam virum adortus fuerit.
4. Quod virum per mulierem vitae ipsius sociam in ejusdem peccati societatem pellexerit.

XXIX   Quo respiciens Apostolus, ait, virum non prius seductum fuisse, sed mulierem, hancque transgressionis ipsius causam fuisse, nimirum, administram atque instrumentalem, 1 Tim. 2, 13. 14.

XXX   Causa lapsus interna, est libera utriusque nostri parentis voluntas,* vel potius deflexio voluntatis, Satanae potius quam Deo auscultantis.

XXXI   Uterque cum sic a Deo conditus fuerit ut posset* non peccare, si nollet peccare, et posset, si vellet.

XXXII   Et quamvis Deus utrumque mutabiliter bonum creaverit, ista tamen mutabilitas in statu ipsorum integro, nec defectus fuit naturae ad imaginem Dei conditae, nec peccatum, nec causa peccati, sed conditio creaturae conveniens; a qua creator hac perfectionis nota incommunicabili* distinguitur, quod per se ac natura* sit immutabiliter* bonus.

We should note that in leading them astray the devil took four actions:* 28
1. He appeared to Eve in the form of a serpent to hide his deception more effectively.
2. He took on the body of the animal which surpassed the others in its cunning and in its talent for creeping into the garden.
3. He attacked the woman before the man because her resolve was weaker.
4. He enticed the man through the woman, his life-partner, into a partnership in the same sin.

In considering this, the apostle says that the first to be seduced was not the man but the woman, and that she was the cause of his transgression, obviously as the instrumental and supportive cause (1 Timothy 2:13, 14).[13] 29

The internal cause of the fall is the free will* of both our parents; better yet, it is the bending of the will that listened to Satan instead of God.[14] 30

Both of our parents were created by God in such a way that they were able* not to sin if they willed not to sin, and that were able to sin if they willed to.[15] 31

And although God created each of them good in such a way that they could change, nevertheless that changeability in their good state was neither a defect in the nature that was created in God's image, nor was it sin or the cause of sin. It was the condition that suited the creature from whom the Creator is set apart by this incommunicable* mark of perfection, that He in himself and by nature* is unchangeably* good.[16] 32

---

13   For the term 'instrumental cause' as distinct from 'principal efficient cause' see the explanation provided in *SPT* 1.13–14 and *SPT* 3.6. The distinction of principal and instrumental causes is employed here to harmonize the different statements by the apostle Paul that trace the first sin back to Adam and to Eve respectively.

14   It seems that the term 'free will' (*voluntas libera*) is chosen here deliberately instead of 'free choice' (*arbitrium liberum*); see for a fuller discussion of these and other cognate terms *SPT* 17.3–8. In an early stage of the Reformed scholastic tradition, Jerome Zanchi argued for the equation of 'free choice' and 'free will' (see *RTF*, 79–80).

15   In theses 30 and 31, the human *will* is identified as the internal and, thus, principal efficient cause of the fall into sin. Besides the fact that the fall therefore cannot be attributed to any external cause, the volitional understanding of sin implies that it should not be viewed as, for example, mental and emotional weakness, mere lack of insight, or tragic fate. Since sin is an act of man's own will, he is held responsible for it. See also thesis 33: Although the devil exerted external persuasion, this influence imposed no coercive necessity, but man still remained free to assent or resist the devil by his will.

16   This thesis points to a difference in the way God and man respectively possess the property of being good. For God, being good is a property that belongs essentially to his nature and, thus, He cannot be otherwise; cf. *SPT* 6.30, where it is stated that the will of God and its adjacent virtues such as goodness are qualified by his attributes of the first sort (simplicity, immutability, etc.). Human beings were created good in a sense that left open the choice

XXXIII	Nec ideo parentes nostri sunt excusabiles, quod Diaboli instinctu mandatum Dei transiliverint, cum Diabolus externa suasione nullam voluntati ipsorum necessitatem* cogentem afferre potuerit.
XXXIV	Peccato illi forma proprie* assignari non potest, cum sit privatio* formae vel deformitas et defectio a perfectione* ac lege quam Deus homini dederat; nec finis,* cum sit aberratio a fine, et ab ordine ad finem, ad quem homo fuit creatus.
XXXV	Effecta peccatum illud consequentia sunt poenae, aut utrique parenti communes,* aut alteri propriae.
XXXVI	Poenae communes sunt, 1. amissio justitiae originalis. 2. sensus nuditatis. 3. terror conscientiae. 4. ejectio ex Paradiso. 5. omnis generis laborum ac cruciatuum congeries. 6. moriendi necessitas.
XXXVII	Errant ergo, qui peccatum utriusque parentis, atque imprimis Adami, exiguum ac veniale fuisse arbitrantur. Quo enim Dei mandatum fuit levius atque observatu facilius, eo magis uterque ob illius transgressionem coram Deo fuit inexcusabilis, ac reus mortis temporariae et aeternae.
XXXVIII	Propria viri poena fuit, singularis quaedam rerum toto vitae suae curriculo gerendarum cura ac sollicitudo.
XXXIX	Propria mulieris poena, fuit summa partus atque educationis liberorum difficultas.
XL	Quemadmodum omnes homines in utroque parente originaliter peccarunt, ac per ejusdem naturae vitiatae propagationem communi lue sunt contaminati, sic ejusdem criminis ac mortis rei sunt constituti, Rom. 5, 12.
XLI	Utrumque interim parentem per fidem in Jesum semen mulieris promissum, Deo fuisse reconciliatum, ac participem factum salutis aeternae, asseverare non dubitamus.

---

between good and evil. The fact that they could develop in morally diverse directions does not diminish the goodness in which they were created; rather it is an implication of the freedom of will with which they were endowed.

Yet it does not therefore mean that our parents are to be excused because they over-stepped God's command by the instigation of the devil; for the devil by his external suggestion could not adduce any coercive necessity* to their will.

One cannot assign a proper* form to sin, because sin is a lack* of form or a distortion of and departure from the perfect* law which God had given to man. Nor does it have an end,* because it is a deviation from the law and from the ordering towards the end for which man was created.[17]

The effects which followed upon that sin were punishments, either shared* by both parents or specific to one or the other.

The shared penalties are: 1. the loss of their original righteousness;[18] 2. their awareness of nakedness; 3. the terror of their conscience; 4. the ejection from Paradise; 5. the mound of all kinds of struggles and sufferings; 6. the necessity of dying.

Therefore those people err who think that the sin of both parents, but chiefly Adam, was minor and pardonable. For the less burdensome and easier it was to observe God's commandment, so much the more without excuse was each of our parents before God on account of that transgression, and guilty of temporal and eternal death.

The punishment specific to the man was a certain singular worry and anxiety for the things that he was to manage throughout the whole course of his life.

The punishment specific to the woman was a very great hardship in child-bearing and in the upbringing of children.

Just as all people sinned in both parents originally and were infected by this common ailment through the proliferation of that same damaged nature, so too were they counted guilty of the same crime and death (Romans 5:12).[19]

We do not, in the meantime, hesitate to assert that both parents through faith in Jesus, the promised seed of the woman, have been reconciled to God and have become partakers of eternal salvation.

---

17 In this thesis, 'form' and 'end' are elements from the theory of fourfold causality (cf. *SPT* 1.13–14 and *SPT* 3.6), employed here as a heuristic device to discuss important aspects of sin. In scholastic thinking, 'form' is a positive, normative category that defines the essential quality of a substance or act. As sin is merely negative and has no existence apart from its deviance from the law of God, such a positive category cannot be assigned to it. Similarly, it is denied that sin has an end, as it consists precisely of missing the end established to man by God.

18 On the original righteousness in which man was created, see *SPT* 13.37–43.

19 The next disputation, *SPT* 15, is devoted to an explication of this sentence.

DISPUTATIO XV

De Peccato Originali

Praeside D. ANDREA RIVETO
Respondente ABRAHAMO ab ELDERE

THESIS I   Homini in creatione duplex vita a Deo data fuit, animalis et spiritualis: illa, in animae et corporis unione sita fuit; haec, in conjunctione animae cum Deo opifice suo. Ut prima amittitur per separationem unionis illius naturalis,* sic per alienationem hominis a Deo, secutus est spiritualis interitus. Qua defectione si reliquas etiam creaturas ita pessum dedit Adam, ut propterea maledictioni factae fuerint obnoxiae, nihil a ratione alienum est, si ad totam ejus sobolem sit propagata, quae peccati hujus per quod mors intravit in mundum, particeps facta, sub illius deformitate et reatu oppressa manet, donec ab alio liberetur.

II   Postquam igitur actum est de primo illo peccato πρωτοπλάστων, postulat methodi ratio, ut de eo quod a primo illo immediate* originem ducit, et ad posteros propagatum est, instituatur disputatio. Quod ut ordine fiat, an sit tale peccatum, nobis erit primo disquirendum. 2. Quid sit? ubi de causis ejus, subjectis* et effectis, sigillatim erit agendum.

III   Id eo accuratius nobis faciendum, quod in causa duorum hominum, Adae videlicet et Christi, quorum per alterum venundati sumus sub peccato, per alterum a peccatis redimimur, proprie fidem Christianam consistere, cum August. censemus, *De pecc. orig.* c. 14.[a] Ideo enim Filius Dei carnem assumpsit humanam, et in ea pati voluit, ut humanum genus* a servitute peccati, in qua ex

---

[a] Erroneous reference; correct to Augustine, *De gratia Christi et de peccato originali* 2.24.28 (CSEL 42:186–187).

DISPUTATION 15

On Original Sin

President: Andreas Rivetus
Respondent: Abraham van Eldere[1]

At creation God granted man a two-fold life: a natural life, and a spiritual life. The former is situated in the union of soul and body, the latter in the linking of the soul to God, who is its craftsman. As natural life is lost by the disjunction of that natural* union, so spiritual death follows man's alienation from God. If by his rebellion Adam also brought the other creatures down so low that therefore they became subject to a curse, it is entirely plausible that the curse was passed down to his whole offspring. Being made partaker of the sin whereby death entered the world, his offspring remains burdened by the deformity and charge of guilt until someone else relieves it.

And so, having treated the first sin of our ancestors, for the sake of proper method we should discuss the sin that has its origin directly* in that first transgression, and that was passed on to his descendants. To do so in an orderly fashion we must first enquire whether a sin of this kind exists, and second, what that sin is.[2] At that point we shall have to give separate treatments of its causes, subjects,* and effects.

We should perform this task all the more meticulously because, with Augustine, we judge "that strictly speaking the Christian belief is founded upon the position of two men, namely Adam and Christ, of whom through the one we were sold under sin, and through the other we are redeemed from sins" (*Concerning Original Sin*, chapter 14). For this is the reason why the Son of God assumed human flesh and willed to suffer in it: To release the human race*

1

2

3

---

1   Born ca. 1598 and coming from Dordrecht, Abrahamus Hermanni ab Eldere matriculated on 15 February 1620 in theology. He defended this disputation on 10 March 1621 and dedicated it to P. van Asperen, a member of the High Counsel of Holland and Zeeland, Joh. Becius and Joh. Dibbetz, pastors in Dordrecht, A. Tyckmannus, pastor in Zwijndrecht, A. Aemilius, rector of the Latin School at Dordrecht (1615) and at Utrecht (1619), and to his friend P. Boelenius. Abraham van Elderen was not ordained as pastor but served as *conrector* of the Latin school in Dordrecht from 1621. He died in 1637. See Du Rieu, *Album studiosorum*, 145, and NNBW 1, 799.

2   The order of "whether it is" and "what it is" stems from Aristotle's theory of science. Aristotle, *Posterior Analytics* II, c.7, 92b4–7. Theses 4 to 7 provide arguments for the factual existence of original sin; from thesis 8 onward, the question "what it is" is answered.

praevaricatione primi parentis detinebatur, liberaret; unde jam olim, et hoc tempore, Ecclesia eosdem gratiae* Christi hostes passa est, et patitur, quos originalis peccati experta est oppugnatores.

IV De naturae* obliquitate et depravatione aliquando conquesti sunt, qui nihil alias supra naturam sapuerunt. Homines natura sua esse malos, et induci non posse* ut justitiam colant, notavit Plato, lib. 2. *de Repub.*[a] Et Cicero lamentatus est, Hominem a natura noverca in lucem edi, corpore nudo, fragili atque infirmo, animo ad molestias anxio, ad timores humili, ad labores debili, ad libidines proclivi, in quo divinus ignis sit obrutus, ingenium et mores. Citatur ab Aug. lib. 4. *contra Jul.* ex. lib. *de Repub.*[b] Sed neque malum satis agnoverunt, neque ad mali causam et fontem, spirituali luce destituti, pervenire potuerunt.

V Ab Adamo in posteros, peccatum vere sic dictum derivari, ex Scriptura Veteris et Novi Testamenti evidentissimum* est; in qua ipse Deus asserit, omne figmentum et cogitationes cordis humani, tantummodo malum esse omni tempore, Gen. 6, 5. idque a pueritia ipsius, Gen. 8, 21. Et Job negat, posse mundum nasci ex immundo conceptum semine, Job. 14,4. Et David agnoscit se in iniquitatibus conceptum, Ps. 51, 7. Et Christus asserit, carnem esse quicquid ex carne natum est, Joh. 3, 6. Et Paulus, per unum hominem peccatum in mundum intrasse, per peccatum mortem, et ita in omnes homines mortem pertransiisse, in quo omnes peccaverunt, etiam ii qui non peccaverunt ad similitudinem Adami, Rom. 5, 12. 13. 14. et nos omnes natura esse filios irae, Eph. 2, 3. Quae pauca e multis selecta, morbum satis detegunt, quem Satan tegendo incurabilem reddere tentat.

---

[a] Plato, *De re publica* 2.358c   [b] Augustine, *Contra Julianum* 4.12.60 (MPL 44:767), citing the lost Cicero, *De re publica* 3.1.

from slavery to sin, in which it was held prisoner following the transgression of the first parent. As a result, already in former times—but also in this age—the Church has suffered and suffers the same enmity against Christ's grace,* which it meets in the opposition against [the doctrine of] original sin.

At various times men who knew of nothing beyond what is natural bemoaned the distortion and perverseness of the natural* state. Plato observed, "by their very nature men are evil, and cannot* be persuaded to cherish justice" (*Republic*, book 2). And Cicero lamented the fact that "man is brought forth to the light of day by his step-mother, nature, with a body that is naked, frail and powerless, with a soul that is anxious over troubles, abject in the face of fears, crippled at the prospect of hard work, inclined towards wanton passion, in whom the divine fire-light, its talent, and character, lie hidden from view." This is quoted from the *Book about the Republic* by Augustine, Book 4, against Julian. But even so they did not acknowledge evil sufficiently, nor could they reach the cause and source of evil, as they lacked spiritual light.

The Scripture of the Old and New Testament most clearly* shows that it is right to say that from Adam sin is passed down to his descendants. In Scripture God himself asserts that every imagination and the thoughts of the heart of man are only evil all the time (Genesis 6:5)—and that from the time of childhood (Genesis 8:21). And Job states that what is conceived from an impure seed cannot possibly be born pure (Job 14:4). David confesses that he was conceived in iniquity (Psalm 51:7). And Christ asserts that "whatever is born from flesh is flesh" (John 3:6). And Paul: "Through one man sin came into the world, and through sin death, and so death came to all men, in whom all sinned,[3] even those who did not sin in the manner of Adam" (Romans 5:12–14). And, "we all by nature are children of wrath" (Ephesians 2:3). These few texts (picked from many) sufficiently expose the disease which Satan tries to make incurable by hiding it.

---

3   The Greek text reads: ἐφ' ᾧ πάντες ἥμαρτον. Rivetus follows the interpretation of Augustine and later theologians, who read ἐφ' ᾧ as *in quo*. Contemporary biblical exegetes agree that ἐφ' ᾧ should not be translated as 'in whom' but as 'because.' The words ἑνὸς ἀνθρώπου ("one man") are so far removed that they do not form an obvious antecedent. Remarkably, the King James Version (1611) reads "for that [i.e., because] all have sinned." For a helpful summary of the difficulties involving *in quo*, see S. Lewis Johnson Jr., 'Romans 5:12: An Exercise in Exegesis and Theology,' in *New Dimensions in New Testament Study, eds*. Richard N. Longenecker and Merill C. Tenney (Grand Rapids: Zondervan, 1974), 298–316, esp. 304–305.

VI   Idem evincitur rationibus firmissimis ex analogia fidei petitis. 1. A circumcisione olim, et baptismo hoc tempore, infantibus administrato: utroque sigillo justitiae fidei et remissionis peccatorum, non certe actualium in illis, cum actualiter peccare non potuerint, ergo originalis. 2. A communi omnibus morte, a qua non excipiuntur infantes. Est autem mors stipendium peccati, Rom. 6, 23. quod juste non potest nisi peccatoribus irrogari, cum omnis poena, si justa sit, poena peccati sit, nec morte pungi debeat, qui ejus aculeum non sensit. 3. A redemptione per Christum facta, et generatione* per Spiritum. Qui enim nascuntur sine peccato, redemptore non egent; nec spirituali regeneratione, quos carnalis non infecit generatio. At Christus pro omnibus mortuus est, ergo etiam pro infantibus. Et nisi quis renatus fuerit ex aqua et spiritu, non intrabit in regnum coelorum, 2 Cor. 5, 14. Joh. 3, 3. 4. Adde, omne genitum gignenti esse simile, Adam genuit filium ad similitudinem suam, Gen. 5, 3. Imago Adami opponitur imagini Dei per peccatum obliteratae; genuit ergo corruptus corruptum, ut leprosus leprosum.

VII   His accinit Orthodoxus antiquitatis consensus, docens, firmissime credendum et nullatenus dubitandum, omnem hominem qui per concubitum viri et mulieris concipitur, cum peccato originali nasci, impietati subditum, mortique subjectum, et ob hoc irae filium. Quae Fulgentii verba, *de fide ad Petr.*[a] exprimunt Ecclesiae fidem etiam ante exortam haeresim Pelagianam, ut prolatis Irenaei, Cypriani, Hilarii, Gregor. Nazianzeni, Basilii, Ambrosii, Hieronymi etc. sententiis contra Julianum probavit* Augustinus.[b] Tempore autem Augustini

---

[a] Fulgentius, *De fide ad Petrum* 69 (CCSL 91A/753).   [b] Augustine, *Contra Julianum* esp. 1.1.1–2.20.37 (MPL 44:641–702).

Similar proof is found in the very convincing arguments drawn from the analogy of faith.⁴ 1. The argument from the circumcision administered to infants in former times, and baptism nowadays: Each is a sign of the righteousness of faith and of the forgiveness of sins. It is not, surely, the forgiveness of actual sins in those children, since they could not have sinned in deed; therefore it is the forgiveness of original sin. 2. The argument based on the fact that death is shared by all people, and from which infants are not exempt. Moreover, "death is the wages of sin" (Romans 6:23), which can be imposed with justice only upon those who have sinned, since every punishment—if the penalty is just—is a punishment for sin, and because one should not be pricked by death who does not feel its sting.⁵ 3. The argument based on the redemption made through Christ and the generation* through the Spirit. For those who are born without sin do not need a redeemer; nor are they in need of spiritual regeneration who have not been affected by carnal generation. But "Christ died on behalf of everyone," and thus on behalf of infants, too. And "unless one is born again from the water and the spirit, he will not enter into the kingdom of heaven" (2 Corinthians 5:14; John 3:3,4). Add to that the fact that everything that is born is similar to that which brought it forth; "Adam bore a son in his own likeness" (Genesis 5:3). Adam's likeness replaced the image of God that sin had wiped out; therefore what was corrupt has produced something corrupt, and the leprous has produced what is leprous.

The orthodox consensus of antiquity is in harmony with these arguments, teaching "that we must believe most firmly, and not doubt in any way whatsoever, that everyone who is conceived through the sexual intercourse of man and woman, is born in original sin, is submersed in unrighteousness, is subject to death, and therefore is a child of wrath." These words of Fulgentius [bishop of Ruspe],⁶ in *On Faith to Peter*, express the Church's belief even before the Pelagian heresy arose, as also Augustine demonstrated* against Julian with passages quoted from Irenaeus, Cyprian, Hilary, Gregory of Nazianzus, Basil, Ambrose, Jerome, etc.⁷ Moreover, at the time of Augustine and in the ages that

---

4   The analogy of faith is "the use of a general sense of the meaning of Scripture, constructed from the clear or unambiguous *loci*, as the basis for interpreting unclear or ambiguous texts." DLGTT, s.v. "analogia fidei."
5   Allusion to 1 Corinthians 15:55–56.
6   Fulgentius of Ruspe (AD 462/467–527/533) was born to a noble family at Carthage, and became a monk under influence of a sermon by Augustine. His defense of the Chalcedonian position on the Person of Christ brought him into conflict with the Arian king Thrasamund.
7   Later in his life Rivetus collected quotations on imputation from the confessions and the writings of the Reformers for the Synod of Charenton (1645). See A. Rivetus, *Testimonia de imputatione primi peccati omnibus Adami posteris*, in: *Opera theologica*, 3 vols. (Rotterdam:

et insecutis seculis, praeter infinitos scriptores, eandem dilucide expresserunt Concilia contra Pelagium et Semipelagianos congregata, Palaestinum,[a] Milevitanum, Carthaginense,[b] Toletanum 6.[c] et Arausicanum.[d]

VIII Cum esse tale peccatum auctoritate constet et ratione, videndum est deinceps quid sit. Et quidem de nomine primum, quod ipsi varium tam in Scripturis, quam in aliorum scriptorum monumentis, inditum est. Appellatur enim a Paulo, peccatum peccans, et malum inhabitans, Rom. 5, 12. et 7, 13. malum adjacens, ibidem versus 17, εὐπερίστατος ἁμαρτία, Hebr. 12, 1. et concupiscentia, lex membrorum, corpus peccati, etc. Rom. 7, 7. 23. A patribus nonnullis, antiqua serpentis plaga, venenum, pondus antiqui criminis, etc. Sed post exortum Pelagium, Augustinus, ut adversariorum strophas et aequivocationes, aliorum nominum occasione arrepta excogitatas, etiam ipso vocabulo praeverteret; peccatum hoc originale, vel originis, passim nominavit, unde hoc nomen* deinceps in Ecclesia frequentatum, a nobis etiam retinetur, ut rei* explicandae satis commodum et conveniens.

IX Dicitur autem *originale*, non ad restrictionem, quasi aequivoce* peccatum appellaretur; sed ad distinctionem actualis peccati. Nec etiam Originale appellatur, quod sit aliorum omnium peccatorum fons et origo, significatione* transitiva, et ratione* effecti, etiamsi id ipsi competat; sed vel quia inest unicuique ab ortu suo, id est, ab ipso conceptionis momento, aut quia contrahitur a prima origine, id est, a primo parente, aut quia omnes jam inde ab initio in Adam peccaverunt; quae tres rationes olim a diversis allatae, in hanc unam contrahi possunt, originale vocari, quia propagatione haereditaria nativitatem nostram maculavit, atque in nobis statim, ut primum homines sumus,

---

[a] The acts of the synod of Palestine (or: council of Diospolis, or of Lydda) of 415 have only been preserved in fragments, and especially in Augustine, *De gestis Pelagii* (cf. NPNF1 5:179). [b] The anti-Pelagian canons are erroneously attributed to the second council of Mileve (in Numidia) in 416, and actually come from the fifteenth synod of Carthage in 418 (DH 222–224, against Pelagius). [c] The acts of the sixth synod of Toledo (638) do not condemn Pelagius directly, but do indirectly address the issue of original sin (DH 491). [d] For the second synod of Orange (529), see DH 371–372.

Leers, 1651–1660), 3:798–826. Translated into English in *Theological Essays: Reprinted from the Princeton Review* (New York: Wiley and Putnam, 1846), 195–217. On the developments in the doctrine of original sin, see Tatha Wiley, *Original Sin: Origins, Developments, Contemporary Meaning* (Mahwah: Paulist Press, 2002), and F.R. Tennant, *The Sources of the Doctrines of the Fall and Original Sin* (Cambridge: Cambridge University Press, 1903), 273–345.

15. ON ORIGINAL SIN

followed, besides countless other writers, the same belief was expressed by the Councils that were held against the Pelagians and semi-Pelagians held at Palestine, Milevis, Toledo (the sixth), and at Orange.

Since by both biblical authority and reason it is agreed that such a sin does exist, we must next see what it is. First, then, about the various names given to it in Scriptures and the works of other writers. For Paul calls it "sin that is sinning," and "indwelling evil" (Romans 5:12, 7:13), "the sin that so easily ensnares" (Hebrews 12:1), and "desire,"[8] "the law of our members," "the body of sin," etc. (Romans 7:7.23). By several church-fathers it is called "the ancient snare of the serpent," "poison," "the burden of the ancient offense," etc. But after Pelagius arose, Augustine, in many places called this sin "original" or "from the origin," so that even by means of the very word he could render useless the adversaries' dodgy tricks, which they had invented when they seized the opportunity to make up other names. From that time on this term* was frequently used in the Church, and we retain it too, as it is suitable enough and convenient for explaining the topic.*

And it is called "original" not to restrict its meaning, as if "sin" is an equivocal term,* but to distinguish it from actual sin.[9] Nor is it called "original" because it is the fount and source of all other sins by transference of meaning* and by reason* of its effect[10] (even though that does also apply to the original sin itself). But it is so called because either it exists in each and everyone from birth, that is, from the very moment of conception, or because it derives from the first origin, that is, from the first parent. Or it is so called because all men sinned already from the beginning in Adam. These three explanations, taken from various previous sources, can be drawn together into this one explanation: It is called "original" because by hereditary propagation it has sullied our birth, and it resides in us straight away, as soon as we are human beings, and it is passed

---

8   The Latin word *concupiscentia*, rendered here as 'desire,' became a technical term in patristic and scholastic doctrine of sin. In that connection it is commonly rendered as 'concupiscence,' which means, in general, any longing of the soul for what is good, or specifically, the desire of the lower appetites, contrary to reason, to satisfy the senses.

9   'Actual sin' is discussed in the next disputation, SPT 16. The Latin term *aequivocatio* or one of its deratives occurs in SPT 7.3,7, 15.8,9, 20.21 and 38.30. It is used for words that can have two or more interpretations, sometimes with the negative connotation of the intention to mislead. Rivetus denies that adding the qualification 'original' to the substantive 'sin' alters the meaning of the word 'sin.'

10 It is true that the sin of Adam is the origin of all other sins, both in the sense that the sinful character of all sins flows from it and that all sins result from it; still 'original sin' does not in the first place refer to the sin of Adam but to the sin inherent in all of his descendants.

insedit, et naturae et originis lege in nos derivatum est; ut ipso nominis etymo opponatur Pelagianorum dogmati, negantium peccatum ullum cum homine nasci, sed in eo solum cum nascitur quod Deus condidit, inveniri. Quam appellationem etiam confirmant loci Scripturae supra memorati, ex Gen. 8. Job 14. Ps. 51. et Eph. 2.

x   Ad rem quod attinet, peccatum originale definimus, ἀνομίαν seu vitiositatem haereditariam, ex defectione omnium hominum naturali modo ab Adamo propagatorum, in ipsius primi parentis lumbis factam; qua toti quanti sunt, corrupti, eoque ab omni bono aversi, et ad omne malum tantum propensi et inclinati, rei sunt irae Dei et morti aeternae obnoxii.

xi   Efficiens hujus peccati causa* est primorum parentum lapsus, quo justo Dei judicio reatus et pravitas naturae attracta est, et in totam posteritatem transfusa. Quia enim in paradiso duplicem Adam gerebat personam,* cum suam ipsius, tum totius posteritatis cujus sustinebat massam; etiam peccatum ejus geminum habuit respectum, tum ad ipsum, et sic erat personalis* et actualis ipsius transgressio, non proprie* originalis sed originans, seu originem praebens omnibus aliis et peccatorum effectibus, tum ad totum posteritatis genus, quod in lumbis ejus latens una peccabat, ut Levi decimatus fuit, dum esset in lumbis Abrahami patris sui, Hebr. 7, 8. et 9., et ita fuit universalis culpa seu peccatum universale et naturae totius vel speciei,* in omnes homines generatione derivandum, ad quos in Adamo sententia illa directa fuerat, Quacumque die comederis de fructu, etc. morte morieris, Gen. 2, 17.

xii   Qua ratione etiam peccatum illud est quodammodo voluntarium. Etsi enim infantes propriae voluntatis* usum nullum habeant, voluntarium tamen etiam in illis dicitur peccatum originale, voluntate primi parentis; ex qua tamquam efficiente causa, malum hoc in posteros propagatum est, velut a radice et origine, qua factum est, ut voluntas singulorum, cum primum incipit esse, inficiatur vitio pravae concupiscentiae, a quo mala, perversa, et a Deo aversa dicitur. Quam utramque voluntarii rationem breviter complectitur Augustinus, dum ait, peccatum originale non absurde vocari voluntarium, quia ex prima hominis mala voluntate contractum, factum est quodammodo haereditarium, lib. 1. *Retract.* c. 13.,[a] sumpta nempe ratione voluntarii communiter, secundum voluntatem primi principii alicujus totius, sive id fuerit individuum, sive specificum.

---

[a] Augustine, *Retractationes* 1.13.5 (CCSL 57:38).

15. ON ORIGINAL SIN

on to us by a law of nature and origin. And so by the very etymology of the word the doctrine of the Pelagians may be opposed, who state that no sin comes with man's birth, but that in man when he is born one finds only what God has created. The passages of Scripture mentioned above also lend support to this naming: for example, Genesis 8, Job 14, Psalm 51, and Ephesians 2.

10 Now concerning the matter proper: We define original sin as inherited lawlessness or vice effected in the loins of that first parent, committed by the rebellion of all men who from Adam have been generated in the natural way. In this all people in existence are corrupt, and so they are hostile to every good thing, and tend or incline to every sort of evil only; they deserve the wrath of God, and are worthy of eternal death.

11 The efficient cause* of this sin is the fall of the first parents, whereby in God's righteous judgment the guilt and depravity of nature was attracted and transmitted to all posterity. For in Paradise Adam bore a two-fold personality* as he carried in him the mass [of humanity] that included all posterity as well as his own. So his sin, too, had two aspects: One looked to himself, and thus was his own, personal* and actual transgression—not original in the proper* sense but originating or giving origin to all other sins and to the effects of sin. The other aspect concerns the whole race of posterity which lay concealed in his loins and sinned along with him, in the same way as Levi paid tithes "while he was in the loins of his father Abraham" (Hebrews 7:8,9). Similarly also the universal guilt or universal sin of the entire nature or species* was to be passed on to all men by generation, to whom in Adam this statement had been directed: "And on whatever day you eat of the fruit, etc. you shall certainly die" (Genesis 2:17).

12 For this reason even original sin is in some way voluntary.[11] For although infants do not exercise a will* of their own, nevertheless even in them original sin is called voluntary, through the will of the first parent. From that will as the efficient cause, this evil was passed on to posterity, as from a root or source, whereby it happens that the will of an individual, as soon as it comes into existence, is infected with the vice of concupiscence. Hence the will is called evil, perverse, and hostile to God. Augustine summarizes both meanings of being voluntary when he says that it is not inappropriate to call original sin voluntary because it was contracted from the first evil will of man and somehow became hereditary (Book 1, Retractations chapter 13), namely taken in the general meaning of voluntary, referring to the will of a first principle of some totality (whether that be individual, or specific).[12]

---

11 Regarding the voluntary character of sin, see *SPT* 14.30–31. The claim that even original sin is voluntary entails the accountability of man for his being sinful from birth.

12 If the first principle of a totality acts voluntarily, the totality itself can be said to act

XIII Quo sensu, peccatum illud non tantum esse contra legem, sed etiam lege fuisse prohibitum, dicendum est. Etsi enim infantes in se* nullius praecepti capaces sint, ut objiciebat Pelagius, tenebantur tamen, etiam priusquam actu essent, aliquo praecepto; non quidem quod voluntate propria exsequi debuerint; sed quod debuerint ac potuerint adimplere voluntate communi* generis humani, ut erat in Adam voluntas naturae seu speciei. Datum enim ipsi fuerat praeceptum ut principio generis humani, ut obedientia non solum personali, sed naturae totius, in ipso conservaret perfectionem* illam, in cujus amissione, et contrariae corruptionis successione, consistit hoc de quo agimus, peccatum.

XIV Cujus propagationis ratio hinc patet, quia non aliter potest intelligi nos in Adamo mortuos esse, quam quod ipse peccando, non sibi tantum cladem et ruinam ascivit, sed naturam quoque nostram in simile praecipitavit exitium. Et quia Dominus quas naturae nostrae collatas dotes voluit, apud ipsum deposuerat, ideo cum acceptas illas perdidit, non tantum sibi, sed nobis omnibus amisit, qui ratione communis naturae humanae, omnes veluti unus ille homo eramus, ut scite August. lib. 3. *De pecc. meritis*, cap. 7.[a]

XV Non est autem necesse ad propagationem illam, animam ab Adamo per traducem derivari, vel a corpore tamquam vase corrupto vitiari, ut videmus pomum vel florem, aut aliud ejusmodi, infici tetro odore ejus corporis quo continetur, quia haec contagio in substantia* carnis aut animae causam non habet, sed sufficit, si homo, cujus pars est anima, sit ab Adamo; quod verum est, etsi anima non sit de substantia parentis. Homo enim vere et proprie dicitur hominem generare, quia generatio* terminatur* ad productionem compositi. Et licet anima rationalis non educatur de potentia* in actum,* virtute generationis, propagatur tamen corpus illi proportionatum, ex quorum unione resultat humana natura; propter quod dicitur humana natura cum semine propagari, non per effectivam productionem animae sed per convenientem et proportionatam materiae dispositionem, ad quam ita dispositam, infallibiliter

---

[a] Augustine, *De peccatorum meritis et remissione* 3.7.13–14 (CSEL 60:139–141).

voluntarily. Adam, being the first principle of the human race, acted voluntarily, and therefore the original sin of all his posterity is voluntary, even in the case of young children.

In this sense, it should be said that this sin is not only opposed to the law but was also forbidden by the law. For although infants are of themselves* not liable to any command (as Pelagius objected), nevertheless, they were bound by a certain command even before they actually existed—not, to be sure, a command which they ought to have followed by their own will, but one which they ought to have fulfilled (and were able to fulfill) by the common* will of the human race, as the will of our nature or species existed in Adam. For to him, as the head of the human race, the command had been given so that by means of an obedience that is both personal and for the entire human race, he would preserve perfection* in himself. The sin which we are here treating exists in the loss of that perfection, and in the subsequent contrary corruption.

The way of this propagation is therefore clear, because our death in Adam can only be understood if Adam, by committing sin, not only brought ruin and destruction upon himself, but also cast our human nature down to similar ruin. And because the Lord had entrusted him with the gifts He willed to be joined to our nature, for that reason when Adam lost what he had received, he lost them not only for himself but for all of us, who by reason of our shared human nature were all as that one man, as Augustine neatly states in *On the Merits and Forgiveness of Sin*, book 3, chapter 7.

However, for this propagation it is not necessary that the soul be transferred from Adam through a physical offshoot,[13] or that it must suffer damage from the spoiled vessel of the body (like a fruit, a flower, or something else of that sort we see spoiled by the foul humors of the organism which contains it), because this infection does not have its cause within the substance* of the flesh or the soul. It suffices to say that man—part of whom is his soul—comes from Adam. This holds true even though the soul is not from the substance of the parent. For man is rightly and properly said to generate man, because the generation* ends* at the production of the thing composed.[14] And although the rational soul is not drawn forth from potency* to act* by virtue of generation,[15] nevertheless a body suitable for that soul is propagated, and human nature results from the union of the two. Therefore it is said that human nature is propagated along with the seed not through the effective reproduction of the soul, but through a suitable and proportionate disposition of matter, which the soul infallibly follows once

---

13 Cf. the discussion of traducianism and creatianism in SPT 13.52–53.
14 The opinion that the process of generation ends at the production of the supposit or the composed thing is derived from Aristotle, *Metaphysics* 5, c. 4 1015a10.
15 The soul does not proceed from potency to act, because it is *forma* (form) without *materia* (substance).

anima consequitur. Sufficit enim ut ratione ultimarum dispositionum quas homo generans inducit, censeatur vere hominem generare.

XVI Ex dictis certum est, hoc peccatum in homines non transiisse per imitationem, sed per propagationem. Quod etiam hac probatur ratione, quod imitatio proprie non sit cujusque rei similis, sed ejus dumtaxat quam quis cognovit et suo facto exprimendam sibi et effingendam proposuit. Quare, cum ex posteritate Adami sint fuerintque plurimi, quibus de primo homine ejusque transgressione nihil auditum nihilque omnino sit cognitum; consequens foret, in eos, etsi gravissimos peccatores, peccatum per primum hominem non transiisse, contra universalem Apostoli sententiam. Si autem imitatio extendatur ad eos qui similia peccata perpetrarunt, etiam incognita, potius dixisset Apostolus, per Diabolum peccatum intrasse in mundum, quam per unum hominem; cum imitationis ratione, filii Diaboli dicantur homines mali, et primus ille peccaverit.

XVII Hic frustra se torquent qui quaestiones movent et curiose rimantur, quid muliere sola vel viro solo labente futurum fuisset? Cum enim uterque in peccatum lapsus sit, nec de eo quod alias, ex suppositione ejus quod non est, eventurum fuisset, quicquam in Scriptura habeatur, praestat μὴ ὑπερφρονεῖν παρ' ὃ δεῖ φρονεῖν, et non definire cum discrimine, quae sine crimine nesciuntur. In quaestione vero, an ab Adamo tantum, an etiam ab Eva derivetur in posteros peccatum, existimamus vere responderi posse, ab Adamo potissimum tamquam a capite et principio generationis activo, eoque capite generis humani, non tantum naturali et politico modo, sed in iis etiam quae ad supernaturalia* gratiae dona felicitatemque spectant, supernaturali, procedere; ut quod fecit, id nos omnes fecisse censeamur. Sed quia generatio non sine muliere perficitur ex ordine naturae, et uterque parens labe illa et tabe maculatus fuit, Evae quoque in ea propagatione mali, suas partes, saltem secundarias, tribuimus.

it is so arranged. The ultimate dispositions which the man who generates brings forth are sufficient reason to consider him as truly generating another human being.

From what has been stated it is clear that this sin was not transmitted to other people through imitation, but through propagation. This point is demonstrated also by the argument that, properly speaking, imitation does not follow each and every thing that is similar, but only that which someone has come to know and has chosen to portray and fashion through his own actions. And therefore, since there have been and are very many people from Adam's descendants who have not heard or known anything at all about the first man and his sin, it would follow that although they are most grievous sinners, the sin of the first man did not cross over to them (which is contrary to the apostle's general judgment). However, if imitation is extended to those who have committed comparable sins—even unbeknownst to themselves—the apostle would have said that sin entered into the world through the devil rather than through one man; because imitation implies that wicked people are called sons of the devil and that he was the first one who had sinned.[16]

At this point people get all twisted up for nothing as they pryingly dig up and pose these questions: "What would have happened if only the woman, or only the man, had fallen?" For since both did fall into sin, and since one cannot find that Scripture contains anything about what would have happened otherwise (assuming what in fact did not occur), it is best not to think more highly than we ought to think, and not to risk making a decision about some matter of which ignorance is not an offense. But concerning the question whether sin is handed down to their descendants only from Adam, or also from Eve, we are of the opinion that a truthful answer can be that it proceeds chiefly from Adam as the head and active principle of the generation (and so from the head of the human race), not only on the level of our human nature and our political life, but also in those things that look to the supernatural* gifts of grace and happiness on the supernatural level—so that we all are considered to have committed what he did. But because in the order of nature generation is not achieved apart from a woman, and because both parents were stained by the fall and corruption, we attribute also to Eve her own role in that propagation of evil, albeit of secondary rank.

---

16 Scripture calls wicked people sons of the devil and says that the devil was the first one to have sinned (1John 3,8–10 and John 8,44). The Latin text here is a little ambiguous; the phrase can also be translated as: "Given that with respect to imitation wicked people are called sons of the devil and he was the first one who had sinned." It is clear that Rivetus warns the reader against interpreting Scripture so that original sin is transmitted by way of imitation of either Adam or the devil.

XVIII Cum autem Dominus noster Jesus Christus homo factus, licet materiam corporis sui ex beata Virgine ab Adamo descendente susceperit, corpus tamen non assumpserit formatum activa seminis virtute, sed vi Spiritus Sancti, qui materiam illam disposuit et sanctificavit; hinc factum est, ut peccatum originale non contraxerit, ut talis esset, qualis nos decebat Pontifex, sanctus, sine vitio, sine labe, segregatus a peccatoribus, et sublimior coelis factus, Hebr. 7, 26.

XIX Hic miraculosus conceptionis modus* cum sit Christo proprius, et hominum nemini praeter eum contigerit, neminem etiam alium a peccati originalis labe eximimus, ne eximiam quidem ac beatam Virginem Θεοτόκον, quam cum Epiphanio censemus, non genitam esse praeter hominum naturam, sed sicut omnes ex semine viri, et ex utero mulieris, contra *Collyrid. Haeres.* 79.[a] ac proinde communi legi fuisse obnoxiam, cum opus habuerit Redemptore Christo, quem servatorem suum agnovit, Luc. 1, 47. aerumnis et tandem morti corporis obnoxia fuerit, et inter OMNES illos reperiatur qui in Adamo peccaverunt, et qui mortui sunt omnes, pro quibus omnibus mortuus est Christus, Rom. 5, 12. 2 Cor. 5, 15.

XX Cum id de Beata Virgine, citra ejus contumeliam sentiamus, absit ut cuipiam alteri hoc privilegium communicemus, quod vel concipiatur vel nascatur sine originali peccato. Id tamen calumniosissime nostris affingunt Pontificii et Pseudo-Lutherani, quasi docerent nullos filios fidelium peccatum hoc contrahere, etsi contrarium saepissime asserant quibus id affingitur. Consequentia autem, quam nectunt eo quod filios fidelium in foedere censere docemus, qui

---

[a] Epiphanius, *Panarion* or *Adversus haereses* 79.5 (MPG 42:748); the Latin translation cited by Rivet is not equivalent to that found in MPG, but can be found in *Contra octoginta haereses opus, pannarium* [...], ed. Janus Cornarius (Paris: n.p., 1544), 314.

15. ON ORIGINAL SIN

Moreover, when our Lord Jesus Christ became man, although He received the physical material for his body from the blessed virgin (who was a descendant of Adam), yet He did not assume a body that had been fashioned by the active power of a man's seed but by the power of the Holy Spirit, who ordered the material and made it holy. Hence it happened that He was not infected by original sin, so that He "should be such a high priest as is fitting for us— holy, without sin, without blemish, set apart from sinners, and exalted above the heavens" (Hebrews 7:26).

Since this miraculous mode* of conception is unique to Christ and applies to no-one besides him, we exempt no other person from the stain of original sin, not even the chosen blessed virgin, bearer of God, whom we (with Epiphanius) "do not consider to have been generated outside of human nature, but, like all people, from the seed of a man and the womb of a woman" (Epiphanius, *Collyridean Heresy* 79).[17] Accordingly she was subject to the law that is common to all, as she was in need of Christ the Redeemer, whom she acknowledged as her Savior (Luke 1:47). She was subject to the hardships of the body and ultimately death, and she is to be found in the company of all who have sinned in Adam, who are all mortal, for all of whom Christ died (Romans 5:12; 2 Corinthians 5:15).

As we intend no affront in forming this judgment about the blessed virgin, far be it from us to bestow on anyone else the special status of being conceived or born without original sin. Nevertheless, the papal theologians and pseudo-Lutherans[18] most slanderously impute to people of our confession as if they taught that no children of believers are infected by this sin, while in fact the ones to whom this is ascribed very often state the opposite. Moreover, the logical consequence which they attach to our teaching that children of believers

18

19

20

---

17   For Epiphanius see 3.24. This reference is to his *Adversus haereses* (*Against Heresies*) wherein he condemns the sect of the Collyridians, an Arabian group of women, who, as priestesses, rendered divine worship to Mary and offered cakes (κολλυρίδες) to her, perhaps in imitation of the worship of Ceres. See Philip Schaff, *Nicene and Post-Nicene Christianity: From Constantine the Great to Gregory the Great, A.D. 311–600* (Edinburgh: T&T Clark, 1891), 417–418. Cf. Hilda Graef, *Mary: A History of Doctrine and Devotion*, vol. 1: *From the Beginnings to the Eve of the Reformation* (London: Sheed and Ward, 1963), 72–73.

18   The Reformed stated that young children did not receive forgiveness at the moment of baptism, but that they ought to be baptized because they are born as children of the covenant. This led the papal and Lutheran adversaries to make the accusation that the Reformed denied the doctrine of original sin. See Fr. Belcarius, *Aduersus impium Caluini, ac Caluinianorum dogma de infantium in matrum uteris sanctificatione & pleraque alia Caluini etiam dogmata breuis commentarius* (Paris: Cl. Fremy 1566), 1: "For however many of us derive our origins from Adam, we are all born unclean (as Paul testifies) from the

propterea sancti dicuntur et sunt, futilis est et captiosa; nec enim sequitur, si reatus peccati ipsis remittatur per gratiam, peccatum eos non contraxisse per naturam. Adde, quod externa illa in foedere recensio et sanctificatio, etsi aliquam societatem cum ecclesia importet, et in interna sanctificatione bene sperare nos jubeat ex probabili quodam indicio divinae benevolentiae, non tamen certam fidem facit verae justificationis et regenerationis omnium et singulorum qui ex piis parentibus originem ducunt, cum habeat Deus sua particularia judicia ipsi relinquenda.

XXI   Alioqui si naturam spectemus, credimus, hominem etiam regenitum, prolem generare non secundum quod regenitus est, sed secundum carnem, ideo prolem nasci peccatricem; quemadmodum ex parente circumciso, generari potuit filius cum praeputio, et ex grano purgato, granum cum gluma, quia non generatio, sed regeneratio, facit Christianos, et a peccatis nemo nascendo, sed renascendo mundatur. Adde, quod nostra sententia, peccatum illud in regenitis ex parte remaneat, etsi reatus sublatus sit, ut infra dicetur.

XXII   Et haec quidem de materia peccati originalis, quae subjecti κατηγορίας rationem habet communiter sumpta, quae in definitione his verbis comprehendebatur, omnium hominum naturali modo ab Adamo propagatorum. Subjectum* autem ὑπάρξεως vel inhaesionis, quando peccatum hoc consideratur non respectu totius speciei de qua praedicatur,* sed individui, cui agnascitur et inhaeret; est non solum hominis corpus, neque sola anima, sed corpus et anima simul, adeoque homo totus quantus, secundum omnes corporis et animae facultates,* secundum se totum, et totum sui: ita tamen ut anima praecipue subjectum sit, tamquam principium* actus,* corpus vero qua instrumentum quo agit. Hinc est quod in Scriptura describitur per caecitatem mentis, malitiam cordis, ἀχρηστίαν corporis et omnium membrorum, 1 Cor. 2, 14. Eph. 4, 18. Gen. 6, 5. et 8, 21. Jer. 17, 9. Ps. 14, 2. 3. Rom. 3, 12. et 6, 12. 13. et 19. Joh. 3, 5.

---

start; Ephesians 2, Romans 5, Augustine, *Against Julian*, book 6, chapter 12 ("Omnes enim quotquot ab Adamo originem ducimus, impuri (ut testatur Paulus) profecto nascimur, Ephes. 2 Rom. 5. August. li. 6. contra Iulian c.12.") And on page 4, Belcarius writes: "For this is what Beza writes: 'For by the form of the covenant children of believers are holy in God's sight from the time of birth, yet it is Baptism that signs and seals this sanctification.'" ("Sic enim scribit Beza. *Nam ab utero coram Deo sancti sunt fidelium pueri ex foederis formula, sed ea sanctificatio Baptismo obsignatur*").

15. ON ORIGINAL SIN 367

are counted as in the covenant, and that therefore they are said to be, and in fact are, holy, is pointless and far-fetched. Neither does this entail that such children had not acquired original sin by nature, because the guilt of sin is forgiven them by grace. Add that this outward inclusion in the covenant and sanctification (even though it brings with it a certain tie to the church) bids us to draw good hope also for their inner sanctification from the plausible signs of God's good favor, yet it does not make for a firm faith in true justification and regeneration for each and every person who traces his birth to righteous parents, since we must leave it to God to make his own particular judgments.[19]

In other respects, if we consider nature, we believe that even a regenerate man begets offspring, not in keeping with the fact that he is regenerate but according to the flesh, and therefore his offspring is born sinful. In this same way a son who is uncircumcised can be generated by a father who has been circumcised, and a kernel with a husk can be produced by a kernel that has been purged; because it is not generation, but re-generation that makes Christians, and no-one is cleansed from sins by being born but by being re-born. Add to this the fact that in our judgment sin partly remains in the regenerate, although the guilt has been taken away, as will be said below.

Concerning the matter of original sin, this matter, generally taken, has the role of subject of a category and this subject of a category is comprehended in the definition with the following words: "All people who issue from Adam in the natural manner." However, the subject* is a subject of inherence,[20] when sin is considered not regarding the species as a whole of which it is predicated,* but regarding the individual with whose birth it comes about and to whom it adheres. In this case, the subject is not only the person's body, nor his soul only, but his body and his soul together. And so it is the person and all that he is, along with all the faculties* of body and soul, according to his whole being and as a complete person in himself. However, it is so in such a way that the soul is the subject especially, as the principle* of action,* while the body is the subject insofar as it is the instrument by which the soul acts. Hence in Scripture original sin is described as the blindness of the mind, the wickedness of the heart, the uselessness of the body and all its limbs (1 Corinthians 2:14; Ephesians 4:18; Genesis 6:5 and 8:21; Jeremiah 17:9; Psalm 14:2,3; Romans 3:12 and 6:12, 13, and 19; John 3:5[-6]).

21

22

---

19   Cf. *SPT* 44.47.
20   The phrase "subject of category" refers to the general species of human being, while "subject of inherence" refers to each individual particularly.

XXIII   Nec tamen propterea sequitur, esse substantiam vel substantialem imaginem diaboli in homine, aut ipsam animam, aut ipsum cor hominis. Non est enim peccatum οὐσιῶδές* τι καὶ αὐτοσύστατον, sed παρακείμενον καὶ ἐνοικοῦν καὶ εὐπερίστατον, Rom. 7, 20. 21. Heb. 12, 1. Quod in homine haeret velut accidens* in subjecto; quae etsi in homine corrupto non sint divellenda, distinguenda tamen asserimus. Nam substantiarum omnium creator Deus est, peccatum autem neque a Deo creatum est, neque omnino creatura aut essentia* est. Et Adamus post peccatum eandem naturae suae essentiam retinuit quam ante habuit, idemque homo fuit. Nostra autem essentia neque peccato, neque gratia, in aliam mutatur essentiam, etiamsi vel inficiatur malo, vel perficiatur bono.

XXIV   Forma peccati originalis consistit in ἀνομίᾳ illa et inobedientia, qua cum Adamo peccaverunt omnes qui in eo fuerunt secundum rationem, ut vocant, seminalem; quae inobedientia et culpa cum reatu consequente, juste a Deo judice omnibus Adami filiis imputatur, quatenus omnes fuerunt et sunt unus cum eo. Si vero consideretur id quod in homine post actum remanet et veram peccati rationem habet, unde proprie et formaliter homo dicitur peccator, nihil est aliud quam depravatio illa et deformitas totius humanae naturae, qua, conformitate cum Deo amissa, labes et foedissima omnium hominis partium corruptio, successit.

XXV   Non igitur significanter satis vim hujus peccati expresserunt, qui eam tantum in justitiae originalis carentia constituerunt; quia per illud, natura nostra non tantum boni inops est, sed etiam malorum omnium adeo fertilis et ferax, ut otiosa esse non possit. Itaque corruptionis hujus duas partes cum Scriptura agnoscimus, nempe defectum et privationem* boni, et pravam ad malum

However, it does not therefore follow that original sin is a substance, or the substantial image of the devil within mankind or that it is man's very soul or heart. For sin is not a thing of essence* that has its own existence, but it is concomitant, dwelling among us, easily ensnaring us (Romans 7:20, 21; Hebrews 12:1). It is something that inheres in human beings as an accident* in the subject. Although these things [essence and sin] cannot be separated within corrupt man, yet we do assert that they should be distinguished. For God is the creator of all substances; yet sin neither was created by God, nor is it a created thing or an essence.* Even Adam, after the fall into sin, kept the same essence of his own nature that he had previously, and he remained the same man. Our essence indeed does not change into another essence either by sin or by grace, even though it is spoiled by evil or made perfect by good.[21]

The form of original sin exists in that lawlessness and disobedience whereby all have sinned with Adam who were in him by virtue of a 'seminal relation' (as they call it).[22] God the judge justly imputes this disobedience and offense, along with the attendant charge of guilt, to all of Adam's children, insofar as all were and are one with him. But if one considers what remains in man after the deed and what has the true nature of sin wherefore man properly and formally is called a sinner—it is nothing else than the perversion and deformity of the whole human nature, whereupon, the likeness with God having been lost,[23] the fall and foulest corruption of all the parts of man followed.

And so those who locate original sin only in the absence of original righteousness do not express the force of this sin meaningfully enough. For our nature not only is destitute of what is good, but it also is so prolific in all things evil that it cannot be idle. And so along with Scripture we recognize two parts to this corruption: the failure and loss* of the good, and a depraved tendency

---

21   The Lutheran theologian Matthias Flacius Illyricus (1520–1575) taught that original sin was the *substantia formalis* or the *forma substantialis* of fallen human beings. F. Bente, *Historical Introductions to the Book of Concord* (St. Louis: Concordia, 1965), 273. He also taught that human beings are transformed from the image of God to the image of the devil (*imago diaboli*); see Jan Rohls, *Reformed Confessions: Theology from Zurich to Barmen* (Louisville: Westminster John Knox Press, 1997), 78. For a comprehensive treatment of the issue see Robert C. Schultz, "Original Sin: Accident or Substance: The Paradoxical Significance of FC I, 53–62 in Historical Context," in *Discord, Dialogue, and Concord: Studies in the Lutheran Reformation's Formula of Concord*, eds. Lewis W. Spitz and Wenzel Lohff (Philadelphia: Fortress, 1977), 38–57.

22   The Augustinian concept of *rationes seminales* not only is related to the doctrine of original sin, but also expresses that God's creation contains the powers or seeds of all things that develop in the course of history. Augustine, *On Trinity*, book VIII, chapter 13.

23   For the distinction between the image and the likeness of God see *SPT* 13.36.

inclinationem; cum praeter ignorantiam in mente, et aversionem a Deo in corde, haereat in omnibus pronitas ad sapiendum et faciendum ea quae lege Dei prohibentur. Hinc quidam e nostris, fomitem peccati non esse absque actuali peccato, imo peccatum actuale esse dixerunt; quod ἀκύρως quidem dictum, in calumniam tamen non debuit ab adversariis trahi, cum nihil aliud voluerint quam peccatum hoc et esse actu, et actuosum etiam et operosum, ut ne in parvulis quidem quiescat, quin vitiosos motus excitet.

XXVI   Scriptura certe quoties peccatum originale nobis insinuat, non meram privationem, sed aliquid quodammodo positivum, id est, affirmativum,* solet inculcare, nimirum tale vitium quo caro concupiscit adversus spiritum, id est, per quod homo ad malum pronus, et divinae legi contrarius fit, ut Rom. 6, 12. Non regnet peccatum in vestro mortali corpore, ut obediatis concupiscentiis ejus. Quae verba indicant, concupiscentiam quandam habitualem esse in homine, cujus proprii actus sunt concupiscentiae actuales, quod malum habituale Apostolus peccatum appellat: Occasione, inquit, accepta peccatum per mandatum, operatum est in me omnem concupiscentiam, id est, omne genus* pravorum desideriorum, tamquam proprios suos actus, Rom. 7, 8.

XXVII   Ex quibus et similibus apparet, quod etsi non sit negandum, peccatum originale esse carentiam justitiae sive rectitudinis, quae unicuique nascenti inesse deberet, plenius tamen ejus rationem exprimi, nomine pravae inclinationis, vel proclivitatis ad omne malum, quam privationis. Nam privationis proprie non sunt actus* aliqui, quos tamen Scriptura passim peccato originali tribuit.

XXVIII   Idem ratione confirmari potest. Nemo enim avertit se a bono quopiam, nisi ductus cupiditate ac desiderio apparentis alterius boni, quod cum priori non consistit. Quod ergo in actibus veritatem habet, idem et in vitio habituali in prima nativitate contracto, conformiter intelligendum est. Ideo enim nascimur aversi ab incommutabili bono, quia nascimur curvi et inclinati ad bona

to evil. For in addition to the ignorance of the mind and a turning-away from God in the heart, there clings in all people a propensity for knowing and doing those things which God's law prohibits. Hence some people of our confession have said that the tinder of sin is not without actual sin, but in fact is actual sin.[24] This is a loose statement, yet it should not have been turned into slander by the opponents, since nothing else was intended than that this sin is also real, and that it is active and busy, too, so that it is at rest not even in little children, but it stirs up sinful behavior.

26 It is certain that whenever Scripture implicates us with original sin it usually drives home the point that it is not merely a lack or deficiency, but something that is somehow positive.[25] That is, it is something affirmative,* some vice whereby the flesh lusts against the spirit, that is, whereby man becomes prone to evil and is turned against the divine law. Thus Romans 6:12: "Let not sin reign in your mortal body that you should obey its desires." These words show that concupiscence is a kind of habit in man, of which the proper actions are actual desires. This habitual evil is called sin by the apostle: "Sin," he says, "having seized the opportunity by the commandment, works every concupiscence in me," that is, every kind* of crooked desires as its own proper actions (Romans 7:8).

27 From these and similar texts it appears that although one cannot deny that original sin is the lack of that righteousness or uprightness which each and every person should possess at birth, yet its nature is more fully expressed by 'an evil tendency,' or 'an inclination toward every wickedness,' rather than 'a lack.' For actions* are not a property of a deficiency, while Scripture in fact does attribute actions to original sin.

28 The same conclusion may be reached by means of reason. For no-one turns himself away from anything good unless he is drawn by a longing or desire for something else that seems good, which cannot co-exist with the former good. Well then, we should think that what holds true in actions holds similarly also for the habitual vice incurred at the time of birth. In fact it is for this reason that we are born averse to the unchangeable good, since we are born crooked

---

24   Roman Catholic theology held that concupiscence acted as *fomes peccati* or tinder for sinful desires. Peter Lombard defines original sin as *concupiscentia* which is not actual sin, but a *fomes peccati* (*Sententiae* II.30.8). It is not clear to which authors Rivetus is referring here. If the 'some of our confession' include Luther, it might be a reference to his statement in *Assertio omnium articulorum*: "Fomes vere est actuale peccatum" (WA 7: 111).

25   The term 'positive' should be understood here in a logical or ontological sense, not as an evaluative statement. For further explanation, see SPT 8.3 note 4, and SPT 11.20 note 22.

commutabilia. Quo utroque malo, tam aversionis, quam conversionis Augustinus definivit peccatum in genere, esse aversionem a bono praestantiori, et conversionem indebitam ad minus bonum; illud autem minus bonum est revera morale malum, quatenus ad id homo convertitur, aversus a Deo, *Quaestione* 2. *ad Simplicium.*[a]

XXIX Hinc est quod ex sanioribus Scholasticis* nonnulli agnoscunt, peccatum originale esse quandam inordinatam dispositionem et σύρραξιν, provenientem ex dissolutione illius harmoniae, in qua consistebat ratio originalis justitiae; exemplum afferentes aegritudinis et morborum, in quibus est aliquid privativum, quatenus tollitur aequalitas sanitatis, et aliquid positivum, nempe humores inordinate dispositi. Sic sentiunt originale peccatum habere privationem originalis justitiae, et cum hac inordinatam dispositionem partium animae, ac proinde non esse privationem puram, sed quendam habitum corruptum. Sic Thomas 1, 2. q. 82. art. 1.[b] Et Cajetanus[c] ibidem affirmat, privationem puram dare solam negationem in subjecto apto nato; corruptionem vero, addere aliquod positivum contrarium, in quo privatio fundatur.

XXX Hunc corruptum habitum qui concupiscentiam dixerunt, late sumpto vocabulo in generali significatione, cum Scriptura locuti sunt; quae carnis et concupiscentiae nomine, quam ut malam et vitiosam insectatur, non intelligit appetitum in genere, ut rationem simul et sensitivum complectitur, neque sensitivum in specie, neque eum qui peculiariter concupiscibilis appellatur, neque omnino naturalem aliquam facultatem, aut conditionem humanae naturae per se. Haec enim in Adam fuerunt initio creationis, et a Christo una cum naturae humanae veritate assumpta sunt. Sed vitium naturae, quod per peccatum in eam subintravit, et culpabiliter (ut ita loquar) infecit.

---

[a] Augustine, *De diversis quaestionibus ad Simplicianum* 1.2.18 (CCSL 44:45). [b] Thomas Aquinas, *Summa theologiae* 1/2.81.1. [c] Tommaso de Vio Catejan, *Summa sacrae theologiae* 1.2 81.1 (Leonine edition 7:94).

and inclined to good things that are changeable. Augustine gives to both of these evils (the aversion as well as the inclination) this general definition of sin: the turning away from the superior good, and the unjust turning towards a lesser good. That lesser good, however, is really a moral evil, insofar as man turns himself to it and away from God (Augustine, *On Various Questions, To Simplician*, question 2).

Hence it happens that some of the more sound schoolmen* recognize that original sin is some disordered disposition and a disruption that results from the break-up of that harmony in which original righteousness consisted. As examples they adduce illness and diseases in which there is something lacking (insofar as the balance of good health is disrupted) and something positive (namely disorderly arranged temperaments). And thus they judge that original sin takes away original righteousness resulting in a disorderly arrangement of the soul's parts. Accordingly, it is not a plain lack but some corrupt habit. Thus Thomas, *Summa theologiae* 1/2.q.82.art.1. And in the commentary on this passage Cajetan asserts that a mere privation only consists in a negation in a subject that was born apt, but that corruption adds some contrary positive thing, on which privation is founded.

Those who said that this corrupt habit is concupiscence (taking the word broadly, in a general sense) spoke in line with Scripture.[26] With the words "flesh" and "concupiscence," which are rejected as evil and sinful, Scripture does not mean desire in general (entailing rational as well as sensual desire); it also does not refer to the senses in particular, nor to him who is especially subject to carnal lust; nor again does it refer to some natural capacity or condition of human nature as such. For those qualities existed in Adam at the beginning of creation, and Christ assumed them along with his true human nature. But the corruption which entered into nature through sin also infected nature itself and made it punishable, so to speak.

---

26 The term *concupiscentia* is a late Latin word that had been used by Tertullian to mean not simply any desire (though he also used it with that meaning) but distorted desire. For Augustine concupiscence has a wide range of meaning, from a good concupiscence of the soul, by which it aspires to wisdom, to the uncontrollable elements of sexuality. While not itself sinful, desire has become disordered in humanity's sinful condition. While Augustine sometimes used it interchangeably with *libido*, he did not exclusively identify it with sexual desire, but with any sinful lust, no matter how noble its object. Especially in his anti-Pelagian works Augustine frequently used *concupiscentia* as a technical term for the volitional disorder inherited from Adam. See Peter Burell, "Concupiscence," in *Augustine through the Ages: An Encyclopedia*, ed. Allan D. Fitzgerald (Grand Rapids: Eerdmans, 1999), 224–227. It seems that in this disputation Rivetus uses concupiscence as a technical term in Augustine's anti-Pelagian sense. See also SPT 15.33–34.

XXXI Versatur autem circa ea omnia quae male et inordinate ab homine expeti possunt. Unde cum dixisset Apostolus, Gal. 5, 17. Carnem concupiscere adversus spiritum, ut ostenderet quam late pateat talis concupiscentia, subjecit catalogum aliquot operum carnis, inter quae non tantum fornicationem, immunditiam etc. enumerat, quae per appetitum sensitivum committuntur, et peculiariter carnalia peccata dicuntur; verum etiam veneficia, inimicitias, contentiones, homicidia, sectas seu haereses et ejusmodi, quae solent spiritualia peccata appellari. Carnis ergo et concupiscentiae nomine Apostolus significavit vitium incitans ad omne peccatum, unde etiam Corinthios carnales esse probat, ex eo quod contentiones et aemulationes essent inter ipsos, 1 Cor. 3, 3. Et omne genus peccati a concupiscentia procedere, satis idem significat, cum de ea ipsa loquens, ait: Peccatum operatum esse in se per mandatum omnem concupiscentiam, Rom. 7, 8. ut intelligamus quam late mandatum patet in prohibendo, tam late patere concupiscentiam in appetendo.

XXXII Hunc generalem vocabuli concupiscentiae sensum, agnovit multis in locis Augustinus praesertim *De civ. Dei*, lib. 14. cap. 3.[a] cum videret vitia quae in Diabolo tenent principatum, Apostolum carni tribuere quam certum est Diabolum non habere; superbiam tamen quae omnium horum vitiorum est origo, in Diabolo regnare. Nec ausus est ipse Bellarminus, *De amiss. grat. et stat. peccati*, lib 5. cap. 15.[b] negare, etiam in animae parte superiore simile vitium inveniri; imo concupiscentiae vim etiam in mente sedem habere. Qua concupiscentiae acceptione probata, ut quicquid in homine est, ab intellectu ad voluntatem, ab anima ad carnem usque, ea inquinatum refertumque esse intelligatur, peccatum originale concupiscentiam dici posse et esse, affirmamus; cujus etiam concupiscentiae genus, non regere ratione, sed omnino exstirpare oportet, qua uti recte non possumus, sed cui semper resistere debemus, quae non poena modo est, inflicta per peccatum, sed verae culpae propriam semper habet rationem. Nihil boni agitur de ipsa, nihil boni agit ipsa, nihil boni concupiscitur ex ea, sed et malum est quicquid concupiscitur per ipsam, Augustinus *contra Jul.* lib. 4. c. 1. et 2.[c]

---

[a] Augustine, *De civitate Dei* 14.3 (CCSL 48:416–418). [b] Bellarmine, *De amissione gratia et statu peccati* 5.15 (*Opera* 5:441b). [c] Paraphrase of Augustine, *Contra Julianum* 4.1.1–4.2.13 (MPL 44:737–743).

31 Nevertheless the corrupt habit does involve all the things man can pursue wickedly and illicitly. Thus when he said "the flesh lusts against the spirit" (Galatians 5:17), in order to show how broad the extent of concupiscence is, the apostle appended a list of some of the works of the flesh, among which he mentions not only sexual immorality, filthiness, etc., which are done through the desires of the senses,[27] and which are called sins of the flesh in particular. But he also mentions witchcraft, hatred, discord, murder, factions or heresies and the like, which are usually called sins of the spirit. Therefore, with the words "flesh" and "lust" the apostle means the vice that gives rise to every sin, whence he demonstrates that even the Corinthians are carnal, from the fact that "there are jealousies and quarreling among them" (1 Corinthians 3:3). And he shows quite clearly that from concupiscence every kind of sin comes forth, when in speaking about that he says: "Through the commandment sin worked every kind of concupiscence in me" (Romans 7:8), to make us understand that in its longing concupiscence reaches as far as the commandment reaches in forbidding it.

32 In many places Augustine acknowledges the general scope of meaning in the word "concupiscence," especially in the *City of God*, book 14, chapter 3, when he sees the apostle attributing the vices that are primarily present in the devil to the flesh—which the devil certainly did not have. But the pride that is the source of all these vices does rule in the devil. Bellarmine himself, in his book *On the Loss of Grace and the State of Sin*, book 5, chapter 15, did not dare to deny that the same vice occurs also in the higher region of the soul—in fact that the power of concupiscence has its abode in the mind.

Having proved the meaning of concupiscence in such a way that whatever is in man, from intellect to will, from soul to body, should be understood as being defiled and crammed with it, we affirm that original sin can be called and actually is concupiscence. The desire of this sort should not be guided by reason, but it should be totally eradicated, because we are unable to use it in a right way but we should always resist it. It is not only a punishment inflicted by sin, but it always has the proper character of true guilt. As Augustine says against Julian (Book 4, chapters 1 and 2): "Nothing good comes from it, it does nothing good, nothing good is desired from it, but whatever is desired by it, is evil."

---

27 An appetite is an internal inclination. Thomas Aquinas distinguishes between *appetitus sensitivus* and *appetitus rationalis*. The first is an organic faculty, the sensual inclination to a concrete object which is useful or pleasant. The second is a faculty of the soul, tending to the good as such. Thomas Aquinas, *Summa theologiae*, 1.80.2.

XXXIII   Nec audiendi sunt, qui in eo Pelagium damnantes quod talem concupiscentiam a Deo esse insitam dicebat, tamquam bonum aliquod naturale,* fatentur quidem eam ad peccatum sollicitare, non tantum suggerendo quod malum est, quomodo sollicitat Diabolus, nec per accidens* aut occasionaliter, quomodo vinum et forma mulieris ad intemperiem vel gulae vel Veneris, sed per se, et suapte natura, et proprio suo actu; proinde non esse amandam, sed odio habendam tamquam vitium, nos abducens et avertens ab eo, quod summe amandum est. Non esse tamen peccatum proprie dictum, audent asserere; ne in non renatis quidem, nisi ratione vel actus* primi peccati imputati, vel effectus sui, cum in actuale peccatum prorumpit.

XXXIV   Quo[a] semel posito fundamento,* non mirum est, si non solum concupiscentiam in renatis, quatenus pro habitu sumitur, veri nominis peccatum esse negent, sed etiam id de ipsius actu affirment, et primis ejus motibus, quos involuntarios vocant; quia reatus in ipsis ablatus est et dominium concupiscentiae sublatum. Quare nec reprehensionem nec poenam mereri, qui concupiscentiam et pravas illas motiones sentiunt; cum in ipsis non sint voluntariae, ac proinde nec peccata sint.

XXXV   Nos vero cum Scriptura, non solum in non renatis depravationem illam naturae et concupiscentiam, veri nominis peccatum esse asserimus, sed etiam in renatis et sanctis quamdiu in corpore mortis hujus habitant, inhabitans peccatum, etsi non regnet, etsi reatus ejus ita sublatus sit ut a Deo ipsis non imputetur, etsi extenuatum sit et imminutum, accedente regenerationis gratia, esse tamen in se proprie dictum peccatum, idque non remanere tantum in appetitu sensitivo et parte animae inferiori, sed etiam in mente et voluntate ex parte sedem habere; cum adhuc ignorantiae, dubitationibus et erroribus mens sit obnoxia, et voluntas φιλαυτίᾳ laboret, ut opus sit, etiam renatis, reformatione per regenerationem mentis suae, renovatione spiritus mentis suae et interioris hominis de die in diem, Rom. 12, 2. 2 Cor. 4, 16. Eph. 4, 23.

XXXVI   Certe Apostolus non semel cap. 7. Epist. ad Rom. malum illud diserte peccatum vocat, non tantum quia ex peccato est, et ad peccatum inclinat, sed etiam quia repugnat legi mentis, et adversus spiritum concupiscit, qua in re consistit vera peccati ratio. Nam quicquid repugnat formaliter spiritui et legi divinae, est,

---

[a] Quin 1625

Neither should we listen to those who, while condemning Pelagius for saying 33
that such concupiscence was implanted by God as something good by nature,*
also admit that it leads to sin, not just by prompting something wicked (in
the way that the devil incites it), nor through some chance event* or occasion
(as wine or a woman's beauty may lead to a lack of self-control in drinking
or sexuality), but by itself, by its very nature, and through its own action.
Accordingly they say concupiscence should not be loved but hated as a sin that
distracts and diverts us from what we should love most dearly. Nevertheless,
they make bold to claim that strictly speaking it is not a sin, not even in those
who have not been born again, except by reason of the action* or effect of the
first sin that was imputed to them, when it bursts forth into actual sin.[28]

Once this basis* is laid it is no wonder if they deny not only that in those who 34
have been born again "sin" is the right word for concupiscence (insofar as it is
taken as a habit), but also make this claim about its action and chief movements, which they call "involuntary"—because the guilt has been removed
from them and the dominion of concupiscence has been taken away. Therefore they claim those people who become aware of concupiscence and those
wrong movements deserve neither censure nor punishment; for these are not
voluntary in them, and consequently are not sins.

But we assert with Scripture that "sin" is the proper name for the perversion 35
of nature and concupiscence, an indwelling sin in people who are not reborn
as well as in the reborn and holy for as long as they live in this mortal body.
For although concupiscence does not rule over them and the guilt of it has
been removed so that God does not impute it to them, and although it is
weakened and diminished as the grace of regeneration increases, nevertheless
it is properly called sin in them. And it remains not only in the desire of the
senses and the soul's lower part, but it also occupies some place in their minds
and wills (since the mind is still subject to ignorance, doubts, and mistakes, and
the will suffers from self-love), so that even in those who have been born again
there is a need for reform "through the regeneration of the mind, the renewal
of the spirit of the mind, and of the inner man day in, day out" (Romans 12:2;
2 Corinthians 4:16; Ephesians 4:23).

To be sure, on more than one occasion in chapter 7 of the Letter to the 36
Romans the apostle clearly labels this wickedness [of concupiscence] "sin,"
not only because it comes from sin and inclines towards it, but also because
it resists the rule of the mind and desires against the spirit, and herein sin's
real nature exists. For whatever formally resists God's spirit and law is properly

---

28   The Council of Trent maintained that *concupiscentia* is from sin and inclines to sin, but has never been understood as truly sin (DH 1515).

peccatum proprie dictum cum vera peccati ratio in ἀνομίᾳ consistat. Nec adversarii negant, remanere in baptizatis carentiam originalis justitiae, quae si vere peccatum sit, naturam non mutavit ubicumque reperitur; neque enim dimissio reatus facit de peccato non peccatum, quia homo a reatu solvitur proprie, non peccatum in se consideratum, nec amittit rationem peccati, eo quod minuatur, quia magis et minus non mutant speciem, etsi graduum inferant discrimen. Denique si poena tantum esset, nec peccati rationem haberet, non diceret Johannes, concupiscentiam non esse ex Patre, 1Joh. 2, 16. a quo poenam esse constat. Et Christus qui omnes naturae nostrae infirmitates, excepto peccato, suscepit, Hebr. 4, 15. concupiscentiam assumpsisset, praesertim cum eam esse materiam exercendarum virtutum, et pertinere ad humanae naturae primam constitutionem, cum Pelagio sentiant adversarii. Vide Dom. Sot. lib. 1. *de Nat. et grat.* cap. 3.[a] Tapper. art. 2.[b] et Bellar. lib. 2. *de amiss. grat.* cap. 2.[c]

XXXVII Hactenus de forma peccati originalis. Jam de fine dicendum esset; sed quia secundum se respectu hominis in quo est, finem* non habet, effecta et consequentia, loco finis, solent considerari. Primum est *Reatus*, quo nomine intelligitur obligatio ad poenam, sive vinculum illud inter peccatum et poenam quasi medium interjectum, quo peccator ad subeundam poenam, et quamdiu durat reatus, ad poenae quam subit, durationem, arctissime obligatur.

XXXVIII Hinc sequitur poena, quae alia temporalis est, alia aeterna. Ad temporalem pertinent mors corporis, aliaeque hujus mortalitatis aerumnae atque miseriae, quibus homo factus ὀλιγόβιος, et satur commotione, ut flos simul ac egressus est, succiditur, Job. 14, 2. juxta illud Apostoli, per peccatum mors. In Adam omnes moriuntur. Corpus mortuum propter peccatum, Rom. 5, 12. 1Cor. 15, 21. Rom. 8, 10. Mors enim, morbi et omnes res adversae ex peccato fluunt,

---

[a] Domingo de Soto, *De natura et gratia: Quod opus ab ipso authore denuo recognitum est, nonnullisque in locis emendatum, et apologia contra reverendum episcopum Catharinum auctum* (Paris: Jean Foucher 1549), 7b–10a. [b] Ruard Tapper, *Explicatio Articulorum viginti, venerandae facultatis Sacrae Theologiae Generalis studii Lovaniensis, circa dogmata Ecclesiastica, nostro hoc tempore controversa, una cum responsione ad argumenta adversariorum*, in *Opera* 1:24–82. [c] Bellarmine, *De amissione gratia et statu peccati* 2.2 (*Opera* 5:250b–251a).

called sin, since the true nature of sin consists in lawlessness. And our opponents do not deny that the loss of original righteousness lingers in those who have been baptized; which, if it is truly sin, did not change its own nature wherever it is found. For also the remission of guilt does not turn sin into non-sin because man is properly freed from guilt (not sin as viewed in and of itself), and it also does not lose the nature of sin by being diminished (because the species of sin is not altered by a greater or lesser amount, even though they do introduce different degrees). And lastly, if it were only a penalty and did not have the nature of sin, John would not say "that the desire is not of the Father" (1 John 2:16), from whom the punishment comes. And Christ, who took upon himself all the "weaknesses" of our nature, "sin excepted" (Hebrews 4:15), would also have assumed concupiscence, especially when our opponents are in agreement with Pelagius that desire is the material object of the virtues that are to be cultivated and belongs to the basic structure of human nature. (See Domingo de Soto,[29] Book 1, *On Nature and Grace*, chapter 3; Ruard Tapper,[30] Art. 2, and Bellarmine, book 2, *On the Loss of Grace*, chapter 2.)

So much for the form of original sin. Now we should discuss the goal of original sin. But because sin does not have a goal* for itself regarding the human being in whom it exists, it is customary to examine its effects and consequences instead of its goal. The first effect is guilt, a word indicating an obligation to punishment, or a link inserted as a means between sin and punishment, whereby the sinner is obliged in the strongest possible terms to undergo the punishment and as long as the guilt remains to undergo the harshness of the penalty.

Following this is punishment, of which one is temporal and the other eternal. To temporal punishment belongs bodily death and the other hardships and miseries of this mortality whereby man has a life that is short-lived and "full of trouble; he comes forth like a flower and withers" (Job 14:2). According to the word of the apostle, "death comes through sin. In Adam all die, the body is dead on account of sin" (Romans 5:12; 1 Corinthians 15:21; Romans 8:10). For death, diseases, and all other hardships flow forth from sin, and those who have

---

[29] Domingo de Soto (1494–1560) was the representative of Emperor Charles V at the Council of Trent. Born in Segovia, he joined the Dominican order and served as a professor of theology at the University of Salamanca.

[30] Ruard Tapper (1480–1559), a Dutch theologian and inquisitor, professor at Louvain, was a delegate to the Council of Trent. Tapper led the trial against Jan de Bakker (Pistorius) from Woerden, one of the first Protestant martyrs of the Netherlands. Reference here is to his commentary on the twenty articles of the university of Louvain condemning Reformed doctrines.

a quibus non liberantur renati in hac vita, ne infantes quidem recens baptisati, qui ad ostensionem debitae miseriae, etiam mortem primam subeunt, quod indicium certum est, in iis adhuc remanere peccatum, etsi reatus aeternae mortis foederatis sit remissus.

XXXIX   Meretur autem per se, non tantum mortem illam temporalem, aut corporis, sed praeterea poenam aeternam, cujus rei sunt omnes qui sine remissione, cum hoc peccato de hac vita decedunt: quae novissima et secunda mors appellari solet, quae non tantum est poena damni, ut loquuntur, et ἀηδονίας, sed sensus etiam et λύπης, ut cum gaudii vacuitate, dolorem et ignominiam importet. Neque enim possunt qui aeterna felicitate privantur, non sentire gravissimum illud damnum, quod secum affert perpetuum a regno coelorum exilium; et cum salvandi, non solum adulti, sed etiam qui in infantia mortui sunt, fruituri sint visione Dei cum pleno sensu gaudii et felicitatis, contrarius status esse non potest sine dolore corporis et animi. Qua in re tamen, ut peccatorum inaequalitatem, sic etiam poenarum et suppliciorum intensiores vel remissiores gradus agnoscimus, quod justi judicis arbitrio relinquimus.

XL   Usus hujus doctrinae est, ut agnoscentes miseriam nostram, qua ab ipso ortu peccato infecti et immunditie polluti, a Deo abalienati sumus, omni arrogantia et praesumptione abjecta, cum vera humilitate ad Christum propitiatorem confugiamus, et cum ipsa generatio nostra vitio sit contaminata, regenerationis nostrae auctorem secundum Adamum, cum gratitudine agnoscamus; ex quo justitia fidei in nos per imputationem derivatur, et nova obedientia per sanctificationem et renovationem inchoatur; ut quod in primo amisimus, in secundo hoc, cum usura, tandem plene recuperemus; et interea e manu inimicorum nostrorum liberati, serviamus ipsi cum sanctitate et justitia in ejus conspectu, cunctis vitae nostrae diebus, Luc. 1, 74. et 75. Ipsi honor et gloria.

August. *De pecc. orig.* cap. 29.[a]

Quisquis contendit, humanam in qualibet aetate naturam, non indigere medico secundo Adam, quia non est vitiata primo Adam; non in aliqua quaestione in qua dubitari vel errari salva fide potest, sed ipsa regula fidei qua Christiani sumus, gratiae Dei convincitur inimicus.

---

[a] Augustine, *De gratia Christi et de peccato originali* 2.29.34 (CSEL 42:193).

been reborn are not in this life liberated from them, not even infants who have just been baptized, and they too suffer the first death "as an indication of the misery deserved." This is a clear sign that sin still lingers in them, although for those in the covenant the guilt of eternal death has been cancelled.

By itself original sin earns not just temporal or bodily death, but also eternal punishment, of which all are guilty who depart from this life without forgiveness and with this sin. This eternal punishment is usually called the last or second death, which is not only a punishment of damnation (as they call it) and unhappiness, but also of feeling pain and sorrow, since together with the loss of joy, it introduces grief and shame. For it is impossible that those bereft of eternal happiness do not feel that most serious injury, accompanied by eternal banishment from the kingdom of heaven. And since those who are to be saved (not only the adults but also those who died in infancy) will delight in beholding God with a full sense of joy and happiness, the opposite state cannot exist without grief for body and soul. In this matter we acknowledge that just as there are different degrees of sinners, so too are there greater and lesser degrees of punishments and sufferings—a matter we leave to the decision of the just judge. 39

The benefit of this doctrine is that while acknowledging the misery in which we have been infected by sin and polluted by filth from the moment of our birth, and in which we have been estranged from God, let us, putting aside every pride and presumption, in true humility take refuge in Christ the propitiator, and since our first generation was contaminated with sin, let us gratefully acknowledge the second Adam the producer of our regeneration. The righteousness of faith is bestowed upon us through imputation from him, and through sanctification and renewal a new obedience has begun. Thus what we have lost in the first Adam we shall at long last regain in this second Adam, with interest, and having been freed from the hand of our enemies, let us ourselves serve in his presence in holiness and justice, for all the days of our lives (Luke 1:74, and 75). To him be glory and honour. 40

Augustine *On Original Sin*, chapter 29

Whoever maintains that human nature at any time did not require the second Adam for its physician because it was not corrupted by the first Adam stands convicted as an enemy to the grace of God—not over some question in which sound faith isn't affected by doubt or error, but over the very rule of faith by which we are Christians.

Bernard. *serm. 1. super Dom. 1. post. 8. Epiphan.*[a]

Aliena est culpa, quia in Adam omnes nescientes peccavimus; nostra, quia etsi in alio, nos tamen peccavimus, et nobis justo Dei judicio imputabatur, licet occulto.

---

[a] Bernard of Clairvaux, *Dominica prima post octava, epiphaniae, sermo prius* 3 (SC 481:206).

15. ON ORIGINAL SIN

From a sermon of Bernard

The blame is another's, because it was unknowingly that we all sinned in Adam; the blame is ours, for although in another we are the ones who sinned, and in God's just but hidden judgment it was imputed to us.

DISPUTATIO XVI

De Peccato Actuali

Praeside D. ANTONIO WALAEO
Respondente LAEVINO COOLMAN

THESIS I   Quandoquidem de primo primorum Parentum lapsu, atque inde exorto peccato originali, praecedentibus disputationibus actum fuit; reliquum jam est, ut de actuali peccato agamus. Cujus primo naturam, deinde vero causas et genera breviter examinabimus.

II   Peccare, sicut et Graecis ἁμαρτάνειν et Hebraeis חטה, proprie* a via vel scopo aberrare; in hac vero materia, a divinae legis praescripto declinare significat.*

III   Peccatum actuale ex Augustino, lib. 22. *contra Faustum,* cap. 27.[a] definiri solet, factum, dictum aut concupitum aliquid contra legem aeternam. Quae definitio tolerari potest, si ad plenam enumerationem vox* *cogitati* addatur, et vox *concupiti* tam de concupiscentia voluntatis,* quam affectuum intelligatur.

IV   Plenior tamen definitio a nostris traditur, quod sit actio contra legem Dei, Deum offendens, et peccatorem reum faciens irae Dei et mortis, nisi remissio fiat propter Christum mediatorem.

---

[a] Augustine, *Contra Faustum Manichaeum* 22.27 (CSEL 25:621).

DISPUTATION 16

On Actual Sin

President: Antonius Walaeus
Respondent: Laevinus Coolmanus[1]

Seeing that in the preceding disputations we have treated the initial fall of our first parents, and the original sin that thereupon arose, it now remains for us to treat actual sin. Of this sin we shall consider briefly its nature first, and then its causes and sorts.[2]

In Latin "to sin," like the Greek *hamartanein* and the Hebrew *ḥattah*, literally* means to wander from the way or to miss the target; but in this case it means* to stray from the precept of God's law.

In defining actual sin it is usual to follow Augustine (*Against Faustus*, book 22, chapter 27): "Some deed, word, or desire against the eternal law." We can accept this definition if we complete the list by adding the word* "thought," and if we understand the word "desire" to include the concupiscence of both the will* and the affections.[3]

Our own people[4] have handed down a fuller definition, that sin is an "action against the law of God, that causes offense to God, and makes the sinner guilty of the wrath of God and death, unless forgiveness is granted on account of Christ the mediator."[5]

---

1 Born ca. 1597 and coming from Zierikzee, Levinus Coolman matriculated on 27 April 1617 in philosophy. There is no further information in other *Alba*, in *Repertorium*, or in BLGNP. See Du Rieu, *Album studiosorum*, 130.

2 The nature of actual sin is discussed in theses 2–28, the causes in 29–34, and the sorts in 35–54.

3 In Augustine's theology 'concupiscence' (*concupiscentia*) is a central, and much-discussed concept; in his writings the word often means 'evil desire,' and often it has sexual overtones. Augustine employs the term to express divine punishment for the Fall and the cause for all evil human actions. Concupiscence occurs both on the level of the rational will and on the level of the sensitive affections or emotions. See further Timo Nisula, *Augustine and the Functions of Concupiscence*, Supplements to Vigiliae Christianae, vol. 116 (Leiden: Brill, 2012), and cf. note at SPT 15.30. In quotations from Scripture, *concupiscentia* is mostly rendered, in a non-technical sense, as 'desire' or 'lust.'

4 I.e., the Reformed theologians or the theologians of the Reformation.

5 Cf. Philip Melanchthon, *Loci praecipui theologici*, 1559, CR 21: 667: "Sin is a defect or an inclination or an act that is in contravention with the law of God, offends God, is condemned by God, and that makes us liable to eternal wrath and eternal punishments, unless forgiveness

v Definitio haec elicitur ex 1Joh. 3, 4. ἡ ἁμαρτία ἐστὶν ἡ ἀνομία, peccatum est legis transgressio, et ex dicto Pauli, Gal. 3, 10. Maledictus omnis, qui non manserit in omnibus, quae scripta sunt in libro legis ut faciat ea, et versus 13. Christus nos redemit a maledictione legis, factus pro nobis maledictio.

vi Ex qua definitione manifestum est, propriam naturam et formam hujus peccati consistere, in absentia seu forma rectitudinis et sanctitatis, quae secundum Dei legem actionibus nostris tam internis quam externis inesse debet; unde et non male August. lib. 11. *de Civit. Dei*, cap. 9.ᵃ mali nulla natura* est, sed amissio boni mali nomen accepit.

vii Quando ergo a nonnullis Reformatae Ecclesiae scriptoribus asseritur, malum non esse meram privationem, id non sic intelligendum est, quasi malum per se aliquam vere positivam naturam habeat seu metaphysicam; cum omne ens tale, bonum sit, et a solo Deo omnis boni auctore, nam in eo vivimus, movemur et sumus, Act. 17, 28. sed hoc ab illis intelligitur, de privatione inefficaci atque otiosa; quales sunt privationes quae potentiam* absolute auferunt, ut caecitas visum.

viii Peccatum vero actuosa privatio* est, qua principium* agens, atque ipsa actio ex eo profecta, privatur sola rectitudine, cum principii ipsius corruptione, non ablatione; qualis est luxatio cruris, a quo motus non aufertur, sed motus ordinatio et rectitudo. Unde fit ut peccatum non tantum negative, sed et affirmative* enuntietur a Scriptura, et efficacia illi tribuatur, sanctitati ac justitiae contraria atque inimica, Rom. 8, 7. Gal. 5, 17. quia motus ille atque actio, cui privatio illa inhaeret, ex vi privationis inhaerentis, adversatur motui atque actioni sanctae et justae, ac proinde et Dei legi.

ᵃ Augustine, *De civitate Dei* 11.9 (CCSL 48:330).

---

is exercised." (Peccatum est defectus vel inclinatio vel actio pugnans cum Lege Dei, offendens Deum, damanata a Deo, et faciens reos aeternae irae et aeternarum poenarum, nisi sit facta remissio.)

This definition is borrowed from 1 John 3:4, "sin is lawlessness" (or sin is the transgression of the law); and from Paul's wording, "cursed is everyone who does not abide by everything that is written in the book of the law, to do them" (Galatians 3:10); and [Galatians 3] verse 13: "Christ has redeemed us from the curse of the law, having been made a curse for us."

It is clear from this definition that the proper nature and form of this sin consists in the absence of righteousness and holiness (or their form),[6] which according to God's law ought to be present in our outward as well as inward actions. For this reason Augustine rightly says: "Evil does not have a nature,* but the loss of the good has been given the name 'evil'" (*On the City of God*, book 11, chapter 9).

Therefore when some writers of the Reformed Church assert that evil is not a mere privation[7] of something, we ought not to understand it as though evil has some truly affirmative or metaphysical nature. For all such being is good and comes from God, who alone is the author of all good, as "in Him we live and move and have our being" (Acts 17:28). But they understand this to mean a privation that is inoperative and idle. Lack or absence of this sort is the kind that removes capabilities* altogether, as when blindness removes sight.

Yet sin is an active privation,* whereby the active principle* and the very action that proceeds from it is deprived only of righteousness by the corruption—not the removal—of the principle. It is like the dislocation of one's leg, which does not lose its ability to move, but its control and correct movement. For this reason one finds in the Scriptures that sin is expressed not only in negative terms but also affirmatively,* and it is granted an efficacy that is contrary and hostile to holiness and justice (Romans 8:7, Galatians 5:7), because the movement and action to which the deficiency clings, by the power of that inherent deficiency withstands the holy and just motion and action, and so it also withstands God's law.

---

6 The meaning of *in absentia seu forma rectitudinis* is unclear; perhaps the text is corrupt. It appears that a theological distinction is being made between the material and the formal aspect of the sin of omission. The material is the thing considered in itself, its virtue or good. The formal is the mode of consideration, what is perceived. Relative to the thing itself, it is bad, corrupt and defective. Walaeus makes use of this distinction in the theses that follow. See Van Asselt and others, *Scholastic Discourse*, 190, 318.

7 In scholastic language a privation (e.g., 'blind,' understood as 'bereft of sight') is distinct from a mere negation (e.g., 'not able to see') and refers to something that is missing whereas it should be there. Cf. *amissio*, 'loss,' in thesis 6 above, and *SPT* 11.21, 14.34, 15.25. See also *DLGTT*, "privatio" and "privatio boni."

IX Subjectum* autem proximum* hujus de quo agimus, peccati quod Scholastici* materiale vocant, est res* seu actio physice bona, cui privatio illa, tamquam moralis forma, vel potius deformitas, cohaeret; unde fit ut non tantum ipsa vitiositas, sed et actio tota cum vitiositate conjuncta, denominative, ut loquuntur in Scholis, peccatum et malum appelletur.

X Ad actuale peccatum hic a nobis refertur non tantum commissio actus* pravi, sed etiam omissio actus boni; quia ejusmodi omissio circa actus ipsos versatur, et quia raro, nisi ex actione mala, actus boni omittuntur; sive voluntas intra se omissionem illam intendat, sive interim occupetur actionibus aliis vitiosis, quae cum actibus illis praeceptis consistere non possunt, nemo enim potest duobus Dominis servire, etc. neque Deo simul et Mammonae, Matth. 6, 24.

XI Differentia tamen aliqua est, inter privationem illam, quae est in peccato omissionis et commissionis; quia in peccato omissionis est totius actus debiti omissio, sicuti Christus, Matth. 25, 42. dicturus est, esurivi et non cibastis me, sitivi et non potastis me; sed in peccatis commissionis est privatio ordinis seu rectitudinis, in ejusmodi actu secundum Dei legem requisitae.

XII Haec autem rectitudinis atque ordinis privatio, vel est respectu substantiae et materiae actus, vel respectu modi, quo is actus a lege praecipitur.

However, the nearest* subject* to the sin we are now treating (which the Schoolmen* call the "material" subject) is a thing* or an action that is physically good, to which that privation clings as though it is a moral form—or rather moral deformity. As a result not only the wickedness itself but also the whole action that is joined to the wickedness is called sin and evil in a denominative way, as they say in the Schools.[8]

At this point we include in actual sin both the commission of an evil deed* and the omission of a good deed. For such an omission concerns the actions themselves and good deeds are seldom omitted except on the basis of a wicked action, whether the will within itself intends that omission or whether it is preoccupied in the meantime with other, wicked actions which cannot co-exist with those actions that have been commanded. For no-one is able to serve two masters, etc., nor God and Mammon at the same time (Matthew 6:24).

However, there is some difference between the privation that is in the sin of omission and the sin of commission, because in the sin of omission it is an omission of the entire deed that is owed, as Christ would say (Mathew 25:42): "I was hungry and you did not feed me; I was thirsty and you did not give me drink." But in sins of commission there is a lack of the order and righteousness that is demanded of such a deed in keeping with God's law.

Well then, this privation of righteousness and order occurs either with respect to the substance and material aspect of the deed, or with respect to the manner wherein the performance of that deed is prescribed by the law.

---

8 See, e.g., John Buridan who defines a denominative predication as a predication in which the predicate connotes something additional or external to the signification of the subject (in contrast to an essential predication where this is not the case). For example, 'Man is white' is a denominative predication and 'Man is an animal' is an essential predication. For the Latin text, see John Buridan (L.M. de Rijk, ed.), *Summulae de praedicabilibus* (Nijmegen: Ingenium, 1995), cap. 1, pars 3. For the English translation, see Gyula Klima, Fritz Allhof, and Anand Jayprakash Vaidya, eds., *Medieval Philosophy: Essential Readings with Commentary*, Blackwell Readings in the History of Philosophy, 2 (Oxford: Blackwell, 2007), 81. "Therefore, everything that is predicated of something is either predicated essentially, so that neither term adds some extraneous connotation to the signification of the other, or it is predicated denominatively, so that one term does add some extrinsic connotation to the signification of the other. This division is clearly exhaustive, for it is given in terms of opposites." (Omne ergo quod praedicatur de aliquo vel praedicatur essentialiter, scilicet ita quod neuter terminus super significationem alterius addat extraneam connotationem, vel praedicatur denominative, scilicet ita quod unus terminus addat super significationem alterius aliquam connotationem; apparet enim quod haec divisio sit sufficiens, quia per opposita.)

XIII   Respectu substantiae* seu materiae, quando committitur id, quod Dei lege expresse vetatur, ut, si homo colat Deos alienos, contra praeceptum primum; si adulteretur, contra praeceptum septimum, etc. Respectu modi, quando res quidem fit quae Dei lege praecipitur aut permittitur, sed non eo modo quo praecipitur aut permittitur; quorum illa peccata per se, haec vero peccata per accidens,* etsi non satis proprie, a nonnullis vocantur, quia modus* ille non minus in legis sententia (quae spiritualis est, Rom. 7, 14.) continetur, quam res et actio ipsa praecepta.

XIV   Modi autem hi ad haec tria genera revocari possunt; ad principium actus, ad finem,* et ad circumstantias alias medias.

XV   Ad principium, ut si res a Deo praecepta, quidem fiat, sed non ex fide vera, aut corde puro, sicut Paulus loquitur,

1 Tim. 1, 5. Finis legis est caritas, ex corde puro, conscientia bona et fide non ficta. Hac conditione destituta fuerunt opera illa de quibus idem Apostolus, Rom. 2, 14. dicit, quod gentes legem non habentes, tamen quae legis sunt, fecerint.

XVI   Ex fine non recto actio alioquin praecepta, fit vitiosa, cum Pharisaei jejunarunt, orarunt, eleemosynas dederunt, ut gloriam ab hominibus aucuparentur, Matth. 6, 1. unde Apostolus Paulus, 1 Cor. 10, 31. monet, ut sive edamus, sive bibamus, sive quippiam aliud faciamus, omnia ad Dei gloriam faciamus.

XVII   Ex vitiosis quoque circumstantiis actio per se licita et bona, mali naturam induit, ut cum filii Aharon ignem alienum intulerunt in altare Domini, Levit. 10, 1. Cum Chusa manus contrectatione arcam a lapsu conservare voluit, 2 Sam. 6, 6. Quum Israëlitae Deo vero sacrificarunt in excelsis, 2 Reg. 12. 3. Quando fideles libertate Christiana utuntur cum infirmorum scandalo, Rom. 14, 20. Et ceteris similibus, quarum diligens ratio in observatione divinorum praeceptorum est habenda.

XVIII   Quemadmodum ergo actio bona non nisi ex omnium illarum conditionum conjunctione nascitur, sic contra actio vitiosa ex defectu vel unius istarum oriri potest,* sicuti exempla thesi antecedenti proposita demonstrant.*

XIX   Ad peccati naturam plenius cognoscendam, cognitio propriorum ejus effectuum plurimum facit.

With respect to substance* (or the material aspect), the lack of righteousness and order occurs when one commits something that is expressly forbidden by God's law, as when a man worships foreign gods contrary to the first commandment. If adultery is committed, it is against the seventh commandment, etc. With respect to the manner, it is when something happens which God's law commands or does allow, but not in the way in which it is commanded or permitted. Some people call the former "sins in and of themselves," and the latter "sins by accident,"* albeit not very accurately. For the latter manner* is included no less in the judgment of the law (which is spiritual—Romans 7:14) than the commanded thing and action itself. 13

The manners, moreover, can be summed up by the following three sorts: by the principle of the act, by its end,* and by other intermediate circumstances.[9] 14

By the principle of the act: When something God has commanded actually happens, but not out of true faith or a pure heart; as Paul says (1 Timothy 1:5): "Love is the end of the law, from a pure heart, a clear conscience, and a sincere faith." About deeds which lacked this condition the same apostle says (Romans 2:14): "For the gentiles, who do not have the law, still perform the things of the law." 15

An action which in other respects is commanded becomes sinful because of an end that is not right. For example, when the Pharisees fast, pray, and give alms, in order to obtain glory from men (Matthew 6:1). For this reason the apostle Paul warns: "So that whether we eat or whether we drink, or whatever else we do, let us do all things to the glory of God" (1 Corinthians 10:31). 16

An action that in itself is permitted and good takes on the nature of evil because of sinful circumstances. This happened when the sons of Aaron brought profane fire to the altar of the Lord (Leviticus 10:1); when Uzzah wished to keep the ark from falling by stretching out his hand (2 Samuel 6:6); when the Israelites made offerings to God on the high places (2 Kings 12:3); when believers use their Christian freedom with offense to those who are weak (Romans 14:20). And there are many similar instances in which careful attention should be given to God's commandments. 17

Therefore just as a good action arises only from the combination of all these conditions, so too on the other hand can* a sinful action arise from the failure of even one of them, as is demonstrated* by the instances presented in the previous thesis. 18

The knowledge of its proper effects makes for a fuller understanding of the nature of sin. 19

---

9 These three sorts are discussed in the next three theses.

XX Effectus peccati (seu, ut alii malunt, proprium consequens) duplex est, proximus et remotus; proximus* appellatur reatus, remotus* vero peccati poena.

XXI Reatus (quem Scholastici quidam, sed perperam, formale peccati vocant, cum unius rei* tantum una sit forma) est relativum* quid, inter peccatum et poenam medium, nempe respectus ille quo peccator per peccatum suum a Deo avertitur et ad poenam obligatur atque ordinatur; quem Sacra Scriptura peccati stipendium, Rom. 6, 23. aculeum mortis, 1 Cor. 15, 56. item maledictionem, Gal. 3, 10. appellat.

XXII Reatus ille non male a quibusdam, in omni peccato ac proinde et actuali, duplex constituitur, nempe culpae et poenae. Reatus culpae est ipsa interna peccati indignitas seu damnabilitas, qua peccator ex se Dei amore et favore fit indignus, quemadmodum ex Ps. 5, 5. Es. 59, 2. et aliis locis Scripturae videre est. Reatus poenae est ipsa ad hunc aut illum poenae gradum actualis ordinatio atque obligatio.

XXIII Posterior per remissionem peccatorum et imputationem justitiae Christi in regenitis et fidelibus plane tollitur. Prior vero, qui in reliquiis carnis ipsorum adhuc haeret, per justitiam et sanctitatem Christi quidem tegitur, et impeditur quominus ulteriores suos effectus producat, ab ipso tamen peccato non nisi cum ipso peccato tolli potest, non magis quam calor ab igne, aut risibile ab homine.

XXIV Quamobrem et Apostolus Paulus, Rom. 8, 1. asserit quidem, nullam nunc esse condemnationem iis qui sunt in Christo Jesu, qui non ambulant secundum carnem, sed secundum Spiritum; non tamen ait nihil in iis esse condemnabile, contra vero testatur Sacra Scriptura, fideles si in se* solis respiciantur prout actu

The effect of sin (or, as others prefer, its proper outcome) is two-fold: immediate, and distant. The immediate* one is called the liability, and the distant* one the punishment for sin.

The liability (called by some Schoolmen the formal aspect of sin, though incorrectly, since one matter* has only one form)[10] is something relative,* located between sin and punishment, namely that aspect whereby the sinner through his sin is turned away from God and is obligated to and destined for punishment; Scripture calls this the wages of sin (Romans 6:23), the sting of death (1 Corinthians 15:56), and the curse of death (Galatians 3:10).

Some suitably locate the liability of every sin—thus also of actual sin—in two places: the liability of guilt, and the liability of punishment. The liability of guilt is the inward unworthiness or very damnability of sin, whereby the sinner of his own accord makes himself unworthy of God's love and favor, as can be seen in Psalm 5:5, Isaiah 59:2, and other places of Scripture. The liability of punishment is being actually destined and obligated to this or that degree of punishment.

The latter effect is removed completely through the forgiveness of sins and the imputation of Christ's righteousness for those who have been reborn and who believe. But the former effect, which still clings to the remnants of their flesh, is surely covered by Christ's righteousness and holiness, and is hindered from producing its effects further, but it cannot be separated from its own sin unless that sin is removed along with it—no more than heat can be removed from a flame, or the ability to laugh from a human being.[11]

For this reason also the apostle Paul asserts in Romans 8:1 that "there is now no condemnation for those who are in Christ Jesus, who do not walk according to the flesh but according to the Spirit." He does not say, however, that there is nothing worthy of condemnation in them. In fact, Holy Scripture testifies the

---

10 A remark of Augustine (*Retractationes* 1.15.2; CCSL 57:46) occasioned this discussion: "Concupiscence is the liability of original sin" (*Concupiscentia est reatus originalis peccati*). Roman Catholic theologians like Domingo de Soto (*De Natura et Gratia*, lib. 1, 9) and Gabriel Vasquez (*Disputationes metaphysicae*, 132 c. 3) held that liability (*reatus*) was the form of sin. A theological consequence of this position is that when the liability is taken away by God's forgiveness, the sin is no longer a sin. Walaeus rejects the opinion with the argument that something can have only one form. He had already identified the form of sin as 'the absence of rectitude' (thesis 6). Therefore 'liability' cannot be the form of sin.

11 'Being able to laugh' is a standard example in medieval logic of a property that always and only belongs to a specific subject, in this case to 'human being,' and cannot be separated from it: cf. SPT 7.27, note 14. Likewise, 'liability of guilt' cannot be separated from 'sin': Removal or negation of the former implies negation of the latter.

sunt, non posse* coram Deo aut ejus judicio justos esse aut consistere, Hiob. 9, 2. Ps. 130, 3. item 143, 2. Dan. 9, 7. 9. 10. et ad Rom. 4, 1. et sequentibus.

XXV Poena peccatis debita est duplex, vel damni vel sensus. Poenam damni hic vocamus (etsi quidam hanc vocem* paulo aliter sumant) noxam illam, quam anima peccatrix ex peccati actu* intrinsecus contrahit, nempe ablationem majorem aut minorem divinae gratiae, prout peccati indignitas vel major vel minor est; item maculam, ut vocant, et labem, quae ex illa aversione in anima haeret; quemadmodum eo referri potest quod Christus Mat. 15, 11. ait: non quod intrat in os, sed quod exit ex ore, illud κοινοῖ, profanum vel impurum reddit hominem; item quod Apostolus Rom. 1, 24. testatur, quod Deus illos, qui mutaverunt gloriam incorruptibilis Dei in similitudinem imaginis corruptibilis hominis, tradiderit concupiscentiis cordium suorum ad impuritatem.

XXVI Poena sensus partim in conscientiae angoribus consistit, partim in aliis cruciatibus animi, aut corporis; quos vel in hac vita vel in futura homines impoenitentes sunt experturi. Ira enim et excandescentia, afflictio et angustia adversus omnem animam hominis, qui malum operatur, Rom. 2, 8. 9.

XXVII Nec vero tantum temporarias, sed et aeternas poenas peccatum meretur, quemadmodum Christus Mat. 25, 41. denuntiabit: Ite maledicti in ignem aeternum. Et sane justum est, ut peccata quae adversus Dei summam majestatem committuntur, summis etiam poenis luantur, quas intensive simul et semel Mediator noster in cruce ut nos ab iis liberaret, nostro loco exhausit; cum vero ceterae nudae creaturae intensive infinitas* sufferre non possint, aequum est ut extensive summas, id est, duratione infinitas, eorum loco perferant.

XXVIII Adde quod peccata, quae per supernaturalem* gratiam,* ac poenitentiam veram nunquam abrumpuntur, etiam nunquam finiantur, unde et eorum poena nunquam finiri potest; et quum Deus obedientibus legi aeterna praemia sit pollicitus, justitiae divinae ratio* etiam postulat, ut poena quae praemio aeterno opponitur, quoque sit aeterna.

16. ON ACTUAL SIN

opposite: That believers, if viewed in themselves* only and just as they really are, cannot* be righteous or even stand before God's presence or judgment (Job 9:2; Psalm 130:3; Psalm 143:2; Daniel 9:7, 9, 10, and to Romans 4:1 and following).

25 The punishment that is owed for sins is twofold, being either the pain of loss, or the pain of sense.[12] The 'pain of loss' (a word* some people use with slightly different meaning) we here call the injury that the sinning soul contracts internally from the act* of sinning; namely, a greater or lesser removal of God's grace proportionate to the degree of the sin's meanness. The penalty is also a blemish or stain, as they call it, which clings to the soul by its turning away from God. What Christ says in Matthew 15:11 can be applied here: "It is not what goes into the mouth, but what comes out of it, that defiles, that renders the man profane or unclean." So too for the witness borne by the apostle in Romans 1:[23–]24: "Those who have changed the glory of the incorruptible God into the likeness of the image of corruptible man, God gave over to the lusts of their hearts for uncleanness."

26 The 'pain of sense' exists partly in the anxieties of the conscience, partly in the other torments of mind or body that unrepentant people will undergo in this life or in the one that is to come. For there will be "wrath and indignation, tribulation and anguish on every soul of man of who does evil" (Romans 2:8,9).

27 Sin, however, merits both temporal and eternal punishment, as Christ will declare: "Depart, you cursed ones, into the eternal fire" (Matthew 25:41). And this is fair, for sins which are committed against the most high majesty of God are also atoned for by the harshest penalties, which our mediator fully endured intensively[13] in our place on the cross once and for all, to set us free from them. But since the other mere creatures cannot endure unending* penalties intensively, it is fair that they instead undergo the highest punishments extensively, that is, endless in duration.

28 Add to this the fact that sins which are never broken off through supernatural* grace* and true remorse also never come to an end; consequently, the punishment for them, too, can never come to an end. And since God has promised everlasting rewards to those who obey the law, the nature* of God's justice demands that also the punishment which forms the opposite to the eternal rewards must be everlasting.

---

12 In medieval theology, 'pain of loss' (*poena damni*) is the infinite pain in hell of the exclusion from the beatific vision as punishment for having turned away from God. The 'pain of sense' (*poena sensus*) is the limited pain in body and soul as punishment for having turned to a created, lesser good than God himself. Cf. DLGTT s.v. "poena."

13 Intensive in the sense of a concentrated quality of action and extensive in the sense of quantity of duration.

XXIX Natura peccati hoc modo satis explicata, restat ut de peccati actualis causis et generibus nonnulla subjungamus.

XXX Causa* peccati efficiens nec in Deo, nec in divina providentia proprie est quaerenda, nam omne quod Deus fecit, erat valde bonum, Gen. 1, 31. atque opus ejus perfectum est, et omnes viae ejus sunt jus, Deut. 32, 4. Imo nec ipse ad malum tentari potest, nec quenquam tentat, Jac. 1. 12.

XXXI Fatemur quidem, omnia quae in mundo fiunt, etiam quae maximorum scelerum rationem habent, secundum Dei arcanam voluntatem et providentiam fieri, Act. 2, 23. et 3, 18. Sed tamen inde non sequitur, Deum ullo modo eorum culpae esse affinem, sicut Libertini blasphemant; quia Dei opus bonum a malo opere creaturae in eadem actione sedulo distinguendum est.

XXXII Nam sicut Deus bonorum omnium causa effectrix est et ordinatrix, ita omnium malorum quae ex ejus permissione fiunt, proprie non effectrix, sed ordinatrix tantum causa est et moderatrix, sicut Josephus loquitur Gen. 50, 20. Vos quidem cogitaveratis contra me malum, sed Deus cogitavit illud in bonum, ut faceret sicut est die hoc. Cui similis locus est Es. 10, 5. 6. 7., ac propter hanc moderationem atque directionem, hae quoque actiones pravae Deo in Scripturis ascribuntur, non ut causae effectrici, sed ordinatrici et moderatrici; scivit enim ad suam omnipotentissimam bonitatem potius pertinere, de malis bene facere, quam mala esse non sinere, ut scite et vere Augustinus dixit.[a]

XXXIII Peccati ergo hujus causa efficiens, seu potius deficiens, est prava hominum mens et voluntas.* Sicut enim Christus Joh. 8, 44. testatur, Diabolum quando mendacium loquitur, ex propriis loqui, quia mendax est et pater mendacii, sic Apostolus asserit, Jac. 1, 14. Unumquemque tentari, cum a propria concupiscentia abstrahitur atque inescatur, et 1 Joh. 2, 16. Concupiscentiam carnis, libidinem oculorum et fastum vitae non esse ex Patre, sed ex mundo.

---

[a] Augustine, *De correptione et gratia* 27 (CSEL 92²:251).

Having explained the nature of this sin sufficiently enough in this way, it remains that we add some observations about the causes of actual sin, and its sorts.

It would not be right to look for the efficient cause* of sin in God or in his divine providence, for "everything which God made was very good" (Genesis 1:31); and "his work is perfect, and all his ways are just" (Deuteronomy 32:4). Indeed, "He cannot be tempted to evil, nor does He tempt anyone" (James 1:13).

We do grant that everything that occurs in the world (including those things which have the character of the greatest misdeeds) occurs by God's secret will and providence (Acts 2:23, 3:18).[14] However, it doesn't follow from this that God is in any way connected to the guilt for them, as the Libertines slanderously claim. For in any one action one must carefully distinguish God's good work from the evil work of the creature.[15]

For whereas God is the cause which effects and ordains all good things, so too He is strictly speaking not the effective cause of all the evils which come about by his permission, but only the cause that ordains and moderates them, as Joseph says in Genesis 50:20: "You indeed meant evil against me, but God meant it for good, in order to bring it about as it is today." Isaiah 10:5–7 is a passage like it, and because of this moderation and direction also these wicked doings in the Scriptures are attributed to God, not as the effecting cause but as the ordaining and moderating one; for as Augustine ingeniously—and rightly—states: "For He knew that to do good from evil redounds more to his own almighty goodness than not to allow evil to exist."

And so the efficient cause of this sin, or rather its deficient cause, is the depraved mind and will* of men.[16] For just as Christ testifies that "the devil, when he speaks a lie, speaks from his own resources, because he is a liar and the father of lies" (John 8:44), so also the apostle states: "But each one is tempted when he is drawn away by his own evil desires and is enticed" (James 1:14); and 1 John 2:16 states: "The lust of the flesh, the lust of the eyes, and the pride of life, are not from the Father, but from the world."

---

14   Cf. *SPT* 14.21–25 and 11.21–24.
15   See the *Belgic Confession*, art. 13 "On Divine Providence": "God neither is the author of, nor can be charged with, the sins which are committed." The reference to the Libertines is probably linked to John Calvin's discussion with these free thinkers; see Paolo de Petris, *Calvin's Theodicy and the Hiddenness of God: Calvin's Sermons on the Book of Job* (Bern: Peter Lang, 2012), chapter 5.
16   Augustine wrote that sin does not have an efficient, but only a deficient cause: *The City of God*, 12, 7. As a privation, sin does not have an efficient cause. There is no real reason why the will would turn away from the highest, divine good. To ask what the efficient cause of sin is, is like willing to see darkness or to hear silence, Augustine explains.

XXXIV Causae vero adjuvantes προκαταρκτικαὶ et προηγούμεναι variae colligi possunt, tum extra nos, tum intra nos. Nam et unum peccatum saepe alterius est causa, Rom. 1, 14. etc. et Diaboli suggestiones, 1 Par. 21, 1. et mundi scandala, Mat. 18, 17. item caligo mentis, 1 Tim. 1. 13. infirmitas carnis, Mat. 26, 69. consuetudo peccandi, Rom. 2, 5. Atque aliae occasiones plurimae, quas Satan et mundus assiduo suggerunt; adversus quae omnia fidelibus sedulo semper orandum est et vigilandum.

XXXV Genera peccatorum actualium ex variis circumstantiis varia constitui possunt et solent; nos iis recensendis contenti erimus quae difficultatem aliquam habent, et quorum discrimen ex iis quae a nobis hactenus dicta sunt, ita perspicue colligi non potest.

XXXVI Peccatum actuale primo dividimus in internum et externum.

XXXVII Internum, quod in mente, voluntate atque affectibus inordinatis subsistit, quales sunt errores et dubitationes mentis de Deo, ejus proprietatibus, aut Evangelii revelati doctrina. In voluntate et affectibus, primi concupiscentiae motus, licet spiritus adversus eos pugnet, eosque superet. Illos enim praecepto decimo directe repugnare asserimus, cum Apostolo Rom. 7, 7. Eos vero quibus voluntas plenum consensum adjungit, etsi opere ipso non compleantur, reliquis praeceptis vetari demonstrat locus, Mat. 5, 22. et 28. item 1 Joh. 3, 15. Quicumque odit fratrem suum, homicida est, etc.

XXXVIII Externum est, quod dictis et factis se foris ostendit, quod tamen sine internis antecedaneis non est; quemadmodum Apostolus Jacobus 1, 15. testatur, concupiscentia postquam concepit, parit peccatum, et peccatum per actum gignit mortem.

XXXIX Utrumque rursum est vel *regnans*, vel *non regnans*; quae divisio sumitur ex Rom. 6, 14. et 17. Regnans definiri solet, cui homo non resistit per gratiam Spiritus, sed plena voluntate indulget et servit; non regnans contra, cui homo per gratiam Spiritus resistit et non indulget. Prius proprie in irregenitis, posterius vero in regenitis locum habet; quemadmodum ex continua disputatione Pauli ad Rom. 6. 7. et 8. capite hoc discrimen est perspicuum.

XL Quaestio satis ardua, et tamen explicatu necessaria, hic movetur, quomodo peccatum regnans et non regnans per hanc resistentiam aut indulgentiam distinguatur; cum in homine naturali,* et sub lege tantum constituto, pugna quoque sit rationis et affectuum, sicut omnes Philosophi testantur, et ipse Apostolus, Rom. 2, 15.

16. ON ACTUAL SIN

But it is possible that various attendant and assistant causes come together from outside of us as well as from within. For one sin is often the cause of another one (Romans 1:24 and following), and then there are the promptings of the devil (1 Chronicles 21:1) and the turmoils of the world (Matthew 18:7). There is also the darkened mind (1 Timothy 1:13), the weakness of the flesh (Matthew 26:69[-75]), and the habit of sinning (Romans 2:5). Satan and the world constantly furnish very many other pretexts; believers must always pray and guard against all of these with dogged concentration.

The types of actual sin can be determined (and usually they are established) from a variety of situations. We shall content ourselves with a summary of those which are challenging in some way, and which cannot be discerned so clearly on the basis of what we have said up to this point.

First we divide actual sin into internal and external.

Internal actual sin: It has its existence in the mind, the will, and the unruly affections, such as the errors and doubts of the mind about God and his properties, or about the doctrine of the revealed Gospel. It exists in the will and the affections, the initial stirrings of concupiscence—although the spirit fights and overpowers them. For we assert (together with the apostle in Romans 7:7) that they are in direct conflict with the tenth commandment. We assert, too, that those affections with which the will fully agrees, even if they do not result in the performance of an actual deed, are prohibited by the other commandments, as Matthew 5:22 and 28 demonstrates, and also 1 John 3:15: "Whoever hates his own brother, is a murderer, etc."

External actual sin displays itself openly in words and deeds, notwithstanding the fact that it does not exist without a prior internal sin, as the apostle James testifies in chapter 1:15: "Evil desire when it has conceived, gives birth to sin, and sin through its actions brings forth death."

Both sorts of sins are either 'reigning' or 'non-reigning' sins—a distinction that is drawn from Romans 6:14 and 17. 'Reigning sin' is usually defined as sin which a man does not resist through the grace of the Spirit, but which he gratifies and serves with his entire will. 'Non-reigning sin,' on the other hand, is that which a man does resist through the grace of the Spirit, and which he does not gratify. The former is found in those who have not been reborn; the latter in those who have been reborn. This distinction is evident from Paul's prolonged argument in Romans Chapter Six, Seven, and Eight.

At this point a rather difficult question arises that we must answer: How reigning and non-reigning sin are distinguished by this resistance or gratification, since there is also a struggle between reason and affections in the natural* man who is established only under the Law, as is attested by all the Philosophers, and by the apostle himself in Romans 2:15.

XLI Sed respondemus, magnam esse differentiam inter pugnam et resistentiam illam spiritus et carnis, quae in solis regenitis locum habet; et inter resistentiam seu pugnam rationis et affectuum, quae in homine quoque animali reperitur. Discrimen vero hisce quatuor capitibus breviter comprehendimus.

XLII Primum discrimen petitur ex 1 Cor. 2, 14. et aliis locis parallelis. Nam cum homo animalis non capiat ea quae sunt Spiritus Dei, sed ea ei sint stultitia, ut et Christus ipse crucifixus; in peccatis quae adversus ea ab ejusmodi homine committuntur, nulla est reluctatio rationis adversus affectus, sed ipsa ratio cum voluntate et affectibus pleno impetu illa reprobat, contemnit et saepe persequitur, ut Evangelica historia passim et ipsa experientia testatur.

XLIII Secundum discrimen sumitur a modo, quo ipsa praecepta caritatis Dei et proximi, ut thesi 15. 16. et 17. explicatum est, exiguntur. Etsi enim opus legis etiam gentilium cordibus inscriptum sit, et cogitationes eorum hic se mutuo accusent aut excusent, Rom. 2, 15. tamen cum verum principium* et verus finis praeceptorum Dei eis ignotus fuerit, hinc necessario fit, ut ratio ipsorum cum affectibus in iis non modo non pugnet, sed potius conspiret.

XLIV Tertium discrimen statuimus in effectu et fructu pugnae utriusque. Etsi enim homo irregenitus in quibusdam ductu rationis adversus affectus pravos pugnet; tamen quia et ipsa ejus ratio, in plurimis caeca, in omnibus infirma est, affectus vero, nisi speciali Dei auxilio refrenentur, vehementes et indomiti, hinc fit ut licet nonnunquam meliora videant, tamen fere deteriora sequantur,[a] et ipsi affectus rationem ipsorum ut plurimum transversam agant; quemadmodum Apostolus testatur, Rom. 1, 32. et Eph. 2, 2. Quum contra in regenitis Spiritus carne sit fortior, et ejus plerumque victor, Rom. 6, 22. ac proinde non ambulant secundum carnem, sed secundum Spiritum, Rom. 8, 14.

---

[a] Allusion to Ovid, *Metamorphoses* 7.20.

16. ON ACTUAL SIN

But we reply that there is a big difference between the struggle and resistance of the spirit and the flesh occurring only in regenerate people, and the struggle and resistance that takes place between reason and affections in the natural man, too. We summarize the difference briefly under these four headings.

The first distinction is taken from 1 Corinthians 2:14, and other similar places: "For the natural man does not grasp the things of the Spirit of God, but they are folly to him, as is also the crucified Christ himself." In the sins that are committed by such a man against the things of the Spirit there is no struggle of reason against the affections, but reason itself, supported by the will and the affections, casts them aside with full force. It despises and often persecutes the spiritual things, as the gospel-history, and experience itself, proves time and again.

The second distinction is drawn from the way in which the very commands of love towards God and the fellow-man are fulfilled, as was explained in thesis fifteen, sixteen, and seventeen. For "what the law requires is written on the hearts of the gentiles also, and their consciences accuse them of this, or perhaps excuse them" (Romans 2:15). Nevertheless since the true starting-point* and end of God's commandments were unknown to them, it necessarily happens that their reason does not struggle against the affections but rather even conspires with them.[17]

The third distinction is placed in the effect and result in either struggle. For although the unregenerate man in some cases struggles against his depraved affections by the guidance of reason, yet because also his reason itself is blind in very many matters and helpless in all of them, and because his affections are volatile and untamed, unless they are reined in by the special help of God, it follows that the affections almost always pursue what is worse (although it does happen that they occasionally sense what is better). The very affections drive their reason into the opposite direction most of the time, as the apostle testifies (Romans 1:32, and Ephesians 2:2). Contrary to this, in those who have been reborn the Spirit is mightier than the flesh, and most of the time He is victorious over it (Romans 6:22); and consequently "they do not walk according to the flesh, but according to the Spirit" (Romans 8:[4,]14).

---

17 The argument of thesis 43 is rather densely formulated. Because the gentiles lack the right motive and intention, they do not experience an internal struggle between spirit and flesh. They may comply 'materially' with what the Law demands, but not in the right way. They act out of the wrong principles and for the wrong ends. For example, they do not act out of love for God and for his honour, but out of self-interest.

XLV   Deinde etsi fideles in hoc certamine, vel ex sua negligentia, vel Dei singulari exploratione nonnunquam in singularibus quibusdam actibus superentur; tamen peccati suavitas et victoria per Spiritus, quem contristant, efficaciam, in ipso peccati actu multum labefactatur, et post peccatum perpetratum victi non manent, sed per veram poenitentiam ac dolorem secundum Deum denuo resurgunt, ac mundo, carni et Satanae deinceps gravius ac constantius bellum indicunt; ut ex Sanctorum, quorum lapsus Scriptura nobis describit, exemplis liquet. Quum contra homines infideles per peccata sua magis ac magis ei se mancipent, Joh. 8, 34. atque animam suam in desiderio ipsius dilaudent, Ps. 10, 3. aut si forte ex conscientiae angoribus ac poenae metu, ad tempus se humilient, metu eo evicto ad ingenium redeant, ut in exemplo Pharaonis, Saulis, Achabi et aliorum videre est.

XLVI   Et haec discrimina, vera sunt τεκμήρια, ex quibus vere fideles apud animum suum certi esse possunt, quod peccatum in ipsis non regnet, ac proinde quod Spiritu regenerationis agantur, et sint non sub lege, sed sub gratia.

XLVII   Tertia peccati divisio est in remissibile et irremissibile. Remissibile est quod veniam consequi potest, qualia omnia sunt, excepto peccato in Spiritum Sanctum, Mat. 12, 31. Irremissibile est quod veniam consequi non potest, quia remedia omnia per quae venia obtinetur, pertinaciter repellit.

XLVIII Remissibile a Pontificiis distinguitur in mortale et veniale. Veniale vocant quod mortem non meretur, sed propter parvitatem suam venia dignum est. Mortale, quod mortem meretur, et cum gratia Dei consistere non potest.

16. ON ACTUAL SIN

Next, although in this strife believers are sometimes overpowered in some particular deeds either by their own carelessness or by God's special testing, even so the appeal and triumph of sin is made to waver greatly even in the very act of sinning by the power of the Holy Spirit, whom they grieve.[18] And after the sin has been committed they do not remain defeated, but through true repentance and grief towards God they rise up once again, and thereupon wage war against the world, their own flesh, and Satan more seriously and steadfastly, as is evident from the examples of those saints whose fall Scripture records for us. People lacking faith, on the other hand, enslave themselves more and more through their own sins (John 8:34), and "boast of the desire of their hearts" (Psalm 10:3). If they happen to humble themselves for a while because their consciences are pricked and they fear punishment, once that fear has been pushed aside they return to their usual temper, as is seen in the case of Pharaoh, Saul, Ahab, and others.

Now these distinctions form reliable indicators whereby true believers can be certain in their own hearts that sin does not have dominion over them, and consequently they are led by the Spirit of regeneration, and they are not under the law but under grace.[19]

The third distinction in sin is between forgivable and unforgivable. Forgivable is the sin that can obtain pardon; all sins are of this kind, except the sin against the Holy Spirit (Matthew 12:31). Unforgivable is the sin that cannot receive pardon, because it obstinately rejects all means of the cure whereby pardon is obtained.

The papal teachers divide forgivable sin into mortal and venial. They call venial sin that which does not deserve death, but which on account of being minor is worthy of pardon. Mortal sin is what deserves death and cannot co-exist with the grace of God.[20]

---

18 Ephesians 4:30.
19 Romans 6:14.
20 To distinguish between a mortal sin, as though it alone deserves death and damnation, and a venial sin, as though it is but a pardonable weakness, was a much debated distinction. In Catholic theology, mortal sin is the sin by which justifying grace is lost. It can only be forgiven through grace given in the sacrament of penance. Venial sin does weaken the theological virtue of charity, but can be overcome by individual effort. Both Lutherans and Reformed considered every sin to be a 'mortal' sin, by its very nature. Protestants customarily denote sins of thought, word, and deed. See *DLGTT*, s.v. "peccata mortalia," and Van Asselt, and others, *Scholastic Discourse*, 192–195.

XLIX Nos quidem fatemur peccata non esse aequalia, ac proinde per unum peccatum Dei justitiam gravius offendi quam per aliud, unde graviores poenas et conscientiae angores meretur; sed tamen negamus ullum peccatum ex sese esse venia dignum, aut non esse mortale, si propter Christum non condonetur.

L Id demonstratur, 1. quia Sacra Scriptura de omni peccato pronuntiat, quod ejus stipendium sit mors, Rom. 6, 23. quod mortis aculeus sit peccatum, 1 Cor. 15, 56. quod eorum finis seu fructus sit mors, Rom. 6, 16. 2. quia omne peccatum est contra legem, cujus violatio omnis maledictionem meretur, Gal. 3, 10. Peccatum autem omne esse contra legem, hinc evincitur, quia lex exigit caritatem ex toto corde, tota anima, et tota cogitatione, Mat. 22, 37., item quia omne peccatum est contra Deum, 1 Reg. 8, 46. et contra legem mentis, Rom. 7, 23.

LI Demonstratur id quoque invicte ex typica remissione peccatorum Veteris Testamenti. Nam non tantum pro gravioribus, sed et pro levioribus peccatis, nempe infirmitatis et ignorantiae, (quae Pontificii venialia esse volunt) sacrificia offerre cogebantur, ut ex Levit. 4, 5. etc. videre est. Sacrificia autem respiciebant unicum Christi sacrificium, per quod omnia peccata nostra expiata sunt, dum pro nobis factus est maledictio, ut nos a maledictione liberaret, Gal. 3, 13.

LII Peccatum irremissibile est peccatum in Spiritum Sanctum. Etsi enim et impoenitentia finalis non remittatur, id fit ex accidenti,* non quia reliqua peccata, de quibus poenitentia non agitur, in se sint irremissibilia, sed quia eorum cursus per fidem et poenitentiam non interrumpitur.

LIII Definimus autem peccatum in Spiritum Sanctum, contemptum et oppugnationem malitiosam Christi, et gratiae Evangelicae per externum verbi auditum cognitae, et per Spiritum Sanctum intus persuasae; sive is sit in iis qui doctrinam Christi nondum sunt professi, quales fuerunt Pharisaei, Mat. 12. sive professi sint et ab ea defecerint, de quibus Heb. 6. et 10.

LIV Et hic est supremus peccati gradus, a quo Christus singulari misericordia vere fideles et regenitos servat, 1 Joh. 5, 18. Scimus enim quod omnis qui ex Deo genitus est, non peccat (nempe peccato ad mortem, pro cujus remissione rogari non debet, ut versibus antecedentibus pronuntiavit) sed qui genitus est ex Deo, conservat seipsum, et malus ille non tangit eum.

We do grant, however, that sins are not all equal and that one sin therefore causes greater offense to God's justice than another; consequently it merits more serious punishment and pangs of the conscience. Nevertheless, we state that not any sin is worthy of pardon in and of itself, or that it is not deadly, unless it is forgiven for Christ's sake.

This is proved, because 1) Holy Scripture declares about every sin that its wages is death (Romans 6:23), the sting of death is sin (1 Corinthians 15:56), and its end or fruit is death (Romans 6:16). 2), because every sin is against the law, of which every violation deserves the curse (Galatians 3:10). That every sin is against the law is proved from the fact that the law demands love from the whole heart, the whole soul, and the whole mind (Matthew 22:37). 3) because every sin is against God (1 Kings 8:46), and against the law of the mind (Romans 7:23).

It is also undeniably proved by the foreshadowing in the forgiveness of sins in the Old Testament. For not only for the more serious, but also for the lighter sins, namely of weakness and ignorance (which the papal teachers argue are venial sins) they were compelled to offer sacrifices, as is seen from Leviticus chapters 4, 5 and following. But, the sacrifices pointed to the one and only sacrifice of Christ which made expiation for all our sins, since He has become the curse for us, to free us from the curse (Galatians 3:13).

Unforgivable sin is the sin against the Holy Spirit. For while the final refusal to repent is not forgiven either, this happens indirectly:* Not because the other sins of which one does not repent are in themselves unforgiveable, but because their course is not halted by faith and repentance.

Well then, we define the sin against the Holy Spirit as the contemptuous and ill-willed resistance to Christ and the evangelical grace that one had come to know outwardly through hearing the Word, and that the Holy Spirit had worked convincingly within one's heart. The contempt arises in those people who have not yet professed the teaching of Christ (such as the Pharisees, Matthew 12) or in those who professed and then defected from it (about which Hebrews 6 and 10 writes).

And this is the greatest degree of sin, from which Christ in his own special compassion protects those who genuinely believe and are reborn (1 John 5:18). "For we know that anyone born of God does not sin" (i.e., the sin unto death, for which one should not ask for forgiveness, as the preceding verses declared) but "he who is born of God, saves himself, and the evil one does not touch him."

DISPUTATIO XVII

De Libero Arbitrio

Praeside D. ANTONIO THYSIO
Respondente JACOBO ADR. TETHRODIO

THESIS I   Quamvis secundum ordinem et seriem disputationum, agendum foret de Libero hominis Arbitrio, ejusque vi, quatenus consideratur a lapsu, attamen ut hoc ipsum tanto plenius percipiatur, communiter et cum respectu ad omnes status hominis de eo agemus.

II   Sejungimus ab hac disputatione cohaerentes quaestiones de infallibili divina Praescientia, moderatrice Providentia, efficaci Praedestinatione; itemque quae inde dependent, de rerum contingentia* et necessitate,* atque causa peccati. Sunt enim illae divinae actiones, et humano arbitrio extraneae; cum de viribus hic proprie* agatur, homini divinitus concessis tributisque, et quid quantumque voluntas* humana in se possit, non autem ut relate se habet ad Dei definitionem rectionemque.

III   Vox* itaque liberi arbitrii Sacrae Scripturae ἄγραφος, a Patribus Latinis usurpata est, ad exprimendum illud, quod Philosophi, et eos secuti Theologi Graeci, αὐτεξούσιον, id est, eam quae a se ipso, seu propriam potestatem, ἐλευθέραν

DISPUTATION 17

On Free Choice

President: Antonius Thysius
Respondent: Jacobus Adrianus Thetrodius[1]

1   Whereas the order in this series of disputations would require us to provide a treatment of man's free choice and its power as seen after the fall, for the sake of a fuller understanding we shall treat free choice in general and as it regards all the states of man.[2]

2   We exclude from this disputation the closely related questions about God's infallible foreknowledge, his governing providence, and his efficacious predestination, and also what depends upon it, the contingency* and necessity* of things, and the cause of sin. For they are divine acts beyond the purview of human choice. Yet it is appropriate* at this point to deal with man's powers, since they were yielded and granted to man by God. The same applies to what and how much the human will* can achieve by itself, but not as the these achievements are related to God's determination and governance.[3]

3   Well then, the word* "free choice," not recorded in Holy Scripture, was used by the Latin church-fathers to express what the philosophers and the Greek theologians who followed them call *autexousios*, that is, 'a power which is of itself'—one's own power; or *eleuthera proairesis*, 'free choice'; and

---

1   Born ca. 1599 and coming from Haarlem, Jacobus Adriani Tetrodius (also: Tetteroo or Tetterode) matriculated on 23 May 1616 in law and philosophy. He was ordained in Krommenie in 1623; he died in 1651. See Du Rieu, *Album studiosorum*, 123, and Van Lieburg, *Repertorium*, 249.

2   The distinction between free choice in general and its functioning in the diverse states of man is common in Reformed scholastic theology. See RTF, 43–46 and *passim*. The Latin word *arbitrium* is rendered here as 'choice' instead of 'will.' The main reason is that *arbitrium* consists of an 'intellectual' component of judging different options in terms of good and bad, and of a 'volitional' component of making a decision between two (or more) options. By affirming a basic freedom of choice, the Reformed scholastics do not suggest that the human will is free in all respects.

3   This thesis notes the relevant connections of human free choice to divine foreknowledge, providence and predestination, and then leaves them aside to focus on the powers of free choice proper. The aforementioned factors occur throughout preceding and subsequent disputations; see in particular SPT 6.32–33, SPT 11 (providence, including several aspects of God's foreknowledge), and SPT 24 (predestination).

προαίρεσιν, liberam electionem, et τὸ ἐφ' ἡμῖν, quod in nobis seu nostra potestatesitum, vocant; quorum illud ab Academia, istud a Peripato, hoc a Stoa est.

IV   Ex his illa αὐτεξουσίου, vox, quae ἀδέσποτον, quod nullius juri, imperio ac directioni subest, a nullo scil. pendens, in humana natura* et fragilitate, quae voluntatis libertate ab obligatione et directione Dei nunquam est libera, sed ejus providentiae et gubernationi subjicitur, arrogantius quiddam notat; ac soli Deo haec juris libertas convenit. Quamvis Origenes in Dialogo cum Magetio[a] inter αὐτεξούσιον et παντεξούσιον distinguat, ut illud etiam creaturae, hoc tantum Deo conveniat. At vero illud ipsum non nisi tropice et respectu quodam, nempe secundum participationem, creaturae tribui potest.

V   Potior et accommodatior hic vox est ἑκουσίου, id est, spontanei et voluntarii, quae quidem ἀκουσίῳ, coacto et invito, non simpliciter ἀναγκαίῳ, necessario, quod sese habet ad τὸ βίαιον, coactionem, ut genus* ad speciem,* opponitur.

Gemina enim necessitas, immutabilitatis* et coactionis; illa cum voluntario consistere potest,* haec non potest. Ita Deus necessario et immutabiliter bonus est, ut qui ad contrarium se habere non potest, non tamen coacte, sed libere. Aliquando vero necessitas lubentiae et libentiae opponitur. Simile hic

---

[a] See the *Adamantii dialogus de recta in Deum fide* 3 (MPG 11:1081), which an old tradition attributes to Origen.

to eph' hēmin, 'what lies within us' or is placed within our power. The first of these expressions comes from the Academy, the second from the Peripatetics, and the last one from the [philosophers of the] Stoa.[4]

Of these the word *autexousios*, which is 'without a master,' means that one is not subjected to the law, rule, or direction of anybody; or, to be dependent on no-one. Given the nature* of man with its fragility and freedom of the will, which is never free from obligation to God and his guidance but is subjected to his providence and governance, this word has a somewhat more presumptuous meaning—this judicial freedom only belongs to God. But Origen, in the *Dialogue with Magetius*, makes a distinction between *autexousios* and *pantexousios*, wherein the former applies to the creature, the latter only to God. The former term, however, can be applied to the creature, but in a metaphorical sense only, and in a certain respect, namely according to participation.[5]

A better and more fitting term here is the word *hekousios*, that is, 'willful' and 'willing,' which is certainly opposed to *akousios*, 'coerced' and 'unwilling,' but is not simply opposed to *anagkaios*, 'necessary,' which is related to *to biaion*, 'compulsion,' as a kind* to its species,* for *necessity* is twofold: the necessity of immutability* and the necessity of compulsion. The former can* be consistent with *willing*, the latter cannot. Thus God is necessarily and immutably good as one who cannot be otherwise; still He is not coerced but free [to be good]. Sometimes, indeed, necessity is opposed to pleasure.[6] Here we have a similar

---

4   The mention of these Greek terms is not uncommon in Reformed scholastic discussions of free choice; see for example Zanchi and Junius in RTF, 53–57, 64–66, 99. On Aristotle's preference for *proairesis*, see *Nicomachean Ethics* III, 1–5. For a review of the ongoing discussion on free will between the Greek philosophical schools see Carlos Steel, "Liberté divine ou liberté humaine? Proclus et Plotin sur ce qui dépend de nous," in: M. Broze and others, eds., *Mélanges de philosophie et de philologie offerts à Lambros Couloubaritsis*. Paris: Vrin, 2008, 525–542. Steel mentions Epictetus and Proclus as the most important Stoic authors on this point.

5   The Greek words *autexousios* and *pantexousios* are derived from *exousia*, 'capacity, authority.' Only God has authority over everything (*pantexousia*); creatures can have authority of themselves (*autexousia*), but only with a limited scope and in a limited sense of 'self.' The term 'participation,' used to indicate the way in which creatures are *autexousios*, appears Platonist, but it need not bear truly Platonic implications in Christian discourse, as it can denote merely the secondary, derivative way in which creatures have certain properties compared to God.

6   The Latin text here uses two synonyms: *lubentia* and *libentia*. In opposition to 'necessity' (*necessitas*), 'pleasure' (*lubentia*) is a common synonym of (rational) 'spontaneity' (*spontaneitas rationalis*). The usage of 'pleasure' instead of 'contingency' might indicate a weaker, compatibilist theory of freedom, in which the human will has no true alternatives to choose from, but is merely able to assent willingly to the course of events established by the divine

discrimen inter liberum et contingens; nam hoc illud comprehendit, ac genus est liberi ac fortuiti. Adeoque optime voluntati et libero arbitrio creaturae convenit cum praescientia et providentia Dei.

VI Ut autem res* Sacris Scripturis est tradita, ita etiam sua hic habet vocabula, dicitur enim θέλημα, voluntas, et ἐλευθερία, libertas, et voluntatis ἐξουσία, potestas, 1 Cor. 7, 36. 37. 39. Quin τὸ ἑκούσιον hic usurpatur 1 Cor. 9, 17. ad Philem. versus 14. Hebr. 10, 26. 1 Pet. 5, 2.

VII Dum porro *Liberum arbitrium** dicitur, ibi libertas adjectum et affectio proprietasque est arbitrii, quod proprie juris et potestatis vocabulum est, unde sane non proprie denotat mentis judicium et libertatis voluntatem, ut volunt Scholastici,* ita ut duae potentiae* simul denotentur, neque potestatem liberam quidvis vel bonum vel malum faciendi, sed potius volendi et nolendi, seu eligendi et repudiandi; liberam, sine coactione, suo ac proprio motu facultatem.

VIII *Subjectum** ergo liberi arbitrii proprie* est voluntas, quamvis mentis consilium et judicium, ut necessario antecedens praeferat (judicium enim rationis consequitur voluntas) et facultatem* prosequendi et faciendi bonum vel malum, ut consequens inferat. Adeo ut si omnia haec complecti velimus, disputatio potius inscribenda fuerit de Viribus humanis.

IX *Objectum seu materia* ejus sunt omnia quae in deliberationem et electionem, actionemque humanam cadunt, seu bona et mala, scilicet non physica quae appetuntur et fugiuntur naturali* appetitu, sed quae mores actionesque

---

will. As Thysius continues with the stronger terminology of 'contingency,' we have reason to take these terms as synonyms.

distinction between *free* and *contingent*; the latter includes the former and is the *genus* (or type) of what is free and accidental. And so necessity is perfectly in accordance with the creature's will and free choice together with God's foreknowledge and providence.[7]

The subject-matter,* however, is transmitted by the Holy Scriptures, and they have their own vocabulary for it. It is called *thelēma*, 'the will,' and *eleutheria*, 'freedom,' and *exousia*, 'the power' of the will (1 Corinthians 7:36, 37, 39). Indeed, *to hekousion* ['voluntary'] is used in 1 Corinthians 9:17, in the letter to Philemon, verse 14, Hebrews 10:26, and 1 Peter 5:2.

Well then, when choice* is called free, then freedom is an addition and an affection or property of the will. Strictly speaking it is a word for one's legal right and power, so that it certainly does not properly denote mental judgment or choice, or the will of freedom as Scholastics* believe—so that two faculties* are indicated at the same time[8]—nor a free power to do any possible good or evil whatsoever. Rather, it is the power of willing and willing not, or of choosing and rejecting;[9] a faculty that is free—without compulsion—and that works by its own movement.

Therefore the will is in a proper* sense the subject* of free choice, although the mind's council and judgement occur first and must of necessity precede, for the will follows the judgement of reason. Following their actions, the faculty* of pursuing (and doing) good or evil occurs. If we wished to include all these processes, it would have been better to give this disputation the title, "concerning the powers of the human being."

The object or the material of free choice is all that is subject to human deliberation, choice, and action; or, all the good and evil things that concern moral behavior and actions (though not the physical things that our natural* desires

---

7   On the accordance of free will and providence, viewed from the opposite side, see *SPT* 11.10–16 above.

8   The view that 'free choice' consists of two co-operating faculties (the intellect and the will) occurs frequently in medieval and Reformed scholasticism. Thysius here argues that its proper seat is the will alone; see also thesis 8.

9   The two expressions "power of willing and willing not" and "power of choosing and rejecting" indicate what in standard scholastic terminology is called the 'freedom of contradiction' (*libertas contradictionis*: freedom to say 'yes' or 'no'). See *RTF*, 45–46, 112–113, for further explanation, and cf. *SPT* 6.35 and 12.34.

spectant; aut ut pressius loquamur, idque in Ecclesia, lex et voluntas Dei, in verbo ejus expressa et postulata, ejus objectum est.

x   Unde distinctio oritur inter objecta. Alia enim spectant naturalem hanc vitam, seu quae vitae praesentis sunt, quae Apostolus τὰ βιωτικὰ vocat, ut edere, bibere, loco moveri, quiescere, etc. Alia vitam honestam et civilem, seu opera politica et domestica, ut familiam et rempublicam curare, et quae eo spectant, a qua justitia civilis et philosophica dicitur. Alia denique vitam spiritualem et religiosam, Deum, legem ejus, cujus rursus vel externa, vel interna opera sunt. Ab illis disciplina et justitia externa, seu carnis; ab his spiritualis justitia, ut motus et actiones spirituales, cultusque Dei internus, denominatur.

xi   Haec distinctio objectorum hic necessaria est, ut non confuse, sed distincte agatur; quam etiam adhibet auctor *de Vocatione gentium*,[a] et alter qui sub nomine Augustini *Hypognostici*[b] nomine venit.

xii   Quaeritur ergo, cum agitur de libero arbitrio in Ecclesia, quomodo se habeat hominis voluntas, ipsiusque voluntatis facultas et actio ad haec objecta? Certe hic communiter respondemus, hominem omnia, quae vult et eligit agitque, non naturae necessitate, neque extrinseca vi coactum, invitum et involuntarium velle et agere, (natura enim, et violentia, et coactionis necessitas voluntati adversa est) sed praevio consilio, spontaneum, voluntarium et liberum (ita ut possit et idoneus sit, intrinseco principio voluntatem suspendere et electionem differre in alterutrum objectorum vel oppositum vel diversum) eligendo vel repudiando ferri, id est, hoc vel illud, et hoc prae illo eligere et velle, idque vel potentia proxima, vel saltem remota.* Atque haec natura proprietasque voluntatis humanae, eaque perpetua est.

xiii   Quamvis autem ita arbitrium semper sit et maneat liberum; attamen cum qualitas* potentiae inhaerens, sive bona, sive mala, proximum* principium* et causa* sit voluntatis et actionum, sive bonarum, sive malarum, hinc fit ut illius principii respectu vere liberum vel non liberum sit et censeatur arbitrium.

---

[a] Prosper of Aquitane, *De vocatione gentium* 1.2 (MPL 51:649–651).   [b] Ps.-Augustine, *Hypognosticon* 3.4 (MPL 45:1623–1624).

pursue or shun).[10] Or, to say it more succinctly, in the Church its object is God's law and will as conveyed and commanded in his Word.

Arising from this is a distinction between the objects of the will. For some things pertain to this natural or present life, which the apostle calls *ta biōtika*, such as eating, drinking, walking, being at rest, etc.[11] Other things pertain to respectable, civic life, or the political and domestic enterprises, such as looking after the family and the common good. And what pertains to them is called civil or philosophical righteousness. And lastly, other things concern the spiritual and religious life, the life of devotion to God and his law—which operations, in turn, are either external or internal. The former of these are called outward (or bodily) discipline and righteousness; the latter are called spiritual righteousness, such as the motions and actions of one's soul, and the inward worship of God.

This distinction here between objects is necessary for an unconfused and clear treatment of the topic. The distinction is made also by the author of the *Calling of the Gentiles*, and the other author, who wrote *Hypognosticon* under the name of Augustine.

And so when free choice is treated in the Church the question arises how man's will (both the faculty of the will itself and its act) is related to these objects. Here, we certainly give the general answer that a human wills (and does everything that he wills and chooses to do) not out of natural necessity; nor does he will and do anything coerced by external force or against his will, unwillingly. For nature, violence and the necessity of compulsion are opposed to the will. But it is upon prior deliberation, spontaneously, voluntarily, and freely (so that he is able and suited by a principle within himself to suspend his will and to delay choosing between one object and another, or its opposite, or a different one). That is, man is capable of choosing and willing this or that, and of preferring one thing over another by means of a direct or indirect* faculty. And this is the nature and property of the human will, and it is perpetual.

Although the will is thus free and always remains so, yet because of the inherent quality* of a faculty (whether good or bad), there is a *proximate* principle* and cause* of the will and its acts (whether good or bad), by which it happens that with respect to that proximate principle the choice truly is free and is judged to be free or not free.

---

10   The expression "moral behavior and actions" conveys two important aspects in view of 'free choice': first, the moral aspect of being good or bad, as opposed to merely 'natural' appetites; second, the intentional aspect of a deed or action that can be performed or refrained from, as opposed to unconscious reflexes and instincts.

11   See 1 Corinthians 6:3–4.

XIV   Atque hoc respectu pro ratione* variantis conditionis et status hominis, varie liberum arbitrium considerandum est, nempe vel in statu creationis et integritatis, vel lapsus et corruptionis, vel gratiae et reparationis, vel denique gloriae et perfectionis.

XV   In *statu* igitur *integritatis*, in quo Deus hominem ad imaginem suam et similitudinem creavit, Gen. 1. qua bonitas omnibus creaturis communis,* Gen. 1, 31. singulariter et peculiariter ad hominem restringitur, quem, ut Salomon inquit, rectum creavit Deus, Eccl. 7. et ut Paulus, in sapientia, justitia et sanctitate, Eph. 4, 24. Col. 3, 10. in eo, inquam, statu integritas fuit omnium virium et interiorum et exteriorum, atque ut bonitas et rectitudo illuxit in mente, ita etiam vera libertas, non tantum naturalis illa homini, qua in utramque partem se habere potuit, sed et libertas seu vacuitas a peccato fuit; seu in arbitrio fuit habitus boni, facultas, propensio et facilitas ad bonum, qua velle et agere bona, malum fugere, et bonum persequi posset,* seu praestare Deo integram obedientiam potuit. Ita ut arbitrium hic fuerit vere liberum, et natura, et naturae bonitate, ad ejus sanctum exercitium.

XVI   Veruntamen talis hic boni in natura insitus fuit habitus, ut tamen homo, quemadmodum natura compositus finitusque creatus erat, ita et mutabilis etiam voluntate foret; neque ita voluntate singulariter confirmata, quin libero arbitrio abutens a bono se avertere, et ad malum convertere, illud velle atque eligere, agereque, id est, objecta bonitatis specie inclinari ad deficiendum, et deficere sponte et proprio motu posset; ut et Deo ita permittente factum est. Cujus voluntarium lapsum, et lex Dei, et comminatio legi addita, et historia lapsus, Gen. 2. et 3. Eccl. 7, 29. evincit.

XVII   Ergo hic arbitrium se habuit libere εἰς τὸ ὁπότερον utrimque, etiam secundum rationem principii et potentiae proximae. Liberum quidem fuit a peccato, sed non a mutabilitate boni, et possibilitate peccati, ac in utrumvis flexile. Unde et a bono deflectendo, et in malum inflectendo, se et libertatem suam amisit, ut ait Augustinus.[a]

---

[a] Augustine, *Enchiridion* 9.30 (CCSL 46:65).

And in this regard, because* of the varying condition and status of man, free choice has to be considered variously, whether in the state of creation and integrity, or of the fall and corruption, or of grace and restoration, or lastly, in the state of glory and perfection.

Well then, it was in the state of integrity that God created man in his own image and likeness, by which the goodness common* to all creatures (Genesis 1) was uniquely restricted to humanity in particular (Genesis 1:31). Solomon says that God created it good (Ecclesiastes 7[:29]); and Paul says: in wisdom, justice, and holiness (Ephesians 4:24; Colossians 3:10). Now in this state, I say, there was an integrity of all the inward and outward capabilities, and just as goodness and righteousness enlightened the mind, so there was also true freedom for mankind—not only that natural freedom whereby he could guide himself into any direction, but there was also a freedom and absence from sin.[12] Or, the will had what was good and there was a faculty, a tendency and facility towards the good, whereby he could will and do what is good, could flee what is evil and pursue the good, or he could* render complete obedience unto God so that both by nature and by the goodness of its nature the will was truly free to exercise it in a holy manner.

Even so, the disposition towards the good that was implanted in our human nature is of such a sort that man, as he was created by nature to be composite and finite, could for the same reason also change his will. And man's nature was not constituted so specifically that he could not turn himself away from good and towards evil by misusing his free will to determine, to choose, and to do evil. Of his own initiative and motion, under the pretext of doing good, he was able to turn aside to rebellion—which in fact happened, with God's permission. The law of God, the severe warning that accompanied it, and the account of the fall offer proof that the fall of man was self-willed (Genesis 2 and 3, Ecclesiastes 7:29).

Therefore the will had the freedom herein to move in a direction that was either good or evil, on account of the principle and its proximate potency. To be sure, it was free of sin, but not free of changing from the good and of the possibility of sinning, and it could be bent into either direction. Whence both by turning away from what is good and by turning towards what is bad, the will ruined itself as well as its freedom, as Augustine states.

---

12 These sentences allude to the distinction of a threefold freedom formulated by Bernard of Clairvaux, *On Grace and Free Choice*, 61–64: freedom of nature or freedom from necessity (*libertas naturae / libertas a necessitate*)—freedom of grace or freedom from sin (*libertas gratiae / libertas a peccato*)—freedom of glory or freedom from misery (*libertas gloriae / libertas a miseria*). Cf. RTF, 82–83.

XVIII In *statu* porro *corruptionis,* seu in homine naturaliter* tantum genito, et originali peccato obstricto, quamvis is (licet totus corruptus) non amiserit, ut in intelligentia intellectionem, ita neque in voluntate naturalem libertatem electionis, sed retinuerit cum animae substantia* naturales ejus facultates, quae actionum sunt principia, et potentiam remotam et passivam suscipiendi contrarii; attamen amisit, ut ab intelligentia, ita et a voluntate rectitudinem et bonitatem, imo contrarium habitum vitiosum accepit.

XIX Adeoque liberum arbitrium potentia proxima et activa, Diabolo instigante, sub cujus potestate et dominio est, non amplius in bonum, quod vere bonum, sed tantum in malum quamvis specie bonum, attamen in generibus et gradibus mali electione remanente, necessario respectu principii proximi, sponte, voluntate et libenter tamen fertur. Eligit enim malum, et bonum repudiat.

XX Verum ut distincte agamus, non eodem modo hic in rebus omnibus pariter se habet voluntas seu arbitrium hominis depravati. In rebus enim quae vitam naturalem et civilem respiciunt, quaeque sensui et rationi subjecta sunt, et ad disciplinam externam et carnalem justitiam, quae non modo externis actionibus, sed et interno motu definitur, spectant, in iis reliquiae et igniculi hic supersunt: adeo ut ea non mente modo intelligere, sed voluntate deligere, affectu expetere, et viribus prosequi et agere quadamtenus possit, Rom. 1, 19. 32. et 2, 14. 15. et 9, 31. et 10, 2. Phil. 3, 6. 7. Gal. 1, 13.

XXI Verum ut sit in homine hic quaedam libertas et agendi facultas, magna tamen ob concupiscentiae vim est infirmitas; et voluntas saepe non dictamen rationis, sed sequiorem partem affectuum et cupiditatum motum et ductum sequitur. Diabolus etiam, qui est efficax in infidelibus, non desinit hanc imbecillam naturam incitare, et praecipitare in varia delicta, unde et civilis hujus justitiae ubique grandis conturbatio apparet, eoque inter homines etiam ea rarissima est.

XXII Ista porro quantulacumque facultas et in apparentia licet eximia interdum sit justitia, ultra politicam et honestam philosophicamque non exsurgit, neque ad verum bonum, Deoque placens assurgere valet. Nam quoad causam efficientem, personae* hujusmodi Deo neutiquam placent; neque actiones ex

Then again, in man's corrupt state, or in man as born only naturally* and bound up by original sin, although he had not lost the intellect in his intelligence (despite being corrupted entirely) nor the natural freedom of choice in his will, he retained his natural faculties (along with the physical substance* of his soul)[13] which form the principle of his actions, and he retained the remote and passive ability to undertake the opposite. Nevertheless, he lost the righteousness and goodness in both his intellect and his will; indeed, he took on the opposite, sinful inclination.

And so by the proximate and active capability,* instigated by the devil (who has power and dominion over it) free choice is drawn no longer towards the good that is truly good, but only towards the evil that only appears good (although a choice remains between the sorts and degrees of evil); with respect to the nearest principle it is necessarily carried off freely, willingly, and of its own accord. For he chooses evil and rejects the good.

But to maintain proper distinctions in this treatise: the depraved man's will or choice here does not behave in the same way in all things. For in affairs that concern the natural and civic life, in affairs subject to the senses and reason, and which concern external discipline and corporal justice (defined not only by outward actions but also by internal movement), remnants and tiny sparks [of goodness] survive. They survive so much that man is able to grasp them with his mind, to choose them with his will, to desire them with his emotions, and to pursue and even perform them to some degree (Romans 1:19,32, and 2:14,15, and 9:31, and 10:2; Philippians 3:6,7; Galatians 1:13).

But although man possesses some freedom and faculty to act, nevertheless because of the force of his desires the freedom is very weak; and often his will follows not the prescripts of reason but the worse part of his passions, the movement and lead of his desires. And the devil, who is powerful in unbelievers, does not stop inciting this weak nature and throwing it headlong into various misdeeds. It is for this reason that the massive upheavals in civil justice appear, and that civil justice occurs rarely in society.

Well then, since man's ability is so small and righteous only occasionally and by exception, it does not extend beyond the political, respectable, and philosophical spheres;[14] nor does it have the power to reach up to what is truly good and pleasing to God. For with respect to the efficient cause, persons* of

---

13 It is not immediately clear what is meant by the 'physical substance' of the soul. The *Synopsis*'s theory of the soul is presented in *SPT* 13.14–32. From that exposition, it is clear that 'physical substance' should not be understood in a material sense. Most probably, the 'physical substance' is distinguished here from the 'moral quality' of the soul.

14 Cf. thesis 10 above.

puro fonte, vera Dei agnitione et fide, ejusque timore oriuntur, neque debito fine* ad Dei gloriam suscipiuntur, aguntur et diriguntur, ex quibus tamen bonum opus censeri debet.

XXIII Ac proinde omnis talis hic actio, etiamsi feratur in bonum, et, si actum* ipsum spectes, in et per se sit bona, attamen, quia non fit bene, peccatum redditur, et peccatis accensetur, Rom. 14, 23. Hebr. 11, 6. Adeoque arbitrium et ab eo fluens actio et opus revera peccatum est. Magis tamen peccat, qui in se, et per se mala vult, cupit et facit, quam qui moraliter et in se bona male facit. Unde Deus etiam illis corporalem mercedem retribuit, 1 Reg. 21, 29. Mat. 6, 2. 5. 16.

XXIV At in spiritualibus et internis naturalis et irregeniti hominis arbitrium, tantum ad mala liberum est. Ut enim intellectus, ea, quae divinae legis sunt, magna parte ignorat, verum scilicet Deum, et quae cum voluntate ejus congruunt, Eph. 2, 12. Rom. 7, 7. maxime vero quae Evangelii, quae plane supranaturalia sunt, adeoque supra intellectum et voluntatem, et sine supranaturali luce et oculo, fidei videlicet, ut oportet, cognosci et firmo assensu apprehendi non possunt: ita etiam voluntas, pravitate devincta, contraria hisce vult, eligit, affectat et efficit, 1 Cor. 2, 14. Rom. 8, 6. 7. etc.

XXV Unde sane homo naturalis, insitis viribus, ac libero voluntatis arbitrio, non potest e peccato emergere, ignorantiam pravasque inclinationes abjicere, se ad Deum convertere, ac novos et spirituales motus, initia verae poenitentiae, fidei, timoris, et dilectionis Dei et proximi,* atque invocationis, ex se recipere et inchoare, eaque efficere. Ad haec enim ἀδυναμία homini naturaliter genito in Scriptura tribuitur, Joh. 3, 3. 5. et 6, 44. et 8, 43. Rom. 8, 3. 7. 2 Cor. 3, 5., immo adversitas et odium.

XXVI Est ergo arbitrium hic liberum, qua ad partem alteram, malum scilicet, redactum est; et non coacta necessitate sed lubentia ad peccatum vergit. Veruntamen quia hominis est sub peccato venundati, eidem servientis et in eo mortui; non tam *liberum* quam *servum* dici debet, liberum, inquam, a justitia, et servum peccati, Joh. 8, 34. Rom. 6, 16. Qualiter eleganter August. in *Enchiridio*,[a] Servi, inquit, addicti, quae potest esse libertas? nisi quando eum peccare delectat, libere enim servit qui sui domini voluntatem libenter facit. Ac per hoc ad peccandum liber est, qui peccati servus est.

---

[a] Augustine, *Enchiridion* 9.30 (CCSL 46:65).

this sort are by no means pleasing to God. Nor do the actions well up from the pure source: the true knowledge of God, faith in him, and reverence toward him. And such actions are not initiated, performed, and directed by the goal* of giving God the glory that is owed to him; and yet it is on these grounds that they should be considered as good works.

23 Hence every action of this sort, even if it does result in good and is good in and of itself (if one considers the action* per se), nevertheless, because it is not done rightly, is rendered sinful and is counted as sin (Romans 14:23; Hebrews 11:6). And so the decision of the will, and the consequent action and result, do in fact constitute sin. However, the person who in and of himself chooses, desires and commits evil is a greater sinner than he who morally and of himself does good deeds wrongly. On these grounds God bestows upon such people a corporal recompense (1 Kings 21:29; Matthew 6:2, 5, 26).

24 In spiritual and inward matters, however, the will of the natural, unregenerate man is free only to do evil. For his intellect is largely ignorant of the substance of God's law, that is, of the true God and what conforms to his will (Ephesians 2:12, Romans 7:7). His intellect is ignorant especially of the substance of the Gospel, which is supernatural (and thus beyond the intellect and the will); it is ignorant of things that can be understood and grasped with firm conviction only by the supernatural light and the supernatural eye—namely, the eye of faith (as it ought to be). So also the will, bound by depravity, wills, chooses, desires, and accomplishes things opposite to the supernatural ones (1 Corinthians 2:14, Romans 8:6,7).

25 As a result the natural man, given his innate abilities, and by the free choice of his will, is surely not able to rise up from sin, to cast off his ignorance and his depraved tendencies, to turn himself towards God, and of his own accord to receive, commence, and effect new and spiritual motions—the beginnings of true repentance, faith, reverence and love of God and one's neighbor,* and of calling upon him. For Scripture ascribes to the natural man the inability to do these things (John 3:3,5, and 6:44, 8:43; Romans 8:3, 7; 2 Corinthians 3:5); in fact opposition to them and disdain are attributed to him.

26 Therefore the will has freedom insofar as it has been restricted to the one side (i.e., the side of wickedness), and it inclines towards sin not by the force of necessity but out of pleasure. But because this is the will of a man who has been sold under sin, who is its slave and dead in it, it should be called bound rather than free. I mean, set free from righteousness and enslaved to sin (John 8:34; Romans 6:16). Augustine, in the *Enchiridion*, says it neatly like this: "What sort of freedom can a bound slave have? None, except when it pleases him to sin, for he serves freely who freely does the will of his master. And in this way the one who is a slave to sin is free to commit sin."

XXVII In *statu* autem *gratiae* et reparationis*, in quo homo naturalis et carnalis, divina gratia, virtute et efficacia Spiritus Sancti ab illo statu vindicatur, et habitu novo infuso renovatur, ac spiritualis efficitur, in vita spirituali promovetur, atque in ea conservatur, liberum ejus arbitrium revera servum liberatur, et liberum vere redditur, Joh. 8, 36. Sed illud pro ratione initii ad bonum, provectionis ac progressus, perdurationis et perseverantiae in bono, aliter atque aliter se habet.

XXVIII Respectu quidem initii ad bonum, seu primi reparationis actus, liberum naturalis hominis arbitrium, pro natura sua, quoad spirituales facultates, revera corrupta, imo et mortua, verum a Deo emendanda et excitanda, non συνεργεῖ, cooperatur, Deo, sed habet se respectu Dei agentis, ad modum* quadamtenus naturae et subjecti, παθητικῶς, passive.

XXIX Non tamen se habet hic homo libero suo arbitrio instar trunci: agit enim Deus in subjecto* homine intelligendi volendique facultate praedito, et quidem per verbum,* Rom. 10, 17. Joh. 17, 20. 1 Cor. 1, 21. Neque etiam ita quasi patiatur ipse homo naturalis Deum agere, qui bonae voluntatis actus* est; quum natura Deo exterius verbo suo, promissione et comminatione, aliisque persuasoriis utenti, resistat ac refractarius sit, Mat. 23, 37. Act. 7, 51. Sed ut is, qui totus mala qualitate* et habitu affectus devinctusque est, Eph. 2, 1. 2. 3. Tit. 3, 3.

XXX Agit autem hic Deus divino modo, et quidem gratia, potentia et efficacia tali ac tanta, ut cum effectu pravitatem a voluntate amoveat, et rectitudinem inserat, ut ita ex nolente volens, ex reluctante Deo obediens reddatur; quae sane solius Dei Omnipotentis est actio, ut quae in Scripturae vocibus recreationis, regenerationis, resuscitationis e mortuis et similibus exprimitur, Eph. 2, 10. Joh. 3, 3. Tit. 3, 5. Eph. 1, 19. 20. et 2, 5. Col. 2, 12. 13.

27 However, in the state of grace* and restoration in which the natural, carnal man is vindicated from the state of depravity by the grace of God and the efficacious power of the Holy Spirit, and in which he becomes spiritual, advancing in the spiritual life wherein he is preserved and renewed by the new disposition infused into him, his free will (actually, his enslaved will) is liberated and rendered truly free (John 8:36). But that will behaves a little bit differently all the time, in view of its beginning towards goodness, its progressive advancement, persistent endurance, and its steadfastness in the good.[15]

28 But as far as the start towards goodness is concerned, or the initial act of restoration, the natural man's free choice, in keeping with its nature, is truly corrupt—dead, in fact, regarding its spiritual faculties. It must be restored and brought to life by God; it does not work in cooperation with God but it behaves to some extent passively towards him as the one who acts, according to the degree* of its nature and subject.[16]

29 Man does not, however, behave with his free choice like some block of wood;[17] for God works in man as a subject* endowed with the faculties of mind and will, and He works through his Word* (Romans 10:17; John 17:20; 1 Corinthians 1:21). Yet it is not as though the natural man himself allows God to be at work in him (for that is an act* of good will). For by nature man is stubborn and opposes God when He uses his own Word outwardly, with its promise, its warning, and its other means of persuasion (Matthew 23:37; Acts 7:51). But God works in man such as he is, entirely weakened and bound by his evil character* and habits (Ephesians 2:1–3; Titus 3:3).

30 Moreover, God herein works in his divine manner, and in fact with a grace, power, and efficacy of such a sort and degree that He effectively takes the depravity out of the will and implants uprightness in it, so that man is changed from unwilling to willing, and from resisting God to obeying Him. This is obviously an act of the almighty God only, as expressed in Scripture by the words recreation, regeneration, awakening from the dead, and the like (Ephesians 2:10; John 3:3; Titus 3:5; Ephesians 1:19, 20 and 2:5; Colossians 2:12, 13).

15　For the "start towards goodness" see theses 28 to 32; the "progressive advancement" in goodness is discussed in theses 33 to 42; the "steadfastness" in doing good, which belongs to the state of glory, is discussed in thesis 43.

16　This statement is directed against the Roman Catholic view of human co-operation in the moment of conversion towards God, as expressed in the Tridentine Decree on Justification (DH 1525). See also the affirmative statement, in thesis 37 below, of co-operation in the subsequent process of renewal.

17　This expression resembles ch. III/IV, art.16 of the Canons of Dordrecht, where it is said that God's grace does not work in man as if in wooden blocks (*non agit in hominibus tanquam truncibus et stipitibus*).

XXXI Proinde ad hanc gratiam nemo quicquam confert, imo ne vel bono gratiae universalis, lucisque naturalis, vel gratiae specialioris, legis scilicet, (quae gratiae nomine* improprie* et catachrestice censetur) sese ad eam, praeparare, disponere et applicare valet, non magis quam ad generationem* et vivificationem suam quisquam quidquam confert.

XXXII Non tamen diffitemur, Deum Antecedaneis quibusdam, utpote tum natura, tum lege, hic uti, quibus peccator ad sui desperationem adductus, ad consolationem Evangelii et spem in Deo manuducatur; at vero vi Spiritus, per Evangelii praedicationem,* opus hoc in nobis efficitur, ne quis arbitretur, nos violentos raptus, et Enthusiasticos et momentaneos motus statuere.

XXXIII Ceterum haec regeneratio, a qua est potentia et principium* bene volendi agendique divinitus tributa, ut sit totalis reformatio et renovatio, et secundum subjectum, totum sc. hominem, et omnes ejus vires, et objectum, universam nempe Dei legem; non tamen est totalis, secundum intensionem graduum, seu excellentissimum gradum qualitatis bonae, sed partialis juxta gradum remissiorem, in quo esse potest et est contrarium: hoc est, in mente, voluntate, affectibus, potentia, viribusque actionis remanent reliquiae peccantis naturae, quae agnitionem faciunt obscuriorem, voluntatem affectusque remissiores, potentiamque infirmiorem, adeo ut non omnia quae volumus, opere compleamus, 1 Cor. 13, 12. Rom. 7, 8. 24. Marc. 9, 24.

XXXIV Proinde in uno eodemque homine renato, respectu diversi principii, non autem subjecti, duae quasi partes oppositae statuuntur, caro et spiritus, Matth. 26, 41. Gal. 5, 17. Imo duo quasi homines, vetus et novus, Eph. 4, 22. Col. 3, 9. externus et internus, apertus et occultus, Rom. 7, 22. 1 Pet. 3, 4. ac denique naturalis seu animalis et spiritualis, 1 Cor. 2, 15. Unde in homine regenito carnis spiritusque lucta exsurgit, Rom. 7. Gal. 5. A praedominante tamen qualitate spiritus, et secundum insignem profectum, simpliciter spiritualis dicitur, 1 Cor. 2, 15. Gal. 6, 1. at secundum defectum et infirmitatem, seu comparative etiam carnalis, 1 Cor. 3, 1.

So then, no-one contributes anything to this grace. In fact, man has no more power to prepare, dispose, and apply himself to that grace than he does to contribute anything to his own conception* and birth—neither by the benefit of universal grace and the light of nature, nor by the benefit of particular grace, namely the law (which is imprecisely* and loosely included in the word* 'grace').

We do not deny, however, that herein God makes use of certain prior preparations, such as nature, or the law, whereby the sinner is drawn to despair in himself and led by the hand to take comfort in the Gospel, and to hope in God. But it is by the power of the Spirit through the preaching* of the Word that this work is achieved in us—lest anyone should think that we recommend violent seizures or sudden, spiritualist movements![18]

Furthermore, this regeneration (whereby the ability and principle* of willing and doing good is divinely bestowed by God) consists of a total reformation and renewal, both in view of the subject (i.e., the entire man and all his powers) and in view of the object (i.e., God's universal law). However, it is not a *total* reformation and renewal, according to the intensity of degrees or the highest degree of good quality; but it is partial, according to a lesser degree, in which the contrary can and does exist. That is, remnants of our sinful nature remain in the mind, the will, the feelings, in the capability and power to act, which cause recognition to be more obscured and the will and feelings to be more limited, and the power weakened—so much so that we do not achieve everything we wish to do (1 Corinthians 13:12; Romans 7:8, 24; Mark 9:24).

So then, with respect to the different principles (but the same subject)[19] two opposing parts have been placed opposite each other, so to speak, in one and the same regenerate person, a natural and a spiritual part, flesh and spirit (Matthew 26:41; Galatians 5:17). Indeed, there are, as it were, two persons, the old and the new (Ephesians 4:22; Colossians 3:9), an outer and inner one, a revealed and a hidden one (Romans 7:22; 1 Peter 3:4), and finally a natural (or physical) and a spiritual one (1 Corinthians 2:[14–]15). Consequently, in the regenerate person a struggle arises between the flesh and the spirit (Romans 7; Galatians 5). From the predominant quality of the spirit, however, and following significant progress, the person is simply called spiritual (1 Corinthians 2:15; Galatians 6:1). But according to the shortcomings and weaknesses, or comparatively, he also is called carnal (1 Corinthians 3:1).

---

18   Thysius distances himself from 'spiritualist' views of conversion, but he does not identify his opponents. For more information on 'spiritualists' see *SPT* 2.8 footnote 9.

19   The two conflicting principles in regenerate man (flesh and spirit) are not viewed as quasi-independent 'persons,' but as contrary forces within the one person.

xxxv   Atque hinc fit, ut homine, Dei Spiritu, et quidem ex parte, renovato, liberum arbitrium se habeat partim ad bonum, partim ad malum. Ad bonum quidem, quod secundum novas vires, novasque inclinationes et motus, a Spiritu Dei in mente et voluntate effectas inditasque, homo hac spirituali potentia, eodem Spiritu praevio et comitante, intelligat, velit, agat spiritualia, id est, Deo vocanti consentiat et obediat, poenitentia, fide, et sanctitate vera; ita ut inchoet, conetur et operetur interiorem et exteriorem obedientiam, seu bona opera Deo placentia; idque tum in spiritualibus et ad Regnum Dei pertinentibus, 1 Cor. 2, 14. tum civilibus, et ad disciplinam externam spectantibus, quas religiosus* ex fide et ad Dei gloriam vult et agit, Rom. 14, 7. 8. 1 Cor. 10, 31. Jac. 4, 15. Quin in illis ipsis eodem Spiritu proficit et perseverat.

xxxvi   Hae tamen actiones et opera, utut secundum rationem principii sui boni, regenerationis scilicet, et Spiritus Sancti assistentiam, ad normam divinae legis edita, sint bona; attamen cum respectu reliquiarum carnis, multis defectibus contaminentur, absolute* bona non sunt. Es. 64, 6. censentur vero ut hujusmodi, divina acceptatione in Christo Salvatore, obtegente infirmitates nostras, et propter Spiritus Sancti operationem, et spiritualis partis praedominium.

xxxvii   Hic ergo homo Dei gratia et Spiritu renatus non tantum παθητικῶς, passive, sed et ἐνεργητικῶς, active, se habet, ac incipit Deo συνεργεῖν, id est, ut loquitur passim Augustinus, gratia Dei praeveniente, praeparante et operante, homo regenitus, ab eadem gratia ducente et comitante, cooperante et adjuvante, actus, vult et agit, et eadem subsequente proficit et perseverat. Non secus quam

And so it happens that when man has been renewed (albeit partly) by the Spirit of God, his free choice relates partly to the good, and partly to the bad. To the good, because following the new powers, inclinations and movements produced and bestowed in his mind and will by God's Spirit, man, by means of this spiritual capability and by the leading and accompaniment of the same Spirit, understands, wills, and achieves spiritual things. That is, man is in harmony with God who calls him and obeys Him in repentance, faith, and true holiness—so much so that he begins, strives, and manages to devote himself to inward and outward obedience, or good works pleasing to God. And this he wills and does in spiritual matters that concern the kingdom of God (1 Corinthians 2:14), and in civil matters that pertain to outward self-discipline, which the devout* person wills and does out of faith and to God's glory (Romans 14:7,8; 1 Corinthians 10:31; James 4:15). In fact, by the Holy Spirit he also improves and perseveres in these matters.

Yet these actions and works, as much as they are in keeping with their own good principle (i.e., the help of regeneration and the Holy Spirit), and because they were brought about by the norm of God's law, they are good. Nevertheless, since in light of the remnants of the flesh humanity is sullied with many blemishes, the works and actions are not good in an absolute* sense (Isaiah 64:6). And yet they are deemed to be of a good sort by virtue of God's acceptance in the Savior Christ (who covers our weaknesses), the working of the Holy Spirit, and the predomination of the spiritual part.

In this matter the person who has been renewed by God's grace and the Spirit behaves not only passively but also actively, and he begins to work together with God. That is, as Augustine says in several places, as God's grace leads the way, prepares, and is at work in him, the regenerate man, driven by the same grace that leads, accompanies, assists and collaborates with him, wills and acts and, while that grace supports him, progresses and persists.[20]

---

20 The precise source of these statements in Augustine's writing is uncertain. The reference *passim* seems to indicate that numerous statements by Augustine are summarized by *dicta* in thesis 37. Probable sources include: *De gratia et libero arbitrio* 17 (MPL 44): "… so that the whole process is ascribed to God, who makes the will in man good to receive aid and then aids it when it is made ready. For man's good will precedes many of God's gifts, but not them all; and of the things that it does not precede is man's will itself …" (… ut totum detur Deo, qui hominis voluntatem bonam et praeparat adiuvandam et adiuvat praeparatam. Praecedit enim bona voluntas hominis multa Dei dona sed non omnia; quae autem non praecedit ipsa, in eis est et ipsa …); *Enchiridion*, 9.32 (MPL 40): "And who was it that had started to grant him that love, however small, except he who prepares the will, and who by his co-operation perfects what he starts by his operation? For just as in starting he works it so that we may have the will, so too in perfecting he works with us as we will."

puellus nutricis manu ductus et suffultus ambulat; et puer, manu a praeceptore ducta, pingere discit et pingit, quia ita agitur ut simul agat.

XXXVIII Non otiosa itaque hic voluntas, sed liberatae voluntatis aliqua est libertas et actio, ut Scriptura confirmat, Phil. 2, 13. 2 Cor. 3, 17. Rom. 6, 18. etc. Atque in eandem sententiam praeclare Augustinus, lib. *de Correptione et gratia*,[a] Intelligant, inquit, si filii sunt Dei, Spiritu Dei se agi, ut quod agendum est, agant, et cum egerunt, illi a quo aguntur, gratias agant. Aguntur enim ut agant, non ut ipsi nihil agant.

XXXIX Ad malum idem, et proh dolor! identidem, se habet liberum arbitrium. Quum enim in renatis, ob inchoatam, non perfectam regenerationem, seu renovationem naturae, id est, mentis, voluntatis, affectuum et potentiae, semper maneant reliquiae carnis seu peccati, magnaque infirmitas, quae objectis (quae caro et mundus suggerit) ac Diaboli variis tentationibus excitantur, neque a Spiritu Sancto semper, aut eadem mensura, ac speciali gratia regantur, atque in bono confirmentur, sed interdum ad tempus aliquatenus, idque certo Dei consilio, deserantur, sibique permittantur, puta ut eos castiget, humilientur, et discant ab eo pendere; pii voluntate et libero suo arbitrio, atque opere, ad peccata, etiam gravia, feruntur et in ea prolabuntur, ut piorum exempla, Davidis, 2 Sam. 11, 2. Ps. 51, 13. 2 Sam. 24, 1. et 1 Par. 21. et Petri, Luc. 22, 31. 55. etc. ostendunt.

XL Atque ex his apparet, hominem regeneratum, in hac vita perfectam gradibus et numeris omnibus obedientiam ob imperfectionem causae proximae,* praestare non valere; neque semper, ob adversantem carnem, inoffensum et constantem pietatis cursum tenere, sed cespitare, cadere et peccare, contra Catharos et Perfectionarios.

---

[a] Augustine, *De correptione et gratia* 4 (CSEL 92²:221).

(Et quis istam etsi parvam dare coeperat caritatem, nisi ille qui praeparat voluntatem, et cooperando perficit, quod operando incipit? Quoniam ipse ut velimus operatur incipiens, qui volentibus cooperatur perficiens.)

It is like a young boy who is led by his nurse and steadied by her hand as he begins to walk; and like a boy who learns how to write as his teacher guides his hand, and then writes on his own, because he both is acted upon and acts himself.

Therefore the will is not idle here, but when liberated it possesses some freedom and action, as Scripture testifies (Philippians 2:13; 2 Corinthians 3:17; Romans 6:18, etc.). And in the same sense Augustine says very clearly in the book *On Corruption and Grace*: "If they are God's children they understand that they are led by God's Spirit to do what they should do, and when they have done it, they give thanks to the one who has done it. For they are led to do them, and not so that they do not do them." 38

Regrettably, time and time again the conduct of free choice relates to evil. For in fact the remnants of the flesh and sin always remain in those who have been reborn, because the regeneration or renewal of their nature (i.e., of their mind, will, feelings, and power) has only begun and has not been perfected. And there remains a great weakness which is also aroused by the attractions supplied by the world and our flesh, and by the different temptations of the devil. And they are not always governed by the Holy Spirit (or, governed to the same extent) and by special grace, nor confirmed in the good. But occasionally and for a period of time they are abandoned and left to themselves (by God's certain decree). This happens so that He may chastise and humble them, so that they learn to rely upon him. The pious by their own will, free choice, and work, are led to sin, even serious sin, and they fall into them, as is shown by the examples of these saints: David (2 Samuel 11:2; Psalm 51:13; 2 Samuel 24:1; and 1 Chronicles 21) and Peter (Luke 22:31, 55, etc.). 39

It is clear from these points that the regenerate man cannot in this life accomplish the perfect obedience to every degree and amount because of the imperfection of the nearest* cause.[21] And because his flesh opposes him, he is not able to maintain an uninterrupted and constant course of piety, but he stumbles, fails, and sins—contrary to the Catharist Heretics and the Perfectionists.[22] 40

---

21 The 'proximate cause' (*causa proxima*) here is man's own will and free choice, which is imperfect because it relates to both good and evil (see thesis 39 above).

22 In the early twelfth century, several groups of Christians outside the Roman Catholic church designated themselves as *cathari* (derived from Greek *katharos*, 'pure.' The word can be traced to German *ketzer*, 'heretic,' which appeared first in 1210) or *perfecti*. They held to a radical dualism of spirit and matter, and propagated a pure, perfect life of the spirit, freed from the bounds of the body. Similar ideas and practices were revived in diverse Anabaptist movements accompanying the Reformation of the sixteenth century.

XLI Veruntamen non eo usque a Deo Patre miseratore, a Christo ipsorum liberatore et capite, a Spiritu Sancto sanctificatore, in regenerationis gratia deseruntur, aut ipsi eam deserunt, ut libero suo arbitrio et opere in malo fatiscant, peccatum in illis regnet, incidant in indolentiam et impoenitentiam, et peccatum ad mortem, seu totaliter et finaliter deficiant; sed divina gratia, Christi cura, et Spiritus efficacia, et seminis illius spiritualis vi, ad et per veram resipiscentiam revocantur, ne peccent finaliter, et pereant, Mat. 24, 24. Luc. 22, 31. 32. 61. Joh. 17, 11. 12. 20. et c. 10, 29. 30. 1. Joh. 2, 27. et 3, 9. et 5, 4. 1 Pet. 1, 4. 5.

XLII Est ergo hic liberum arbitrium in gratiae et reparationis statu liberandum et liberatum: scilicet non simpliciter liberum a peccato, sed a servitute seu mancipio peccati, et servum justitiae, et divina gratia praeservatum a periculo excidii.

XLIII In *statu* denique *gloriae et perfectionis*,* seu post hanc vitam in altero seculo, ac vita aeterna, hominis beati ac glorificati (quoniam ibi, tum, ac in illo, perfecta erit restitutio ac regeneratio, et quidem secundum gradum excellentissimum, in quo nihil contrarii cadit aut cadere poterit, id est, lucebit in mente perfectissima Dei et voluntatis ejus cognitio, judicii sine ignorantia et dubitationibus integritas, in voluntate et corde affectibusque et omnibus viribus, omnibus modis perfecta vigebit sine ulla repugnantia inclinatio, propensio, alacritas et studium, ad Deo obediendum; tumque ille a Deo perpetuo et efficaciter regetur et confirmabitur) erit arbitrium ejus vere quidem liberum, imo liberrimum, ut quod non natura quidem simpliciter, sed gratia erit immutabiliter* bonum. Libertatis autem hujus qualitatis et quantitatis considerationem, referimus ad coelestem illam scholam, Rom. 8, 21. 1 Cor. 13, 10. 12. et 15, 28.

XLIV Ergo homo libero suo arbitrio, in primo quidem statu, potuit non peccare, sed in bono consistere; in secundo vero, liberi arbitrii abusu factus malus non potuit non peccare, nedum viribus arbitrii ad bonum resurgere; in tertio autem

17. ON FREE CHOICE

But even so, in the grace of regeneration they are not abandoned by God their compassionate Father, nor by Christ their Redeemer and Head, nor by the sanctifying Holy Spirit. They are not abandoned, nor do they themselves abandon grace to the point where they acquiesce in evil by their own free choice and work, where sin rules in them, and where they fall into indifference and unrepentance, and into sinning unto death; or where they fall away totally and finally. But by God's grace, Christ's care, and the Spirit's power, and by the strength of that spiritual seed, they are called back to, and through, a genuine change of heart, lest they sin unto the end and so perish (Matthew 24:[22–]24; Luke 22:31, 32, 61; John 17:11, 12, 20, and chapter 10:[28]29, 30; 1 John 2:27 and 3:9 and 5:4; 1 Peter 1:4, 5). 41

On this point therefore, in the state of grace and restoration, free choice must be set free and it has been freed. In other words, the will is freed not simply from sin, but from slavery or servitude to sin;[23] it is in the service of righteousness, and kept safe by God's grace from the risk of total destruction. 42

Lastly, there is the state of glory and perfection* in the next age of eternal life, after the current age, when man will be blessed and glorified. For there, then, and in that man the restoration and regeneration will be perfect and actually match the highest degree in which nothing adverse can or does befall him. Then in the mind of man there will shine forth the most perfect knowledge of God and of his will, an integrity of judgement that has no ignorance or doubts. In the will, the heart, the feelings and in all the powers, being perfect in every way, and without any opposition, there will thrive an inclination, a tendency, an eagerness, and a desire to obey God. And then that man will be ruled and established by God for evermore and to good effect. His will shall be truly free—indeed, most free, as it shall be invariably* good, not absolutely by nature (to be sure) but by grace.[24] A consideration of the quality and amount of this freedom, however, we shall defer to that heavenly school (Romans 8:21, 1 Corinthians 13:10, 12; and 15:28). 43

Well then, when he was in the first state, man was able with his free choice not to sin but to stand firm in the good. In the second state, having become wicked by the abuse of his free choice, man could do nothing but sin—let alone to ascend to the good by the powers of his will. In the third state, created anew 44

---

23 See thesis 26 above for the terminology of 'slavery,' based on texts like John 8:34 and Romans 6:16.

24 Cf. *SPT* 14.32 for the distinction between God's unchangeable goodness and man's changeable goodness. There, the difference stated in terms of man's initial position before the Fall holds also for his final state of glory: though man will be invariably good, this is not a natural quality, but a gift of grace.

divina gratia et efficacia recreatus, et eadem in bono confirmatus, non potest libero arbitrio totaliter et finaliter peccare, sed in bono provehitur et perseverat; in quarto denique statu a Deo glorificatus, non poterit amplius peccare, ut ait Augustinus,[a] sed sine ulla mutatione liberum arbitrium a peccato et miseria liberum perpetuo remanebit.

XLV Rejicimus Orthodoxae doctrinae contrarias has Antitheses: Pelagianorum unam, qui liberum arbitrium in rebus omnibus illaesum statuebant, ac sibi sufficere ut Deo obediat, si velit, adeoque totum sibi tribuentes, in Deum sacrilegi erant; Semipelagianorum alteram, qui liberum arbitrium in rebus spiritualibus laesum, attenuatum et inclinatum quidem, non autem corruptum asserebant, ac conversionem, partim gratiae, partim libero arbitrio tribuebant, inter Deum et homines partientes. Haec enim ipsorum erant axiomata: Est ubi voluntas hominis voluntatem Dei antevertit, est ubi illa ab hac antevertitur, ut Cassianus[b] voluit; item, Gratia Dei est quae nos salvat, liberum vero arbitrium est, quo, vel in quo, ut Faustus[c] speciose dicit, salvamur. Cui Orthodoxi opposuerunt, uniformem esse salutis rationem, et liberum arbitrium esse quod salvatur.

XLVI Quos errores renovarunt varie Scholastici, et Concilii Tridentini Patres; nec non ex Evangelicis quidam pigmento συνεργίας interpolarunt, maxime illi, quorum errores in Dordracena Synodo a Reformatis Ecclesiis rejecti sunt.

---

[a] Augustine, *De civitate Dei* 22.30 (CCSL 48:863–864).   [b] This appears not to be an actual quotation, but rather a paraphrase of John Cassian's view; Thysius may have had in mind the discussion in John Cassian, *Collationes* 13.11 (CSEL 13²:375–378).   [c] This too does not appear to be an actual quotation from Faustus, but an allusion to the title of one his works now known as *De gratia Dei libri duo* (CSEL 21:1–98) as reported by Gennadius of Massilia (or Marseille) in the older editions of his *De viris illustribus* 86: "Edidit quoque opus egregium de Gratia Dei qua salvamur, et libero humanae mentis aribitrio in quo salvamur" (Helmstadt, 1612), 27. Note that this reading is not supported in either MPL 58:1109 ("Edidit quoque opus egregium de Gratia Dei qua salvamur, et libero arbitrio. In quo opere docet …") or W. Herding, ed., *Hieronymi de viris inlustribus liber. Accedit Gennadii Catalogus virorum inlustrium* (Leipzig: B.G. Teubner, 1924), 106 ("Edidit quoque opus egregrium de gratiae Dei qua salvamur; in quo opera docet …").

by God's grace and power, and established by it in the good, man is not able with his free choice to sin totally and finally, but he advances and stands firm in what is good. And finally, in the fourth stage, glorified by God, man will no longer be able to sin, as Augustine says, but his free choice forever will remain free of sin and misery, without change.[25]

45 We reject the following contrary theses that oppose the orthodox teaching: the first is of the Pelagians, who held that in everything free choice is undamaged and self-sufficient to obey God if it wishes to. And so, by assigning the power of the will entirely to themselves, they committed sacrilege against God. The second contrary thesis is that of the semi-Pelagians, who assert that whereas free choice is indeed wounded, weakened, and worsened, it is not corrupted, and they attribute conversion partly to grace and partly to the freedom of the will, thus splitting it between God and men. For these were their fundamental propositions: "That there is a point at which the will anticipates the will of God, and another point at which it is anticipated by God's will," as Cassian held.[26] Similarly: "God's grace is what saves us, but it is free choice by which, or in which, we are saved," as Faustus says with deceptive attraction. Against him the orthodox posited: "The ground of salvation is uniform," and "free choice is that which is saved."

46 These errors were renewed in various ways by the Schoolmen and by the fathers of the Council of Trent,[27] and also some of the Evangelicals who refurbished them with a coloring of human co-operation, in particular those whose errors were rejected by the Reformed churches at the Synod of Dordrecht.[28]

---

25   Cf. also the footnote on thesis 15 above for Bernard of Clairvaux's elaboration of 'freedom' in terms of necessity, sin, and misery.
26   John Cassian (360–435) probably was born in the Provence. He became a monk in Palestine and Egypt. His major works are *De institutis coenobiorum* (*Institutes of the Coenobia*) and *Collationes patrum* (*Conferences of the Fathers*). He is known chiefly as the first representative of semi-Pelagianism, which is the reason why Cassian is mentioned in the disputation on free choice. Cassian opposed Augustine, who deemed the will to be dead, in his treatise *On Corruption and Grace*. Cassian stated that the will was sick, but not dead. Cassian believed that God's grace needed to cooperate with human free will, thus relinquishing the Augustinian *sola gratia*.
27   See the Tridentine Decree on Justification (DH 1521, 1554–1555).
28   Besides the explicitly mentioned Arminian errors rejected by the Synod of Dordrecht, the reference to "some of the Evangelicals" might include the alleged "synergism" of Philip Melanchthon and his followers such as Johann Pfeffinger and Victorinus Strigel.

DISPUTATIO XVIII

De Lege Dei

Praeside D. JOHANNE POLYANDRO
Respondente ARNOLDO SCHOMANTIO

THESIS I Quanta homo in peccatum prolapsus, virium liberi arbitrii* laboret defectione, quantaque ejus sit miseria, ex lege Dei cognosci potest.

II Lex Latinis sic dicta, quod publice legi soleat, a Graecis νόμος appellatur, quod suum cuique tribuat, ab Hebraeis תורה, id est, doctrina, quod nos de voluntate* Dei nostroque erga ipsum ac proximum* nostrum officio doceat.

III In Sacra Scriptura lex diversis significationibus* accipitur, primum pro qualibet Dei institutione, Ps. 1, 2. et 19, 8.

IV Hinc nomen* legis, tam Novi, quam Veteris Testamenti doctrinae attribuitur, Es. 2, 3. Jer. 31, 33. Rom. 3, 27.

V Secundo speciatim sumitur, aut pro lege morali, ut Luc. 10, 26., aut pro ceremoniali, ut Luc. 2, 22., aut pro forensi, ut Joh. 19, 7.

VI Tertio per metonymiam subjecti* accipitur pro libris Mosis doctrinam legis complectentibus, ut Luc. 24, 44.

VII Quarto sumitur synecdochice, pro omnibus libris Veteris Testamenti, ut Joh. 10, 34.

DISPUTATION 18

Concerning the Law of God

President: Johannes Polyander
Respondent: Arnoldus Schomantius[1]

It is from the law of God that one can learn how much man, after the fall into sin, suffers from the failure of the powers of his free choice,* and how great his misery is. 1

The law, called *lex* by the Latins because it used to be read [*legi*] publicly, is called *nomos* by the Greeks because it renders [*nemein*] to each his due, and *Torah* by the Hebrews, that is, instruction, because it instructs [*yarah*] us about the will* of God and our duty towards him and our neighbor.* 2

In Holy Scripture "law" is used with different meanings,* and firstly for anything that has been instituted by God (Psalm 1:2, and 19:8). 3

Hence the word* "law" is applied to the teaching of the New as well as the Old Testament (Isaiah 2:3; Jeremiah 31:33; Romans 3:27). 4

Secondly, the word is used with particular meaning for moral law (as in Luke 10:26), ceremonial law (as in Luke 2:22), or forensic law (as in John 19:7).[2] 5

Thirdly, as a metonym of the subject,* it is used for the books of Moses that contain the teaching of the law, as in Luke 24:44. 6

Fourthly, it is used by synecdoche for all the books of the Old Testament, as in John 10:34. 7

---

1 Born ca. 1599 and coming from Tiel, Arnoldus Schoemantius matriculated on 19 February 1619 in law. He was ordained in Ingen in 1623. He was admonished by the classis Tiel for indecent behaviour several times, but was restored in the ministry after showing repentance. He retired in 1666. It seems unlikely that Schoemantius lived until 1699, as Van Lieburg, *Repertorium* 221, suggests. See Du Rieu, *Album studiosorum*, 139, Van Lieburg, *Repertorium*, 221. See Menno Potjer, "Machtsverhoudingen in de classis Tiel," *Bijdragen en Mededelingen van Gelre, Vereeniging tot Beoefening van Geldersche Geschiedenis, Oudheidkunde, en Recht* 90–91 (1999): 67–93, esp. 68–69, 93 n. 52.

2 The distinction of the moral, ceremonial, and political or forensic sides of the law was common in Reformed orthodoxy. Cf. Theodore Beza, *Lex Dei, moralis, ceremonialis et politica, ex libris Mosis excerpta & in certas classes distributa* (Genève: Pierre de Saint-André, 1577). In *SPT* 18.32 the word 'political' is used instead of 'forensic'; in this context they are synonymous. The tripartition occurs as early as Thomas Aquinas, who divides all precepts of the Old Law into these three categories: *Summa theologiae*, 1/2.99.4–5. The distinction is reiterated in thesis 33 below, and then elaborated in theses 34 to 51.

VIII Quinto per metonymiam adjuncti, vel pro Ministerio Levitico, ut Heb. 7, 12., vel pro legis rigore et maledictione, ut Rom. 6, 14.

IX Sexto, metaphorice pro naturali* rationis humanae praeceptione, Rom. 2, 14.

X Ex quibus apparet, legem in sacris literis non accipi pro aeterna lege, vel rationis forma, quae in conceptu divino, tamquam in ἀρχετύπῳ exsistit, sed pro legitima ordinatione a Deo, tamquam a perfectissimo exemplari, ad genus humanum in tempore derivata, huicque variis modis communicata ac declarata.

XI Nos ergo intra limites Sacrorum Bibliorum consistentes, legem sumimus pro informatione ac praeceptione temporaria, qua Deus res* juri suo consentaneas, hominibus ad imaginem suam conditis praecipit, dissentaneas prohibet, cum promissione praemii, ac comminatione supplicii, ut eos ad voluntatis suae obsequium flectat.

XII Haec pro principiorum suorum proximorum* diversitate, distribuitur in legem naturalem, humanas ac divinas.

In the fifth place, as a metonym of the adjunct,³ it is used for the Levitical ministry, as in Hebrews 7:12, or for the severity and curse of the law, as in Romans 6:14.

In the sixth place it is used figuratively for the natural* directive of human reason (Romans 2:14).

From these usages it appears that "law" in the sacred writings is not used for the eternal law, or for the essential conceptual content that exists in the divine understanding as in an archetype, but for a legal rule that is drawn down by God, as the most perfect exemplar, for the human race within time, and communicated and declared to it in various ways.⁴

Well then, staying within the boundaries of the sacred books, we employ the word "law" for the instruction and rule in history whereby God commands people created in his image to do anything* that agrees with his judgment and forbids them to do what is contrary to it, with the promise of reward and the threat of punishment, so that He may direct them to obey his will.

According to the diversity of its closely* related principles, this law is divided into natural law, human laws, and divine laws.⁵

---

3   A metonym substitutes the name of a related thing for the thing itself. When the subject is put for anything that belongs to it, for instance when the container is put for the contents, it is called a metonym of the subject. Thus 'law' can refer to the Pentateuch, because it contains the law. A metonym of the adjunct is a metonym whereby that which belongs to anything is put for the subject; for instance when the contents are put for the container. Thus 'law' can refer to the Levitical ministry or to the curse of the law, because they are contained in the law. A synecdoche is more general and exchanges one idea for another associated idea, here a part—the law—is put for the whole. Cf. Lausberg, *Handbook*, §§ 568, 572.
4   For archetypal and ectypal theology, see *SPT* 1.3–4.
5   The remainder of this disputation, theses 13–51, is dedicated to the law as defined in thesis 11 (where the law, as God's instruction and rule in time is carefully distinguished from the eternal law in thesis 10). The discussion is arranged by the trichotomy here introduced: natural law (or the common notions), in thesis 13–25; human law (or civil law), in thesis 26–29; divine law, in thesis 30–51. Thomas Aquinas has the fourfold division into eternal, natural, human (positive) law and divine (Old and New) law: *Summa theologiae*, 1/2.91. Polyander left the eternal law out of further discussion (thesis 10), but retained the other three types of law. The detailed structure of this disputation is presented the Introduction ("Genres and Structures").

XIII   Lex naturalis* est lumen et dictamen rectae rationis in intellectu, hominem κοιναῖς ἐννοίαις, seu communibus notionibus,* ad justi et injusti, honesti ac turpis discretionem informans, ut quid faciendum sit vel fugiendum, intelligat.

XIV   Istarum notionum aliae sunt primariae, quas principia* practica, aliae secundariae, quas conclusiones ex principiis illis ratiocinationis adminiculo exstructas vocamus.

XV   Utraeque notiones ante hominis lapsum fuerunt incorruptae, ac suavi harmonia conjunctae, cum vi juxta ipsarum consilium decernendi in voluntate, jussaque voluntatis recte exsequendi in affectibus.

XVI   Post hominis lapsum, priores quidem notiones in ipsius intellectu immotae permanent, ac perspicue relucent; posteriores vero cum a generalibus ad particularia acceditur, miserandum in modum vacillant, et a sincera aequitatis regula deflectunt, ut docent iniquissimarum legum, ac corruptissimorum morum exempla, quae in Ethnicorum historiis inveniuntur.

XVII   Quamvis communes istae notiones post transgressionem Adami, partim naturae vitio, partim consuetudinis atque educationis pravitate, valde sint obscuratae, ac pene exstinctae, quae tamen earum supersunt scintillae, peccato, etiam in maxime obtenebratis, redarguendo ac condemnando sufficiunt.

18. CONCERNING THE LAW OF GOD

13 Natural law* is the light and direction of sound reason in the intellect, informing man with common notions*[6] to distinguish right from wrong, and honorable from shameful—so that he may understand what he should do or shun.

14 Some of those notions are of a primary sort, and we call them practical principles;* others, which are secondary, we call conclusions constructed from those principles with the help of reasoning.

15 Before the fall of man, both sorts of notions were unspoiled and coupled together in delightful harmony, together with the power in the will to make decisions according to their directions, and to carry out the commands of the will properly in the affections.[7]

16 After the fall of man, however, the first, primary notions in his intellect remained unchanged, and they shine forth clearly; but the latter, secondary notions stagger with wretched hesitation whenever one goes from general things to particular ones, and they deviate from the sound rule of equity, as is shown by the examples of the very unfair laws and overly corrupt customs that are found in the histories of gentile peoples.

17 After the transgression of Adam those notions were completely covered up and nearly wiped out, partly because of the corruption of his nature and partly because of the depravity of his behavior and upbringing. And yet the little sparks of these common notions that do remain are sufficient to convict and condemn sin, even in those who have been darkened completely.

---

6 The concept of common notions may be traced to ancient mathematics. Euclid divides the first principles into definitions, postulates, and common notions (*koinai ennoiai*), of which only the common notions are undeniable. Theologians applied this idea to the general and undeniable knowledge of the existence of God. For use of the term by Polyander see Platt, *Reformed Thought and Scholasticism*, 10–33. Here Polyander states that all human beings by nature have some undeniable beams of the light of natural law. In the following theses Polyander distinguishes the *principia* from the *conclusions* and argues that after the fall the human mind is no longer able to draw the correct conclusions from the moral principles, although the principles remain intact.

7 The terminology used in this thesis reflects that of Aristotelian 'faculty psychology,' which conceives the human mind or soul as consisting of several faculties, in this case intellect, will and affections. In order to accomplish an act, a complete and therefore effective will is needed, which is the result of unanimity of all three faculties. Thysius in *SPT* 13.32 and 38 first divides the faculties of the soul into the intellect and the will, but later says that the affections were so composed that they complied with the intellect and the will. Within Reformed Orthodoxy the affections were sometimes seen as part of the will and sometimes as an independent faculty. Cf. *RTF*, 43–44.

XVIII Idcirco Paulus ait, jus Dei ab Ethnicis olim impietati atque injustitiae deditis, fuisse agnitum, Rom. 1, 32. atque opus legis cordibus ipsorum inscriptum, Rom. 2, 14. hocque duplici probat* testimonio, externo et interno.

XIX Externum testimonium* est legum ab ipsis conditarum, quibus eos sibimetipsis legem fuisse asserit; ea scilicet jubendo, aut vetando, quae Deus in lege sua scripta jubet aut vetat, Rom. 2, 14.

XX Internum est conscientiae, suis cogitationibus injustas ipsorum actiones accusantis, justas ex juris animo concepti auctoritate defendentis, Rom. 2, 15.

XXI Duplicia juris istius vestigia in hominis natura* apparent, quorum alia videntur ipsi cum brutis animalibus aliquo modo esse communia, alia vero ipsi sunt propria.

XXII Ea homini cum ceteris animalibus videntur esse communia, ad quae omnes creaturae, vita ac sensu animali praeditae, στοργῇ, atque affectione naturali ad sui suorumque conservationem proclives, spontali instinctu feruntur; qualia sunt vitae suae defensio, prolis suae propagatio, educatio ac dilectio.

XXIII Hinc Jurisconsulti jus naturale καταχρηστικῶς ac latiore significatione nuncupant, quod natura omnia animalia docuit.

XXIV Homini propria sunt, ad quae affectiones ipsius, dictamine ac ductu rationis (cujus reliquae animantes sunt expertes) secundum normam boni et aequi sibi divinitus attributam, diriguntur; qualia sunt, Deum esse colendum, magistratus, parentes et bene meritos esse honorandos, pacta esse servanda et similia.

XXV Cum autem homo non seorsim in sacro Codice consideretur, ut animal, sed conjunctim, ut animal rationale, vel potius ut creatura ad imaginem Dei condita, ideo nostri Theologi jus illud naturale ad hominem tamquam ad verum et proprium illius subjectum cum Apostolo restringunt, Rom. 1. et 2.

XXVI Etsi hoc jus hominum animis insitum, communi omnium gentium judicio atque assensu comprobetur, ipsi tamen gentiles sapientiores illud externarum legum auxilio indigere agnoverunt, ut et melius intelligatur et rectius observetur.

For this reason Paul says that God's judgment was known to the gentiles who in former times had been given over to godlessness and unrighteousness (Romans 1:[26–]32) and that the requirement of the law was inscribed upon their hearts (Romans 2:14[15]). He demonstrates* this with a twofold testimony, external and internal.

The external testimony* is the law they themselves set up, and Paul asserts that they were a law unto themselves, namely by commanding or prohibiting the very things that God commands or forbids in the law which He had written (Romans 2:14).

The internal testimony is that of the conscience, which by its deliberations confronts their wrong actions and defends the right ones by the authority of the law that has been laid up in their hearts (Romans 2:15).

Evident in the nature* of mankind are two-fold traces of this law, some of which he appears to share with irrational living beings, while others belong properly to him.

The ones mankind seems to share with the other created living beings are those to which all creatures endowed with animate life and perception are inclined by natural instinct, in order to protect themselves and their offspring by innate affection and natural feeling. Traces of this kind are: guarding their own lives, propagating, nurturing, and cherishing their own offspring.

For the reason that it has taught all living beings, this law is loosely (and with a rather broader meaning) called "natural law" by the lawyers.

Traces of the law that properly concern mankind are the ones to which his affections are directed by the bidding and guidance of reason (which the other creatures lack), in keeping with the norm of good and right that God has granted to him. Traces of this kind are: that God should be worshipped, parents and others who rightly deserve it respected, and agreements kept, and the like.[8]

However, since the sacred Book does not consider mankind separately as a living being, but jointly, as a living being endowed with reason—better yet, it offers a treatment of him as a creature made in God's image—therefore our theologians restrict that natural law to mankind as its true and proper subject. This is what Paul does in Romans 1 and 2.

Although in the judgment and consensus common to all peoples it is agreed that this law is implanted in the souls of men, nevertheless the wiser heathens acknowledge that for a better understanding and proper keeping of it, this internal law needs the help of external laws.

---

8 *Pacta sunt servanda* has always been a basic principle of civil law. For some historical remarks on the issue see Hans Wehberg, *"Pacta Sunt Servanda," The American Journal of International Law* 53 (1959): 775–786.

XXVII   Unde effectum est, ut tam inter Ethnicos, quam inter Christianos, quam plurimae leges civiles quorundam prudentum arte, ac Magistratuum auctoritate in Respublicas sint introductae.

XXVIII   Leges illae sunt definitae* juris sententiae, solenni ac peculiari legitimi Magistratus mandato stabilitae, quae ex notionibus communibus tamquam ex principiis ac fontibus, conclusiones aliquas ac determinationes* particulares, seu rivulos pro opportunitatibus personarum,* rerum, temporum et locorum, ad commune et privatum civium bonum producunt; hasque promissione praemii, ac comminatione poenae stabiliunt.

XXIX   Hae leges subditorum conscientias, vel ad observationem, vel ad poenam obligant, si in omnibus suis edictis legis divinae exemplari sint prorsus conformes; non obligant, si huic adversentur.

XXX   Legis divinae exemplar est, quod Deus ipse per Angelos suos coelestes, ac per servum suum Mosem ab ipso immediate inspiratum digito suo conscriptum populo Israëlitico in monte Sinai tradidit, Exod. 19, 20. et 20, 1. et seqq. Act. 7, 53. Gal. 3, 19.

XXXI   Hoc legis divinae exemplar modum bene beateque coram Deo et proximo nostro vivendi summatim decem praeceptorum cancellis circumscribit, quamobrem a Mose, Deut. 4, 13. עשרת הדברים, id est, decem verba, a nobis Decalogus appellatur.

XXXII   Tametsi finis* legis divinae maxime proprius et proximus sit unicus, nimirum caritas secundum praecepta Dei ordinata, in qua conscientia tuto acquiescat; media tamen huic inservientia sunt triplicia, quorum primum consistit in statutis moralibus, secundum in ceremonialibus, tertium in politicis.

XXXIII   Inde est quod lex Dei, in moralem, ceremonialem et politicam distinguitur.

XXXIV   Lex moralis est quae praeceptis generalibus, perpetuo et reciproce veris, cum jure divino et naturali consentientibus, cuilibet homini absolute

18. CONCERNING THE LAW OF GOD

Hence it came about that thanks to the skills of a few wise individuals and the authority of the magistrates in the commonwealth, as many civil laws as possible were introduced among both gentile and Christian nations.

These laws are the pronouncements* of what is just, established by the solemn and specific order of a legitimate magistrate, and they issue from commonly-held notions that are like principles and sources. And like little streams, they produce certain conclusions and particular provisions* according to the needs of persons,* things, times, and places, for the public and private good of citizens; and they establish these by promising reward and by threatening with punishment.

If in all their edicts these laws conform entirely to the exemplar of God's law, they bind the consciences of their subjects to keeping them or to suffering punishment; if the laws contradict God's law, then they do not bind their subjects.[9]

The exemplar of God's law is the one that God himself, through his heavenly angels and through his servant Moses, directly inspired and recorded with his own finger, and that He himself handed to the people of Israel on Mount Sinai (Exodus 19:20, and 20:1 ff.;[10] Acts 7:53; Galatians 3:19).

This exemplar of God's law describes in a summary fashion and encompassed in ten commandments the way to live well and in blessedness before God and our neighbor. Therefore Moses calls it 'Aseret Hadᵉvarim, that is, the ten words, and we call it the Decalogue.

The goal* that is most appropriate and closest to God's law is a single one, namely, the love ordained according to God's precepts wherein the conscience rests securely. However, the means that serve this goal are three-fold, of which the first exists in statutes that are moral, the second ceremonial, and the third political.[11]

Hence the law of God is divided into the moral, the ceremonial, and the political.

The moral law is the one which by means of general commands that are perpetually and mutually true[12] (commands that are in harmony with the

---

9 Cf. Acts 5:29: "We must obey God rather than men."
10 Cf. also Exodus 31:18.
11 See note on thesis 5 above.
12 *Reciproce vera* expresses that the truth of these commands is universal. The statement, "if there is a human being, then there is an *animal rationalis*," is mutually true, because if there is a rational animal there is also a human being. The statement, "if there is a human being, then there is an *animal*," however, is not mutually true, because not every *animal* is a

necessariis et utilibus, justam et accuratam secundum Dei voluntatem vivendi formam praescribit; adhibitis promissis vitae praesentis et futurae, si quis ejus praecepta servaverit, minisque mortis primae ac secundae, si quis illa violaverit.

XXXV Tres ergo illius sunt partes:
1. Mandata quibus aliquid vel praecipitur, vel vetatur.
2. Promissiones de benedictione temporaria et aeterna.
3. Comminationes de maledictione, Exod. 19, 5. Deut. 27, 26. Luc. 10. Rom. 10, 5. Gal. 3, 10.

XXXVI Duae illius sunt tabulae, quarum prioris quatuor praecepta definiunt officia pietatis Deo ex summa atque integra illius dilectione primario loco praestanda; posterioris sex, officia justitiae indicant erga proximum, ex sincera erga eum caritate secundario exercenda, Mat. 22, 38.

XXXVII Summa prioris tabulae a Christo nominatur primum et magnum mandatum; posterioris, secundum, ac superiori simile, ut doceat, ad exactam utriusque observationem requiri:
1. Ut cultus pietatis Deo debitus, et voluntati et majestati ipsius supremae sit consentaneus.
2. Ut Deum primo, et per se immediate,* cetera vero omnia propter Deum amemus, atque imprimis pios homines propter spiritualem ipsorum atque arctiorem cognationem cum Deo.
3. Ut officia caritatis erga proximum cedant officiis pietatis erga Deum, ac propter ipsius cultum, injusta proximi odia, omnesque acerbitates et injurias fortiter ac constanter perferamus.

XXXVIII Legem hanc non minus ad Christianos pertinere sub Novo, quam ad Judaeos sub VetereTestamento, probamus his argumentis:
1. Quod externa sit effigies internae legis naturae nostris protoplastis ante lapsum impressae per creationem eorum ad Dei imaginem, quae posita est in sanctitate et justitia; quarum virtutum munia Decalogus quibuslibet hominibus repraesentat, atque Evangelium a fidei domesticis ad imaginem Dei per Spiritum Dei renovatis efflagitat.

---

human being. In line with Aristotle, Peter Ramus defined a so-called 'catholic axiom' as one of which the consequent is always true of the antecedent, not only always and *per se*, but also reciprocally. See Petrus Ramus, *Dialectics* (Paris: Andreas Wechelus, 1572), 63, and cf. Aristotle, *Posterior Analytics*, 73a27. This idea was applied to necessary precepts. According to John Althusius the precepts that are not mutually true (i.e., true only in specific places and times) should be sifted out. Cf. Frederik S. Carney, ed., *The Politics of Johannes Althusius* (London: Eyre & Spottiswoode, 1964), xviii, 6.

divine and natural right and that are absolutely necessary and useful for each and every human being) prescribe the just and precise way of living according to God's will. Added to this moral law are promises for the present and future life if one keeps its precepts; added also are the threats of the first and second death if one breaks them.[13]

35 Therefore it consists of three parts: 1) commandments whereby something is required or forbidden; 2) promises of temporal and eternal blessing; 3) threats of damnation (Exodus 19:5; Deuteronomy 27:26; Luke 10[26–28]; Romans 10:5; Galatians 3:10).

36 The moral law consists of two tables, in the former of which four precepts define the duties of piety that we must present to God in the first place, out of the highest and sincere love that we have for Him. Of the latter table there are six that show the duties of righteousness that we must carry out towards our neighbor in the second place, out of true love towards him (Matthew 22:38[-39]).

37 Christ calls the summary of the former table "the first and great commandment"; He calls the summary of the latter "the second and like the first," in order to teach us that we are required to keep both of them carefully: 1) So that the pious worship that is owed to God may be in harmony with his supreme will and majesty. 2) So that we first love God directly* for who He is, and then everything else for his sake (in particular the devout people for their spiritual and closer connection to God). 3) So that the duties of love we have toward our neighbor may yield to the duties of piety to God, and so that we may endure the unjust hatred of our neighbor and every affliction and injustice with constant steadfastness for the sake of our service to Him.

38 We prove, with the following arguments, that this law is as relevant to Christians in the New Testament as it was to Jews in the Old Testament: 1) It is the outward representation of the internal law of nature that before the fall was impressed upon our first parents as they were created in God's image; this law is grounded in holiness and justice.[14] The Decalogue portrays to people one and all the duties that accompany these virtues, and the Gospel urgently demands these duties from the members of the household of faith, who have

---

13   The terms "first and second death" are derived from Revelation 2:11 and 20:5–6,14.
14   For Adam's disobedience to the moral law as summary of the natural law implanted in him cf. *SPT* 14.7.

2. Quod haec lex primis nostris parentibus revelata, per Mosem repetita et restaurata, non tantum a Prophetis, sed etiam a Christo et Apostolis fuerit exposita, ab ipsis observata, aliisque stricte commendata, Mat. 5, 17. et seqq. Luc. 10, 27. Rom. 6, 13. et 7, 25. et 12. et 13.

3. Quoniam filii Dei ab observatione mandatorum hujus legis, tamquam a τεκμηρίῳ, atque infallibili germanae cum Deo conjunctionis testimonio, describuntur, 1Joh. 1, 6. 7. et 2, 3. 4. 5. 6.

4. Quia caritas ex fide non ficta et bona conscientia (quae est finis Decalogi) Timotheo veluti scopus objicitur, ad quem omnes suas actiones referre debeat, 1Tim. 1, 5.

XXXIX Tam perfecta est haec lex, ut nihil ei in praeceptis moralibus, aut a Christo, aut ab Apostolis ipsius additum fuerit, quo ad exactiorem bonorum operum normam sub Novo Testamento sit adducta; sed quae falsarum interpretationum ac malorum corruptelis ante Christi adventum fuerat obliterata et antiquata, genuina Christi, Judaeisque seductis nova atque inaudita interpretatione, iteratisque ad universalem mandatorum ejus observationem commonefactionibus, pristino suo nitori plene fuit restituta.

XL Legis hujus usus aut est communis quibuslibet hominibus in contumacia conclusis, aut electorum saluti peculiariter destinatus.

XLI Prior usus est triplex:

1. Ut freno externae suae disciplinae effrenatas hominum quorumlibet affectiones cohibeat.

2. Ut in se tamquam in speculo, tum amissionem originalis generis humani in Adamo justitiae, tum carnis seu naturae corruptae ἀδυναμίαν, id est, impotentiam ad mandata sua praestanda, pravasque ad ea violanda inclinationes quibuslibet peccatoribus demonstret. Unde per eam agnitio peccati fieri dicitur, Rom. 3, 19. 20. et 4, 15. et 5, 20. et 7, 7. et seqq.

3. Ut sit nuntia justi judicii divini adversus ejus transgressores. Unde vocatur ministerium mortis, iram operans ac terrorem incutiens, 2Cor. 3, 7. Rom. 4, 15. Hebr. 12, 29.

18. CONCERNING THE LAW OF GOD

been restored to God's image through God's Spirit. 2) This law, which had been revealed to our first parents and was restated and reinforced through Moses, was promoted not only by the prophets but also by Christ and his apostles, who observed them and strongly recommended them to others (Matthew 5:17 ff.; Luke 10:27; Romans 6:13 and 7:25, and chapters 12 and 13). 3) The observance of this law's precepts is like a token or emblem whereby those who keep them are described as sons of God; it is infallible testimony of their genuine union with God (1 John 1:6,7 and 2:3,4,5 and 6). 4) The love that comes from a unfeigned faith and a good conscience (which is the goal of the Decalogue) is put before Timothy as the target to which all his actions should be directed (1 Timothy 1:5).

This law is so complete that nothing has been added to it in any moral injunctions (either by Christ or by his apostles) to raise it up to a more exacting norm of good works under [the dispensation of] the New Testament. But because it had fallen into disuse and had been cast aside by false interpretations and evil corruption before the coming of Christ, Christ fully restored its pristine lustre by his true interpretation (new and unheard of to the Jews who had been misled) and by the repeated admonitions that its commands be observed universally.[15]

The use of this law is general for any and all people who are trapped in their willful disobedience and it is intended specifically for the salvation of the elect.

The first use is three-fold:

1. To check all the unbridled passions of people with the reins of its own external control.
2. To reveal in its own reflection (like a mirror) to sinners one and all the loss of the original righteousness of the human race in Adam, and the powerlessness of the corrupted flesh or nature; that is, the inability to perform what it has been commanded, and the crooked tendencies to violate those commands. Therefore knowledge of sin is said to come about through the law (Romans 3:19, 20; 4:15; 5:20; and 7:7 ff.).
3. To be the herald of God's righteous judgment against those who transgress it. Therefore it is called the ministry of death, working wrath and striking with fear (2 Corinthians 3:7; Romans 4:15; and Hebrews 12:29).[16]

---

15 Similar statements on the relation between Christ and the Mosaic law are made in *SPT* 23.22–23.

16 The *Synopsis* reflects the Reformed threefold use of the law as best known from Calvin's *Institutes*, 2.7.6–14 (*usus paedagogicus/elenchticus, usus politicus/civilis, usus didacticus/ normativus*). Formally, however, *SPT* chooses a format based on a distinction between 'all people' and 'the elect only,' and divides the traditional first and third uses into three uses each. So thesis 41 begins with the original *usus secundus* (check of unbridled passions), and

XLII Posterior usus electorum saluti peculiariter destinatus, est quadruplex:
1. Est, ut adhibito subsidio ministerii Evangelici, eos sensu peccati ac reatus sui dejectos, ad Christum Salvatorem nostrum deducat, finem legis ad justitiam omni credenti, Rom. 10, 4.
2. Est, ut ipsis in Christum credentibus sit agendorum et omittendorum regula atque index viae ad vitam ducentis; ob quem usum appellatur lex operum, Rom. 3, 27., via Dei, Ps. 119, 3., via veritatis, Ps. 119, 30, et lucerna pedum nostrorum, Ps. 119, 105.
3. Ut sancta atque honesta ipsorum secundum praescriptionem legis conversatio sit testimonium verae ipsorum cum Deo communionis, 1Joh. 1, 6. 7. et 2, 2. 3. 4. 5. 6.
4. Ut lex eos suo stimulo ad studium sincerae caritatis erga Deum et proximum indies magis impellat, 1Tim. 1, 5.

XLIII Ad reprobos contumaces quod attinet, hi non legis illius, sed perversae suae cupiditatis vitio in vetitum petulanter nitentes, se adversus ejus interdicta obdurant, eoque semetipsos magis reddunt coram Deo damnabiles.

XLIV Huic legi operum Apostolus legem fidei ex diametro opponit, qua omnis operum gloriatio excluditur, Rom. 3, 27. Ex qua exclusione necessario sequitur, legem illam operum a nemine posse* in hac vita, quantumvis regenito, perfecte servari, ac proinde neminem posse suis operibus coram Deo justificari.

XLV Interim Deus officium perfectae caritatis sibi ac proximo nostro debitum, a nobis jure exigit, cum ejus praestandi facultatem* naturae nostrae in primis nostris parentibus dederit.

XLVI Lex ceremonialis est σκιαγραφία, ac delineatio externa cultus divini, quem Deus in quatuor primae tabulae praeceptis efflagitat, ad formam Reipublicae Israëliticae olim accommodata, variis constans umbris typicis, quarum corpus est in Christo, qui mandata illius per carnem suam abolevit, ut sublato illo intergerivi inter Judaeos et Gentiles parietis septo, utrosque in uno corpore per crucem Deo reconciliaret, Col. 2, 17. Eph. 2, 15. 16.

---

distinguishes two types of the original *s usus primus* (reflection of loss of righteousness and law as herald of God's judgment). Thesis 42 ascribes a third type of the original *primus usus legis* to the elect only, namely the law's task to lead to Christ (with the help of the Gospel), and distinguishes three types of the original *tertius usus legis*, namely its function as a guide to life for believers, as a witness of their true communion with God, and as a stimulus to pursue sincere love of God and one's neighbor. As a consequence, one aspect of the original *primus usus legis*, namely leading convinced sinners to Christ, is now limited to the elect.

18. CONCERNING THE LAW OF GOD

The second use, ordained specifically for the salvation of the elect, is fourfold:

1. It is, with the additional help of the ministry of the Gospel,[17] to lead those who have been humbled by their sense of sin and guilt, to Christ our Savior, who for every believer is the goal of the law unto righteousness (Romans 10:4).
2. It is, for those people who believe in Christ, to be the rule for what must be performed and what must be left aside, and the guide on the road that leads to life. For this use it is called the law of works (Romans 3:27), the way of God (Psalm 119:3), the way of truth (Psalm 119:30), and a light for our feet (Psalm 119:105).
3. So that the holy and honorable behavior according to the precepts of the law may be a witness of the believers' true communion with God (1 John 1:6,7; 2:3; and 3:4,5, and 6).
4. So that the law, by its own stimulus, may drive them on more every day to pursue sincere love towards God and their neighbor (1 Timothy 1:5).

As far as stubborn reprobates are concerned, these people are not of that law; but, insolently hastening by the sin of their own perverse desire into what is forbidden, they harden themselves against its commands, and so they render themselves more worthy of damnation in God's sight.

The apostle places the law of faith diametrically opposite this law of works, so that all boasting in works is excluded (Romans 3:27). From this exclusion of boasting it necessarily follows that no-one (however much regenerated he may be) is able* to keep that law of works perfectly in this life, and thus no-one can be justified before God by means of his own works.

Meanwhile God rightly demands from us the duty of perfect love that we owe him and our neighbor, since in our first parents He has bestowed upon our nature the ability* of performing it.

The ceremonial law is the 'shadow painting,' the sketched outline of the divine worship which God demands in the four commandments of the first table. This law was once arranged to suit the structure of the Israelite nation, and it consisted of a variety of figurative foreshadowings, of which the bodily substance is in Christ, who in his own flesh abolished its commandments. He did so in order to take away the dividing wall of hostility between Jews and gentiles, and so that through the cross He might reconcile with God the two parties in one body (Colossians 2:17; Ephesians 2:15, 16).

---

17 No independent function, apart from the gospel, is attributed to the law in leading the elect to Christ. Cf. also Gal. 3:24: "So the Law was our guardian until Christ came that we might be justified by faith" (NIV).

XLVII De hac verum est illud axioma: Lex ceremonialis est mortua, et si postliminio revocetur, fit mortifera.

XLVIII Varius legis illius usus fuit sub Veteri Testamento:
1. Ut populus Israëliticus hujus observatione, tamquam parietis intergerivi septo, ab aliis Gentibus profanis sejungeretur, ne familiari cum his consuetudine in eandem cum ipsis impietatem atque idololatriam prolaberetur.
2. Ut ex externis illius ritibus intelligerent, non tantum internum animae, sed etiam externum corporis cultum Deo esse consecrandum.
3. Ut nervus esset et retinaculum sacri ministerii Levitici in Ecclesia Judaica usque ad Christi adventum conservandi.
4. Ut esset chirographum ipsis occulte contrarium, quo suum reatum atque obligationem ad poenam mortis aeternae, ob legis divinae transgressiones adversus semetipsos obsignarent, Col. 2, 14.
5. Ut esset paedagogia ad Christum, Gal. 3.
6. Ut typica illius sacrificia essent symbola oblationis Christi expiatoriae, nostraeque sanctificationis per aspersionem ipsius sanguinis, Hebr. 9. et 10.

XLIX Lex politica est, quae officia magistratuum ac subditorum Reipublicae Israëliticae certis constitutionibus civilibus determinat, easque poenis corporalibus in rebelles sancit, juxta normam utriusque tabulae Decalogi, atque imprimis secundae.

18. CONCERNING THE LAW OF GOD

Regarding this law that axiomatic statement is true: "The ceremonial law is dead, and if it is returned to its former privileged status, it would be deadly."[18]

There were various uses of that ceremonial law during the Old Testament period:

1. So that by observing it the people of Israel might be segregated from the other, pagan peoples as if by the enclosure of a wall that separates them; lest through familiar interaction with them they should fall headfirst and together with them into the same impiety and idol worship.
2. So that they might understand from its outward ceremonies that they must dedicate not only the inward worship of their soul to God, but also the outward worship of their body.
3. So that it might be the nerve and tether of the holy Levitical ministry that was to be preserved in the Jewish church until the coming of Christ.
4. So that it might be a public record of the debts that had been held against them in an invisible way; by this law they seal their guilt against themselves, as well as their obligation to the punishment of eternal death on account of their transgressions of God's law (Colossians 2:14).
5. So that it might be a tutor to lead them to Christ (Galatians 3[:24]).
6. So that its characteristic sacrifices might be symbols of Christ's atoning sacrifice and of our sanctification through the sprinkling of his blood (Hebrews 9 and 10).

The political law is what determines the duties of the governing officials and the subjects of the Israelite nation by means of certain civil regulations. It lends authority to them through the corporal punishment of those who rebel, in keeping with the norm of the Decalogue's two tables, and in particular the second one.

---

18 The law, after Christ fulfilled it, is not merely dead but also deadly. It is a dangerous thing for Christians to keep the Jewish ceremonies. According to Jerome they are *perniciose et mortiferae Christianis* (Jerome *Epist.* 112.14.2, CSEL 55. 382). Augustine had a more nuanced view about the period of transition, but he agreed that after that period the ceremonies of Judaism are *perniciosae et mortiferae*. His letter to Jerome on this issue is included among the latter's correspondence (Jerome *Epist* 116.18.1; CSEL, 55. 409). Polyander might have been drawing on the summary of the discussion offered by Thomas Aquinas, who says that according to Augustine the legal ceremonies were *neque mortifera neque mortua* ('neither imparting death nor deadly') before the passion of Christ; they were *mortua et mortifera* ('deadly and imparting death') after the gospel was proclaimed; they were *mortua non tamen mortifera* ('deadly but not imparting death') in the middle period. See Aquinas, *Summa theologiae*, 1/2.103.4; cf also *Super Galatas lectiones* cap. 2, lect. 3.86–89.

L   Hujus praecipuus usus fuit, ut accurata mandatorum legis moralis ac ceremonialis observatione, justitia cum pietate conjuncta inter Judaeos peculiariter vigeret.

LI   Quae in hac lege sunt juris communis, illa omnis generis magistratus et subditos etiamnum obligant; quae vero sunt juris particularis Judaici, illa una cum Mosis politia exspirarunt.

50 The foremost use of this political law is that by the precise keeping of the precepts of the moral and ceremonial laws, justice might thrive in conjunction with piety especially among the Jews.

51 Even to the present day governing officials and their subjects one and all are obliged to obey those precepts in this political law that belong to the universal law; however, the ones that belong to the particular Jewish [political] law have become obsolete along with the Mosaic system of government.

DISPUTATIO XIX

De Idololatria

Praeside D. ANDREA RIVETO
Respondente SAMUELE BOCHARTO

THESIS I Lex divina, de qua proxime actum est, unicum illum Legislatorem qui potest servare et perdere, Jac. 4, 12. nobis colendum proponit, eo cultu interno et externo, quem ipse in verbo suo revelavit et praescripsit; qui communiter Ebraeis עבדה Ex. 12, 26. Graecis θρησκεία, Act. 26, 5. Latinis *Religio* dictus est, quam vocem Augustinus, *de vera Religion.*[a] post Lactantium, *Institut.* Lib. 4. cap. 48.[b] a religando deducit, quia per religionem uni Deo religamus animas nostras; ut religio* a vinculo pietatis sit dicta, quo homo Deo constringitur; et non male a Cicerone, lib. 2. *de invent.*[c] descripta, quae superioris cujusdam naturae, quam divinam vocant, curam ceremoniamque affert.

II Religioni in excessu opponitur, quam Graeci δεισιδαιμονίαν, Latini superstitionem dixerunt; non quod in religione possit aliquis in excessu peccare secundum absolutam* quantitatem, sed secundum eam tantum, quam vocant proportionis; quae in ea re duo requirit, 1. Ut non colatur quod coli non debet. 2. Non exhibeatur ei qui debet coli, cultus praeter ejus voluntatem* superinductus.

---

[a] Augustine, *De vera religione* 55.111 (CCSL 32:259). [b] Erroneous reference; correct to Lactantius, *Institutiones divinae* 4.28 (CSEL 19/1:389). [c] Cicero, *De inventione* 2.22.66 and 53.161 does speak about *religio*, but not in the way it is used in this disputation. For the latter, one should consult Cicero's *De natura deorum* 2.28.72 instead, where a connection is indeed drawn between *religio* and *religare*.

DISPUTATION 19

On Idolatry

President: Andreas Rivetus
Respondent: Samuel Bochartus[1]

The Law of God,[2] which was treated in the previous disputation, puts before us that we must worship only that "Lawgiver who has the power to save and to destroy" (James 4:12) and that we must do so by the inward and outward worship which He himself has revealed and commanded in his Word. This worship is commonly called *ʿevada* in Hebrew (Exodus 12:26), *thrēskeia* in Greek (Acts 26:5), and *religio* in Latin, a word which Augustine (*On True Religion*), following Lactantius (*Institutes* Book 4, chapter 28) derives from *religare* ['to bind, tie'] because through religion* "we bind our souls to the one God," so that 'religion' is the word for the fetter of piety which fastens man to God. And Cicero, in Book 2 of *On Invention*, rightly described it as "that which offers homage and reverence to anything of a higher nature that is called divine."

Over against 'religion,' and by way of excess, is placed what the Greeks called *deisidaimonia* ['fear of demons'] and the Latins 'superstition'; not because someone can sin in religion by excess according to absolute* quantity, but only according to so-called quantity of proportion.[3] In this case the latter requires two things: That no worship is given to what should not be worshiped, and that to him who ought to be worshiped no worship is shown beyond what he wills.*

---

1   Born in 1599 in Rouen (France), Samuel Bochardus matriculated on 24 November 1620 in theology. He defended this disputation on 23 June 1621 and dedicated it to P. Molinaeus, theologian and pastor at Paris, and Joh. M. Langlaeus, pastor at Rouen. Thereafter he also studied in Sedan, Saumur, and Oxford. He was ordained in Caen in 1628 and became a distinguished scholar and polyglot; he died in 1667. See Du Rieu, *Album studiosorum*, 151 and http://en.wikisource.org/wiki/1911_Encyclopædia_Britannica/Bochart,_Samuel (accessed February 27, 2014).
2   Here and in the subsequent three disputations reference is made only to commandments from the first table of the law. The choice of these topics (idolatry, the oath, the Sabbath) seems to reflect the religious and social questions of the early seventeenth century.
3   In other words, we can never worship God too much (absolute quantity), but we can worship other things that should not be worshiped, or worship God in ways He does not wish to be worshiped (quantity of proportion).

III Hinc duae superstitionis species* distinguuntur; quarum illam, quae eo modo quo non oportet, cultum Deo instituit, ἐθελοθρησκείαν Scripturae vocant; alteram, qua colitur quod coli non debet, εἰδωλολατρείαν, sub qua aliquando utraque comprehenditur; quamvis non negemus illam praecise sumptam, ab hac distingui, cum non omnis superstitiosus sit proprie* idololatra, etsi omnis idololatra sit superstitiosus. De hac postrema nobis jam ex ordine agendum.

IV Dicitur Idololatria, nomine* ex duobus composito εἴδωλον et λατρεία, quasi Idoli cultus vel servitus; εἴδωλον autem, si vocis* etymum spectemus, ab εἴδεσθαι, quod Graecis sonat videri vel assimilari, ortum habet; et in genere apud auctores linguae Graecae probatos simulacrum et imaginem quamlibet significat,* sive mente conceptam, sive manu effictam, sive rei* exsistentis, sive non exsistentis. Non igitur est diminutivum, ut volunt adversarii, ab εἶδος propter defectum repraesentationis, quasi esset Idolum, rei quae non est, repraesentativum. Quod etiamsi contendat Bellarminus,[a] fatetur tamen Lorinus[b] et ipse Jesuita in cap. 17. Act. vers. 16. vocem hanc inter profanos auctores aeque late patere posse atque τοῦ εἰκόνος, et si latinitate utramque donemus, eandem esse significationem *Idoli et Iconis*, sive imaginis.

V Quod autem addit, usu ecclesiastico in malam semper partem accipi, id et nos agnoscimus, et pro Idolo habemus, non solum externam imaginem arte factam, ad repraesentandum et colendum numen, sive verum, sive fictum, sed etiam omne numen falsum, sine imagine, vel ab hominibus excogitatum, cum non sit; vel etiamsi res* aliqua sit subsistens, sed creatura cui divina aestimatio, vel cultus divinus tribuitur. Ideo recte Patres Concilii Francofurtensis[c]

---

[a] Bellarmine, *De ecclesia triumphante* 2.5 (= *De reliquiis et imaginibus sanctorum*; *Opera* 3:213a)
[b] Jean Lorin, *In Actus Apostolorum commentaria* (Cologne: Hierat, 1621; first ed. 1605), 523.   [c] See the corresponding note with the English translation.

Hence two sorts* of superstition are distinguished, of which the one establishes the worship of God in an inappropriate manner (which the Scriptures call 'self-willed worship'), and the other occurs when something is worshiped that ought not to be worshiped (which the Scriptures call 'idol-worship,' and which sometimes includes both sorts). We do not deny, however, that the former, strictly speaking, is distinguished from the latter, since not every superstitious person is strictly* an idol-worshiper (although every idolater is superstitious). We shall now treat this latter topic of idolatry.[4]

Idolatry is called by a name* made up of two parts, *eidōlon* and *latreia*, like the worship of, or slavery to an idol. Moreover the Greek word *eidōlon*, if we consider the word's* etymology, comes from *eidesthai*, which in Greek means "to seem; or to represent [as something]." And in general among respected writers in the Greek language it means* some likeness and image, whether conceived in the mind or fashioned by hand; and a likeness of something* that does or does not exist. Therefore the word *eidolon* is not, as our opponents would have it, a diminutive of *eidos* for its lack of representation, as though an idol is representative of something that doesn't exist. Even though this is what Bellarmine contends, still [Jean] Lorin,[5] himself also a Jesuit, on Acts 17:16 admits that this word can have a range of meaning among the pagan authors equally broad as the Greek word *eikōn*, and if we render both of them in Latin, the meaning of 'idol' and 'icon,' or image, would be the same.

But when he adds that in ecclesiastical usage the word is always understood in a negative sense, we agree; and we consider an 'idol' not only an external image that is skillfully made to represent a real or imaginary deity for worship, but also any false deity that has no image or that is the figment of man's imagination (since it is not real). It is an idol also if it is something* that exists but is a creature deemed to be a god, or on which divine worship is bestowed. Accordingly the fathers of the Council of Frankfurt rightly said that "they do not

---

4 First the term 'idolatry' is discussed (theses 4–6), then its substance or real definition (theses 8–9). Formal subdivisions are treated next (10–14), and then the (historical) origin of idolatry (15) and the need of its abolition (16). This is followed by a long discussion of five kinds of contemporary Roman-Catholic idolatrous practices (17–26). Finally, there is a discussion of the lawful use of images (27–29), new heresies (30) and the punishments for idolatry (31–32).

5 Jean de Lorin (Joannes Lorinus, 1559–1634) was a French Jesuit who taught philosophy, exegesis and theology in Rome, Paris and Milan. He wrote extensive biblical commentaries, in which he often adapted patristic interpretations. Lorinus was also involved in the conversion of Jews in France and Italy.

dicebant, Se imagines Sanctorum non idola nuncupare, sed ne idola nuncuparentur, adorare se eas et colere, iisque servitium impendere nolle, *Capitularis* cap. M. lib. 2. c. 18.

VI Idolum etiam cum Apostolo, 1 Cor. 8, 4. nihil esse in mundo dicimus; non quidem, ut nonnulli male interpretantur, quod res in rerum natura* non exsistens idolo repraesentetur, Daemonia enim exsistunt, ipsorum tamen idolum nihil est; sed quia nihil tale est pro quali colitur, ut divinitatis opinionem vel cultum promereatur, aut ad salutem quicquam prodesse possit, quemadmodum idem Apostolus negat, 1 Cor. 10, 19. idolis immolatum, esse aliquid, quasi diceret, consecrationem ejus vanam esse. Haec igitur nihil dicuntur ratione* efficaciae, et quia nullius sunt momenti, et nihili facienda, ut nihil esse dicitur qui se putat esse aliquid, Gal. 6, 3., quo sensu in Scriptura idola dicuntur vanitates, falsitates, mendacium; ἐστὶ μὲν ἀλλ' οὐκ ἔχει τινὰ ἰσχύν, inquit Chrysostomus, *Hom.* 20. *in 1. ad Corinthos*.[a]

VII Nomen* autem λατρεία, etsi cum solum ponitur, saepe ad homines referatur, imo, ut Valla[b] notavit et exemplis probavit,* magis ad homines pertinuerit, et vana sit, si voces spectemus, λατρείας et δουλείας, in sensu ab adversariis

---

[a] John Chrysostom, *Homilia in Epistulam primam ad Corinthios* 20.1 (MPG 61:162).   [b] Lorenzo Valla, *Annotationes in Novum Testamentum* (Basel: n.p., 1526), In Matthaeum ch. 4, pp. 17–18.

call the images of the saints 'idols,' but that they did not wish to worship and honour them, or to pay homage to them, lest they be called 'idols'" (*Capitularis*, Chapter M, Book 2 heading 18).[6]

With the apostle [Paul] (1 Corinthians 8:4) we state also that an idol "is nothing in the world," though not, as some wrongly explain, because something that does not exist in reality* is portrayed by an idol; for demons do exist, yet an idol of them is nothing. But an idol is nothing in the world because it is not at all like the thing for which it is worshiped, that it should earn the recognition or worship as a god, or be of any benefit for salvation. The same apostle, in 1 Corinthians 10:19, denies that sacrifice to idols is anything, as if to say that the consecration of it is useless. Thus they are called "nothing" because* they lack effectiveness and carry no weight, and should be considered as nothing, in the same manner as he "who considers himself to be something" is "nothing" (Galatians 6:3), and in this sense the idols in Scripture are called "vanities," "falsehoods," "a lie." Chrysostom says: "It may exist, but it has no power" (*Homily* 20, on 1 Corinthians).

But the word* *latreia* ['due service'], even when it occurs by itself, often refers to what is owed to human beings; in fact, as Valla has observed and demonstrated* by means of examples, it applied more frequently to human beings.[7] And the distinction between *latreia* and *douleia* ['bondage, servitude'],

---

6 The Council of Frankfurt (794), presided over by Charlemagne, dealt with the decisions of the Second Council of Nicea (787) about the veneration of icons. The Council of Nicea had distinguished between *latreia* (adoration), which is owed only to God, and *proskunēsis*, the equivalent of *duleia* in the sense of veneration or reverence paid to icons or to saints (cf. DH 601). Later Western theologians used the Latinized term *latria* for the adoration of God and *dulia* for the worship of saints (and sometimes *huperdulia* for the worhip of Mary). How the veneration of images related to that of their prototypes (i.e., of God, Christ, Mary, saints, angels) was a matter of discussion among theologians: see thesis 23.

The Council of Frankfurt used a Latin translation of the original Greek acts of the Second Council of Nicea that missed the crucial distinction in Greek between *latreia* and *proskunēsis*, as it rendered both with the Latin '*adoratio*.' Contrary to what Rivetus suggests, the quotation is not from the acts of the Frankfurt Council, but from the *Opus Caroli Regis contra synodum* (formerly known as the *Libri Carolini* or as the *Caroli Magni Capitulare de Imaginibus*), a set of four books composed around 790 by order of Charlemagne, in order to refute the decisions of the second Council of Nicea; See Ann Freeman and Paul Meyvaert, eds., *Opus Caroli contra synodum*. Monumenta Germania Historiae, Leges, Concilia, 2, Suppl. 1 (Hannover: Hahnsche Buchhandlung, 1998), lib. IV, c. 18, p. 532. See further Thomas F.X. Noble, *Images, Iconoclasm, and the Carolingians* (Philadelphia: University of Pennsylvania Press, 2009), 158–206.

7 Lorenzo (Laurentius) Valla (c. 1406–1457), Italian humanist, rhetorician, and educator. After a brief stint as professor of rhetoric at the University of Padua, Valla became a travelling scholar. He was famous for his elegant style, and for unmasking some erroneous attributions

excogitato, distinctio; tamen in compositione τοῦ εἰδώλου, fatemur accipi pro cultu religioso, et omnibus ad eum pertinentibus, qualia sunt adoratio, invocatio, fiducia, eucharistia, sacrificium, juramentum, vota, Templorum, Altarium et Festorum consecrationes, etc, quae Augustinus his verbis comprehendit: Cultus divinitati, vel si expressius dicendum, Deitati debitus, est cum sacra facimus, sacrificamus, vel aliqua nostra, seu nos ipsos, religiosis ritibus consecramus, *De Civ. Dei*, lib. 10. c. 1.[a]

VIII Est igitur Idololatria, ad rem quod attinet, σεβάζεσθαι καὶ λατρεύειν τῇ κτίσει παρὰ τὸν κτίσαντα, id est, colere ac servire rebus creatis, praeterito creatore, Rom. 1, 25. Superstitio, qua debitus soli Deo cultus, religiosus nempe quivis ei exhibetur, cui non debet exhiberi, sive creatura sit, sive figmentum humanum; qua significatione, salva nominis proprietate, Idololatriae vox hanc habet extensionem, ut sit in genere, religiosa latria creaturae, sive ea animo tantum fiat, sive corporali et externo cultu, sive in imagine, sive sine ea; nam et dracones et serpentes, item ignem, ventum, aërem, solem, lunam et stellas, alioqui religiose coluerunt; nec ab Idololatriae crimine absolvuntur Romani toto illo tempore, nempe centum septuaginta annorum ab urbe condita, quo apud eos Templa sine imaginibus aut simulacris fuisse testatur Plutarchus in

---

[a] Augustine, *De civitate Dei* 10.1 (CCSL 47:272).

of authorship, most notably the so-called Donation of Constantine. During the last decade of his life, he served as secretary to pope Nicholas V.

in the sense that has been thought up by our opponents, is pointless if we consider the actual words.⁸ Even so, we grant that in conjunction with the words 'of an idol,' *latreia* is used for religious worship and all that pertains to it (things such as adoration, invocation, the placing of trust, the eucharist, sacrifice, oath, vows, the dedication of temples, altars and feasts, etc.). All this Augustine summarizes with these words: "Worship that is owed to the divinity, or, to express it more precisely, to the deity, occurs when we render things sacred, make sacrifices, or when we dedicate something that belongs to us, or even ourselves, by means of religious rites" (*On the City of God*, book 10, chapter 1).⁹

And so a real definition of idol-worship is "worshiping and paying homage to the created thing while ignoring the Creator" (Romans 1:25). Superstition occurs when any worship that is owed to God only is shown in a religious way to something that ought not to receive it, whether it be a creature or a figment of the human mind.¹⁰ By this definition (and keeping the proper force of the word) 'idolatry' has the extended meaning that it is 'the religious worship of a creature' generally, either in the heart only or in outward, physical worship (with or without an image). For people have bestowed religious worship also upon dragons and snakes, as well as fire, wind, air, sun, moon and stars. Nor are the Roman people absolved from the charge of idolatry for that whole period of time, namely the one hundred and seventy years after the founding of the city, when, Plutarch testifies in the *Life of Numa*,¹¹ their temples were without images

8

---

8   See note 6 above.
9   Augustine plays upon the words *sacra facere* (to make sacred things) and *sacrificere* (to sacrifice).
10 Rivetus adopts the Greek verb *latreuein* from Rom. 1:25. In doing so, he seems to suggest that the distinction between *latreia* and *douleia* also is not warranted by Scripture. See also thesis 9.
11 Plutarch (c. AD 46–120), from Chaeronea in Greece, studied at Delphi during the reign of Nero. He attempted to revive and purify popular pagan religion. According to him, there is but one God and all other gods are but personifications of this one God (*De Iside et Osiride* 377F; *Isis and Osiris* [Loeb Classical Library, vol. 5, 1936], section 67). Besides philosophical writings, he produced biographies (*Bioi Paralleloi*) of distinguished Greeks and Romans, such as king Numa, which is referenced in SPT 19.8. According to George Karamanolis, Plutarch is the first "to distinguish different levels of ethical life, namely the civic/practical and the theoretical/purified ones, depending on whether virtue pertains to the soul as organizing principle for one's daily life, or to the intellect as one's guide to knowledge of Forms." See George Karamanolis, "Plutarch," *The Stanford Encyclopedia of Philosophy* (Fall 2010 Edition), ed. Edward N. Zalta, accessed February 27, 2014, http://plato.stanford.edu/archives/fall2010/entries/plutarch/.

vita Numae,ᵃ quia nondum tunc ingenia Graecorum atque Tuscorum fingendis simulacris urbem inundaverant, ut scite Tertul. *Apol*. c. 25.ᵇ

IX   In hac definitione Genus* est *Superstitio*, de qua dictum est. Objectum est, quicquid non est Deus verus. Forma sive differentia, consistit in cultu religioso qualicumque, de quo nihil aut parum refert, quocumque vocabulo aut phrasi exprimatur, nempe verbo λατρεύειν, vel δουλεύειν, vel σέβειν, vel προσκυνεῖν, dummodo ex re ipsa constet, religiosum et divinum esse cultum, qui soli Deo debeatur, cum Scriptura promiscue et indifferenter haec verba, colere, adorare, servire, invocare, etc. usurpet, ubi de solo Deo rite colendo disserit.

X   Nec opus est addere ad perfectam definitionem, clausulam sicut Deo, qua Idololatriam velare nonnulli ex Jesuitis conantur, quasi Idololatria non committeretur, nisi ab eo qui divinum cultum creaturae exhiberet hoc animo, ut existimatio talis creaturae conciliaretur, qualis in solum Deum vere competit. Hoc enim falsum esse, patet ex eo, quod ipsi Pontificii fatentur, multos inter Ethnicos, non unum Spiritum in idolis coluisse, sed diversos, gradibus quasi inter se distantes, ut iis quidem fuerit unus Deus supremus, sed sub ipso alii minores Dii, substantiae* nimirum spirituales a summo Deo creatae; in quarum tamen cultu Idololatriam commiserunt, etsi eos non coluerint cum summa voluntatis inclinatione et prostratione, cum apprehensione Dei ut primi principii* et ultimi finis,* atque adeo summi boni, quae ad essentiam cultus divini requirit Bellarminus, *De Sanct. beat*. l. 1. c. 12.ᶜ quam paucis et melius describit Nazianz. τὴν μετάθεσιν τῆς προσκυνήσεως ἀπὸ τοῦ πεποιηκότος ἐπὶ τὰ κτίσματα, translationem cultus creatoris ad creaturam, *Orat*. 38.ᵈ Alioqui Dominus non recte respondisset Satanae, eum ad προσκύνησιν religiosam invitanti, scriptum esse, Dominum Deum tuum adorabis et ei soli λατρεύσεις, Luc. 4, 8. cum Satan non peteret ab eo ut se agnosceret primum principium, sed talem tantum cui potestas et gloria regnorum mundi data erat.

ᵃPlutarch, *Vita Numae* 8.8.2.   ᵇTertullian, *Apologeticus* 25.13 (CCSL 1:137).   ᶜBellarmine, *De Ecclesia triumphante* 1.12 (= *De beatitudine et canonizatione sanctorum*; *Opera* 3:168a).   ᵈGregory of Nazianzus, *Oratio* 38.13 (SC 358:132).

or likenesses, because "at that time the Greeks' and Etruscans' inventions for making likenesses had not yet flooded the city," as Tertullian (*Apology* 25) nicely states.

According to this definition the *genus** is 'superstition,' about which we spoke. The *object* is anything that is not the true God. The *form* or the difference exists in the religious worship, however that may be, for it makes little or no difference with what word or phrase it is expressed (*latreuein, douleuein, sebein* or *proskunein*)[12] so long as it is clear from the matter itself that it is religious and divine worship that is owed only to God; for Scripture uses these verbs 'to worship,' 'to adore,' 'to serve,' 'to call upon,' etc., loosely and indiscriminately when dealing with the proper worship of God alone.

For a complete definition it is not necessary also to add the phrase 'as to God,' whereby some of the Jesuits try to cover up idolatry, as if idolatry is committed only when someone shows divine worship to a creature with the intent "that such estimation as befits God alone be granted to a creature."[13] The falsehood in this is clear from the fact that the papal teachers themselves admit that many heathens did not worship one spirit in their idols, but several different ones, as if they were distinguished from each other by degrees; thus they did indeed have one supreme God, but below him other, lesser gods (namely spiritual beings* created by that supreme God). In worshiping these gods they did commit idolatry, even though they did not honour them with "the utmost inclination and prostration of the will, and with the intellectual understanding of God as the first principle* and the final goal,* and so as the highest good"—which things Bellarmine considers essential requirements for divine worship (*On the Blessedness of the Saints*, Book 1, chapter 12). All of this [Gregory of] Nazianzus presents concisely and better as "the transference of worship from the Creator to the creature" (*Oratio* 38). If this were not so, the Lord's response would not have been correct when Satan invited him to religious prostration [*proskunēsis*], that it is written: "You shall worship the Lord your God and him only shall you serve (*latreuseis*)" (Luke 4:8). For Satan had not asked Jesus to acknowledge him as "the first principle," but only as the one "to whom had been given the power and the glory" of the kingdoms of the world.

9

10

---

12   These terminological distinctions—though deemed irrelevant by Rivetus—were very important for the Orthodox and Roman Catholic Church: see note 6 above and thesis 28.

13   Here Rivetus seems to be paraphrasing the position of the Jesuit theologian Gregory of Valencia (ca. 1550–1603), in his *Apologeticus de Idolatria adversus impium libellum Iacobi Heerbrandi lutherani* (Ingolstadt: Sartorius, 1579), 26–28.

XI   Non ergo excusatur ab Idololatria, qui cultum religiosum tribuit rei quam novit Deum non esse; nam, quicquid contra sentiat, cum adorat, invocat et genu flectit, id dicitur pro Deo habere in Scriptura, quod alioqui secundum suam opinionem pro Deo non habet; quod etiam agnoscunt Scholastici,* qui distinguunt inter speculativam et practicam Divinitatis attributionem creaturis. Qui enim illis Divinitatem negant speculative, quantum ad cognitionem pertinet; practice tamen, id est, actu et re ipsa illis independentiam a Creatore suo attribuunt. Sic Idololatra fuit Varro, qui exterius Idola colebat, non ex opinione insitae iis Divinitatis, sed voluntate conformandi se populo, ut testatur August. Cujus etiam judicio, eo damnabilius agebat Seneca, quod illa quae mendaciter agebat, sic agebat ut eum populus veraciter agere existimaret, *De Civit. Dei*, lib. 1. cap. 6. et ejus. lib. cap. 10.ᵃ

XII   Ad Idololatriam pertinet etiam cultus Divinus, non solum cum creaturae exhibetur relicto Deo, sed etiam cum colitur religiose creatura simul cum Deo, sive sit imago manufacta, sive res alia artificialis vel naturalis* extra Dei praescriptum ad adorationem assumpta: non solum quia cum homines novum et fictitium constituunt cultum, novum etiam et fictitium constituunt Deum; quo sensu idem Augustinus dicit, lib. 1. *De Consen. Evang.* c. 15.ᵇ renuisse gentes Ebraeorum Deum colere, quoniam si alio modo Deum colere vellent quam se colendum ipse dixisset, non utique illum colerent, sed quod ipsi finxissent; quae ratio ad secundam superstitionis speciem magis pertinet, nempe ad modum* colendi Deum; sed praesertim, quia quod non debet coli, religiose adoratur, etiamsi factum sit ad repraesentandum Deum. Ibi enim dupliciter peccatur, 1. quia contra expressum Dei Verbum,* quo prohibet ne quis eum ulla specie exprimat, effingitur Deo figura, infinita ipsius Majestate prorsus indigna. 2. quia in societatem cultus cum Deo admittitur.

ᵃ Erroneous reference; correct to Augustine, *De civitate Dei* 6.10 (CCSL 47:183). Seneca's work itself is no longer extant.   ᵇ Erroneous reference; correct to Augustine, *De consensu evangelistarum* 1.18.26 (CSEL 43:24–25).

19. ON IDOLATRY 463

Therefore whoever bestows religious worship on something which he knows is not God is not excused; for whatever contrary thoughts he may be having when he worships, invokes, and kneels, Scripture calls that "to consider as God," despite the fact that in his own opinion he does not consider it as God. This is acknowledged by even the schoolmen,* who make a distinction between the "speculative" and the "practical" attribution of divinity to creatures. For people who deny creatures the status of divinity "in a speculative way" as far as their understanding is concerned, nevertheless do bestow it "in practice"; that is, by their action and in reality, they do bestow on them a state of independence from their Creator. Thus Varro[14] was an idolator, as he was worshiping idols outwardly, not from the conviction that they possessed an innate Divinity, but for the purpose of conforming to the common people, as Augustine testifies, in whose judgment "also the conduct of Seneca was all the more damnable because what he did falsely he did in such a way that the people thought that he was doing it truthfully" (*On the City of God*, book 1, chapter 6; and of the same book, chapter 10).

Besides idolatry in the form of religious worship shown to a creature after God has been rejected, there is also the worship of a creature who is honoured alongside and with God, whether that creature be a hand-made image or some other thing (either artificial or natural*) chosen for worship without God's command. Firstly, because when men make up and establish a new form of worship, they also make up and establish a new God. In this sense the same Augustine says, that the Hebrew tribes refused to honour God, "because if they wanted to honour God in a way different than He had said he should be honoured, they would not at all be honouring Him but whatever they had invented" (*On the Harmony of the Gospels*, Book 1, chapter 15). This manner of idolatry belongs more to the second kind of superstition (i.e., to the mode* of honouring God). Secondly, and more fundamentally, because it is idolatry when something that should not be honoured is worshiped in a religious manner, even though it is made as a representation of God. For then two sins are being committed: 1. Because contrary to the expressed Word *of God which prohibits anyone from portraying any likeness of Him, a figure of God is being fashioned that is entirely unworthy of his infinite majesty. 2. Because it introduces a worship in association with the worship of God.

11

12

---

14 Marcus Terentius Varro (116–27 BC). Born into a noble family, Varro pursued a political and military career. He also was a prolific writer of more than 74 works. For our knowledge of history of Roman culture, especially his *Nine Books of Disciplines* and his *Chronology* are important.

XIII   Frustra enim et falso contendunt Pontificii, in Vetere Testamento non reperiri exemplum, in quo ad Idololatriam revocata sit adoratio veri Dei, in imagine, cum imagine, vel per imaginem facta; cum Scriptura diserte testetur, vituli adoratores in deserto publicasse festum Jehovae, Ex. 32, 1. et Micham post effictam fusilem imaginem quae Teraphim vocatur, Jud. 17, 4. ex argento quod diserte scribitur dedicatum fuisse Jehovae, dixisse, nunc novi Jehovam benefacturum esse mihi, ibid. versus 13. et cultum vitulorum Jeroboam, dictum fuisse timorem Jehovae, 2 Reg. 17, 28. adeo ut Jehu qui vitulorum fuit patronus, et non recessit a peccatis Jeroboam, gloriaretur tamen apud Jonadabum de zelo suo pro Jehova, 2 Reg. 10, 16.

XIV   Nec obstat quod Scriptura vitulos illos alienos Deos appellat, quod Judaeos dicit Daemoniis non Deo immolasse, obtulisse sacrificium Idolo, etc, non agitur enim illis locis, de hominum adorantium sensu et existimatione aut intentione, sed de veritate rei ex judicio Dei, verbo et facto testantis, cultum illum contra verbi praescriptum usurpatum, sibi displicuisse, et Daemonem auctorem habuisse; etsi secundus hic Idololatriae modus a primo quo creatura pro Deo directe colitur, gradibus differat, quos gradus etiam Scriptura distinguit in Achabo, cum ait, 1 Reg. 16, 31. leve illi fuisse ambulare in peccatis Jeroboam, abiisse et servivisse Baal, incurvavisseque se ei, quae graduum distinctio locum non haberet, si Jeroboam statuisset directam vitulorum adorationem sine relatione* ad Deum Israëlis.

XV   De origine Idololatriae non est quod longum contentionis funem ducamus, si originem referamus ad tempus quo coepit. Si de Idololatria, ut ita dicam, spirituali, quaestio intelligatur, non dubitamus, eam a daemonibus suggestam hominibus illis qui veri Dei ignorantia primum laborarunt, et vanis affectibus sese dediderunt. Si de Idololatria externa, per signa et imagines quaeratur; de tempore etiam nihil potest certi responderi. De occasione, fere omnes ex libro Sapientiae, primos existimant fuisse Idolorum auctores qui hunc honorem detulerunt mortuis, ut eorum memoriam superstitiose colerent, cum acerbo luctu dolens pater, cito rapti filii sibi fecit imaginem, etc., quem locum varii

19. ON IDOLATRY

For it is a pointless and wrong contention of the papal theologians that no instance is found in the Old Testament where the worship of the true God in an image, or with or through an image, is referred to as idolatry. For Scripture clearly testifies that those who worshiped the calf in the desert had declared a public feast to the Lord (Exodus 32:1) and that Micha, after the molten image (which was called *Terafim*, Judges 17:4) was fashioned from the silver [money] that is recorded explicitly as dedicated to the Lord, had said: "Now I know that the Lord will prosper me" (Judges 17:13). And Scripture states that the worship of the calves of Jeroboam was called "the fear of the Lord" (2 Kings 17:28).[15] Indeed Jehu, who was a defender of worshiping the calves, and "who did not depart from the sins of Jeroboam," nevertheless boasted to Jonadab about his zeal for the Lord (2 Kings 10:16).

The fact that Scripture calls those calves "foreign gods" is not an objection; nor that it states the Jews had made offerings to devils and not to God; that they "had offered sacrifice to an idol," etc. For these passages are not concerned with the thinking and intentions of the people who are worshiping, or with their motivations; but they concern the fact of the matter from the perspective of God's judgment, who testifies in word and deed that this worship, undertaken contrary to the prescript of his Word, was displeasing to Him and that it was the devil who had started it. Even so, this second mode of idolatry differs by degrees from the first, wherein a creature is directly honoured as God. Scripture, too, distinguishes these degrees in the case of Ahab when it says (1 Kings 16:31): "It was a light thing for him to walk in the sins of Jeroboam; to have gone and served Baal, and to have bowed down before him." This difference in degrees would be out of place if Jeroboam had established a direct worship of the calves, without any reference* to the God of Israel.

Concerning the origin of idolatry there is no need for us to pursue a long line of controversy if we take 'origin' to mean the time in which it began. If the question is understood to be about spiritual idolatry (to put it that way) then we do not doubt that devils suggested it to people who first struggled in their ignorance of the true God, and who gave themselves over to false emotions. If the question concerns outward idolatry through "signs and images," then too nothing certain can be said about the time. About the opportunity for idolatry nearly everyone thinks from the book of Wisdom that the first makers of idols were those who bestowed this honour upon the deceased, in order to give superstitious honour to their memory—when "a father mourning with bitter grief, made for himself an image of the child who suddenly had been taken

---

15 The reference is most likely to 1 Kings 12:28.

varie exponunt, inter quos ii rem acu tangere videntur, qui non primum Idololatriae principium, sed magis tritum et publicum auctorem indicasse referunt; ubi tamen notandum, auctorem illum, imagines filii a patre factas, Idola appellare, c. 14, 15.

XVI   Sed cum de re ipsa constet, non tam de origine litigandum, quam de abolitione laborandum, et iis liberandis qui hoc errore detinentur, saltem convincendis, qui verbis et exemplo Idololatriam promovent et stabiliunt; quales hoc tempore affirmamus esse Pontificios omnes, illos quidem seductos, hos vero seducentes, idque multis nominibus, et in variis capitibus.

XVII   Primum et praecipuum est in cultu Sacramentalis Panis in Eucharistia, quem illi non negant a se exhiberi plane Divinum, cum signo ad elevationem Hostiae dato, omnes, genibus flexis, aut toto corpore prostrato Sacramentum* adorant tamquam Deum suum; quam Idololatriam duplicant in circumgestatione Panis, praesertim in proprio ad id dicato festo, pronuntiantes anathema contra omnes, qui Sacramentum hoc latriae cultu, etiam externo, adorandum aut in Processionibus circumgestandum, aut publice ut adoretur, proponendum esse negant, *Concil. Trid.* Ses. 3. Can. 6.[a]

XVIII   Falsum enim est quod supponunt, vi Transubstantiationis nullum aliud hic esse suppositum* praeter Christum; cum, ipsis etiam fatentibus, accidentia* maneant, quae a Christo in personae* unitatem non sunt assumpta; et quae etsi merae creaturae sunt, ita adorantur, ut ad ea se referat primum adoratio et cultus omnis, qua ratione etiam agunt de adoratione Sacramenti; Deus autem non est Sacramentum. Accedit, quod certi esse non possunt de consecratione

---

[a] DH 1656 (read session "13" for "3").

from him" (*Wisdom of Solomon* 14:15). Different people explain this passage in different ways; of them the ones who seem to reach the gist of the matter tell us that the author had meant not the initial starting-point of idolatry but rather the well-worn, common one. On this point it should be noted that the author calls the images which the father made of the son "idols" (*Wisdom of Solomon* 14:15).

But seeing that there is certainty about the matter itself, we should work more towards abolishing idolatry than to enter into controversy over its origin. And we should seek to free (or at least convince) both those who are in the grip of the error of idolatry, and those who by their speech and example encourage and establish it. We affirm that all the papal theologians of our own day are such people, both those who are led astray and certainly those who mislead them by means of many names and in different chief points.

First and foremost is the worship of the sacramental bread in the Eucharist, which they admit they clearly portray as divine when all the people, after the signal has been given at the elevation of the host,[16] worship the sacrament* as if it is their god, and their knees are bent or their entire bodies are stretched out on the ground. They perpetrate a second act of idolatry in the ceremonial procession of the bread, particularly at the feast devoted specifically to it,[17] as they pronounce curses upon everyone "who states that this sacrament should not be adored with the worship of adoration (*latria*) (even outwardly), nor carried around in ceremonial procession, nor displayed in public for adoration" (Council of Trent, session 3, canon 6).[18]

For what they suppose is wrong, that by virtue of the transubstantiation there is no other 'supposit'* except Christ; while, as even they themselves admit, the accidents,* which Christ had not taken up into the unity of his person,* do remain present, and although they are merely created things, they are worshiped in such a way that adoration and all worship is directed primarily at them.[19] This is the reason for their adoration of the sacrament—but God is not a sacrament! And then there is the fact that they cannot be certain about

---

16   The 'signal' refers to the bell that is rung when the priest elevates the Host, after the words of consecration.

17   Here reference is made to the feast of Corpus Christi, which usually includes a procession of the Blessed Sacrament after the Mass.

18   DH 1656 (session 13—not 3—canon 6).

19   According to the doctrine of transubstantiation, the substance changes into the body and blood of Christ, while the accidents (size, shape, color, taste etc.) of the bread and the wine remain the same. The philosophical technical term 'supposit' signifies a subsistent individual substance.

vera Panis, quae pendet a ministri intentione, de qua cum apud illos non possit esse certitudo Fidei, cum Samaritanis adorant quod nesciunt, Joh. 4, 22.

XIX 2. Idololatriam committunt in cultu Sanctorum, tam Angelorum quam hominum, quos constat ab ipsis adorari, invocari, iis donaria cum religiosis ceremoniis offerri; iisdem, saltem ad praxin quod attinet, Deitatem affingi; cum ubique invocentur quasi essent infiniti; etiam mentis oratione, ac si cordium essent scrutatores, iis vota nuncupentur, quod Deo tantum competit; templa, altaria et festi dies in eorum honorem consecrentur. Quibus actionibus, aut ipsis opinionem Deitatis conciliare volunt, aut praecipuum Orthodoxorum argumentum pro Filii et Spiritus Sancti Deitate evertunt, imo in utrumque labuntur incommodum.

XX Quam Idololatriam in cultu B. Virginis Mariae ita conduplicant, ut nihil sive in verbis, sive in factis, Deo proprium relinquant: imo supra Christum Deum in aeternum benedictum, eandem evehant, tamquam quae ipsi etiam in hoc statu gloriae imperet. Sic enim illi: Quid est esse Matrem Dei. Mater est causa* Filii, Mater superior est Filio, Matri debetur honor a Filio, Matri tenetur morem gerere Filius.[a] Costerus (*in Hymn. Ave Maris Stella.*) qui etiam omnipotentiam in coelo et in terra eidem tribuit,[b] et alii, misericordiae regnum ejusdemque

---

[a] Franciscus Costerus, *Meditationes in Hymnum Ave Maris Stella* (Cologne: Hierat, 1600), 10.
[b] Costerus, *Meditationes*, 62.

the true consecration of the bread, which depends on the intention of the one who administers it; but since they cannot have any certainty of faith about the intention, they (along with the Samaritans) "worship what they do not know" (John 4:22).

Secondly, they commit idolatry by worshiping saints, both angels and humans, and everyone knows they adore and call upon them, and they present votive offerings to them in religious ceremonies. And they attach the status of deity to these saints, at least as far as the practice is concerned, because they are invoked everywhere as though they are infinite. And as if saints are able to search the hearts, they are vowed promises in the silent prayer of the soul, which befits God alone. Temples, altars, and holy days are consecrated to their honour. By these deeds, they either wish to acquire for them [i.e., the saints] the reputation of deity, or they overturn the principal argument of the orthodox for the divinity of the Son and the Holy Spirit.[20] Indeed, they slip and fall into both of these hazards.

They commit twice as much idolatry in worshiping the blessed virgin Mary—so much so that they leave nothing proper to God alone, in word or in deed. In fact they exalt her beyond the Christ, the God who is blessed unto eternity,[21] as though she rules over him even in this state of glory. For thus they speak: "What does it mean to be the Mother of God? The Mother is the cause* of the Son, the Mother is superior to the Son; honour is owed to the Mother by the Son, the Son is bound to comply with the Mother's wishes." [Francis] Coster[22] in the [*Meditations*] *upon the Hymn 'Hail, Star of the Sea'*, ascribes to her also "almighty power in heaven and on earth,"[23] and others state that God himself bestowed upon her "the realm of compassion, and the distribution of

---

20   Cf. *SPT* 8.30 and 9.27, where it is argued that only because the Son and the Holy Spirit are truly God, they are worthy of the veneration peculiar to God.
21   Romans 9:5. Note the difference between ancient and modern translations; see *SPT* 8.27, note 23.
22   Francis Coster (1531–1619) was born in Malinnes and died in Brussels. At the age of twenty-one he was one of the first to join the newly-formed Society of Jesus, and was welcomed by its founder, Ignatius of Loyola, who also appointed him as a lecturer in biblical theology in Cologne. He published sermons, meditations, a catechism, and other works in Latin, Dutch, and German. One of his opponents was Francis Gomarus. See Arie-Jan Gelderblom, Jan L. de Jong, and Marc van Vaeck, eds., *Yearbook for Early-Modern Studies*, 3–2003, *The Low Countries as a Crossroads of Religious Beliefs* (Leiden: Brill, 2004).
23   Costerus, *Meditationes*, 62.

dispensationem, Biel in *Can. Missae* lect. 80.ᵃ ipsi a Deo mandatam, reservato sibi justitiae regno. Unde factum est, quod post Bonaventuram, in Psalmo in eum finem composito, omnia quae in Psalmis Deo et Christo tribuuntur, *Domini* nomine in *Dominae* mutato, per summum sacrilegium adjudicent.

XXI 3. Ejusdem criminis rei sunt, cum Sanctorum, praesertim Martyrum corporibus (si tamen Martyrum, ut cum Augustino, *de opere Monach.* cap. 28.ᵇ excipiam) corporum particulis aut reliquiis quibusvis, vim quandam supernaturalem* affixam statuunt, qua in modum physicarum causarum, et non solum efficacia, ut loquuntur, morali, proprie morbos abigere, daemonia ejicere, et contactu suo benedictiones corporis et animae conferre contendunt; eorundem Sanctorum membra, cineres, vestes, etc. religiose colunt et adorant, eadem ad cultum e sepulcris eruunt, asservant in templis, includunt aureis et argenteis thecis, in processionibus circumgestant. Quibus cum divinam virtutem ascribant, in iisdem fiduciam collocent, in loco religioso easdem ad cultum proponant, iis suffitum offerant, adorabundi coram iis procidant, dies festos ad earum cultum consecrent, ad earum tactum juramentum praestent, ut religionem iis majorem concilient, votivas peregrinationes instituant; apertam ab iis et multiplicem Idololatriam committi, non est quod dubitemus; cujus horrendae profanationis, hoc jam de ipsis sumpsit supplicium Deus, quod excaecati, falsis et suppositis reliquiis delusi sint, et acciderit saepe ut eorum corpora adoraverint in terris, quorum animae torquentur in inferis; praeter socordiam illam

---

ᵃ Gabriel Biel, *Sacri canonis missae expositio* (1499), lectio 80.   ᵇ Augustine, *De opere Monachorum* 28.36 (CSEL 41:585).

it" while keeping for himself the realm of justice ([Gabriel] Biel,[24] Lecture 80 of the *Canon of the Mass*). Hence it happened that after Bonaventure, in a psalm composed for this purpose, they assign to her everything that in the Psalms is attributed to God and Christ, through the greatest sacrilege—by changing the word "Lord" to "Lady."[25]

Thirdly, they are guilty of that sin when they think of the bodies of saints and especially martyrs (that is, if they even were martyrs, as I would object, with Augustine [*On the Work of Monks*, chapter 28]) that some supernatural* power is attached to them, or to their body-parts, or to whatever remains. By this power that acts like a physical cause and not merely, as they say, by moral effectiveness, they claim properly to cure diseases, drive out demons, and by touching them bestow blessings upon one's body and soul. They devotedly worship and adore the limbs, ashes, clothing, etc., of these saints, and they dig them out of their graves to worship them, and preserve them in churches, and lock them up in gold and silver boxes, and carry them around in processions. And because they assign divine powers to them, they place their trust in them, and put them on display in sacred places to worship them; they offer them incense, and fall down before them in order to adore them; they consecrate holy days for worshiping them, swear oaths by touching them, and, to obtain greater reverence for them, they undertake promised pilgrimages. There is no reason for us to doubt that these people commit blatant and repeated idolatry, and in return for this horrible profanity God has already exacted punishment from them. For in their utter blindness they have been deceived by these false and supposed relics, and it has often happened that "they adore on earth the bodies of those whose souls are being tormented in hell." Besides that there is

21

---

24   Gabriel Biel (c. 1410–1495), German theologian. He joined the Canons Regular of the Congregation of Windesheim, an order affiliated with the Brethern of the Common Life. After completing his philosophical and theological studies in Heidelberg, Erfurt, and Cologne, Biel served his Congregation in several positions. In the early 1480's, Biel cooperated with Duke Eberhard of Württemerg in founding the University of Tübingen. In 1484 he was appointed as the first professor of Theology, a position he held until his death in 1495. His theology is nominalistic, but also indebted to Thomas Aquinas. His major works are the *Canonis Missae Expositio* (*Exposition of the Canon of the Mass*) a theological commentary on the Mass and the *Collectorium*, a commentary on the *Sentences* of Peter Lombard. Biel's works played an important role in the theological training of the young Luther.

25   During the Middle Ages, Psalters of the Blessed Virgin Mary were formed by adding to each psalm a phrase (antiphone) that referred it to Mary. In a later stage the psalms were omitted so that only the antiphones remained. A well-known Mary Psalter was attributed to Bonaventure, but his authorship is (correctly) denied by Rivetus. See also the article "Rosary," in *New Catholic Encyclopedia* (2nd ed.; Detroit: Gale, 2003), 12: 373–376.

qua brutorum etiam animalium ossa, non raro pro humanis deosculati sunt, ut Genevae ante lucis ortum, cervinum membrum pro Antonii brachio, et pumicem aridum pro Petri cerebro.

XXII 4. Multiplicis item Idololatriae convincuntur in efformatione et cultu variarum imaginum Dei et Sanctorum. Imagines enim s. s. Trinitatis effingere praesumunt, contra expressam Dei prohibitionem, caventis serio, ne ullam ei similitudinem exprimamus, Deut. 4, 15. quod etiam fieri non posse* testatur Scriptura, Es. 4, 18. Act. 17, 29. Rom. 1, 13. cui Patres omnes qui de hac re scripserunt, consentiunt usque ad Damascenum[a] alias Iconolatram, qui tamen summae esse insipientiae et impietatis Deum figurare fatetur, eumque sequentes inter Pontificios: Abulensis, Peresius, Hesselius et alii, agnoscente ipso Bellarm.

---

[a] John of Damascus, *De fide orthodoxa* 89 (= 4.16; SC 540:238).

the dimwittedness wherein they have lovingly bestowed kisses upon the bones of even dumb animals, thinking that they were human (as happened in Geneva before the light dawned there); so too for a deer-limb mistaken for the arm of Anthony, and a wrinkled pumice-stone for the brain of Peter.[26]

Fourthly, convicted of manifold idolatry are those who fashion and worship various images of God and of the saints. For they make so bold as to create images of the most holy Trinity, contrary to the explicit prohibition of God, who earnestly warns us not to make any likeness of him (Deuteronomy 4:15). Scripture even testifies that this cannot* be done (Isaiah 40:18; Acts 17:29; Romans 1:23), and all the church-fathers who have written about this matter are in agreement on this, even including John Damascene, who is also known as 'the icon-worshiper' and nevertheless admitted that "it is an act of utmost folly and impiety to make an image of God." And so too those among the papal teachers who followed him: Abulensis,[27] Peresius,[28] Hesselius,[29] and others, as

22

---

26   The examples are taken from Calvin's 'A Treatise on Relics,' originally published in 1543. See: John Calvin, *Traité des reliques*, (reprint; Geneva: Labor et Fides, 2000), 24.

27   Abulensis ('someone from Avila') is Alonso (Tostado) Fernández de Madrigal (1400–1455), a Spanish exegete. In 1441 he obtained the degrees of Master of Arts and Bachelor of Theology from the University of Salamanca. He was appointed bishop of Avila in 1449. As an exegete, Abulensis commented on the historical books of the Old Testament, and wrote four tomes on the Gospel of Matthew. Bellarmine, in the chapter "On Images," refers to his comments on the worship of images in Deuteronomy 4 in a discussion of Calvin's opinion that some Catholics oppose the making of images of God. The three authors mentioned are Abulensis, Durandus, and Peresius, but not Hesselius, who is named by Rivetus. Bellarmine concedes that the making of images of God is a matter of opinion, not faith. Nevertheless, he disagrees with Calvin's reasoning from this kind of prohibition to a general condemnation. See Richard Viladesau, *The Triumph of the Cross: The Passion of Christian Theology and the Arts, From the Renaissance to the Counter-Reformation* (Oxford: Oxford University Press, 2007), 213.

28   Peresius, or Martin Perez d'Ayala (1504–1566), was bishop of Cadix and later archbishop of Valencia. He studied in Alcalá, Salamanca and Louvain and was professor in philosophy and theology in Granada. He attended the Diet of Worms in 1545, where the Protestants turned down the idea of a general council of the whole Church. Perez participated in several sessions of the general Council of Trent (1545–1563) and advocated a reformation of the Catholic Church. In his doctrine, he stressed the divine origin of the episcopacy and argued for 'Tradition' as the comprehensive source of faith. His most famous work is *De divinis, apostolicis atque ecclesiasticis traditionibus* (*On Divine, Apostolic, and Ecclesiastical Traditions*, 1549).

29   Johannes Hesselius (1522–1566), or Jan Hessels, was a Louvain professor in theology and participant in the final session of the Council of Trent. He was critical of scholastic speculations and supported a positive theology based on Scripture and the Fathers. Among his

De Imag. lib. 3. cap. 8.[a] qui etsi sacrilegium illud palliare conetur, adductis quibusdam locis ex Scriptura, in quibus membra humana Deo tribuuntur, vel apparitiones quaedam describuntur, in quibus effectus, judicia, vel opera Dei metaphorice adumbrantur, quae ab hominibus non possunt aut debent exprimi, eo tandem deducitur ut dicat in Ecclesia Romana non esse tam certum, an sint faciendae imagines Dei sive Trinitatis, quam Christi et Sanctorum, quia hoc ad fidem pertinet, illud est in opinione. Si in opinione tantum sit, an sint faciendae, certe multo magis an sint colendae. At non potest* esse cultus Deo gratus qui fit sine fide; ingratissimus autem est qui fit contra fidem, qualis hic est de quo agimus.

XXIII In cultu imaginum Sanctorum hominum, quas Synodus Nicaena[b] sub Irene perfecte adorandas decrevit, etsi inter recentiores Papistas varii sint loquendi modi, quibusdam rotunde profitentibus, Imagines Trinitatis et Christi eadem esse adoratione colendas, qua prototypi, nec duas sed unam et eandem esse adorationem, quod docuit Thomas, part. 3. q. 25. art. 3.[c] aliis, et praesertim novis Jesuitis, varias distinctiones excogitantibus; convenit tamen inter omnes, 1. lmagines apud eos ad cultum religiosum consecrari. At Imaginum consecratio est Idololatria, inquit Tertul. lib. *De Idolol.* cap. 4.[d] 2. Conjuncte concipi cum exemplari quod adoratur, easque adorari non solum per accidens* vel improprie,* sed etiam per se et proprie, ita ut terminent venerationem, ut in se considerantur, eoque cultu qui analogice* et reductive pertinet ad speciem ejus cultus qui debetur exemplari; neque dicendum eas improprie esse venerandas, quia quod non dicitur nisi improprie, simpliciter negari potest. Quae omnia sunt Bellarmini *De imaginibus*, cap. 21. Et cap. 25.[e] qui propterea cum Baronio,[f] Ecclesiae Gallicanae Episcopos, qui Ludovico Pio regnante, in Synodo

---

[a] Erroneous reference; correct to Bellarmine, *De Ecclesia triumphante* 2.8 (= *De reliquis et imaginibus sanctorum*; *Opera* 3:219a).   [b] DH 601.   [c] Thomas Aquinas, *Summa theologiae* 3.25.3.   [d] Tertullian, *Liber de idolatria* 4.2 (CCSL 2:1103).   [e] Bellarmine, *De Ecclesia triumphante* 2.21, 25 (= *De reliquis et imaginibus sanctorum*; *Opera* 3:248b, 253b).   [f] See note 33 with the English text below.

---

works are several New Testament commentaries and apologetic writings against Protestants, in particular concerning the Eucharist. He was a colleague and close friend of Michael Baius (1513–1589), whose interpretation of the theology of Augustine was condemned as Pelagian in 1567.

Bellarmine himself acknowledges (*On Images*, book 2 chapter 8). It is true that he tried to disguise that sacrilege by adducing some passages of Scripture which attribute human limbs to God or portray some appearances wherein God's accomplishments, judgments, or works are represented figuratively (which mankind cannot or should not express); yet finally he takes it to the point where he says that in the church of Rome "whether images of God or the Trinity ought to be made is not as certain as of Christ and the saints, because the latter pertains to faith, and the former is a matter of opinion."[30] If the making of images is only a matter of opinion, then surely the worship of them even more so. But worship that occurs apart from faith cannot* be pleasing to God; yet one that is contrary to faith is very displeasing to him—and such is the kind that we are handling here.

23 In worshiping images of men who are saints, which the Synod of Nicaea under [the empress] Irene determined "must be adored in a perfect way," the more recent papal teachers speak about it in different ways, as some make the facile declaration that images of the Trinity and of Christ should be worshiped with the same adoration with which the prototypes are worshiped, and that there are not two adorations but only one and the same, as Thomas taught (Part 3, Question 25, article 3). Others, in particular the more recent Jesuits, think up a variety of distinctions. Nevertheless, they all agree to the following: 1. That they consecrate images for religious worship—but "the consecration of images is idolatry," says Tertullian (*Book on Idol-Worship*, chapter 4). 2. That "the images are conceived jointly with the original model that is being adored; and that they are adored not only accidentally* and improperly,* but also in and of themselves and properly, so that the images themselves become the object of reverence, as they are considered in themselves." "And [the images are to be worshiped] with a worship which by analogy* and reduction belongs to the type of worship that is owed to the original model."[31] "And we should not say that they must be worshiped indirectly, because whatever is said only indirectly simply can be denied." All these words come from Bellarmine (*On Images*, chapter 21 and 25). Therefore, together with Baronius, he accuses the bishops of the French Church of error, who at the synod of Paris that was held

---

30 Denying matters that pertain to faith (*de fide*) implies heresy; matters of opinion (*de opinione*) are open.

31 In contrast with Thomas Aquinas, Bellarmine states that the images should not be worshiped with exactly the same kind of worship as the original, i.e., the worship of *latria* in the case of God or Christ, the worship of *hyperdulia* in the case of Mary, and the worship of *dulia* in the case of the saints, but with a sort of worship that is related to and can be reduced to the worship paid to the original.

Lutetiae congregata decreverunt, imagines non esse adorandas, sed in Ecclesiis conservandas ad ornatum et populi instructionem historicam, erroris arcessit.

XXIV Cum autem haec adoratio aut veneratio Imaginum, quocumque tandem distinctionum fuco pallietur, religiosa inter cultores habeatur, qui etiam suppliciter se coram iis prosternunt, capita aperiunt, genua flectunt, sertis, corollis, vestibus pretiosis, eas exornant, iisdem cereos accendunt, suffitus adolent, oscilla et anathemata appendunt, easdem circumgestant ut pluvias e coelo eliciant, et alias Divini cultus species ipsis exhibent; non tam audiendum quid dicant, quam conspiciendum quid agant. Nam quod Cajetano objicit Bellarm. de ipso etiam et sodalibus verum est, cogi eos subtilissimis uti distinctionibus, quas vix ipsimet intelligunt, nedum populus imperitus; ubi supra, c. 20.[a] At, qui non intelligunt distinctiones, facta diligenter imitantur, et eodem Idololatriae crimine involvuntur, praesertim cum etiam audiunt imaginem consecrari

---

[a] Error in reference; correct to Bellarmine, *De Ecclesia triumphante* 2.22 (= *De reliquis et imaginibus sanctorum*; *Opera* 3:250a).

during the reign of Louis the Pious decreed that images should not be adored, but should be stored in the churches only for decoration and as an illustration of history[32] for the common people.[33]

Well then, since this adoration or veneration of images (regardless of whatever disguise of distinctions one uses to cover it up) is considered religious by its worshipers—those who humbly prostrate themselves before them, uncover their heads, bend their knees, bedeck them with wreaths, crowns, or precious garments; those who light candles for them, burn incense, and plant kisses or curses on them, and carry them about in procession in order to draw rain down from heaven, and who display other forms of divine worship before them— then we must not so much listen to what they say as observe what they do. For Bellarmine's objection to Cajetan is true of himself and his associates, that "they are forced to use the most subtle distinctions, which they themselves— not to mention the uneducated populace—hardly understand" (*On Images*, chapter 22).[34] But those who do not understand the distinctions copy the deeds scrupulously, and so they are implicated in the same crime of idolatry, especially when they hear that an image is consecrated for "a holy expulsion of

---

[32] "Illustration of history" means the catechetical instruction in the important events of the history of salvation. 'Historical images' remind the viewer of the biblical stories and, for Catholics, also of the legends of the saints. The narrative 'historical image' is contrasted with the cultic image. The Council of Trent acknowledged not only the cultic, but also the catechetical and edifying functions of images: cf. DH 1824.

[33] Caesar Baronius (1538–1607), Italian church historian and cardinal, member of the Oratory of St. Philip Neri. His main works are the *Annales Ecclesiastici* (*Ecclesiastical Annals*) 12 volumes, 1588–1607), which covers the history of the church until 1198, and was later supplemented by others. It was a comprehensive survey of the history of the church at the time and was intended as an alternative to the 'Magdeburg Centuries,' a church history by a group of Lutheran scholars led by Matthias Flacius. Baronius sought to show the apostolic origin of Catholic doctrines and practices like celibacy and the veneration of images. See also Cyriac K. Pullapilly, *Caesar Baronius: Counter-Reformation Historian* (Notre Dame: University of Notre Dame Press, 1975). Baronius described the Parisian Synod or Colloquy of 825 in *Annales Ecclesiastici*, vol. 9 (Mainz: Ioannes Gymnicus and Antonius Hieratus, 1601), 902–928. The Colloquy was summoned by Louis the Pious in response to signs of a resurgence of iconoclasm in the Eastern Church. See Thomas F.X. Noble, *Images, Iconoclasm and the Carolingians* (Philadelphia: University of Pennsylvania Press, 2009), 263–286.

[34] In chapter 7 of *On Images*, Bellarmine stated that in a specific passage Cajetan did not express his position clearly because he did not differentiate between 'image' and 'idol.' According to Rivetus, Bellarmine himself acknowledges in chapter 22 that it is hardly possible to come up with a clear, unambiguous formulation of how images are to be worshiped.

ut sit Daemonum sancta expulsio, Angelorum advocatio, fidelium protectio, etc, quae verba habentur in consec. Imag. B. Joh. Evang. *Pontif.* p. 172. parte 2.

XXV Huc etiam pertinet multimoda σταυρολατρεία Pontificiorum. Crucem enim quam veram esse existimant, latriae cultu adorari debere definiunt duplici nomine, quatenus repraesentat Christum crucifixum, et propter contactum Christi membrorum. Aliam vero quamlibet etiam λατρείᾳ adorant propter repraesentationem; spem et fiduciam in cruce collocant, et a ligno crucis benedicto exspectant remedium generi humano salutare, fidei soliditatem, bonorum operum profectum, et redemptionem animarum, *Pontific. part. 2 tit. de benedict. novae crucis.*[a] Et in die Parasceues omnes a summo ad minimum, crucem latria venerantur, tamquam spem unicam, augentem piis justitiam et reis veniam donantem. Suaves etiam odores cruci offerunt, fatente Bellar. *de Eccles. triumph.* lib. 1. cap. 13.[b] At Helena invenit titulum, Regem adoravit, non lignum; utique quia hic gentilis est error et vanitas impiorum, Ambr. in *Orat. funeb. Theodos.*[c]

XXVI 5. Ad multiplicem illam Ecclesiae Romanae Idolomaniam pertinet efficacia quam rebus a se consecratis tribuunt, aquae, sali, oleo, ramis palmarum, cereis, agnis et similibus, quas consecratione adipisci quandam spiritualem virtutem praetendunt, eamque Divinam, si Bellarmino fides adhibeatur, *de Sanct. beat.*

---

[a] See the corresponding note with the English text. [b] Bellarmine, *De Ecclesia triumphante* 1.13 (= *De beatitudine et canonizatione sanctorum*; Opera 3:171b). [c] Ambrose, *De obitu Theodosii oratio* 46 (CSEL 73:395–396).

demons, a call to angels for assistance, and a defense of believers," which words are used in the consecration of an image of John the Evangelist (Pontif. p. 172, p. 2).[35]

Here belong also the various forms of cross-worship by the papal teachers. For they determine that the cross which they think is the true one ought to be adored with the worship of *latria* for two reasons: Because it represents the crucified Christ, and because it came into contact with the limbs of Christ. But they also offer adoration (*latria*) to every other cross for what it represents. They place their hope and trust in the cross, and from the wood of the cross that has received blessing they expect "healthy remedies for the human race, strengthening of the faith, progress in doing good works, and the redemption of souls" (Pontif. Part 2, entitled, *On the Blessing of a New Cross*).[36] And on Good Friday everyone, from the greatest to the least, offers adoration (*latria*) to the cross as it "is their only hope, increases righteousness in the pious, and grants forgiveness to the guilty."[37] "They even offer pleasant fragrances to the cross," as Bellarmine admits (*On the Church Triumphant*, book 1, chapter 13).[38] But, "Helena has found a pretext: She worshiped the King and not the wood; certainly so, because it is a pagan deception and a folly of the impious" (Ambrose, *Funeral Oration on the Death of Theodosius*).

In the fifth place, to those various forms of idol-mania of the Roman Church belongs also the power which they ascribe to things they have consecrated: water, salt, oil, palm-tree branches, candles, lambs and similar objects, which they claim "acquire certain spiritual, even divine powers by virtue of their consecration," if Bellarmine is to be trusted (*On the Blessedness of Saints*, Book 3,

---

35   The reference is to some *Pontifical*, a liturgical book for bishops. However, the blessing of an image of John the Baptist is neither in the *Roman Pontifical* as it was revised after Trent, nor in its thirteenth-century precursor, the *Pontifical* of William Durand, bishop of Mende. However, there were many local *Pontificals* with their own rituals and blessings. The blessing quoted here by Rivetus is found, for example, in the *Samson Pontifical* (Cambridge, Corpus Christ College MS 146, 27–28) and in the *Canterbury Pontifical* (Cambridge, Corpus Christi College, MS 44, 141–142).

36   This blessing of a new crucifix is included in the standard text of the Roman Pontifical as it was revised under pope Clement VIII, after the Council of Trent. There are many editions of the text. See, for example: *Pontificale Romanum, Clementis VIII Pont. Max. iussu restitutum atque editum* (Paris: Rolinus Thierry & Eustachius Foucault, 1615), part 2, p. 283.

37   The hymn '*O Crux ave, spes unica*' was sung in the liturgy of Good Friday as part of the larger hymn '*Vexilla Regis*,' composed in the sixth century on the occasion of the arrival of a relic of the True Cross in Poitiers.

38   Bellarmine talks here about offering incense to "images and relics," but does not explicitly mention the cross.

lib. 3. c. 7. prop. 3.ᵃ unde fiduciam suam in illis rebus collocant, et ab iis sperant remedia contra insultus Diaboli, morbos et alia pericula. De agnis Dei Pontifex petit in eorum consecratione, ut agni immaculati virtutem accipiant eandem quam Agnus innocens immolatus in ara crucis, contra omnes Diaboli versutias, et fraudes maligni Spiritus, ut eos devote ferentibus nulla tempestas praevaleat, nulla adversitas dominetur, nulla aura pestilens, nullus morbus caducus, etc. partus incolumis servetur, *Cerem. Eccles. Rom.* lib. 1. cap. 7.ᵇ Eadem exempla in plerisque aliis proferri possunt ex ritualibus libris; ex quibus constat apertissime, eos creaturis ascribere quae Dei propria sunt, idque ex humana institutione, sine ullo Dei verbo; ut minus mirum sit, si ipse Pontifex, primarius harum rerum consecrator, qui sanctos ipsos apotheosi donat, divinis honoribus apud eos colatur, et in abominandum Idolum degeneret.

XXVII   Quod de imaginibus dictum est, non ita accipiendum, ut in universum existimemus omnem imaginum usum esse illicitum; id enim tantum de imagine Trinitatis absolute* intelligimus. Ad creaturas quod attinet, extra Idololatricum cultum contra primam legis tabulam; aut obscoenitatem, turpitudinem, et alium similem abusum contra secundam; artem imagines effingendi non damnamus, quam ad historiam et ornatum in communi vita aliquid conducere non negamus. In locis autem sacris ubi Deus colitur, non solum necessarias non esse, etiamsi ad usum historicum, doctrinalem, aut memoriae subsidium in iis collocentur, censemus; sed etiam periculosas esse, ac proinde illicitas, nec ferri debere in templis Christianorum, sed tolli et aboleri, quantumvis non adorentur: ne errare mereantur qui Christum et Apostolos ejus, non in codicibus scriptis, sed in parietibus pictis quaerunt, Augustinus, *de Cons. Evang.* lib. 1. c. 9.ᶜ

ᵃ Bellarmine, *De Ecclesia triumphante* 3.7 (= *De iis ritibus*; *Opera* 3:294b).   ᵇ *Sacrarum cerimoniarum sive rituum ecclesiasticorum Sanctae Romanae Ecclesiae libri tres* (Cologne: Birckmann, 1572), 1.7 (p. 89v°).   ᶜ Erroneous reference; correct to Augustine, *De consensu evangelistarum* 1.10.16 (CSEL 43:16).

chapter 7, proposition 3). As a result, they place their trust in those consecrated things and hope that they will grant immunity from the attacks of the devil, from diseases and other perils. When the 'lambs of God' are consecrated, the pope prays that "the spotless lambs may receive the same power as that of the innocent Lamb, sacrificed on the altar of the cross, power against all the trickeries of the devil and the deceits of the evil spirit, that no storm may prevail over those who piously bear these lambs, and that no adversity may overtake them, nor any noxious airs, or debilitating disease, etc.; that the offspring may be kept from harm" (*The Ceremonies of the Roman Church*, Book 1, chapter 7).[39] The same examples can be produced from numerous other places in the books on rituals; from these it is very obvious that they attribute to creatures what properly belongs to God, and that they do so on the basis of human institutions and without any word from God. And so it should be of little surprise to us if they were to worship the pope himself with divine honours, since he is foremost in consecrating these things and in canonizing people as saints; and that he has degenerated into an accursed idol.

27 What we have said about images should not be taken to mean that we generally consider every use of images to be unlawful; in our view this applies in an absolute* sense only to images of the Trinity. As far as creatures are concerned, apart from idolatrous worship that is contrary to the first table of the Law, and apart from indecency, shamefulness or other similar abuse contrary to the second commandment, we do not condemn the art of making images; and we don't deny that it brings about some good for the sake of the illustration of history in public life. But we do think that in the sacred places where God is worshiped images are not necessary, even if they do contain some historical or doctrinal use, or help to commemorate something.[40] What is more, we think that they are dangerous, and for that reason unlawful, and that they should not be brought into Christian churches but removed and banished from them, even if they are not adored, and lest people "who seek Christ and his apostles not in the written books but on the painted walls meet up with error" (Augustine, *On the Harmony of the Gospels*, Book 1, chapter 9).

---

39   Rivetus refers to a papal liturgical book of which many editions exist: *Sacrarum Cerimoniarum sive Rituum Ecclesiasticorum Sanctae Romanae Ecclesiae Libri Tres*, (Cologne: Birckmann, 1572), book I, section 7, 89b. The *agni Dei* or 'Lambs of God' are discs made of the wax of old paschal candles and impressed with the figure of a lamb. They were blessed by the pope in the first year of his pontificate and every seventh year afterward. The discs were worn in a gold or silver frame for protection against all kinds of evil.
40   On the "illustration of history," see footnote 33 on thesis 23 above.

XXVIII Neque etiam omnes cultus aut honoris distinctiones absolute rejicimus, etsi πολυθρύλλητον illam λατρείας et δουλείας; sensu Pontificio, approbare non possimus. Nam si nominum non solum significatio spectetur, sed etiam Scripturae usus, utraque tribuitur Deo et hominibus. ἔργον λατρευτὸν appellant LXX. omne opus servile, Lev. 23, 7. 8. 21. quod opponitur operi religioso; cum hic agatur de iis operibus, quae die Sabbati fieri non debebant, et Paulus Gal. 4, 8. δουλείας cultum vindicat soli Deo vero, cum Galatas culpat quod illum reddiderint iis qui natura* Dii non sunt. De ὑπερδουλείᾳ nihil in Scriptura, neque etiam in ullo vetere scriptore reperitur. Creaturis igitur reddere possumus Latriam et Duliam. Creatori etiam Latriam et Duliam praestare debemus, i. servire debemus creatori et creaturae.

XXIX Sed ne eodem cultus genere, quod fas non est, id fiat, distinguenda sunt diversa membra cultus religiosi et civilis aut dilectionis et societatis; quam distinctionem probavit maxime Augustinus, qui satis vidit non sufficere simplicem illam λατρείας et δουλείας, quia, ut idem ait, *In Exodum* qu. 94.[a] δουλεία debetur Deo tamquam Domino, quam non deberi Sanctis defunctis, idem docet, cum ait, *De vera relig.* cap. 1.[b] eos a nobis honorari caritate, non servitute. Et Martinus Peresius Ajala scriptor Pontificius, *De Tradit. part.* 3. *de cult. Sanct.*[c] profitetur, se nescire an hoc officium appellari debuisset δουλεία, cum veneratio illa quae communiter Sanctis debetur, minime in signum servitutis exhibeatur. Omnes enim servi Dei sumus, quanquam meritis et sanctitate dispares. Deum igitur solum religiose colimus, Fideles autem et Sanctos caritate, non servitute, dilectione et societate, quae omnia sanctis Angelis et hominibus reddimus modo conveniente, iis qui nobiscum familiariter non conversantur, saltem (de Angelis dico) visibili modo, et qui infiniti non sunt: nempe memoriam eorum sancte recolentes et eorum excellentiam agnoscentes et praedicantes. Denique civilem servitutem et honorem reddimus iis quibuscum in societate humana

---

[a] Augustine, *Quaestionum in Heptateuchum libri VII* 2.94 (CCSL 33:117).   [b] Erroneous reference; correct to Augustine, *De vera religione* 55.110 (CCSL 32:258).   [c] Martin Pérez de Ayala, *De divinis, apostolicis et ecclesiasticis traditionibus* (Cologne: Jaspar Gennepeus, 1560), 194r° (= *pars* 3, *consideratio* 7).

And we do not even reject outright all forms of worship or honorary decorations, although we cannot commend that notorious differentiation between *latreia* and *douleia* in the sense used by the papal party.[41] For if one regards not only the meaning of these words but also the way they are used in Scripture, both words are applied to God and to men. The Septuagint calls all laborious work [*ergon latreuton*] 'servile labour' (Leviticus 23:7, 8, 21). It is the opposite of religious service, since it concerns those tasks which ought not to be performed on the Sabbath-day. And Paul (in Galatians 4:8) claims the worship of veneration [*douleia*] only for God, since he finds fault with the Galatians because they bestowed it upon those who by nature* are not gods. One finds nothing about *huperdouleia* [high veneration] in Scripture, nor in any of the ancient writers.[42] Therefore we can render *latria* and *dulia* to creatures. And to the Creator we must offer both *latria* and *dulia*; that is, we ought to serve the Creator and the creature.

But in order for that service to happen by a different sort of worship (one which is not against the law of God), different parts must be distinguished of religious and civil worship, or of goodwill and fellowship. This distinction was very strongly commended by Augustine, who saw adequately that it is not enough to distinguish simply between *latreia* and *douleia*, because, as he himself says (*On Exodus*, question 94), "*douleia* is owed to God because He is Lord." And that this should not be owed to deceased saints, Augustine also teaches when he says (*On True Religion*, chapter 1) that these saints should be "honoured through our love, not our service." And Martin Perez d'Ayala, a papal writer, admits (*On Tradition*, part 3, *On the Worship of Saints*) that he does not know "whether this duty ought to have been called *douleia*, because the veneration that is commonly owed to saints is least of all an indication of servitude. For we all are servants of God, although unequal in our merits and holiness." Therefore we should worship only God in a religious manner, but believers and saints "with love, not with servitude; with goodwill and fellowship." All these latter things we render to holy angels and men in a befitting manner, to those who do not keep our company in a familiar way—at least in a visible way (I am speaking about angels)—and who are not infinite. And we do so by piously keeping them in our memory, and by recognizing and declaring their surpassing worth. And lastly we render civil service and honour to those people with whom we dwell in human fellowship, according to the

---

41   See note 6 above and also thesis 9.
42   After Albertus Magnus it was common to distinguish the high veneration of Mary (*hyperdouleia*) from the common veneration of saints. See also note 6 above.

vivimus secundum uniuscujusque gradum et ordinem. Hoc modo perspicue distinguuntur, quae Deo et hominibus debentur.

xxx   Cum autem Domino nostro Jesu Christo, aeterno Dei Filio, omnimodum religionis cultum aequaliter cum Patre et Spiritu Sancto tribuamus, hoc ipso profitemur, nos eum agnoscere pro Deo in aeternum benedicto. Ac proinde detestamur Idololatriam novorum Samosatenianorum, qui sibi Idolum Christi fabricarunt; cum, sublata ipsi Divinitate, eoque in ordinem creaturarum redacto, eidem nihilominus Divinos honores tribuunt, abominandae sectae antesignani, etsi gregalium quorundam ingratia, qui necessariam ἀκολούθησιν Nazianzeni[a] agnoscunt, εἰ δὲ προσκυνητὸν, πῶς οὐ σεπτὸν, εἰ δὲ σεπτὸν, πῶς οὐ θεός. Hinc Patres et Concilia Arium et Nestorium Idololatriae condemnarunt, quod Christum adorarent; quem ille Deum creatum, hic hominem a persona τοῦ λόγου divisum existimavit; imo ipsa Nicaena Synodus secunda,[b] et 7. in *Epist. Synod. ad Const. et Iren.* Nestorii in homine Idololatriam anathemate ferit, et Arrianos Deum ut creatum adorantes, juste a Basilio[c] Idololatras fuisse appellatos pronuntiat. Et recte Nazianz. Qui creaturam adorat, etiamsi in nomine Christi id facit, est Idololatra, Christi nomen Idolo imponens, vid. Athan. *contra Arrian. orat.* 1.[d] Nyssen. *in laud. Basil.*[e] Eund. *orat. Funeb. de Placilla*[f] Nazianz. *orat.* 40.[g]

---

[a] Gregory of Nazianzus, *Oratio* 31.28 (SC 250:332).   [b] Mansi 13:742 (NPNF2 14:572).   [c] This reference is difficult, but may well be to Basil the Great, *Comm. in Isaiam prophetam* 13:4 (MPG 30:573D; the attribution of this work to Gregory is no longer widely accepted).   [d] Athanasius, *Contra Arianos Oratio* 1.42 (AW 1/1:152).   [e] Gregory of Nyssa, *In laudem Basilii* (GNO 10/1:115).   [f] Gregory of Nyssa, *Oratio funebris de Placilla* (GNO 9:489).   [g] Gregory of Nazianzus, *Oratio* 40.42 (SC 358:296). The reference to this oration can be found beginning with the 1642 edition. It is absent in the original disputation pamphlet and the 1625 edition of the *Synopsis*, which instead refer to actio 6 of the second synod of Nicaea (see Mansi 13:203–364).

degree and rank of each. In this way a clear distinction is made between what is owed to God and what is owed to men.

But when we ascribe to our Lord Jesus Christ, the eternal Son of God, all manner of religious worship in a measure equal to that of the Father and the Holy Spirit, we thereby proclaim that we acknowledge him as the God who is praised for ever and ever. And accordingly we loathe the idolatry of the new Samosatenians[43] who have made for themselves an idol of Christ, because after depriving him of his divinity and lowering his status to that of a creature they nevertheless bestow divine honours upon him. They form the front line of an accursed sect, although they are but common footsoldiers, who admit to this necessary consequence drawn by [Gregory of] Nazianzus: "If He is to be adored, how can He not be worshiped? And if He is to be worshiped, how can He not be God?" Hence the church-fathers and the councils condemned Arius and Nestorius[44] for their idolatry, because they gave adoration to Christ. The former considered him a created God, the latter a man separated from the person of the Word. In fact, the second Synod of Nicaea, and the seventh [ecumenical council] in the *Letter of the Synod to Constantine* [the sixth] *and Irene* strikes "Nestorius' idolatry of a man" with the curse of anathema, and declares that the Arians who worshiped God as created being were rightly called idolaters by Basil. "Whoever worships a creature, even though he does so in the name of Christ, is an idolater, for he imposes the name of Christ upon his idol" (see Athanasius *Against the Arians*, Oration 1; Nyssen, *In Praise of Basil*; the same, *Funeral Oration for Placilla*, Nazianzus, *Oration* 40).

---

43 On the 'new Samosatenians' see *SPT* 8.15, note 13. Rivetus, who probably learned the views of this sect during his study at Bern, accuses them in this disputation of giving divine honour to Christ despite the fact that they denied he is God.

44 Nestorius (AD 386–450), a disciple of Diodorus, and presbyter and monk in Antioch, appointed patriarch of Constantinople in 428, belonged to the Antiochene school of theology. His view of the full reality and completeness of the human and the divine in Christ implied the conjunction of both a human person and divine person in one. In Constantinople, early in his career he preached against the popular notion of Mary as "Mother, or Bearer of God" (*theotokos*), and advocated a more proper form, "Mother of Christ" (*Christotokos*). His opponent was Cyril of Alexandria, and the controversy was set to be decided at the General Council of Ephesus convened by Emperor Theodosius II, in 431. By approving a letter composed by Cyril, the fathers condemned the Christology of Nestorius, and affirmed the use of the term *theotokos*. The Second General Council of Constantinople (553) reiterated the condemnation of the Nestorian view as heresy.

XXXI   Gravissimum autem esse peccatum Idololatriae, Scripturae omnes testantur et ipsa rei natura, cum spirituale sit adulterium simulque sacrilegium, quo amor, timor et honor soli Deo debitus, ad Idola, quibus Deus gloriam suam dare non vult, Es. 42, 8. tamquam ad corrivales injuste transfertur, Hos. 1, 2. et seq. Maximum est uxoris crimen, si sacram conjugii fidem violet: subditi, si alteri honorem Regi debitum deferat; ut non immerito Deus praecepto de Idololatria vitanda addiderit, se Zelotem esse, visitantem iniquitatem patrum in filios in tertiam et quartam generationem, eorum qui oderunt se, etc.

XXXII   Merito igitur gravitatem peccati sequitur poenae pondus, tam in hac vita quam in futura. In hac vita, caecitas mentis, spurcities corporis, et punitiones aliae temporales, divinitus immissae, quorum longus texitur catalogus, Deut. 28. a v. 16. usque ad finem. Sed quod maxime metuendum est, foris erunt omnes Idolis servientes, id est, a regno coelorum exclusi, et pars eorum erit in stagno ardenti igne et sulphure, quod est mors secunda, Apoc. 22, 15. 1 Cor. 6, 9. Apoc. 21, 8. Quapropter Filioli custodite vobis a simulacris, Amen. 1 Joh. 5, 21.

COROLLARIA.

Cum nulla sit consensio templi Dei cum Idolis, merito ab Ecclesia Romana secessionem fecerunt Orthodoxi, obtemperantes Patris mandato: Exite e medio eorum et separamini, dicit Dominus, et impurum ne attingatis; et ego suscipiam vos, 2 Cor. 6, 16. 17.

But all the Scriptures, and the nature of the matter itself, testify that the sin of idolatry is a very serious one, since it is spiritual adultery and sacrilege, whereby the love, reverence, and honour that is due to God alone is wrongly shifted to idols as his rivals (Hosea 1:2–3), to whom God is unwilling to grant his own glory (Isaiah 42:8). It is a very grave offense of a wife to break the sacred trust of marriage; so too for a subject who transfers to another the honour that is owed to his king. Therefore God deservedly added to the commandment about avoiding idolatry that He "is jealous, visiting the sins of the fathers upon the children to the third and fourth generation of those who hate" him, etc.

The burden of punishment rightly follows upon the gravity of this sin, both in this and the future life. In this life it is the darkening of the soul, the filthiness of the body, and other temporal punishments that are sent by God's permission. A long list of these punishments is provided in Deuteronomy 28, from verse 16 to the end. But what we must especially fear is that "outside will be all those who serve idols" (Rev. 22:15); that is, they will be barred from the kingdom of heaven (1 Corinthians 6:9), and "their lot will be in the lake burning with fire and sulphur, which is the second death" (Revelation 21:8). Therefore, "little children, keep yourselves from idols, Amen." (1 John 5:21).

Corollary.

Since there is no harmony between the temple of God and idols, the orthodox rightly separated themselves from the Roman church, in obedience to the Father's command: "'Therefore come out from their midst and be separate,' says the Lord, 'and touch nothing unclean; and I shall receive you'" (2 Corinthians 6:16, 17).

DISPUTATIO XX

De Juramento

Praeside D. ANTONIO WALAEO
Respondente PETRO LAOVICO

THESIS I Juramentum (quod Graeci ὅρκον ab ἕρκος, quia veritatis est firmamentum, vocant) a jure derivari, manifestum est, quoniam id quod juratur, instar legis alicujus ratum esse debet, quemadmodum clarius ex Jurisjurandi voce* liquet, quae idem quod Juramentum notat; etsi nonnulli velint illud ab hoc differre, quod Jusjurandum in re controversa interponatur, Juramentum vero generalius etiam in re non controversa usurpetur.

II Significat* autem Juramentum, ut Cic. lib. 3. *Officiorum*[a] testatur, religiosam veritatis affirmationem,* unde et sacramentum* Latinis vocatur, quia Juramenti interventu veritatis confirmatio, sacra et religiosa redditur.

III De hujus Juramenti usu legitimo, aut abusu, jam nobis agendum. Quod ut ordine et compendiose fiat, primo Juramentum Christianis esse licitum demonstrabimus, deinde quodnam et quale illud sit, ex Scriptura Sacra videbimus, ac denique quaestiones nonnullas, quae circa usum aut abusum Juramenti versantur, examinabimus.

IV Inter veteres Judaeos primi omnium Esseni Juramentum omne aeque atque perjurium condemnabant, ut Josephus, lib. 2. *de Bello Jud.* c. 7.[b] refert. Eos olim secuti sunt quidam Monachi Humiliati dicti, et hodie Anabaptistae. Imo vero

---

[a] Cicero, *De officiis* 3.104. [b] Erroneous reference; correct to Josephus, *De bello judaico* 2.8.

DISPUTATION 20

Concerning the Oath

President: Antonius Walaeus
Respondent: Petrus Laovicus[1]

It is clear that *iuramentum*, 'oath' (which the Greeks call *horkos*, from *herkos*, because it is the mainstay of the truth), derives from *ius*, 'law,' because that which is sworn should be just as valid as a law. This is even more clear from the word* *ius-iurandum*, which has the same meaning as *iuramentum*. Yet there are some who think that the former differs from the latter on the grounds that *iusiurandum* is introduced in the context of a matter that is disputed, whereas *iuramentum* is used more generally, also in undisputed matters.

Well then, *iuramentum*, as Cicero avers (*On Moral Duties*, book 3), means* "a religious confirmation* of truth"; wherefore in Latin it is also called a 'sacrament'* because the assertion of the truth is rendered sacred and binding by the intervention of an oath.

It is our task now to treat the lawful and the unlawful use of the oath. So that this may be done in an orderly and profitable manner, we shall first demonstrate that the oath is permissible for Christians; then we shall see from Holy Scripture what an oath is and what its qualities are; and lastly we shall investigate some questions that arise concerning the use and abuse of the oath.

Among the ancient Jews it was the Essenes who were foremost in condemning every true and false oath equally, as Josephus reports (*On the Jewish War*, book 2 chapter 7). Their followers in former days were certain monks called the Humble Ones, and today it is the Anabaptists. The truth is that many papal

---

[1] Born in ca. 1598 and coming from Middelburg, Petrus Lodovicus (or Laovicus) matriculated on 21 April 1618 in philosophy. He was ordained in Grijpskerke in 1624, Arnemuiden and Kleverskerke (1626), Veere (1640) and Essequebo (1658; now: Georgetown in Guyana). He died in 1659. See Du Rieu, *Album studiosorum*, 135, Van Lieburg, *Repertorium*, 145, and L.J. Joosse, *Geloof in de Nieuwe Wereld: Ontmoeting met Afrikanen en Indianen (1600–1700)* (Kampen: Kok, 2008), 101.

et multi Pontificii abstinentiam a Juramento inter consilia referunt, et majorem perfectionem* in ea constituunt.

V Nos vero sicuti plurima Juramenta plane illicita esse asserimus, sic quoque Jusjurandum aliquod esse legitimum, ac proinde non tantum licitum sed et nobis non minus sub Novo quam sub Veteri Testamento in verbo Dei praescriptum, contra omnes illos asserimus.

VI Prima demonstratio* sumitur ex eo, quod Juramentum sit legis naturae,* sicuti ex omnium gentium usu liquet, unde et Aristoteles Jusjurandum in *Rhetor. ad Alex.* cap. 18.ª definit, φᾶσιν ἀναπόδεικτον μετὰ θείας παραλήψεως, et Ciceroᵇ affirmationem religiosam Deo teste adhibito. Etsi enim in falsorum numinum attestatione errarint, tamen in rebus seriis, et magni momenti assertionibus, illud quod pro Deo colebant, in testimonium* vocandum esse universi agnoverunt.

VII Quod argumentum tanto est firmius, quia legi morali, divinae et aeternae innititur. Quum enim Deus nomen* suum in vanum usurpari vetat, ex contrario sensu nomen suum cum debita religione* ac reverentia etiam usurpari in Juramentis concedit. Quemadmodum Moses et Prophetae id ipsum saepius inculcant, ut Deut. 6, 13. et 10, 20. Jehovam Deum tuum timeto, eum colito et ei adhaereto, ac per nomen ejus jurato, ipse enim est laus tua, etc. et Ps. 63, 12. Rex ipse laetabitur in Deo, gloriabitur quisquis jurat per eum, quia obturabitur os loquentium mendacium, atque alibi passim.

ª Aristotle, *Rhetorica ad Alexandrum* 1432a33; the reference to ch. "18" in the disputation text should be corrected to "17." ᵇ Cicero, *De officiis* 3.104.

teachers also reckon refraining from oaths among their counsels[2] and they place a greater perfection* in refraining.

As for us, just as we affirm that very many oaths are clearly made in a way that is not permissible, so also do we affirm over against all of them that the oath itself is a permissible thing, and accordingly it is not only lawful for us but even commanded in God's Word, in the New Testament no less than the Old.

The first clear demonstration* is drawn from the fact that the oath belongs to the law of nature,* as is evident from the use that all peoples make of it, whence also Aristotle (in the *Rhetorica ad Alexandrum* Chapter 18) defines it as "an affirmation without proof accompanied by an invocation of the gods," and Cicero as "a religious confirmation to which God is summoned as witness." For although they went wrong in calling on false deities as their witnesses, they all agreed that in serious matters, and in claims of great consequence, what they worshiped as God should be called upon as witness.*

This argument is much more solidly grounded by the fact that it rests upon the moral, divine, and eternal law.[3] For while God forbids that his name* be used in vain, he does, on the other hand, allow his name to be used—with the appropriate awe* and respect—in oaths. Moses and the prophets drive this point home quite frequently, as in Deuteronomy 6:13 and 10:20: "You shall fear the Lord your God, him you shall serve and you shall cling to him, and you shall swear by his name, for he is your praise," etc. And Psalm 63:12: "The king himself shall rejoice in the Lord, whoever swears by him shall glory, because the mouth of those who speak lies shall be stopped," and in very many other places.

---

2 The term 'counsels' evokes an important distinction employed in Roman Catholic moral and spiritual theology. In addition to the 'precepts' or 'commandments' (*praecepta*) to be observed by all Christian believers in order to attain eternal life, the 'counsels' (*consilia*) represent a higher ethical and religious standard for those who strive for Christian perfection. The three principal instances of 'evangelical counsels' are poverty, chastity (celibacy), and obedience. As the text above indicates, also the avoidance of swearing oaths could be counted among them. See also the extensive discussion of the 'vows' (*vota*) in theses 26–46 below. An important difference between the 'precepts' and the 'counsels' is that the former are *necessary* for salvation, while the latter are *optional*. The distinction originates in the ascetic tradition of the Early Church, was expounded among others by Origen, and became a standard element of Catholic teaching. For a recent discussion see Hans Urs von Balthasar, *The Laity and the Life of the Counsels: The Church's Mission in the World* (San Francisco: Ignatius, 2003).

3 On these distinctions of the law, see SPT 18.10,12,33.

VIII Legis autem naturae ac moralis usum ad Christianos sub Novi Testamenti statu constitutos spectare, inter omnes Christianos pro confesso habendum, nam Christus Mat. 5. legem in hoc quoque praecepto, a falsis Pharisaeorum interpretationibus vindicaturus testatur, se non venisse, ut legem solveret, sed ut impleret, versus 17. imo vero, eum qui vel unum ex minimis illis praeceptis solveret et ita homines doceret, minimum futurum esse in regno coelorum, docet versus 19.

IX Secunda demonstratio sumitur ex praedictionibus Propheticis; quae singulari Dei beneficio inter gentes ad Christum conversas sub Novo Testamento futurum promittunt, ut per solum Deum verum juretur. Tale vaticinium est Es. 45, 2. Respicite ad me et servemini omnes fines terrae, etc. per me juravi, prodiit ex ore meo verbum, quod non revocabitur, mihi incurvatum iri omne genu, juraturam omnem linguam. Et Es. 65, 16. de tempore Novi Testamenti agens, Qui sibi benedicturus est in terra, benedicat sibi per Deum firmi, et juraturus in terra, juret per Deum firmi. Tale vaticinium etiam exstat Jer. 5, 2. et 12, 16. Ecquis vero ausit asserere, illud interdictum esse fidelibus Novi Testamenti, quod Deus tamquam singulare beneficium iis se praestiturum promittit?

X Tertio idem invicte probatur* ex exemplis, quae non tantum in Veteri Testamento occurrunt, sed etiam in Novo. Exempla Veteris Testamenti a Deo ipso praestita, aut probata, sunt ubique obvia et controversia carent; exempla quae in Novo exstant, non sunt minus illustria. Apostolus Rom. 14, 11. demonstrat, nos omnes comparituros esse coram tribunali Christi, quia scriptum est, Vivo ego, dicit Dominus, mihi se flectat omne genu, et in Epistola ad Heb. cap. 7, 20. colligit Apostolus, Christi sacerdotium esse praestantius, quam Leviticum, quia interposito Dei jurejurando, sacerdos Novi Testamenti est factus, quae verba etsi ex Veteri Testamento citentur, tamen cum vis et effectus eorum sub Novo demum Testamento plene fuerit exhibendus, ipsum illud juramentum ad Novi Testamenti tempus omnino spectat. Quum autem Deus Pater Christum sacerdotem Novi Testamenti per jusjurandum constituerit; Christus vero ipse omnes sibi subjectum iri, in Novo Testamento aperte juraverit, sequitur evidenter,* et Deum Patrem et Christum juramenti usum suo exemplo confirmare.

20. CONCERNING THE OATH

It should be generally acknowledged by all Christians that the use of the natural and moral law pertains to Christians living in the New Testament state, for Christ in Matthew 5, in order to uphold also this commandment of the law in the face of the Pharisees' false interpretations, bears witness that "he has not come to abolish the law but to fulfill it" (5:17). In fact, "he who relaxes even one of the least of these commandments and teaches other men so, will become least in the kingdom of heaven" (5:19).

The second clear demonstration is taken from the predictions of the prophets, which foretell that by a unique act of God's kindness it would happen among those people who have turned to Christ under the New Testament that oaths will be made only in the name of the true God. A prophecy of this sort is Isaiah 45:22: "Turn to me and be saved, all the ends of the earth, etc.; I have sworn by myself, the word has gone forth from my mouth, which will not be recalled, that every knee shall bow to me, and every tongue shall swear." And Isaiah 65:16, dealing with the time of the New Testament: "He who blesses himself in the land shall bless himself by the God of truth, and he who takes an oath on the land shall swear by the God of truth." A prophecy of this sort occurs also in Jeremiah 5:2[4] and 12:16. Well then, would anyone be so bold as to claim that the very thing which God promises He will provide as a special benefit to them is forbidden to believers in the New Testament?

In the third place, the same thing is demonstrated* irrefutably by the instances that occur in the Old Testament as well as in the New. God himself has furnished or approved instances in the Old Testament, and these are obvious everywhere and beyond debate. The examples on record in the New Testament are no less evident and clear. In Romans 14:11 the apostle draws attention to the fact that we shall all appear before the judgement-seat of Christ, because it is written: "As I live, says the Lord, every knee shall bow before me," and in the Letter to the Hebrews chapter 7:20[-21] the apostle comes to the conclusion that the priesthood of Christ is more excellent than the Levitical one because "by the insertion of an oath by God, he was made priest of the New Testament" [Psalm 110:4]. Although these words are quoted from the Old Testament, nevertheless, since the force and effect of them would be made fully manifest only in the New Testament, that oath looks entirely to the time of the New Testament. Moreover, since it is through the taking of an oath that God the Father appointed Christ as priest of the New Testament, and since Christ himself in the New Testament clearly stated by an oath that all would be subjected to him, it evidently* follows that both God the Father and Christ by their own example affirm the use of the oath.

---

4 More correctly: Jeremiah 4:2.

XI   Alia exempla Novi Testamenti idem quoque confirmant. Nam ut solennem illam asseverationem Christi, Amen, Amen, jam praeteream, Apostolus Paulus Rom. 9, 1. plenam juramenti formam exprimit, quum inquit: Veritatem dico in Christo, non mentior, conscientia mea mihi attestante per Spiritum Sanctum, et 2 Cor. 1, 23. Ego Deum testem, invoco in animam meam. Quemadmodum et ad Rom. 1, 9. et Phil. 1, 8. Testis est mihi Deus cui servio. Sic denique Angelus jurat per viventem in secula seculorum Apoc. 10, 6.

XII   Idem denique evincit juramenti legitimi natura ac finis.* Quum enim verum juramentum sit quaedam divini nominis invocatio, in qua Deus et cordium cognitor et veritatis vindex agnoscitur ab iis qui jurant, ut exempla et loca supra proposita ostendunt; et cum finis legitimi juramenti ab Apostolo Hebr. 6, 16. laudetur, quod sit πάσης ἀντιλογίας πέρας εἰς βεβαίωσιν, omnis controversiae finis ad confirmationem inter homines: inde necessario colligitur, ejus usum inter homines laudabilem esse et a Deo probatum.

XIII Primo igitur hoc nostrae disputationis membro monstrato,* jam nobis legitimorum juramentorum natura* ac conditio diligenter est inquirenda, ut licita ab illicitis, ex Dei verbo possimus distinguere.

XIV   Juramentum ergo legitimum esse asserimus, actionem religiosam, qua Deum in testem eorum quae dicimus aut promittimus, invocamus, ut de eorum veritate ac certitudine alios securos reddamus, quando gloria Dei, Ecclesiae aedificatio, patriae salus, aut proximi* caritas id a nobis postulant.

XV   Actionem esse religiosam, ex invocatione divini nominis patet; unde et in solennibus juramentis ritus quidam religiosi observari inter homines semper fuerunt soliti; in quorum tamen observatione superstitio et idololatria diligenter cavenda est.

XVI   Forma hujus invocationis est duplex: vel enim simpliciter Deus in testem veritatis invocatur, quemadmodum ex Rom. 1, 9. et Phil. 1, 8. antea visum est; vel invocationi illi simplici exsecratio adjungitur, qua Dei in nos vindictam si fallamus, vel auxilium aut beneficium si vera juremus, imprecamur: cujusmodi diversae formulae passim in Scripturis occurrunt, vide Ruth 1, 17. 1 Reg. 1, 29. et 2, 23. 24. Item 2 Cor. 1, 23. etc.

20. CONCERNING THE OATH

Other examples in the New Testament confirm the same point. For, leaving aside for now that solemn assertion by Christ, "truly, truly," the apostle Paul in Romans 9:1 expresses the oath in its full form, when he says: "I am speaking the truth in Christ, I am not lying, my conscience bears me witness in the Holy Spirit," and, in 2 Corinthians 1:23: "I call upon God as witness to my spirit." In a similar fashion also in Romans 1:9 and Philippians 1:8: "God is my witness, whom I serve." So too, finally, the Angel "swears by him who lives for ever and ever" (Revelation 10:6). 11

And lastly, the same point is brought out by the nature and intended goal* of the legitimate oath. For since a true oath is a certain calling upon God's name whereby those who swear acknowledge God as the one who knows the hearts and upholds the truth (as the instances and passages presented above show), and since the goal of a lawful oath is praised by the apostle in Hebrews 6:16 because "in every dispute an oath is final for confirmation" for people, it must be concluded that the use of it by human beings is commendable and approved by God. 12

Now that the first element of our disputation has been shown,* we must next conduct a careful investigation into the nature* and conditions of lawful oaths, in order to be able, by God's Word, to distinguish between ones that are permissible and ones that are not permissible. 13

We affirm, therefore, that a lawful oath is a religious act whereby we call on God to be witness of the things we say or promise, in order to render others confident in the truth and certainty of these things, whenever God's glory demands it from us, or the upbuilding of the church, the safety of the fatherland, or the love of our neighbor.* 14

The invocation of God's name reveals that it is a religious act; therefore people of all times have been accustomed to follow some religious rituals in taking solemn oaths. However, in observing them one must be careful to guard against superstition and idolatry.[5] 15

This invocation takes one of two possible forms: Either God is called upon simply as witness to the truth, as was observed earlier from Romans 1:9 and Philippians 1:8, or a curse is added to that simple invocation, whereby we call down on our heads the punishment by God if we lie, or his support and blessing if we swear the truth. Various formulae of this kind of oath occur in the Scriptures: see Ruth 1:17, 1 Kings 1:29 and 2:23, 24. Similarly, 2 Corinthians 1:23, etc. 16

---

5   On superstition and idolatry, see Disputation 19 above.

XVII   In utroque hoc jurandi modo, sive simplici, sive cum imprecatione conjuncto, solius Dei nomen esse invocandum, asserimus; cum et ille solus sit καρδιογνώστης, et supremus veritatis occultae vindex, et sacrae literae in omnibus qui de vero juramento agunt, locis, solius veri et viventis Dei nomen sonent.

XVIII   Unde perspicuum est, assertiones nonnullas a viris etiam sanctis nonnumquam usurpatas, ut a Joseph. Gen. 42, 15. Ita vivat Pharao; ab Anna, matre Samuëlis, 1 Sam. 1, 26. Ut vivit anima tua, Domine mi, etc. non esse juramenta proprie* dicta, quia nulla hic est annexa invocatio; sed tantum collatio cum rebus, quarum incolumitas ac dignitas illis erat cordi, aut de quarum veritate inter ipsos constabat.

XIX   Impie ergo quidam sacrificuli, et alii, gentilium diras imitati, ut veritatem suae religionis aut assertionis coram obstupefacto populo affirment, Satanam vel inferni diras adversus sese invocant; cum solus Deus veritatis occultae judex et vindex in sacris literis nobis proponatur. Impie quoque Pontificii in juramentis suis cum invocatione nominis divini, Sanctorum defunctorum invocationem conjungunt; contra aperta mandata Dei, Deut. 6, 13. et 10, 20. item Es. 45, 22. et 65, 16. quorum Thes. 7. et 9. a nobis expressa est mentio.

XX   Subjectum* circa quod juramenta legitima versantur, sunt, ea quae dicimus, aut promittimus. Nam factorum veritas per juramenta asseritur, futurorum vero certitudo per juramenta promittitur, unde et juramenti in assertorium et promissorium divisio est orta.

XXI   Utrumque sine dolo aut fraude, per verba secundum communem* hominum consuetudinem intellecta fieri debet, contra Jesuitarum mentales reservationes, et Anabaptistarum fraudulentas aequivocationes. Nam si in omni

20. CONCERNING THE OATH

17   In either of these forms of swearing (whether the simple one or the one accompanied by a curse) we affirm that one should call upon the name of God only, since He is the only one who knows the heart and supremely upholds the hidden truth; and in all the passages dealing with the true oath, the sacred writings mention only the name of the true and living God.

18   From this it is clear that some statements of affirmation which even saintly people sometimes used (like Joseph in Genesis 42:15, "as Pharaoh lives"; and like Hannah, Samuel's mother, in 1 Samuel 1:26, "as your soul lives, my lord," etc.) are not strictly* speaking oaths, because no invocation was attached to them. A statement of this sort only draws a comparison with things of which their wellbeing and worth were dear to their hearts, or the truth of which they all agreed upon.

19   Therefore it is impious of some sacrificers (and others too) to imitate the threats that heathens make, in order to reinforce the truth of their seeming piety or their claim in the presence of the people they have shocked. They call on Satan or hellish threats to witness against them,[6] even though the holy writings present to us God as the only judge and upholder of hidden truth. In their oaths the papal teachers also impiously add the invocation of deceased saints to their calling on God's name, contrary to God's explicit command in Deuteronomy 6:13, and 10:20; likewise Isaiah 45:22 and 65:16, which we cited in theses seven and nine.

20   Lawful oaths have as their subject* the things we say or promise. For through the oath we assert the truth of things in the past and promise the certainty of future things, and from this arises the division of oaths into one of assertion and one of promise.

21   Both oaths ought to be by means of words understood according to the common* usage of people, without deceit and trickery—contrary to the 'mental reservations' of the Jesuits[7] and the Anabaptists' deceitful ambigui-

---

6   Namely, in case they do not speak the truth.
7   The concept of 'mental reservations' became famous through its adoption by the Jesuit order. In earlier Roman Catholic casuistry, the notion of 'wider mental reservation' covered the use of equivocal expressions and cases in which a qualification of a statement could be inferred from specific circumstances known to the speaker but not to the hearer. The concept of 'strict mental reservation' was developed in the sixteenth century and approved by several theologians, mainly of the Jesuit order. Besides the equivocation implied in the wider mental reservation, the strict mental reservation means that one's statement is contrary to his or her intention; for example, when a man says to a woman, "I take you for my wife," but has no intention to marry her. The Jesuit moralists approve such a 'lie' if the speaker has good reasons for misleading the hearer; in that case, one is not guilty of perjury

sermone nostro, nostrum etiam debet esse etiam, et non, non, ut Christus praecipit, Matth. 5, 37. et Apostolus Paulus repetit, 2 Cor. 1, 18. quanto magis hoc in jurejurando est observandum.

XXII Quod ea speciatim attinet, quorum veritas jurejurando asseritur, ea certo oportet esse cognita ac perspecta. Temerarium enim est, Deum in testem ac vindicem veritatis nobis incertae, tamquam certae vocare, sicut jurisjurandi verus usus quoque ostendit; est enim πάσης ἀντιλογίας πέρας, ut ex Apostolo Heb. 6, 16. audivimus.

XXIII Quod porro rerum futurarum promissiones attinet, jurandum hic nobis ex praescripto Dei, Jer. 4, 2. in veritate, in judicio et in justitia.

XXIV *In veritate*; quia non tantum lingua ac verbis, sed et animo ac sincero proposito est promittendum, contra infidum hoc hominum genus, qui lingua jurant, sed mentem injuratam gerunt. *In judicio*; quia nihil leviter ac temere, et quod nullo modo est in nostra potestate, promittendum; alioqui enim nomen Domini in vanum assumitur. *In justitia* denique; quia nihil nisi honestum ac justum est jurejurando promittendum; illicita enim male jurantur, ac pejus observantur.

XXV Ex quibus patet, juramenta, ex iracundia aut simili affectu profecta, non esse legitima; quale fuit Davidis, cum internecionem domui Nabalis iratus juravit, 1 Sam. 25, 22. Aut de rebus incertis, quale fuit Herodis, qui puellae saltatrici

---

or lying. In the strict mental reservation the speaker mentally adds some qualification to the words which he utters, and the words together with the mental qualification make a true assertion in accordance with fact. Despite the adoption of this strategy by the Jesuit order, the 'mental reservation' remained controversial within the Catholic Church, and was eventually condemned in 1679. See also Perez Zagorin, *Ways of Lying: Dissimulation, Persecution, and Conformity in Early Modern Europe* (Cambridge: Harvard University Press, 1990).

ties.[8] For if in all our speech our "'yes' should be 'yes' and our 'no' 'no'," as Christ teaches in Matthew 5:37 and the apostle Paul repeats in 2 Corinthians 1:18, how much more must we keep this command in the swearing of oaths.

22 When it comes to the specific things about which the truth is asserted by means of the oath, they surely must be well-understood, and transparent. For it is rash to call God as the witness and upholder of a truth about which we are unsure as if it is certain. The true usage of oath-swearing shows this too, for "it is final in every dispute," as we have heard from the apostle in Hebrews 6:16.[9]

23 As far as the promise of future things is concerned we must swear in accordance with the precept God gives in Jeremiah 4:2: in truth, in uprightness, and in justice.

24 In truth: Because the promise must be made not only with our tongue and our words, but also from the heart and with genuine intent—quite unlike that unreliable type of people who swear with their tongue only but not in their heart. In uprightness: Because we should promise nothing lightly and too hastily, or promise what is not in any way under our control; for otherwise the Lord's name is used in vain. Lastly, in justice: Because nothing should be promised in an oath unless it is honest and just. For it is bad to swear things that are not permissible, and even worse to keep them.

25 From these things it is clear that oaths which proceed from a hot temper or a similar emotion are not lawful. Of such a sort was David's oath when in anger he swore total destruction on the household of Nabal (1 Samuel 25:22). Nor should one swear about matters that are uncertain, such as Herod did when he swore

---

8 In the Dutch language, the expression 'menistenleugen' (Mennonite lie) recalls the practice ascribed to the Anabaptist leader Menno Simons and his followers. The 'menistenleugen' is defined as "a half-truth, or a phrase or sentence formulated in such a way that the listener can interpret it in a different way from what has been said in fact." A frequently told anecdote about Menno Simons reveals his tactic of dealing with the truth (see C.J. Dyck, "Menno Simons and the White Lie," *Mennonite Encyclopedia*, Scottsdale: Herald Press, 1990, 5:555): "It was illegal to be an Anabaptist in the Netherlands, and the authorities had put a price on Menno's head. Menno was an itinerant pastor and networker among hidden groups, and he was very influential—so he was a prime target. One day Menno was traveling from one church to another, riding on a stagecoach. Instead of getting into the coach, he decided to ride up front, up high, with the driver. Suddenly policemen dashed up on horses; they were hunting for Menno. One of them shouted, 'Is Menno Simons in that coach?' So Menno leaned down and asked: 'Is Menno in there?' Someone from inside replied, 'No he's not in here.' So Menno told the policemen, 'They say Menno's not in the coach.' Foiled, frustrated, the horsemen rode away."

9 See thesis 12 above.

daturum se juravit, quicquid petiisset, Matth. 14, 7. Aut de rebus impiis, quale fuit Judaeorum illorum, qui se cibum non sumpturos conjurarant, nisi occiso Paulo, Act. 23, 13.

XXVI Ad promissorium hoc juramenti genus,* *vota* pertinent, ad quorum rectum usum, conditiones in omni legitimo juramento requisitae quoque pertinent.

XXVII Unde liquet, omnia illa vota esse condemnanda, quae vel creaturis fiunt, vel temere, et de rebus vetitis, aut in nostra potestate non sitis, nuncupantur. Ad quae referimus vota, quae inter Pontificios Sanctis voventur, item tria illa quae Monachatui communia sunt, nempe paupertatis voluntariae, caelibatus et obedientiae, ut vocant, regularis.

XXVIII Legitima vero vota proprie circa res* divinum cultum spectantes versantur, sive per se et directe, sive per accidens* et indirecte.

XXIX Quae per se et directe divinum cultum spectant, sunt vel universalia vel particularia.

XXX Universalia rursum sunt vel ordinaria et perpetua in Ecclesia Dei, vel extraordinaria et certis tantum casibus renovata.

XXXI Ordinaria sunt, per quae singuli fideles ad totum cultum divinitus institutum, observandum, a se, aut parentibus suis obligantur; quae obligatio in Novo Testamento per Baptismum inchoatur, per Sacram vero Coenam renovatur ac confirmatur. Unde et illius obligationis signacula, Sacramenta* a veteri Ecclesia sunt appellata.

to give to his dancing daughter whatever she asked (Matthew 14:7). Nor about wicked things, such as those Jews did who swore that they would not eat food unless Paul was killed (Acts 23:13).

26 The conditions that are requisite in every lawful oath pertain to the right use of the vows that belong to this promissory kind* of oath.[10]

27 From this it is clear that we must condemn all vows that are made to creatures, or that are spoken rashly or about things that are forbidden or not within our control. Among these we place those vows that the papal teachers make to saints; so too the three that are common to the state of being a monk, namely the vows of voluntary poverty, celibacy, and the obedience which befits regular clergy (as they call it).

28 Lawful vows, however, are those that properly concern matters* that look to the worship of God, whether of themselves and directly, or by accident* and indirectly.

29 The ones which of themselves look directly to the worship of God are either universal or particular.

30 Again, the universal ones are either ordinary and continuous in the church of God, or they are extraordinary and renewed only in certain cases.

31 Ordinary vows are ones through which individual believers obligate themselves or their parents to keep the whole worship that God has ordained. In the New Testament this obligation begins at Baptism and is renewed and confirmed at Holy Supper. For this reason the early church called the signs of that obligation 'sacraments.'*[11]

---

10 The discussion of the 'vows' is structured as follows:
   I. vows made to creatures—always to be condemned (th. 27)
   II. lawful vows that look to the worship of God (th. 28)
      a. either of themselves and directly (th. 29–39),
      b. or by accident and indirectly (th. 47–51), such as oaths in political and non-religious affairs.
   Concerning the vows made directly to God, a further distinction is made between vows of universal scope (e.g., the sacraments, the reforms by Judah's king Josiah, th. 30–32), and particular vows made by individual persons (th. 33–39). A critical discussion is provided of the question whether one should impose limits on one's own and other people's freedom by means of such particular vows (th. 40–46).
   In addition to the discussion of the vows provided here, Disputation 38 is entirely devoted to this theme, which was obviously of theological and social relevance at the time of the *Synopsis*.

11 For the use of the word 'sacrament' in this connection, see also thesis 2 above. The connection of the terms 'oath' and 'sacrament' is traced back to Tertullian's *An Address to the Martyrs*, 3.1 (CCSL 1: 5), where Tertullian urges the Christian prisoners to die like brave soldiers, because "we were drafted into the army of the living God immediately

XXXII Extraordinaria voco, quae certis casibus aut temporibus nonnunquam a tota Ecclesia, aut ab illius optima parte renovantur, adversus aliorum a vero Dei cultu defectionem, aut corruptionis futurae metum, qualia vota publice a Josua, Jos. 24, 25. a Josia, 2 Reg. 23, 3. ab Esdra, Esd. 10, 5. et nonnullis aliis, inter Dei populum fuerunt instituta.

XXXIII Particularia vota appello, quae a particularibus Ecclesiae membris fiunt, idque vel in rebus necessariis et per se sanctis, vel in rebus mediis et per se adiaphoris.

XXXIV In rebus sanctis et bonis pii nonnunquam novo voto se obstringunt, ut calcar sibi ad virtutem aliquam a Deo praeceptam addant; vel adversus nonnulla vitia, a quibus maxime infestantur, remedia validiora inveniant. Non quo per ejusmodi vota obedientiam suam Deo magis gratam, et ut volunt Pontificii, meritoriam constituant, aut majoris perfectionis gradum acquirant; sed quo infirmitatis suae sibi conscii, pluribus adminiculis se adversus Satanae ac carnis impetum confirment.

XXXV Sic Job. 31, 1. testatur, se pepigisse foedus cum oculis suis, ne adverteret ad virginem, et Nehemias cum primoribus populi speciatim juramento se obstrinxerunt, quod porro non essent filias suas vicinis gentibus in matrimonium daturi, nec merces ab iis venales allatas, Sabbatis empturi.

XXXVI Praecipua vero difficultas consistit in votis illis, quae de rebus mediis atque adiaphoris concipiuntur.

XXXVII Sunt ea autem duplicia, vel enim res ipsae votis subjectae, quoad operis substantiam,* verbo Dei praeceptae sunt, ac solae earum circumstantiae liberae atque arbitrariae; vel tam res quam rerum circumstantiae libero usui humano sunt relictae.

XXXVIII Prioris generis exempla, sunt vota de jejunio et sui ipsius afflictione, Num. 30, 13. Vota de eleemosynis in pauperes, aut aliis sumptibus in Ecclesiae necessarios usus faciendis, Gen. 28, 20. Vota de seipso, aut suis Ecclesiae ministerio consecrandis, quale fuit votum Annae, 1 Sam. 1, 11.

XXXIX Posterioris generis exempla, sunt in votis plane arbitrariis Veteris Testamenti; item in Rechabitis de abstinentia a vino, uvis, etc. item de non conserendis agris aut vineis, de non aedificandis domibus, de Tabernaculis habitandis,

---

when we repeated the words in the oath [*sacramentum*]." At the time of the Reformation, Ulrich Zwingli took up Tertullian's idea of the sacraments as a parallel to the soldier's oath in *Statement of Faith* (*Fidei ratio*; 1530), p. 11, and *True and False Religion* (*De vera et falsa religione*; 1530), pp. 196–197. In article 34 of the *Belgic Confession*, the description of baptism as the "mark and sign" of Christ (more pointedly in Dutch: "merk en veldteken") recalls the context in which Tertullian used the term 'sacrament.' For a general discussion of the function of signs and sacraments in the era of the Reformation see Edward Muir, *Ritual in Early Modern Europe* (2nd ed.; Cambridge: Cambridge University Press, 2005).

32 I give the name extraordinary vows to those which the entire church (or the better part of it) sometimes renews in certain cases or situations over against others who have defected from the true worship of God, or out of a fear of imminent decay, such as the public vows pledged in the midst of God's people by Joshua (Joshua 24:25), Josia (2 Kings 23:3), Ezra (Ezra 10:5), and some others.

33 I give the name 'particular vows' to those which are made by individual members of the church, and which happen either in matters that are urgent or sacred in themselves, or in matters that are intermediate and indifferent in themselves.

34 In sacred and noble matters the pious sometimes subject themselves to the obligation of a new vow in order to give themselves an incentive to keep some precept of God, or to find stronger remedies against some vices that are harassing them greatly. They do so not because through this kind of vow they might make their obedience more pleasing to God, and, as some papal teachers would have it, more meritorious, or to obtain a greater degree of perfection. Rather, deeply aware of their own weakness, by these additional supports they seek to strengthen themselves against the onslaught of Satan and their own flesh.

35 In this way Job testifies that "he made a covenant with his eyes not to look lustfully at a girl" (Job 31:1); and Nehemiah and the leaders of the people bound themselves with an oath that from that time onward they "would not give their daughters into marriage to the neighboring peoples" and that "on the Sabbath-day they would not purchase goods that they have brought to sell" [Nehemiah 10:30–31].

36 A special difficulty exists, however, in those vows that are uttered about intermediate matters, or matters of indifference.

37 And these matters are of two kinds, for either the Word of God commands that the matters themselves are subject to vows insofar as the nature* of the work is concerned (while only their circumstances are unrestricted and voluntary), or the matters as well as their circumstances are left to be used according to human freedom.

38 Examples of the first kind are: vows of fasting and self-affliction (Number 30:13), vows of giving alms to the poor, or of other expenses that must be assumed when the Church has need of them (Genesis 18:20[-22]), vows of dedicating oneself or one's loved ones to the service of the Church; such was Hannah's vow, in 1 Samuel 1:11.

39 Examples of the second kind are found in vows of the Old Testament that are obviously voluntary, like the vows of the Rechabites to abstain from wine, grapes, etc.; and like the vows of not sowing fields and vineyards, of not building

etc., quorum mentio fit et obedientia a Deo laudatur Jer. 35., etsi haec de obedientia politica a nonnullis explicentur.

XL Prioris generis libertatem voto constringere, non existimamus illicitum. Tum quia res illae sunt perpetui usus in Ecclesia et per Christi adventum non abolitae; tum quia ejusmodi vota inter Patriarchas quoque usitata ante legem latam fuerunt, unde et inter omnes gentes ex lege naturae usurpata videntur.

XLI Quod inde quoque suaderi potest; quod rerum illarum modus* aliquis, exemplis et praeceptis Apostolicis, in genere saltem fuerit constitutus. Quemadmodum in jejuniis frequens fuit Apostolus, 1 Cor. 7, 5. et 2 Cor. 11, 27. de liberalitate in sanctos, pro divinae erga nos benedictionis modo, praecepta dat, 1 Cor. 16, 2. et Stephanae familiam testatur se addixisse sanctis, in ministerium, id est, ministerio sanctorum se totos devovisse. Etsi enim hic votorum non fiat mentio, quum tamen certum cordis propositum in iis laudetur, non erit illicitum hoc cordis propositum, etiam *voto*, ad calcar nostrae negligentiae addendum, confirmare.

XLII An vero posterioris generis vota sint licita in Novo Testamento, per quae, nimirum, rerum per se indifferentium usus ad unam partem perpetuo restringatur, difficilior est quaestio; nec de iis inter scriptores Orthodoxos convenit, quibusdam non licere, quibusdam licere affirmantibus, modo absit opinio cultus et adsit finis bonus.

XLIII Nos ergo, salvo aliorum judicio, nemini licere existimamus sibi aut aliis absolute* per votum interdicere usu earum rerum, quem Christus liberum esse voluit. Pugnat enim hoc cum praecepto Apostoli ad Gal. 5, 1. Perstate in illa libertate, qua Christus nos liberavit, et ne regredientes implicamini servitutis jugo. Item, ad Col. 2, 20. Si mortui estis cum Christo ab elementis mundi; quid ut viventes in mundo, ritibus oneramini, ne ederis, neque gustaris, neque attigeris, etc. Imo vero ut doctrina Daemoniorum condemnatur, abstinere a cibis quos Deus creavit, 1 Tim. 4. Si vero eorum discrimen aliis obtrudere non possumus, ergo nec nobis ipsis.

XLIV Secundum quid* tamen, et aliquo respectu id licere existimamus; nempe eo modo et in eum finem, quem Sacra Scriptura ipsa nobis praescribit, si,

houses, and of dwelling in tents, etc. These were mentioned in Jeremiah 35 [:1–11], and God commends adherence to them—although some people explain these as being about obedience of a political nature.

We deem that it is allowed to place restrictions on one's freedom by means of the first kind of vow. This is so because those matters are for perpetual use in the Church and were not abolished with Christ's coming, and also because the patriarchs, too, had used vows of this sort before the Law was introduced, and hence it appears that all peoples also make use of them by the law of nature. 40

This can be shown convincingly also from the fact that, in a general way* at least, the apostles established those vows in some form or other by their own example and instruction. Accordingly, the apostle often fasted (1 Corinthians 7:5; 2 Corinthians 11:27), and he gives instruction about our generosity towards fellow believers, according to the measure of God's blessings to us (1 Corinthians 16:2). And it is testified of Stephanas' family that they committed themselves to service [1 Corinthians 16:15]; that is, that they devoted themselves entirely to serving the saints. For although no mention is made here of vows, nevertheless since the firm resolve of their hearts is commended, it will be allowed to confirm this heart's resolve also with a vow, to spur us on in our slothfulness. 41

A more difficult question, however, is whether vows of the latter sort are permitted in the New Testament; that is to say, those vows whereby the use of things that of themselves are indifferent is continuously restricted to one party. Nor is there any agreement among the orthodox writers about these vows, as some of them assert that they are not permitted, and others that they are, provided that not any notion of worship accompanies them and that they serve a good goal. 42

And so, without slighting the opinion of others, it is our view that no one is permitted by means of a vow to forbid himself or others completely* from using those things which Christ has willed to be unrestricted. For this is in conflict with the teaching of Paul in Galatians 5:1: "Stand fast in that freedom in which Christ has set you free, and do not return to being tied up with a yoke of slavery." Likewise, in Colossians 2:20: "If you have died with Christ from the elements of the universe, why as though living in the world do you submit yourselves to regulations—do not eat, do not taste, do not touch, etc.?" In fact, to abstain from foods which God has created is condemned as the devils' own teaching (1 Timothy 4[:1–3]). Well then, if we cannot foist that distinction upon others, then we cannot foist it upon ourselves either. 43

However, in a relative* sense, and in some respects we deem that it is permitted to forbid oneself. That is to say, when it is done in a way and for a purpose which sacred Scripture itself prescribes for us: Namely, if their use 44

nimirum, eorum usus sit aliis futurus scandalo, aut cessurus nobis in licentiam carnis; has enim duas conditiones proponit Scriptura, Rom. 14, 20. Gal. 5, 13.

XLV	Et in hoc vovendi modo non praejudicatur libertati Christianae, quia Sacra Scriptura libertatem illam sic ipsa restringit. Alio vero modo aut fine hoc audere, superstitio est Christianis fugienda.

XLVI	Atque hinc quoque sequitur, quando metus scandali aut licentiae carnis ex earum rerum mediarum usu cessat, tum vim voti hujus quoque cessare; quia tum finem a Deo praescriptum non habet, ac proinde in ἐθελοθρησκείαν verbo Dei vetitam transit.

XLVII	Et haec quidem sufficiant de juramenti objectis in rebus sacris aut cultum Dei spectantibus; restant nonnulla de materia juramenti in rebus politicis et profanis.

XLVIII	Requiritur ergo, ut illa quae juramento asserenda aut promittenda sunt, non sint res leves aut vulgares; quales in communem hominum vitam quotidie incidunt, in quibus sermo noster esse debet, Etiam et non, ut Christus, Matt. 5, 37. jubet, sed ut sint res graves atque arduae, et in quibus Reipublicae salus aut proximi caritas singulariter versatur, sicut exempla Scripturae omnia ostendunt, et finis juramento propositus, Heb. 6.

XLIX	Sunt autem ea vel publica, vel privata. Publica sunt, confoederationes inter principes aut populos, inter Abrahamum et Abimelecum, ut Gen. 21, 31., et inter Isaacum et Abimelecum, Gen. 26, 28. et inter Nebuchadnesarem et Tsedekiam, 2 Chron. 36, 13. etc. Huc referimus juramentum fidelitatis inter Principes et subditos, item sacramentum* militare, cujus utriusque exemplum 2 Reg. 11, 4. Huc quoque referimus juramenta judicialia, Ex. 22, 11., et alibi, item foedera conjugalia, Mal. 2,14.

were to become a stumbling-block for others, or if it were to end up as a license for the flesh for ourselves. For these are the two conditions that Scripture puts forward in Romans 14:20 and Galatians 5:13.

And in this manner of making vows no prejudice is intended against Christian liberty,[12] because sacred Scripture itself limits that freedom in this way. But daring to do this in a different way or for a different purpose is a superstition that Christians ought to shun.

Hence it follows also that when the fear of stumbling-blocks or of licenses of the flesh from the use of those intermediate things ceases, then the force of this vow also comes to an end. For then it does not have the purpose that was prescribed by God, and consequently it becomes a self-willed religion that is forbidden by the Word of God.

And so let these comments be sufficient about the objects of the oath in matters that are holy or that look to the worship of God. It still remains to make some observations about the substance of the oath in political and non-religious affairs.

It is required therefore that those things which are to be confirmed or promised by means of an oath be not trivial or mundane. Things of this sort occur every day in the common course of human life, in which our speech should be "yes and no," as is the bidding of Jesus in Matthew 5:37. Instead they should be serious and demanding matters, and matters in which there is a special concern for the wellbeing of the nation or love for the neighbor, as is shown by all the Scriptural examples and the purpose for oaths stated in Hebrews 6.[13]

Well then, these matters are either public or private in nature. The public ones are: treaties among rulers or nations, such as between Abraham and Abimelech (Genesis 21:31), between Isaac and Abimelech (Genesis 26:28), and between Nebuchadnezzar and Zedekiah (2 Chronicles 36:13), etc. In this category we also place oaths of fidelity between rulers and their subjects, as well as military oaths;* an example of each occurs in 2 Kings 11:4. In this place we also put oaths of a judicial sort (Exodus 22:11 and elsewhere), likewise vows of marriage (Malachi 2:14).

---

12 Christian liberty was an important theme in the theology of the Reformers; see Martin Luther's treatise *Von der Freiheit eines Christenmenschen* (WA 7, 12–38), and John Calvin's *Institutes*, 3.19.

13 See theses 12 and 22 above.

L   Privata vocamus quae inter privatos privatim fiunt. Quale exploratores Terrae Canaan Rachabae meretrici de ipsa et cognatione ejus a caede conservanda praestiterunt, Jos. 2, 12. Jacob et Laban de injuria aut noxa invicem non inferenda, Gen. 31, 53. David et Jonathan de mutua amicitia et cura, 1 Sam. 20, 12.

LI   Hoc tamen hic interesse videmus, quod inter personas* aequales et sibi mutuo nondum subjectas, jusjurandum non nisi ex mutuo consensu fiat; inter eas vero quarum aliae aliis subjectae sunt, juramentum etiam imperari atque exigi possit, ut exempla supra allata evincunt.

LII   Hisce ad hunc modum breviter explicatis, subjiciemus jam aliquot quaestiones, quae in juramentorum praxi versantur et inter Theologos disputantur, ex quibus reliquarum, quas hic non memoramus, solutiones fere pendent.

LIII   Et *primo* quaeritur, An juramentum deferri possit iis, qui per falsos Deos, aut per creaturas jurant; cum per ejusmodi delationem peccandi occasiones suggerere videamur.

LIV   Ad hoc respondemus, inter personas quae sibi mutuo subjectae non sunt, quum alia ratione caveri non potest, id posse permitti; sicut exemplum Jacobi, qui per Deum verum, et Labanis, qui per Deos Nachoris juravit, Gen. 31, 53. ostendit. Nam non ideo probatur vitium jurijurando adhaerens, etsi juramenti fides et veritas probetur.

LV   *Secundo* quaeritur, an juramenta per falsos Deos aut creaturas facta, servanda sint ab iis, qui postea melius edocti, errorem in juramento admissum agnoscunt. Respondemus, si res jurejurando promissae sint bonae et justae, omnino servanda esse ejusmodi juramenta arbitramur, ex Analogia loci Matt. 23, 16. et seqq.

LVI   *Tertio* quaeritur, an omnia juramenta et vota servanda sint, quae de rebus futuris concepta aut nuncupata sunt. Respondeo, omnia ea juramenta ac vota esse servanda, quae conditiones supra a nobis allatas habent, licet ea gravia nobis aut damnosa sint, ut David testatur, Ps. 15, 4. et exemplum, quod exstat Jos. 9. de Gibeonitis, et Jud. 21, 1. de Benjamitis, etc.

LVII   Si quae tamen jurejurando promissa sunt, quae cum Dei verbo pugnant, tum valebit illud vulgare, In turpi voto muta decretum, in malis promissis rescinde fidem, quemadmodum exemplum Davidis, 1 Sam. 25, 33. et Christi reprehensio, Marc. 7, 11. demonstrant. Nam nullum juramentum, quamlibet

We give the name 'private' to those vows that are made between individuals privately. The spies of the land of Canaan offered such a vow to Rahab the harlot, to save her and her family from slaughter (Joshua 2:12). Jacob and Laban promised each other that they would cause no injury or harm to each other (Genesis 31:53). David and Jonathan made a vow of friendship and mutual care (1 Samuel 20:12).

Moreover, here we see that there is a difference: The taking of oaths between persons* who are of equal status and not yet subject to each other should occur only when it is by mutual consent. However, between persons of which one is subject to another, the oath may even be demanded and required, as the examples that were adduced above prove.

Having briefly explained these matters to this extent, we shall now add a few questions which are brought to bear in the practice of making oaths and which are debated by theologians; the solutions to other questions (which we are not bringing to mind here) are generally derived from these.

And in the first place the question is asked whether the making of oaths can be entrusted to those who swear by false gods or by creatures, since we seem to be providing opportunities to sin by offering an oath of this kind.

Our answer to this is that when it cannot be avoided by another means, the taking of such oaths can be permitted between people who are not subject to one another. This is illustrated by the example of Jacob, who swore by the true God, and Laban, who swore by the gods of Nahor (Genesis 31:53). For it is not so that hereby the fault accompanying the oath is being confirmed, although the truth of the vow and its dependability is being confirmed.

Secondly, the question is posed whether oaths made in the name of false gods or creatures must be kept by those people who, when they are better informed at a later point in time, realize that an error was inserted in the oath. We respond that in our judgment such an oath should be kept in its entirety, if the things promised by swearing are good and just, on analogy of Matthew 23:16 f.

In the third place the question is asked whether all the oaths that are devised or uttered about future events must be kept. My answer is that all those oaths and vows must be kept which have the conditions we introduced earlier, even though they may be harmful or detrimental to us, just as David testifies (Psalm 15:4), as well as the example found in Joshua 9 about the Gibeonites, and Judges 21:1 about the Benjamites, etc.

However, if in making oaths promises are made which conflict with the word of God, then that well-known saying applies: 'In a shameful vow alter your decision; in evil promises break your trust.' This is what the example of David (1 Samuel 25:33) and the reprimand by Christ (Mark 7:11) demonstrate. For no

sacrum et vehemens, hominem potest solvere ab obedientia quam Deo debet, nec juramentum potest* esse iniquitatis vinculum.

LVIII   *Quarto* quaeritur, an latroni aut piratae fides data sit servanda. Respondeo, latroni ac piratae servandam esse fidem in promissis quae damnum tantum privatum secum trahunt, ex dicto Davidis Ps. 15. Si quid vero adversus rempublicam, aut boni civis officium juramento promissum sit, id servari non potest, quia id contra legem Dei pugnat.

LIX   *Quinto* quaeritur, an fides haereticis sit servanda. Negant id Romanenses, quia lex Dei haereticos punire jubet. Sed respondeo, nec omnium haereticorum poenam mandat Deus, et si quorum poenam mandat, non mandat eorum poenam quibus fides publica in contrarium est data. Quemadmodum licet maledicentes principi divina lege puniebantur, noluit tamen David Simei propter hoc crimen, contra fidem datam poena commerita affici.

LX   *Sexto* quaeritur, an frangenti fidem fides quoque frangenda sit. Respondeo, in juramentis reciprocis aut conditionalibus, conditione ab una parte violata, alteram partem non amplius teneri, certum est. Sed si absolute quis quippiam alteri jurarit, et si alter suam fidem non praestet, non ideo perfidia ab altera parte est utendum.

LXI   *Denique* quaeritur, an a jurejurando praestito quispiam per alium solvi possit. Respondeo: de minoribus, aut sub aliorum potestate constitutis, Deus legem tulit, Num. 30. alios vero juramenta legitima solvendi aut dispensandi modos Sacra Scriptura ignorat.

20. CONCERNING THE OATH

oath, however sacred and forceful it may be, has the power* to free a man from the obedience that is owed to God, nor can any oath bind us to sin.

58 Fourthly it is asked whether one must keep the promise of trust that has been given to a robber or pirate. I answer that one must keep the trust promised to a robber or pirate in those vows which bring in their wake damage only for the individual person, in keeping with David's statement in Psalm 15. However, if anything is promised by oath that is contrary to the common good or an upright citizen's duties, then it cannot be kept, because it is in conflict with the law of God.

59 In the fifth place the question is asked whether the trust that is sworn to heretics must be kept. The followers of Rome state that it should not be kept, on the grounds that God's law bids heretics be punished. But I reply that God does not order the punishment of all heretics, and if he does demand their punishment, he does not demand punishment of those who were granted the public promise to the contrary. It is in this way that those who maligned a ruler were punished by God's law; nevertheless David did not want Shimei to be punished for this crime with a just penalty, since that would violate the promise given to him.

60 It is asked in the sixth place whether we should break the trust that is placed in someone who breaks his trust. My answer: It is obvious that in mutual or conditional oaths, when one party breaks the condition, the other party is no longer bound. But if someone has made an unconditional oath to another, and if the other does not make good on his trust, then that is not a reason for the other party to act in faithlessness.

61 And finally the question is posed whether one can be released by someone else from a given oath. I respond that God has given a law concerning minors or those under the control of others in Numbers 30;[14] however, Holy Scripture does not know of other ways to resolve or discharge legitimate oaths.

---

14 Numbers 30:4–17 describes the validity of oaths made by women in their relationship to men. In cases in which a woman is subjected to a man's rule (as a daughter or a wife), the man can make void her (thoughtless) oath as soon as he learns about it and thereby release the woman from her oath. If a man, however, hears about the oath, but does not oppose it, the oath remains valid and he is not allowed to annul it in the future.

DISPUTATIO XXI

De Sabbatho et die Dominico

Praeside D. ANTONIO THYSIO
Respondente SAMUELE DAMBRINO

THESIS I Posteaquam de Idololatria deque Juramento, ad explicationem prioris Tabulae Decalogi est actum, sequitur, ut de Sabbatho et Die Dominico συζήτησιν similiter instituamus.

II Ac primo vocem* quod attinet, שבת Sabath, idem valet quod cessare, quiescere, desinere. Unde שבת Shabbath, contracte, quasi שבתת ut vult Kimchi,[a] et שבתון Shabbathon omnis cessatio sc. ab opere, et quies, nempe a motu et labore; quae relata ad Deum est speciatim cessatio Dei, et quidem ab opere creationis die septimo; ad hominem, ejusdem similiter cessatio hebdomadatim eodem die repetita, ei fini benedicto sanctificatoque. Unde utrumque, et ipsa cessatio et hic dies, Sabbathi nomine* venit. Ac dicitur hic dies, dies Sabbathi, seu dies quietis, et שבת, שבתון Shabbath, Shabbathon, Sabbathum quietis, Ex. 31, 15. et simpliciter, Sabbathum. Quin dies septimus et Sabbathum pro eodum sumuntur.

---

[a] See R. David Kimchi, *Sefer ha-Shorashim* (Berlin: G. Bethge, 1847), 369. Thysius probably used the following work based on Kimchi: *Thesaurus linguae sanctae, ex R. David Kimchi Libro Radicum [...] contractior et emendatior* (Paris: Robert Estienne, 1548), 1348, of which a copy is found in the university of Leiden library.

DISPUTATION 21

On the Sabbath and the Lord's Day

President: Antonius Thysius
Respondent: Samuel Dambrinus[1]

Now that in explaining the first table of the Decalogue we have treated Idolatry and the Oath, it follows that we similarly hold a disputation on the Sabbath and the Lord's Day.[2] 1

In the first place, as far as the verb* *Shabbat* is concerned, it has the same force of meaning as 'to cease,' 'to be at rest,' 'to stop.' Whence *Shabbat* (in contracted form), like *Shabbatat* (as Kimchi[3] would have it), and *Shabbaton*, means any form of 'cessation,' that is, from work; and it means 'rest,' namely rest from movement and work. With reference to God it means in particular God's being at rest, namely from the work of creation on the seventh day. Similarly with reference to man, it means the repeated weekly stoppage on the same day, a day which has been blessed and hallowed for this very purpose. From there both the stoppage itself and the particular day go by the name,* 'Sabbath.' And so this day is called 'the Sabbath day' or 'the day of rest,' and *Shabbat, Shabbaton*, the *Sabbath of rest* (Exodus 31:14[15]), and simply *Sabbath*. In fact, 'the seventh day' and 'Sabbath' are taken to mean the same thing. 2

---

1 Born ca. 1599 in Goes, Samuel Dambrinus matriculated on 24 September 1620 in theology. He was ordained in Munster (now: Borssele), Zeeland in 1627; he died in 1640. See du Rieu, *Album studiosorum*, 149, Van Lieburg, *Repertorium*, 46, and J.H. Hessels, *Archives of the London Dutch Church* (London: Nutt, 1892), 27, 239.

2 In this disputation Thysius first discusses the etymology and meaning of the Hebrew term 'Sabbath' (theses 1–7), and after offering a definition (theses 8–9) he turns to its origin, institution and its efficient cause (theses 8–16). After this he treats the goals of the Sabbath: universal, civic, and special, with its subdivisions (theses 17–21). This is followed by an extensive explanation of the Fourth Commandment and its observance (theses 23–40), its duration (theses 41–49), and its continuity and discontinuity with the institution of the Sunday in the New Testament era (theses 50–58). Finally, several forms of Sabbatarianism and its counterparts are rejected (theses 59–60). Thysius concludes this disputation by listing the most important feast days of the Christian Church: Nativity, Eastern, Pentecost.

3 David Kimchi (1160–1235) was a Jewish rabbi also known by the acronym Radak. His philological treatise on the Hebrew language, *Michlol*, was used by Christian Hebraists in the sixteenth century.

III Praeterea Sabbathi et Sabbathorum vox toti septimanae tribuitur, 2 Reg. 11, 7. Luc. 18, 12. scilicet, quod in hebdomade Sabbathum est, a quo reliqui dies censentur; etiam singuli dies a Sabbatho denominantur, prima, secunda, etc. Sabbathi, id est, a Sabbatho; atque hi Gentilibus quibusdam, planetarum et idolorum, puta Saturni, Solis, Lunae, etc. nominibus indigitantur. At prisca Ecclesia, forte ut sese ab utrisque, Gentilibus et Judaeis, disjungeret, singulos septimanae dies ferias appellavit: quamvis Scaliger obtinuisse id velit, praecipuo quodam principis septimanae Paschatis (cujus dies omnes antiquitus feriati, teste Hieronymo, erant) auspicio, lib. 1. *De Emend. temporum*.[a]

IV Id autem Sabbathum suo ambitu complectitur, praeter vulgare illud Hebdomadarum seu dierum, quod proprie* Sabbathum est, etiam annorum; nempe tum anni septimi recurrentis, quod Sabbathum terrae dicitur, Ex. 23, 11., quia eo terra quiescebat inculta, et inde prognata pauperibus cedebant, unde et ad desolationem terrae Sabbathum transfertur; tum septies septem annorum expletorum, quinquagesimi scilicet, qui Jubilaeus, ac liberationis et remissionis appellatur, ob libertatis possessionumque restitutionem, Lev. 23, 15. Quae quidem ab eodem sunt principio,* quietis nempe divinae, et synecdochice sub ea comprehenduntur. Sabbathum vero Thalmudicum septem millenariorum, quod mundi vocant, hic missum facimus.

V Adhaec quaelibet tempora sacra et feriata, etiamsi in septimum diem non inciderent, generali notione etiam Sabbatha dicuntur, et sub illo synecdochice continentur, Ezech. 20, 22. et 23. cap. tum menstruum, ut Neomenia seu Novilunium, Num. 28,11. tum anniversarium, nempe tria festa maxime solennia; ut

---

[a] Joseph Justus Scaliger, *Opus novum de emendatione temporum in VIII. libros tributum* (Paris: Sebastien Nivelle, 1583), 5A.

Moreover, the words 'Sabbath' and 'Sabbaths' are given to the entire week (2 Kings 11:7, Luke 18:12); this means that the other days of the week are counted from the Sabbath. Individual days, too, receive their name from the Sabbath: the first, the second day of the Sabbath etc., which means [the first, the second day] after the Sabbath. By some Gentile people these days are indicated by the names of planets and idols, such as Saturn, Sun, Moon, etc. But the early church, perhaps to distinguish itself from both the Gentiles and the Jews, gave the name 'holidays' to the individual days of the week—although Scaliger in book 1 of his *On the Correction of Chronologies* is of the view that the early church did this as a special token of the first week of the Passover (of which every day was a holiday in antiquity, according to Jerome).[4]

Moreover, besides the common one of '[the Sabbath] of weeks' or '[the Sabbath] of days' (which is properly* what 'Sabbath' is), 'Sabbath' includes in its range of meanings also '[the Sabbath] of years.' That is to say, it means also the Sabbath of the recurring seventh year, which is called 'the Sabbath of the land' (Exodus 23:11), because in that year the land was left to rest uncultivated; and whatever did grow upon it was left for the poor. From this the word is also transferred to the devastation of the land (Jeremiah 25:29[5]). It is used also of the completion of seven times seven years, that is, the fiftieth year, which is called the year of Jubilee, the year of freedom and of release because of the restoration of freedom and property (Leviticus 25:8, 10) They too stem from the same principle,* namely the divine rest, and are included in it through synecdoche.[6] As for the Talmud's 'Sabbath of the seven millennia,' which they call the 'Sabbath of the universe,' we do not trouble ourselves with that here.[7]

Additionally, all sacred days and holidays, even when they do not occur on the seventh day, are called Sabbath in a general sense and are included by it through synecdoche (Ezekiel 20, 22, and 23). These include the monthly (as in the 'Neomenia' or 'the New Moon') (Numbers 28:11) as well as the yearly

---

4   Joseph Justus Scaliger (1540–1609), was a French protestant humanist known for expanding the notion of classical history from Greek and Ancient Roman history to include Persian, Babylonian, Jewish and Ancient Egyptian history. After St. Bartholomew's massacre in 1572, Scaliger fled to Geneva, but returned to France in 1574. After two decades as a private scholar, he was appointed professor at Leiden in 1593, as the successor of Justus Lipsius.
5   Jeremiah 25:11–13, cf. 2 Chronicles 36:21.
6   For 'synecdoche,' see note at *SPT* 4.17.
7   The expressions 'sabbath of the world' or 'sabbath of the seven millennia' as references to the seventh era of the world, the age of Messiah, are found in Jewish commentaries on the Talmud: "Just as the seventh year is one year of release in seven, so is the world," Babylonian Talmud, *Sanhedrin*, fol. 97.

Paschatis, quod primi mensis anni, et septem diebus in Azymis, (unde festum infermentatorum dicitur) in memoriam transitus Angeli liberationisque ex Aegypto, et ad novarum frugum gratitudinem testandam, peragebatur; Pentecostes, quod expletionis septem a Paschate septimanarum, (unde et festum Hebdomadarum vocatur) in legis latae, et messis primitivorum (unde et denominationem habet) celebrationem; denique Scenopegiorum (cum quo conjungebantur etiam festa tubarum et expiationis) quod mensis septimi a Paschate erat et octo diebus, ad testandum ipsos in deserto in tabernaculis degisse, et ob fructus reliquos perceptos (quare et collectionis appellatur) celebrabatur: ex quibus et illius et hujus primus et ultimus Sabbathum erat et vocabatur, Exod. 23, 14. Lev. 23. Deut. 16.

VI Haec autem festa solennia, si in Sabbathum inciderent, ob duplicem festivitatem magnus dies Sabbathi vocabatur, Joh. 19, 31. At Scaliger simpliciter refert ad ipsam festivitatem, quod מועד, Moēd, seu חג, Chag, id est, statum seu solenne festum, septuaginta interpretes μεγάλην ἡμέραν vertant, Es. 1. Si vero plurium dierum, ut Paschatis et Scenopegias ultimus, puta septimus infermentatorum, et octavus Tabernaculorum, δευτερόπρωτον, secundoprimum Sabbathum dicebatur, Luc. 6, 1. quasi primum secundario repetitum, δεύτερον ὡς πρῶτον, id est, secundum primo par et aequale. At Scaliger esse vult, ἀπό δευτέρας πρῶτον, id est, a secunda die Paschatis, unde inibatur computus in Pentecostem. In *Prolegom.* ad I. *De Emend. temp.* et 1. 6.[a]

VII Quinimo et passim, totus externus iste divinus cultus, seu excercitium publicum, Sabbatho continetur et intelligitur, nempe Res, Loca, Tempora, et Personae sacrae, Deo ejusque cultui, Divina praescriptione, consecrata dedicataque.

VIII Attamen Sabbathi Hebdomadarii hic singularis est praeceptio, quod reliquis sit antiquius, excellentius, eorumque fundamentum:* ac proinde singulariter hic mandatur, et a nobis considerandum est.

---

[a] Scaliger, *Opus novum*, a-v v°- a-vi v°, and 259B–260D.

feasts, namely the three most solemn feast days. One of these is Passover, which was held in the first month of the year and by seven days of unleavened bread (whence it is called the Feast of Unleavened Bread) to commemorate the passing-over by the Angel and the deliverance from Egypt, and also to testify to their thankfulness for the new harvest. Another is Pentecost, which falls after the completion of seven weeks from Passover (whence it is called also the Feast of Weeks) and which was held to celebrate the giving of the Law, and of the harvest of the first fruits (from which it also gets its name).[8] And lastly there is the Feast of Booths (to which also the feast of trumpets and the feast of atonement are connected), which happened in the seventh month after Passover and lasted for eight days. It was celebrated as a testimony to their dwelling in tents in the wilderness, and for receiving the left-over harvest (whence it is also called the Feast of Ingathering). Of these both the first and the last days were, and were called, Sabbath-days (Exodus 23:14[15], Leviticus 23, Deuteronomy 16).

Moreover, if these solemn feast days should fall on the Sabbath, they were called the "great Sabbath-day" (John 19:31) because of the double celebration. But Scaliger simply applies the term to the feast day itself, because the translators of the Septuagint render *moʿed*, or *ḥag* (that is, the appointed or solemn feast day) as great day [*megalē hēmera*] (Isaiah 2). But if there was more than one sabbath day, such as the last of the Passover or of the Feast of Booths, namely the seventh day of the Feast of Unleavened bread, or the eighth day of the Feast of Booths, then it was called the second-first [*deuteroprōtos*] Sabbath (Luke 6:1), as though the first was repeated on the second, or *deuteron hōs prōton*, that is, the second equal to and the same as the first. But Scaliger thinks that it is *apo deuteras prōton*, that is, after the second day of Passover, from which point in time one started counting the days to Pentecost (in *On the Correction of Chronology*, the Prolegomena I, and 1.6).

6

In fact, 'Sabbath' throughout entails and assumes the entire outward religious worship, or the public practice of it; that is, the holy things, holy places, holy times, and holy people that have been consecrated and dedicated to God, along with worship of him, by divine decree.

7

But what we are discussing here is the commandment peculiar to the weekly Sabbath, since it is older and more special than the other Sabbaths and is the basis* for them. For this reason it receives its own commandment here, and that is what will be considered by us in what follows.

8

---

8 Pentecost is not only called the Feast of Weeks but also the Feast of Harvest. In the Vulgate Pentecost is called *messis primitivorum*; see Ex. 23:16; cf. Lev. 23:16.

IX   Est porro Sabbathum solenne et ordinarium Festum a Deo institutum, Hebdomadarium scilicet seu septimus et quidem a creatione dies, ad imitationem Dei, eo die ab operibus creationis cessantis, a servilibus et quotidianis operibus externa similiter cessatione et quiete a Judaeis religiose ex Dei mandato observandus; sanctisque exercitiis divini cultus occupandus.

X   Sabbathi autem praeceptio haec non est a naturae necessitate,* ut reliqua praecepta, quae menti insita ac per se cognita sunt, sed κατὰ συνθήκην, ex voluntaria Dei institutione, seu positivi (ut loquuntur) juris. Nam ut naturae sit, certa stataque tempora divino cultui dicanda, et quae ex divina praescriptione sunt, immote servanda esse, attamen hunc diem, et quidem huic parti divini cultus, puta memoriae creationis et ob hanc causam, quod Deus eo tempore cessaverit; et simili modo quiete scilicet et otio, singulariter observari et celebrari, non naturae, sed instituti est. Potuisset enim hoc ipsum non sigillatim commemorandum hoc die proponi, sed creationis memoria aut initio ejus, aut termino,* id est, diei primo aut ultimo deputari.

XI   Atque hinc etiam esse videtur, quod praeceptum hoc non negative, ut tria antecedentia, sed affirmative,* et singulariter hac forma proponatur, Memento ut diem Sabbathi sanctifices; causaque ejus subjiciatur, Quia cessavit die septimo ab opere suo; secus quam in ceteris, quae menti insita et per se cognita sunt, fieri videmus.

Well then, the Sabbath is a solemn, regular—namely, weekly—feast day 9
established by God, or the seventh day from creation, which, in imitation of
God who on that day ceased his work of creation, the Jews were commanded
by God to observe similarly by ceasing and resting externally from their servile
and everyday work in order to be occupied with the sacred activities of divine
worship.

Moreover, this precept for the Sabbath does not arise from a natural neces- 10
sity,* unlike the other commandments which are implanted in the heart and
are known through themselves; it exists by design, by the willful institution
of God, or the positive law, as it is called.[9] It is natural that certain set times
must be assigned for worshipping God, and that whatever comes from a commandment of God must be kept unchanged. However, it is by decree and not by
nature that this day in particular was established for this purpose of worshiping
God: in order to remember the creation, and for the fact that God ceased from
his work at that time; and for observing and celebrating it in precisely the same
way—that is, by resting and not working. For it could have been possible for this
[resting and not working] to be assigned for commemoration not specifically
on this day of the week, whereas the remembrance of creation could have been
assigned to either the start or finish,* that is, on the first or last day of the week.

Hence one sees also that this commandment is presented not negatively 11
(as are the three that come before it) but positively* and in a special way,
with this formula: "Remember to keep the Sabbath-day holy." And the reason
for it follows: "Because God rested from his work on the seventh day"; this is
different from what we see happening in the other commandments, which are
implanted in the heart and are known through themselves.

---

9 Here Thysius refers to a fundamental distinction between divine natural law, and positive law. The latter comprises commandments that are positive, that is, posited by the free will of God. Therefore they are not absolutely necessary but free and contingent: It is possible for them to be abrogated. In contrast to the first and second commandments, the commandment of the Sabbath with its observance of specific times cannot be deduced from God's nature (*ius divinum*). It can only be traced back to a free decision of God's will. See also thesis 42 on the cause of the Sabbath and theses 45–46 on the abrogation of ceremonial aspects of the Sabbath in the New Testament—which however does not imply abolition of its moral content. For the distinction between *ius divinum* and *ius positivum* in Reformed theology, including its roots in John Duns Scotus, see Beck, *Gisbertus Voetius*, 359–380; Aza Goudriaan, *Reformed Orthodoxy and Philosophy, 1625–1750: Gisbertus Voetius, Petrus van Mastricht, and Anthonius Driessen*, Brill's Series in Church History, vol. 26 (Leiden: Brill, 2006), 287–324.

XII   Atque hic dies, non humanae est institutionis, aut ex ἐθελοθρησκείᾳ, spontaneo cultu susceptus, sed Lege divinitus praeceptus imperatusque. Unde omnem necessitatem a Dei auctoritate accipit.

XIII   Is autem quando sit institutus, quibusque imperatus nempe, an jam inde ab initio, etiam ante lapsum, ab orbe scilicet condito, universim tum hominibus sit praestitutus, ut creationi coaevus, an vero post, Legis latae per Mosen tempore, Judaeis institutus, non perinde certum. Dicitur quidem Deus, sexto creationis die operibus suis absolutis, septimo ab illis quievisse, et ei benedixisse, eumque sanctificasse, Gen. 2, 2. 3. id est, non tantum augustum habuisse, sed et reliquorum numero exemisse ac religiosum homini esse voluisse; verum an ut destinatione, usu quoque a primordio fuerit an potius προλήψει anticipatione, inde certo non constat.

XIV   Certe Sabbathi ante legem Mosis nusquam ulla fit mentio, neque quisquam Sanctorum ejus cultor refertur, ut notat Tertul. lib. *adversus Judaeos*,[a] nisi quod ante Decalogum nomen, ratio* et usus ejus declaretur Exod. 16, 5. etc, forte ut tum institutum vel quod complura externi cultus a Mose potius sunt restituta et

---

[a] Tertullian, *Liber contra Judaeos* 2.12–14 (CCSL 2:1343–1344)

This day also was not founded by humans or from self-willed service,[10] nor undertaken as an unprompted worship, but it was commanded and ordered by God's Law. Thus it derives all its necessity from the authority of God.

But it is not entirely clear when that day was established, or to whom it was commanded; that is, whether it was presented to mankind as a whole already from the very beginning, even before the fall into sin (i.e., when the world was created), or whether in fact it was ordained later for the Jewish people, at the time when the Law was given through Moses. It states in Genesis 2:2,3 that after he had completed his work on the sixth day of creation, God rested from his works on the seventh day and blessed it, and hallowed it. That is to say, he considered the day not just worthy of honour, but he set it apart from the group of other days and determined that for mankind it be devoted to worship. However it is not altogether certain from this whether the use of that day was designed from the very beginning, or whether it was rather an idea awaiting realization.[11]

At any rate, before the Law of Moses no mention is made of the Sabbath-day anywhere, nor is any of the saints referred to as being a keeper of it, as Tertullian observes in his book *Against the Jews*; except that before the Decalogue was provided the name, reason,* and use of the Sabbath were manifested (Exodus 16:5, etc.). Perhaps this is so because the Sabbath was established at that time; or else it is so because Moses revived and augmented many features of its outward

---

10   On self-willed worship, see also SPT 19.3.
11   Apparently Thysius leaves the issue of the origin of Sabbath-keeping undecided. In the years immediately after the publication of the *Synopsis*, a debate arose on this question. In his "Investigatio sententiae et originis Sabbati" [Investigation into the Meaning and Origin of the Sabbath] (*Opera Omnia* [Amsterdam 1664] 2:256–276, first published in 1628), Franciscus Gomarus argued that the Sabbath as a recurring, weekly day of rest was not instituted in Paradise but during Israel's sojourn in the desert. Rivetus presented the opposite view in his *Praelectiones in cap. xx. Exodi* [Lectures on Exodus 20] (2nd ed.; Leiden: F. Heger, 1637), 107–123. Gomarus replied to Rivetus in 1632 with "Defensio investigationis originis Sabbati" [Defense of the Investigation into the Origin of the Sabbath] (*Opera Omnia*, 2:299–312). Rivetus responded in 1633 to Gomarus with "Appendix ad disquisitionem de origine primae observationis Sabbathi," [Appendix to the Discussion of the Origin of the First Sabbath Observance] in *Praelectiones*, 123–158. See G.P. van Itterzon, *Franciscus Gomarus* (The Hague: Martinus Nijhoff, 1930), 301–309. For an overview of the diverse Reformed interpretations of the Fourth Commandment, see Hugo B. Visser, *De Geschiedenis van de Sabbatsstrijd onder de Gereformeerden in de Zeventiende Eeuw* (Utrecht: Kemink en Zoon, 1939), and Richard J. Bauckham, "Sabbath and Sunday in the Protestant Tradition," in *From Sabbath to the Lord's Day: A Biblical, Historical, and Theological Investigation*, ed. D.A. Carson (Grand Rapids: Zondervan, 1982)

amplificata, quam primitus instituta; ut ante diluvium sacrificia, Gen. 4. mundorum et immundorum animalium discrimen, Gen. 7. post diluvium, comestio carnis cum sanguine prohibita, Gen. 9., circumcisio, Gen. 17. Joh. 7, 22. aliaque, ita et hoc verisimile est.

xv   Attamen Deus Israëlitis Sabbathum dedisse singulariter dicitur, Ezech. 20,12. illudque iis notum fecisse, Neh. 9,14. videlicet, vel ut rem cujus scientia aut usus ante non fuerit, vel quam intermissam et exoletam revocaverit et pristino usui restituerit. Sed parum interest, quid sit de temporis, aut personarum,* quoad institutionem, circumstantia: tametsi prior sententia probabilior videri potest.

xvi   Rationalis interim et divinae sapientiae conveniens institutionis ejus assignatur causa, a jubentis auctoritate et conformitate exempli, videlicet Dei, duplicato ad obediendum vinculo. Congruum enim fuit, ut quemadmodum ipse a primo opere suo, Creationis scilicet, die septimo cessavit et quievit, ita et homines eo ipso recurrente die, a suis operibus quiescerent, ut ita Creationis cessationisque divinae celebraretur memoria. Non primum selegit, in quo creationis fuit inchoatio; neque postremum seu sextum, in quo consummatio, sed septimum in quo operum fuit complexio et ab iis cessatio. Ita ut septimus in numeri dierum creationis complexu censeatur. Ex Gentibus quidam, septimum similiter diem coluerunt, vel prisco usu, vel Judaeorum imitatione, vel, ut Hesiod. 2. *Dierum*,[a] Linus,[b] item Joseph. 2. *cont. App.*[c] Clemens Alexand. 5. *Strom.*[d] Euseb. *De Praepar. Evang.*[e] Lampr. *In Alexandro Severo*,[f] aliam forte ob

---

[a] Hesiod, *Opera et dies* 2.770.   [b] Linus is an apocryphal writer mentioned, and quoted from a collection of philosophical sayings by Aristobulus in Eusebius, *Praeparatio evangelica* 13.12.16 (SC 307:324).   [c] Josephus, *Contra Apionem* 1.209.3 and 2.21.2.   [d] Clement of Alexandria, *Stromata* 5.14.107 (SC 278:202).   [e] Eusebius, *Praeparatio evangelica* 8.12.10 (SC 369:132).   [f] Lampridius, *Historia Augusta* on Alexander Severus 43.5.

worship rather than establishing it for the first time then—like the offering of sacrifices before the flood (Genesis 4[:3–5]), the distinction between clean and unclean animals after the flood (Genesis 7[:2]), the prohibition against eating flesh with its blood (Genesis 9[:4]), circumcision (Genesis 17; John 7:22), and also other things. It is likely that this also applies in the present case.

But Ezekiel 20:12 states specifically that God gave the Sabbath to the Israelites, and Nehemiah 9:14 that he made it known to them, evidently as something of which there was no prior knowledge or use, nor as something that he had recalled and restored to its former use after it had been interrupted and disappeared. But as far as its institution is concerned, it makes little difference what the circumstances of the time or the people* were—although the former interpretation seems more likely.

At the same time, a cause for the institution of the Sabbath that is reasonable and in harmony with divine wisdom is indicated by the authority of him who commands it and by conforming to the precedent for it, namely God, thus binding us to obedience in two ways. For it was fitting that just as he himself ceased his first work (that is, creation) on the seventh day and rested, so also mankind should rest from his works on that same day, whenever it recurs, in order to celebrate the remembrance of creation and God's resting from it. He chose not the first day, on which creation started; nor did he choose the last, sixth day, on which it was completed. But he chose the seventh day when he surveyed his labours and ceased from them, so that the seventh day is counted among those included in the days of creation. Some of the heathens similarly honoured the seventh day, either from age-old practice or from imitating the Jews. Or, as reported by Hesiod (*Works and Days*), Linus, and Josephus (*Against Apion* 2), Clement of Alexandria[12] (*Stromata* 5), Eusebius (*Preparation for the Gospel*), and Lampridius in *The Life of Alexander Severus*,[13] they honoured the

---

12   Clement of Alexandria (c. AD 150–c. 215) was a Christian convert influenced by Hellenistic philosophy, especially by Plato and the Stoics. Probably born in Athens, he was a teacher at the Catechetical School of Alexandria. One of his most important writings is the *Stromata* (*Miscellanies*), an apologetic work. Cf. Eric Osborn, *Clement of Alexandria* (Cambridge: Cambridge University Press, 2008).

13   The *Historia Augusta* is a collection of biographies on the Roman emperors from Hadrian to Numerian (i.e., AD 117–284), presented as the product of six different authors—among whom is Aelius Lampridius (c. AD 310)—composed during the reigns of Diocletian and Constantine I. However, the current consensus is that both the identification of the authors and the date are spurious, and that the collection was actually written by a single author in the late fourth century. Cf. Ronald Syme, *Ammianus and the Historia Augusta*

causam, scilicet ob septem Planetarum revolutionem. Alii tamen nonum, alii decimum sacrum habuerunt.

XVII   *Fines** porro ejus plures sunt, ac distingui possunt, ut unus sit universalis, specialis alter. *Universalis* quidem, qui communiter totum humanum genus spectat; estque is primarius, nempe stato hoc Judaeis a Deo die, memoria absolutionis opificii Dei, atque ab eo requietis, seu Dei qua Creatoris agnitio et professio, Gen. 2, 2. Exod. 20, 10. in quo fidei exercitatio est, Hebr. 11, 3. Atque hoc fine cessatur a propriis operibus, ut divinis tanto melius vacare liceat.

XVIII   Assignatur et *Politicus* finis, refocillatio seu recreatio corporis a laboribus; etiam ejus qui sub alterius est potestate, servi ancillaeque, imo et jumentorum, Exod. 23, 12. Et respiret filius ancillae tuae. Deut. 5, 14. Ut requiescat servus tuus et ancilla tua sicut et tu. Memineris quod et ipse servus fueris in Aegypto. Scilicet, ne continuis laboribus fatigentur et conficiantur, sed eorum remissione fessa membra leventur et vires reficiantur. Non enim Deus tantum Creator, sed et Conservator est creaturarum, Ps. 36, 7. Atque hic finis secundarius, ut sit alius a priori, ei tamen subordinatur et ad eum refertur, tamquam actus* quidam caritatis, ita ut haec refectio etiam ad Dei cultum suo modo spectet.

XIX   *Specialis* vero est, qui Judaeos peculiariter, nempe per accessionem quandam spectat, seu accessorius et extrinsecus accedens: estque duplex. Primus est memoria eductionis ex Aegypto, Deut. 5, 15. Et memineris quod servus fuisti in terra Aegypti, et eduxit te Deus tuus inde manu valida et brachio extento; idcirco praecepit tibi Dominus Deus tuus ut faceres diem Sabbathi. Atque ita Sabbathum signum requietis in terra Canaan, in quam induxit illos Josua, Heb. 4, 8.

XX   Alter *finis* sublimior, *spiritualis* scilicet, aeternam hominis salutem spectans, Israëlitarum nempe sanctificatio; qui quidem ceremonialis et sacramentalis, imo et typicus est. Hoc enim signo corporalis quietis et otii testatum facere voluit Deus, se ipsorum esse Deum et sanctificatoreni; segregando illos tum externe a reliquis populis, tum interne ab omnibus peccatis. Exod. 31, 13. 17. Sabbatha mea custodietis, quia signum est inter me et vos in generationibus vestris, ut sciatis quod ego Dominus sanctificans vos; ac servabitis Sabbathum, quia sanctitas est vobis; ubi et foedus seculi vocatur, 16. Similia sunt in

---

(Oxford: Oxford University Press, 1968); *Emperors and Biography: Studies in the 'Historia Augusti'* (Oxford: Oxford University Press, 1971); *Historia Augusta Papers* (Oxford: Oxford University Press, 1983).

seventh day for another reason, perhaps such as the rotation of the seven planets. Some, however, consider the ninth day sacred, and others the tenth.

17 And as for the goals* of the Sabbath-day, these are many, and can be divided into two groups, of which one is world-wide in scope and the other specific. The world-wide goal concerns the whole human race together, and it is the primary one, namely that this day was appointed by God for the Jews to remember that God completed his handiwork and took his rest from it, or to acknowledge and confess God as creator (Genesis 2:2; Exodus 20:10)—wherein the exercise of faith consists, according to Hebrews 11:3. And mankind ceases from his own works so that he can be freed so much the better for the works of God.

18 A civic goal is indicated also: to reinvigorate and refresh the body after its labours. This includes those whose bodies are owned by another, slave and handmaid, even the beasts of burden. Exodus 23:12 states: "And the son of your handmaid shall have respite"; Deuteronomy 5:14: "So that your slave and your handmaid may rest as well as you. You shall remember that you were a servant in the land of Egypt." In other words, in order that they not be worn out and destroyed by constant hard work, but rather by relaxing from it, they lift their drooping limbs and regain their strength. For God is not only the one who has made his creatures, he also preserves them (Psalm 36:7). And this secondary world-wide goal, too, although it is different from the first, is subordinate and responds to it, as an act* of love, so that in its own way this recovery also looks to the worship of God.

19 The special goal of the Sabbath is one that pertains to the Jews in particular, that is, through an additional application or as an adjunct goal that happens outwardly, and it is two-fold. The first is to commemorate the deliverance from Egypt; Deuteronomy 5:15 [states]: "You shall remember that you were a servant in the land of Egypt, and that your God led you out from there with a mighty hand and an outstretched arm. Therefore the Lord your God commanded you to keep the Sabbath day." And so the Sabbath is a symbol of the rest in the land of Canaan into which Joshua led them (Hebrews 4:8).

20 The second specific goal is a more lofty one, namely a spiritual one that looks to the eternal well-being of man: the sanctification of the people of Israel. This goal is ceremonial and sacramental, and typical, too. For by this sign of physical rest and relaxation God wanted to testify to them that he is their God and the one who sanctifies them. He did so by separating them outwardly from the other nations and inwardly from all their sins. Exodus 31:13, 17: "You shall keep my Sabbaths, because it is a sign between me and you throughout your generations, that you may know that I the Lord sanctify you. And you shall keep the Sabbath, because it is holy for you." And in verse 16 it is called

Ezechiele, cap. 20, 12. 20. ut sciatis, quia ego sum Dominus Deus vester, ac proinde publica illis professio totius religionis* fuit. Adeoque Christum ejusque beneficia designat, ita ut perpetuum et spiritualem Sabbathismum, et coelestem con sequentem perfectumque figuret, quod fideles a propriis malis que operibus feriantes, Deum hic in se operari sinant, cujus consummatio in altera vita futura est, Es. 66, 23. Hebr. 4, 3. 9.

XXI Ex horum autem finium consideratione constat, quantum et quale hoc Sabbathum sit, ut quod non usu tantum sanctificatum et sanctum, quatenus facit ad exercitationem externam, sed et sacramenti* ratione, qua promissionem et effectum sanctificationis fidelibus adjunctum habuit et attulit. Unde etiam videmus in Scriptura Sacra totum divinum cultum eo comprehendi. Atque ideo haec Lex tam saepe in Scripturis repetitur, diligenter inculcatur, graviter urgetur, obedientia ejus plurimum laudatur, et neglectus et violatio severe vindicatur, Es. 56, 2. etc.

XXII Tantum de diei septimi seu Sabbathi institutione, ejusque causa* efficiente et finibus; sequitur ejus observatio, quae est in Sabbathi ipsius sanctificatione, Deut. 5. Observa diem Sabbathi, ut sanctifices eum. Sanctificationi enim divinae, qua Deus illum sanctum habuit facto suo, quando is quievit a suo opere, sanctumque haberi voluit eique benedixit, id est, a reliquis segregavit et exemit, respondet sanctificatio hominum, quae et observatio et factio Sabbathi, Deut. 5, 15. Sabbathizatio seu Sabbathismus, Lev. 25, 2. et glorificatio Sabbathi, Es. 58, 13. dicitur.

XXIII Formula hujus edicti singularis est. Non simpliciter, ut in aliis, praecipitur, Sanctifica Sabbathum, sed praemittitur haec monitio, Recordare diem Sabbathi, ut sanctifices eum, quo significatur* res* talis, quae facile (utpote in natura* non insita) in oblivionem abire posset, adeoque jugi memoria recolenda, neque

also "a perpetual covenant." There are similar words in Ezekiel 20:12, 20: "That you may know that I am the Lord your God"; and so keeping the Sabbath was to them the public profession of their entire religion.* The Sabbath is even a symbol of Christ and his benefits, in such a way that it points to the eternal and spiritual Sabbath-day[14] and the heavenly perfection that is to come, because the believers rest from their own evil works, allow God on this earth to perform his work in them—work that will be accomplished fully in the next life (Isaiah 66:[22–]23; Hebrews 4:3,9).

A consideration of these goals makes it plain how important and significant this Sabbath is: The fact that it is hallowed and sacred not just in practice (insofar as it makes for an outward exercise), but also by virtue of being a sacrament* whereby it held out and conveyed to believers the additional promise and effect of sanctification. Hence we also observe in sacred Scripture that the Sabbath comprises the whole worship of God. Therefore this law is repeated in the Scriptures time and again, it is driven home with great care, it is impressed on us with serious urgency, and for obeying it praise is given frequently, while neglecting or breaking it is punished severely (Isaiah 56:2 etc). 21

So much for the institution of the seventh day (or the Sabbath) and what its efficient cause* and goals are. What comes next is the keeping of the seventh day, which exists in hallowing the Sabbath itself, Deuteronomy 5[:12]: "Observe the Sabbath-day, to keep it holy." For the divine sanctification whereby God, by his own doing, deemed it holy when he rested from his work and wanted it to be held holy (that is, by separating it from the other days and setting it apart), and blessed it, corresponds to the sanctification of it by man, which is called the "keeping and making of the Sabbath-day" (Deuteronomy 5:15), "Sabbath-keeping" or "Sabbath-observance" (Leviticus 25:2) and "honouring the Sabbath-day" (Isaiah 58:13). 22

The wording for this commandment is unique. For one is not given a simple command, "Hallow the Sabbath" (as in the others), but the following warning precedes it: "Remember the Sabbath-day, that you keep it holy." This shows* that the matter* is of a sort that can fade easily into oblivion (because it is not engraved into our nature*);[15] therefore we must cultivate it constantly in 23

---

14 In Hebrews 4:9 the rest that remains to the people of God is *sabbatismos* in Greek, which is Latanised here: *Sabbathismum*.
15 Cf. thesis 10 above.

insuper habenda, sed summa cura servanda. Sanctificatur autem, dum illo die fiunt similia iis quae hoc ipso fecit Deus, et ab hominibus fieri praecepit; contra solvitur, polluitur et profanatur, dum avertuntur oculi a Sabbatho, Ez. 22, 26. eaque eo die geruntur quae non licet eo die facere, et omittuntur quae fieri debent, Mat. 12, 2.

XXIV Parasceue seu praeparatio Sabbathi, est tum apparatus ad Sabbathum, tum dies ipse Sabbathum antegrediens, qui et προσάββατον vocatur, Marc. 15, 42. quo sexta Feria ea fiebant et ordinabantur, quae Sabbatho fieri nefas erat, omniaque disponebantur quae ad ejus observationem cultumque requirebantur, 1 Par. 9, 32. Luc. 23, 54. Imo vero, ut aliqua diei antecedentis portiuncula ad Sabbathum a Judaeis anticipabatur, ita ad Sabbathi exitum subsequentis diei particula assumebatur, nempe ut Sabbathum omnino et quam religiosissime servaretur. Sed hoc ex Judaica superstitione fuit.

XXV Incipit ejus observatio a vespera, ac desinit in vesperam. Ut enim in creatione Universitatis prima, creati mundi facies tenebricosa fuit, cui inde lux allata, atque ita ex tenebrarum et lucis duratione dies constituta, ita et hic ex divina institutione res habet, Lev. 23, 32.

XXVI Observatio in eo generaliter sita est, ne ullum eo die מלאכה, opus, seu עבודה, servitium, et מלאכה עבדה, id est, servile opus, Lev. 23, 8. faciat homo, nempe opus suum. Sex, inquit, diebus operaberis et facies omne opus tuum, at septimus dies est Sabbathum Dei tui, tunc non facies ullum opus, neque tu, uxor, filius, filia, neque servus ancillaque, neque inquilinus seu peregrinus, qui in portis tuis. Id est, toti domui tuae, imo vero et omnibus animantibus domesticis, ut bovi et asino, quae laboriosa maxime (non quod sanctificatio ejus ad bruta spectet, sed ne adhibiti ad laborem homini quietem impediant) quin et civitatis incolis et advenis, ne suo exemplo publicam quietem interturbent, opus interdicitur, Ex. 20. Deut. 5. Atque ita sub negotii prohibitione, otium externum praecipitur religiose servandum; ipsumque adeo tale otium in parte divini cultus ponitur.

XXVII Prohibetur ergo opus seu negotium, et quidem nostrum, scilicet servile, mechanicum, laboriosum, quaestuosum, quotidianum atque ordinarium; idque tum privatum, tum publicum, id est, quod privatim aut publice a nobis

our memories, and we should not make light of it but guard it very carefully. Moreover, the Sabbath is hallowed so long as on that day we do things similar to those God did on that day and which he commands men to do. On the other hand, the Sabbath-day is lost, polluted, and desecrated when our eyes are distracted from the Sabbath (Ezekiel 22:26) and we do things on that day which we are forbidden, and we omit what we ought to do (Matthew 12:2[, 11, 12]).

24 The Paraseve or getting ready for the Sabbath refers to the trappings required for the Sabbath as well as the actual day that precedes the Sabbath. It is also called the "day-before-the-Sabbath" (Mark 15:42), when on the sixth day of the week one performs and sets in order those things that are not permitted to be done on the Sabbath, and everything necessary for its observance and worship is arranged (1 Chronicles 9:32, Luke 23:54). In fact, just as the Jews consider a small portion of the preceding day as the Sabbath, so too do they add a small part of the following day to the conclusion of the Sabbath: for the sake of keeping the Sabbath day in its entirety and as religiously as possible. But this practice arose from Jewish superstition.

25 Keeping the Sabbath begins and ends with the setting of the sun. For as at the first creation of the universe the appearance of the created world was covered in darkness, whereupon light was then brought to it, and just as day was established by the length of darkness and light, so in this case too does this matter come by the establishment of God (Leviticus 23:32).

26 In general Sabbath-keeping rests in the fact that on that day one does not perform any work (*meˡlakhah*), servile work (*ʿavodah*), that is, laborious work (*meˡlakhah ʿavodah*) (Leviticus 23:8). He says: "Six days you shall labour and do all your work, but the seventh day is the Sabbath of your God; then you shall not do any work, neither you, your wife, son, daughter, nor your man-servant and handmaid, nor the lodger or foreigner who is within your gates." This means that work is prohibited for your entire household, which includes also all your domestic animals—like the ox and donkey—that are mostly beasts of burden (not because the hallowing of the day applies to animals, but lest they become a hindrance to man's rest by being put to work) and even the strangers and foreigners in your towns, lest by their example they cause a disruption to the public rest (Exodus 20, Deuteronomy 5). And so by prohibiting work in this manner we are instructed to keep the outward rest as a religious duty; and in this way even such rest is considered as part of the divine worship.

27 And so what is forbidden is any work or business that we undertake: work that is servile, that involves machinery, that is laborious, brings in a profit, work that is daily and ordinary. Both private and public work are included, that is,

fieri solet, Es. 58, 3. quae quum et prohibita fuerint in festis aliis solennioribus, Lev. 23, 7. 8. 25. 32. 36. Num. 28, 25. multo magis Sabbatho. Ut Israëlitis Sabbatho domo egredi ad colligendum Manna, Ex. 16, 22. item Ligna, Num. 15, 32., quin accendere ignem, Ex. 35, 3. coquere et lixare, Ex. 16, 14. ita ut non nisi pridiana edere et reposita bibere liceret, ut ait Ignatius *ad Magn.*[a] et continuus usus comprobat, arare et metere, Ex. 34, 21. Torcularia calcare, Neh. 13, 15. ferre et efferre onus, Jer. 17, 21. 22. inferre res venales, Neh. 13. vendere et emere, Neh. 10, 31. pugnare, 1 Mac. 2, 36. sepelire, 2 Mac. 12, 30. et similia.

XXVIII His accedunt quae in Novo Testamento recensentur; ut sunt, tum ea quae ex opinione Judaeorum ab ipsis, quasi Sabbathi profanatio, Christo improperantur; puta, discipulos ejus cum eo Sabbatho per sata euntes, vellere et manibus atterere spicas, Mat. 12, 2. quasi in eo quidam apparatus cibi esset; ipsum curare seu sanare aegros, Mat. 12, 10. sanatum ejus jussu lectum tollere et ambulare, Joh. 5. collyrium ex sputo et terra facere, et caeci oculis illinere; ejusdem imperio caecum abire se ablutum, Joh. 9. tum alia, utpote iter facere et extra praescripta spatia ambulare, (unde iter Sabbathi dicitur, quod fuit circiter duorum millium passuum, ut definiverant Judaei) Act. 1, 12. Sabbatho fugere, Mat. 24. Sinere in cruce pendere corpora interfectorum, Joh. 19, 31. Mortuos sepelire et aromatis condire, Luc. 23, 36.

---

[a] Pseudo-Ignatius, *Epistula ad Magnesios* 9.3; Thysius thus cites a passage from the longer, spurious version of the letter to the Magnesians, which is not found in the shorter, authentic version. For the longer text, see Franciscus X. Funk and Franciscus Diekamp, eds., *Patres apostolici*, 2 vols. (Tübingen: H. Laupp, 1901–1913), 2:112–132, there 124.

what we are used to perform either on our own or in public (Isaiah 58:3[, 13]). Since these have been prohibited for other solemn feast-days (Leviticus 23:7, 8, 25, 32, 36; Numbers 28:25), so much the more are they prohibited for the Sabbath-day. Thus it was forbidden for the Israelites on the Sabbath-day to leave their homes to gather Manna (Exodus 16:22), or wood (Numbers 15:32), or even to kindle a fire (Exodus 35:3), to cook or bake (Exodus 16:14[23–25]). And as a result they were permitted to eat and drink only what had been laid up the day before, as Ignatius[16] says (in his *Letter to the Magnesians*), and as the uninterrupted practice confirms. They were forbidden to plough and to sow (Exodus 34:21), to tread the winepress (Nehemiah 13:15), to bear or carry out burdens (Jeremiah 17:21, 22), to import goods for sale (Nehemiah 13[:15–16]), to sell or buy (Nehemiah 10:31), to go out to battle (1 Maccabees 2:[34–35]36), to bury the dead (2 Maccabees 12:30[38, 39]), and similar activities.[17]

To these prohibitions are added the ones listed in the New Testament, such as the ones with which the Jews upbraided Christ out of their own conviction that it was a desecration of the Sabbath: As when his disciples were going through the grain fields on a Sabbath-day and they plucked heads of grain and rubbed them in their hands (Matthew 12:2)—as if doing this was preparing a meal. Or when he himself healed and cured the sick (Matthew 12:10); when he commanded the man who was healed to "take up your mat and walk" (John 5:8); when he made an ointment from his spittle and earth and anointed the eyes of the blind man; and when he commanded the blind man to "go and wash himself" (John 9[:7]). And there are other prohibitions: To make a journey and to walk distances that are beyond what is prescribed (it is from this that the saying comes, "a Sabbath-day's journey" (Acts 1:12), which was about two thousand feet, according to the calculation of the Jews); to take to flight on the Sabbath (Matthew 24[:20]); to leave the bodies of those who have died hanging on a cross (John 19:31); or to bury the dead and embalm them with spices (Luke 23:56).

28

---

16 Ignatius (c. AD 35–108) was a disciple of the apostle John, and became the third bishop of Antioch. While en route to his martyrdom in Rome he wrote a series of letters.

17 It is remarkable that here and in theses 34 and 61, Maccabees is mentioned in conjunction with the canonical books. In general, Thysius was of the opinion that the apocryphal books do not have the same authority as the canonical books and should not be mixed with them, although they can be read with benefit privately, *SPT* 3.37. This might be an exception, because the references describe how the Sabbath functioned in a historical sense. There is also a reference to Maccabees in *SPT* 40.15.

XXIX Missas hic facimus multas et superstitiosas, Pharisaicas observatiunculas, quibus divinum mandatum magis strinxerunt, quales Judaei etiam hodie multas habent; ut de non assando pomo, corticando allio, interficiendo pulice, etc, quae merae humanae corruptelae sunt hujus a Deo imperatae observationis.

XXX Sed universalitas illa de nullo opere faciendo, suam habuit interpretationem, exceptionem et oeconomiam seu dispensationem.* In hoc ergo censu operum neutiquam sunt opera divina et miraculosa, et quae ad illorum demonstrationem imperata, ut quae Dei potius, imo revera ejus sunt, quamvis per hominem gesta, externum et operosum quiddam prae se ferant; ut dum circumgestatione arcae et clangore tubarum a Sacerdotibus septimo die Jericho concidente, omnia a populo excisa sunt; et Christus Sabbatho curavit virum aridam manum habentem, Mat. 12, 9. mulierem laborantem morbo invaletudinis a Satana inflicto, Luc. 13, 11. hydropicum, Luc. 14. aegrotum e morbo diuturno ad piscinam decumbentem, quem insuper jussit grabatum tollere et ambulare, Joh. 5. caecum, cujus oculos collyrio a se facto et oculis imposito aperuit, et jussit abire se ablutum, Joh. 9, 14.

XXXI Unde Judaeis, facta haec Christi sub praetextu Sabbathi ad calumniam rapientibus, opponit illud, Pater meus operatur usque adhuc, et ego operor, Joh. 5. eo innuens, opus divinitus editum, quale suum, nunquam censendum esse Sabbathi violationem, ut quod auctoritate, vi atque potentia* effectrice Patris sit effectum; deinde et illud, Dico autem vobis, Majorem templo hic esse, et Filius hominis est etiam Dominus Sabbathi, Mat. 12, 6. 8. id est, Sabbathum habet in sua potestate, ita ut possit ei, prout vult, dominari, quo se Christus a communi hominum sorte eximit, dum se majorem templo et Dominum Sabbathi dicit, et opera sua a consuetis disjungit.

XXXII Excipiuntur praeterea opera, quae animam et Dei cultum ejusque gloriam spectant, ut sunt omnia opera, extra cultum servilia, ac ministeria, quae Sabbatho a Sacerdotibus in templo fiebant, quibus dicit Christus, eos sine crimine Sabbathum profanare, Mat. 12, 5., ut sunt sacrificia aliaque, et nominatim circumcisio, de qua Christus, Sabbatho circumciditis hominem, ita tamen ut non solvatur lex Mosis, Joh. 7, 22. 23. Unde Christus suorum operum divinorum assertionem capit.

21. ON THE SABBATH AND THE LORD'S DAY

Here we leave aside the Pharisees' many and superstitious detailed little observances whereby they have further curtailed God's commandment; even the Jews of today have very many of this sort. They include: roasting apples, husking garlic, killing fleas, etc. They are mere human perversions of the observance God commanded.

Yet that general injunction about not performing any work did have its own interpretation, exceptions, and economy or dispensation.* Therefore excluded entirely from this listing of doing work are the deeds of God and his wonders, as well as the works ordered to display them, since these are of God (in fact, they are his work) although they are performed by men and give the outward impression of being somewhat laborious. Such as when the priests carried the ark and blew the trumpets on the seventh day when Jericho fell, and the people razed everything; and when, on the Sabbath, Christ healed the man with the withered hand (Matthew 12:9[-13]); the woman suffering from the disease of infirmity that Satan had inflicted (Luke 13:11); the man afflicted with dropsy (Luke 14[:2–4]); the man smitten with a long-lasting disease and lying by the pool, whom Christ ordered to take up his mat and walk (John 5[:8]); the blind man whose eyes he opened with the ointment he had prepared, and whom he ordered to go and wash himself (John 9:14).

Therefore Christ responded to the Jews, when they seized upon these actions to slander him on the pretext of the Sabbath-day, by saying, "My father is working still, and I too am working" (John 5[:17])—thereby implying that his own work, proceeding as it is from God, should never be deemed a violation of the Sabbath, since it is accomplished by the Father's authority, force, and effective power.* And then he added this: "Moreover I say to you: one greater than the temple is here; and the Son of Man is also Lord of the Sabbath (Matthew 12:6, 8)." That is, he holds the Sabbath in his power to such a degree that he can rule over it as much as he pleases; hereby Christ separates himself from the common lot of men, because he says that he is greater than the temple and Lord of the Sabbath, and he distinguishes his own works from those of the common kind.

Moreover, exception is made for the works that pertain to life and to the worship of God and his glory. Such works are all the humble, menial tasks which the priests carry out on the Sabbath-day apart from the worship, in the temple. About these priests Christ says that "they desecrate the Sabbath without penalty" (Matthew 12:5). These include sacrifices and other duties, in particular circumcision, about which Christ says: "You circumcise a man on the Sabbath-day so that the law of Moses still is not broken" (John 7:22, 23). It is from this that Christ derives his defense of his divine works.

XXXIII   Quinimo et omnes actiones quae praesentem necessitatem communem* circa creaturas earumque conservationem habent, ac speciatim: Primo, mutorum animalium curatio, ut solvere Sabbatho bovem aut asinum praesepi et aquatum ducere, Luc, 13, 11. ovem, asinum aut bovem cadentem in foveam inde extrahere, Mat. 12. Luc. 13, 11 et 14, 1. (quae quidem hodie Judaeis habentur in illicitis, at non olim) adeoque praeservare bestias ab interitu licebat, ac omnia agere quae ad necessariam omnino creaturarum Dei conservationem faciebant.

XXXIV   Deinde et hominum; quod Sabbathum, ut ait Christus, sit propter hominem, non homo propter Sabbathum, Marc. 2, 23. Unde quies et cessatio ab opere quae homini ejusque statui et saluti obest, non simpliciter vetatur, ut Sabbatho vellere spicas et comedere, Luc. 6, 1. pugnare, seu hostibus bellum inferentibus resistere, 1 Reg. 20, 29. 1Macc. 2, 40. 41., quamvis a persequendo hoste, et praeda distribuenda tum abstinuerunt, 2Macc. 8, 27. Quod simili necessitatis casu, exemplo Davidis edocet et comprobat Christus, quia cum esuriret, ipse et comites ederint de panibus propositionis, quibus vesci ipsis non erat licitum, sed solis Sacerdotibus, Lev. 24. Mat. 12, 3. 4.

XXXV   Neque caritatis atque misercordiae debita necessariaque officia, hac ipsa Sabbathi observantia sistuntur, utpote Sabbatho homini benefacere, sanare et similia, prout Christus fecit, et a Judaeis exquirit: Licetne Sabbatho benefacere an malefacere, hominem servare an trucidare seu perdere? Luc. 6, 9. ac concludit, licere Sabbatho benefacere, Mat. 12, 12. Sabbathi enim lex, ut reliquae cerimoniae, cedit caritati proximi, secundum illud quod ex Osea Christus in eum sensum affert, Misericordiam volo et non sacrificium, nempe comparate, potius quam sacrificium.

XXXVI   Denique non prohibentur ea quae moderatam corporis refocillationem et recreationem spectant, utpote quae inter fines Sabbathi sit, modo praecipuum Sabbathi usum cultumque non impediant, sicuti est praeter quietem a laboribus, Ex. 23, 12. adire ad convivium, Luc. 14, 1. 7. ambulare, Luc. 24, 13. ac similia. Et sane Sabbathum festus dies cum fuerit, eo hilaria agere Judaeis consuetum

In fact exception is made for all activities that concern the immediate needs 33
common* to living creatures and their well-being; and in particular, first, the
care of animals that are dumb, like freeing the ox and donkey from their stalls
and leading them to water (Luke 13:11[15]), or pulling up a sheep, donkey, or
ox that has fallen into a pit (Matthew 12[:11]; Luke 13:15, 14:5). (Unlike former
times, nowadays the Jews consider these actions illegal.) Thus it was permitted
to preserve animals from death—to do anything that promoted the necessary
preservation of everyone of God's creatures.

And then there is the well-being of mankind; for "the Sabbath," as Christ 34
says, "is made for man, not man for the Sabbath" (Mark 2:27). Hence man is
not commanded outright to rest or cease from work if doing so harms his
prosperity or health, like plucking heads of grain and eating them (Luke 6:1),
conducting warfare, or defending against the enemy when they attack (1 Kings
20:29; 1 Maccabees 2:40, 41), although they did then refrain from pursuing the
enemy and sharing the spoils (2 Maccabees 8:27). Christ teaches and approves
of this by means of a similar case of need, namely the example of David, because
when he was hungry "he and his comrades ate of the bread of the presentation,
which it was not lawful for him to eat, but only for the priests" (Leviticus 24[:9];
Matthew 12:3,4).[18]

Nor does this keeping of the Sabbath put a stop to performing duties that are 35
needed or required out of charity and compassion; such as acts of kindness to
someone on the Sabbath, healing and similar deeds that Christ performed and
of which he asked the Jews: "Is it lawful on the Sabbath to do good or to do evil,
to save a man or to destroy and slaughter him?" (Luke 6:9). And he concludes
that it is lawful to do good on the Sabbath (Matthew 12:12). For the law of
the Sabbath, like the other ceremonies, yields to charity for the neighbor;[19]
and in keeping with that, Christ refers to that statement from Hosea: "I desire
compassion and not sacrifice," obviously in the comparative sense of "rather
than sacrifice."

And finally, activities aimed at modest bodily invigoration and relaxation 36
are not prohibited, since they belong to the purposes of the Sabbath-day, provided they do not hinder the chief function and worship of the Sabbath. Thus,
besides resting from our labours (Exodus 23:12), there is going to a dinner (Luke
14:1,7), going for a walk (Luke 24:13), and similar activities. To be sure, when
there was a feast-day of Sabbaths, the Jews were accustomed to make merry,

---

18 The story of David and his men is found in 1 Samuel 21:4–7.
19 For the connection of loving God and loving one's neighbor, see *SPT* 18.37.

fuit, quae eo demum abierunt, ut illo ad insanas saltationes et plausus etiam abuterentur; testis est Ignat. *ad Magn.*[a] et Aug. *in Joh.*[b]

XXXVII   Verum hac ipsa die Sabbathi ab omnibus operibus cessatione et vacatione non praecipitur tantum et per se, otium corporale, sed insuper et propter hoc, negotium religiosum, occupationes scilicet, exercitia officiaque sancta. Unde dicitur Sabbathum Domini, Ex. 20. vel Domino, Lev. 23. et Sabbathum sanctitatis, et sanctitas Domini, Es. 28, 12. quia non modo Dei sancti, sed et sanctum, et rebus Domini ac sanctis, publice et privatim dicatum et impendendum, et ad nominis ejus sanctificationem dirigendum est.

XXXVIII Talia erant in templo, panum propositionis singulis diebus Sabbathi dispositio, Lev. 24, 8. sacrificium Sabbathi duplicatum, duorum scilicet agnorum anniculorum, et duarum decimarum similae oleo commixtae, ac duplex libamen ejus, Num. 28, 9. 19. Ez. 26. convocatio sancta, totius nempe populi in templo aut Synagogis conventus solennis, Lev. 23, 13. Mat. 12. Luc. 4, 16. et 13, 10. Cantica singularia Sabbatho occinenda, ut Ps. 92. etc. Verbi Dei, Mosis nempe et prophetarum lectio, Neh. 8. Act. 13, 14. ejus praedicatio, Marc. 1, 21. Act. 15, 21. ad populum exhortatio, Luc. 4, 16. Act. 13, 14. de rebus divinis dissertatio, Act. 17, 2. aliaque pietatis officia Sabbathis singulariter praestanda.

XXXIX Sed nondum in quiete et observatione horum externorum exercitiorum, Sabbathi plena erat sanctificatio, nisi eo fine, quo institutum, usurparetur, et pie sancteque interius haec gererentur, sine quo, ut externa omnia, conventus, sacrificia, incensum, ita et Sabbathum, quin et Kalendas et festivitates, se abominari et odisse, sibi molesta et fatigationi esse, testatur Dominus; ac requirit ad hoc lotionem, munditiem et ablationem malarum cogitationum, et quietem a perverse agendo, bonique actionem, Es. 1, 11. etc. Amos 5, 21. scil. ut non faciat quis voluntatem suam, neque vias suas, neque eloquium suum, Es. 58, 13. Qui est Sabbathismus internus, sine quo res per se sancta non erat. Totus ergo dies,

---

[a] Pseudo-Ignatius, *Epistula ad Magnesios* 9.3 (Funk and Franciscus Diekamp, eds., *Patres apostolici*, 2:124); for the 'longer' version of this letter, see the note with SPT 21.27 above.   [b] Augustine, *In Ioannis Evangelium tractatus* 3.19 (CCSL 36:28–29).

something that they eventually ended up abusing with wild dances and clapping, as attested by Ignatius (*Letter to the Magnesians*) and Augustine (*On the Gospel of John*).

In fact, on the actual day of the Sabbath what is commanded by the stoppage and freedom from all labour is not merely the physical rest in and of itself; but beyond it and on account of it, religious activity is commanded, that is to say, the religious business, the sacred exercises and duties. For this reason it is called "the Sabbath of the Lord" (Exodus 20), or "unto the Lord" (Leviticus 23), and the "Sabbath of holiness" and "the holiness of the Lord" (Isaiah 28:12),[20] because it is not only of the holy God, but is itself holy; it is dedicated publicly and privately for the things of the Lord, sacred things, and is to be spent to these things and directed to the sanctification of his name.

In the temple, activities of this sort included setting out the bread of presentation on each Sabbath-day (Leviticus 24:8), the Sabbath-day's double sacrifice, that is, of the two one-year old lambs, and of the two-tenths of fine flour mixed with oil, and the double outpouring of it (Numbers 28:9, 10; Ezechiel 26[21]), the sacred assembly, that is the solemn gathering of the entire people in the temple or synagogue (Leviticus 23:13; Matthew 12[:5]; Luke 4:16 and 13:10). The psalms special to the Sabbath-day were to be sung (such as Psalm 92, etc.); there was the reading from the Word of God, that is from Moses and the Prophets (Nehemiah 8; Acts 13:14), and the preaching of it (Mark 1:21; Acts 15:21), the exhortation to the people (Luke 4:16; Acts 13:14), the exposition of the ways of God (Acts 17:2), and other pious tasks that must be performed especially on the Sabbath.

But the hallowing of the Sabbath would not be complete by resting and keeping these outward practices alone, unless the Sabbath was spent for the purpose for which it was instituted, and unless these practices were undertaken with inner piety and reverence. Without that, God testifies, all the outward things, assemblies, sacrifices, incense-burning, even the Sabbath-day and the New Moons and festivals are abhorrent, hateful, tiresome, and a source of grief for him. And for this he demands washing, cleansing, the removal of evil thoughts, and resting from doing evil, and doing good (Isaiah 1:11, etc.; Amos 5:21); that is, "if anyone does not do his own will, nor go his own way, nor speak his own words" (Isaiah 58:13). That was internal Sabbath-keeping, without which it would not of itself be a sacred event. Therefore the entire

---

20 It is not clear why Thysius refers to Isaiah 28:12 here. One would rather expect a reference to Exodus 16:23, which literally reads "the Sabbath of holiness for the Lord."
21 Rather: Ezekiel 46:4–5.

ex toto animo, quantum fert humana necessitas et imbecillitas, rite ac pie Deo servandus erat.

XL Huic autem sanctificationi Sabbathi promittitur Judaeis benedictio, tum privata, tum publica, ac pronuntiatur custodiens illud beatus, Es. 56, 2. et 58. Ac contra ejus profanationi pollutionique maledictionem comminatur Deus, Ex. 31, 14. Lev. 26, 14. Jer. 17, 26. 27. Neh. 13, 15. etc. poenisque gravissimis et morte ulciscitur, Num. 15, 32. etc, utpote cujus profanatio contemptus esset totius legis Dei et divini cultus.

XLI Tantum de diei septimae a creatione, seu Sabbathi, id est, quietis a Deo ad suum exemplar imperatae, institutione et observatione. Sequitur ejus duratio, quae, ut ejus institutio, a Deo pendet. Nempe sanxisse hanc Sabbathi legem, in generationibus suis pacto seu foedere seculi, et quod signum sit לעולם, in seculum, pronuntiavit Deus, Ex. 31, 16. 17. quod qualiter accipiendum sit, porro considerabimus.

XLII Certe, ut quae sparsim diximus, simul colligamus; cum Sabbathum sub hac notione speciali, si *causam* spectes, sit ex instituto divino, nitens voluntario Dei arbitrio; si *rem et materiam* respicias, cessationem et quietem Dei a creatione et operibus creationis, ac Dei, qua creatoris, singularem celebrationem; si *circumstantiam temporis*, die a creatione recurrente septimo, scilicet a vespera in vesperam, fuerit celebrandum; si *modum*,* quiete, et quidem praecisa observatione, cum inhibitione accendendi ignem et coquendi, etc, ita ut etiam ipsa quies censeatur in pietate; si *finem*, accesserit et acceperit finem peculiarem, videlicet populi Israëlitici ex Aegypto, seu quietis ab illa servitute, atque signi significationis ejus; si *genus* denique, reliquis Judaicis festivitatibus ac ceremoniis, (quae sub hoc praecepto continentur) passim conjungatur, quae omnia juris positivi sunt, (quare etiam praecepto monitio et causa additur); omnino in eo rerum genere est, quae mutationi et abolitioni subjecta sunt.

XLIII Imo vero et reipsa, ipsius, ut reliquarum cerimoniarum Veteris Testamenti (quae futurorum bonorum fuerunt typi et exemplaria, Heb. 9, 9. et 10. 1., sive Christi, sive beneficiorum ejus; et umbrae, quorum corpus est Christus, Col. 2, 17., imo paedagogia ad Christum, Gal. 4, 2.) duratio, usque ad tempus προθεσμίας et διοθώσεως, id est, praedefinitionis et emendationis, Gal. 4. Heb. 9, 10.

day was to be observed, as much as human condition and weakness allowed, entirely from the heart and with due custom and devotion, to God.

40 For this hallowing of the Sabbath-day the Jews are promised blessings, private as well as public ones, and he is declared "blessed, who observes it" (Isaiah 56:2, and 58). On the other hand, God threatens a curse for desecrating and polluting it (Exodus 31:14; Leviticus 26:14[15, 16]; Jeremiah 17:26, 27; Nehemiah 13:15, etc.), and he punishes it with the gravest penalties, and death (Numbers 15:32, etc.), since profaning the Sabbath-day was despising the whole law of God and divine worship.

41 Thus far about the institution and observance of the seventh day after creation, or the Sabbath, that is of the rest commanded by God according to the pattern he set. Next comes its duration, which, like its institution, depends upon God. God has certainly declared that he has confirmed this law for the Sabbath "throughout your generations as an everlasting treaty or covenant, and that it should be a sign forever [*le'olam*]" (Exodus 31:16, 17). It is how this command should be interpreted that we shall consider next.

42 Well then, let us gather together what we have said in diverse places: The Sabbath in the restricted sense of considering what caused it, was established by God's ordinance, and rests on his voluntary will. So too, if you look to the matter and substance of it: God's stopping and resting from creation and the works of creation, and the unique celebration of God as creator. And, if you regard the circumstance of time, it was to be celebrated on the recurring seventh day after creation; to be precise, from the setting of the sun until it sets again. And as to the manner* of it, by resting, and also by its exact observance (with the prohibition of starting a fire or cooking, etc.), so much so that even the rest itself is pious. Regarding the goal for it, the Sabbath has received and taken on a special goal, namely of the rest for the Israelite people coming out of Egypt, or the rest following that state of slavery and what it represents. Finally, regarding its *genus*, the Sabbath is everywhere linked to the other Jewish festivals and ceremonies which this commandment encompasses and which all belong to the positive law (for which reason a warning and a cause are added to the commandment). For these reasons, the Sabbath belongs entirely to the category of things that are subject to change and abolition.

43 Yes indeed, the duration of the Sabbath itself is like that of the other ceremonies of the Old Testament, which were "types and examples of good gifts to come" (Hebrews 9:9 and 10:1), or of Christ or his benefits; and they were "shadows whose substance is Christ" (Colossians 2:17), and "guardians leading the way to Christ" (Galatians 4:2). It should be taken to mean that it endures until the time *prothesmias* and *diorthōseos*, that is, the time 'pre-ordained' 'for the right order' (Galatians 4[:5–7]; Hebrews 9:10), and that it, along with the

intelligenda est, ipsumque cum reliquis Veteris Testamenti ritibus et umbris Christi Domini adventu abolitum est.

XLIV Proinde quae de duratione לעולם, id est, in seculum, dicuntur, non de aeterna proprie, sed diuturna continuaque (qualiter vox illa non raro in Scriptura accipitur, Gen. 17, 7. 8. Ex. 21, 6. et 29, 9.) usque ad tempus a Deo designatum, Messiae videlicet, accipiendum est, quo tempore promittitur, Neomenia ex Neomenia, et Sabbathum ex Sabbatho, Es. 66., id est, Sabbathismus spiritualis et perpetuus, qui reliquus est populo Dei, ad Heb. 3. et 4. cap.

XLV Et sane Christus, dum dicit, se, ut majorem templo, ita et Dominum Sabbathi, Marc. 2, 28. indicat Sabbathum sic in sua potestate esse, ut de eo non dispensare, sed et illud abolere possit. Imo Apostolus abolitum indicat; tum universe, sub dierum, mensium, temporum et annorum nomenclatura, Rom. 14, 5. Alius aestimat diem prae die, alius peraeque aestimat. Gal. 4, 10. Dies observatis, et menses et tempora et annos, vereor ut frustra laboraverim inter vos, tum speciatim et diserte, Col. 2, 16. Nemo, inquit, vos damnet ob cibum et potum, aut respectum festi aut novilunii, aut Sabbathorum, quae sunt umbrae rerum futurarum, corpus autem est Christi. Itaque Sabbathum, et re et nomine, speciali illa acceptione in Christi regno, abrogatum est: adeo ut in Novo Testamento in legis commemoratione, sub ratione* praecepti Christianis nulla usquam ejus fiat mentio.

XLVI Neque tamen ex Sabbathi hujus abrogatione sequitur, quartum praeceptum (quod suo modo morale) omnino abolitum esse. Nam in eo duo sunt, generale quiddam et speciale. *Generale* est, quod, ut reliqua moralia praecepta, naturae est insitum; videlicet:

other rituals and shadows of the Old Testament, was abolished at the coming of Christ the Lord.

Accordingly, what is stated about its duration as *l^eolam*, that is, 'unto the age,' must be understood not in the strict sense of 'eternal,'[22] but 'lasting a long time' and 'continuously' (in which way that word is frequently used in Scripture: Genesis 17:7,8; Exodus 21:6 and 29:9), until the time determined by God, namely the time of the Messiah, a time when (it is promised) there will be "New Moon following upon New Moon, and Sabbath following upon Sabbath" (Isaiah 66[:23])—which means the spiritual and everlasting Sabbath-keeping that remains for the people of God (according to Hebrews chapters 3 and 4).

Surely, when Christ says that he is a greater one than the temple and thus also "Lord of the Sabbath" (Mark 2:28), he means that the Sabbath is so within his power that not only is he able to have control over it but even to do away with it altogether. In fact, the apostle points out that it is abolished, in the general sense of names that are assigned to days, months, seasons, and years. Thus Romans 14:5: "One man considers a day as more important than another, and another man considers them alike"; and Galatians 4:10: "You are observing the days, months, seasons, and years. I fear that I have laboured in vain among you"; and, most to the point and expressly, Colossians 2:16: "Let no-one," he says, "condemn you on account of food and drink, or regarding a religious festival, a New Moon or Sabbath-days, which are shadows of things to come, of which their substance is Christ." And so in reality as well as in name, in its special meaning the Sabbath is annulled in the kingdom of Christ, to the extent that when the Law is recalled in the New Testament, no mention at all is made of the Sabbath in the sense* of being a commandment for Christians.

However, it does not follow from the repealing[23] of this Sabbath-day that the fourth commandment (which is a moral one, in a way) was entirely done away with. For there are two aspects to it, a general and special one. The general one is that, like the other moral commandments, it has been implanted in nature, namely

---

22 For this strict sense, indicating eternity as an attribute of God, see *SPT* 6.28.
23 In this thesis both the terms *abrogatio* and *abolitio* are used for denoting the repealing of the ceremonial aspects of the Sabbath-day. In classical Latin the first term has a juridical connotation, indicating the annulment of a law in all its parts, while the second refers to 'suspension' or 'casting into oblivion.' See Charlton T. Lewis and Charles Short, *A Latin Dictionary* (Oxford: Clarendon Press, 1958), 11.

1. Ut quamvis toto vitae tempore pietati sit studendum, tamen propter negotia hujus seculi, quibus haec vita est obnoxia, a quotidianis laboribus aliquod tempus singulariter divino cultui et publico ministerio verbi, ceremoniisque sacris divinitus traditis, formandae alendaeque pietati, segregetur et assignetur.
2. Imo ut certus sit dies, quem vel Deus definiverit, vel ad ordinem et decorum libertati Ecclesiae definiendum permiserit, ad cujus observationem tota Ecclesia obligetur.
3. Et quidem accommodus, id est, qui toties repetito in se calculo revolvatur, atque proportionata humanae naturae fragilitas, cultusque divini necessitas exigit; quem septimum (qui numerus perfectionis est, et fere toti naturae respondet, et aliis etiam gentibus observatus) Judaeis a creatione Deus instituit, et Apostoli in ordinatione diei Dominicae, ἀναλόγως recurrentem secuti sunt.
4. Ut rationabilis sit institutionis causa, ac operibus beneficiisque Dei generalibus ac specialibus commemorandis publice dicetur.
5. Ut usu et observatione sit et habeatur sanctus.
6. Adeoque animus totus ab aliis curis avocetur totusque dies pietatis ac caritatis officiis impendatur, idque quantum fert humana imbecillitas et vitae praesens necessitas.
7. Ne opera quae impediunt ejus sanctificationem, sine causa et contumaciter exerceantur.
8. Denique humanitatis et caritatis officia erga subditos, imo et bestias, hic praestentur. Quae usque adeo naturali lege* traduntur, ut et universae gentes stativas ferias universo populo communes, et rebus sacris obeundis consecratas, habuerint.

XLVII *Speciale vero*, quatenus divina institutione, hoc generale revocatur ad hanc speciem,* puta septimum a creatione diem, seu Sabbathum, et quidem qua imperatum Judaeis; et per hanc ipsam illud explicatur, ac otium stricte mandatur.

XLVIII Atque ita omnia Decalogi praecepta omnibus communia, ad Judaeos speciatim accommodantur. Sic enim Deus praefatur: Audi Israël, Ego Dominus sum Deus tuus, qui eduxi te e terra Aegypti, e domo servitutis; cujus tamen beneficii commemorationem, novo accepto, immutandam praedicit, ita ut non dicatur

1. That although we must strive for piety the entire time of our lives, yet because our lives are subject to the busy activities of this current age, some time should be set aside from the daily labours and allocated specifically to the worship of God and the public administration of the Word, to the ceremonies and the sacred things that God has granted us, and to develop and foster a pious life.
2. That there be a specific day which God has either determined or allowed to the freedom of the church for an orderly and befitting time which the entire church is bound to observe.
3. That there be a suitable day, that is, after a recurring number of days have rolled around, when our fragile human nature (being proportionate to the recurrence) and the need for worshiping God require it. For this worship God has, from the time of creation, ordained the seventh day for the Jewish people (which is the number of completeness, and which corresponds almost to all of nature and was kept also by other peoples). The apostles, too, kept to this recurring seventh day analogously in ordaining the Day of the Lord.
4. That the cause for this day be reasonable, and that it should be dedicated publicly to the purpose of recalling both the general and the particular deeds and benefits of God.
5. That in its use and observance this day be sacred, and be deemed sacred.
6. And that also the entire soul be diverted from its other cares and that the whole day be spent in the duties of piety and charity—and to do so as much as our human weakness and our present need of life can bear.
7. That no tasks which hinder the sanctification of that day be performed without cause or in defiance of it.
8. And finally, that here we practice our duty to be humane and charitable towards those placed under us, including even the dumb animals. The law of nature* has passed on these duties to such an extent that races all around the world have set holidays shared by all their folk, as well as days that are dedicated to attending to their religious affairs.

The special aspect of the Sabbath, insofar as God's ordinance has reduced the general aspect to this special* one, is "the seventh day after creation" or the Sabbath, and even the one "commanded to the Jews." It is by means of this specific aspect that the general one is explained and the Sabbath-rest strictly demanded.

And so in this way all the commandments of the Decalogue that are common to everyone are applied in a particular way to the Jews. For God's first words are: "Hear, o Israel, I the Lord am your God, who led you out of the land of Egypt, out of the house of slavery." In so doing, however, he foretells that their commemoration of this benefit will change when they receive the new

ultra, Vivens qui eduxit Israël e terra Aegypti, sed e terra Aquilonis, etc. Jer. 16, 14. Similiter in αἰτιολογίᾳ, Sabbathi specialiter subjicitur, Memineris quod servus fuisti in terra Aegypti, et eduxit te Dominus Deus tuus inde in manu valida, et brachio extento. Idcirco praecepit tibi Dominus Deus tuus ad faciendum diem Sabbathi. Etiam in quinti praecepti promissione, Ut sis longaevus in terra, quam tibi Dominus Deus tuus daturus est. Ubi intelligitur terra Canaan, populo Israëlitico promissa. Ita ut genus* ad speciem* hic accommodetur.

XLIX   Ut ergo speciale praesupponit generale, quod ad speciem revocatur: ita divinitus speciali abolito, generale manet immotum et immutabile,* specificandum tamen secundum singularem rationem et novam ordinationem.

L   In Novo itaque Testamento, quamvis Sabbathum Judaicum cum reliqua lege mandatorum, quae in ritibus posita erat, per carnem Christi ejusque crucem essent abolita, Eph. 2. Col. 2. fidelesque ab eorum servitute liberati, Gal. 5.; attamen Apostoli cum Judaeis conversantes, Sabbathi diem, ut et alia Legis, non necessitate,* sed pro Christiana libertate, et oeconomia certoque consilio ne imbecillibus essent scandalo, aliquamdiu retinuerunt, cum Judaeis, non tamen Judaice, usurparunt, conventumque sollennem agitarunt, Act. 13, 14. 44. et 16, 13. et 17, 2. et 18, 4. scilicet ut cum honore, ut loquuntur Veteres, Synagoga sepeliretur.

LI   Verum postquam a Judaeis secesserunt et ad gentes transierunt, Act. 18, 6. et 19, 8. ac fratres quidam e Judaeis eorum urgerent necessitatem, et observationem salutarem facerent, Gal. 2, 4. 5. ad declarandam et firmandam libertatem Christianam, ut loca Judaeorum deseruerunt, ita et tempora alia conventus habere coeperunt, Act. 18, 7. et 19, 8.

LII   Et quidem ob novum recreationis et reparationis Christi opus et beneficium, solemniter celebrandum, praeterito Sabbatho creationis monumento (quamvis eo toto Dominus in sepulcro quievisset, quae quies Sabbatho creationis respondere poterat), Resurrectionis Domini diem (in qua est Redemptionis nostrae

21. ON THE SABBATH AND THE LORD'S DAY

covenant, so that it will no more be said: "The Living one who led Israel from the land of Egypt, but from the land of the North, etc." (Jeremiah 16:14). Similarly, when the reasons for the Sabbath are given, a special statement is added: "You shall remember that you were a slave in the land of Egypt, and the Lord your God brought you out from there with a mighty hand and an outstretched arm. Therefore the Lord your God commanded you to keep the Sabbath day." Also in the promise of the fifth commandment: "That you may live long upon the land, which the Lord your God will give to you." Here it means the land of Canaan, promised to the people of Israel, so that the *genus** here is applied to the *species*.*

49 And so just as the particular aspect assumes the general one that is reduced to the species, so too when God annuls the particular, the general aspect remains unaltered and unchangeable,* although it must be specified according to the ground that is unique to the newly established one.

50 Therefore in the New Testament, although the Jewish Sabbath along with the law of other commandments comprising rituals was abolished in the body of Christ and his crucifixion (Ephesians 2; Colossians 2), and although believers were freed from their bondage to them (Galatians 5), nevertheless the apostles, in conversing with the Jews, for a period of time maintained "the Sabbath-day," along with the other elements of the Law—not out of necessity,* but out of Christian liberty, economy, and a steadfast resolution not to be a cause for scandal among those who were weak. They practised it with the Jews, but not in a Jewish manner, and they conducted solemn assemblies (Acts 13:14, 44; 16:13; 17:2; 18:4), obviously so that, as the ancients say, "the synagogue might be buried with due respect."[24]

51 The apostles, however, after they separated themselves from the Jews and went over to the gentiles (Acts 18:6, 19:8[9]), and when some brothers from the Jews pressed upon them the need for keeping the Sabbath and considered the observance a matter of salvation (Galatians 2:4,5), began to have different times for their assemblies for the sake of declaring and confirming Christian freedom, in the same way as they had abandoned the meeting-places of the Jews (Acts 18:7, 19:8[9]).

52 And in fact, in order to celebrate solemnly the benefit of Christ's new work of recreation and restoration, the apostles left aside the Sabbath's function of commemorating creation (although for that entire day the Lord had rested in the grave, which could correspond to the Sabbath-rest following creation), the apostles chose for their public assemblies (Acts 20:7) the day of the resurrection

---

24 The common expression of 'the ancients' appears to have been coined by Augustine (Jerome, *Epist.* 116.20.4 CSEL, 55. 412).

consummatio, quae incidit in octavam a creatione, seu unam, id est, primam Sabbathorum seu Hebdomadae, Joh. 20, 1. Mat. 28, 1. Marc. 16, 1. 2. 9. Luc. 24, 1. 2. quaque se vivum mulieribus, discipulis Apostolisque publice exhibuit, Luc. 24, 24. Joh. 20, 19. 26.) Apostoli ad publicum conventum usurparunt, Act. 20, 7., et consueto observandum ordinarunt, 1 Cor. 16, 1. 2, ubi κατὰ μίαν σαββάτων, distributive, pro, per primam cujusque Sabbathi accipitur. Quo ordinaria et continua et eadem recurrens priscae Ecclesiae observatio significatur.

LIII Unde et hic dies relative non Κυρίου tantum, sed et denominative cum articulo ἡ κυριακὴ ἡμέρα nominari coepit, Apoc. 1, 10., nempe non solum, quod eo resurrexerit Dominus et vivum se exhibuit, sed etiam quod ei rei, imo universim Domino, imo a Domino sacratus dedicatusque esset. Qualiter et coena Domini δεῖπνον κυριακὸν, 1 Cor. 11, 20. appellatur, et locus conventus κυριακὴ et precatio sollemnis κυριακὴ εὐχή, ut scite declarat Augustinus. *De verbis Apost. serm.* 15.[a] Si autem Apostolicae institutionis, divinae quoque fuerit auctoritatis.

LIV Fidem etiam facit perpetua testificatio, praxis et usus, jam inde ab initio Ecclesiae Dei priscorum patrum ut testatur Euseb., *Hist. eccl.* lib. 3. cap. 21.[b] Ignatius, *Epist. ad Magnes. et Trall.*[c] (quae Eusebio[d] et Hieron.[e] ejus genuinae censentur) Justin. in *Apolog.* 2.[f] Dionys. Corinth. Episc. apud Euseb. lib. 4. cap. 22.[g] Theoph. Antioch. lib. 1. *De Allegor. in Mat.*[h] Melito apud Euseb. lib. 4.

---

[a] Augustine, *Sermo* 169.2.3 (= *Sermo de verbis Apostoli* 15; MPL 38:916).   [b] Erroneous reference; correct to Eusebius, *Historia ecclesiastica* 3.27.5 (SC 31:137).   [c] Pseudo-Ignatius, *Epistula ad Magnesios* 9.4 (Funk and Franciscus Diekamp, eds., *Patres apostolici*, 2:124); Thysius uses the 'longer' version of this letter (see the note with SPT 21.27 above), but the passage cited here is also found in the authentic, 'shorter' version as *Epistula ad Magnesios* 9.1 (SC 10²:102). And Pseudo-Ignatius, *Epistula ad Trallianos* 9.5–6 (*Patres apostolici*, 2:104–106); once again, Thysius cites the longer, spurious version of the letter.   [d] Eusebius, *Historia ecclesiastica* 3.36.5 (SC 31:148).   [e] Jerome, *De viris illustribus* 16 (Herding, ed., *Hieronymi de viris inlustribus liber*, 20).   [f] Erroneous reference; correct to Justin Martyr, *Apologia* 1.67.3 (SC 507:308).   [g] Erroneous reference; correct to Eusebius, *Historia ecclesiastica* 4.23.11 (SC 31:205).   [h] Theophilus of Antioch was a first century church father, and is mentioned in Eusebius, *Historia ecclesiastica* 4.24 (SC 31:206–207). In his *Magna bibliotheca veterum patrum*, Marguerin (or: Margarin) de la Bigne published a commentary whose first volume bears the title *s. p. nostri Theophili patriarchae Antiocheni commentariorum sive allegoriarum in sacra quatuor Evangelica*. A fifteen volume edition of de la Bigne's *Magna bibliotheca* (Cologne: e sumptibus Antonii Hierati, 1618–1622) is held by the Leiden University library, and may well have been used by Thysius; the quoted passage can be found in 2:152C–D. In his letter to Algasia, Jerome cites a passage also found in this commentary, noting that it comes from Theophilus's harmony of the gospels ("Theophilus Antiochenae Ecclesiae [...] qui quatuor Evangelistarum in unum opus compingens"); see Jerome, *Epistulae* 121.6 (CSEL 56/1²:24). Following Adolf von Harnack, the majority of scholars today no longer believe the text de la Bigne published to be the authentic commentary from Theophilus mentioned by Jerome.

of the Lord (when our redemption was completed which happened on the eighth day following creation, or on day one, i.e., the "first day of the Sabbaths" or first day of the week [John 20:1, Matthew 28:1, Marc 16:1,2,9, Luke 24:1,2] and on which day he openly showed himself alive to the women, the disciples, and the apostles [Luke 24:34, John 20:19, 26]), and ordained it to be the one customarily observed. See 1 Corinthians 16:1,2, where *kata mian sabbatōn*, "on the first of the sabbaths," is taken in a distributive sense: "the first day of each week." Hereby is meant the observance by the early Church that became ordinary, continuous, and occurring repeatedly.

For this reason people began to call this day not only "of the Lord" (in a relative sense), but also "the Lord's day" (denominatively, with the definite article; Revelation 1:10). The reason, surely, is not only because on that day the Lord arose from the dead and showed himself alive, but also because that day was hallowed and consecrated to that very fact; indeed it was sacred entirely to the Lord and by the Lord. In the same manner also the supper of the Lord is called "the Lord's Supper" (1 Corinthians 11:20), and the place for assembly is called "the Lord's," and that solemn prayer is called "the Lord's prayer," as Augustine neatly explains (Sermon 15, *On the Words of the Apostle*). What is more, while the day has been instituted by the apostles, it was also authorized by God.

What also lends credence to this day of the week is the perpetual attestation, practice, and use of it already from the very beginning of God's church of the early fathers, as witnessed by Eusebius (*Ecclesiastical History* Book 3 chapter 21), Ignatius (*Epistles to the Magnesians, Epistle to the Trallians*, which are judged to be genuinely his by Eusebius and Jerome), Justin (*Apology* 2), Dionysius bishop of Corinth[25] (in Eusebius Book 4 chapter 22), Theophilus of Antioch[26] (*On Allegory in Matthew* Book 1), Melito [of Sardes] (in Eusebius Book 4

---

25 Dionysius († AD 171) was bishop of Corinth. Eusebius knew a collection of his letters and says that Dionysius wrote a letter to Rome about the custom of sending gifts to the poor churches, and he refers also to a letter from Rome that he read on the 'holy Lord's Day.'

26 Theophilus succeeded Eros as patriarch of Antioch c. AD 169, and probably died 183/185. The only writing by him that remains is *Apology to Autolycus*, although Eusebius and Jerome mention other works, including some catechetical writings and commentaries.

cap. 25.ᵃ Irenaeus apud Euseb. lib. 5. cap. 24.ᵇ Clemens Alex. *Strom.* lib. 7.ᶜ Orig. *in 15. cap. Exod. Hom.* 3.ᵈ et lib. 8. *Contra Celsum*.ᵉ Tertul. *De Coron. mil.*ᶠ Cypr. *epist.* 33. et 59.,ᵍ aliique. Accedit lex de eo lata Constant. Imp. apud Euseb. lib. 4. *vitae* ejus,ʰ et Sozom. lib. 1. cap. 8.ⁱ ac reliquorum succedentium Imperatorum, ut videre est C. de Feriis.

LV Est ergo hic dies, etsi Apostolicae institutionis ususque, non tamen ita in se et per se sanctus, quasi mysterium, figuram et symbolum sanctum habeat, aut pars, aut instrumentum pietatis per se sit, (ut in Vetere Testamento nominatim Sabbathi dies) sed tantum secundum Christianam libertatem, sapienter ab Apostolis definitus* ordinatusque est, disciplinae, ordinis et politiae gratia, directusque ut subserviat pietati sanctitatique. Atque cum hac determinatione constare potest dierum inter se aequalitas, Rom. 14, 5. Gal. 4, 10. Col. 2, 16.

LVI Neque proinde observandus, qua Sabbathum a veteri populo ratione, per se et absolute otio et quiete, quae in parte pietatis ponebatur, sed pro modo Christianae libertatis, propter aliud, ut divino cultui vacare publice privatimque tanto expeditius possimus; unde neque tali, aut tam rigida et praecisa

---

ᵃ Erroneous reference; correct to Eusebius, *Historia ecclesiastica* 4.26.2 (SC 31:208). ᵇ Eusebius, *Historia ecclesiastica* 5.24.11 (SC 41:69). ᶜ Clement of Alexandria, *Stromata* 7.12.76.4 (SC 428:234–236). ᵈ Origen, *In Exodum homilia* 7.5 (SC 321:222). ᵉ Origen, *Contra Celsum* 8.22 (SC 150:222). ᶠ Tertullian, *De corona* 3.4 (CCSL 2:1043). ᵍ Cyprian, *Epistulae* 38.2.2 (= *Ep.* 33 in the Pamelius and Baluzius editions; CCSL 3B:185) and *Epistulae* 64.4.3 (= *Ep.* 59 in Pamelius and Baluzius; CCSL 3C:422–423). ʰ Eusebius, *De vita Constantini* 4.18.1 (GCS 7/1:126 = *Eusebius Werke* 1/1). ⁱ Sozomen, *Historia ecclesiastica* 1.8.11 (SC 306:146).

chapter 25), Irenaeus (in Eusebius Book 5 chapter 24), Clement of Alexandria (*Stromata* Book 7), Origen (*Homily 7*, on Exodus chapter 15; and in *Against Celsus*, Book 8), Tertullian (in *Of the Soldier's Garland*), Cyprian[27] (*Letter 33 and 59*), and others. In addition, there is the law concerning it introduced by the emperor Constantine (in Eusebius Book 4 of *Life of Constantine*), and by Sozomen[28] (Book 1 chapter 8), and the laws of the other emperors who succeeded him, as can be seen in the *Codex on Holidays*.

Well then, this day, although it was instituted and employed by the apostles, nevertheless is not "holy in and of itself," as though it forms some sacred mystery, figure, or symbol; or as if it is *per se* a part of or means of piety (as nominally the Sabbath-day in the Old Testament[29]). Rather, according to Christian freedom this day was fixed* upon and ordained wisely by the apostles, for the sake of discipline, order, and polity. And it was intended that the day be of service to piety and holiness. Understood in this way, then, there can be an equality in the week-days (Romans 14:5, Galatians 4:10, Colossians 2:16).

And consequently the day ought not to be observed in the manner of the Sabbath-day of the people of old, "for its own sake and in utter rest and quiet" (something that was considered part of the piety), but "in the manner of Christian freedom" on account of another reason: That we should be able much more readily to make room for the public and private worship of God. Hence we should celebrate the Sabbath not in such a manner (nor with such a strict and

---

27   Cyprian (or Thascius Caecilius Cyprianus, c. AD 200–258), bishop of Carthage from 249 until his death as a martyr. Cyprian took a strict position on the question of re-admitting those who had lapsed, i.e., Christians who had renounced their faith under pressure of persecution. His most important work is *De unitate ecclesiae* (*On the Unity of the Church*). He wrote several letters, of which Epistle 33 and 59 are mentioned in this thesis. However, in the letters usually marked with these numbers, no reference to the observance of the first day of the week as Lord's Day occurs. In Epistle 58 on infant baptism Cyprian mentions the eighth day, the first day after the Sabbath, as the Lord's Day (the day of Christ's resurrection).

28   Salminius Hermias Sozomenus (c. AD 400–450) was born near Gaza and educated at Beirut and Constantinople. He wrote two works on church history, of which only the second one is extant. He relates many events not recorderd elsewhere. See H. Leppin, "The Church Historians (1): Socrates, Sozomenus, and Theodoretus," in *Greek and Roman Historiography in Late Antiquity*. ed. Gabriele Marasco (Leiden: Brill, 2003), 219–254; and Peter van Nuffelen, "Sozomen's Chapter on finding the True Cross (HE 2.1) and His Historical Method," in *Papers Presented at the Fourteenth International Conference on Patristic Studies Held in Oxford 2003: Other Greek Writers, John of Damascus and Beyond, the West to Hilary*, eds. F. Young and others, Studia Patristica, vol. 42 (Leuven: Peeters, 2006), 265–272.

29   Cf. thesis 21 above.

observantia, qualem Judaismus exigebat, aut superstitio imposuerat, sed moderata religiosaque, qualis scilicet quies necessario ad divinum cultum deponcitur, celebrandus est.

LVII   Atque huc revocanda sunt ἀναλόγως communia pietatis et caritatis officia, quae Sabbatho a Judaeis fieri debebant, et a Christianis cum Judaeis adhuc conversantibus praestita fuerunt, ut sunt, conventus publicus et sollemnis, et in eo Scripturarum Sacrarum lectio et praedicatio,* precatioque, Act. 13. 15. 16. 17. et 18. cap. Ac post, paulatim evanescente Sabbatho, die Dominico sunt usurpata, nempe in conventu publico, Doctrina Apostolorum, Communio scilicet pauperum, Fractio panis, nempe mystici, seu coenae Dominicae administratio, Precesque sollemnes et publicae (quibus quatuor totus fere Dei cultus absolvitur, Act. 2, 42.) quae hoc die Apostolicae Ecclesiae solennia fuerunt, Act. 20, 7. 1 Cor. 16. ut etiam ab iis graphice hunc diem describit Justin. *Apol.* 2.[a]

LVIII   Verum non publice modo, sed et privatim hunc ipsum sanctis pietatis exercitiis, quales sunt, Sacrae Scripturae lectio et meditatio domestica, colloquium de rebus sacris, etc, atque caritatis officiis transigendum censemus, secundum illud Clementis: Neque Dominicis diebus, qui sunt hilaritatis, praeter sanctitatem aliquid dicere aut facere concedimus. Neque tamen omnis corporis recreatio hic omnino prohibetur, ut quae etiam inter fines Sabbathi est; scilicet quae divinum cultum non impedit, et sacris peractis, honeste, decenter, moderate et sine offensione et scandalo fit.

LIX   Rejicimus ergo in Christianitate Sabbathum illud primordiale et Judaicum, et Sabbatharios seu Sabbathizantes Christianos; quorum alii Sabbathum diei Dominico pari observantia celebrandum adjungebant, ut Ebionaei, Euseb. l. 3. c. 21.[b] et quidam alii, quorum mentio fit a Gregor. lib. 11. *epist.* 3.[c] Alii illud similiter, non tamen Judaice otiantes, festum habebant; quod etiam videre est apud Clem. Rom. Episc. lib. *Constit. Apost.* 2. cap. 63.[d] et 7. cap. 24.[e] Sabbathum,

---

[a] Erroneous reference; correct to Justin Martyr, *Apologia* 1.67.3 (SC 507:308).   [b] Erroneous reference; correct to Eusebius, *Historia ecclesiastica* 3.27.5 (SC 31:137).   [c] Erroneous reference; correct to Gregory the Great, *Epistulae* book 13, *Ep.* 1 (CCSL 140A:991–993).   [d] The reference appears to be erroneous; corrected to Clement of Rome, *Constitutiones apostolicae* 2.62 (SC 320:33–36).   [e] Erroneous reference (for more, see corresponding note with English text); correct to Clement of Rome, *Constitutiones apostolicae* 7.23 (SC 336:50). The Apostolic Constitutions are no longer thought to have been collected by Clement.

exact observance) as was required by Judaism or as superstition had imposed, but with a moderate, reverent rest of the sort that is needed for the worship of God.

And in an analogous way we should also recall the duties of piety and charity that were common to Jews and Christians: The Jews had to perform them on the Sabbath, and those Christians who still interacted with the Jews performed them, too. Such duties were the public and solemn assembly, and during it the reading and preaching* of the sacred Scriptures, and prayers (Acts 13:15, 16, 17, and chapter 18[:19, 20, 26]). And later, when the Sabbath-keeping declined, the following duties were undertaken on the Day of the Lord: in the public assembly the apostolic teaching, sharing with the poor, the breaking of the bread (i.e., the mystical bread) or the administration of the Lord's Supper, and the solemn and public prayers. The worship of God is summed up by these four duties together (Acts 2:42). These are the solemnities of the apostolic church which took place on this day (Acts 20:7, 1 Corinthians 16[:2]); they are also vividly depicted on that day by Justin (*Apology* 2). 57

We deem, however, that the Lord's Day should be spent in the holy duties of piety not only in public but also privately. Such duties are the reading and contemplation of sacred Scripture at home, conversations about sacred matters etc., and acts of charity, just as Clement says: "On the Lord's Days, which are days of joy, we permit nothing to be said or done that is not holy."[30] Even so, not all bodily recreation is entirely prohibited, as this also belongs to the goals of the Sabbath. Thus activities may be done that pose no hindrance to the worship of God; activities following the completion of the sacred rites, honourable, decent, moderate things that cause no offense or scandal. 58

Therefore, being in the Christian era, we reject the idea of an "original Jewish Sabbath," and Sabbatarians or Sabbath-keeping Christians.[31] Some of these joined the Sabbath to the Day of the Lord, to celebrate it with equal observance; such were the Ebionites (Eusebius Book 3 chapter 21) and some others mentioned by Gregory (Book 11 letter 3). Others kept the feast in a fashion similar to the Jews, yet without observing rest in the Jewish manner, as can be seen in Clement bishop of Rome (*Apostolic Constitutions* book 2, chapter 63, and book 7, chapter 24). He says: "We keep the Sabbath and the Day 59

---

30   Clement of Rome, *Apostolic Constitutions*, book 5, chapter 10 (MPG 1:853).
31   In the sixteenth century some groups of Anabaptists and Unitarians became Sabbatarians, imitating early Jewish Christians; some even adopted Jewish dietary laws. On this, see Williams, *Radical Reformation*, 478, 624–627.

inquit is, et Dominicum diem festum agimus, quoniam illud naturae conditae est monumentum, hic resurrectionis. Contra quos est Can. 29. Synodi Laodic.[a]

LX Quin diei Dominicae, tum sub libertatis Christianae praetextu eversores, ut hodie sunt Anabaptistae; tum eos, qui Sabbathum illud non tantum abolitum, quam in diem Dominicum tantum translatum atque mutatum statuunt, eumque revera sanctionem, non tantum ordinatione usuque, sed et significatione et effectu, ut Scholastici* et Pontificii quidam. Denique graviter incessimus Dominicae diei profanatores, qui non modo non necessariis et alienis actionibus, ut spectaculis, ludis scenisque, sed et intemperantia, luxu omnique genere flagitiorum, eum violant in irreparabile infirmorum scandalum, et horrendum dedecus Christiani nominis.

LXI Quod ad reliqua festa attinet, quae postera Ecclesia, non superstitiose Sanctis, sed ad Christi et singularium operum redemptionis nostrae memoriam adhibet, qualia sunt anniversaria festa: Nativitatis Domini, in qua salutis

---

[a] Mansi 2:580 (NPNF2 14:148).

of the Lord as a feast-day, because the former is a remembrance of the creation of the world, and the latter of the resurrection." Contrary to this statement is Canon 29 of the Synod of Laodicea.[32]

But we reject entirely those who overturn the Lord's Day under the pretext of Christian liberty, such as the Anabaptists of today.[33] We also reject those who hold that the Sabbath-day of old is not so much abolished as merely transferred and altered into the Day of the Lord, and that it is actually a holy day not because of the ordinance and use of it, but because of its significance and effect; such are some of the Scholastics* and papal theologians.[34] And finally, we seriously reproach those who profane the Lord's Day, those who violate it not just by performing unnecessary or irrelevant activities (such as entertainments, games and plays) but also by their licentiousness, extravagance and every sort of disgrace, with the consequence of irreparable scandals to those who are weak, and horrendous infamy to the Christian reputation.

As far as the other feast-days are concerned, which the later Church devoted not superstitiously to the saints but to the remembrance of Christ and his special deeds for our redemption, they are the following annual feasts:

---

32   Canon 29 of the Synod of Laodicea: "Christians must not judaize by resting on the Sabbath, but must work on that day, rather honouring the Lord's Day; and, if they can, resting then as Christians. But if any shall be found to be judaizers, let them be anathema from Christ."

33   It is not clear to which views exactly Thysius is referring, but in general there were two extremes at the beginning of the seventeenth century. Kenneth L. Parker summarizes them thus: "One view, held by Anabaptists and the Family of Love, was that the Sabbath was abrogated and that no difference should be made between days or times. Advocates of this view asserted that the fourth commandment was merely ceremonial and that Christian liberty put an end to such bondage. At the other extreme were Jews and 'Sabbatary Christians' who claimed that the seventh day Sabbath of the Jews was established from creation and remained as binding on Christians as Jews, because of the perpetuity of the moral law," (*The English Sabbath: A Study of Doctrine and Discipline from the Reformation to the Civil War*, Cambridge: Cambridge University Press, 1988, 97). He moreover refers to John Sprint, *Propositions, Tending to Proove the Necessarie Vse of the Christian Sabbaoth* (London: H. Lownes, 1607).

34   Thysius refers to Bellarmine, *De cultu sanctorum*, book 3 chapter 10. The point became important in the Reformed debate on the Sabbath. Criticizing "the trifling of the false prophets, who in former centuries instilled Jewish ideas into the people," Calvin stated (*Inst.* 2.8.34) that the ordinance of the Sabbath is no longer bound to the number of seven days. Walaeus tried to explain Calvin's position, *Opera Omnia* 1:297–298. On the reception of Calvin's passage in later Reformed theology, see Visser, *Sabbatsstrijd*, 302–308. For the view on the Sabbath before the Reformation, see F.W.J. van den Berg, *De viering van den Zondag en de Feestdagen in Nederland vóór de Hervorming* (Amersfoort: Van Amerongen 1914).

nostrae reparatae est initium; Resurrectionis, seu Paschatis, in qua ejus complementum et ratificatio; ac denique Missionis Spiritus Sancti, seu Pentecostes, in qua est regni et Ecclesiae Christianae fundamentum: non eodem censu habemus. Attamen dum habentur pro humanitus institutis, et abest divini cultus opinio, omnisque superstitio, necessitate eorum libertas Christiana non premitur, multitudine Ecclesia non oneratur, sed ad ordinem usumque illustrem Ecclesiae tenentur; utiliter usurpari posse arbitramur, qualiter et festum Purim a Mardochaeo, Esth. 9, 19. et Encaeniorum a Maccabaeo, 1 Macc. 4, 59. institutum observatumque, Joh. 10, 22. legimus.

the Birth of the Lord, wherein lies the starting-point of our renewed salvation; the Resurrection, or Passover, in which our salvation was made complete and confirmed; and lastly the Sending of the Holy Spirit, or Pentecost, wherein lies the basis of the kingdom and Christian church. These feasts we do not hold in the same regard. Nevertheless, as long as it is understood that they are human institutions, and that any notion of divinely prescribed worship—or superstition—is absent from them; and so long as Christian freedom is not suppressed by the necessity of having them, and the great number of them is not a burden to the church, but that they are held for the good order and the distinguished use of the Church we do think that they may be put to good use.[35] A feast of this sort was Purim, ordained and observed at the time of Mordecai (Esther 9:19), and the Feast of the Dedication of the temple in Maccabeus' day (1 Maccabees 4:59), as we read in John 10:22.

---

35 The Reformed tradition originally saw the feast days as a matter of Christian liberty (Calvin, *Institutes* 2.8. 34). The Presbyterians in general rejected the feast days; for the Reformed in the Netherlands, however, an original rejection of the feast days gradually changed into acceptance. In 1618–1619 the Synod of Dordrecht decided that 'Next to the Sundays, the congregations would also celebrate Christmas, Easter and Pentecost with the next day and because most cities and provinces held the day of circumcision (New Year) and of the day of ascension, the ministers ought to persuade the magistrates to confirm to the common use where this is not yet the case.' (article 67) H.H. Kuyper, *De Post-acta of Nahandelingen van de Nationale Synode van Dordrecht in 1618 en 1619 gehouden* (Amsterdam-Pretoria: Höveker & Wormser, 1899), 146. It is worth noting that Thysius only mentions Christmas, Easter and Pentecost and not the other days prescribed by the Synod. As for 'Good Friday' the Synod did not prescribe observance of it, although was customary to preach on the passion of Christ during the seven weeks before Easter. See Willem J. van Asselt and Paul H.A.M. Abels, 'De zeventiende eeuw' in *Handboek Nederlandse Kerkgeschiedenis*, ed. H.J. Selderhuis (2nd, revised edition; Kampen: Kok, 2010), 437.

DISPUTATIO XXII

De Evangelio

Praeside D. JOHANNE POLYANDRO
Respondente PETRO DOORNYCK

THESIS I   Quemadmodum per legem, de qua supra disputavimus, morbi nostri spiritualis, nimirum peccati, contagium ac labes, sic ejus remedium per Evangelium cognoscitur.

II   Vox,* *Evangelium*, denotat apud classicos auctores profanos, 1. Quodvis bonum ac laetum nuntium de re qualibet grata atque exoptata, Aristoph. in *Plut.*[a] Augustinus lib. 2. *Contra Faustum*,[b] et 18. *De Civitate Dei* c. 35. 2.[c] Praemium quod hujusmodi nuntium afferentibus olim dari solebat, Hom. *Odyss.* x.[d] Cicer. l. 2. *ad Att. ep.* 12. 1.[e] Sacrificia ac preces quae pro re feliciter gesta decernebantur, Plutarchus in *Phocione*.[f] Xenoph. lib. 2.[g] Isocrat. in *Areop.*[h]

---

[a] Aristophanes, *Plutus* 765.   [b] Augustine, *Contra Faustum Manichaeum* 2.2 (CSEL 25:254–256).
[c] Augustine, *De civitate Dei* 18.35 (CCSL 48:630).   [d] Homer, *Odyssey* 14.152.   [e] Cicero, *Epistulae ad Atticum* 12.1.   [f] Plutarch, *Phocio* 23.4.   [g] Xenophon, *Hellenica* 1.6.37.2 and 4.3.14.1.   [h] Isocrates, *Areopagiticus* 10,4.

DISPUTATION 22

On the Gospel

President: Johannes Polyander
Respondent: Petrus Doornyck[1]

While it is from the Law (about which we disputed above) that we come to know the contagion and defect of our spiritual illness, that is, of sin, it is from the Gospel that we learn of the remedy for it.[2]

Among the pagan classical authors the word* *evangelion* means 1) any good and happy news about some pleasant and longed-for matter (Aristophanes, *Plutus*;[3] Augustine, *Against Faustus* Book 2, and 18 *The City of God* chapter 35); 2) the reward that used to be given to those who brought news of this good sort (Homer, *Odyssey* 14; Cicero *Letters to Atticus*, Book 2, Letter 12); 3) the sacrifices and prayers that were decreed for some happy outcome (Plutarch in the *Life of Phocion*, Xenophon Book 2, Isocrates[4] in *Areopagiticus*).

---

1   Born ca. 1601, Petrus Jacobi Doornick matriculated on 21 January 1619 as an alumnus of the Leiden States College. He was ordained in Oudenbosch in 1622, Poortvliet (1624), and he was enlisted from 1640 until 1643 in the Dutch West Indies Company in Paraïba, Brazil; he died in 1655. See Du Rieu, *Album studiosorum*, 138, Van Lieburg, *Repertorium*, 51, and Joosse, *Geloof in de Nieuwe Wereld*, 447–478.
2   Throughout the New Testament the word used for Gospel is εὐαγγέλιον; it is rendered into Latin as *evangelium*.
3   Aristophanes (c. BC 446–c. 386) was a comic Athenian playwright. Eleven of his 40 plays survive. The extant version of the comedy *Plutus* (*Wealth*) is the second version, dating to BC 388. On the use and meaning of the term 'gospel,' which is the point of the SPT 22.2 text, in Aristophanes's play, the leader of the chorus says, at one point, "My good fellow, what has happened to your friends? You seem the bearer of good tidings." And a few lines later, Chremylus's wife asks, "What mean these shouts? Is there good news?" And, line 765, which is the reference in parentheses in SPT 22.2, contains the Greek word (*evangelia*): "I wish to wreathe you with a garland of loaves for good tidings, on your reporting such news as this." For a discussion of the use of classical sources to explain 'gospel' see Faber, "Scholastic Continuities," 572.
4   Isocrates (BC 436–338) was an ancient Greek Athenian rhetorician and one of the ten Attic orators. He was also a champion of the written word. The sense of 'good news,' as used in the Areopagiticus, conveys the image of offering sacrifice on account of good news, or a succesful message. On his *Areopagiticus*, see the translator's Introduction in Isocrates (trans. George Norlin), volume II: *On the Peace, Areopagiticus, Against the Sophists, Antidosis, Panathenaicus*, Loeb Classical Library, vol. 229 (London/New York: Heinemann/Putnam, 1929), 100–103.

III In sacris literis κατ' ἐξοχὴν significat* felicissimum nuntium ac jucundissimum de salutari Redemptoris nostri Jesu Christi adventu. Ibique interdum generatim, interdum speciatim sumitur.

IV Generatim sumpta, ipsam de Christo promissionem Evangelicam ejusque impletionem complectitur, ut Gal. 3, 6.

V Speciatim sumpta atque ad Christi exhibitionem restricta, primo historiam denotat de Christo, in carne manifestato, ut Marc. 12.

VI Secundo, pro laeta usurpatur doctrina ac praedicatione* de hominum peccatorum reconciliatione cum Deo, per gratuitam peccatorum remissionem morte Christi expiatoria ipsis partam, quibuslibet indefinite oblatam, pauperibus spiritu atque infantibus revelatam, credentibus vero singulariter applicatam, ad horum salutem et misericordiae divinae cum justitia conjunctae patefactionem laudemque sempiternam, 1 Cor. 9, 14. 15. et seqq.

VII Causa* efficiens principalis Evangelii est Deus, Pater, Filius et Spiritus Sanctus, tum decreti divini de illo hominibus nuntiando, tum nuntiationis ipsius respectu.

VIII Decreti respectu, quoniam hoc mysterium Evangelicum absconditum fuit in Deo a seculis secundum propositum aeternum quod constituit in Christo Jesu Domino nostro, ut docet Apostolus, Eph. 3, 9. 10. 11. Unde et Evangelium ipsum, aeternum vocatur, Apoc. 14, 6.

IX Respectu nuntiationis Evangelicae, quia haec Dei actio, cum fit ad extra,* est actio Trinitatis indivisa. Unde Evangelium aliquando vocatur absolute,* verbum* et potentia Dei, ut Rom. 1, 16. 1 Pet. 1, 23., aliquando relate* ad primam personam divinam, Evangelium Dei, nempe Patris, Rom. 1, 7. ad secundam,

22. ON THE GOSPEL

3 In the sacred writings the most prominent meaning* of the word "Gospel" is: the very blessed and highly welcome message about the salvific coming of our Redeemer Jesus Christ. They sometimes use the word in a general sense, and other times with specific meaning.

4 When taken in a general sense, the word includes in its scope of meaning the evangelical promise itself about Christ, and the fulfillment of it, as in Galatians 3:6.[5]

5 When taken in a specific way, limited to presenting Christ, it means firstly the account of Christ manifested in the flesh, as in Mark 12.[6]

6 Secondly, the word is used for the joyful teaching and preaching* of the reconciliation of sinful people with God through the free remission of sins obtained for them by the expiatory death of Christ. It is offered to one and all without restriction; it is revealed to the poor in spirit and to little children, and actually applied individually to those who believe, for their salvation and the revelation of God's mercy and accompanying justice, and for his eternal praise (1 Corinthians 9:14, 15, etc.).

7 The principal efficient cause* of the Gospel is God, the Father, Son, and Holy Spirit, with respect to both the divine decree of declaring it to mankind and the declaration itself.

8 Regarding the decree God is the efficient cause, because this mystery of the Gospel was hidden with God before all ages according to the eternal purpose which he accomplished in Christ Jesus our Lord, as the apostle teaches in Ephesians 3:9,10, and 11. Whence also the Gospel itself is called eternal (Revelation 14:6).

9 Regarding the declaration of the Gospel God is the efficient cause, because this action by God, since it occurs toward the outside,* is an action that is not divided among the Trinity.[7] And so the Gospel is sometimes called "the word* and power of God" in an absolute* sense, as in Romans 1:16 and 1 Peter 1:23. Sometimes it is used in a relative* sense for the first person of the Godhead, "the Gospel of God," namely of the Father (Romans 1:1), or for the second

---

5 More correctly: Galatians 3:8 or 3:16.
6 The reference is probably to Mark 1:1.
7 Polyander here follows a common Trinitarian rule according to which the works of the Trinity 'toward the outside' are undivided and thus common to the Father, the Son, and the Holy Spirit (*Opera Trinitatis ad extra indivisa sunt*). This axiom goes back to Augustine and Gregory of Nyssa. See *SPT* 7.21,26; 9.10.

Evangelium Christi, ut 2 Cor. 9, 13. ad tertiam, ministerium Spiritus, ut 2 Cor. 3, 6.

x   Verum ratione* ordinis personarum* divinarum ad actionem illam diverso cooperandi modo concurrentium, nuntiatio Evangelii, alio respectu Patri, alio Filio, alio Spiritui Sancto attribuitur.

xi   Nam Patri attribuitur ut primario Evangelii auctori, cum hoc ex sinu ipsius productum fuisse dicitur, Joh. 1, 18. Filio, ut fidissimo Patris legato, qui verba a se prolata non sua, sed Patris sui esse asseverat, Joh. 14, 10. 24. Spiritui Sancto, ut intimo verborum Filii interpreti, cum Christus ait, eum novi nihil Apostolis renuntiaturum, sed eadem declaraturum quae jam ab ipso audiverant, Joh. 16, 13. 14.

xii   Causa προηγουμένη, Deumque in se movens ad Evangelii nuntiationem, est gratuita Dei misericordia ac benevolentia, qua miserum genus* humanum Adami culpa in peccata prolapsum complecti voluit.

xiii Objectum Dei misericordiam suam ac benevolentiam gratuitam Evangelio suo patefacientis, est humani generis miseria in peccatum mortale Diaboli seductione praecipitati, cui Deus interdum immediate, interdum mediate, Redemptionis suae gratiam* annuntiavit.

xiv   Immediate* Deus Pater eam annuntiavit sub Vetere Testamento familiis Adami et Abrahami, Gen. 3, 15. et 12, 7. et 15, 2. sub Novo Judaeis, Mat. 3, 17. et 17, 5.

xv   Mediate* Deus eandem gratiam annuntiavit per Prophetas et Apostolos, quorum illi Redemptorem nostrum Jesum Christum venturum praenuntiarunt; hi eum venisse testati sunt.

person, "the Gospel of Christ" (as in 2 Corinthians 9:13), or for the third person, the "administration of the Spirit" (as in 2 Corinthians 3:6).⁸

But with regard* to the order in which the divine persons* come together for that action in the different ways that they cooperate, the declaration of the Gospel is ascribed in different respects to the Father, the Son, and the Holy Spirit.⁹

For it is ascribed to the Father as the foremost author of the Gospel, since it is from his bosom that it is said to have proceeded (John 1:18). It is ascribed to the Son as the most trustworthy ambassador of the Father, who earnestly declares that the words he brings forward are not his own but those of his Father (John 14:10, 24). And it is ascribed to the Holy Spirit as the most closely related interpreter of the Son's words, since Christ says that the Spirit would declare nothing new to the apostles, but that he would announce the same things that they had heard from himself (John 16:13, 14).

The impelling cause whereby God within himself moves to declare the Gospel¹⁰ is God's unrestricted mercy and goodwill with which he purposed to embrace the wretched human race* that had fallen into sin by the guilt of Adam.

The object to which God reveals his unrestricted mercy and goodwill in his Gospel is the wretched human race that had fallen headlong into deadly sin by the Devil's deception, and to which God announced the grace* of his redemption, sometimes directly and sometimes indirectly.¹¹

Under the old covenant God the Father declared his grace directly* to the families of Adam and Abraham (Genesis 3:15, 12:7, and 15:5); under the new covenant he did so to the Jews (Matthew 3:16 and 17:5).

God declared the same grace indirectly* through the prophets and the apostles, of whom the former announced beforehand that our Redeemer Jesus Christ was going to come, while the latter bore witness that he had come.

---

8   In an 'absolute sense,' 'Gospel' is predicated of the Godhead as such. In a 'relative sense,' it can be predicated to each of the divine persons. See also SPT 7.26.

9   Polyander here complements the axiom *Opera Trinitatis ad extra indivisa sunt* (see th. 9) with the traditional doctrine of appropriation: although the works 'toward the outside' are works of the Trinity taken as a whole, they can be attributed or 'appropriated' in different respects to the Father, the Son, and the Holy Spirit.

10 This inward impulsive cause excludes any cause external to God: see SPT 10.18 note 12.

11 Directly, if by God himself (see th. 14); indirectly, if through somebody else (see th. 15).

XVI   Idcirco Apostolus Paulus ad novitatis suspicionem ab Evangelio removendam, asserit, Deum jam ante, illud promisisse per Prophetas in Scripturis Sacris, Rom. 1. 2. In cujus rei fidem, illorum profert testimonia* ex Veteri Testamento adversus Judaeos Evangelii contemptores, Act. 13. Quemadmodum etiam Christus, Minister circumcisionis, ac nostrae professionis Apostolus, Rom. 15, 8. Hebr. 3, 1.

XVII   Tanta interim est inter Christum θεάνθρωπον, atque inter alios Evangelii praecones, quibus Johannes Baptista, atque ipsi Angeli coelestes annumerantur, inaequalitas, quanta est inter Dominum supremum ac servos, Domini sui nomine, ministerii Evangelici causa, emissos, propter eos qui haeredes erunt salutis per ipsum Dominum acquisitae.

XVIII   Ab his tamen ob auctoritatem et virtutem extraordinariam qua Deus eos divinitus instruxit, Evangelium suam quoque denominationem interdum participat, ut Rom. 2, 16. et 2 Cor. 4, 3. ubi Dei Evangelium etiam, Pauli et coapostolorum ejus Evangelium nuncupatur.

XIX   Proprium Evangelii ὑποκείμενον vel subjectum* est Christus ἐνσαρκωθεὶς seu incarnatus. In hujus enim Redemptione, satisfactione pro nostris peccatis, ac reliquis beneficiis enarrandis totum occupatur. Quo sensu nominatur Evangelium Jesu Christi Filii Dei, id est, de Jesu Christo Filio Dei, Marc. 1, 1. Rom. 1, 3. 16. et 15, 19. 1 Cor. 9, 12. 2 Cor. 9, 13. Gal. 1. Similiter sermo Christi, Col. 3, 16. et Testimonium ejus, 2 Tim. 1, 2.

XX   Objectum Evangelii indefinitum sunt omnis generis homines peccatores, sive sint viri, sive foeminae, sive domini, sive servi, sive Judaei, sive Graeci.

XXI   Objectum Evangelii definitum* sunt filii Dei ordinati ad vitam aeternam, qui a priore vocantur electi Dei, a posteriore, nunc fideles seu credentes in Christum, nunc infantes et pauperes spiritu, peccati mole defatigati.

XXII   Forma est, plena atque evidentissima* gratiae salutiferae per Prophetas in Christo promissae patefactio et publicatio, Dei ordinationi omnibus modis in se tota atque in omnibus suis partibus conformis.

16. Therefore the apostle Paul, in order to avert from the Gospel any suspicion of novelty, states that "already beforehand God had promised it through the prophets in the sacred Scriptures" (Romans 1:2). To add credence to this matter he brings forward testimonials* from the Old Testament against the Jews who despised the Gospel (Acts 13). In the same way Christ is "servant to the circumcision"[12] and "the apostle of our confession" (Romans 15:8, Hebrews 3:1).

17. In the meantime, the difference in equality between Christ, who is "God and man," and the other heralds of the Gospel (among whom are reckoned John the Baptist and the heavenly angels themselves) is as vast as it is between a most high Master and the servants sent forth to administer the Gospel in their Master's name for the sake of those who will be heirs of the salvation, obtained through the Master himself.

18. Nevertheless, the Gospel does, on occasion, take its name from these heralds because of the authority and exceptional ability whereby God has divinely taught them, as in Romans 2:16 and 2 Corinthians 4:3, where God's Gospel is called even the Gospel of Paul and his co-apostles.

19. The proper substance or subject* of the Gospel is Christ 'in the flesh,' or the incarnate Christ. For the Gospel is entirely occupied with telling about his redeeming work, his satisfaction for our sins, and his other benefits. In this sense it is called "the Gospel of Jesus Christ the Son of God," i.e., the gospel about Jesus Christ, God's Son (Mark 1:1; Roman 1:3, 16; Romans 15:19; 1 Corinthians 9:12; 2 Corinthians 9:13; Galatians 1[:7, 11, 12]). In similar fashion it is called "the Word of Christ" (Colossians 3:16) and "his testimony" (2 Timothy 1:8).

20. The indefinite object of the Gospel is sinful people of every kind, whether they are men or women, masters or slaves, Jews or Greeks.

21. The definite* object of the Gospel are God's children who have been ordained unto eternal life, who beforehand are called God's elect and afterward are called sometimes the faithful or the believers in Christ, and at other times little children and poor in spirit, weighed down as they are by the burden of their sin.

22. The form of the Gospel is the full and very clearly evident* revelation and proclamation of the saving grace promised in Christ through the prophets, which in every way (in its entirety and in all its parts) is in harmony with God's ordained purpose.

---

12 In this text "circumcision" is used as metonym for the Jewish people.

XXIII Finis* ultimus est Dei gloria, cui summae misericordiae et justitiae laus hoc Evangelii testimonio tribuitur, quod vadi nostro, proprio suo Filio non pepercerit, sed eum pro nobis morti crucis maledictae tradiderit, ut nos a legis maledictione liberatos, sibi in aeternum reconciliaret.

XXIV Proximus* Evangelii finis est fidelium salus ac vita aeterna, ideoque definitur potentia* Dei ad salutem omni credenti, Rom. 1, 16. atque odor vitae ad vitam, 2 Cor. 2, 16.

XXV Perditio vero infidelium non est Evangelii finis, sed ex illorum vitio eventus adventitius. Deus enim Evangelio suo declarat, quod nullius peccatoris exitio delectetur, sed salutari cujuslibet per resipiscentiam ac fidem translatione e potestate tenebrarum in regnum Filii sui dilecti Jesu Christi.

XXVI Haec ergo salutaris in regnum Filii Dei translatio est proprium Evangelii effectum, atque idcirco Evangelium Regni appellatur, Marc. 1, 14.

XXVII Hujus translationis duo sunt gradus; quorum priore in regnum gratiae in hoc seculo transferimur, posteriore in regnum gloriae in altero seculo evehemur.

XXVIII Prior translationis modus* fit secundum Dei propositum, beneficio vocationis ad fidem, justificationis per fidem, et sanctificationis ex fide, sese per bona opera manifestantis.

XXIX Posterior fiet beneficio glorificationis, qua in Domini nostri Jesu occursum rapti, cum eo longe super omnes coelos ascendemus, ut in domo Patris ipsius proxima immediataque ipsius visione ac communitate beatissima in aeternum fruamur.

XXX Ob hoc effectum distincte consideratum, Evangelium varia nomina* in Sacra Scriptura sortitur; quod nimirum sit verbum veritatis, Col. 5, 5. fidei, Rom. 10, 8. reconciliationis, 1 Cor. 5, 19. pacis, Eph. 6, 15. justitiae, Heb. 15, 13. gratiae Dei, Act. 14, 3. et 20, 32. Verbum regenerans, 1 Pet. 1, 23. Evangelium salutis, Eph. 1, 13. et vitae, Phil. 2, 15.

22. ON THE GOSPEL

23 The ultimate goal* of the Gospel is the glory of God, to whom praise of his highest mercy and justice is ascribed in this Gospel's testimony, because he did not spare his own Son, our surety, but gave him up to an accursed death on the cross for us, in order that he might reconcile us to himself for ever, freed from the curse of the law.

24 The nearest* goal of the Gospel is salvation and eternal life for those who believe, and so it is defined as "the power* of God unto salvation for all who believe" (Romans 1:16) and the "aroma of life unto life" (2 Corinthians 2:16).

25 The destruction of unbelievers, however, is not a goal of the Gospel; that is an unconnected outcome from elsewhere, from their sins. For in his Gospel God declares that he takes no delight in the destruction of any sinner, but he delights in transferring everyone to salvation through repentance and faith from the power of darkness into the kingdom of his beloved Son, Jesus Christ.[13]

26 Therefore this saving transfer to the kingdom of God's Son is the proper effect of the Gospel, and therefore it is called the "Gospel of the Kingdom" (Mark 1:14).

27 There are two stages to this transfer; in the first one we are led, in this age, into the kingdom of grace, and in the second we are carried up into the kingdom of glory in the age that is to come.

28 The former kind* of transfer happens by God's ordained purpose and through the gift of being called to faith, of being justified through faith, and of being made holy by faith that gives evidence of itself through good works.

29 The latter kind of transfer will take place by the gift of being glorified, whereby we shall be taken up to meet our Lord Jesus and we shall ascend with him far above all the heavens, so that in his Father's house we shall have the joy of beholding him close and in full, and we shall have blessed communion in eternity.

30 When considered separately in light of this effect, the Gospel acquires a variety of names* in Sacred Scripture; to be precise, that it is the word "of truth" (Colossians 1:5), "of faith" (Romans 10:8), "of reconciliation" (2 Corinthians 5:19), "of peace" (Ephesians 6:15), "of justice" (Hebrews 5:13), "of the grace of God" (Acts 14:3 and 20:32); the "regenerating Word" (1 Peter 1:23); the Gospel "of salvation" (Ephesians 1:13), and "of life" (Philippians 2:15[16]).

---

13 Polyander is alluding to Col. 1:13: "He has rescued us from the power of darkness and transferred us into the kingdom of his beloved Son."

XXXI Mala quae pravorum hominum culpa ex Evangelii praedicatione eveniunt, non sunt ejus effectis annumeranda, qualia sunt infidelium scandalum, 1 Cor. 1, 23. 1 Pet. 2, 8. hostium gladius, Mat. 10, 34. pertinacium excaecatio, 2 Cor. 4, 4. et major condemnatio, Mat. 11, 21. 2 Thes. 1, 7. 8.

XXXII Ceterum Evangelium aliquando Legis titulo insignitur, quoniam sua quoque habet mandata suasque promissiones ac comminationes.

XXXIII Mandata Evangelii sunt duo, unum de poenitentia, alterum de fide in Jesum Christum, Marc. 1, 15. Resipiscite et credite Evangelio.

XXXIV Ad prius mandatum pertinent conciones Novi Testamenti, tam legales, quam Evangelicae; ad posterius Evangelicae potissimum adhibentur.

XXXV Quae vero exstant Mat. 5. Joh. 13. et alibi, non sunt nova mandata Evangelii proprie* sic dicti, praeceptis legis moralis addita, hisque exactiora, sed sunt eadem quae Moses populo Dei tradiderat, a Christo repetita, a corruptelis Pharisaicis repurgata, pristinoque suo nitori genuina interpretatione restituta.

XXXVI Errant ergo Scholastici* ac Jesuitae, asserentes, novam legem a Christo latam esse, ejusque praecepta Mosaicis esse longe perfectiora, excellentiora et severiora. Lombard. 3. *sent. dist.* 4.[a] Thom. Aquin. *in cap.* 5. *Mat.*[b] et 1. 2. q. 91. art. 5.[c] Scot. 3. *sent. dist.* 40.[d] Biel. 3. *sent. dist.* 4.[e] Bellarm. l. 4. *de Justificat.* cap. 3. et 4.[f]

XXXVII Errant quoque Sociniani, qui duplicia statuunt Christi mandata, quorum alia singulis decalogi praeceptis ab ipso addita, alia Apostolis ab ipso sigillatim tradita fuisse, asseverant.

---

[a] Lombard, *Sententiae* 3.40. [b] Thomas Aquinas, *Super Evangelium s. Matthaei Lectura*, ed. R. Cai (Turin: Marietti, 1951), 76–86 (esp. #474–558). [c] Thomas Aquinas, *Summa theologiae* 1/2.91.5. [d] Scotus, *Ordinatio* 3.40.1 (*Opera omnia* 10:343–354). [e] Gabriel Biel, *Collectorium circa quattor libros Sententiarum*, ed. Wilfrid Werbeck and Udo Hofmann, 5 vols. (Tübingen: Mohr, 1973–1992), 3:698–704 [f] Bellarmine, *De iustificatione* 4.3–4 (*Opera* 6:301a–306b).

The evil consequences that come about by the guilt of depraved people from the preaching of the Gospel should not be numbered among its effects. Evils of this sort are the offense caused to unbelievers (1 Corinthians 1:23; 1 Peter 2:8), the sword-wielding by enemies (Matthew 10:31), the complete blindness of those who are hard-hearted (2 Corinthians 4:4), and a harsher judgment (Matthew 11:21[-24]; 2 Thessalonians 1:7, 8).

And furthermore, the Gospel sometimes receives the distinguishing title of Law, because it also contains its own commands, promises, and warnings.

There are two commands in the Gospel; one is the command of repentance, the other of faith in Jesus Christ; Mark 1:15: "Repent and believe the Gospel."

To the former demand belong the New Testament appeals, both legal and evangelical. To the latter demand the evangelical appeals are applied above all.[14]

But those that are found in Matthew 5, John 13, and elsewhere, are not new commandments of the Gospel in the proper* sense of the word Gospel, as if added to the precepts of the moral law and more precise than these.[15] Rather, they are the same commandments which Moses had delivered to God's people, and which Christ repeated and cleansed of the Pharisees' corrupting influences, and which were restored to their former splendor by authentic interpretation.

Therefore the Scholastics* and the Jesuits go astray when they claim that Christ gave a new law, and that his commandments are by far more perfect, surpassing, and severe than those of Moses (Lombard, *Sentences* Book 3, dist. 40; Thomas Aquinas on Matthew chapter 5, and *Summa theologiae* 1/2, question 91, art. 5; Duns Scotus, *Sentences* Book 3, dist. 40; Biel, *Sentences* Book 3, dist. 40; Bellarmine, *On Justification* Book 4, chapters 3 and 4).

Going astray also are the Socinians, who think that the commandments of Christ are two-fold: They claim that Christ added some of these commandments to the individual precepts of the Decalogue and handed down others separately to the apostles.[16]

---

14   The first sentence of thesis 34 refers to the 'demand of repentance' (thesis 33), and the second to the demand 'of faith in Jesus Christ' (thesis 33).

15   The Old Testament was said to consist of ceremonial, judicial and moral laws. According to the medieval Scholastics, only the moral laws of the Old Testament remained in force after the coming of Christ (cf. thesis 46). See *SPT* 18.5.

16   Theses 38–45 discuss the first type of the commandments of Christ according to the Socinians, and theses 46–51 discuss the second type. The notion of these so-called 'precepts of Christ that he added to the Decalogue' belonged to the earliest Socinian writings and catechisms. In 1608, Valentinus Smalcius wrote of "the added precepts of Christ" in

XXXVIII	Mandata quae asserunt primo legis moralis praecepto a Christo fuisse addita, sunt duo. 1. Quo Christus certam orandi rationem nobis praescripsit. 2. Quo jussit ut eum pro vero Deo, id est, (secundum pravam eorum interpretationem) pro tali, qui divinum in nos habet imperium, agnoscamus, adoremus et invocemus. Quorum utrumque ad primum legis praeceptum referri debet.
XXXIX	Non enim Christus ista precandi formula novam aliquam Deum invocandi rationem, sed sub Veteri Testamento usitatae conformem instituit, primo quidem legis praecepto generaliter a Deo imperatam, et variarum orationum compositione a Davide atque aliis viris Dei ad populi usum specialiter accommodatam.
XL	Nec Christus, cum pro vero Deo agnosci atque invocari voluit, novum Dei cultum praescripsit, sed primo mandato expressum, quo Deus Pater prohibens ne Deos alienos coram ipso habeamus, eum vult adorari qui unus est idemque cum ipso Deus, qualem, non tantum (ut volunt Sociniani) auctoritatis, sed etiam ejusdem naturae divinae respectu, Christum esse tota Scriptura attestatur.
XLI	Idem de ceteris ad sequentia praecepta additionibus, quas Christo affingunt, judicandum est. Nam fugienda esse idola, non tantum Apostoli ex secundo praecepto docuerunt, 1 Cor. 10, 14. et 1 Joh. 5, 21. sed etiam Moses hujus praecepti interpres, Deut. 7, 5. ubi jubet populo Israëlitico, ut Gentium altaria diruat ac statuas earum confringat.
XLII	Deinde quod nobis non solum non liceat pejerare, verum etiam ne in veris quidem jurare, nisi ob causas longe gravissimas, easque quibus gloria Dei nititur, non tantum Christus docuit, Mat. 5, 34., sed etiam Oseas 4, 15. juxta hoc tertii praecepti interdictum, Ne assumito nomen Domini Dei tui in vanum.

On the Divinity of Christ (Racovie, 1608). Although Polyander does not directly mention the Socinian catechism which later became known as the *Racovian Catechism*, the ensuing discussion clearly addresses the issues it raises about the "precepts of Christ, which he added to the Law." The following English translation is based on an enlarged edition in 1680: Thomas Rees, ed., *The Racovian Catechism, with Notes and Illustrations, Translated from the Latin: To Which is Prefixed a Sketch of the History of Unitarianism in Poland and the Adjacent Countries* (London: Longman, Hurst, Rees, Orme, & Brown, Paternoster Row, 1818), section V, chapters 1, 2. The catechism was first published in Latin in 1609. Several revised and enlarged editions ensued, such as in 1660 and 1680. Hereafter, it is cited as *RC*. On Socinus and Socinians, see *SPT* 2.28 and 7.50.

38 There are two commandments that they claim Christ added to the first precept of the moral law: 1) the one whereby Christ directs us to pray in a certain manner; 2) the other whereby he orders us to acknowledge, worship, and call upon him as true God, that is (according to their faulty interpretation) as such a one who wields his divine supreme power over us.[17] Both of these should be referred to the first precept of the law.

39 For by that prayer-formula[18] Christ did not establish some new manner of calling upon God, but one that conforms to the one used in the Old Testament, one that actually had been ordered by God in a general way in the first precept of the law, and that God adapted specifically for use by his people through the composition of diverse prayers by David and other godly men.

40 And Christ, when he willed to be acknowledged and called upon as true God, did not prescribe a new worship of God, but the one expressed in the first commandment. For in it God the Father, when he prohibits us from having any strange gods before him, wills him to be worshiped who is one and the same with God himself. And all Scripture bears witness that such a one is Christ—not only regarding his authority (as the Socinians would have it) but also regarding his divine nature.[19]

41 We should make the same assessment of the other additions to the subsequent commandments that they wrongly claim as Christ's. For it is not only the apostles who taught from the second commandment that we must flee from idols (1 Corinthians 10:14, and 1 John 5:21)[20] but Moses, too, when he interprets this commandment in Deuteronomy 7:5, where he orders the Israelite people to demolish the altars of the heathens and to smash their images into pieces.

42 Next, the fact that we are not permitted to swear falsely, nor even to swear in true matters unless the reasons for so doing are very serious and advance God's glory, is something that was taught not only by Christ (Matthew 5:34) but also by Hosea (chapter 4:15), according to this prohibition in the third commandment: "You shall not take the name of your God in vain."[21]

---

17 On the claim that Jesus added precepts about prayer and authority, cf. RC 185–186, 189, 193–194.

18 On the 'prayer formula,' see RC, 185–186.

19 The RC asks a series of leading questions about inducements to worship Christ, claiming that the first commandment of the decalogue permits the worship of God alone. Cf. RC, 190, 192, 194–195. In SPT 8.30, it was argued that precisely because of his truly divine nature, Christ as the Son of God is worthy of divine worship.

20 Cf. RC, 211 which refers to these same two New Testament texts concerning idolatry.

21 Cf. RC, 212–213 on the prohibition in the third commandment.

XLIII Sic quae in Novo Testamento de officio subditorum erga Magistratum quinto praecepto addita esse existimant, in Veteri quoque Testamento imperata inveniuntur, Lev. 19, 32. Prov. 14, 11. Eccl. 33, 25.

XLIV Neque irae ac vindictae prohibitio in Evangelio, ut censent, tantummodo repetitur, sed etiam apud Mosem, Lev. 19, 17. 18. et Salomonem, Prov. 24, 24.

XLV Libidinosum praeterea aspectum, gestus et sermones obscoenos, septimo, avaritiam, octavo, omnis generis mendacium, etiam ex levitate profectum, nono, denique pravae cupiditatis motum etiam involuntarium, decimo praecepto prohiberi, Judaei ante Christi adventum ex Prophetarum monitis intellexerunt, quae exstant, Prov. 6, 25. et 23, 31. et 5, 20. et 7, 13. 14. Ps. 62, 11. Prov. 15, 27. Es. 56, 11. et 57, 17. Prov. 6, 18. 19. et 19, 5. Ps. 9, 8.

XLVI Mandata quae Sociniani a Christo sigillatim tradita autumant, aut mores, ut loquuntur, aut externos actus religiosos respiciunt, quae vulgo ceremoniae vocantur.

XLVII Moralia nuncupant abnegationem sui ipsius, tolerantiam crucis seu perpessionem et imitationem Christi.

XLVIII Horum primum, ex propria Socinianorum interpretatione, referendum est, tum ad septimum et octavum praeceptum, tum imprimis ad decimum; quandoquidem per abnegationem sui ipsius intelligunt renuntiationem concupiscentiae carnis, oculorum et fastus hujus vitae, ex 1 Joh. 2, 15. 16.

XLIX Secundum comprehenditur sub primo legis praecepto, ad cujus observationem etiam patientia ac crucis tolerantia requiritur.

The same goes for the precepts they think were added in the New Testament to the fifth commandment about the duties of subjects towards the civil magistracy, for these orders are found also in the Old Testament (Leviticus 19:32; Proverbs 14:11[21, 35]; Ecclesiasticus 33:25).[22]

Nor is the prohibition against wrath and revenge to be found only in the Gospel, as they suppose;[23] it is given also by Moses (Leviticus 19:17,18) and Solomon (Proverbs 24:24[24]).

Furthermore, before the coming of Christ the Jews understood from the admonitions of the prophets that the seventh commandment forbids gazing lustfully, indecent gestures and foul-mouthed speech; that the eighth forbids greed, the ninth deceit of any kind (even that which comes from frivolity), and, finally, that the tenth commandment forbids even the unwilled emotions that arise from our corrupt desires. These are found in Proverbs 6:25, 23:31, 5:20, 7:13–14, Psalm 63:11, Proverbs 15:27, Isaiah 56:11 and 57:17, Proverbs 6:18–19 and 19:5, Psalm 10:8.[25]

The commandments which the Socinians say Christ delivered separately refer to moral matters (as they call them) or outward religious actions, commonly called ceremonies.[26]

By moral commandments they mean: self-denial, bearing the cross or endurance, and the imitation of Christ.[27]

The first of these, according to the Socinians' own explication, must be in reference to the seventh and eighth commandments, and mainly to the tenth, since by the self-denial they understand putting aside the lusts of our flesh and eyes, and the haughtiness of the present life, from 1 John 2:15, 16.[28]

The second of these is included under the first precept of the law; for in order to keep it, too, endurance and bearing the cross are required.

---

22 Cf. *RC*, 229 which addresses the issue of the duty of subjects towards the magistrate.
23 Cf. *RC*, 233 on the claim that Christ adds a precept to the sixth commandment.
24 Rather: Proverbs 24:1, 8, 19, 29.
25 The original references to the Psalms in this thesis follow the numbering of the Vulgate.
26 Theses 46–51 discuss the second type of the commandments of Christ according to the Socinians, i.e., those that are handed down separately to the apostles; see thesis 37. The precepts of Christ, delivered by him separately, according to the *RC*, are of two kinds, relating to morals and external religious acts, that is, ceremonies. See *RC*, section V, chapter 2, page 239.
27 Cf. *RC* and its claims on three kinds of morals, 239.
28 Cf. *RC* on the precepts which relate to contempt of the world, 241–242.

L   Christi imitatio nihil aliud est, ut iidem eam definiunt, quam compositio vitae nostrae ad regulam vitae Jesu Christi, qui perfecta sua erga Deum ac proximum caritate legis mandata implevit, ac proinde Christi imitatio, non in alius legis, quam in moralis observatione consistit.

LI   Coena Domini non tantum est mandatum Evangelii ceremoniale, prout statuunt Sociniani, sed etiam Sacramentum* εὐχαριστικὸν ad gratiae salutaris nobis morte Christi partae atque Evangelio annuntiatae celebrationem institutum, ut colligi potest ex Christi commonefactione, Luc. 22, 19. Hoc facite in mei commemorationem, et Pauli, 1 Cor. 11, 16. Quotiescumque ederitis panem hunc, et poculum hoc biberitis, mortem Domini annuntiabitis, usque quo venerit.

LII   Quamvis Evangelii et legis mandata in eo consentiant, quod eandem vitae regulam nobis praescribant, ut nimirum sobrie, nostri ratione, religiose* erga Deum, juste erga proximum vivamus, Tit. 2, 12. in hoc tamen inter se discrepant, quod Lex hominem reum peccati ad hujus detestationem excitet; Evangelium vero eundem suis ad fidem et resipiscentiam exhortationibus ad Christum Redemptorem deducat.

LIII   Promissiones Evangelii sunt potissimum duae: 1. De justificatione coram Deo per fidem. 2. De haereditate vitae aeternae, Rom. 1, 17. 1 Joh. 2, 25.

LIV   Etsi lex non minus quam Evangelium Deo obedientibus vitam aeternam polliceatur, Mat. 19, 16. in eo tamen hoc ab illa differt, quod lex vitam aeternam cuilibet homini promittat, sub conditione propriae justitiae perfectae; Evangelium sub conditione alienae justitiae, nempe Christi, per fidem applicati.

LV   Comminationes sunt, de infidelium Christo non obtemperantium coram Deo condemnatione, ac poena mortis aeternae, Joh. 3, 18. 36. Heb. 2, 2. 3.

LVI   Usus Evangelii praecipuus est, ut Christum legis finem esse ostendat ad justitiam omni credenti, Rom. 10, 4. Reliqui ex ejus finibus atque effectibus, quos supra indicavimus, cognosci possunt.

The imitation of Christ (according to their definition of it)[29] is nothing other than structuring our lives by the rule of the life led by Jesus Christ, who fulfilled the law's commandments with his own perfect love towards God and the neighbor. Accordingly, the imitation of Christ consists in the keeping of no law other than the moral one. 50

The Supper of the Lord is not just a ceremonial demand of the Gospel, as the Socinians think,[30] but it is also a eucharistic sacrament* that has been ordained as a celebration of the saving grace obtained for us by Christ's death and declared in the Gospel. This can be deduced from Christ's admonition in Luke 22:19: "Do this in remembrance of me"; and Paul's, in 1 Corinthians 11:26: "Whenever you eat this bread and drink of this cup, you proclaim the Lord's death until he comes." 51

To be sure, the things that are commanded in the Gospel and the Law are in agreement as they prescribe for us the same rule of life, namely, that we live soberly, as befits us, in pious devotion* towards God and justly towards our neighbor (Titus 2:12). Nevertheless, they differ from each other in this, that the Law stirs up the man guilty of sin to despise it, but the Gospel, with its encouragements to faith and repentance, leads the same man to Christ his Redeemer. 52

The promises of the Gospel are especially about these two things: 1) the justification in the presence of God through faith; 2) the inheritance of eternal life (Romans 1:17; 1 John 2:25). 53

Although the Law holds forth the promise of eternal life to those who obey God no less than the Gospel does (Matthew 19:16), the latter differs from the former in that while the Law promises eternal life to each and every man on the condition of one's own perfect righteousness, the Gospel does so on the condition of an alien righteousness, namely of Christ, and applied through faith.[31] 54

The threats of the Gospel concern the condemnation of unbelievers who do not obey Christ in the presence of God, and the punishment of eternal death (John 3:18, 36; Hebrews 2:2,3). 55

The foremost use of the Gospel is to show that Christ is the goal of the Law unto the righteousness of everyone who believes (Romans 10:4). The other uses of the law can be learned from the goals and effects that we have pointed out above. 56

---

29   Cf. RC on following Christ, 248–249.
30   Cf. RC, and its view on "commemoration" in "the breaking of holy bread," 263, 265.
31   See also SPT 23.5–6, 29.

DISPUTATIO XXIII

De Veteri et Novo Testamento

Praeside D. ANDREA RIVETO
Respondente DANIELE PAIN

THESIS I   Postquam praecedentibus disputationibus actum est seorsim de Lege et de Evangelio, et utriusque natura descripta est; sequitur, ut conferantur etiam inter se, secundum convenientiam et discrepantiam, seu differentiam. Et quoniam eaedem res* variis nominibus comprehenduntur, inter quae, cum de collatione illa agitur, satis frequentia sunt nomina Veteris et Novi Testamenti, de eorum significatione* dicendum est; qua nisi prius declarata et restricta, nihil proclivius est quam impingere, in hac de qua agitur, convenientia assignanda, et discrimine designando, aliis aliud intelligentibus, et pro ratione acceptionum quibus adhaerent, diversa potius loquentibus quam sentientibus.

II   Nomen* Ebraicum ברית ab eo verbo dictum volunt quod purgare et mundare significat, quia in foedere aut pacto sine omni Sophistica utrimque declaretur ratificeturque fides, adhibita publica ceremonia. Hoc nomen Graeci interpretes Veteris Testamenti ubique per διαθήκην reddiderunt, uno loco excepto Deut. 9, 15. ubi per μαρτύριον, testimonium,* verterunt. Apud Graecos autem διαθήκη ut plurimum accipitur in ea significatione singulari, in qua apud Latinos Testamenti nomen, quae tamen est interpretatio speciei,* alioquin ut nomen Ebraeum, sic etiam Graecum dispositionem sonat in genere, sed eam tamen dispositionem cui implicata est promissio, sive sit pactio inter viventes, quam

DISPUTATION 23

On the Old and the New Testament

President: Andreas Rivetus
Respondent: Daniel Pain[1]

Now that we have given individual treatments of the Law and the Gospel (and their natures) in the preceding disputations, it follows that we should compare them regarding their similarities and dissimilarities, or differences. And because people use different names to speak about the same matters* (among them being the terms "old" and "new testament," which are used most commonly when Law and Gospel are compared), we should speak about their meaning. If the meaning* is not made clear definitively in advance, nothing is easier than to force things by indicating similarities and noting differences, as one person understands one thing, and another something else, and, depending on the assumptions that each clings to, they differ in wording rather than in content.

Some people wish to derive the Hebrew word* *b^erit* ['covenant'] from a verb that means 'to cleanse' or 'to make clean,' because in a covenant or treaty both parties reveal and endorse their trust without any filthy sophistry, with an added ritual open to the public. The Greek translators of the Old Testament[2] rendered this word with *diathēkē* ['covenant, testament'], the only exception being in Deuteronomy 9:15, where they translated it as *marturion*, 'testimony.'* In the Greek writers, then, *diathēkē* is used mostly with that singular meaning for which the Latin writers use the word 'testament.' This Latin word, however, has a specific* denotation that differs from the Hebrew and Greek words, which mean *disposition* or *arrangement* generally. Yet a promise is implied in *disposition*, whether it be a treaty between two parties that are alive (they

1

2

---

1 Born ca. 1600 and coming from the province of Poitou (France), Daniel Pain (or Pin) matriculated on 17 April 1621 in theology. He defended this disputation on 14 November 1621 and dedicated it to Theophylus Brachetus, also known as Théophile Brachet de la Milletière (1588–1665), who wrote books and pamphlets propagating union between Protestants and Roman Catholics. Before his stay in Leiden, Pain had studied in Geneva in 1620 with Benedict Turretini, and he is mentioned also as one of the students who followed John Cameron to Glasgow. He served the church of Châtellerault in 1626. See Du Rieu, *Album studiosorum*, 152.
2 In this disputation the words "Old Testament" and "New Testament" (beginning with upper case letters) refer to the books of the Bible. With lower case letters, reference is to the subsequent administrations of the covenant.

συνθήκην vocant, sive Testamentum proprie* dictum, suprema nempe morientis dispositio de rebus relictis, legitime vel verbis nuncupata, vel tabulis consignata.

III Hanc vocem* in hoc, de quo agimus, argumento τῆς παλαιᾶς ἢ καινῆς διαθήκης, Apostolus in propria hac significatione accipit Hebr. 9, 15. et seqq. pro testamento in quo mors intercedit testatoris, ideoque notat, prius testamentum sine sanguine non fuisse dedicatum. Nos ejus auctoritatem sequentes, in eadem materia Veteris et Novi Testamenti speciale nomen foederis generico nomini praeferimus, cum agatur de pacto inter Deum et homines inito, quod morte Christi, primum quidem sanguine victimarum significata, deinde ipso facto obita, sanciri oportuerit.

IV Nec tamen foederis nomen propterea rejicimus, quia si conventionis et pactionis modum* spectemus, ut in humanis partes dissidentes certis conditionibus mutuo praestandis conveniunt, easque caesis victimis ritu veterum (unde non solum apud Latinos icere aut ferire foedus, sed etiam apud Hebraeos כרת ברית, scidit aut feriit foedus, Gen. 15, 18.) aut datis obsidibus, tabulis insuper et signis confirmant: sic inter Deum et homines facta est conventio de aeterna reconciliatione et pace, mediatore victima pro hominibus facto; Tabulis foederalibus confectis, et additis signis Sacramentalibus ad confirmationem. Sed quia mirando modo effectum est, ut idem qui victima fuit mediator, tamquam testator etiam morte sua ratum haeredibus fecerit testamentum, ut tota pacti hujus ratio significetur, hanc vocem specialiter usurpamus.

call it *sunthēkē*), or a 'testament' in the proper* sense of the word, that is, the final arrangement a dying man makes for the things that he will leave behind. This kind of arrangement is made legal by the spoken word or by recorded documents.³

In Hebrews 9:15–22 the apostle employs this word* with this proper meaning for the subject of the old or new testament that we are treating here, to denote a testament that came to pass by the death of the testator. For this reason he observes that "the former testament was put into effect not without blood." Following his authority, when dealing with the same subject-matter, we prefer the specific terms 'old and new testament' to the general word 'covenant,' as it concerns a treaty that was undertaken between God and man and was to be put into effect by the death of Christ, having been foreshadowed first by the blood of slaughtered animals and actually executed by his death.

And yet we do not therefore reject the name 'covenant' if we look at it in the way* an agreement or treaty is reached in human affairs: Parties that differ with each other make an agreement on the basis of certain conditions that each side must meet, and they make these conditions binding by slaughtering animals according to the custom of their ancestors (whence comes the saying, in Latin, 'to strike' or 'slay' a covenant, as well as the Hebrew *karat bᵉrit*, 'to cut' or 'smite' a covenant, Genesis 15:18), or by exchanging hostages in addition to sealed documents. In the same manner an agreement is made between God and man about the everlasting reconciliation and peace that was achieved for them by the mediator who became the victim on man's behalf. Records of their covenant were drawn up to confirm it, along with additional sacramental signs.⁴ But we employ especially this word 'testament' so that it signifies this treaty with its full meaning, because in a wondrous way it happened that the same mediator who was the victim was also the testator who put the testament into effect for his heirs by means of his own death.

---

3   D.A. Weir, *The Origins of the Federal Theology in Sixteenth-Century Reformation Thought* (Oxford: Clarendon, 1990), 51–61 provides information on the lexical and biblical evidence that was available to late sixteenth and early seventeenth century theologians, and that may underlie Rivetus's discussion of *bᵉrit*, *diathēkē*, and *testament*. Among the probable sources are the important *Lexica* produced by Hebrew scholars Johannes Reuchlin, Robert Stephanus, and Johannes Buxtorf Sr. Critical qualifications to Weir's exposition, and additional information on the exegetical discussions of the relevant biblical terms by Reformed authors from Bullinger to Piscator are provided by Brian J. Lee, *Johannes Cocceius and the Exegetical Roots of Federal Theology: Reformation Developments in the Interpretation of Hebrews 7–10*, Reformed Historical Theology, vol. 7 (Göttingen: Vandenhoeck and Ruprecht, 2009), 23–56.
4   The word 'sacramental' may contain the connotation 'oath of allegiance'; see thesis 8 below, and cf. SPT 20.2,31.

v   Dicuntur autem Vetus et Novum Testamentum, vel proprie, vel figurate. Deinde significatione lata, vel stricta. Proprie, nomine Testamenti Veteris significatur Lex, quatenus per Mosem data est Judaeorum populo, vitam promittens sub conditione perfectae obedientiae et comminatione maledictionis contra transgressores, una cum onere intolerabili rituum legalium, et jugo strictissimae politiae, quod propterea dicitur litera occidens, ministerium mortis et condemnationis, generans ad servitutem, Agaris instar, 2 Cor. 3, 6. 7. Gal. 4, 23. et 24. Huic opponitur in propria significatione Novum Testamentum, doctrina nempe spiritualis gratiae et salutis, ab ipso Filio Dei e sinu Patris plene revelata, et Apostolorum praedicatione* divulgata, qua promittitur gratuita justitia et vita aeterna, per et propter mortem testatoris Christi, omnibus in eum credituris per gratiam* quam est largiturus.

vi   In hac significatione differunt Vetus et Novum Testamentum non solum circumstantiis quibusdam et accidentibus,* sed essentialiter,* et ut cum Paulo loquamur, duo testamenta sunt, Gal. 4. 24. in utroque enim diversa prorsus salutis ratio* instituitur, cum illud promittat vitam sub conditione operum, hoc autem remissionem peccatorum et vitam aeternam, innitenti Christo per

Moreover, they may be called the "old" and "new" testaments in a literal sense or a figurative one. And the words may be used with wide or narrow meaning.[5] When the sense is literal, the word "old testament" stands for the Law, insofar as it was given to the Jewish people through Moses. It promised life to them on condition of perfect obedience, with the provision of a curse upon the transgressors, and it brought with it an unbearable burden of legal rituals and the yoke of a highly restrictive political order. For this reason it is called "the letter that kills," "the dispensation of death and condemnation," "bearing children for slavery, like Hagar" (2 Corinthians 3:6,7; Galatians 4:23, 24). Placed opposite to this is the "new testament" (in the strict sense), the teaching of spiritual grace and salvation fully revealed by the Son of God himself from the bosom of the Father and spread abroad by the apostles' preaching.* It promises righteousness without price, and life everlasting through and for the sake of Christ the testator unto all who believe in him through the grace* that he will lavish on them abundantly.

In this sense the old and new testaments are different not only in some circumstantial qualities and contingencies,* but also in essence,* and (to use the words of Paul) "there are two testaments" (Galatians 4:24).[6] For each one established an entirely different ground* for salvation, as the former holds forth the promise of life on the condition of works, while the latter promises the forgiveness of sins and life everlasting to everyone who relies on Christ through

---

5   A twofold division is introduced here. First, the old and new testaments are understood in either a literal or a figurative sense. The literal sense is discussed in theses 5 to 7, and here the two testaments stand for the substantially different administrations of God's covenant with man, expressed as Law and Gospel respectively. In the figurative or metonymical sense, 'old testament' and 'new testament' refer to the books that contain the proclamation of both the Law and the Gospel, together with the sacramental signs of each. This meaning of the terms is discussed in theses 8 to 10. Interfering with this basic distinction, the second division is between a strict and a wider sense. The strict sense is equivalent to the literal understanding of the two testaments (thesis 12), while in a wider sense the books of 'old' and 'new' testaments, contain elements of both the Law and the Gospel (theses 10 to 11).

6   This statement seems inconsistent with the substantial identity of the old and new testaments stated in theses 14 and 15. The contradiction can be solved with help of the distinction between the strict and the wider sense of the words 'old and new testament': In the strict sense, these indicate Law and Gospel as opposite ways to salvation, one by demanding obedience, the other by promising forgiveness and eternal life on account of Christ's satisfaction; in the wider sense, 'Old Testament' and 'New Testament' are understood as two subsequent administrations of the one covenant of grace established by God with humankind. Theses 5 and 6 argue along the strict sense in which old and new testament are opposed; theses 14 and 15 take them in the wider sense in which they differ gradually but not essentially.

fidem. Ideo dicuntur excidisse a gratia, qui per legem volunt justificari, Gal. 5, 4. Et lex promissioni ita opponitur, ut si ex illa sit haereditas, ex hac esse non possit, Gal. 3, 18. Eadem est ratio oppositionis Legis operum, et Legis fidei, Rom. 3, 27. quarum prima intelligitur, doctrina qua salus promittitur, sub conditione si omnia feceris; altera vero, doctrina qua eadem salus proponitur sub conditione si credideris, quam ipsam conditionem gratis dat Deus ut impleant quicumque justificantur.

VII   Hoc igitur sensu, Vetus Testamentum dicitur Ministerium mortis, litera occidens, 2 Cor. 3, 6. intolerabile jugum servitute cultores premens, Act. 15, 10. Umbra tantum futurorum bonorum, Heb. 10, 1. imperfectum, abolendum, etc. Cui oppositum Novum Testamentum ea qua diximus significatione, est ministerium Spiritus vivificantis, lene Christi jugum, donans nos spiritu adoptionis, et libertate filiorum Dei, Matt. 11, 29. Rom. 8, 17. habens veram imaginem rerum, perfectum et aeternum.

VIII Figurate* per Metonymiam Vetus et Novum Testamentum appellantur libri qui codice Veteris Testamenti continentur, et Apostolorum atque Evangelistarum scripta, quo modo in rebus humanis, tabulae et signa testamentorum, Testamenta vocantur, qua ratione etiam signa Sacramentalia,* eandem Testamenti denominationem assumunt. Sic Apostolus 2 Cor. 3, 14. loquitur de velamine manente in lectione Veteris Testamenti. Ex cujus dicti analogia, lectio Evangelii potest dici lectio Novi Testamenti, quo sensu, vulgo Novi Testamenti nomen pro Evangeliorum codice usurpatur. Nam quod in eodem cap. vers. 6. loquitur de Ministris Novi Testamenti id ad codicem sacrum non pertinet. Ad signa vero quod attinet, Poculum Eucharistiae Christus ipse, μετωνυμικῶς, Novum Testamentum in sanguine suo appellavit, Luc. 22, 20. et Apostolus Testamentum seu foedus circumcisionis, Act. 7, 8.

IX   Horum librorum et signorum convenientia et discrimen, pendet a materiis subjectis et revelationis modis, de quibus quia in aliis acceptionibus dicendum erit, levi negotio quid de utrisque sentiendum sit, quivis judicabit, cui nota erit natura* rerum de quibus in unoquoque agitur, et earum inter se vel discrepantia, vel harmonia.

X   Late sumpto Διαθήκης vocabulo, comprehenditur cum additione παλαιᾶς, Lex per Mosem data, de qua dictum est, et promissio de semine mulieris

faith. Therefore those people are said "to have fallen away from grace, who wish to be justified through the Law" (Galatians 5:4). And the Law is placed over against the promise in such a way that if the inheritance comes by the former, then it cannot come by the latter (Galatians 3:18). The same reason exists for the contrast between the Law of works and the Law of faith (Romans 3:27). The first of these is understood as teaching salvation that is promised on the condition "that you do all these things," while the second teaches that the same salvation is offered on the condition "that you believe." God freely grants that condition so that whoever is justified fulfills it.

In this sense, therefore, the old testament receives the names "administration of death, the letter that kills" (2 Corinthians 3:6), "the unbearable yoke" that oppressed its supporters with slavery (Acts 15:10), "a mere shadow of so many good things yet to come" (Hebrews 10:1), lacking in perfection, intended for abolition, etc. The new testament is placed opposite it in this strict sense (as we called it). It is the "ministry of the life-giving Spirit," "the easy yoke of Christ," bestowing on us the spirit of adoption and the freedom of being God's children (Matthew 11:29, Romans 8:[15–]17), having "the true image of things," perfect and eternal. 7

Figuratively* and as metonyms the names "old and new testaments" are given to the books that make up the codex of the Old Testament and the writings of the apostles and evangelists, in the same way as in our human affairs the sealed records of our last wills are called "testaments." For this reason also the signs of the sacraments* receive the same name of "testaments." In this sense, in 2 Corinthians 3:14 the apostle speaks of a "veil that remains over the reading of the old testament." And by the analogy of this statement the reading of the Gospel can be called the reading of the new testament; in this sense the word "new testament" is employed generally for the Gospel-books. But what is said in verse six of the same chapter about "ministers of the new testament" does not concern the sacred book. As far as the signs of the sacrament are concerned, Christ himself calls the cup of blessing by the metonym "new testament in his blood" (Luke 22:20), and the apostle speaks of a testament or covenant of circumcision (Acts 7:8). 8

The similarities and differences between these books and the representation of them depends on the subject-matter and the ways in which it has been made known. And when these will be employed in a different sense, anyone who knows the nature* of each topic treated (and their differences or similarities) will decide with little trouble what to think of it. 9

When the word "testament" [*diathēkē*] is used with wider meaning and accompanied by the word "old" [*palaia*] it embraces the Law given through Moses (about which we spoke) and the promise made to Adam about the seed 10

Adamo facta, eademque Abrahamo in semine suo repetita, in quo benedicendae erant omnes nationes. Hanc promissionem diserte Apostolus Gal. 3, 17. διαθήκην προκεκυρωμένην, Testamentum ante sancitum seu ratum habitum appellat, et ad Eph. 2, 12. διαθήκας τῆς ἐπαγγελίας, foedera promissionis. Sed eidem promissioni jungitur Lex per Mosem data, quatenus sub Veteri Testamento significatione lata comprehenduntur, eatenus tantum, ut lex sit Paedagogus ad Christum, Gal. 3, 24., quia quod lex moralis ab humano genere severissime efflagitabat, id in Christo solum et sacrificio illius exhiberi, lex ceremonialis clamitabat; politica utrique ancillante, et ordinem externum, prout ex utriusque usu erat, procurante.

XI   Sic etiam Novum Testamentum late sumitur, pro doctrina tum gratiae et fidei, tum resipiscentiae et gratitudinis, sive novae obedientiae. Quia Evangelii vox* est, Resipiscite et credite Evangelio, Marc. 1, 15. ac proinde fidem Evangelii et resipiscentiam postulat, quae duo secum necessario trahunt novam obedientiam, qua Deo digne vivitur. Quo sensu Evangelium accipitur, cum Apostolus dicit, se separatum ad praedicandum Evangelium Dei, Rom. 1, 1. Deum judicaturum secundum Evangelium suum, Rom. 2, 16. et similibus.

XII   Stricte autem utrumque sumitur, in ea significatione quam propriam diximus, et qua ita directe opponuntur, ut conciliari non possint; ac proinde non opus est ut prolixam inter ea collationem instituamus. Nam etsi conveniant generali auctoris unius, qui Deus est, consideratione, qui legem tulit, ut legislator, Evangelium, ut parens misericors; generali etiam ratione materiae, quia utraque doctrina mandato obedientiae, et remunerationis promissione constat; generali finis* proposito, nempe gloria sapientiae et bonitatis Dei; item subjecto* communiter* considerato, nempe hominum genere; est tamen differentia maxima in speciali horum omnium respectu, de qua dictum est supra Thesi sexta. Eo autem sensu quo hic intelligitur Vetus Testamentum, fatemur, nunquam in Sacra Scriptura hoc nomen pro foedere gratiae usurpari.

XIII   Sed nihil obstat, quo minus foedus gratiae, seu promissio patribus facta, circumstantiis suis paedagogicis vestita, Testamenti Veteris nomine veniant, quia

of the woman, and the same promise made again to Abraham about his own offspring, in whom all the nations were to be blessed. The apostle expressly calls this promise a "testament considered to have been ratified or confirmed previously" (Galatians 3:17), and at Ephesians 2:12 "the covenants of promise." But "the Law given through Moses" is joined to that same promise insofar as they are understood in a broad sense under the old testament. But only to the extent that the Law is "our custodian unto Christ" (Galatians 3:24), because the ceremonial law cried out that what the moral law most urgently demanded from the human race was achieved only by Christ and his sacrifice.[7] And the law of the political order provided support to each of the other laws, and attended to them with an outward arrangement that each could use.

11 In this way also "new testament" is taken in a broader sense for the teaching of grace and faith, as well as repentance and thankfulness, or the new obedience. For the call* of the Gospel is: "Repent and believe in the Gospel," and so it demands faith in the Gospel and repentance—two things that are necessarily accompanied by the new obedience whereby one lives a life worthy to God. This is the sense of the word "Gospel" when the apostle says that he "was set apart to preach the Gospel of God" (Romans 1:1), and "God is going to judge according to his Gospel" (Romans 2:16), and similar texts.

12 Both "old" and "new testament" are, however, used with strict and literal meaning (as we called it) and then they are opposed to each other so diametrically that they cannot be reconciled. Thus there is no need for us to undertake a lengthy comparison of them. They are similar from the general perspective of their single authorship, namely God. As lawmaker it was he who gave the law, while as merciful Father it was he who gave the Gospel. They are similar also from the general perspective of content, for the teaching in both testaments consists in the command to obedience and the promise of rewards. They agree in the general intent of their goals,* namely the glory of God's wisdom and goodness. So too when we consider the subject* that they share:* the human race. On the other hand, however, a very large difference occurs when one considers each of all these things in particular—we spoke about this particular aspect above, in thesis six. We do admit, however, that the word "old testament," in the sense that it is understood here, is never used in Holy Scripture for the covenant of grace.

13 But there is nothing that prevents the covenant of grace or the promise made to the patriarchs (when dressed in the circumstantial qualities of its role as custodian) from going by the name "old testament," because it contained

---

7 On the relation between the moral law and the ceremonial law see also *SPT* 18.32–34, 46–48.

aliquid in eo erat innovandum et antiquandum. Sic enim Paulus, Ebr. 8, 13. et 9, 1. πρώτην διαθήκην ἣν πεπαλαίωκε, primum Testamentum quod antiquavit Deus, accipit pro toto Religionis* cultu veteris tabernaculi, in quo certe promissio continebatur et confirmabatur. Etsi, ut diximus, ἁπλῶς operum foedus proprie designet; novi autem appellatione non nisi foedus gratuitum intelligatur. Verum ut omnis ambiguitas tollatur. nobis instituenda est comparatio Veteris Testamenti cum Novo; quae Testamentum Vetus considerat, quatenus sumitur pro foedere gratuito, qualiter post lapsum statim cum primis parentibus initum est, et cum Abrahamo pactum, et cujus, lex per Mosem data, fuit adminiculum; Novum vero qualiter fuit a Christo innovatum et confirmatum.

XIV His positis, dicimus duo haec Testamenta unum et idem esse ad substantiam* quod attinet, ut patet in consideratione causarum* omnium. Nam si efficientem spectemus, utriusque, quam προηγουμένην vocant, fuit sola Dei misericordia qua id pepigit, nullis hominum meritis permotus, solum Christum tamquam mediatorem constituens, in quo erat reconcilians mundum sibi, 2 Cor. 5, 19. Si materiam, una eademque est; utrobique enim eadem fides et obedientia requiritur, eadem haereditas vitae aeternae promittitur, per imputationem justitiae fidei, et gratiosam adoptionem in Christo. Si formam, in utraque est pactio inter partes dissidentes confirmata sanguine mediatoris, aut venturi, aut exhibiti. Si finem proximum,* neutrum ad carnalem seu terrenam felicitatem

23. ON THE OLD AND THE NEW TESTAMENT

something that had to be renewed and was to become obsolete. For when Paul says "the first testament which God has made obsolete" (Hebrews 8:13 and 9:1), he takes it to mean the entire religious worship* of the old tabernacle—which surely contained the promise, and confirmed it. And although strictly speaking, as we have said, "testament" means simply the covenant of works, nevertheless by adding the name "new" it means only the covenant of grace. But in order to remove any doubt as to its meaning, we ought to undertake a comparison of the old testament with the new. As far as the old testament is concerned, it is taken for the covenant of grace insofar as immediately after the fall it began with our first parents and was made with Abraham; and to support it there was the law given through Moses. And as for the new testament, it is taken for the covenant of grace insofar as Christ renewed and confirmed it.[8]

Having made these points, we state that these two testaments are one and the same as far as their substance* is concerned, as is evident when we consider all their causes.*[9] For if we look at the efficient cause for each (which some call 'impelling cause'),[10] then it was brought about by God only because of his mercy and not because he was moved by any human merits. He ordained Christ alone as the mediator, "in whom he was reconciling the world unto himself" (2 Corinthians 5:19). If we look at the material cause of each, it is one and the same, for both of them demand the same faith and obedience; both promise the same inheritance of eternal life through the imputation of the righteousness of faith, and the same gracious adoption in Christ. If we look at their form, then in both of them an agreement between two differing parties is established by the blood of the mediator, as one who is coming or as one who has been revealed. If we look at their nearest* goal, then neither of them was calling people to

14

---

8 Apart from the statements made in the present disputation, the *Synopsis* has no elaborate doctrine of the covenant of works and the covenant of grace. The origin and the importance of the idea of a twofold covenant in early Reformed theology are highly debated. It can be traced back, probably to Calvin and Bullinger, but certainly to the authors of the Heidelberg Catechism, Zacharias Ursinus and Caspar Olevianus. A brief survey of the various hypotheses on the origin of federal theology is provided by Willem J. van Asselt, *The Federal Theology of Johannes Cocceius (1603–1669)*, Studies in the History of Christian Thought, vol. 100 (Leiden: Brill, 2001), 325–332. See also Lyle D. Bierma, *The Covenant Theology of Caspar Olevianus* (Grand Rapids: Reformation Heritage Books, 2005).

9 The scheme of fourfold causality is used here to cover the most important aspects of the substantial agreement of old and new testament in terms of its author (God), its content (promise of eternal life; demand of faith), form (agreement between two parties), and goal (man's happiness and God's glory).

10 On *causa impulsiva, causa impellens* see SPT 10.18 and note there.

praesentisque vitae potissimum bona, sed multo magis ad aeternae felicitatis spem revocabat. Si ultimum, utrobique fuit laus gloriosae gratiae Dei in Christo.

xv Duo tamen Testamenta dicuntur, non per divisionem generis* in species,* sed subjecti secundum accidentia;* quia eadem res specie et substantia manens, variatur secundum diversam oeconomiae* rationem, et administrationis* modum, tam ex parte Dei, quam ex parte hominum. In administratione interna Dei, licet unus idemque sit Spiritus electis communicatus, ad unam et eandem υἱοθεσίαν, qui tantam cognitionis lucem effundit, quanta sufficit ad salutem, id tamen constat, in Novo Testamento majorem refulgere Spiritus Sancti efficaciam, et illustriorem donorum varietatem et amplitudinem, si ipsum corpus Ecclesiae spectetur communiter: tunc enim effudit de Spiritu suo super omnem carnem, qui antea parcius communicabatur, Joel. 2, 28.

xvi Externae etiam administrationis consideratio, discrimen praebet non exiguum. Est enim, si qualitatem* revelationis spectemus, in Veteri Testamento minor perspicuitas, cum Christus tamquam venturus offeratur, qui in Novo praedicatur exhibitus. In illo, sub terrenis beneficiis coelestis haereditas contemplanda praebetur, et Patribus degustanda exhibetur, et judicii contra in reprobos magis conspicua documenta in poenis corporeis dantur: quae causa fuit cur benedictiones illas temporales majoris, quam nunc deceret, aestimarint. Jam vero mentes nostrae recte ad coelestem haereditatem diriguntur,

23. ON THE OLD AND THE NEW TESTAMENT 587

fleshly or earthly happiness or especially to the good things of this current life, but instead much more to the hope of everlasting happiness. If we consider the ultimate goal: For each it was the praise of God's glorious grace in Christ.

15 And nevertheless they are called two testaments, not by dividing their kind* into species* but according to the accidental* qualities of their subject-matter.[11] For the same thing that remains in their species and substance varies according to the different grounds for their arrangement* and the way each is administered* (from both the side of God and of man). God, in administering the testaments inwardly, imparts to the elect (for one and the same sonship) the one and the same Spirit who pours forth as much light of knowledge as is needed for salvation. Nevertheless it is quite obvious that in the new testament the Holy Spirit shines forth with greater efficacy, and the diversity and abundance of gifts shines more brilliantly, if we consider the body of the Church as a community. For then "he poured out upon all flesh his Holy Spirit" who before was imparted more sparingly (Joel 2:28).

16 A consideration of their outward administration, too, produces no small difference.[12] For if we look at the quality* in which the testaments are revealed, it is less transparent in the old, since Christ is proffered as yet to come, while in the new he is preached as already revealed. In the former, the heavenly inheritance is put forth as something to be viewed in terms of earthly benefits, and displayed as something whereof the patriarchs were to have a foretaste. And contrary to that, the old testament gives much more obvious demonstrations of the judgment of the ungodly, in the form of bodily punishments. This was the reason why they considered those temporary blessings more valuable than would be fitting today. But as it is now, our hearts are aimed straight and directly

---

11   This sentence indicates different levels of distinction between old and new testament. The denied division into two species would imply an overly strong difference between old and new testament, comparable with the difference between 'dog' and 'horse' as two species of the common genus 'animal.' The difference, therefore, is to be found in accidental and relative qualities of arrangement, transparency, abundance, and so on. The weaker distinction of the two testaments asserted here seems to contradict the strong difference stated in thesis 6 above: a difference "not only in some circumstantial qualities and contingencies, but also in essence" (but see the explanation given in the footnote at thesis 6).

12   The differences between the old and the new testament listed in theses 16 to 20 follow in large part the exposition by John Calvin in his *Institutes*, 2.11. To the five differences mentioned by Calvin, Rivetus adds the "length of time" (thesis 20). The third difference in Calvin, labeling the old testament as a "letter that kills" and the new testament as the "Spirit who vivifies," was placed at the front by the *Synopsis* in theses 5 to 7.

clarius et liquidius revelata per Evangelium futurae vitae gratia, omisso inferiori illo exercitationis modo.

XVII   Tertium hoc discrimen additur, quod Vetus Testamentum umbratili et per se inefficaci ceremoniarum observatione involutum tradebatur, et Christus eo variis ritibus et figuris, venturus adumbrabatur; at in Novo, revelata facie nobis inspiciendus offertur, et ipsarum rerum veritas et corpus tamquam praesens exhibetur; et quae in eo sunt instituta signa, non jam rem futuram promittunt, sed ante promissam, et suo tempore impletam testantur, ejusque efficaciam majorem obsignant; neque sunt cruenta, neque tot numero, neque adeo onerosa aut obscura; sed ἀναίματα, pauciora, facilioris observationis, et majoris perspicuitatis; in illo umbra erat futurorum bonorum, in hoc vera et viva imago rerum, Hebr. 10, 1.

XVIII   Quarta differentia cernitur, in amplitudine populi et universitate receptorum in foedus, quia cum sub Veteri Testamento terminaretur* promissio in Abrahamo et posteritate ejus, exclusis ceteris gentibus, aut paucis admissis, gratia quadam extraordinaria, qua in familiam Abrahae quodammodo inserebantur; jam sub Novo Testamento diruta maceria, quae tamdiu misericordiam Dei intra Israëlis fines conclusam tenuerat, pax annuntiata est iis qui procul erant, ut cum iis qui erant prope, in unum Dei populum coalescerent. Hinc vocatio gentium, praeclarum Novi Testamenti beneficium, Mysterium a seculis et generationibus absconditum, et ipsis Angelis mirabile, Col. 1, 26.

XIX   Quinta consistit in administrationis varietate ex parte hominum. In Veteri enim Testamento non tantum legis moralis observatio exigebatur, sed etiam haeres parvulus tamquam nihil differens a servo, sub oeconomica servitute legis ceremonialis detinebatur. Gal. 4, 2. 3. 4. Hinc etsi haeres, qua talis, spiritu adoptionis donatus fuerit, ac proinde libertatis, tamen qua infans, actu nondum plena libertate fruebatur, sed etiam servitutis spiritu, in eo libertas contemperabatur. At in Novo Testamento fideles non sunt amplius hisce observationum vinculis et oneribus obnoxii, non acceperunt spiritum servitutis iterum ad timorem, sed spiritum adoptionis per quem clamant, Abba Pater, Rom. 8, 13.

at the heavenly heritage, as the grace of the life to come is more clearly and transparently revealed through the Gospel, and as the inferior way of exercising it was abandoned.

A third difference is added in this, that when the old testament was handed down it was wrapped up in a shadowy keeping of ceremonies that possessed no efficacy of itself; and the various rites and figures in it were a means of foreshadowing Christ as yet to come. But in the new testament we are offered to behold him with his face uncovered, and the truth of the things themselves and his body are displayed in the here and now. And the signs that were instituted in the new testament no longer promise some future thing, but they bear witness to one that had been promised earlier and was fulfilled in due time. They form signs and seals of its greater efficacy. And these signs are not bloody, nor so great in number, nor so burdensome or difficult to perceive. In fact, these signs are bloodless, fewer in number, easier to discern, and of greater clarity. In the former testament "there was a shadow of good things that were going to come, while in the latter there is a true, living form of real things" (Hebrews 10:1). 17

A fourth difference is seen in the quantity of people and the universal scope of those who are received into the covenant. For whereas under the old testament the promise was limited* in scope to Abraham and his descendants to the exclusion of other peoples—or with the inclusion of a very few who were somehow engrafted into Abraham's family through some extraordinary grace. But now, in the new testament, when the wall that divided them has been broken down—the wall that for so long a time kept God's mercy confined within the boundaries of Israel—peace has been proclaimed for those who were far off, that they might join with those who were close by into the one people of God. Hence the calling of the gentiles, that most precious gift of the new testament, is called "the mystery hidden for ages and generations," and the angels themselves marvel at it (Colossians 1:26). 18

The fifth difference exists in the changed ways in which they are administered on the part of man. For in the old testament it was required not only to keep the moral law, but even "the heir, as long as he is a little boy, being no different from a slave" is kept in practical slavery to the ceremonial law (Galatians 4:2,3,4). Hence, even though the heir, as heir, was granted the "spirit of adoption," and so "of freedom," nevertheless, as a "little child" he could not yet actually enjoy complete freedom; the freedom he possessed was moderated even by a spirit of slavery. But in the new testament, those who believe are no longer subject to these chains and burdens of observances; "they did not receive the spirit of slavery again unto fear, but the spirit of adoption through which they cry out, 'Abba, Father'" (Romans 8:13[15]). 19

xx   Ultima differentia est in duratione utriusque administrationis. Prima enim cessare debuit, postquam venisset plenitudo temporis; mutationi proinde obnoxia fuit. Lex enim et Prophetae usque ad Johannem, Luc. 16, 16. Sed translato Sacerdotio, necesse est ut Legis translatio fiat, Heb. 7, 12. Et lex transgressionum causa addita est, donec veniret semen, ibid. vers. 18. At semine hoc jam manifestato, nulla amplius exspectanda est mutatio Sacerdotii, quia Christus manet Sacerdos in aeternum, Psalmo centesimo decimo, versu quarto.

xxi   Ex dictis colligimus, gratiae beneficium non esse separandum a Veteri Testamento, hoc modo considerato, cum in eo concio gratiae de remissione peccatorum per Christum mediatorem audita fuerit, qua non minus omnes fideles fuerunt justificati et salvati, quam Novi Testamenti tempore. Una semper fuit salutis ratio; et per gratiam Domini nostri Jesu Christi credimus salvari καθ' ὃν τρόπον, quemadmodum patres nostri, Act. 15, 11. Nec per legem facta est promissio Abrahamo et semini ejus, ut esset haeres mundi, sed per justitiam fidei, Rom. 4, 13. Quia Jesus Christus heri et hodie, idem etiam in secula, Ebr. 13, 5. Ideo Paulus Rom. 4, 1. et 6. ita diligenter adducit exempla Abrahami et Davidis in justificationis negotio, ut evincat, neminem aliter fuisse ab initio mundi justificatum, quam fide in Christum.

xxii   Detestanda est igitur eorum audacia, qui cum impuro Serveto non aliter de populo Israëlitico senserunt, quam de porcis ex Epicuri grege,[a] qui in hac terra a Deo saginati, citra ullam spem coelestis immortalitatis vixerint. Nec minus aliorum error rejiciendus est, qui verum discrimen Veteris et Novi Testamenti tollentes, in utroque praeceptorum a Mose et Christo traditorum observatio-

---

[a] Horace, *Epistles* 1.4.15–16.

23. ON THE OLD AND THE NEW TESTAMENT

20 The final difference lies in the length of time taken for the administration of each. For the first testament had to cease after the fullness of time had come; therefore it was subject to change. For it says "the Law and the prophets until the time of John" (Luke 16:16); "for when there is a change in the priesthood, there must be a change also in the law" (Hebrews 7:12). And, "the law was added because of sin, until the seed should come" (Hebrews 7:18). But now that this seed has been revealed, we should no longer expect a change in the priesthood, since Christ remains as "priest forever," Psalm 110:4.[13]

21 From these words we gather that the benefit of grace is not to be segregated from the old testament, if it is considered in this way, since the announcement of grace concerning the remission of sins through Christ the mediator was heard in it, and all believers were no less justified and saved than in the time of the new testament. For there always was but one way to salvation, and "through the grace of our Lord Jesus Christ we believe that we are saved in the same way as our fathers were" (Acts 15:11). "And it was not through the law that the promise was made to Abraham and his seed that he should inherit the world, but through the righteousness of faith" (Romans 4:13). For "Jesus Christ is the same yesterday, and today, and even to the end of the age" (Hebrews 13:8). And thus Paul, in Romans 4:1 and 6, brings forward the examples of Abraham and David in his dealing with justification so attentively that he succeeds in proving that from the beginning of the world no-one has been justified in any other way than by faith in Christ.

22 Therefore we must detest the presumption of those who together with the vile Servetus felt no differently about the Israelite people than about the swine of Epicurus' herd who have lived beyond any hope for heavenly immortality, being fattened up by God for this earth.[14] We should equally reject the error of others who take away the real difference between the old and the new testaments, and who make keeping the precepts handed down by Moses and

---

13   The reference to Hebrews 7:18 seems to be mistaken; in fact, the quotation is from Galatians 3:19. As the previous thesis (19) referred to Galatians, and thesis 20 closes with a reference to Psalm 110 that plays such an important role in the argument of the Letter to the Hebrews, the mistake is understandable.

14   The combined reference to Servetus and Epicurus' herd is probably derived from Calvin, *Institutes*, 2.10.1. The phrase "swine of Epicurus' herd" was coined by Horace (*Epistles* 1.4.15–16: *me pinguem et nitidum bene curata cute vises, / cum ridere voles, Epicuri de grege porcum* ("When you need a laugh, you can see me, fat and shiny, with well-cared-for hide, a hog from the flock of Epicurus"). He used it to express his contempt of the hedonism practiced by the followers of the Greek philosopher Epicurus (341–270 BC). Cf. Faber, "Scholastic Continuities," 574–575.

nem causam salutis constituunt, et fidem cum exsecutione mandatorum legis sub Veteri Testamento, et Evangelii sub Novo (quae perfectiora fuisse fingunt, sive numerum spectes, quia plura addita, sive uniuscujusque excellentiam, quia ampliata) confundentes, justitiam operum utrobique inducunt, eamque in potestate nostra sitam et viribus humanis paratam.

XXIII Falsum est enim, Christum Legi Mosis aliquid addidisse, ut ex imperfecta perfectam redderet, cum lex, cum primum a Deo lata fuit, semper fuerit perfectissima bonorum operum regula, quando nihil perfectius requiri possit, quam dilectio Dei ex toto corde, quae totius naturae integritatem, et omnium cogitationum, verborum et actionum, cum norma justitiae conformitatem requirit. Hinc est quod qui vitam ex operibus quaerunt, ad legem Christus remittit, Matt. 19, 17. Luc. 10, 28. Quodsi lex impleta habet efficaciam conferendi vitam aeternam, ad ejus perfectionem* nihil addi potest.* Et Bellarminus ipse sui oblitus, recte notat, Christum, Matt. 5. non dixisse, nisi abundaverit justitia vestra plus quam Prophetarum, sed plus quam Scribarum, etc. ut significaret, se non tam velle addere ad onera praeceptorum Legis, quam tollere de medio corruptelas Scribarum et Pharisaeorum, *De justific*. lib. 4. cap. 4.[a]

XXIV Hos errores novi Photiniani a Pelagianis mutuati sunt, in eo tantum a Pontificiis distantes, quod gratiae necessitatem* non agnoscant, ut possint impleri praecepta illa tam vetera interpolata, quam nova promulgata. Hi enim etsi utramque legem, tam veterem quam novam, quam in praeceptis constituunt, justitiae regulam statuant; fatentur tamen, non tantum necessariam esse gratiam revelationis externae per praedicationem, sed etiam operationis inter-

---

[a] Bellarmine, *De iustificatione* 4.4 (*Opera* 6:306b).

Christ into the cause for salvation. They confuse faith with performing the commandments of the old testament Law and the new testament Gospel. In their imagination these commandments are more perfect because if you look at their number, more have been added, and because if you look at the excellence of any of them, they have been intensified And they introduce into both testaments the righteousness by works, a righteousness placed under our control and supplied by our human strength.

23 For it is false to state that Christ added anything to the law of Moses in order to render the imperfect perfect, because the Law, when God first gave it, always has been the most perfect rule for good works, since nothing can be required that is more perfect than to love God entirely from the heart. This love demands the integrity of our entire nature and a conformity of all our thoughts, words, and actions, to the Law of righteousness. Hence it happens that Christ sends those who seek their life from works back to the Law (Matthew 19:17; Luke 10:28). Because if a fulfilled Law has any power to bestow eternal life, then nothing can* be added to its perfect* quality. Even Bellarmine, forgetting his own position, rightly points out that Christ, in Matthew 5[:20], "did not say: 'Unless your righteousness exceeds that of the prophets,' but he said: 'that of the scribes, etc.'; hereby he meant that he wished not so much to increase the burdens of the Law's precepts, as to deprive the Scribes and Pharisees of their wrong teaching" (*On Justification*, Book 4, chapter 4).

24 The modern Photinians[15] have adopted these false notions from the Pelagians, differing with the papal teachers only in that they do not acknowledge that grace is necessary* for them to be able to fulfill both those old precepts that have been refurbished as well as the ones that have been newly made known. For these people [= the papal teachers], although they make both the old and the new law (which they designate as commandments) into the rule of righteousness, nevertheless they do admit that not only is the grace of outward revelation that comes by the preaching necessary, but also of its inward

---

15 The reference to 'modern Photinians' is unclear. Photinus († AD 376) was a pupil of Marcellus of Ancyra, and became bishop of Sirmio in 343. In the post-Nicene Arian controversy, Photinus took a radical stance by denying the deity of Christ altogether, and by describing him as mere man adopted by God. Apparently, the understanding of the Gospel in terms of a moral law that should and can be fulfilled by man in the imitation of Christ is viewed by Rivetus as a consequence of the Christological heresy of Photinus. This could explain why the 'Photinians' are mentioned together with the 'Pelagians.' In SPT 25.2, Photinus is mentioned again, in the company of Servetus and Socinus. During the seventeenth century, polemical books against the 'Photinians' were published, mainly by Lutheran authors such as Jacob Martini and Abraham Calov.

nae, cujus actus* tamen a voluntate* humana suspendantur aut determinentur.*

xxv In quo non solum falluntur, quod nimium arbitrio* humano tribuant, sed quod justificationis gratiam non intelligant, duas matres, liberam et servam, confundant, carnem et promissionem pro eodem habeant, Legem operum cum Evangelio componant, ut res, quoad substantiam easdem, diversas tantum secundum magis et minus, vel perspicuitatis vel perfectionis, aut assistentiae spiritus, cum natura* et genere* duae res sint, quae in negotio justificationis componi non possunt. Nam qui sunt sub lege, non sunt sub gratia, Rom. 6, 14. Christus igitur qui gratiam attulit, novam legem non condidit, ut in ejus observatione justitiam constituerit.

xxvi Neque tamen dicimus, quod illi calumniantur, Christum per Evangelium legem moralem sustulisse; nec negamus eandem legem Christum perfecisse, non solum implendo obedientia perfecta, sed etiam nativae suae perfectioni eam restituendo, et a corruptelis seniorum vindicando, non alia praecepta legalia addendo, aut jam data prolatando: quod factum ab eo fuisse, frustra ex cap. 5. 6. et 7. Matth. probare* contendunt Pontificii et Sociniani.

xxvii Neque etiam inficiamur, Novo Testamento contineri doctrinam operum et varia mandata, imo urgeri omnia mandata Legis moralis, nempe tamquam necessaria ad novam obedientiam et sanctificationis exercitia; sed hoc negamus, quod illi volunt, Novum Testamentum proprie dictum, quatenus est promissionis gratiae in Christo datae doctrina, requirere conditionem totius legis implendae, quod vult Bellarminus, *De justif.* lib. 4. cap. 2.[a] aut justos, non esse liberos ab observatione legis divinae, quatenus illa exigit obedientiam perfectam, qua ex debito justus aliquis pronuntiatur.

---

[a] Bellarmine, *De iustificatione* 4.2 (*Opera* 6:296b).

working—although they make its actions* dependent on the human will* or determined* by it.

They go wrong in this matter not only because they ascribe too much to the human will,* but because they do not understand the grace of justification. They confuse the two mothers, "free and slave,"[16] and they consider flesh and promise to be one and the same thing; they join the Law of works with the Gospel, as though these are similar things in substance, being different only in quantity, clarity, completion, or assistance by the Spirit. In actual fact, they are two different matters in nature* and in kind,* matters that cannot be joined together in the working of justification. For "those who are under the Law are not under grace" (Romans 6:14). Therefore Christ who brought grace did not found a new law, as though he ordained that righteousness comes by keeping it.

However we do not say, as they falsely claim, that through the Gospel Christ has done away with the moral law. Nor do we deny that Christ has made perfect the same law, by fulfilling it with his perfect obedience, and also by restoring it to its original perfection. He did so by liberating it from the corrupting influences of the elders, but not by adding other precepts of the law to it or by extending those that already had been given. The papal teachers and the Socinians strive in vain to prove* that Christ had done this from Matthew chapters five, six, and seven.[17]

We also do not deny that the doctrine of works and a variety of commands are contained in the new testament; in fact, all the commands of the moral law are impressed upon us as needful for the new obedience and the exercise of sanctification. But we do deny this, which they hold, that the new testament strictly speaking, insofar as it is the teaching of the promise of grace given in Christ, demands "the condition of fulfilling the entire law," as Bellarmine would have it (*On Justification* Book 4 chapter 2); or that the righteous are not free from observing the divine law insofar as it demands complete obedience, whereby someone is declared righteous as he deserves.[18]

---

16   Cf. Galatians 4:21–31.
17   For the Socinians, see the reference to the Racovian Catechism, given in the footnote at SPT 22.37. In SPT 22.36, some Roman Catholic authors are quoted who state that Christ gave a new law, with commandments that are more perfect than those of Moses.
18   Cf. Romans 4:4 (Vulgate): "Ei autem qui operatur merces non inputatur secundum gratiam sed secundum debitum." ("Now to the one who works his wage is not credited as grace but as his due.")

XXVIII   Nam quas opponunt nobis conditiones Pontificii in Novo Testamento ad vitam requisitas, ut, nisi abundaverit justitia vestra plus quam Scribarum et Pharisaeorum, etc. Mat. 5, 20. item, si vis ad vitam ingredi, serva mandata, Mat. 19, 17, sunt comminationes aut promissiones legales, non Evangelicae, et quae proprie* ad Novum Testamentum non pertinent, sed ad foedus operum et Vetus Testamentum stricte acceptum; et in Evangelio proponuntur, ut arguatur justitiariorum hypocrisis; et legis ἀδυναμίᾳ indicata, via sternatur ad promissionem gratiae quae propria est Novi Testamenti. Sic juvenem ex operibus justitiam quaerentem prius docere voluit Dominus, neminem coram Deo censeri justum, nisi qui legi satisfecerit (quod impossibile est) ut infirmitatis suae convictus ad fidei subsidium se conferret.

XXIX   Deinde, non omnem conditionem negamus in Evangelio et Novo Testamento requiri ad salutem, requiritur enim conditio fidei et novae obedientiae, quae ubique urgetur. Sed hae conditiones a Deo gratis donantur, neque imperfectione sua, si modo sincerae sint, impediunt salutem, quae ab alia causa manat. At non ita sentiendum de conditione totius legis implendae, quam statuunt illi salutis causam, et quae a Deo nemini in hac vita donatur talis, ut judicium Dei sustinere possit; cum in multis labamur omnes, et qui deliquit in uno, factus sit omnium reus, Jac. 3, 2. et 2, 10. Etsi enim Christus etiam regenerantem gratiam attulerit, qua legem suorum cordibus inscribit, non tamen in ea, salutis causa versatur, aut proprie Novi Testamenti ratio, sed in hac promissione, propitiabor iniquitati eorum et peccati eorum non memorabor amplius, Jer. 31, 31.

XXX   Quae cum ita sint, intolerabilis est Pontificiorum arrogantia, qui non solum perfectiorem illam legem quam sibi imaginantur, prae morali lege a Deo per Mosem tradita, se posse implere, idque facili negotio, praesumunt, eam cum Christi leni jugo confundentes; sed praeterea contendunt, addita esse legi a Christo in Novo Testamento consilia quaedam, quae ipsi Evangelica appellant, quibus se abundantiorem operum justitiam consequi posse pertendunt, quam quae in lege praescripta est, et ex ea gradus in coelo promereri praeter beatitudinem essentialem; ita ut non servata, poenam non afferant, servata majus

For the conditions raised by the papal teachers in objection to us as required in the new testament for eternal life—such as, "unless your righteousness exceeds that of the Scribes and Pharisees" (Matthew 5:20), and, "if you would enter life, keep my commandments" (Matthew 19:17)—these are threatening warnings or promises of the Law and not of the Gospel. They are not relevant or proper* to the new testament but to the covenant of works and the old testament (strictly understood). And they are put forward in the Gospel in order to demonstrate the hypocrisy of those who would be righteous in themselves. And when the incapability of the Law has been demonstrated, they pave the way for the promise of grace appropriate to the new testament. And in this way our Lord determined first to teach the young man who sought righteousness from works that no-one is deemed righteous before God unless he has met the requirements of the Law (which is impossible), so that, being convinced that he is not capable in himself, he would turn to faith for his reliance.

Furthermore, we do not say that the Gospel and the new testament demand no condition at all, for the condition of faith and new obedience (which is everywhere impressed on us) is demanded. But God provides these conditions freely, and their imperfect quality forms no hindrance to salvation (which flows from another source), so long as they are genuine. But this is not how we should view the condition of fulfilling the entire Law, which they make into a cause of salvation. God does not bestow it in this life on anyone in such a way that they can bear God's judgment. For "we all err in many ways" and "he who fails in one commandment is guilty of them all" (James 3:2 and 2:10). For although Christ has brought also regenerating grace whereby he "writes the law upon the hearts of those who belong to him," nevertheless the cause for salvation does not reside therein, nor does the reason proper for the new testament. But the cause for salvation resides in the following promise: "I shall forgive their iniquity and I shall no more remember their sin" (Jeremiah 31:34).

This being the case, we should not tolerate the pride of the papal teachers, who presume that they are able to fulfill that more perfect law which they fancy for themselves, beyond the moral law God handed down through Moses, and to keep it with little trouble, as they confuse it with the "easy yoke" of Christ. But they also make the additional claim that Christ added certain "matters of advice," which they describe as "belonging to the gospel"[19] and whereby they insist upon being able to achieve a more abundant righteousness of works than the one contained in the prescribed law. They claim that from them they can merit higher steps in heaven beyond the essential blessedness, in such a

---

19 On these *consilia evangelica* see the footnote at SPT 20.4

praemium mereantur: qualia sunt tria illa quae vocant perfectionis substantialia, continentia, paupertas et obedientia, et alia plura, ut, non vindicare se ipsum, injurias patienter ferre, etc.

XXXI Haec doctrina legi divinae injuria est, perfectionem in hominum traditionibus potius quam in praeceptis Dei constituens, aut libere observari vel violari posse insinuans, quae vere Dei praecepta sunt in utroque Testamento tradita, omnesque homines obligantia; qualia sunt privatae vindictae abstinentia, dilectio inimicorum, juramentorum temere susceptorum detrectatio, et si quae similia sint, aut praecepta singularia, pro ratione donorum et vocationis Dei suscipienda. Quicquid enim homo habet boni, cum id a Deo habeat, ei debitor est a quo habet, et inutilem servum se profiteri debet, qui quod debuit facere, fecit, Luc. 17, 10.

XXXII His corruptelis rejectis, acquiescimus divinae huic dispensationi,* qua ita legem et promissionem disposuit Deus, ut illam respiceremus condemnantem, hanc quaereremus consolantem; illam reposcentem, hanc ignoscentem, illam plectentem, hanc amplectentem: et in utroque Testamento nihilominus, eandem et unicam salutis viam proposuit per gratiam in Christo mediatore, mutatis tantum circumstantiis, et dispensationis modis, sine ulla dispensantis mutatione. παρ' ᾧ οὐκ ἔστι παραλλαγὴ, ἢ τροπῆς ἀποσκίασμα, apud quem non est transmutatio, aut conversionis obumbratio, Jac. 1, 17. qui variis seculis, variis quoque modis pro summa sua sapientia, suis prospexit, pro uniuscujusque conditione, ut nota nunc fiat per Ecclesiam imperiis et potestatibus quae in coelis sunt, ἡ πολυποίκιλος σοφία τοῦ Θεοῦ, multiformis illa sapientia Dei, Eph. 3, 10. Ὧ μόνῳ δόξα.

way that if they don't keep them they will not incur punishment, but if they do keep them they will earn a greater reward. There are three such matters of advice, which they call the three essential [vows] of [the state of] perfection: abstinence, poverty, and obedience.[20] And there are many others also, such as not taking revenge for one's self, bearing injury with patience, etc.

31   This teaching does harm to God's law, as it places perfection in the traditions of man rather than in the precepts of God, by implying that one can keep or transgress freely what in fact was handed down by God in the two testaments and is binding for everyone. Such precepts include: withholding from taking personal revenge, loving one's enemies, recanting oaths that were taken rashly. We must also perform other similar, individual precepts, according to God's gifts and calling. For whatever good a man possesses, since he has received it from God, he is a debtor to the one from whom he has it, and he must confess that he is "an unworthy servant, who has done what was his duty" (Luke 17:10).

32   Having rejected these false teachings, we take our repose in this dispensation* of God, whereby God has arranged the law and the promise in such a way that we regard the former as one that condemns and we seek the latter for the comfort it brings. The former demands while the latter forgives, the former finds blame while the latter embraces in love. Nevertheless in both the old and the new testaments he has offered the same, the only way to salvation through his grace in the mediator Christ, having changed only their circumstantial qualities and the ways in which he dispensed them. But there was not any change in the one who dispenses them, "with whom there is no variation or shadow due to change" (James 1:17). It is the same Christ who in different ages and in different ways by his own great wisdom provided for those who were his (according to their own individual conditions), and now "through the church has made known to the powers and principalities in the heavenly places that manifold wisdom of God" (Ephesians 3:10). To him alone be the glory.

---

20   Reference here is to the three vows by which one enters the so-called 'state of perfection' of a religious order, as distinguished from secular clergy. The other 'state of perfection' is the one of the bishops. It does not connote moral perfection. On Calvin's position on the religious vows, see David Steinmetz, "Calvin and the Monastic Ideal," in *Anticlericalism in Late Medieval and Early Modern Europe*, eds. Peter A. Dykema and Heiko A. Oberman, Studies in Medieval and Reformation Thought, vol. 51 (Leiden: Brill, 1993), 605–617.

COROLLARIUM.

Inter Veteris et Novi Testamenti dispensationem medium intercessit Johannis Baptistae ministerium, quod ut excellentia cessit Apostolico, sic praecelluit Prophetico; cujus baptisma a Deo institutum, remissionem peccatorum obsignasse, idemque substantia* et significatione* fuisse cum baptismate jam in Ecclesia recepto, statuimus.

Corollary.

The ministry of John the Baptist came between the dispensation of the old and the new testaments; as in merits it yielded to the apostolic ministry, so too did it surpass that of the prophets. We posit that his baptism, being ordained by God, signed and sealed the remission of sins, and was the same in substance* and meaning* as the baptism that is now received in the Church.

Glossary of Concepts and Terms

Absolute (adv.): independently, existing without being dependent on something else (gr.); referring to values or principles that may be viewed without relation to other things. Cf. *absolutus* (adj.): without qualification, restriction; free.

Accidens (n.): a property of a thing that is not essential to its nature; an incidental property, or property of a material substance not contained or entailed by its definition (Aristot.). Regarding God, it is commonly denied that God has 'accidents' since all his properties are entailed in his being God.

Actus (n.): act; actuality. That which exists or is actualized, in distinction from that which has the potential to exist in the future (cf. *potentia*). Compared to the Aristotelian duality of 'act' and 'potency,' Christian thought abandons the notion of necessary realization of potencies. *Actus* is also used as distinct from *facultas*, as the specific act that is distinct from the general capacity.

Ad intra/extra: toward the inside/outside; inward/outward. For classic Reformed theology, the Augustinian distinction between the internal and external works of God (*opera ad intra/ad extra*) is decisive. The *opera ad intra* are the internal Trinitarian relations; the *opera ad extra* are the eternal, contingent acts of the divine knowledge and will. What is *ad intra* is essential and necessary, what is *ad extra* is eternal and contingent.

Administratio (n.): see *dispensatio*.

Aequivocus (adj.): ambiguous, having like but not identical significations; equivocal. Diction can be univocal, equivocal, or analogous. Different uses of the same word can have different meanings, causing semantic ambiguity. See also *analogia*.

Affirmatio (n.): an affirmed, asserted, and confirmed proposition. Also called *propositio positiva* as opposed to a negated proposition (*propositio negativa*). See also *negatio* and *privatio*.

Analogia (n.): a relation of likeness; analogy. It is primarily a concept that refers to the theory of predication. The same term can be attributed to different sub-

jects in ways that are univocal (having the same meaning), equivocal (having a different meaning) and analogous (having a similar meaning).

Arbitrium (n.): see *voluntas*.

Attributum (n.): specific property, attribute; proper quality. In theological Latin *attributum* indicates what is essential *for God*. It is a property that is entailed by God's individual essence.

Causa (n.): cause; that which effects motion or change (Gk. *aition*). In the Aristotelian system there are four kinds of cause: material, formal, efficient, final. This theory of causality excludes the Christian notion of creation and contingency, since the 'Aristotelian' causes operate in a necessary way. In medieval Latin, *causa* was not necessarily a heavily-laden concept; its basic meaning is *condition*: that which is required for the existence of something. For the Protestant scholastics the productive or effective cause (*causa efficiens*) becomes the foremost concept; it is further divided in the principal and the instrumental cause. The pattern of fourfold causality continues to be employed as a structure to cover the most important aspects of a given entity. For example: A carpenter is the efficient cause of a bed and his saw is an instrumental cause. Wood and metal are the material cause, and a specific structure of wood and metal is the formal cause of the bed. Sleeping is the final cause, or goal, of the bed. The efficient and final causes are extrinsic, while matter and form are intrinsic causes. See also *finis*.

Communis (adj.): common; shared; general. It refers to something shared by two or more parties, or what has been communicated. It is the opposite of *singularis*, what is individual or singular.

Communicabilis (adj.): that which can be or is shared in common; communicable. A property that is *communicable* may be held by more than one other entity or persons. An *incommunicable* property cannot be shared between entities or persons.

Contingentia (n.): see *necessitas*.

Definitus (adj.): limited; definite, determinate. In the doctrine of God the term is connected with what God wills; *definitum* is what rests on God's free decision. Applied to the attribute of God's knowledge, it means that God's indefinite knowledge (*scientia indefinita*) comprises what God *can* know, whereas his

definite knowledge (*scientia definita*) regards the factual world, that is the whole of factual reality, the created universe.

Demonstrare (v.): to show, demonstrate; to deliver a proof. It is the most strict form of an argument and of a proof: both the premises of the argument and the deductive relation between the propositions have to be necessary and self-evident. See also *probare* and *monstrare*.

Determinare (v.): to define, determine, prescribe; to decide. The term may be used specifically to indicate the eternal and contingent act of will whereby God selects the possibilities to be actualized in the actual history of the world. His definite knowledge (*scientia definita*) is his determinate knowledge of the actual. If a proposition is *determinata*, it has a truth value. See also *definitus*.

Dispensatio (n.): administration, arrangement; dispensation; economy (Gk. *oikonomia*). As a theological term dispensation may indicate the economy of salvation (*oeconomia salutis*) and its divisions, or the various stages of God's covenant with humankind. In the theology of the Trinity, the classic tradition distinguishes between the *essential* and the *economical* Trinity.

Emanans (part.): see *immanens*.

Essentia (n.): essence, being, existence; intrinsic, indispensible quality of a thing (Gk. *ousia*). The term has a wide range of usages. In the Aristotelian tradition *essentia* has the same meaning as *substantia secunda*, indicating the essence or form of a material thing.

Essentialis (adj.): essential; the quality that makes a being, and apart from which a being cannot be conceived (Gk. *ousiodos*). In the theology of the Trinity what is essential is contrasted with what is personal (*personalis*, or *hupostatikos*). *Essentialis* pertains to what proceeds characteristically from the nature or the essence of God.

Evidentia (n.): evidence. In scholastic discourse it points to the certainty of a proposition.

Facultas (n.): ability, capacity; authority; branch of studies; faculty. It can also mean (financial) resources. It is the talent by which one is able to do something, and as such is distinct from the concrete act.

Figuratus, figurativus (adj.): Figurative, non-literal. In the traditional view, theological language is mainly used literally, not figuratively. In the proposition 'God is good,' 'good' is used literally. In the proposition 'God is my rock,' 'rock' is used figuratively, for God *is* not a rock.

Finis (n.) aim, goal; end. *Finis* answers the question *Why*? It plays a main role in the Reformed doctrine of God because of the decisive significance of the aim or goal God pursues—knowingly and willingly—in his works and actions. This approach differs from Aristotle's philosophy of causality which is a philosophy of necessary and impersonal change. See also *causa*.

Fundamentum (n.): foundation, basis. This term plays also a crucial part in the theory of relation. In the relation *aRb*, for example 'God creates the world,' *a*, or God is called the foundation (*fundamentum*) of the relation R. In an epistemological context the word indicates the theoretical basis of an argument.

Generatio (n.): fertility; production, birth; kind; generation. It is the opposite of corruption. In the Trinitarian language of the church fathers, the Father *begets* (generates) the Son while he himself is *unbegotten*. *Generatio* became a key term in the theology of the Trinity: there are two processions in God, the Son proceeds from the Father, while the Holy Spirit proceeds from the Father and the Son. From the viewpoint of the Father the first procession is called *generatio*, from the perspective of the Son it is called sonship (*filiatio*). See also *processio*.

Genus (n.): class. It is a taxonomic category ranking above *species* (kind) and below family, wherein individual items are identified as a group by shared universals (e.g., 'animal' is the *genus* common to man and beast; 'man' and 'beast' are the *species* distinguished by 'mind-gifted' as the *differentia specifica*). In Aristotle's philosophy the distinction belongs to the theory of the forms which constitute reality; in Christian thought, however, the forms have no creative power. See also *species* and *substantia*.

Gratia (n.): grace. It is used of God's benevolence towards sinful humanity, and the divine working of regeneration. Faith and trust in God are created and given by God. A person is justified, if by God's grace and favor faith and love are working in her heart and life. By grace a Christian is justified (*justus*), not a sinner (*peccator*) although he still commits sins. In this respect the Reformed tradition differs from the Lutheran view (*simul justus, simul peccator*).

Hupostasis (n. Gk.): see *persona*.

Hupostatikoos (adv. Gk.): see *personalis*.

Immanens (adj.): existing or operating within; inherent. It is opposed to *transiens*: what is directed at an external object. This distinction parallels that of *opera ad intra* and *ad extra*. What is called *immanens*, is also called *ad intra*, *inter se*.

Immediate (adv.): see *mediate*.

Immutabilitas (n.): immutability, changelessness. Originally, usage of the term assumed that immutability is equivalent with necessity. In this respect it functions in the doctrine of incommunicable properties of God. A second meaning of 'immutability' is 'unchanging': if God's eternal knowledge of reality is called immutable, this does not imply that this knowledge is necessary, but that it does not change over time. God's eternal knowledge does not change diachronically, but it is contingent synchronically.

Improprie (adv.): see *proprie*.

Incommunicabilis (adj.): see *communicabilis*.

Infinitas (n.): boundlessness; infinity; endlessness. Being finite is having an end, being limited; being infinite is having no end, being un-ending, unlimited, limitless. When applied to number, infinity indicates an immense number. In the doctrine of God the term acquires a specific meaning: if God is infinite, He is infinite not potentially but actually—which was an impossible notion in Greek philosophy. The concept of actual infinity runs parallel to the notion of God's perfection (*perfectus*, complete). God's infinite knowledge is complete knowledge. See also *perfectio*.

In se: in itself. The distinction *in se / secundum quid* (according to something) parallels the distinction between *absolute* (q.v.) and *relative*. The *secundum quid* identifies a specific point to which a predicate applies, and not something as it is in itself.

Lex naturae (n.): law of nature; natural law. In Greek philosophy this is a cosmological concept, the justice embodied in the cosmos (not an ethical concept). In Christian thought, the law of nature becomes a personal and ethical notion. It is usually considered to be a self-evident rule.

Mediate (adv.): involving an intermediate agent; connected indirectly. What is immediate, does not require any deliberation or mediation. What is mediate requires mediation so that at least one or several steps are needed to arrive at the aim.

Modus (n.): way, manner; mode, form. *Modus* is both a general word (way, manner) and a technical term (mode, form). Scholasticism is characterized by a wealth of distinctions and thus it also distinguishes between many kinds of *modi*. The basic *modi*-distinction relates to the levels of existence and language: *modi essendi* and *modi significandi*. A property can be predicated of a thing, and a property or quality can be an essential or an accidental property.

Monstrare (v.): to indicate; to show. Not, in the first instance, a technical term. Delivering proofs is *monstrare*. Cf. *demonstrare* and *probare*.

Natura (n.): nature, natural reality; essence. In Christian thought, nature is created nature; in the middle ages a distinction was made between what is so in a *natural* way ('non-rational') and what is *willed* ('rational'). In theology, *natura* may be used as a synonym of *essentia* (q.v.). God's nature is dealt with in terms of essential properties which are communicable or incommunicable. See also *attributum* and *communicabilis*.

Naturalis (adj.): of or belonging to the nature of things; natural. It is opposed to what is super-natural. In medieval theological Latin, *supernaturalis* indicated that God is above natural reality: he is the creator. In the second half of the fifteenth century the idea of the *duplex ordo* of reality was developed: nature and super-nature. In creation reality has received its own order which suffices, in principle, to arrive at its own perfection. This means that a human person can, in principle, arrive at her own happiness and goodness. Grace and sin are then additional, 'supernatural' aspects which enrich or impoverish life, but they are not crucial and decisive in having impact for what a human person really is.

Necessitas (n.): necessity. It is the opposite of contingency (*contingentia*). In ancient philosophy the notions of necessity and immutability coincide. What is necessary, is always the case; the contingent is sometimes the case and sometimes not. In Christian thought something is considered to be necessary if it not possible that it is not the case. Similarly, 'contingent' is not conceived in terms of different moments of time but as synchronically alternative.

GLOSSARY OF CONCEPTS AND TERMS   609

Nomen (n.): name; noun. The basic functions of a noun are to have a meaning or signification so that something can be said or predicated of something. The disputations in the *Synopsis* usually start with explaining the meanings of the terms involved terms, so that a *nomen* usually is: a meaning-bearing noun.

Notio communis (n., adj.): an insight shared by a number of people.

Notitia practica (n.): see *notitia theoretica*.

Notitia theoretica (n.): Theoretical knowledge, as distinct from practical knowledge. God's theoretical knowledge (*notitia theoretica*) contains what God necessarily knows, including all possibilities. This form of knowledge does not rest on an act of God's will, and it does not entail the actual existence of the objects of knowledge. God's *theoretical* knowledge is his absolute knowledge. God's practical knowledge (*notitia practica*) comprises all that He knows contingently, including the whole of created reality. This knowledge rests on an act of God's will. In the second half of the seventeenth century the distinction between God's theoretical and practical knowledge was superseded by the parallel distinction between God's natural knowledge (*scientia naturalis*) and God's free knowledge (*scientia libera*), which became the standard term for God's practical knowledge. These distinctions run parallel to each other. See also *potentia absoluta/ordinata*.

Oeconomia (n.): see *dispensatio*.

Ousia (n. Gk.): essence; substance. Greek terms in the *Synopsis* do not play an independent role. The authors translated Greek terms back into Latin theological terms. See *essentia*.

Ousiodoos (adv. Gk.): see *essentialis*.

Partes essentiales (n.): essential parts; main constituents. According to the scholastics, a material entity consists of matter of which it is made, but it has also a *form* in virtue of which it is *what* it is. Thus, matter and form are the essential parts or the main constituents of reality and real things.

Partes integrales (n.): integral parts; quantitative constituents. Distinct from *essential parts*, the integral parts indicate the material components of an entity. For example, 'arms' and 'legs' are the integral parts of a body.

Perfectio (n.): perfection, completeness. A term derived from the Latin verb *perficere* which means: to make up, to finish; to complete. *Perfectio* refers to the complete condition of a thing or an attribute. In the *Synopsis* it is mostly used as a divine attribute or as the property of the results of divine actions (e.g., Scripture).

Persona (n.): mind-gifted individual; person. In theological discourse, the term first appeared in discussions of the doctrine of the Trinity, as a translation of the Greek word *hupostasis* that distinguishes the three divine 'Persons' from the divine nature. In its broader application, it means a rational person or *suppositum*, in contrast with animals, trees, stones, things, which are not *rational*. This use of 'rational' does not follow the modern usage; it means: gifted with the faculty of thinking and arguing, and of willing and choosing.

Personalis (adj.): belonging characteristically to a person. Applied specifically to the persons of the Trinity, *personalis* ('personal') refers to the incommunicable personal attributes of each member.

Posse (v.): to be able; can. In scholastic Latin a logical and ontological concept of *posse* was developed which was based on the principle of non-contradiction. When it is said that a proposition is possible (*possibilis*), this means that it is free from contradiction: it is consistent. In Aristotelian philosophy the possible refers to what has potency: now it is not the case, but it will be. See also *potentia*.

Potentia (n.): power; potency. It refers to that which can exist or has the potential to exist (cf. *actus*). The term *potentia* can also be used as a synonym of *facultas*. See also *posse* and *necessitas*.

Potentia absoluta (n.): absolute power. By the term 'absolute power' (as distinct from 'ordained power') the scholastics pointed out that it does not depend on God's will, for it is not determined by God's actual will. What is possible consists of what is consistent in terms of what God *can* will. The whole of these possibilities is not defined by God's will. 'Ordained power' (*potentia ordinata*) is constituted by, and rests on, an act of God's will. While *potentia absoluta* focuses on what God *can* do, the *potentia actualis* or *ordinata* pertains to what God in fact *does*. The distinction of *potentia absoluta* and *potentia actualis* runs parallel to the distinction of the *notitia Dei theoretica* and *practica*.

Potentia actualis (n.): see *potentia absoluta*.

Praedicare (v.): to preach; to predicate. It is used to affirm or attribute a property or an act to a subject.

Praescientia (n.): see *notitia*.

Principium (n.): beginning, source, origin; fundamental principle. In scholastic argumentation, a primary, self-evident proposition on which further reasoning is based.

Privatio (n.): deprivation; the removal of a positive attribute.

Probare (v.): to prove. *Proof* (*probatio*) is a rather broad notion that covers several kinds of proofs. *Demonstratio*, by contrast, is a strict kind of proof in which necessarily true conclusions are necessarily derived from evident premises. Thus, the notion of *probatio* is similar to the modern concept of *proof*. See also *demonstrare*.

Processio (n.): procession. The term refers to the property or act by which the Holy Spirit proceeds from God the Father and God the Son as from a single principle. In a wider sense, it is also used for the *generatio* by which God the Son eternally proceeds from God the Father. Although the process may also be called a production, it is essentially different from any causal production, because the *processiones* are essential to God. Like the *generatio* of the Son, the *processio* or *spiratio* of the Holy Spirit is conceived as an essential, necessary relation on the level of the immanent Trinity.

Proprie (adv.): properly; strictly. A word is used *proprie*, if it is used according to its literal and original meaning. So, when the use of a word develops into new meanings, the word is used *improprie*.

Proximus (n., adj.): neighbor; neighboring; very near; proximate. *Proximius* means 'more closely' and *de proximo* 'soon.' A *causa proxima* (or *principium proximum*) is the direct, nearby cause of something, as distinct from the more remote factors (*causae remotae*) that are involved. See also *causa*.

Qualitas (n.): Quality. One of the crucial Aristotelian categories, qualitas is an accident that affects the substance. The traditional list of Aristotle's category is: quantity, quality, relation, place, time, position, state, action and passivity.

Ratio (n.): computation, account; reason, (logical) account; amount, proportion; ground, underlying principle, aspect; argument, method. In contrast to the modern use of 'rational' a *ratio* regards the objective side of something: for this reason, on this ground.

Relatio (n.): relation. In a general sense, beings can be related in an intrinsic or extrinsic way (a mother is intrinsically related to her child; the passengers are extrinsically related to the train). In scholastic language, *relatio* has a conceptual rather than a real status. The development of the theory of relation served in particular to explain the nature of the relationships among the Father, Son, and Holy Spirit in the Trinity.

Religio (n.): religion. Unlike the modern usage of 'religion,' in medieval Latin *religio* indicates the religious or monastic life. Later it meant the dedicated and committed Christian life, arising from the knowledge, love and reverence of God. Compared to *religio*, *cultus* means 'worship,' 'service.'

Remotus (part.): see *proximus*.

Res (n.): thing; an actual, real thing. Whatever exists, exists as a really distinct entity. In classical Latin *res* was also used to translate the Greek *to on*, for classical Latin has no present participle of *esse*. *Ens* is an invention of medieval Latin. *Res* indicates what exists according to its essential aspects.

Sacramentum (n.): a holy rite; mystery; sacrament. A *sacramentum* is a *thing* (*res*) which is used to convey hidden meaning or significance. In classical Latin *sacramentum* can also refer to a military oath. In Christian contexts it was used both of rites, prayers and objects in general, and of the sacraments in particular. Next to the sacraments proper, the *sacramentalia* denote sacred actions in a wider sense. In theology *sacramentum* became a technical term in the twelfth century, and referred to one of the seven (Catholic) sacraments. The *Synopsis* defends two sacraments: actions which receive their special significance in virtue of divine words.

Scholasticus (n.): schoolman. When used in a general sense, *scholastici* refers to contemporary scholastic theologians or scholastic thinkers. It is not a technical term referring to medieval scholastics.

Scientia (n.): see *notitia*.

Secundum quid: see *in se*.

Significare (v.): to signify; to have meaning. Most scholastic philosophy of language distinguishes between two fundamental uses of nouns: predicating and referring. Predication is executed in virtue of the meaning of the involved word. See also *praedicare*.

Simplicitas (n.): the quality of being uncomplicated, uncompounded, or unmixed; simplicity. A simple act is one that does not consist of components. In Aristotelian philosophy, reality is not simple: it is composed of form and matter, act and potency. In Christian philosophy, God is simple, not consisting of form and matter. The ascription of 'simplicity' to God does not extinguish the 'formal' or 'conceptual' distinctions between the attributes of God. See *attributum*.

Species: see *genus*.

Spiratio (n.): breathing, breath; spiration. *Spiratio* becomes a key term in the theology of the Trinity, and expresses the act by which Holy Spirit (*Spiritus sanctus*) proceeds from the Father and the Son. From the viewpoint of the Father and the Son the procession of the Holy Spirit is called *spiratio*.

Subjectum (n.): foundation of a proposition; subject; topic of a predication. *Subjectum* can be the substrate that functions as the bearer of a specifying form, but usually *subjectum* has to be understood on the logical level as the subject of a proposition.

Subsistentia (n.): subsistence. The property by which an entity is capable of existing *per se*, in itself, or in its own right. It focuses on the aspect of the independence of the existence of what there is. It is mainly said of substances, *supposita* and persons. See *essentia* and *persona*.

Substantia (n.): that which exists; substance. In theological contexts, *substantia* was originally used to render the Greek term, *ousia*. The distinction between first and second substances (*substantia prima, secunda*) derives from Aristotle's metaphysics: a first substance is a material, individual entity we experience in reality, and the second substance is the essence of that first substance that makes it to be *what* it is. On the level of the second substance the distinction between *genus* and *species* operates.

Supernaturalis: see *naturalis*.

Suppositum (n.): a self-existent, self-subsistent thing. Literally, substrate or subsisting reality. In the history of logic *supponere* ('to place as subject') came to mean 'to refer'; thus *suppositum* also means: referent.

Terminus (n.): end; term; fixed period of time. In the philosophical theory of relation, the *terminus* is that which the relation is related to.

Testimonium (n.): witness, testimony; text, passage; proof; last testament. The verb *testare* means 'to bear witness to.' Generally not a technical term, apart from the context of a law suit.

Verbum (n.): word, more specifically: a verb. *Verbum* is also the divine Word, or the second Person of the Trinity. See *nomen* and *vox*.

Voluntas (n.): will. *Voluntas* is the substantive form of the verb *velle* ('to wish, to want'). In the Middle Ages, the term obtains the specifically Christian meaning of 'to will decidedly,' in terms of alternatives. For the latter meaning, *arbitrium* is also used. *Arbitrari* is what a referee (*arbiter*) does: to decide on the basis of what one knows. For Erasmus and Melanchthon, *arbitrium* and *voluntas* are interchangeable. Later, *arbitrium* refers to choice. Both concepts, 'will' and 'choice,' presuppose the contingent nature of reality.

Voluntas necessaria (n.): the necessary or natural will. God knows himself, wills and loves himself by a certain necessity, by his will (not antecedently, but concomitantly). It is impossible that God does *not* will himself, since he is the Supreme Good, and therefore the proper object of his own perfect will. The necessary will is contrasted with the free will (*voluntas libera*). Similarly, the Father cannot will contingently that He generates or loves the Son, for then it is possible that He does not generate or does not love the Son. The necessary will is related to the *opera ad intra*, and the free and contingent will to the *opera ad extra*.

Vox (n.): word. In early modern Latin, *vox* and *sermo* are often synonyms. Originally *vox* indicated a word insofar as it is a physical item expressed (voiced) by the voice—it is a word as a spoken word; *vox* also means *voice*. *Sermo* is a *vox* laden with semantic meaning; speech.

Bibliography

Primary Sources

a *Manuscripts*
Canterbury Pontifical. Cambridge, Corpus Christi College, MS 44.
Samson Pontifical. Cambridge, Corpus Christi College MS 146.

b *Printed Sources Quoted in the Synopsis*
Adamantius. *Dialogus de recta in Deum fide*. MPG 11.
Ambrose. *De obitu Theodosii oratio*. CSEL 73.
———. *Epistulae*. CSEL 82/1–3.
———. *Hexameron*. CSEL 32/1.
Aristophanes. *Plutus (Wealth)*. LCL 180 (new edition), edited by Jeffrey Henderson, 2002.
Aristotle. *De anima (On the Soul)*. LCL 288, edited by W.S. Hett, 1957.
———. *De coelo (On the Heavens)*. LCL 338, edited by W.K.C. Guthrie, 1939.
———. *De Interpretatione (On Interpretation)*. LCL 325, edited by H.P. Cooke and Hugh Tredennick, 1938.
———. *Metaphysica (Metaphysics)*. LCL 271, 287, edited by Hugh Tredennick and G. Cyril Armstrong, 1933, 1935.
———. *The Nicomachean Ethics*. LCL 73, edited by H. Rackham, 1962.
———. *Physica (Physics)*. LCL 228, 255, edited by P.H. Wicksteed and F.M. Cornford, 1934, 1957.
———. *Posterior Analytics*. LCL 391, edited by Hugh Tredennick and E.S. Forster, 1960.
———. *Rhetorica ad Alexandrum (Rhetoric to Alexander)*. LCL 317, edited by Robert Mayhew and David C. Mirhady, 2011.
Arrianus. Lucius Flavius. *Anabasis Alexandrou (Anabasis of Alexander)*. LCL 236, 269, edited by P.A. Brunt, 1976, 1983.
Athanasius. *Contra Arrianos Oratio*. AW 1/1.
———. *Synopsis sacrae scripturae*. MPG 28.
Augustine. *Confessiones*. CCSL 27.
———. *Contra Faustum Manichaeum*. CSEL 25.
———. *Contra Julianum*. MPL 44.
———. *Contra Maximum haereticum*. MPL 42.
———. *Contra Priscillianistas*. CCSL 49.
———. *De baptismo contra Donatistas*. CSEL 51.
———. *De civitate Dei*. CCSL 47, 48.
———. *De consensu evangelistarum*. CSEL 43.

———. *De correptione et gratia.* CSEL 92.
———. *De diversis quaestionibus ad Simplicianum.* CCSL 44.
———. *De doctrina christiana.* CCSL 32.
———. *De fide et symbolo.* CSEL 41.
———. *De Genesi ad litteram.* CSEL 28/1.
———. *De gestis Pelagii.* CSEL 42.
———. *De gratia Christi et de peccato originali.* CSEL 42.
———. *De opere Monachorum.* CSEL 41.
———. *De peccatorum meritis et remissione.* CSEL 60.
———. *De symbolo sermo ad catechumenos.* CCSL 46.
———. *De trinitate.* CCSL 50.
———. *De vera religione.* CCSL 32.
———. *Enchiridion ad Laurentium.* CCSL 46.
———. *Ennarrationes in Psalmos.* CSEL 94/1.
———. *Epistulae.* CCSL 31B; CSEL 44.
———. *In Ioannis Evangelium tractatus.* CCSL 36.
———. *Quaestionum in Heptateuchum libri VII.* CCSL 33.
———. *Retractationes.* CCSL 57.
———. *Sermones.* MPL 38, 39.
Ayala, Martin Perez de. *De divinis, apostolicis et ecclesiasticis traditionibus.* Cologne: Jaspar von Gennep, 1560. (VD16 P 1367)
Balsamon, Theodore. *Commentaria in Epistolas canonicas sanctorum Patrum.* MPG 138.
Baronius, Caesar. *Annales Ecclesiastici.* 12 vols. Roma, Stamperia Apostolica Vaticana: Tipografia della Congregazione dell'Oratorio; Giacomo Tornieri; Luigi Zanetti, 1588–1607 (USTC 812356). Repr. Paris: Guerin, 1864–1883.
Basil the Great. *Commentarius in Isaiam prophetam.* MPG 30.
———. *De fide.* MPG 31.
———. *Epistulae (Lettres de Saint Basile).* Edited by Yves Courtonne. 3 vols. Paris: Les Belles Lettres, 1957–1966.
Bellarmine, Robert. *Disputationes de controversiis christianae fidei adversus hujus temporis haereticos.* Ingolstadt: David Sartorius, 1587–1593 (VD16 B 1606). Repr. Paris: A.L. Vives, 1870–1874.
Bernard of Clairvaux. *De diligendo Deo.* MPL 182.
———. *Dominica prima post octava epiphaniae, sermo prius.* SC 481.
———. *De gratia et libero arbitrio.* MPL 182. [English edition: *On Grace and Free Choice.* Translated by Daniel O'Donovan. Kalamazoo: Cistercian, 1988.]
Biel, Gabriel. *Collectorium circa quattor libros Sententiarum.* Edited by Wilfrid Werbeck and Udo Hofmann. 5 vols. Tübingen: Mohr (Siebeck), 1973–1992.
———. *Sacri canonis missae expositio.* Tübingen: Johann Otmar, 1499 (USTC 743471).
Cajetan, Thomas de Vio. *Commentaria in Summam Theologicam D. Thomae.* In Thomas

Aquinas, *Opera omnia iussu impensaque Leonis XIII Pontificis Maximi edita*, vol. 7: *Prima secundae Summae theologiae qq. 71–114*. Rome: ex Typographia Polyglotta S. C. de Propaganda Fide, 1892.

———. *In S. Scripturam commentarii*. Lyons: Jacques and Pierre Prost, 1639.

Cassian. *Collationes*. CSEL 13².

Cassiodorus. *Expositio Psalmorum*. CCSL 97.

———. *Variarum*. CCSL 96.

Chrysostom, John. *Homilia in Acta*. MPG 60.

———. *Homilia in Epistulam primam ad Corinthios*. MPG 61.

———. *Homilia in Genesin*. MPG 53.

Cicero. *Academica (Academics)*. LCL 286, edited by H. Rackham, 1933.

———. *De inventione (On Invention)*. LCL 386, edited by H.M. Mubbell, 1949.

———. *De natura deorum (On the Nature of Gods)*. LCL 286, edited by H. Rackham, 1933.

———. *De officiis (On Duties)*. LCL 30, edited by Walter Miller, 1913.

———. *Epistola ad Atticum. (Letters to Atticus)*, vol. 1. LCL 7 (new edition), edited by D.R. Shackleton Bailey, 1999.

———. *Pro Archia poeta*. In *Orations*. LCL 158, edited by N.H. Watts, 1923.

Clement of Alexandria. *Stromata*. SC 278, 428

Clement of Rome [attrib.]. *Constitutiones apostolicae*. SC 320, 336

Clement of Rome. *Epistola Clementis ad Jacobum*. MPG 1.

Costerus S.J., Franciscus. *In Hymnum Ave Maris Stella Meditationes*. Cologne: Anton Hierat, 1600 (VD16 C 5561).

Cyprian. *Epistulae*. CCSL 3B–C.

(Pseudo-)Dionysius. *De coelesti hierarchia*. PTS 36.

———. *De divinis nominibus*. PTS 33.

Domingo de Soto. *De natura et gratia: Quod opus ab ipso authore denuo recognitum est, nonnullisque in locis emendatum, et apologia contra reverendum episcopum Catharinum auctum*. Paris: Jean Foucher, 1549 (USTC 200428).

Donatus. *Ars Grammatica*. CCCM 40D.

Empedocles 31 Fr. B105. Edited by Hermann Diels and Walther Kranz, *Die Fragmente der Vorsokratiker*, vol. 1. 10th edition, Berlin: Weidmann, 1960. Edited by M.R. Wright, *Empedocles the Extant Fragments*. London: Bristol Classical, 1995.

Epiphanius of Salamis. *De mensuris et ponderibus*. MPG 43.

———. *Panarion Haeres 69 adversus Arrianos*. MPG 42. [Latin edition: *Contra octoginta haereses opus, pannarium* [...]. Edited by Janus Cornarius. Paris: Jean Foucher, 1544 (USTC 200537).]

Eusebius. *De vita Constantini*. GCS 7.

———. *Historia ecclesiastica*. SC 31, 41.

———. *Praeparatio evangelica*. SC 206, 307, 369.

Faustus. *De gratia Dei*. CSEL 21.

Fulgentius. *De fide ad Petrum*. CCSL 91A.

Génébrard, Gilbert. *De Sancta Trinitate*. Paris: Jean Bienné, 1569 (USTC 140612).

Gerson, Jean. *De examinatione doctrinarum* [*etc.*]. Nürnberg: Johann Sensenschmidt & Andreas Frisner, 1474 (USTC 745255). Repr. *Oeuvres Complètes*, vol. 9. Paris: Desclée, 1973.

Gregory the Great. *Epistulae*. CCSL 140A.

Gregory of Nazianzus. *Orationes theologicae*. SC 250, 358.

———. *Poemata theologica (dogmatica)*. [= *De veris Scripturae libris*] MPG 37.

Gregory of Nyssa. *In laudem Basilii*. GNO 10/1.

———. *Oratio funebris de Placilla*. GNO 9.

Hermes Trismegistus. *Pimander*. Corpus Hermeticum, vol. 1. Paris: Les Belles Lettres, 1960.

Herodotus. *Historiae (Histories)*. LCL 454, edited by C.R. Whittaker, 1969.

Hesiod. *Opera et dies (Works and Days)*. LCL 57 (new edition), edited by Glenn W. Most, 2007.

Homer. *Odyssey*. LCL 105, edited by A.T. Murray, 1919.

Horace. *Epistolae (Epistles)*. LCL 194, edited by H. Rushton Fairclough, 1926.

Hosius, Stanislaus. *Confutatio Prolegomenoon Brentii* [*etc.*]. Cologne: Cholinus, 1560 (VD16 H 5167).

(pseudo-) Ignatius. *Epistula ad Magnesios*. [Spurious, 'longer' versions in Franciscus X. Funk and Franciscus Diekamp, eds. *Patres apostolici*. Vol. 2. Tübingen: H. Laupp, 1913; authentic, 'shorter' versions in SC 10^2.]

Irenaeus. *Adversus Haereses*. FC 8/1–3, 5.

Isidore of Pelusium. *Epistulae*. MPG 78.

Isidore of Seville. *Etymologiae*. Edited by W.M. Lindsay. Oxford: Clarendon, 1911.

Isocrates. *Areopagiticus*. LCL 229, edited by George Norlin, 1929.

Jerome. *Apologia contra Rufinum*. CCSL 79.

———. *Commentaria in evangelium Matthaei*. CCSL 77.

———. *Commentaria in Jeremiam prophetam*. CCSL 74.

———. *Commentaria in Michaiam prophetam*. CCSL 76.

———. *De viris illustribus*. Edited by W. Herder. Leipzig: B.G. Teubner, 1924.

———. *Epistulae*. CSEL 54^2, 56/1^2.

———. *Praefatio in librum Tobiae*. MPL 29

———. *Prologus galeatus in libro Regum*. MPL 28^2.

John of Damascus. *De fide orthodoxa*. SC 535, 540.

Josephus, Flavius. *Antiquitates judaicae (Jewish Antiquities)*. LCL 433, 456 edited by Louis H. Feldman, 1965.

———. *Contra Apionem (Against Apion)*. LCL 186, edited by H. St.J. Thackeray, 1926.

———. *De bello judaico (The Jewish War)*. vol. 1. LCL 203, edited by H. St.J. Thackeray, 1927.

Justin Martyr. *Apologia*. SC 507.

———. *Dialogus cum Tryphone*. Edited by Philippe Bobichon. 2 vols. Paradosis 47/1–2. Fribourg: Academic Press Fribourg, 2003.

Kimchi, R. David. (Trans. and ed. Santi Pagnino.) *Thesaurus linguae sanctae, ex R. David Kimchi Libro Radicum [...] contractior et emendatior*. Paris: Robert Estienne, 1548 (USTC 150097). [Hebrew edition: *Sefer ha-Shorashim*. Berlin: G. Bethge, 1847.]

Lactantius. *De ira Dei*. CSEL 27.

———. *Institutiones divinae*. CSEL 19/1.

Lampridius [attrib.]. *Historia Augusta: On Alexander Severus*. LCL 140, edited by David Magie, 1924.

Lombard, Peter. *Sententiae in IV libris distinctae*. 3rd edition by Collegium S. Bonaventurae ad Claras Aquas, Rome 1971, 1981.

Lorin, Jean de. *In Actus Apostolorum Commentaria [etc.]*. Cologne: Hierat, 1621 (VD17 12:120975Y).

Origen. *Ad Romanos*. SC 539.

———. *Contra Celsum*. SC 150.

———. *De Principiis*. [Peri archōn.] SC 252, 268.

———. *In Exodum*. SC 321.

———. *In Jeremiam homiliae*. SC 232

Ovid. *Metamorphoses*. LCL 042, edited by Frank Justus Miller, 1916.

Philo. *De vita Mosis (On the Life of Moses)*. Edited by L. Cohn: *Philonis Alexandrini opera quae supersunt*, vol. 4. Berlin: Reimer, 1902. Repr. Berlin: De Gruyter, 1962.

Plato. *Cratylus*. LCL 167, edited by Harold North Fowler, 1926.

———. *De re publica (Republic)*, vol. 1. LCL 237, edited by Chris Emlyn-Jones and William Preddy, 2013.

———. *Leges (Laws)*, vol. 2. LCL 192, edited by R.G. Bury 1926.

———. *Timaeus*. LCL 234, edited by R.G. Bury, 1929.

Plautus. *Aulularia (The Pot of Gold)*. LCL 60, edited by Wolfgang de Melo, 2011.

Plinius Caecilius Secundus, Gaius. *Epistulae (Letters)*, vol. 2. LCL 59, edited by Betty Radice, 1969.

Plotinus. *Enneads*, vol. 6. LCL 468, edited by A.H. Armstrong, 1988.

Plutarch. *Phocio (Life of Phocion)*. In *Lives*, vol. 8. LCL 100, edited by Bernadotte Perrin, 1914.

———. *Vita Numae. (Life of Numa)*. In *Lives*, vol. 1. LCL 46, edited by Bernadotte Perrin, 1914.

Porphyry. *De Philosophia Ex Oraculis Haurienda (Philosophy from Oracles)*. Edited by Gustav Wolf, Berlin: Julius Springer, 1856.

Prosper of Aquitaine. *De vocatione gentium*. MPL 51

Pseudo-Augustine. *Hypognosticon*. MPL 45

Rufinus. *Commentarius in symbolum apostolorum*. MPL 21.

Salvian of Marseille. *De gubernatione Dei.* CSEL 8

Scaliger, Josephus Justus. *Opus novum de emendatione temporum in octo libros tributum.* Paris: Sebastien Nivelle, 1583 (USTC 170688).

Scotus, John Duns. *Ordinatio.* In *Ioannis Duns Scoti Opera omnia*, edited by Commissio Scotistica, vols. 1–7. Vatican, 1950–1973.

Simmler, Josias. *De aeterno Dei Filio Domino et Servatore Nostro Iesu Christo* (…) Zürich: Christoph Froschauer Jr., 1568 (VD16 S 6498).

Socinus, Faustus. *Praelectiones theologicae.* In: *Fausti Socini Senensis Opera omnia in duos tomos distincta.* Amsterdam: 1656. [Original edition: 1609.]

Sophocles. *Electra.* LCL 20, edited by Hugh Lloyd Jones, 1994.

Sozomen. *Historia ecclesiastica.* SC 306.

Statius. *Thebais (Thebaid).* LCL 207 (new edition), edited by D.R. Shackleton Bailey, 2004.

Strabo. *Geographica (Geography)*, vol. 7. LCL 241, edited by Horace Leonard Jones, 1930.

Suetonius. *Vita Domitiani (Life of Domitian)* in *Life of the Caesars*, vol. 2. LCL 38, edited by J.C. Rolfe, 1914.

Tapper, Ruard. *Explicatio Articulorum viginti, venerandae faultatis Sacrae Theologiae Generalis studii Lovaniensis, circa dogmata Ecclesiastica, nostro hoc tempore controversa, una cum responsione ad argumenta adversariorum.* In *Ruardi Tapperi Opera*, vol. 1. Köln: Gottfried von Kempen; Birckmann, Arnold d.Ä. (Erben), 1582, 24–82 (VD16 T 183).

Tertullian. *Ad Martyras.* CCSL 1.

———. *Apologeticus.* CCSL 1.

———. *De baptismo.* CCSL 1.

———. *De corona.* CCSL 2.

———. *De pudicitia.* CCSL 2.

———. *Liber adversus Hermogenem.* CCSL 2.

———. *Liber adversus Praxeam.* CCSL 2.

———. *Liber contra Judaeos.* CCSL 2.

———. *Liber de anima.* CCSL 2.

———. *Liber de idolatria.* CCSL 2.

———. *Liber de praescriptionibus.* CCSL 1.

Theodoret of Cyrus. *Historia ecclesiastica.* SC 501.

———. *Quaestiones in Josuam.* MPG 80.

Thomas Aquinas. *Summa Theologiae.* 60 vols. Cambridge: Blackfriars / New York: McGraw Hill, 1964–1973.

———. *Super Evangelium s. Matthaei lectura.* Edited by R. Cai. 5th ed. Turin-Rome: Marietti, 1951.

———. *Super Galatas lectiones.* In *Super Epistolas s. Pauli lectura*, vol. 1: *Super Epistolam ad Galatas lectura.* Edited by R. Cai, 563–649. 8th ed. Turin-Rome: Marietti, 1953.

Valla, Lorenzo. *Annotationes in Novum Testamentum.* Basel: Andreas Cratander, 1526 (USTC 671738). Repr. Turin: Eugenio Garin, 1962.

Varro, Marcus Terentius. *De Lingua Latina (On the Latin Language),* vol. 1. LCL 333, edited by Roland G. Kent, 1938.

Xenophon. *Hellenica,* vol. 2. LCL 88, edited by Carleton L. Brownson, 1921.

c   **Early Modern Prints**

Altenstaig, Johannes, edited by Johannes Tytz. *Lexicon theologicum quo tanquam clave theologiae fores aperiuntur, et omnium fere terminorum et obscuriorum vocum, quae s. theologiae studiosos facile remorantur, etymologiae, ambiguitates, definitiones, usus, enucleate ob oculos ponuntur, & dilucide explicantur.* Cologne: Henning, 1619 (VD17 384:717260F).

Ames, William. *Medulla sacrae theologiae.* Franeker: Ulderik Balck, 1623; London: Thomas Cotes; Robert Allot, 1630.

Bayle, Pierre. *Dictionnaire historique et critique.* 2 vols. Amsterdam: Reinier Leers, 1697.

Belcarius, Franciscus [François de Beaucaire-Péguillon]. *Adversus impium Calvini, ac Calvinianorum dogma de infantium in matrum uteris sanctificatione et pleraque alia Calvini etiam dogmata brevis commentarius.* Paris: Cl. Fremy, 1566 (USTC 158195).

Beza, Theodore. *Lex Dei, moralis, ceremonialis et politica, ex libris Mosis excerpta et in certas classes distributa.* Genève: Pierre de Saint-André, 1577 (USTC 450159).

Brenz, Johannes. *In divi Joannis Evangelion Exegesis.* 2nd edition. Hagenau: Johannes Secerius, 1534 (VD16 B 7711).

Bronchorst, Everard. *Diarium sive adversaria omnium quae gesta sunt in Academia Leydensi, 1591–1627.* Edited by Jacob Cornelis van Slee. The Hague: Martinus Nijhoff, 1898.

Calvin, John. *Commentarii in Epistolas canonicas.* Edited by Kenneth G. Hagen. COR II, vol. 20. Geneva: Droz, 2009.

———. *Contre la secte phantastique et furieuse des libertins qui se nomment spirituelz.* Edited by M. van Veen, 9–41. COR IV, vol. 1. Geneva: Droz, 2005.

———. *Impietas Valentini Gentilis.* CR 37, 361–420.

———. *Brevis admonitio Joannis Calvini ad fratres Polonos, ne triplicem in Deo essentiam pro tribus Personis imaginando, tres sibi Deos fabricent.* CR 37, 629–638.

———. *Institutio christianae religionis.* OS, vol. 3 [English edition: *Institutes of the Christian Religion.* Translated and annotated by Ford Lewis Battles. Rev. ed. Grand Rapids: Eerdmans, 1994.]

Campanus, Johannes. *Göttlicher und Heiliger Schrift, vor vielen Jahren verdunkelt und durch unheilsame Lehre und Lehrer … verfinstert, Restitution und Besserung.* Strasbourg: Jakob Cammerlander, 1532 (VD16 C 633).

Concilia generalia ecclesiae catholicae Pauli V pont. max. auctoritate edita. 4 vols. Rome: Vatican, 1608–1612.

Erasmus of Rotterdam. *Adages*. In R.A.B. Mynors, ed., *Collected Works of Erasmus*, vol. 34. Toronto: University of Toronto Press, 1982.

———. *De Copia*. In C.R. Thompson, ed., *Collected Works of Erasmus*, vols. 23–24. Toronto: University of Toronto Press, 1982.

Goclenius, Rudolph. *Lexicon philosophicum quo tanquam clave philosophiae fores aperiuntur*. Frankfurt: Musculus and Becker, 1613 (VD17 23:289117S). Repr. Hildesheim: Olms, 1980.

Gregory of Valencia. *Apologeticus de Idolatria adversus impium libellum Iacobi Heerbrandi lutherani* [etc.]. Ingolstadt: David Sartorius, 1579 (VD16 V 59).

Luther, Martin. *Assertio omnium articulorum*. WA 7, 94–151.

———. *Von der Freiheit eines Christenmenschen*. WA 7, 12–38.

Maimonides. *Moreh Nebuchim: The Guide for the Perplexed*. Translated by M. Friedländer. New York: Dover Publications, 1956.

Polanus von Polansdorf, Amandus. *Syntagma theologiae christianae* [etc.]. Hanau: Aubrius, 1615 (VD17 12:113268M).

Pontificale Romanum, Clementis VIII Pont. Max. iussu restitutum atque editum. Paris: Apud Rolinum Thierry, & Eustachium Foucault, via Iacobrae, 1615.

Ramus, Petrus. *Dialecticae Libri Duo*. Paris: Andreas Wechelus, 1572 (USTC 170086).

Rees, Thomas, ed. *The Racovian Catechism, with Notes and Illustrations, Translated from the Latin: To Which is Prefixed a Sketch of the History of Unitarianism in Poland and the Adjacent Countries*. London: Longman, Hurst, Rees, Orme, & Brown, 1818.

Rivetus, A. *Testimonia de imputatione primi peccati omnibus Adami posteris*. In *Operum theologicorum*, vol. 3, 798–826. 3 vols., Rotterdam: Reinier Leers, 1651–1660. [Translated into English in *Theological Essays: Reprinted from the Princeton Review*, 195–217. New York: Wiley and Putnam, 1846.]

Sacrarum cerimoniarum sive rituum ecclesiasticorum sanctae Romanae ecclesiae libri tres. Cologne, Birckmann, 1572 (VD16 R 2586).

Sprint, John. *Propositions Tending to Proove the Necessarie Vse of the Christian Sabbaoth*. London: H. L[ownes], 1607.

Viret, Pierre. *Instruction chrestienne en la doctrine de la loy et de l'evangile*. Geneva: Jean Rivery, 1564 (USTC 746).

Voetius, Gisbertus. *Disputationes Selectae*. 5 vols. Utrecht: Joannes à Waesberge, 1648–1669.

———. *Syllabus problematum theologicorum*. Utrecht, 1643.

Walaeus, Antonius. *Loci Communes*. In *Opera Omnia*, vol. 1, 115–558. 2 vols. Leiden: Adriaen Wijngaerden, 1647.

Whitaker, William. *Disputatio de Sacra Scriptura* [etc.]. Cambridge: Thomasius, 1588 (USTC 511100).

Zanchi, Girolamo. *De natura dei, seu de divinis attributis, libri V* [etc.]. Neustadt an der Weinstraße, Josua Harnisch & haer. Wilhelm Harnisch, 1598 (USTC 662742).

———. *De operibus Dei intra spacium sex dierum creatis opus: tres in partes distinctum [etc.]*. Neustadt an der Weinstraße, Matthaeus Harnisch, 1591 (USTC 662737). Repr. in *Opera theologica*, vol. 3. 8 vols. Geneva: Gamonet, 1613.

Zwingli, Ulrich. *De vera et falsa religione*. Zürich: Christoph Froschauer, 1525 (USTC 631774).

———. *Ad Carolum Romanorum imperatorem Germaniae comitia augustae celebrantem, fidei ratio*. Zürich: Christoph Froschauer, 1530 (USTC 608804).

Secondary Literature

Aasgaard, Reidar. "Among Gentiles, Jews and Christians. Formation of Christian Identity in Melito of Sardis." In *Religious Rivalries and the Struggle for Success in Sardis and Smyrna*. Edited by Richard S. Ascough. Studies in Christianity and Judaism, vol. 14. Waterloo: Wilfrid Laurier University Press, 2005, 156–174.

Adam, Alfred. *Lehrbuch der Dogmengeschichte*. 2 vols. Darmstadt: Gerd Mohn, 1965, 1968.

Allert, Craig D. *Revelation, Truth, Canon, and Interpretation: Studies in Justin Martyr's Dialogue With Trypho*. Supplements to Vigiliae Christianae, vol. 64. Leiden: Brill, 2002.

Althaus, Paul. *Die Prinzipien der deutschen reformierten Dogmatik im Zeitalter der aristotelischen Scholastik*. Leipzig: Deichert, 1914.

Arlig, Andrew. "Medieval Mereology." *The Stanford Encyclopedia of Philosophy* (*Winter 2008 Edition*). Edited by Edward N. Zalta, accessed February 27, 2014. http://plato.stanford.edu/archives/win2008/entries/mereology-medieval/.

Asselt, Willem J. van. "Bonae Consequentiae: Johannes Maccovius (1588–1644) and the Use of Reason in Explaining Scripture and Defending Christian Doctrine." In *Vera Doctrina: Zur Begriffsgeschichte der Lehre von Augustin bis Descartes / L'idée de doctrine d'Augustin à Descartes*. Edited by Philippe Bütgen, Ruedi Imbach, Ulrich Johannes Schneider and Herman J. Selderhuis, 283–296. Wiesbaden: Harrassowitz Verlag, 2009.

———. *The Federal Theology of Johannes Cocceius (1603–1669)*. Studies in the History of Christian Thought, vol. 100. Leiden: Brill, 2001.

———. "The Fundamental Meaning of Theology: Archetypal and Ectypal Theology in Seventeenth-Century Reformed Thought." *Westminster Theological Journal* 64 (2002): 319–335.

Asselt, Willem J. van, and others. *Introduction to Reformed Scholasticism*. Grand Rapids: Reformation Heritage Books, 2011.

Asselt, Willem J. van, J. Martin Bac, and Roelf T. te Velde (eds.). *Reformed Thought on Freedom: The Concept of Free Choice in Early Modern Reformed Theology*. Texts

and Studies in Reformation and Post-Reformation. Grand Rapids: Baker Academic, 2010.

Asselt, Willem J. van, Michael D. Bell, Gert van den Brink, and Rein Ferwerda. *Scholastic Discourse: Johannes Maccovius (1588–1644) on Theological and Philosophical Distinctions and Rules*. Publications of the Institute for Reformation Research. Apeldoorn: Instituut voor Reformatieonderzoek, 2009.

Asselt, Willem J. van, and Paul H.A.M. Abels. "De zeventiende eeuw." In *Handboek Nederlandse Kerkgeschiedenis*, edited by H.J. Selderhuis. 2nd rev. ed. Kampen: Kok, 2010.

Baars, A. *Om Gods verhevenheid en Zijn nabijheid: De Drie-eenheid bij Calvijn*. Kampen: Kok, 2004.

Badewien, Jan. *Geschichtstheologie und Sozialkritik im Werk Salvians von Marseille*. Forschungen zur Kirchen- und Dogmengeschichte, vol. 32. Göttingen: Vandenhoeck & Ruprecht, 1980.

Balthasar, Hans Urs von. *The Laity and the Life of the Counsels: The Church's Mission in the World*. San Francisco: Ignatius, 2003.

Barnstone, Willis, and Marvin Meyer, eds. *The Gnostic Bible*. London: Shambhala, 2003.

Bauckham, Richard J. "Sabbath and Sunday in the Protestant Tradition." In *From Sabbath to the Lord's Day: A Biblical, Historical, and Theological Investigation*, edited by D.A. Carson. Grand Rapids: Zondervan, 1982.

Bavinck, H. *Reformed Dogmatics: God and Creation*. Edited by John Bolt. Reformed Dogmatics, vol. 2. Grand Rapids: Baker Academic, 2006.

Beck, A.J. *Gisbertus Voetius (1589–1676): Sein Theologieverständnis und seine Gotteslehre*. Göttingen: Vandenhoeck & Ruprecht, 2007.

Belt, Henk van den. *The Authority of Scripture in Reformed Theology: Truth and Trust* Studies in Reformed Theology, vol. 17. Leiden: Brill, 2008.

Bente, F. *Historical Introductions to the Book of Concord*. St. Louis: Concordia, 1965.

Benz, E. *Die Ost-Kirche im Lichte der protestantischen Geschichtsschreibung bis zur Gegenwart*. Freiburg/Munich: Alber, 1952.

Bierma, Lyle D. *The Covenant Theology of Caspar Olevianus*. Grand Rapids: Reformation Heritage Books, 2005.

Bijdragen en mededelingen van Gelre, Vereeniging tot Beoefening van Geldersche Geschiedenis, Oudheidkunde, en Recht. Vol. 90–91 (1999).

Bok, Nico den. *Communicating the Most High: A Systematic Study of Person and Trinity in the Theology of Richard of St. Victor (†1173)*. Bibliotheca Victorina, vol. 7. Paris: Brepols, 1996.

Bonevac, Daniel. "Two Theories of Analogical Predication." Chapter 2 in *Oxford Studies in Philosophy of Religion*, vol. 4, edited by Jonathan L. Kvanvig. Oxford: University Press, 2012.

Breimer, Douwe D., and others. *Hora Est! On Dissertations.* Kleine Publicaties van de Leidse Universiteitsbibliotheek, vol. 71. Leiden: Universiteitsbibliotheek, 2005.

Carney, Frederik S., ed. *The Politics of Johannes Althusius.* London: Eyre & Spottiswoode, 1964.

Chadwick, Henry. *Priscillian of Avila: The Occult and the Charismatic in the Early Church.* Oxford: Clarendon, 1976.

Coffey, David. *Deus Trinitas: The Doctrine of the Triune God.* Oxford: Oxford University Press, 1999.

Colish, Marcia L. *Peter Lombard.* Brill's Studies in Intellectual History, vol. 41. Leiden—Köln—New York: Brill, 1993.

Cross, Richard. "The Condemnations of 1277 and Henry of Ghent on Angelic Location." In *Angels in Medieval Philosophical Inquiry: Their Function and Significance*, edited by Isabel Iribarren and Martin Lenz, 73–88. Aldershot: Ashgate, 2008.

Denzinger, Heinrich. (Edited by Peter Hünermann, based on the 32th edition by Adolf Schönmetzer, 1963.) *Enchiridion symbolorum definitionum et declarationum de rebus fidei et morum.* 43rd ed. Freiburg: Herder, 2010. [English translation, edited by Robert Fastiggi and Anne Englund Nash: *Compendium of Creeds, Definitions, and Declarations on Matters of Faith and Morals.* San Francisco: Ignatius Press, 2012.]

Dick, Steven. *Plurality of Worlds: The Origins of the Extraterrestrial Life Debate From Democritus to Kant.* Cambridge: Cambridge University Press, 1982.

Dyck, C.J. "Menno Simons and the White Lie." In *Mennonite Encyclopedia*, edited by Cornelius J. Dyck and Dennis D. Martin, 5:555. Scottdale: Herald Press, 1990.

Ehrman, Bart D., ed. and trans. *The Writings of the Apostolic Fathers*, volume 1: *I Clement, II Clement, Ignatius, Polycarp, Didache.* Loeb Classical Library. Harvard: Harvard University Press, 2003.

Faber, Riemer A. "Scholastic Continuities in the Reproduction of Classical Sources in the *Synopsis Purioris Theologiae*." *Church History and Religious Culture* 92.4 (2012): 561–579.

Feingold, Mordechai. *History of Universities.* Vol. 21, bk. 1. Oxford: Oxford University Press, 2006.

Finger, Thomas N. *A Contemporary Anabaptist Theology: Biblical, Historical, Constructive.* Downers Grove: IVP Academic, 2004.

Finkenzeller, Josef. *Offenbarung und Theologie nach der Lehre des Johannes Duns Skotus.* Munster: Aschendorff, 1961.

Fitzgerald, Allan D., ed. *Augustine through the Ages: An Encyclopedia.* Grand Rapids / Cambridge UK: Eerdmans, 1999.

Frank, Günter. *Die Vernunft des Gottesgedankens: Religionsphilosophische Studien zur frühen Neuzeit.* Quaestiones, vol. 13. Stuttgart: Frommann-Holzboog, 2003.

Freeman, Ann, and Paul Meyvaert, eds. *Opus Caroli regis contra synodum.* Monumenta Germania Historiae, Leges, Concilia, 2, Suppl. 1. Hannover: Hahnsche Buchhandlung, 1998.

Gamble, Richard C. "The Sources of Calvin's Genesis Commentary: A Preliminary Report." *Archiv für Reformationsgeschichte* 84 (1993): 206–221.

Gelderblom, Arie-Jan, Jan L. de Jong, and Marc van Vaeck, eds. *Yearbook for Early-Modern Studies*, 3–2003, *The Low Countries as a Crossroads of Religious Beliefs*. Leiden: Brill, 2004.

Glare, P.G.W. *Oxford Latin Dictionary*. Repr. Oxford: Clarendon, 2006.

Goudriaan, Aza. *Reformed Orthodoxy and Philosophy, 1625–1750: Gisbertus Voetius, Petrus van Mastricht, and Anthonius Driessen*. Brill's Series in Church History, vol. 26. Leiden-Boston: Brill, 2006.

Graef, Hilda. *Mary: A History of Doctrine and Devotion*, vol. 1: *From the Beginnings to the Eve of the Reformation*. London: Sheed and Ward, 1963.

Hanson, R.P.C. *The Search for the Christian Doctrine of God: The Arian Controversy 318–381*. Edinburgh: T & T Clark, 1988.

Haykin, Michael A.G. *The Spirit of God: The Exegesis of 1 and 2 Corinthians in the Pneumatomachian Controversy of the Fourth Century*. Leiden: Brill, 1994.

Heppe, Heinrich. *Die Dogmatik der evangelisch-reformierte Kirche dargestellt und aus den Quellen belegt*. 2nd edition by Ernst Bizer. Neukirchen: Neukirchener Verlag, 1958. [English edition: *Reformed Dogmatics: Set Out and Illustrated from the Sources*. Trans. G.T. Thomson. Grand Rapids: Eerdmans, 1978.]

Heine, Ronald E. *Origen: Scholarship in the Service of the Church*. Oxford: Oxford University Press, 2010.

Hessels, J.H. *Archives of the London-Dutch Church, 1568–1872*. London: Nutt, 1892.

Honders, H.J. *Andreas Rivetus als invloedrijk theoloog in Hollands bloeitijd*. The Hague: Martinus Nijhoff, 1930.

Hoven, René. *Lexique de la prose latine de la Renaissance / Dictionary of Renaissance Latin from Prose Sources*. Revised edition. Leiden: Brill, 2006.

Itterzon, G.P. van. *Franciscus Gomarus*. The Hague: Martinus Nijhoff, 1930.

Johnson, S. Lewis Jr. "Romans 5:12: An Exercise in Exegesis and Theology." In *New Dimensions in New Testament Study*, edited by Richard N. Longenecker and Merill C. Tenney, 298–316. Grand Rapids: Zondervan, 1974.

Karamanolis, George. "Plutarch." In *The Stanford Encyclopedia of Philosophy* (Fall 2010 Edition). Edited by Edward N. Zalta, accessed February 27, 2014. http://plato.stanford.edu/archives/fall2010/entries/plutarch/.

Kelly, J.N.D. *Early Christian Creeds*. 3rd edition, London: Longman, 1972.

———. *Early Christian Doctrine*. 5th edition, London: Continuum, 1985.

Kenny, Anthony. *Medieval Philosophy: A New History of Western Philosophy*. Vol. 2. Oxford: Clarendon, 2005.

Kingdon, Robert M. "Social Control and Political Control in Calvin's Geneva." In *Die Reformation in Deutschland und Europa: Interpretationen und Debatten*. Edited by Hans R. Guggisberg, 521–532. Gütersloh: Gütersloher Verlagshaus, 1993.

Kooij, A. van der. "The Canonization of Ancient Books Kept in the Temple at Jerusalem." In *Canonization and Decanonization*. Studies in the History of Religions, vol. 82. Edited by A. van der Kooij and K. van der Toorn, 17–40. Leiden: Brill, 1997.

Kooten, G.H. van. "The Two Types of Man in Philo and Paul: The Anthropological Trichotomy of Spirit, Soul and Body." In *Paul's Anthropology in Context: The Image of God, Assimilation to God, and Tripartite Man in Ancient Judaism, Ancient Philosophy and Early Christianity*. Wissenschaftliche Untersuchungen zum Neuen Testament, vol. 232. Tübingen: Mohr Siebeck, 2008, 269–312.

Lane, Anthony N.S. "Scripture, Tradition and Church: An Historical Survey." *Vox Evangelica* 9 (1975): 37–55.

Langston, Douglas. "Medieval Theories of Conscience." *The Stanford Encyclopedia of Philosophy* (Fall 2010 Edition). Edited by Edward N. Zalta, accessed February 27, 2014. http://plato.stanford.edu/archives/fall2010/entries/conscience-medieval.

Lanham, Richard A. *A Handlist of Rhetorical Terms*. 2d ed. Berkeley: University of California Press, 1991.

Latham, R.E., and others. *Dictionary of Medieval Latin from British Sources*. Oxford: Oxford University Press, 1976–.

Lausberg, H. *Handbook of Literary Rhetoric*. Edited by D.E. Orton and R.D. Anderson. Leiden: Brill, 1998.

Lee, Brian J. *Johannes Cocceius and the Exegetical Roots of Federal Theology: Reformation Developments in the Interpretation of Hebrews 7–10*. Reformed Historical Theology, vol. 7. Göttingen: Vandenhoeck and Ruprecht, 2009.

Leppin, H. "The Church Historians (1): Socrates, Sozomenus, and Theodoretus." In *Greek and Roman Historiography in Late Antiquity*, 219–254. Edited by Gabriele Marasco. Leiden: Brill, 2003.

Lewis, Charlton T., and Charles Short. *A Latin Dictionary*. Oxford: Clarendon, 1958; revised edition Oxford: Clarendon, 1980.

Lieburg, F.A. van. *Repertorium van Nederlandse hervormde predikanten tot 1816*. 2 vols. Dordrecht: Van Lieburg, 1996.

Loux, Michael J., trans. and intro. *Ockham's Theory of Terms: Part I of the Summa Logicae*. Notre Dame: University of Notre Dame Press, 1974.

Lubac, Henri de. *Exégèse medieval: les quatre sens de l'Écriture*. 4 vols. (Paris: Aubier, 1959–1964) [English translation: *Medieval Exegesis: The Four Senses of Scripture*. 4 vols. Grand Rapids: Eerdmans, 2009].

MacCormick, Chalmers. "The 'Antitrinitarianism' of John Campanus." *Church History* 32/3 (1963): 278–297.

Mateo-Seco, Lucas Francisco, and Giulio Maspero, eds. [trans. Seth Cherney] *The Brill Dictionary of Gregory of Nyssa*. Supplements to Vigiliae Christianae, vol. 99. Leiden: Brill, 2009.

McDonald, Paul. *History of the Concept of Mind: Speculations about Soul, Mind and Spirit from Homer to Hume*. Aldershot: Ashgate, 2003.

McGuire, Brian Patrick. *Jean Gerson and the Last Medieval Reformation.* University Park: Pennsylvania State University Press, 2005.

Metzger, B.M. "The Punctuation of Rom. 9:5." *New Testament Studies: Philological, Versional, and Patristic.* Edited by B.M. Metzger, 57–74. New Testament Tools and Studies, vol. 10. Leiden: Brill, 1980.

Muir, Edward. *Ritual in Early Modern Europe.* 2nd ed. Cambridge: Cambridge University Press, 2005.

Muller, Richard A. *Dictionary of Latin and Greek Theological Terms: Drawn Principally from Protestant Scholastic Theology.* Grand Rapids: Baker, 1985.

———. *Post-Reformation Reformed Dogmatics: The Rise and Development of Reformed Orthodoxy, ca. 1520 to ca. 1725.* 4 vols. Grand Rapids: Baker Academic, 2003.

———. "The Debate over the Vowel Points and the Crisis in Orthodox Hermeneutics." In *After Calvin: Studies in the Development of a Theological Tradition.* Edited by Richard A. Muller, 146–155. Oxford: University Press, 2003.

Niermeyer, J.F. *Mediae Latinitatis Lexicon Minus*: A Medieval Latin-French/English Dictionary. Leiden: Brill, 1954–1976.

Nisula, Timo. *Augustine and the Functions of Concupiscence.* Supplements to Vigiliae Christianae. Vol. 116. Leiden: Brill, 2012.

Nuffelen, Peter van. "Sozomen's Chapter on finding the True Cross (HE 2.1) and His Historical Method." In *Papers Presented at the Fourteenth International Conference on Patristic Studies Held in Oxford 2003: Other Greek Writers, John of Damascus and Beyond, the West to Hilary*, 265–272. Edited by F. Young and others. Studia Patristica, vol. 42. Leuven: Peeters, 2006.

Noble, Thomas F.X. *Images, Iconoclasm, and the Carolingians.* Philadelphia: University of Pennsylvania Press, 2009.

Oberman, Heiko A. *The Harvest of Medieval Theology: Gabriel Biel and Late Medieval Nominalism.* Cambridge: Harvard University Press, 1963.

O'Donnell, James Joseph. *Cassiodorus.* Berkeley: University of California Press, 1979.

Osborn, Eric. *Clement of Alexandria.* Cambridge: Cambridge University Press, 2008

Panaccio, Claude. *Le discours intérieur: De Platon à Guillaume d'Ockham.* Paris: Editions du Seuil, 1999.

Parker, Kenneth L. *The English Sabbath: A Study of Doctrine and Discipline from the Reformation to the Civil War.* Cambridge: Cambridge University Press, 1988.

Pettegree, Andrew. "Michael Servetus and the Limits of Tolerance." *History Today* 40 (1990): 40–45.

Platt, John. *Reformed Thought and Scholasticism: The Arguments for the Existence of God in Dutch Theology, 1575–1650.* Studies in the History of Christian Thought, vol. 29. Leiden: Brill, 1982.

Poppi, Antonino. "Fate, Fortune, Providence and Human Freedom." In *The Cambridge History of Renaissance Philosophy*, edited by Charles B. Schmitt, Quentin Skinner and Eckhard Kessler, 641–667. Cambridge: Cambridge University Press, 1988.

Potjer, Menno. "Machtsverhoudingen in de classis Tiel." *Bijdragen en Mededelingen van Gelre, Vereeniging tot Beoefening van Geldersche Geschiedenis, Oudheidkunde, en Recht* 90–91 (1999): 67–93.

Pullapilly, Cyriac K. *Caesar Baronius: Counter-Reformation Historian*. Notre Dame: University of Notre Dame Press, 1975.

Quasten, Johannes. *Patrology*. 6th print, Westminster, Maryland: Christian Classics, 1992.

Ramminger, Johann. *Neulateinische Wortliste: Ein Wörterbuch des Lateinischen von Petrarca bis 1700*. Accessed February 27, 2014. http://ramminger.userweb.mwn.de/.

Rieu, W.M. du, ed. *Album studiosorum academia Lugduno-Batavae MDLXXV–MDCCCLXXV*. The Hague: Martinus Nijhoff, 1875.

Rijk, L.M. de. *Middeleeuwse wijsbegeerte: Traditie en vernieuwing*. Revised edition. Assen: Van Gorcum, 1977.

———. *La philosophie au Moyen Age*. Leiden: Brill, 1985.

Rohls, Jan. *Reformed Confessions: Theology from Zurich to Barmen*. Louisville: Westminster John Knox Press, 1997.

Roth, John D., and James M. Stayer, eds. *A Companion to Anabaptism and Spiritualism, 1521–1700*. Brill's Companions to the Christian Tradition, vol. 6. Leiden: Brill, 2006.

Santoro, G., and others. "The Anatomic Location of the Soul from the Heart, through the Brain, to the Whole Body, and beyond: A Journey through Western History, Science, and Philosophy." *Neurosurgery* 65 (2009): 633–643.

Schaff, Philip, and David S. Schaff, eds. *Creeds of Christendom: With a History and Critical Notes*. 4 vols. 6th ed. Grand Rapids: Baker, 1998.

Schaff, Philip, and Henry Wace, eds. *Nicene and Post-Nicene Fathers*. First and second series. Reprint; Peabody: Hendrickson, 1995.

Scheck, Thomas P. *St. Jerome's Commentaries on Galatians, Titus, and Philemon*. Notre Dame: University of Notre Dame Press, 2010.

Schultz, Robert C. "Original Sin: Accident or Substance: The Paradoxical Significance of FC I, 53–62 in Historical Context." In *Discord, Dialogue, and Concord: Studies in the Lutheran Reformation's Formula of Concord*, edited by Lewis W. Spitz and Wenzel Lohff, 38–57. Philadelphia: Fortress, 1977.

Schweizer, Alexander. *Die protestantischen Centraldogmen in ihrer Entwicklung innerhalb der Reformirten Kirche*. 2 vols. Zurich: Orell, Fues1li & comp., 1854, 1856.

Sinnema, Donald, and Henk van den Belt. "The *Synopsis Purioris Theologiae* (1625) as a Disputation Cycle." *Church History and Religious Culture* 92.4 (2012): 505–537.

Smalley, Beryl. *The Study of the Bible in the Middle Ages*. 3d rev. ed. Oxford: Blackwell, 1983.

"Socinianism." In *The Dictionary of Historical Theology*. Edited by Trevor A. Hart and Richard Bauckham. Grand Rapids: Eerdmans, 2000.

Sorabji, Richard. *Time, Creation and the Continuum: Theories in Antiquity and the Early Middle Ages.* Ithaca: Cornell University Press, 1983.

Steel, Carlos. "Liberté divine ou liberté humaine? Proclus et Plotin sur ce qui dépend de nous." In *Mélanges de philosophie et de philologie offerts à Lambros Couloubaritsis,* edited by M. Broze and others, 525–542. Paris: Vrin, 2008.

Steinmetz, David. "Calvin and the Monastic Ideal." In *Anticlericalism in Late Medieval and Early Modern Europe,* edited by Peter A. Dykema and Heiko A. Oberman, 605–617. Studies in Medieval and Reformation Thought, vol. 51. Leiden: Brill, 1993.

Stelling-Michaud, Suzanne. *Le livre du recteur de l'Academie de Genève: (1559–1878).* Vol. 1: *Le texte.* Geneva: Droz, 1959.

Syme, Ronald. *Ammianus and the Historia Augusta.* Oxford: Oxford University Press, 1968.

———. *Emperors and Biography: Studies in the 'Historia Augusti'.* Oxford: Oxford University Press, 1971.

———. *Historia Augusta Papers.* Oxford: Oxford University Press, 1983.

Tavard, George H. "Tradition in Early Post-Tridentine Theology." *Theological Studies* 23 (1962): 377–405.

Tzamalikos, P. *Origen: Philosophy of History and Eschatology.* Supplements to Vigiliae Christianae, vol. 85. Leiden: Brill, 2007.

Van den Kerchove, Anna. *La Voie d'Hermè: Pratiques, rituelles et traités hermétiques.* Nag Hammadi and Manichaean, vol. 77. Leiden: Brill, 2012.

Velde, Dolf te. *The Doctrine of God in Reformed Orthodoxy, Karl Barth, and the Utrecht School: A Study in Method and Content.* Studies in Reformed Theology, vol. 25. Leiden: Brill, 2013.

———. "Eloquent Silence: The Doctrine of God in the *Synopsis of Purer Theology.*" *Church History and Religious Culture* 92.4 (2012): 581–608.

Veldhuis, Henri. "God is liefde: Over de voortbrenging van de Heilige Geest (*Lectura* I 10, q.1)." In *Geloof geeft te denken: Opstellen over de theologie van Johannes Duns Scotus,* edited by Andreas J. Beck and Henri Veldhuis, 173–182. Scripta Franciscana, vol. 8. Assen: Van Gorcum, 2005.

Viladesau, Richard. *The Triumph of the Cross: The Passion of Christian Theology and the Arts; From the Renaissance to the Counter-Reformation.* Oxford: Oxford University Press, 2007.

Visser, Hugo B. *De Geschiedenis van de Sabbatsstrijd onder de Gereformeerden in de Zeventiende Eeuw.* Utrecht: Kemink en Zoon, 1939.

Vos, Antonie, and others. *Contingency and Freedom: John Duns Scotus Lectura I 39.* Dordrecht: Kluwer Academic: 1994.

Vos, Antonie. *The Philosophy of John Duns Scotus.* Edinburgh: Edinburgh University Press, 2006.

Wallace, William A. *The Elements of Philosophy: A Compendium for Philosophers and Theologians.* New York: Alba House, 1977.

Wehberg, Hans. "Pacta Sunt Servanda." *The American Journal of International Law* 53, (1959): 775–786.
Weir, D.A. *The Origins of the Federal Theology in Sixteenth-Century Reformation Thought.* Oxford: Clarendon, 1990.
Wetter, F. *Die Trinitätslehre des Johannes Duns Scotus.* Münster: Aschendorff, 1967.
Wigelsworth, Jeffrey R. *Deism in Enlightenment England: Theology, Politics, and Newtonian Public Science.* Manchester: Manchester University Press, 2009.
Williams, George Huntston. *The Radical Reformation.* 3rd rev. ed. Kirksville: Truman State University Press, 2000.
Wissink, J.B.M., ed. *The Eternity of the World in the Thought of Thomas Aquinas and His Contemporaries.* Leiden: Brill, 1990.
Zagorin, Perez. *Ways of Lying: Dissimulation, Persecution, and Conformity in Early Modern Europe.* Cambridge: Harvard University Press, 1990.
Zijlstra, S. *Om de ware gemeente en de oude gronden: geschiedenis van de dopersen in de Nederlanden 1531–1675.* Hilversum: Fryske Akademy & Verloren, 2000.

Scripture Index

Genesis
1	10.6, 10.9, 10.10, 10.Cor2, 17.15
1:1	7.29
1:2	9.3
1:3	10.13
1:26	7.42, 10.11
1:27	13.4, 13.36, 13.48,
1:31	10.Cor3, 12.7, 16.30, 17.15
2:2	21.17
2:2–3	21.13
2:7	13.9, 13.16
2:15	13.47
2:16–17	14.6, 17.16
2:17	14.12, 15.11
2:19	13.38
3:1	14.15
3:3	17.16
3:5	14.16
3:15	1.27, 22.14
3:19	13.11, 13.12
3:22	7.42
4:3–5	21.14
5:1	13.16
5:2	13.11
5:3	15.6
6:5	15.5, 15.22
6:7	13.4
7:2	21.14
8	15.9
8:1	9.2
8:21	15.5, 15.22
9	13.23
9:4	21.14
11:7	7.42
12:7	22.14
14	7.43
14:19–20	6.29
14:22	6.29
15:1	1.16
15:5	22.14
15:18	23.4
17	6.37, 21.14
17:7–8	21.44
18:13	1.16
18:20–22	20.38
19	12.39
19:11	12.44
20	7.43
21:31	20.49
21:33	6.28
22:18	1.27
26:28	20.49
31:53	20.50, 20.54
32:29	6.10
41	7.43
42:15	20.18
45:8	11.9
48:16	7.48
50:20	16.32

Exodus
3:6	6.14, 6.15
3:14	6.16, 6.24
3:14–15	6.15
4:11	11.9
6	6.14
6:3	6.16
12:23	12.40
12:26	19.1
14:19	7.48
16:5	21.14
16:22	21.27
16:23	21.37
16:23–25	21.27
17:14	2.5, 3.6
19:5	18.35
19:16	6.8
19:20	18.30
20	21.26, 21.37
20:1–17	18.30
20:2	6.15
20:3	6.25
20:7	6.15
20:10	21.17
20:11	10.2
20:19	6.8
21:6	21.44
22:11	20.49
22:28	6.13
23:11	21.4
23:12	21.18, 21.36
23:14–16	21.5

23:20–21	7.48	**Numbers**	
23:21	1.16	6:23–26	7.45
23:23	7.48	12:6	1.16
23:27	7.48	12:8	1.16, 6.20
24:4	4.10	14:21	6.31
24:12	2.5	14:22	8.23
24:16	6.20	15:32	21.27, 21.40
29:9	21.44	16:22	6.20
31:13	21.20	21:14	3.1
31:14	21.40	23:19	6.26, 6.41
31:15	21.2	27:16	6.20
31:16–17	21.20, 21.41	28:9–10	21.38
31:18	18.30n10	28:11	21.5
32:1–5	19.13	28:25	21.27
32:15	3.6	30:4–17	20.61
32:16	3.3	30:13	20.38
33:18–20	6.20		
33:18	6.43	**Deuteronomy**	
33:19	6.40	4:2	2.28, 3.20, 4.10
33:22	6.43	4:6	4.18
33:23	6.20	4:12	6.20
34:5–7	6.40	4:15	19.22
34:6	6.17	4:35	6.25
34:21	21.27	5	21.26
34:27–28	2.5, 3.7	5:12	21.22
35:3	21.27	5:14	21.18
		5:15	21.19, 21.22
Leviticus		5:26	6.31
4	16.51	6:4	6.25
5	16.51	6:13	20.7, 20.19
10:1	16.17	7:5	22.41
17	13.23	8:3	11.15
19:17–18	22.44	9:15	23.2
19:32	22.43	10:4	3.6
23	21.5, 21.37	10:14	6.29
23:7–8	19.28, 21.27	10:17	6.14, 6.17, 6.29
23:8	21.26	10:20	20.7, 20.19
23:13	21.38	16	21.5
23:15	21.4	17:18	3.10
23:21	19.28	17:19	5.12
23:25	21.27	27:26	18.35
23:32	21.25, 21.27	28:16–65	19.32
2336	21.27	28:58	4.10
24:8	21.38	29:4	13.22
24:9	21.34	29:21	3.4
25:2	21.22	29:29	5.16
26:15–16	21.40	30:11	5.16
		31	3.38
		31:9	3.10, 4.10

Deuteronomy (*cont.*)
31:11	3.11
31:11–12	5.12
31:24	3.10
31:26	3.10, 3.12
32:4	4.8, 16.30
32:39	6.25
32:40	6.31

Joshua
1:13	3.1
2:12	20.50
9	20.56
10:13	12.38
24:25	20.32

Judges
17:4	19.13
17:13	19.13
21:1	20.56

Ruth
1:17	20.16

1 Samuel
1:11	20.38
1:26	20.18
16:15	12.45
20:12	20.50
21:4–7	21.34n18
25:22	20.25
25:33	20.57
28	12.42
28:11	13.25

2 Samuel
6:6	16.17
11:2	17.39
14:20	12.13
16:20	7.44
23:1–2	3.7, 9.23
24:1	17.39
24:16	12.40

1 Kings
1:29	20.16
2:23–24	20.16
8:39	12.22
8:46	16.50
16:31	19.14
17:12	16.15
17:21	13.25
20:29	21.34
21:29	17.23
22:20–24	12.44

2 Kings
10:16	19.13
11:4	20.49
11:7	21.3
12:3	16.17
12:28	19.13
19	12.40
19:15	6.25
22:8	3.10
22:13	3.10
23:3	20.32

1 Chronicles
9:32	21.24
16:14	6.29
16:19	6.29
17:20	6.30
21	17.39
21:1	12.45, 16.34

2 Chronicles
6:14	6.30
6:32	6.15
19:7	6.41
19:8	5.27
33:19	3.1
34:14	3.10
36	7.34
36:13	20.49

Ezra
1	7.43
6	7.43
7	7.43
10:5	20.32

Nehemiah
8	21.38
8:8–9	3.11
8:14	3.11
8:18	3.11
9:14	21.15

10:30–31	20.35	25:12	5.26
10:31	21.27	25:14	5.26
13:15	21.27, 21.40	29:10	6.28
13:16	21.27	33:6	9.13, 10.6, 10.9, 10.10, 12.3
		33:9	10.13

Esther

9:19	21.61	33:14–15	11.9
		36:7	21.18
		36:10	6.31

Job

		44:22	6.32
1:16	12.39	45:7	7.41, 8.27
1:19	12.39	45:7–8	1.5
2:7	12.40	49:16	13.25
4:18	12.33	50:4	5.26
9:2	16.24	51	15.9
11:8–9	6.29	51:7	15.5
12:7–9	6.5	51:13	17.39
14	15.9	53:2	6.3
14:2	15.38	62:11	22.45
14:4	15.5	63:12	20.7
15:3	7.44	72:18	6.8, 12.43
15:15	12.33	81:13	11.22
22:14	11.6	82:6	6.13
31:1	20.35	86:10	6.25
33:4	9.3, 9.26, 10.6, 10.9, 10.10, 13.7	89:35	6.35
34:21	6.32	90:2	6.28, 12.5
36:26	6.28, 6.29	90:4	6.33
38:7	12.6	92	21.38
38:31	12.37	94:7–9	6.42
		95:8	8.23

Psalms

		102:13	6.26, 6.28
1:2	4.8, 5.14, 18.3	102:19	3.16, 13.4
2	7.48	102:25	6.26
2:7	8.9, 8.11	102:25–26	8.23
5:5	16.22	102:27–28	6.28
8	10.19	103:19	11.8
9:8	22.45	103:20	12.13, 12.35
10:3	16.45	104	10.19
10:4	6.3	104:4	12.49
11:7	6.40	104:19–23	12.37
14:1	6.3	104:28–30	11.12
14:2–3	15.22	104:30	9.5, 13.7
15	20.58	110:1	7.47, 8.27, 20.10, 23.20
15:4	20.56	115:3	6.36
19	4.11, 6.5	119	3.3, 4.8, 5.10
19:2	6.9	119:3	18.42
19:2–3	10.21	119:30	18.42
19:5	12.37	119:73	13.11
19:8	3.3, 4.8, 5.17, 6.9, 18.3	119:105	5.16, 18.42
19:8–9	4.9	119:130	5.17

Psalms (cont.)

119:137	6.40
130:3	16.24
136	10.19
136:1	6.40
136:4	12.43
139:1	6.32
139:7	6.29, 9.24
143:2	16.24
145:13	6.40
145:17	6.40
147:4–5	6.33
147:9	11.8

Proverbs

1	1.11
1:1	5.17
2:6	6.33
3:13–15	5.4
5:20	22.45
6:18–19	22.45
6:23	5.16
6:25	22.45
7:13–14	22.45
8	7.18, 8.9, 9.14
8:1	7.48, 8.17
8:12	7.48
8:14	7.48
8:22	8.9, 10.Cor2, 12.5
8:22–30	13.7
8:24	8.9
14:21	22.43
14:35	22.43
15:27	22.45
19:5	22.45
20:24	11.9
21:1	11.9, 12.46
23:31	22.45
24:1	22.44
24:8	22.44
24:19	22.44
24:29	22.44

Ecclesiastes

1:5	12.37
7:29	17.15, 17.16
12:7	9.2, 13.16, 13.25

Song of Solomon

1:4	7.44

Isaiah

1:11	21.39
1:24	6.14
2	21.6
2:22	9.2
2:3	3.3, 18.4
2:6	11.22
6	8.23
6:3	7.46
6:8	7.16, 7.17
6:9	9.23
8:20	3.18, 4.21, 5.12, 5.26
10:5–7	16.32
11:4	9.13
12:2	7.18
14:27	6.35
31:3	6.20
37:36	12.52
38:7	12.38
40	10.17
40:13	10.13
40:14	6.33
40:18	6.20, 19.22
41:23	6.8
42:8	6.15, 19.31
43:13	6.24
44:7	12.22
45:5	6.25
45:21	6.25
45:22	20.9, 20.19
46:10	6.35
48:11	6.43
53:11	1.10
56:2	21.21, 21.40
56:11	22.45
57:17	22.45
58	21.40
58:13	21.22, 21.27, 21.39
59:2	16.22
61:1	9.3, 9.18
61:1–2	9.26
63:9	7.48
63:10	8.23, 9.3, 9.5
64:6	17.36
65:16	20.9, 20.19
66:1	6.29

66:22–23	21.20	**Hosea**	
66:23	21.44	1:2–3	19.31
		1:7	7.47
Jeremiah		4:15	22.42
3:15	1.10		
4:2	20.9, 20.23	**Joel**	
10	10.17	2:28	23.15
10:6	6.27		
10:23	11.9	**Micah**	
12:16	20.9	5:1	9.11
16:13	11.22	5:1–2	8.9
16:14	6.16, 21.48		
17:9	15.22	**Haggai**	
17:21–22	21.27	1:14	9.2
17:26–27	21.40	2:6	7.48
23:6	8.27	2:8	7.48
23:24	6.29		
25:11–13	21.4	**Zechariah**	
25:29	21.4	3:7	5.27
31:33	18.4		
31:34	23.29	**Matthew**	
35:1–11	20.39	1:18	9.26
36:1–4	3.6	1:20	9.26
36:2	2.5	2:13	12.9
36:4	3.8	3:9	6.36
36:28	2.5	3:16	7.17, 9.5, 9.6, 22.14
		3:16–17	7.49
Ezekiel		4	12.40
9:4–6	12.24	5	22.35
20:12	21.15, 21.20	5:17	3.26, 20.8
20:20	21.20	5:17–20	18.38
20:22–23	21.5	5:18	2.28
22:26	21.23	5:19	20.8
44:24	5.27	5:20	23.23, 23.28
46:1–5	21.38	5:22–28	16.37
		5:33–37	20.8
Daniel		5:34	22.42
1:17	3.29	5:37	20.21, 20.48
2	7.43	6:1	16.16
2:20–22	6.33	6:2	17.23
2:36	7.44	6:5	17.23
3	12.39	6:24	16.10
4:17	12.13	6:26	17.23
5:5	3.6	7:15	5.29
5:24	3.6	8:16	12.9
7:9	6.28	10:20	9.17
7:13	6.28	10:27	4.35
9:7	16.24	10:28	13.16, 13.25
9:9–10	16.24	10:29–30	11.5

Matthew (*cont.*)

10:31	22.31
11:22	22.31
11:24	22.31
11:25	8.4
11:26	1.10
11:29	23.7
12	16.53, 21.33
12:2	21.23, 21.28
12:3–4	21.34
12:5	21.32, 21.38
12:6	21.31
12:8	21.31
12:10	21.28
12:10–13	21.30
12:11	21.23
12:12	21.23, 21.35
12:28	9.14, 9.26
12:29	12.35
12:31	16.47
12:31–32	9.5
12:32	9.27
12:45	12.9
13:41	12.24
14:7	20.25
15:11	16.25
15:19	13.22
16:17	5.8
16:18	5.39
17	12.10
17:5	8.13, 22.14
18:7	16.34
18:10	12.16, 12.52
18:20	8.28
19:16	22.54
19:17	6.40, 23.23, 23.28
19:26	6.36
20:15	6.35, 6.38
22:29	3.16
22:32–33	1.30
22:37	13.22, 16.50
22:39	18.36
22:43	3.7
23:16–22	20.55
23:37	17.29
24:15	3.29
24:20	21.28
24:22	17.41
24:24	17.41
25:41	12.11, 12.50, 16.27
25:42	16.11
26:41	17.34
26:69–75	16.34
28	8.30
28:1	21.52
28:19	3.40, 4.35, 7.16, 7.49, 8.5, 9.6, 9.7, 9.27
28:20	8.28

Mark

1:1	22.5n6, 22.19
1:14	22.26
1:15	22.33
1:21	21.38
2:27	21.34
2:28	21.45
7:11	20.57
9:24	17.33
12:29	6.25
12:32	6.25, 12.22
13:27	12.24
15:42	21.24
16:1–2	21.52
16:9	21.52
16:20	8.29

Luke

1:1	3.7, 3.14
1:1–2	3.33
1:1–3	3.1
1:3	3.7, 3.14
1:3–4	4.15
1:4	3.16
1:35	8.17, 9.14, 9.26
1:37	6.36
1:47	15.19
1:74–75	15.40
2:22	18.5
3:4	3.4
4:8	19.10
4:16	21.38
4:18	9.18, 9.26
6:1	21.6, 21.34
6:9	21.35
8:30	12.9, 12.49
10:18	12.49
10:26	18.5
10:26–28	18.35

10:27	18.38	3:34	1.5
10:28	23.23	3:36	22.55
11:20	9.14	4:22	6.44, 19.18
13:10	21.38	4:24	6.12, 6.20, 6.24, 9.3
13:11	21.30	5	2.7
13:11–15	21.33	5:8	21.28, 21.30
14:1	21.33, 21.36	5:17	21.31
14:2–4	21.30	5:18	8.9, 8.14
14:7	21.36	5:19	8.32
16	2.7	5:20–23	8.14
16:16	23.20	5:21	8.29, 8.32
16:29	3.18, 3.26, 4.23	5:23	8.30
17:10	23.31	5:26	6.31, 8.14, 8.32
18:12	21.3	5:39	3.3, 3.18, 4.22, 5.13
20:36	12.11	5:45	3.18
22:19	22.51	6:40	8.29
22:20	23.8	6:44	17.25
22:31	17.39	6:45	1.13, 5.26
22:31–32	17.41	7:22	21.14
22:55	17.39	7:22–23	21.32
22:61	17.41	7:29	1.3
23:43	13.16	8:6	3.6
23:46	9.2	8:8	3.6
23:54	21.24	8:34	16.45, 17.26, 17.41n23
23:56	21.28	8:36	17.27
24:1–2	21.52	8:43	17.25
24:13	21.36	8:44	12.7, 12.27, 15.16n16, 16.33
24:27	4.15	8:54	8.4
24:34	21.52	8:58	8.32
24:39	6.20, 12.9	9:7	21.28
24:44	18.6, 3.26	9:14	21.30
		10	2.31, 5.31

John

1	8.9, 9.14, 10.17	10:3	5.29
1:1	8.17, 8.27	10:5	5.39
1:2–3	10.9	10:15	1.3
1:3	8.29, 10.10, 13.7	10:18	8.32
1:9	5.6	10:22	21.61
1:14	8.9	10:28–29	13.11, 17.41
1:16	1.5	10:29	8.28
1:18	6.20, 22.11	10:30	8.12, 8.14
2:24	8.28	10:33	8.14
3:3	17.25, 17.30	10:34	6.13, 18.7
3:3–4	15.6	10:35	3.3
3:5	17.25, 9.26	10:38	8.12
3:6	9.3, 15.5, 15.22	12:14	7.17
3:8	9.2, 9.26	12:41	8.23
3:13	8.28	13	22.35
3:18	22.55	14	9.5
		14:1	8.30

John (*cont.*)

14:6	6.24
14:10	8.12, 22.11
14:11	7.20
14:16	7.49, 9.6
14:17	2.12, 7.18
14:24	22.11
15	9.5
15:16	9.19
15:26	7.49, 9.6, 9.11, 9.12
16	9.5
16:7	8.29
16:13	9.24
16:13–14	22.11
16:14	8.14
16:14–15	9.17, 9.19
16:27–28	9.11
17:3	1.10, 4.17, 6.2, 6.25, 7.50
17:5	8.28, 10.Cor2, 12.4
17:11–12	17.41
17:17	4.18
17:20	17.29, 17.41
19:7	18.5
19:31	21.6, 21.28
20:1	21.52
20:19	21.52
20:22	9.18
20:26	21.52
20:28	8.27
20:30–31	3.1
20:31	2.7, 3.9, 4.17, 5.13
21:17	8.28, 8.32
21:20	3.33
21:24	3.14, 3.33

Acts

1:1	3.33, 4.15
1:2	3.33
1:7	10.26
1:12	21.28
1:20	3.4
2:2–4	9.5
2:4	3.11
2:6	3.11
2:11	3.11
2:23	16.31
3:18	16.31
5:3–4	9.23
5:4	6.12, 7.29
5:12	12.39
5:29	18.29n9
7:8	23.8
7:30	1.16
7:42	3.27, 3.4
7:51	17.29
7:53	18.30
7:59	8.30, 13.16
8	5.19
8:14	8.4
8:39	12.40
9:14	8.30
10:34	7.3
10:43	1.27
12:7	12.9
12:23	12.40
13	22.16
13:14	21.38, 21.50
13:15–17	21.57
13:44	21.50
14:3	22.30
14:15	6.9, 6.31
14:16	11.22
14:17	6.9
15:8	6.33
15:10	23.7
15:11	1.27, 23.21
15:18	6.33, 8.8
15:21	21.38
16:13	21.50
17	5.19
17:2	4.15, 21.50, 21.38
17:10–11	3.18
17:11	5.14
17:16	19.4
17:22–23	1.26
17:24	6.9, 6.17, 6.19
17:25	6.31, 6.43, 11.5, 11.7
17:26	6.5, 13.49
17:27	6.4
17:28	6.4, 6.31, 11.5, 13.18, 16.7
17:29	6.19, 6.30, 13.18, 19.22
17:30	1.26
18:4	21.50
18:6	21.51
18:19–20	21.57
18:26	21.57
19:9	21.51
19:28	6.29

19:34	1.26	3:12	15.22
20:7	21.57	3:19–20	18.41
20:27	1.14, 4.35	3:27	18.4, 18.42, 18.44, 23.6
20:28	6.12, 7.29, 8.27	4:1	16.24, 23.21
20:32	22.30	4:6	23.21
23:8	12.8	4:13	23.21
23:13	20.25	4:15	18.41
26:5	19.1	5:12	13.39, 14.5, 14.40, 15.8, 15.19, 15.38, 14.4
26:22	4.15		
28:23	3.26	5:12–14	15.5
28:25	7.16, 7.17, 9.23	5:20	18.41
28:26	9.23	6:12	15.26
		6:12–13	15.22
Romans		6:13	18.38
1	1.18	6:14	16.39, 16.46n19, 18.8, 23.25
1:1	6.12, 22.9, 23.11	6:16	16.50, 17.26, 17.41n23
1:1–2	3.21	6:17	16.39
1:2	3.3, 18.25, 22.16	6:18	17.38
1:3	22.19	6:19	15.22
1:7–8	2.10	6:22	16.44
1:9	20.11, 20.16	6:23	13.39, 15.6, 16.21, 16.50
1:16	22.9, 22.19, 22.24	7	15.36, 17.34
1:17	22.53	7:7	15.8, 17.24, 16.37
1:19	1.8, 6.4, 6.9, 17.20	7:7–11	18.41
1:19–20	7.34, 11.4	7:8	15.26, 15.31, 17.33
1:20	1.8, 1.10, 6.5, 6.9, 6.19, 6.20, 6.21, 6.37, 10.21	7:13	15.8
		7:14	16.13
1:21	1.26, 6.43, 13.22	7:20–21	15.23
1:23	6.20	7:22	17.34
1:23–26	19.22	7:23	15.8, 16.50
1:24	16.25, 11.22	7:24	17.33
1:24–28	16.34	7:25	6.12, 18.38
1:25	19.8	8:1	16.24
1:26	18.18	8:3	6.12, 17.25
1:28	11.22, 12.46	8:4	16.44
1:32	16.44, 17.20, 18.18	8:6–7	17.24
2	1.18	8:7	16.8, 17.24
2:4	6.40	8:9	9.17
2:5	16.34	8:10	15.38
2:8–9	16.26	8:11	9.26
2:14	16.15, 18.9, 18.19	8:13	23.19
2:14–15	17.20	8:15	23.19
2:15	1.18, 6.4, 16.40, 16.43, 18.18, 18.20	8:15–17	23.7
		8:21	17.43
2:16	22.18, 23.11	8:27	12.23
2:17–20	3.20	8:28	10.27
3:2	3.3, 3.12, 3.14	8:32	8.9
3:3–4	6.40	9:1	20.11
3:5	6.41	9:5	8.27

Romans (*cont.*)

9:11	12.32
9:14	6.41
9:19	6.35
9:21	6.38
9:31	17.20
10:2	17.20
10:4	3.21, 18.42, 22.56
10:5	18.35
10:8	22.30
10:14	12.23
10:17	5.31, 17.29
11:29	6.35
11:33	6.33
11:35–36	12.31
11:36	11.7, 12.3
12	18.38
12:2	15.35
12:6	5.34
13	18.38
13:1	6.38
14:3	17.23
14:5	21.45, 21.55
14:7–8	17.35
14:11	20.10
14:20	16.17, 20.44
15:4	2.28, 3.9, 3.16, 4.24, 5.17
15:8	22.16
15:19	22.19
16:21–22	3.14
16:22	3.8
16:26	3.6, 3.22, 3.38, 6.28

1 Corinthians

1:1	3.14
1:2	2.10
1:5–6	4.35
1:11	3.13
1:21	1.11, 6.9, 17.29
1:23	22.31
1:23–24	5.8
1:24	8.17
1:25	6.37
2:8	8.27
2:10	9.5, 9.24
2:11	9.2, 9.3, 12.16
2:13	3.9
2:14	5.6, 5.8, 15.22, 16.42, 17.24, 17.35
2:14–15	17.34
2:15	5.27, 5.30, 17.34
3:1	17.34
3:3	15.31
3:7	1.13
3:16	9.23, 9.24
5	3.13
5:9	3.1
6	3.13
6:3–4	17.10n11
6:9	19.32
6:19	9.24
6:19–20	9.23
7	3.13
7:5	20.41
7:25	3.7
7:36–37	17.6
7:39	17.6
7:40	3.7
8	3.13
8:4	6.25, 19.6
8:4–5	6.13
8:4–6	6.17
8:6	7.50, 10.9, 10.10
9	3.13
9:9	11.8
9:12	22.19
9:14–15	22.6
9:17	17.6
10:9	1.16, 8.23
10:14	22.41
10:15	2.10, 5.27, 5.29
10:19	19.6
10:31	16.16, 17.35
11:7	13.48
11:8	13.49, 14.5
11:20	21.53
11:26	22.51
12:4	3.14
12:6	11.7
12:7	3.14
12:8	1.11
12:8–9	9.25
12:11	7.18, 9.5, 9.25
13:9	6.2
13:10	17.43
13:12	12.16, 17.33, 17.43
14	5.18
14:3	5.34

14:29	3.14, 5.27, 5.34	13:5–6	2.34
14:32	3.14	13:13	7.49, 9.27
15:1–2	4.35		
15:3–4	3.4	**Galatians**	
15:14	13–31	1:7	22.19
15:19	8.30	1:11–12	22.19
15:20–22	1.30	1:13	17.20
15:21	15.38	2:4–5	21.51
15:28	17.43	3	18.48
15:56	16.21, 16.50	3:1–2	2.34
16:1–2	21.52	3:6	22.4
16:2	20.41, 21.57	3:8	3.21
16:7	11.22	3:10	16.5, 16.21, 16.50, 18.35
16:15	20.41	3:10–13	4.10
16:19	3.14	3:13	16.5, 16.51
		3:15	4.12
2 Corinthians		3:17	8.4, 23.10
1:11	7.3	3:18	23.6
1:18	20.21	3:19	18.30
1:19	4.32	3:24	23.10
1:23	20.11, 20.16	4:2	21.43
2:16	22.24	4:2–4	23.19
3:2–4	2.34	4:5–7	21.43
3:3	2.9	4:6	9.17
3:5	17.25	4:8	6.19, 19.28
3:6	22.9, 23.7	4:10	21.45, 21.55
3:6–7	23.5	4:21–31	23.25n16
3:7	18.41	4:23–24	23.5
3:8–9	5.25	4:24	23.6
3:14	3.3, 3.21, 5.16, 23.8	5	17.34, 21.50
3:17	17.38	5:1	20.43
3:18	9.26, 13.42	5:4	23.6
4:2	5.16	5:6	1.24
4:3	22.18	5:7	16.8
4:4	12.35, 12.46, 22.31	5:13	20.44
4:16	15.35	5:17	15.31, 17.34
5:14	15.6	6:1	17.34
5:15	15.19	6:3	19.6
5:19	22.30, 23.14	6:11	3.14
6:16–17	19.Cor	6:16	3.17, 4.13
8:7	1.10		
9:13	22.9, 22.19	**Ephesians**	
10:10	3.7	1:4	8.8, 10.27, 10.Cor2, 12.4
10:10–11	3.9	1:5	1.10
10:13	3.17	1:10	12.33
10:16	3.17	1:11	6.35, 6.36, 11.5
11:6	3.7	1:13	22.30
11:27	20.41	1:19	6.37
12:4	6.2	1:19–20	17.30

Ephesians (cont.)

2	15.9, 21.50
2:1–3	17.29
2:2	12.24, 12.39, 12.46, 16.44
2:3	15.5
2:5	17.30
2:10	17.30
2:12	6.44, 17.24, 23.10
2:15–16	18.46
2:20	2.7, 3.22
3:5	3.22
3:9–11	22.8
3:10	12.18, 23.32
3:20	6.37
4:6	7.50
4:11	3.22
4:11–13	5.32
4:18	15.22
4:22	17.34
4:22–24	13.42
4:23	15.35
4:24	17.15
4:30	9.3, 9.5, 16.45n18
5:28	13.50
6:15	22.30

Philippians

1:8	20.11, 20.16
1:10	5.30
1:19	9.17
1:22–23	13.25
2:6	6.19, 6.27, 8.14
2:13	11.9, 17.38
2:16	22.30
3:1	4.15
3:6–7	17.20
3:13–15	5.26
3:15	2.10
3:16	3.17, 4.13
3:21	8.28

Colossians

1	8.9
1:5	22.30
1:13	22.25n13, 8.13
1:15	6.20, 8.9, 8.17, 10.9
1:16	10.10
1:16–17	8.29, 12.3
1:17	8.28
1:20	12.33
1:26	23.18
2	21.50
2:3	1.5
2:9	6.19, 7.6
2:12–13	17.30
2:14	18.48
2:16	21.45, 21.55
2:17	18.46, 21.43
2:18	12.23
2:20	20.43
3:9	17.34
3:9–10	13.42
3:10	17.15
3:16	1.22, 3.11, 22.19
4:16	3.13

1 Thessalonians

1:3	1.24
1:5	4.35
2:13	1.14
4:8	1.14
4:9	1.13
5:23	13.9, 13.32n17

2 Thessalonians

1:7	12.35
1:7–8	22.31
2:2	3.14, 4.33
2:4	6.10
2:9	12.43
2:11	12.46
2:13–15	4.35
2:15	4.15
3:17	3.13, 3.14

1 Timothy

1:3	1.13, 1.25
1:5	16.15, 18.38, 18.42
1:6	1.25
1:13	16.34
1:17	6.17, 6.20, 6.26, 6.28, 6.332:13–14 14.29
3:15	2.30
3:16	6.12, 8.27
4:1–3	20.43
4:4	10.Cor3
4:6–7	1.25
4:7–8	1.22

4:8	1.20	4:8	21.19
5:21	12.32	4:9	21.20
6:3–4	1.13	4:12	5.25
6:4	1.25	4:13	6.33, 12.21
6:15	6.43, 6.38	4:15	15.36
6:15–16	6.17, 6.37	5	5.31
6:16	6.20, 6.43	5:13	22.30
		5:13–14	5.30
2 Timothy		6	16.53, 20.48
1:8	22.19	6:3	11.22
3:15	1.20, 3.3, 4.8, 5.17	6:16	20.12, 20.22
3:16	1.13, 2.5, 2.28, 3.4, 3.6, 4.8, 4.24	7:8–9	15.11
		7:12	18.8, 23.20
3:16–17	3.16	7:18	23.20
3:17	4.20	7:20–24	20.10
4:11	3.33	7:26	15.18
		8:8	8.4
Titus		8:13	23.13
1:1	1.10, 1.18, 1.22, 4.18	9	18.48
1:2	6.41	9:1	23.13
1:9	5.35	9:9	21.43
1:16	6.43, 6.45	9:10	21.43
2:12	22.52	9:14	9.24
2:13	8.27	9:15–17	4.12
3:3	17.29	9:15–22	23.3
3:4	6.40	10	16.53, 18.48
3:5	9.26, 17.30	10:1	21.43, 23.7, 23.17
		10:26	17.6
Philemon		11:3	21.17
14	17.16	11:6	6.7, 6.19, 17.23
		12:1	15.8, 15.23
Hebrews		12:29	18.41
1	8.9	13:8	8.28, 23.21
1:1	1.16, 3.7	13:23–24	3.35
1:2	10.10, 10.17, 10.26		
1:3	8.17, 8.29, 11.5	**James**	
1:6	8.30	1:13	6.41, 16.30
1:7	9.2	1:14	16.33
1:10	8.23, 10.10	1:15	16.38
1:11	6.26	1:17	6.24, 11.9, 23.32
1:12	8.28	1:22–25	1.24
1:14	9.2, 12.9, 12.24, 12.37	2:10	23.29
2:2–3	22.55	2:19	6.3
2:16	7.17	3:2	23.29
3	21.44	4:12	19.1
3:1	22.16	4:15	17.35
4	21.44		
4:2	3.21	**1 Peter**	
4:3	21.20	1:4–5	17.41

1 Peter (cont.)

1:11	1.14, 9.17, 9.24
1:11–12	1.13
1:12	12.13
1:20	8.8, 12.4
1:23	22.9, 22.30
2:8	22.31
3:19	13.25
3:4	17.34
5:2	17.6
5:8	12.24
5:13	3.33

2 Peter

1	2.5
1:1	2.10
1:4	6.19
1:19	3.20, 3.22, 5.13, 5.16
1:20	2.28, 3.6
1:21	1.13, 1.14, 4.8, 9.24
2:1	1.25
2:4	12.27
3:8	6.33
3:15	3.13, 3.35
3:16	3.3

1 John

1:3–4	4.15
1:5	6.24
1:6–7	18.38, 18.42
2:2	18.42
2:3–6	18.38
2:12–14	2.10
2:13	5.17
2:15–16	22.48
2:16	15.36, 16.33
2:25	22.53
2:27	17.41
3:2	1.4, 12.16
3:4	14.1, 16.5
3:4–6	18.42
3:8–10	15.16n16
3:9	17.41
3:15	16.37
4	4.20
4:1	5.29
4:8	6.24
5:4	17.41
5:7	7.5, 7.49
5:18	16.54
5:20	6.31, 8.27
5:21	19.32, 22.41

Jude

1	2.10
6	12.7, 12.11

Revelation

1:1	3.6, 12.19
1:3	5.14
1:4	9.27, 6.16
1:4–5	7.49
1:8	6.16, 6.37
1:10	21.53
1:19	2.5
2	3.6
2:1	3.7
2:7	13.45
2:11	18.34n13
2:23	8.27
4:7	6.40
4:8	6.16, 6.17, 6.19, 6.28
5:5	12.19
5:9	8.30
5:11	12.49
5:12	8.30
6:9	13.25
7	12.39
7:3	12.24
7:9	13.25
10:6	20.11
11:17	6.16
12	12.28
12:7	12.50
12:8	12.47
12:20	12.47
13:13	12.39
14:6	22.8
16:5	6.16
17:14	8.27
19:6	8.27
19:10	12.23
20:5–6	18.34n13
20:14	18.34n13
21:8	19.32
22:13	8.27
22:9	12.23

22:15	19.32	**1 Maccabees**	
22:18–19	4.14, 2.28	2:34–36	21.27
		2:40–41	21.34
Wisdom of Solomon		4:59	21.61
14:15	19.14		
		2 Maccabees	
Ecclesiasticus		8:27	21.34
33:25	22.43	12:38–39	21.27

General Index

Aasgaard, Reidar   89n13
Abelard, Peter   319n9
Abels, Paul H.A.M.   555n35
Absolute   603, *See Glossary*
Abulensis   473
Academics   323n14, *See* Plato
Accidens   603, *See Glossary*
actus purus   297, 297n17
Actus   603, *See Glossary*
ad intra / ad extra   12, 191n11, 175n29, 207n7, 233n4, 241, 249, 251, 603, 607, 614, *See Glossary*
Adam, Alfred   218n22
Administratio   603, *See Glossary*
Aequivocus   603, *See Glossary*
Affirmatio   603, *See Glossary*
Alexander the Great   59
Alexandria   45n18, 79n5, 85n9, 283n28
Allert, Craig D.   65n26
Alsted, Johann Heinrich   41n15, 313n33
Altenstaig, Johannes   261n4
Althaus, Paul   72n35
Amama, Sixtus   75n1
Ambrose   119, 119n16, 323, 355, 479
Ames, William   43n17, 107n1, 108n4, 129n1, 235n8, 319n7, 329n18, 333n22
Amphilochius of Iconium   101, 101n25
Amsterdam   47n20, 107n1, 129n1, 308n28, 521n11
Anabaptists   2, 8, 9, 16, 53n9, 211n13, 245n15, 317n5, 489, 497, 551n31, 553, 553n33
Analogia   603, *See Glossary*
analogy   169n21, 213, 229
 of faith   355, 355n4
angels   14, 33, 41, 285
Anselm of Laon   341n5
Anselm of Canterbury   12
Anthropomorphism   183, 319n8
anthropopathy   181, 235
Anti-Trinitarians   201, 245
Antichrist   25, 67
Antioch   45n18, 101n26, 119n15, 211n13, 217n21, 485n45, 531n16, 547n26
Antiochene school   485n45
Antiochus, Epiphanes   69
Apollinaris   335n23

Apollinarius   318n5
appropriation   13, 207n7, 561n9
Aquinas, Thomas   151n2, 163n15, 169n21, 195n16, 225n28, 253n10, 255n15, 269n12, 281, 297n17, 299n19, 305n26, 311n29, 313n31, 373, 375n27, 433n2, 435n5, 449n18, 471n25, 475, 475n32, 567
Arbitrium   604, *See Glossary*
Arianism   13, 32n4, 85n9, 91n14, 97n19, 121, 209, 209n12, 211, 215n19, 217, 217n22, 249, 249n6, 485
Aristophanes   557
Aristotle   5, 37n9, 37n10, 39n13, 49n4, 111, 111n8, 115n11, 125n24, 151n2, 153, 187n6, 221n24, 249n5, 255n16, 277n22, 289n7, 293n13, 295n16, 297n17, 305n26, 315n2, 323, 323n14, 327n15, 345n11, 351n2, 361n14, 409, 409n4, 437n7, 442n12, 491, 603–606, 610, 611, 613
Arlig, Andrew   115n11
Arminius, Jacobus   1, 215n17
Arnobius   321, 321n11
Arrianus, Lucius Flavius   59, 59n20
Artaxerxes   101
ascension   67
Asselt, Willem J. van   3n5, 19n16, 33n5, 37n10, 87n11, 175n28, 175n29, 263n5, 269n11, 271n15, 329n18, 339n3, 347n14, 387n6, 403n20, 407n2, 409n4, 411n9, 415n12, 437n7, 555n35, 585n8
Athanasius   79n6, 85n9, 103, 185n2
Atheism   181
Athens   3n3, 523n12
atonement   63, 517
attributes of God   10, 37, 151, 163, 165, 195n17, 221, 241
 communicable   10, 163n15, 165, 165n17, 171n22
 eternity   167, 195, 203, 207, 211, 233, 255, 263n6, 287, 541n22
 foreknowledge   173, 183, 207, 343, 345, 345n10, 407, 407n3, 411
 immensity   167, 169
 immortality   161, 171
 immutability   165, 167, 175n29, 195, 223, 347n16

incommunicable   10, 159, 165, 165n17, 187, 187n7, 191, 347
infinity   161n13, 165, 165n17, 167, 189, 195, 211, 297
justice   177, 179, 277, 303, 355, 395, 405, 443, 559, 565
omnipotence   195, 223, 247, 269
omniscience   223, 241
potency   171, 175, 177
simplicity   165, 175n29
Attributum   604, *See Glossary*
Augustine   12, 14, 15, 39, 75, 101, 103, 105, 113, 119, 121, 133, 213n14, 249n7, 253, 253n13, 255, 255n6, 257n17, 261n3, 269, 279, 287n5, 289n9, 303n22, 305n26, 321, 323, 333n22, 337, 351, 353, 353n3, 355, 355n6, 357, 359, 361, 366n18, 369n22, 373, 373n26, 375, 381, 385, 385n3, 387, 393n10, 397, 397n16, 413, 415, 419, 425, 425n20, 427, 431, 431n26, 449n18, 453, 459, 459n9, 463, 471, 474n30, 481, 483, 537, 545n24, 547, 557, 559n7
Augustus   60n23
authority of Scripture   49
autopistos   57, 87n10, 221n24
Ayala, Martin Perez de   5n7, 473n29, 483

Baars, A.   11n10, 218n22, 235n7
Babylon   67
Bacchus   63
Badewien, Jan   261n3
Balacus, Jesuita   69n33
Balsamon, Theodore   101, 101n26
Balthasar, Hans Urs von   491n2
Balthazar   79
baptism   105, 121, 205, 225, 355, 365n18, 379, 381, 501, 502n11, 549n27, 601
Barnabas   65n27, 99, 99n23, 103
Barnstone, Willis   197n18
Baronius, Caesar   475, 477n34
Baruch   79
Basil the Great   31, 31n3, 31n4, 113, 119, 155, 355, 485
Bauckham, Richard J.   201n24, 521n11
Bavinck, Herman   17, 239n9, 289n9, 295n16, 335n23
Bayle, Pierre   13n12
Becius, Carolus   261, 261n1

Becius, Joh.   351n1
Beck, Andreas J.   152n2, 175n29, 213n16, 264n7, 279n23, 295n16, 519n9
Belcarius, Franciscus   365n18, 366n18
Bell, Michael D.   3n5
Bellarmine, Robert   11, 5n7, 53n8, 71n34, 107, 107n4, 108n4, 109, 121, 125, 125n22, 125n24, 139n9, 141, 215, 215n19, 281, 281n27, 341n5, 375, 379, 455, 461, 473n28, 475, 475n32, 477, 477n35, 479, 479n39, 553n34, 567, 593, 595
Belt, Henk van den   1n1, 2n2, 41n15, 87n10
Bente, F.   369n21
Benz, E.   239n10
Berg, F.W.J. van den   553n34
Bernard of Clairvaux   15, 383
Beroea   135, 139
Bethlehem   45n18
Beza, Theodore   211n13, 215n18, 281n27, 303n22, 303n23, 366n18, 433n2
Biel, Gabriel   5n7, 471, 471n25, 567
Bierma, Lyle D.   585n8
Bithynia   59n20
Bochartus, Samuel   453
Boethius   187n7, 207n9, 225n28
Bok, Nico den   187n7
Bologna, Roland of   341n5
Bonaventure   99n24, 195n16, 471, 471n26
Bonevac, Daniel   169n21
Breda   151n1, 247n1
Breimer, Douwe D.   4n7
Brenz, Johannes   109, 341, 341n6
Brielle   285n1
Brink, Gert van den   3n5
Bronchorst, Everard   49n1
Bruno, Giordano   107n4
Brussels   469n23
Bullinger, Heinrich   211n13, 339n3, 577n3, 585n8
Burell, Peter   373n26
Buridan, John   389n8
Bütgen, Phillippe   87n11
Buxtorf, Johannes   577n3

Caen   453n1
Caesarea   31n3, 79n6
Cajetan, Tommaso de Vio   123, 123n21, 373, 477, 477n35
Calov, Abraham   593n15

Calvin, John   11, 11n10, 13, 13n11, 53n9, 87n10, 97n18, 155n6, 215, 215n18, 215n19, 218n22, 235n5, 235n7, 279n24, 281n27, 289n6, 303n22, 313n33, 315n2, 329n19, 333n22, 339n3, 397n15, 445n16, 473n27, 473n28, 507n12, 553n34, 555n35, 585n8, 587n12, 591n14, 599n20
Cameron, John   575n1
Campanus, Johannes   243, 243n14
Cano, Melchior   52n7, 125n23
Canon   531n17
Canons of Dordrecht   421n17
Carney, Frederik S.   442n12
Cassian, John   431, 431n26
Cassiodorus   97, 97n19, 319n9
causa   5, 39, 39n13, 41, 111, 175, 249, 253, 267n10, 315n3, 343, 345n11, 359, 413, 559, 604, *See Glossary*
Celsus   57
Ceres   63, 365n17
Chadwick, Henry   57n13, 287n5
Chaeronea   459n11
Chamier, Daniel   313n33
Chiliasm   127
Chremylus   557n3
Chrysostom, John   119, 119n15, 131, 283n28, 303n22, 457
Church, Fathers   3, 8, 9, 79, 105, 109, 121, 123, 137, 187, 205n5, 209, 211, 213, 215, 235, 237, 257, 287, 289, 303, 313n33, 321, 329, 333, 335, 357, 407, 473, 483, 485, 606
Cicero   25n6, 27n9, 81, 153, 295n16, 353, 453, 489, 491, 557
circumcision   67, 355, 367, 523, 533, 555n35, 581
Clement of Alexandria   523, 549
Clement of Rome   99, 103, 551
Cocceius, Johannes   15n2, 585n8
Coffey, David   239n9
Colish, Marcia L.   341n5
Cologne   471n25
Communicabilis   604, *See Glossary*
communicatio idiomatum   166n18
Communis   604, *See Glossary*
concupiscentia   15, 303n24, 341n5, 357n8, 359, 371, 371n24, 373, 373n26, 375, 377, 377n28, 379, 385, 385n3, 399
concurrence   271, 271n14, 281, 281n26

conscience   25n6, 63, 67, 135, 153, 225, 325, 327, 327n16, 329n18, 349, 391, 395, 401, 403, 405, 439, 441, 445, 495
Constantine   31n2, 79n6, 458n7, 485, 523n13, 549
Constantinople   31n3, 32n4, 45n18, 101n26, 105, 119n15, 123n20, 239n10, 243n13, 485n45, 549n28
contingency   9, 37n10, 175n29, 209n12, 269, 273n18, 297, 407, 409n6, 411
Contingentia   604, *See Glossary*
Coolmanus, Laevinus   385
Costerus, Franciscus   469
Council
   Fourth Lateran   289n9
   of Constantinople   123n20, 243n13, 485n45
   of Ephesus   485n45
   of Florence   239n9
   of Frankfurt   455
   of Milevis   357
   of Orange   357
   of Palestine   357
   of Toledo   357
   of Trent   45n18, 51n7, 81, 81n8, 99, 107n4, 109, 109n5, 125n23, 140n9, 377n28, 379n29, 379n30, 421n16, 431, 431n27, 467, 473n29, 473n30, 477n33, 479n37
   of Trullo   123n20
covenant   16, 61, 77, 121, 137, 143, 303n23, 333n22, 339, 339n3, 365n18, 367, 381, 503, 527, 539, 545, 561, 575, 575n2, 577, 579n5, 579n6, 581, 583, 585n8, 589, 597, 605
   diatheke   575, 577n3, 581
   of grace   16, 339n3, 585, 585n8
   of works   339n3, 585
creatianism   335n23
creation   7, 12, 39, 63, 163n15, 193, 205, 223, 231, 243, 247, 251, 369, 525, 529, 539
creator   9
Creed the Apostles'   121, 247, 251
Cross, Richard   311n29
Crucius, Johannes   49
curse   351, 387, 393, 405, 435, 435n3, 485, 495, 497, 539, 565, 579
Cyprian   355, 549, 549n27
Cyril of Alexandria   283n28, 485n45

GENERAL INDEX   651

Damascenus, Johannes   473
Dambrinus, Samuel   513
Dammanus, Tobias   185
Danaeus, Lambertus   151n2
death   349, 355, 379, 385
    eternal death   449
    first and second   381
    of Christ   559, 577
Decalogue   6, 16, 65, 79, 341n4, 441, 443, 449, 513, 521, 543, 567, 567n16
decrees   233, 263, 263n6, 267, 427, 559
Definitus   604, *See Glossary*
deism   13
Dekker, Eef   3n5
Delphi   459n11
Delumeau, J.   333n21
Demonstrare   605, *See Glossary*
Determinare   605, *See Glossary*
devil   561, *See* Satan
Dick, S.   257n18
Didymus the Blind   45n18
Diocletian   31n2, 57n14, 523n13
Dionysius of Corinth   547
Dionysius the Pseudo-Areopagite   264n7, 313, 313n31
Dispensatio   605, *See Glossary*
distinctio realis   163n16, 233n4
Domitian   97n20
Donatus   319n9
Doornyck, Petrus   557
Dordrecht   261n1, 351n1, 431, 431n28
Driedo, John   51n7
Dulians   249
Durand, William   479n36
Dyck, C.J.   499n8
Dykema, Peter A.   599n20

Ebionites   551
Egypt   49, 59, 67, 161, 161n11, 431n26, 517, 525, 539, 543
Ehrman, Bart D.   99n21
Eldere, Abraham van   351
elect   97, 115, 139, 155, 161, 207, 281, 299, 301, 303, 445, 445n6, 447, 447n17, 563, 587
Emanans   605, *See Glossary*
Empedocles   323
emperichoresis   199, 199n21, 209, 209n10
endiathetos   41, 41n15
enhypostasis   191

Epictetus   409n4
Epicurus   13, 31n2, 183, 591n14
Epiphanius of Salamis   91, 91n14, 95, 101, 121, 365, 365n17
Episcopius, Simon   1
equivocity   169n21, 187, 357n9, 497n7
Erasmus, Desiderius   23n4, 25n6, 27n9, 69n32, 313n30
Erfurt   471n25
Erpenius, Thomas   75n1, 151n1
essence of God   10, 33, 151, 161, 163, 171, 185, 187, 205, 229, 231, 243, 325
Essenes   489
Essentia   605, *See Glossary*
Essentialis   605, *See Glossary*
Euphrates   333
Eusebius of Caesarea   45n18, 79, 79n6, 85, 89, 97, 99, 99n22, 101n27, 103, 127, 155, 523, 547, 547n25, 547n26, 551
Eutyches   283n28
Evidentia   605, *See Glossary*
existence of God   10, 58n18, 151, 151n2, 153, 437n6

Faber, Riemer   307n27, 319n9, 557n3, 591n14
Facultas   605, *See Glossary*
fall of Adam   15, 339
Family of Love   553n33
Faustus   431
Feingold, Mordechai   308n28
Ferwerda, Rein   3n5
Figurativus   606, *See Glossary*
Figuratus   606, *See Glossary*
filioque   12, 237, 239, 239n9, 251n8
Finger, Thomas N.   317n5
Finis   606, *See Glossary*
Finkenzeller, Joseph   51n7
first cause   269, 271, 273, 273n16, 273n18
Fitzgerald, Allan D.   373n26
flesh and spirit   401, 423
forgiveness   16, 67, 355, 365n18, 381, 385, 385n5, 393, 393n10, 403, 405, 479, 559, 579, 579n6
Franck, Sebastian   53n9, 245n15
free choice   15, 69n31, 263n5, 301, 329n18, 347n14, 407, 407n2, 407n3, 409n4, 411, 411n8, 413, 413n10, 415, 417, 419, 421, 425, 427, 427n21, 429, 431, 431n26, 433

free will   15, 37n10, 210n12, 241, 247, 269, 269n12, 273, 285, 299, 299n19, 301, 329, 347, 347n14, 359, 409n4, 411n7, 415, 421, 431n26, 519n9, 614
Freedman, Joseph S.   4n7
freedom
  from misery   415n12
  from necessity   415n12
  from sin   415n12
  of contradiction   303n25, 411n9
  of contrariety   304n25
  of exercise   303
  of glory   415n12
  of grace   415n12
  of nature   415n12
  of specification   303, 303n25
Freeman, Ann   457n6
Fulgentius of Ruspe   355, 355n6
Fundamentum   606, *See Glossary*
future contingencies   297, 297n18

Galerius   57n14
Gallasius, Nicolaus   215n18
Gamble, Richard C.   315n2
Génébrard, Gilbert   215
generatio   207, 209, 211, 213, 235, 233n4, 606, *See Glossary*
Geneva   211n13, 218n22, 229n1, 473, 515n4, 575n1
Gentile Giovanni Valentino   211n13, 215n18
genus   37, 37n9, 39, 43n17, 165, 339n2, 411, 461, 539, 545, 587n11, 606, *See Glossary*
Gerson, Jean   113, 113n9
Ghent, Henry of   311n29
Gisberti, Theodorus   75
Giustiniani Marco Antonio   93n16
Glare, P.G.W.   19n13
glorification   223, 565
Gnosticism   65n27, 103n28
Goclenius, Rudolph   26n4
Gomarus, Franciscus   1, 469n23, 521n11
good pleasure   77, 255, 265
good works   269, 275, 419, 425, 445, 479, 565, 593
Goodyear, Hugh   107n1
Gospel   5, 557
Goudriaan, Aza   519n9

Graef, Hilda   365n17
Gratia   606, *See Glossary*
Gratian   123, 123n19
Gregory of Nazianzus   31, 31n3, 31n4, 89, 95, 101, 101n25, 121, 355, 461, 485
Gregory of Nyssa   255n16, 335n23, 485, 559n7
Gregory of Valencia   71n34, 461n13
Gregory the Great   313n31, 551
Grotius, Hugo   313n33

Haarlem   49n2
habit   119, 371, 373, 375, 377, 399, 421
Hadrian   59n20, 523n13
Hamers, Henricus   247, 247n1
Hanson, R.P.C.   243n13
Hart, Trevor A.   201n24
Hasius, Adrianus   285, 285n1
Haykin, M.A.G.   243n13
Heidelberg   341n6, 471n25, 585n8
Heine, Ronald E.   79n5
Heppe, Heinrich   335n23
heretics   45, 103, 141, 209, 217, 227, 511
Hermann, Wolfgang   69n33
Hermas, Shepherd of   103
Hermes Trismegistus   197
Herodotus   155
Hesiod   523
Hesselius, Johannes   473
Hessels, J.H.   513n1
heterodidaskalia   45
Heukelum   75n1
Hilary of Poitiers   355
Hoffmann, Tobias   299n19
Holy Spirit   229, 405
Homer   327n15, 557
homoousios   121, 217, 217n20, 217n21, 221n23, 241
Honders, H.J.   239n10
Honorius   341n5
Hoogvliet   285n1
Horace   591n14
Hosius, Stanislaus   51n7, 69n33, 109, 109n5
Hove, Martin van den   308n28
Hoven, R.   19n15
Hubmaier, Balthasar   317n5
Hupostatikoos   607, *See Glossary*
hypostasis   11, 185n3, 187, 203, 215n18, 231, 289, 607, *See Glossary*

GENERAL INDEX   653

Iconium   101n25
idolatry   16, 453, 513
Ignatius of Loyola   469n23
Ignatius   531, 537, 547
illumination   37n11, 131, 133
Illyricus, Matthias Flacius   369n21, 477n34
image of God   14, 15, 153, 213, 315, 355, 369
imitation of Christ   571, 573, 593n15
Immanens   607, *See Glossary*
immanent acts   171, 175, 175n29, 207, 233, 233n4, 271n13
Immediate   607, *See Glossary*
immortality   291, 325, 327, 329, 331, 591
Immutabilitas   607, *See Glossary*
immutability   409
Improprie   607, *See Glossary*
imputation   15, 355n7, 369, 377, 381, 383, 393, 585
In se   607, *See Glossary*
Incommunicabilis   607, *See Glossary*
Infinitas   607, *See Glossary*
inspiration   31, 39, 41, 113
Irenaeus of Lyons   103, 103n28, 119, 119n17, 127, 217n21, 329n19, 355, 549
Isidore of Pelusium   283, 283n28
Isidore of Seville   319n9
Islam   63
Isocrates   557, 557n4
Itterzon, G.P. van   521n11

Jerome   45, 45n18, 89, 91, 93, 99, 101n27, 103, 119, 257, 257n18, 321n11, 355, 449n18, 515, 545n24, 547, 547n26
Jesuits   57, 107n4, 215, 455, 461, 475, 497, 567
Jews   45, 59n21, 61n24, 63, 65, 67, 69n28, 81, 85, 89, 89n13, 91, 93, 95, 101, 117, 121, 131, 135, 139, 159, 159n9, 161n11, 181, 197, 199, 211, 443, 445, 447, 449, 449n18, 451, 455n5, 465, 489, 501, 513n3, 515, 515n4, 515n7, 519, 521, 523, 525, 529, 531, 533, 535, 539, 543, 545, 551, 551n31, 553n33, 553n34, 561, 563, 563n12, 571, 579
John of Damascus   95, 151n2, 264n7
Johnson, S.L. jr   353n3
Jones, H.L.   60n23
Jong, Jan L. de   469n23
Joosse, L.J.   489n1, 557n1
Joris, David   53n9, 245n15, 289n6

Josephus, Flavius   59, 59n21, 59n22, 61n24, 85, 89, 91, 101, 333, 489, 523
Josius, Franciscus   229
Julian the Apostate   57, 57n15, 69, 355
Junius, Franciscus   35n7, 41n15, 303n22, 409n4
justification   16, 367, 421n16, 431n27, 565, 573, 581, 591, 595
Justin Martyr   41n15, 65, 65n26, 119, 551

Karamanolis, George   459n11
Keckermann, Bartholomaeus   43n7
Kelly, J.N.D.   41n15, 217n21
Kenny, Anthony   87n11, 293n14
Kerchove, Anna van den   197n18
Kerstemannus   107n1
Kessler, Eckhard   26n4
Kimchi, David   513, 513n3
kingdom of glory   565
kingdom of grace   565
Kingdon, Robert M.   218n22
Klima, Gyula   389n8
knowledge
    acquired   293
    discursive knowledge   47
    innate   295, 325, 439
    intuitive knowledge   47
    of God   173
    practical   263, 263n5, 281, 281n25, 345
Kooij, A. van der   91n15
Kooten, G.H. van   317n5
Kralingen   285n1
Kretzmann, Norman   87n11
Kuyper, H.H.   555n35

Lactantius   31, 31n2, 453
Lampridius   523
Lane, A.N.S.   52n7
Langston, Douglas   327n16
Laovicus, Petrus   489
Lardet, P.   257n18
Lausberg, Heinrich   199n20, 435n3
Law and Gospel   7, 16, 87, 117, 567, 573, 575, 579n5, 579n6, 595
law of God   135, 339, 341n4, 349n17, 385, 385n5, 415, 433, 441, 483, 511, 539
law   47, 51, 53, 69, 111, 339, 349, 385, 405, 413, 557
    ceremonial   433, 441, 447, 449, 583, 583n7, 589

divine   73, 371, 435, 435n5, 491, 595
eternal   385, 435, 435n5, 491
forensic   433, 441, 449, 451
law of works   447
moral   341, 341n4, 433, 441, 443, 443n14, 491, 493, 553n33, 567, 569, 583, 583n7, 589, 593n15, 595, 597
natural   35, 47, 341, 359, 435, 439, 443, 493, 505, 543
laws of nature   271n13
Lee, Brian J.   577n3
Leeuwarden   285n1
Leiden   1, 1n1, 2, 4, 29, 31n1, 41n15, 47n21, 49n1, 49n2, 54n9, 58n18, 65n26, 75n1, 91n15, 107n1, 129n1, 197n18, 199n20, 203n1, 215n17, 222n26, 229n1, 243n13, 255n15, 257n18, 261n1, 299n19, 341n5, 385n3, 469n23, 515n4, 519n9, 549n28, 557n1, 575n1, 585n8
Leppin, H.   549n28
Lerinum   261n3
Lewis and Short   19n13, 541n23
Lex naturae   607, *See Glossary*
Libertines   2, 8, 53, 53n9, 57, 245, 245n15, 289, 289n6, 397, 397n15
Lieburg, F.A. van   31n1, 49n2, 75n1, 107n1, 151n1, 185n1, 203n1, 229n1, 247n1, 261n1, 285n1, 315n1, 339n1, 407n1, 433n1, 489n1, 513n1, 557n1
life   171
eternal   16, 53, 115, 115n12, 135, 151, 303, 429, 491n2, 563, 565, 573, 579, 579n6, 585, 585n9, 593, 597
natural   351
spiritual   333, 351, 421
Linus   523
Lipsius, Justus   515n4
logica modernorum   47n21
logomachia   45
Lombard, Peter   253n10, 341n5, 371n24, 471n25, 567
Longenecker, R.N.   353n3
Lord's Supper   121, 342n6, 459, 467, 474n30, 547, 551, 573
Lorin, Jean   455, 455n5
Louis the Pious   477
Loukaris, Cyrillus   239n10
Louvain   107n4, 379n30, 473n29, 473n30
Loux, Michael J.   193n15
Lubac, Henri de   149n16

Lubbertus, Sibrandus   108n4
Lucretius   327n15
Luther, Martin   124n21, 315n2, 335n23, 371n24, 471n25, 507n12

Maarssen   151n1
Maccabees   69n28, 99, 531, 531n17, 535, 555
MacCormick, Chalmers   244n14
Maccovius, Johannes   75n1, 87n11, 279n23
Macedonius   243, 243n13
Magnus, Albertus   483n43
Maimonides, Moses   161, 161n11, 161n12
Manichaeans   183, 287
Marcellus of Ancyr   593n15
Marcion   205, 205n5
marriage   335, 487, 503, 507
Marseille   261n3
Martini, Jacob   593n15
mataiologia   45
materia   33, 39, 255, 315, 317
McDonald, Paul   327n15
McGuire, Brian Patrick   113n9
Mediate   608, *See Glossary*
Mediator   241, 303, 303n22, 385, 395, 577, 585, 591, 599
Meerkerk   75n1
Melanchthon, Philip   335n23, 385n5, 431n28
Melito of Sardes   89, 89n13, 547
Melun, Robert of   341n5
merit   25, 81, 241, 301, 395, 405, 503, 585, 597
Mesopotamia   60n23, 333
Metzger, B.M.   222n26
Meyer, Marvin   197n18
Meyvaert, Paul   457n6
Middelburg   229n1, 489n1
Migne, J.P.   101n25, 166n18, 249n6, 253n13, 264n7, 305n26, 333n22, 425n20, 551n30
Modus   608, *See Glossary*
Molinaeus, Petrus   453n1
Monstrare   608, *See Glossary*
Montepulciano   107n4
Morocco   161n11
Muir, Edward   502n11
Muller, Richard A.   3n5, 4n6, 19n16, 33n5, 41n15, 43n17, 49n3, 57n18, 75n2, 82n8, 115n11, 129n2, 149n16, 149n17, 152n2, 161n13, 163n16, 165n17, 167n19, 171n22, 174n27, 181n31, 191n11, 195n16, 201n24, 207n7, 207n8, 209n10, 215n17, 217n21, 218n22,

225n28, 235n5, 263n5, 264n7, 331n20, 341n4
Münster, Sebastian 93n16
Musculus, Wolfgang 151n2
Mynors, R.A.B. 23n4

Natura 608, *See Glossary*
natural law 35n8, 341n4, 435n5, 437n6, 443n14, 519n9
natural man 131
Naturalis 608, *See Glossary*
necessary doctrines 147
Necessitas 608, *See Glossary*
necessity 9, 12, 37, 37n10, 49, 51, 53, 65, 75, 109, 115, 125, 137, 165n17, 173, 207, 210n12, 221, 263n6, 305, 329, 349, 407, 409, 417, 447, 491n2, 521
Neoplatonism 57n15, 313n30, 315n2
Nero 459n11
Nestorius 283n28, 485, 485n45
Nicea 31n3, 79n6, 85n9, 103, 105, 215n19, 217n21, 249n6, 457n6, 475, 485
Niclaes, Hendrik 245n15
Nieuwpoort 261n1
Nisula, Timo 385n3
Noble, Thomas F.X. 457n6, 477n34
Nomen 609, *See Glossary*
Norlin, George 557n4
Notio communis 609, *See Glossary*
Notitia practica 609, *See Glossary*
Notitia theoretica 609, *See Glossary*
Nuffelen, Peter van 549n28
Numa 459n11

O'Donnell, James Joseph 97n19
oath 489
Oberman, Heiko A. 51n7, 599n20
Ockham, William of 41n15, 193n15, 299n19
Oeconomia 609, *See Glossary*
Olevianus, Caspar 339n3, 585n8
Olivarius, Johannes 315, 315n1
Origen 57n13, 79, 79n5, 79n6, 89, 91n14, 97, 99, 101n27, 119, 121, 215n18, 257, 257n18, 287, 335, 409, 491n2, 549
original righteousness 331, 331n20, 349, 349n18, 369, 373, 379, 445
original sin 351, *See* sin
Osborn, Eric 523n12
ousia 11, 605, 613, 609, *See Glossary*

Ousiodoos 609, *See Glossary*
Ovezande 185n1
Oxford 453n1

pagans 31, 45, 57, 57n14, 57n15, 63, 67, 131, 285, 449, 455, 557
Pain, Daniel 575
Panaccio, Claude 41n15
papal teachers (Catholic theologians) 8, 9, 51, 53n9, 57, 69, 71, 81, 99, 109, 119, 121, 123, 125, 127, 129, 133, 139, 309, 341, 365, 403, 405, 461, 465, 467, 473, 475, 479, 491, 497, 501, 503, 553, 593, 595, 597
Papias 127
Paradise 305, 331, 333, 333n21, 339, 339n3, 349, 359, 521n11
Parker, Kenneth L. 553n33
Partes essentiales 609, *See Glossary*
Partes integrales 609, *See Glossary*
Patripassianism 218n22
Pelagius 355, 357, 359, 361, 377, 379, 431, 593, 593n15
semi-Pelagians 357, 431, 431n26
Perfectio 610, *See Glossary*
Peripatetics 323n4
permission by God 13, 14, 277, 279, 281, 345
perseverance 299, 299n19, 301, 303
Persona 610, *See Glossary*
Personalis 610, *See Glossary*
Petris, Paolo de 397n15
Pettegree, Andrew 218n22
Pfeffinger, Johann 431n28
Pharisees 493, 533, 567
Philo 99, 99n24, 159n9, 315n2, 317n5
Photinus 593n15
Pinborg, Jan 87n11
Piscator, Johannes 577n3
Plato 18, 37n9, 155, 197, 267, 313n33, 323, 353, 409n5, 523n12
Platt, John 3n5, 58n18, 437n6
Plautus 25n6
Pliny the Younger 61, 61n25
Plotinus 57n14
Plutarch 459, 459n11, 557
pneumatomachians 241
Poitiers 479n38
Polanus, Amandus von Polansdorf 10, 10n9, 108n4, 233n4
Polsbroek 75n1

Polyander, Johannes 1, 2, 11, 29, 31, 37n10, 39n13, 49n2, 107, 107n1, 123n20, 151n1, 185, 187n7, 203n1, 247, 249n7, 261n1, 339, 341n4, 433, 435n5, 437n6, 449n18, 557, 559n7, 561n9, 565n13, 568n16
Polycarp of Smyrna 103n28
Polytheism 181
Poortugaal 285n1
Poortvliet 557n1
pope 18, 25, 123n18, 139, 141, 458n7, 479n37, 481, 481n40
Poppi, Antonino 261n4
Porphyry 57
Posse 610, *See Glossary*
Potentia absoluta 610, *See Glossary*
Potentia actualis 610, *See Glossary*
Potentia 610, *See Glossary*
Potjer, Menno 433n1
practical judgment 309
Praedicare 611, *See Glossary*
Praescientia 611, *See Glossary*
predestination 301n21, 407, 407n3
principium 37, 37n11, 47, 49, 49n3, 73, 85, 151, 153, 213, 239, 273, 295n16, 413, 611, *See Glossary*
Priscillian of Avila 287, 287n5
privatio boni 14, 277, 369, 387, 387n7
Privatio 611, *See Glossary*
Probare 611, *See Glossary*
Processio 611, *See Glossary*
procession 193, 197, 233, 233n4, 235, 235n5, 235n7, 237, 239, 239n9, 467
Proclus 409n4
propagation 333, 357, 361, 363
prophecy 51, 71, 83, 85, 97, 99, 101, 113, 145, 241, 313, 493
prophorikos 41, 41n15
Proprie 611, *See Glossary*
providence 261, 305, 317
Proximus 611, *See Glossary*
pseudepigraphs 83
Pullapilly, Cyriac K. 477n34
punishment 67, 135, 153, 289, 349, 379, 381, 385n5, 393, 395, 435, 449, 455n4, 471, 487, 511, 573, 587

quadriga 129n2
Qualitas 611, *See Glossary*
Quasten, Johannes 217n21

Racovian Catechism 201n24, 568n16, 569n17, 569n18, 569n19, 569n20, 569n21, 571n22, 571n23, 571n26, 571n27, 571n28, 573n29, 573n30, 595n17
Ramminger, J. 19n15
Ramus, Peter 442n12
Ratio 612, *See Glossary*
reconciliation 559
redemption 193, 251
Rees, Thomas 568n16
regeneration 15, 231, 329n18, 355, 367, 377, 381, 401, 403, 419, 421, 423, 425, 427, 429, 597
Relatio 612, *See Glossary*
Religio 612, *See Glossary*
Remotus 612, *See Glossary*
Renesse, Ludwig 151
Res 612, *See Glossary*
Reuchlin, Johannes 577n3
revelation 7, 16, 33, 35, 41, 51, 245n15, 249, 257, 293, 293n15, 295, 587
  natural 35, 41
  supernatural 35, 35n8, 41, 73, 151, 195, 563
Ridderkerk 261n1
Rieu, W.M. du 31n1, 49n2, 75n1, 107n1, 151n1, 185n1, 203n1, 229n1, 247n1, 261n1, 285n1, 315n1, 339n1, 351n1, 385n1, 407n1, 433n1, 453n1, 489n1, 513n1, 557n1, 575n1
Rijk, L.M. de 47n21, 49n3, 389n8
Rijsoord 261n1
Rivetus, Andreas 1, 2, 29, 211n13, 239n10, 261, 261n1, 261n2, 263n5, 263n6, 351, 353n3, 355n7, 357n9, 363n16, 371n24, 373n26, 453, 457n6, 459n10, 461n12, 461n13, 471n26, 473n28, 477n35, 479n36, 481n40, 485n44, 521n1, 575, 577n3, 587n12, 593n15
Rohls, Jan 369n21
Rome 45n18
Roth, John D. 53n9
Rotterdam 285n1
Rufinus, Tyrranius 101, 101n27, 103, 257n18, 335n23
rule of faith 73, 381

sabbatarians 513n2, 551
Sabbath 16, 513
Sabellius 217, 217n22, 218n22, 225
Sacramentum 612, *See Glossary*
Sadducees 289
Salvian of Marseille 261, 261n3, 283

Samosatenians 211, 211n13, 217, 217n22, 485, 485n44
sanctification 193, 223, 229, 231, 251, 381, 429, 525, 527, 565
Santoro, G. 323n14
Sardes 89n13
Sasima 32n4
Satan 51, 67, 105, 151, 279n24, 289n6, 299, 301, 305, 307, 309, 311, 342n6, 343, 345, 347, 347n15, 349, 353, 363, 363n16, 369, 369n21, 375, 377, 397, 399, 403, 417, 427, 461, 465, 481, 497, 503, 533
satisfaction 563, 579n6
Saturn 63, 515
Saumur 453n1
Scaliger, Joseph Justus 515, 515n4, 517
Schaff, Philip 87n11, 185n2, 365n17
Scharpius, Johannes 41n15
Scheck, Thomas P. 45n18
Schiedam 107n1
Schmitt, C.B. 261n4
Scholastics 95, 149, 293, 299, 299n19, 301, 303, 313, 411, 553, 567, 567n15
  Scholasticus 612, *See Glossary*
Schomantius, Arnoldus 433
School of Alexandria 523n12
schoolmen 209, 211, 233, 253, 255, 281, 333, 373, 389, 393, 431, 463
Schultz, Robert C. 369n21
Schweizer, Alexander 3n4
science 37n10, 39
Scientia 612, *See Glossary*
Scotus John Duns 12, 35n8, 213n16, 263n6, 519n9, 567
Scripture 7
  apocrypha 65n27, 75, 89, 99, 103, 107, 531n17
  authority 8, 53n9, 57n18, 71, 75, 87n10, 107
  Canon 49, 75
  interpretation 129
  perfection 8, 107
  perspicuity 107, 129, 129n2
Scriverius, Antonius 203, 203n1
secondary causes 265n8, 271, 273, 273n16, 307
secundum quid 607, *See Glossary In se*
Sedan 453n1
Seneca 463
Septuagint 81, 99, 159, 483, 517, 575

Serafim 199
sermo 614, *See Glossary*
Servet, Michael 217, 217n22, 218n22, 225, 591, 591n14, 593n15
Significare 613, *See Glossary*
Simmler, Josias 211n13
Simons, Menno 499n8
Simplicitas 613, *See Glossary*
sin 7, 15, 277, 341, 345, 349, 351, 419
  actual 15, 355, 357, 371, 371n24, 377, 385, 385n2, 389, 393, 397, 399
  original 317n5, 331, 331n20, 349, 351, 351n2, 353, 355, 356n7, 357, 357n10, 359, 359n11, 360n12, 363n16, 365, 365n18, 367, 369, 369n21, 369n22, 371, 371n24, 373, 375, 379, 381, 385, 393n10, 417
Sinai 51
Sinnema, Donald 1n1, 2n2
Sirach 99
Skinner, Q. 261n4
Slee, Jacob Cornelis van 49n1
Smalcius, Valentinus 567n16
Smalley, Beryl 149n16
Smoutius, A. 107n1
Smyrna 89n13, 103n28
Socinians 3, 47n20, 201, 217, 217n21, 217n22, 244n14, 567, 567n16, 569, 571, 571n26, 573, 595, 595n17
Socinus, Faustus 47n20, 69, 69n31, 69n32, 201n24, 568n16, 593n15
Socrates 37n9, 221n24, 549n28
Sodom and Gomorrah 307
Sophists 47, 557n4
Sorabji, Richard 255n16
Soto, Domingo de 379, 379n29, 393n10
soul 321, 323, 327
Sozomen, Salminius Hermias 549
Species 613, *See Glossary*
Spiratio 613, *See Glossary*
spiration 193, 195n16, 205, 205n6, 231, 233, 233n4, 235, 237, 239, 239n9
spiritual man 131
spontaneity 409n6
Sprint, John 553n33
Stapleton, Thomas 51n7
States of Holland 23, 129n1
States of West-Friesland 23, 129n1
States-General 23, 23n1

Stayer, James M.   53n9
Steel, Carlos   409n4
Steinmetz, David   599n20
Stelling-Michaud, Suzanne   229n1
Stellingwerf, Rombert   129
Stephanus, Robert   577n3
Stoics   13n11, 31n2, 41n15, 295n16, 323, 409, 523n12
Strabo   59, 59n23
Strigel, Victorinus   431n28
Subjectum   613, See Glossary
subsistence   185, 189, 191n10, 195, 195n16, 199n21, 203, 205, 207, 209n10, 215, 215n18, 225n28, 227, 231, 233, 239, 289n8
  Subsistentia   613, See Glossary
Substantia   613, See Glossary
Sudduth, Michael   153n3
Suetonius   97, 97n20
Supernaturalis   614, See Glossary
superstition   453, 455, 461, 463, 495, 495n5, 507, 529, 551, 555
Suppositum   614, See Glossary
Swalmius, Abraham   107
Swalmius, Johannes   31, 31n1
syllogism   221, 221n24, 289n7, 327, 327n16
Syme, Ronald   523n13
Synod
  of Alexandria   243n13
  of Carthage   101
  of Chalcedon   105
  of Dordrecht   1, 2, 25, 431, 431n28, 555n35
  of Ephesus   105
  of Laodicea   85, 101, 103, 105, 553, 553n32
  of Paris   475

Talmud   515, 515n7
Tapper, Ruard   379, 379n30
Tatian   41n15
Tavard, George H.   125n23
Tennant, F.R.   356n7
Tenney, Merill C.   353n3
Terminus   614, See Glossary
Terneuzen   229n1
Tertius   79
Tertullian   65, 65n27, 99, 103, 119, 125, 205n5, 218n22, 321, 329n19, 335, 335n23, 373n26, 461, 475, 501n11, 521, 549
testament   77, 111, 137
Testaments Old and New   16, 55, 575

Testimonium   614, See Glossary
theanthropos   65
Theodoretus of Cyrus   75, 75n3, 121, 249n6, 549n28
Theodosius   32n4, 485n45
theology   7, 31
  theologia archetypa   33, 33n5, 33n6, 81n7, 115, 175n29, 435
  theologia ectypa   33, 33n5, 35n7, 175n29, 435n4
  theologia falsa   45
  theologia unionis   33
  theologia viatorum   33n5
Theophilus of Antioch   41n15, 547
theopneustos   59, 77, 79, 111
Thetrodius, Jacobus Adrianus   407
Thompson, C.R.   25n6
Thrasamund   355n6
Thysius, Antonius   1, 2, 11, 12, 29, 75, 75n1, 75n2, 87n11, 151, 174n27, 229, 233n4, 235n5, 244n14, 315, 315n2, 327n15, 407, 410n6, 411n8, 423n18, 437n7, 513, 513n2, 519n9, 521n11, 531n17, 537n20, 553n33, 553n34, 555n35
Tigris   333
tradition   53, 107
traducianism   335n23
Trajan   61, 61n25
tree of knowledge   333, 341, 341n4
tree of life   333
Trelcatius, Lucas Jr   215n17
Trigland, Jacobus   107n1, 129n1
Trinity   6, 7, 9–11, 13, 33, 41, 65, 77, 151n2, 157n7, 161, 185, 203, 475, 481, 485, 559
  anti-trinitarians   3, 11, 11n10
Tübingen   471n25
Turretin, Franciscus   151n2
Turretini, Benedict   575n1
Tzamalikos, P.   257n18

universe   153, 161, 257n17, 265, 275, 505, 515, 529
univocity   169n21
Urim and Thummim   71
Ursinus, Zacharias   151n2, 585n8
Utrecht   351n1

Vaeck, Marc van   469n23
Valkenburg   31n1

GENERAL INDEX

Valla, Lorenzo   313n30, 457, 457n7
Varro   319n9, 463, 463n14
Vasquez, Gabriel   393n10
Veen, M. van   53n9, 289n6
Velde, Dolf te   171n24, 279n24
Veldhuis, Henri   213n16
Venus   63
Verbum   614, *See Glossary*
Vergil   307n27
Victor, Hugh of St.   12, 341n5
Victor, Richard of St.   12, 187n7, 225n28
Viladesau, Richard   473n28
Viret, Pierre   13n12
visio Dei   33
Visser, Hugo B.   521n11, 553n34
Vlissingen   315n1
Voetius, Gisbertus   43n17, 151n2, 235n8, 279n23, 313n33
Voluntas   614, *See Glossary*
Voluntas necessaria   614, *See Glossary*
Volusianus   39
Vos, Antonie   35n8, 49n3, 263n6
Vossius, G.J.   289n9, 313n33
vows   121, 459, 491n2, 501, 501n10, 503, 505, 507, 509, 511, 599, 599n20
Vox   614, *See Glossary*
Vulgate   45n18, 81, 81n8, 143n11, 159, 517n8, 571n25, 595n18

Walaeus, Antonius   1, 2, 2n3, 9, 11, 12, 29, 49, 49n1, 49n2, 53n9, 59n20, 69n30, 69n32, 69n33, 71n34, 129, 129n1, 143n11, 203, 209n12, 210n12, 245n15, 261n1, 285, 285n2, 287n4, 289n7, 291n11, 293n15, 303n22, 303n23, 304n25, 305n26, 313n31, 385, 387n6, 393n10, 489, 553n34
Wallace, William A.   37n9
Warmia   109n5
Wehberg, Hans   439n8
Weijers, Olga   4n7
Weir, D.A.   577n3
West Indies Company   557n1
Westminster Confession of Faith   87n11
Wetter, F.   213n16
Whitaker, William   52n7, 99n24, 108n4
Wiley, Tatha   356n7
will of God   12, 14, 37, 37n10, 47, 133n4, 173, 175n29, 177, 179n30, 191, 209, 235, 255, 263, 263n5, 271n14, 279n23, 279n24, 291, 345, 431, 443, 519n9
Williams, George Huntston   53n9, 551n31
Wissink, J.B.M.   255n15
Woerden   379n30

Xenophon   557

Zaandam   49n2
Zagorin, Perez   498n7
Zanchi, Jerome   10, 10n9, 151n2, 165n18, 166n18, 269n11, 289n9, 295n16, 313n33, 347n14, 409n4
Zelius, Johannes   339, 339n1
Zephyrinus   123, 123n19
Zierikzee   185n1, 385n1
Zijlstra, S.   53n9
Zwingli, Huldrich   281n27, 502n11